MW01078114

Archaeology, Volcanism, and Remote Sensing in the Arenal Region, Costa Rica

Archaeology, Volcanism, and Remote Sensing in the Arenal Region, Costa Rica

PAYSON D. SHEETS
BRIAN R. MCKEE
EDITORS

UNIVERSITY OF TEXAS PRESS, AUSTIN

Printed in the United States of America
First edition, 1994

∞ The paper used in this publication meets the minimum requirements of American National Standard for Information Sciences—Permanence of Paper for Printed Library Materials, ANSI Z39.48-1984.

The publication of this book was assisted by funds from the Committee on University Scholarly Publications of the University of Colorado and from the Stennis Space Center of NASA.

Library of Congress Cataloging-in-Publication Data
Archaeology, volcanism, and remote sensing in the Arenal Region, Costa Rica / Payson D. Sheets and Brian R. McKee, editors. — 1st ed.
p. cm.
Includes bibliographical references and index.
ISBN 0-292-77667-5 (alk. paper)
1. Indians of Central America—Costa Rica—Arenal, Lake, Region—Antiquities. 2. Arenal, Lake, Region (Costa Rica)—Antiquities. 3. Archaeology—Remote sensing. 4. Volcanism—Costa Rica. I. Sheets, Payson D. II. McKee, Brian R. (Brian Ross), date.
F1545.1.A7A73 1994
972.8601—dc20 93-15655

For Fran

Contents

Archaeology, Volcanism, and Remote Sensing in the Arenal Region, Costa Rica

1

The Proyecto Prehistórico Arenal: An Introduction

PAYSON D. SHEETS

INTRODUCTION

The general theoretical framework for the Proyecto Prehistórico Arenal research is human ecology, the study of the dynamic interrelationships between people, their natural and social environments, and their cultures. Central America (Fig. 1-1) is an excellent laboratory in which to study human adaptation to volcanically active areas, as it provides a significant range of climates, many active volcanoes, and the full range of human societies from hunter-gatherer bands to highly centralized, stratified states. The Arenal Project is directed toward understanding aboriginal settlements and adaptations in the Cordillera de Tilarán area, as residents were affected by the periodic eruptions of Arenal Volcano (Fig. 1-2) and the subsequent soil formation and vegetative recovery processes. A sudden airfall deposit of volcanic ash, formally called *tephra*, initially can be detrimental to natural vegetation, animals, and crops of all kinds if it is thicker than a few centimeters. After the ash has weathered, however, it can become a very fertile soil for intensive or extensive cultivation. Tropical rain forest vegetation on a fertile soil can have a very high biomass and species diversity, offering numerous subsistence alternatives to cultivation. Well-weathered volcanic materials can form very good clays for pottery making or for construction. Volcanic activity and weathering can produce iron oxides, which are useful for pigments, with colors ranging from yellow to orange and red to black. Basalts and andesites are excellent materials for making tough cutting edges for stone tools. Thus, there are obvious benefits to living in volcanically active areas.

There are detrimental factors as well. Although big explosive eruptions of Arenal occurred only on the average of every four centuries, they were very destructive to flora and fauna near the volcano. Studying the risks and benefits of living near Arenal Volcano in prehistoric times is among the research objectives of the project.

Tropical areas are often depicted as uniform, redundant environments. Microenvironmental differences exist, however, and many of them may have been critical for prehistoric land use and choice for settlement location. This chapter presents information on variation in the natural environment, the research background and objectives, and chronology. Other chapters explore variation in settlement, artifacts, remote sensing, and other topics.

CLIMATE

Costa Rica (Fig. 1-3), located between 9° and 11° north latitude, falls within the latitudinal tropics. Tropical seasonality is more pronounced in precipitation than in temperature variation, in contrast to temperate climates (West and Augelli 1966:35; MacArthur 1972). The annual temperature variation in Tilarán is minimal; the January mean temperature of 22.5°C is only 2.1° cooler than that of the hottest month, May, with 24.6°C, according to data supplied by the Instituto Meteorológico. On the other hand, the diurnal range is relatively great, averaging about 8°C. throughout the year.

Some striking climatic gradients can be observed in the research area (Fig. 1-4), in spite of its small size. At the western end of the area, particularly around Tilarán and westward, the climate is a Pacific regime characterized by lower precipitation (under 2,000 mm) and greater seasonality. Cañas, 15 km west of Tilarán, receives only 1,300 mm mean annual precipitation. The eastern end, around the volcano, is much wetter (over 6,000 mm) with minimal seasonal variation in rainfall, more typical of the Atlantic climatic regime. The area to the north of Lake Arenal is wetter and less seasonal than the area south of the lake; however, variables such as slope, aspect,

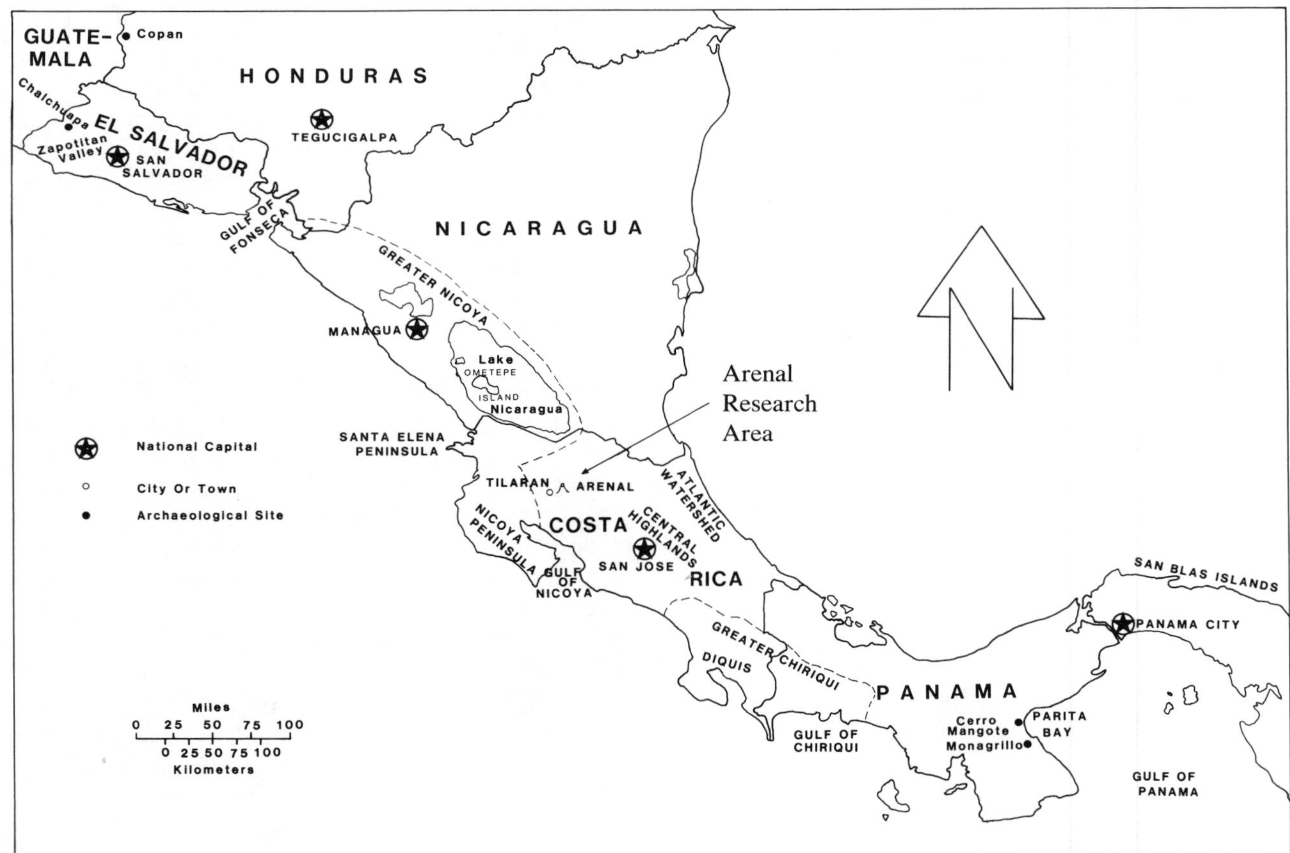

Figure 1-1.
Central America. Map by Brian McKee.

Figure 1-2.
Arenal Volcano from the town of Fortuna. The upwind side of Arenal is still heavily vegetated, in spite of the 1968 eruption and the emission of lava, gasses, and occasional tephra. The consistent northeast trade winds blow gasses and tephra over the Laguna de Arenal and toward Tilarán. Photograph by Payson Sheets.

exposure, and nearby topographic features create microclimates. Certainly, the meteorological data do not support the "uniform, redundant climate" view of the tropics for the Arenal area.

A note of explanation is needed here. Occasional reference to the ICE hydroelectric project will be found in this volume. ICE, the Instituto Costarricense de Electricidad, contracted with Tosi and the Tropical Science Center for a study of climate, soils, topography, hydrology, flora, fauna, and other aspects of the area. That study, completed in 1980, is the primary source of environmental information available to the Proyecto Prehistórico Arenal and is the major source consulted for climatic and biologic information presented in this chapter. Other sources are referenced as they appear.

The ICE hydroelectric project began with construction of a large, earth-fill dam across the Arenal River, just WNW of Arenal Volcano. Construction of the dam, tunnels, and other facilities was largely completed by 1980. The dam greatly enlarged the lake from what was a shallow, largely swampy body of water to a lake with

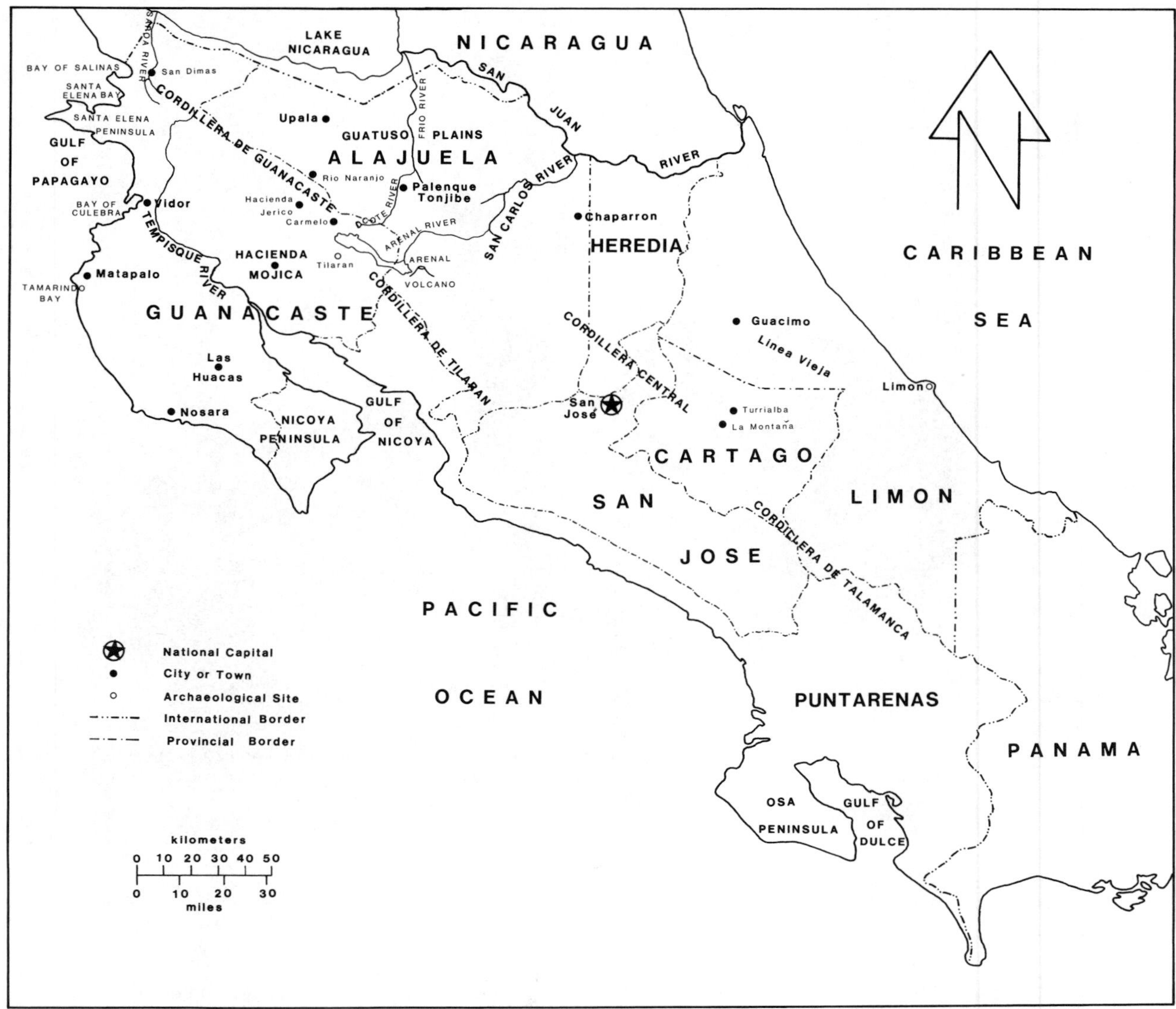

Figure 1-3.
Costa Rica. Map by Brian McKee.

a surface of some 80 km². The lake level was raised from 512 m to a maximum of 545 m. The lake level fluctuates seasonally, and it often drops to about 535 m in the drier months of April or May, exposing an eroded and unvegetated zone along the shore. Eight towns were flooded by the impoundment, along with many archaeological sites, and twenty-five hundred people had to be relocated. The water is diverted under the Continental Divide to two hydroelectric stations between Tilarán and Cañas. Some of the water is used for irrigation in dry, lowland Guanacaste.

A thermal gradient can be seen from east to west. The more rainy and cloudy areas near the volcano have mean temperatures between 22° and 23°C, while areas near the old Lake Arenal to Tilarán average about 24°C. Mean temperatures increase rapidly as elevations drop to below 100 m

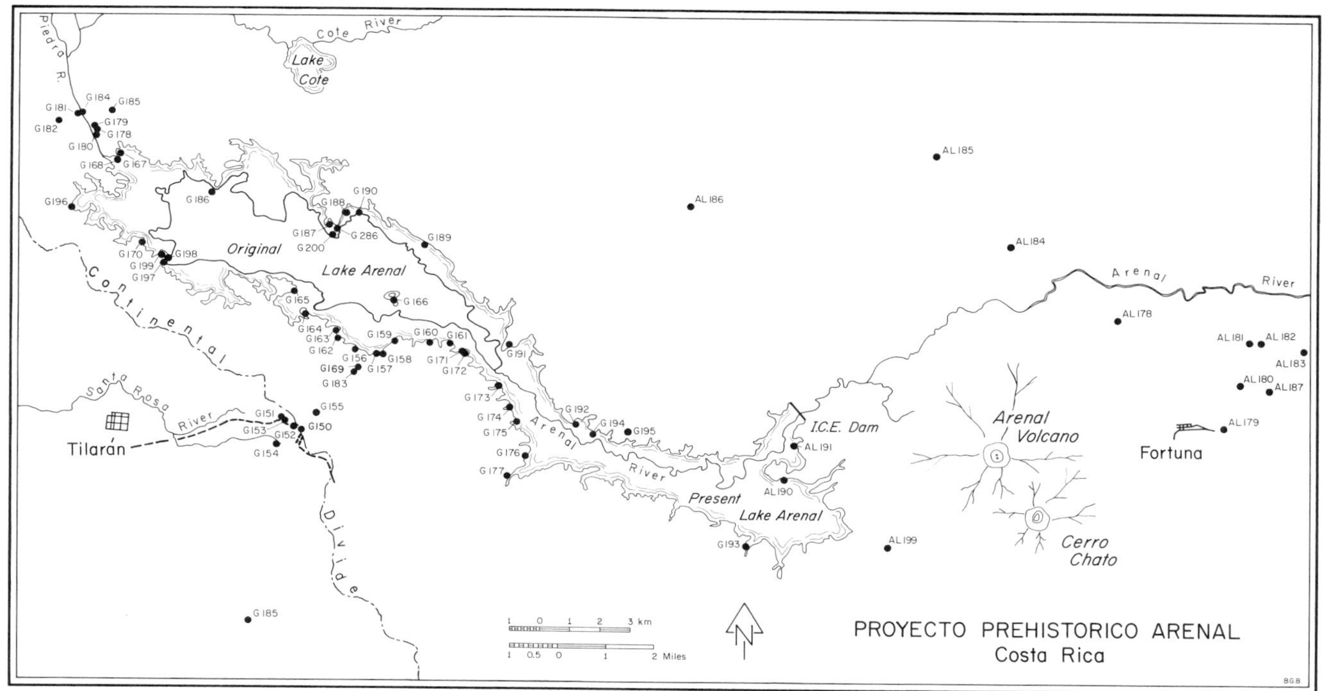

Figure 1-4. The research area, Proyecto Prehistórico Arenal. Note the enlargement of Lake Arenal by the construction of the ICE dam. Map by Barbara Bolton.

Figure 1-5. Evidence of the strong northeast trade winds in the Arenal area. The winds are sufficiently strong, particularly from September to March, to deform vegetation. Photograph by Payson Sheets.

to the west of Tilarán, as exemplified by the 27°C mean at the Corobici power plant, where maxima as high as 38°C have been recorded. The coolest areas are the tops of mountains or ridges; for example, Cerro Amigos, at 1,840 m, has a mean of 16°C, and often a 10°C day-night range (Tosi 1980). Even at this high elevation, there is no frost hazard, but upland areas above 1,500 m in the Cordillera de Tilarán generally were not inhabited prehistorically.

The Tilarán-Arenal area is very windy. Mean annual wind speed is 14.5 km per hour at Tilarán, and wind is consistently from the northeast in all months. Winds are greatest from November through April, with all these months registering mean wind speeds of 15 km per hour or more. January is the windiest month, with an exceptionally high mean wind speed of 28 km per hour. The rainy season months have mean wind speeds of 8 to 14 km per hour. Other areas in the *cuenca* (drainage basin) are even windier; La Toma has an average annual wind speed of 23 km per hour, with a mean of over 30 km per hour in January. For comparison, Chicago has a mean annual wind speed of 16 km per hour, according to the U.S. National Weather Service. Gusts at La Toma reach 100 km per hour or more, yet it is not the windiest point in the basin, as areas facing northeast are buffeted by even higher winds.

The wind negatively affects contemporary vegetation, agriculture, land use, and construction, and presumably it would have been an important factor in the past. Stunted, wind-deformed trees are common in the area (Fig. 1-5). The wind probably affected the stable climax forest less, however, as it is interlocked at the top with vines and stabilized at the bottom by roots. Thus, the wind would have passed over the tops of the trees, with greatly reduced impact at the ground surface. Some shallow-rooted plants, including maize, are very susceptible to wind throw. Isolated tropical trees, with their shallow roots and lack of upper-level support, also are very vulnerable. Thus, in the context of the basin's vegetation and the wind factor, an appropriate land use would have been an extensive tropical forest swidden, making use of particularly small partial clearings on a rotating basis.

Meteorological data are particularly detailed from the Tilarán station, at 562 m, with 33 years of records. An average of 180 days per year have rain, with a minimum of 5 days each in March and April, and a maximum of 20 days from June through October. The wettest months are May, June, August, and September, with means between 105 mm and 125 mm. The driest months (with their average precipitation figures in mm) are January (60), February (28), March (19), and April (34). The fact that the standard deviation exceeds the mean for March and April indicates a less-than-predictable precipitation pattern (and difficulties for archaeologists needing predictable dry months for sensitive excavations).

Tosi (1980) divides the Arenal area into three precipitation provinces: humid (1,400–2,000 mm), perhumid (2,000–4,000 mm), and superhumid (over 4,000 mm). The classification is aided by data from 40 meteorological stations in the area, making it one of the best-documented tropical zones in the world for studying climatic microvariation. The humid area, according to Tosi, is almost ideal for agriculture. The dry months generally have enough soil moisture to maintain crops, and the erosion risk is low, particularly compared to the two other precipitation provinces. The humid province has the highest solar radiation figures and the lowest relative humidity. The soil acidity is the lowest of the three provinces (i.e., higher pH figures), and Tosi feels this is the best of the three for short-term cultigens.

The perhumid province takes up the greatest percentage of the Arenal area and includes virtually all the sites recorded by our research. It is intermediate in all conditions. There are 3 to 6 months of excessive precipitation, and soils are often saturated, and thus anaerobic. Soils are moderate to poor in fertility and are rather acidic. Agriculture is rated as marginal except along shallow slopes or along alluvial areas. Tosi feels permanent or semi-permanent crops are more appropriate than annual crops.

The superhumid province is inappropriate for agriculture (Tosi 1980). There is excessive water in most months, creating leaching and erosional hazards. Soils are the most acid and have the lowest fertility. Soil saturation inhibits oxygen contact with plant roots, and nitrogen fixation is greatly reduced. This area experiences the lowest sunlight (solar radiation) because it has the highest number of cloudy and rainy days of the three provinces.

The Arenal area is exceptionally cloudy (ibid.). Based on 11 years of data from Arenal Viejo, 12 km west of the volcano, the average day has only 4.4 hours of sunlight. The lack of solar radiation is a limiting factor for many cultigens, particularly in the more humid zones in the eastern half of the research area. This would have less of an effect toward the west end of the lake and around Tilarán.

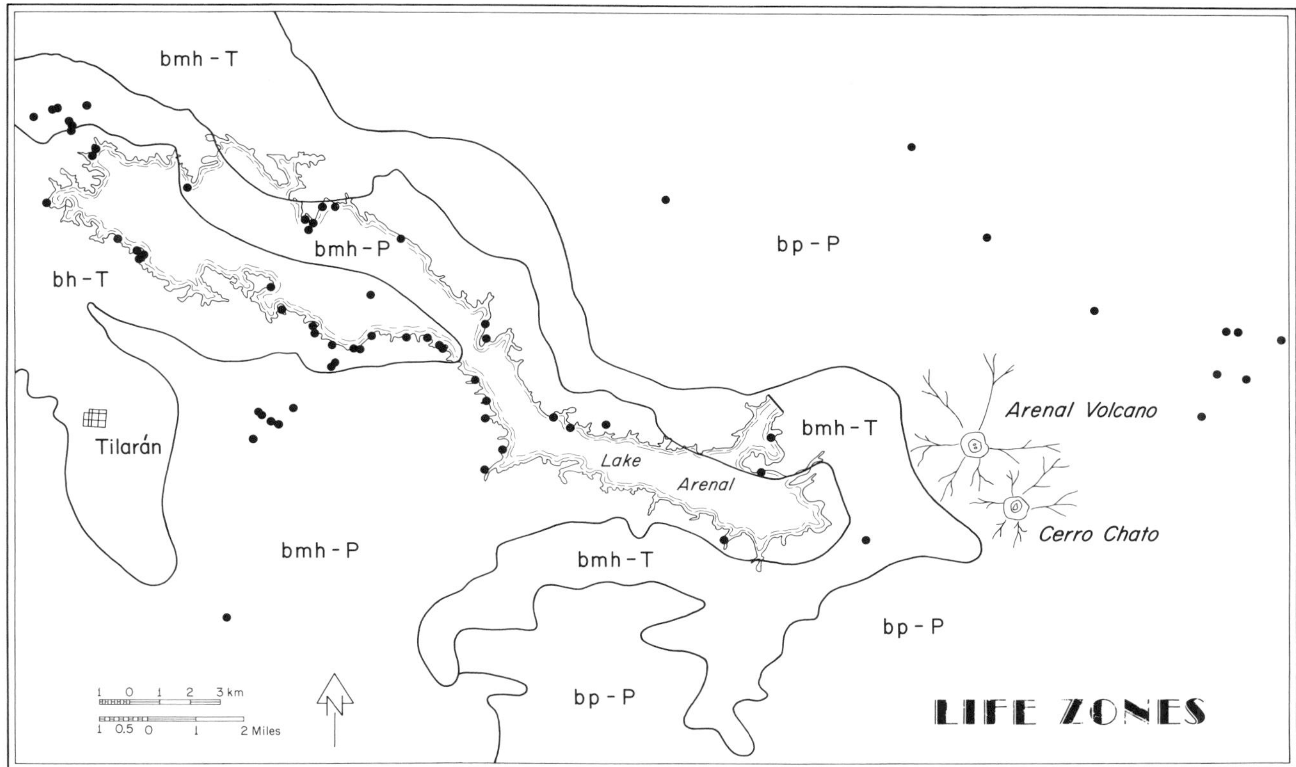

Figure 1-6.
Holdridge Life Zones in the research area, based on Tosi (1980). Map by Barbara Bolton.

LIFE ZONES

The Holdridge "life zones," from Tosi (1980) and mapped on Figure 1-6, probably are the most useful analytic system to describe bioclimatic variation, although they are limited because they do not include soil variation. The Holdridge system emphasizes factors such as elevation, temperature, and the amounts and the timing of precipitation, and how those factors affect vegetation. There are five primary life zones in the area; they are described here beginning with the wettest.

The Tropical Wet Forest (bp-P on Fig. 1-6) has the highest species diversity as well as the greatest standing biomass of all these life zones. It is located in the eastern end of the research area, around Arenal Volcano and extending eastward toward Fortuna. Mean annual precipitation ranges from 4,200 mm at the Sangregado Dam to over 6,000 mm near the volcano, giving new significance to the term "mean precipitation." Some of the area is so wet that laws have been passed forbidding all deforestation because of extreme erosional potential. There is no true dry season, and soils generally are saturated for 11 months of the year. Tosi (1980) recommends against agriculture, as few cultigens can tolerate waterlogged soils, and forest clearance can result in extreme soil erosion and leaching, particularly in sloping areas. The erosional potential can be indicated by data from the Jilguero station, where only 1,340 mm of the annual mean of 5,500 mm is used by vegetation in evapotranspiration; the remaining 3,160 mm is runoff (ibid. 1980) or throughflow. It is unlikely that much agriculture was practiced in this area prehistorically. Compared to the other life zones, the soils here are quite acid and weak in nutriments. We have found a few sites in this life zone, indicating that prehistoric peoples were able to overcome the environmental challenges, but people preferred the drier zones to the west. It should be noted that only a small percentage of this area has been systematically surveyed, due partly to the heavy vegetation cover and partly to the fact that areas near the volcano are buried under very deep deposits of volcanic ash.

The Wet Tropical Forest, Premontane Transition (bmh-T on Fig. 1-6) occupies a fairly narrow zone just to the east of the wettest life zone. Caño Negro is an example, with 4,440 mm of precipitation and 8 months of excessive precipitation. Soils are thoroughly saturated from June through January. During all months more moisture falls than is sent upward by evapotranspiration. Seventy percent of the precipitation must pass through or over the soil, resulting in almost as great an erosional or leaching hazard in this zone as in the wettest life zone. Agriculture is not recommended, but careful silviculture can be practiced, as is done today (ibid. 1980). The seed crops, which require aeration for germination and growth, such as maize and beans, do poorly in this environment. Only three sites have been found in this zone, but survey in this zone has been minimal.

The Premontane Wet Forest (bmh-P in Fig. 1-6) includes the upper Arenal River Valley and some of the Sábalo and Piedra valleys. It also extends into the Silencio area. The mature vegetation is a medium to tall evergreen rain forest. Mean precipitation figures include 2,800 mm at the town of Arenal Viejo and 3,333 mm at Río Chiquito, with only slight seasonality. One-half to two-thirds of the precipitation leaves the area as runoff or throughflow. The remainder is used in evapotranspiration. Although the erosional potential is lower than in the previously described areas, it was and still is a significant problem for inhabitants. There are nine very wet months in which precipitation exceeds evapotranspiration. The months of February, March, and April are drier, however, so evapotranspiration exceeds precipitation, and seed crops can be grown where local soil and slope conditions are suitable. This life zone includes many archaeological sites, including the Silencio cluster, the sites west of Río Chiquito along the south shore of the lake, and the sites around the east and north shore to near the town of Arenal Nuevo. Specifically, the site count is five in and near Río Chiquito, fourteen at the east end of the lake and around the north shore to Arenal Nuevo, six in the Silencio area, and seven past the west end of the lake along the Piedra River, for a total of thirty-two.

The Tropical Moist Forest, Premontane Transition (bh-T on Fig. 1-6) is drier than the other zones, and thus is more suitable for most crops, particularly seed crops. Only rarely is this zone found above 700 m in the research area. The climax vegetation is a medium-to-tall, multistoried evergreen to semideciduous forest (Hartshorn 1983). Areas included here extend from Tilarán to the west end of the lake, and continue along the southern shore of the lake past Tronadora. Twenty-three sites have been found within this life zone, including four near the town of Piedras and nineteen along the south shore of the lake, stretching some 8 km on both sides of Tronadora Nueva. Seasonality is more developed here, with an 8 to 10 month wet season, and a 2 to 4 month drier season. Precipitation means range from 2,100 mm at the western end to about 2,600 mm in the Tronadora area. Tilarán has mean precipitation of 2,200 mm ($\pm$ 500), mean evapotranspiration of 1260 mm, and a mean annual temperature of 23.8°C. Soils are dry enough for germination and growth of seed crops, yet they are wet enough during the drier season to sustain growth. Soils are more fertile and less acid than in the three above-mentioned life zones, and some fertile alluvial floodplains are available along the Sábalo River and the Piedra River. The land can tolerate clearing better than the wetter life zones, because erosional hazards are lessened.

The Humid Premontane Forest (bmh-T on Fig. 1-6) is located to the west of Tilarán and is the driest and warmest of the various life zones in the research area. The zone has a monsoon climate, with a well-defined 4 to 5 month dry season, and a rainy season with only 2 markedly moist months. Mean annual precipitation figures are as low as 1,300 mm. Soils are too dry during the dry season for seed crops to grow without irrigation. There are sites in the zone, known to us by owners' reports or seen by us in brief visits, but we have yet to survey the area systematically. We have formally recorded only one site in this life zone. The zone is entirely on the Pacific side of the continental divide, largely below 500 m.

FLORA, FAUNA, AND LANDFORMS

Tropical forests in general have long been known to harbor the most diverse and abundant flora of any terrestrial biome. Indeed, the numbers of species and the magnitude of the standing biomass of yet-uncut forest in the Arenal area is impressive, even to those familiar with tropical forests elsewhere. The Cordillera de Tilarán is one of the richest and most diverse of tropical forest areas in Costa Rica, based on the species Tosi (1980) and his research team recorded. Many native plants provide edible fruits, nuts, seeds, berries, and roots. As people affect the natural vegetation by selective cutting and burning or clearing, they often leave productive species alive, thus improving the density of desired yet undomesticated flora. The disturbed areas are then opened to a wide variety of successionals, which often are edible directly, or provide forage for animals. Thus, the exploitable animal biomass can increase in a modified environment, as long as the adaptation remains extensive and human population density remains low and dispersed. Unfortunately, the opposite often occurred prehistorically and in recent times in so many areas of the tropics, as overpopulation and intensive adaptations result in habitat destruction, erosion, oxidation, and a host of concomitant problems.

Native flora in the area today that provide edible foods include ceiba, many palms (e.g., corozo, coyol, and pejibaye), ramón, papaya, jícaro, zapote, jocote, nance, guanábana, marañón (cashew), sapodilla, pineapple, and numerous epiphytes. The woods useful for construction of housing, boats or rafts, and wooden implements are too numerous to mention. In addition to selective clearing, the simple act of deliberate planting and minimal tending of productive wild species can markedly increase the life support capacity of the rain forest with very little increase in labor inputs and with minimal detrimental impact on soils.

Proyecto Prehistórico Arenal members have found carbonized macrofossils of numerous wild and domesticated species. Many of those species have been duplicated by analyses of pollen and phytoliths. Species include nance, avocado, coyol and corozo palms, squash, maize, and jícaro (see Chaps. 14–16).

The fauna in the Cordillera de Tilarán are abundant in species diversity, if not in density, in the unmodified forest. The region, according to Tosi (1980), is more diverse than most areas of Costa Rica, with about half the country's known bird species, mammal species, and reptilian species represented there. Many of the estimated 100 mammal species (including deer, armadillo, opossum, rabbit, coyotes, and large felines) could have benefited from an extensive adaptation to people living in the area, as abandoned slash-and-burn plots provide forage. Manatee, the large, slow, and eminently exploitable aquatic mammal, lived in the lake until about 1950, when they finally succumbed to overhunting (ibid. 1980). Of the estimated 150 species of reptiles and amphibians, the turtles and iguana likely were economically important. The 25 fish species probably provided food for near-lake residents. The present estimate of over 100 species of birds probably is greatly reduced from prehistoric numbers. The quetzal is still found in higher elevations; its iridescent long blue-green tail feathers were highly prized by Mesoamerican populations, but we do not know if similar values were held by Arenal-area residents. It is possible that quetzal feathers from this area were exchanged for the occasional Mesoamerican trade good. If there were such trade, however, it probably was intermittent, and not part of a regular system.

Landforms are quite variable in the area. They range from alluvial flats and gently sloping piedmonts to low and high mesas, and include numerous valleys, hills, some recent volcanic structures, and some very steep slopes. These are presented here in descending order of suitability for habitation. Flat areas, or areas with minimal slopes, which had relatively easy access to year-round fresh water, were preferred for housing. In contrast, the tops of steep hills or ridges were preferred for funerary areas. Topography was a major factor in the routing of footpaths, in a manner quite different from the routing of contemporary roads. Roads sacrifice distance to maintain low grades. In contrast, prehistoric paths followed surprisingly straight routes, sometimes ascending and descending slopes of over 35° and preferring to remain high on ridges and away from valley bottoms.

Landforms and features have varied in the past. The drainage of Arenal River prior to the emergence of Arenal and Chato volcanoes was more directly toward the east, to Fortuna and beyond (ibid. 1980). The volcanic structures of Chato and Arenal have diverted that drainage. Prior to the construction of the Sangregado Dam in the late 1970s, the lake water level was 512 m above sea level. Previous lakeshore sediments, unfortunately undated, were seen by Tosi (ibid.: 17) on aerial photographs as high as 530 m. Although Tosi feels Arenal Volcano blocked the valley and created the lake, we feel that may be an error. We now know that Arenal Volcano was born almost 4,000 years ago. If Tosi were correct, that Arenal Volcano blocked the Arenal River sometime in the past 4 millennia and created a lake with a shore at about 530 m, the area under that lake should be devoid of archaeological sites. The fact that Aguilar (1984) found numerous archaeological sites of varying ages in the Arenal River Valley, dating to the last three millennia, and located between the historic lake and the volcano, indicates that no such lake existed as envisioned by Tosi, at least during the last 3,000 years. Also, Murray surveyed the western end of the lake in 1974, and found numerous Zoned Bichrome sites near the 512 m shoreline. Had there been a greatly enlarged Lake Arenal, I suspect it would have had to have been prior to the Fortuna Phase, and that would leave Cerro Chato as a possible blocking agent. As Melson notes (personal communication, 1988), the lake is in a graben and could have existed long before Arenal Volcano. He dates wood from a marsh near the western end of the lake at about 12,000 BP, and feels that older and higher lake levels may antedate human occupation of the area.

Arenal Volcano is a relatively small and very recent strato-volcano, with a peak currently at 1,633 m and a base covering about 12 km^2. Compared with most Costa Rican volcanoes, it has a very symmetrical cone. The cone is composed largely of coalescing basaltic andesite lava flows. A sizeable volcanic ash apron has developed on the downwind side (to the WSW) as airfall deposits have fallen from the approximately ten large prehistoric explosive eruptions (Melson 1982). Arenal erupted explosively most recently in 1968, but the magnitude of tephra (airfall volcanic ash, lapilli, and so on) was much less than the large prehistoric eruptions (Saenz and Melson 1976; Melson 1978; Chap. 2).

The 1968 eruption is unusual for Arenal and for Costa Rican volcanoes in that lava has been emitted continuously for more than two decades and was still being emitted in summer 1991. The earliest eruption, until recently believed to date to about 1000 B.C., has now been revised backward to about 1800 B.C., based on data from the 1985 excavations at the site of Tronadora Vieja (site G-163). In much of the area covered by the research described in this volume, the individual ash layers from these eruptions are fairly thin, usually between 5 cm and 20 cm, with soils formed on top of them. Below the layers of Arenal ash and soils is the Aguacate Formation and older tephra units. That formation is a complex of Miocene and Pliocene volcanic rocks (Castillo-Muñoz 1983), capped by a well-weathered and highly clay-laden tropical soil with a consistent orange color. This project found evidence of people living in the area during Paleo-Indian and Archaic times. Thus, although population densities apparently remained very low, the earliest inhabitants of the Arenal area had adapted to soils and botanical resources prior to the birth of Arenal Volcano and its downwind tephra deposits.

The tectonic depression in which the lake rests dates to the end of the Miocene. It is delimited by two large faults, one along the northern and one along the southern shore (Tosi 1980). That the region remains tectonically active is evidenced by the great earthquake of 1973, and the fact that in only 4 years (1973–1977) twenty-four hundred earthquakes were recorded with magnitudes up to 4.0 on the Richter scale. The 1973 earthquake was one of the largest to have occurred in Central America in recorded history.

Topographically, the research area is dominated by the Continental Divide. Quite high to the north and south (reaching over 1,500 m), it dips between Tilarán and Tronadora (Fig. 1-4) to only 700 m, thus providing a pass for human communication and transportation linking the Atlantic and Pacific drainages. Millennia of alluvial deposition in the tectonic depression helped form a moderately large amount of fertile, flat-lying land around the old Lake Arenal, and downstream along the upper reaches of the Arenal River. Apart from those areas, flat-lying land was scarce. There is an abundance of steeply to moderately undulating terrain, with intermittent, small flat-lying areas on ridges and hilltops or along small drainages. This contrasts markedly with the extensive moist plains of San Carlos to the east and the extensive dry plains of lowland Guanacaste to the west.

SOILS

Tosi (1980) directed a detailed study of soils in the Arenal-Tilarán area. His staff found that 93% of the area had soils developed from volcanic ash, with the rest from basalts. They classified the soils into four types, each unfortunately labeled with pedological jargon approaching opacity.

The "Typic Hydrandept" covers 67% of the area and is derived from recent volcanic ashfalls. Most sites found by this project fall within this soil type. These soils are low in density, high in water-retention capacity, and fairly fertile. They possess high to very high percentages of organic matter and have pH readings from 4.5 to 6.6, depending on moisture. The available phosphorus and potassium are low, as are zinc and manganese, which would have limited the agricultural potential of these soils. Iron, copper, calcium, and magnesium are relatively abundant.

"Andic Tropudult" soils cover 12% of the area and are formed on older volcanic ashfalls. They are found to the north and south of Arenal Volcano, outside of the zone of Arenal tephra deposition. Their fertility is low. It is possible that some of them may have formed on tephra from the earlier but yet-undated eruption(s) of Cerro Chato.

"Udic Argiustoll" soils are derived from basic igneous rocks and cover 6% of the area. They are without significant tephra from Arenal, because they lie outside the downwind zone where significant deposition occurred. They are found in the southwestern part of the study area, in the Pacific drainage between Tilarán and Cañas. They have a high clay content, a low organic content, and are moderate in inherent fertility.

Soils on alluvial or lacustrine sediments account for 3% of the area. Most of these areas have been inundated by the enlarged Lake Arenal during the late 1970s. The soils are very heterogeneous, and they were studied very little by Tosi's group. That is unfortunate for our purposes, as an understanding of them related to the sites found by Aguilar (1984) and by Murray's survey of low-lying areas prior to the dam construction could have shed considerable light on prehistoric choice of settlement location and contributed pertinent data on maximum lake levels over the past few millennia.

PREVIOUS ARCHAEOLOGICAL RESEARCH IN NORTHWESTERN COSTA RICA

Archaeological research in northwestern Costa Rica (Fig. 1-3) has been a microcosm of the changes in method and in theory that have occurred in the discipline during the past century, as outlined by Willey and Sabloff (1971). The early days of exploration and unfettered speculation shifted to classification and description in the early twentieth century, culminating in explanatory and processual concerns, and some symbolic research, in the past couple of decades. Some of the disappointment with the "New Archaeology," that some of its objectives were unreasonable or unreachable, can be seen in the volume *American Archaeology Past, Present, and Future* (Meltzer, Fowler, and Sabloff 1986). These criticisms are also applicable to northwestern Costa Rica. Numerous detailed histories of Costa Rican archaeology have been published (Lothrop 1966; Willey 1971; Aguilar 1972; Stone 1977; Ferrero 1981; Lange 1984b; and Snarskis 1984a), making only a brief summary necessary here.

Following the early explorations directed toward recovery of complete vessels, sculptures, jades, and gold artifacts came Hartman's well-published pioneering research (1901, 1907) in various locations in Costa Rica, including grave excavations at Las Huacas in the Nicoya Peninsula. Lines (1936) continued Hartman's interests, and Lothrop (1926) surveyed the ceramics of the country. Stone has descriptively summarized the prehistory of the region, most recently in 1977. The era of modern archaeology was initiated in the early 1960s by Baudez and Coe (Coe and Baudez 1961).

The 1970s witnessed a veritable explosion of research, involving scholars such as Abel-Vidor, Accola, Aguilar, Dillon, Drolet, Fonseca, Hurtado, Lange, and Snarskis. In northwest Costa Rica, the most intensive research has been conducted along the coast, particularly in the bays of Salinas, Culebra, Santa Elena, and Tamarindo, and in the Gulf of Nicoya, generally under the direction of Lange. The second most intensely studied area is inland in lowland Guanacaste. The third area, the Cordillera, has received much less attention, and it is in the Cordillera that we have focused our efforts.

The Guanacaste–San Carlos Corridor Project was conceived in the late 1970s by Lange and others to investigate a presumed trade route between the Atlantic and the Pacific drainages as it passed over the Cordillera between volcanic massifs (Lange 1982–1983:93). Transisthmian trade and communication routes had already been demonstrated in Panama, so it was logical to extend that model to Costa Rica for testing. Creamer's work failed to document significant long-distance trade, however, at least viewed from the Gulf of Nicoya (Lange 1982–1983). Lange notes the paucity of jade or other imports at the large Hacienda

Mojica graveyard located on the plains of Guanacaste, some 30 km WSW of Tilarán. Lange concludes that the areas on either side of the Divide underwent largely independent developmental sequences in their ceramics. It appears that the data generated from this project, as well as from the Arenal Project, indicate that there was some commerce and communication between the two areas, but it was intermittent and largely inconsequential, in contrast to trade systems in Mesoamerica or the Andes.

Finch (1982–1983) surveyed Hacienda Jerico, some 20 km NW of Tilarán, at an elevation from 300 m to 600 m, on the Pacific slope, in a climate virtually identical to that of Tilarán. Virtually all sites he encountered dated to late Zoned Bichrome and Early Polychrome periods, but surveyed areas were covered by pasture grass and, as we shall see, introduced a strong bias toward finding cemeteries with sufficient architecture to be visible through that vegetation. Funerary architecture includes stone mounds similar to those dating to our Arenal Phase and laja (flat volcanic rocks) tombs similar to those dating to our Silencio Phase, both considered Atlantic or Meseta Central characteristics. In contrast, the ceramics recovered appear to be predominantly related to Greater Nicoya.

Hacienda Mojica, located on the Guanacaste Plains 27 km WSW of Tilarán, also yielded largely late Zoned Bichrome ceramics, with very little later material (Ryder 1982–1983a). Ryder found eight habitation sites and seven cemeteries, all close to rivers. The cemeteries were of the large cobble burial mound–type, similar to our Arenal Phase cemeteries. Habitation sites were located a short distance from the rivers, while cemeteries were found immediately adjacent to the rivers. A thin layer of volcanic ash was found in one excavation, postdating the funerary structure, and thus is probably post-AD 500. If it came from Arenal Volcano, Units 41–40 are likely candidates, but it could be from another source. Notable for their absence are jade and greenstone pendants, mace heads, and elaborately carved metates (ibid.), characteristics that show up in contemporary cemeteries farther to the west. Ryder recovered some sherds and whole vessels of the Atlantic style, but most ceramics appear to be in the Greater Nicoya tradition.

The Guayabo de Bagaces region, located on the western side of Miravalles Volcano, between 450 m and 700 m, is some 35 km NW of Tilarán and in a similar ecozone. Ryder (1982–1983b) found twenty-three sites, of which nineteen were late zoned Bichrome stone funerary mounds (the others included two cemetery-habitation sites, two apparent habitation sites, and two petroglyph sites). The largest mound measured 50 m in diameter and 6 m in height. Most cemeteries were on hills or ridge tops. Some use of laja was noted. Ceramics apparently were predominantly Greater Nicoya in style.

Norr (1979, 1982–1983) conducted surveys and test excavations in the Río Naranjo area about 25 km NW of Tilarán. Both the Tilarán and the Río Naranjo areas are low passes between mountain complexes, and they share many characteristics of climate, topography, and vegetation. Río Naranjo has a slightly lower pass (500 m versus 700 m) and is slightly moister (3,000 mm rather than 2,500 mm annual precipitation) than Tilarán, but otherwise the two settings are nearly identical. Norr's sites were predominantly Zoned Bichrome, and most were discovered by finding stone funerary mounds. She found some ceramics dating to the earlier part of the Zoned Bichrome Period (800–300 BC), but most sites dated to between 300 BC and AD 500. Based on her findings, "the use of the Río Naranjo–Bijagua Valley as a corridor for Precolumbian communication and exchange is not supported archaeologically for any of the Polychrome Periods" (Norr 1982–1983: 143). The predominant external connections with Zoned Bichrome ceramics were westward, with Greater Nicoya. Some very early connections with the Atlantic area are indicated by two pottery types, also found in the Arenal area.

Creamer's survey (1979; Creamer and Dawson 1982–1983) at Upala, about 30 km NE of Río Naranjo, enountered significant occupation during the late Zoned Bichrome Period, but, in contrast to the above-mentioned areas, even larger occupations dating to the Early and Middle Polychrome periods. Stone cobble burial mounds were common. Ceramic affiliations were strongly with Greater Nicoya, with Atlantic characteristics being rare.

Three previous projects in the Arenal area have explored the prehistory of the *cuenca*. The first was the work of Metcalf with William Melson (Chap. 2) in 1969, shortly following the 1968 eruption of Arenal. Metcalf spent three weeks excavating a site found during construction of an observatory north of the volcano. Some 428 sherds were recovered, along with a mano, a celt, and a

Figure 1-7.
Various soils formed volcanic ash deposits in the town of Tronadora, with Tom Sever for scale. Units 65, 60, 50, 30, and the dark zones above Units 20 and 10 are soils. The following Units are volcanic ash layers, with their approximate date of the eruption in parentheses: 61 (1800 BC), 55 (800 BC), 41 and 40 (AD 800–900), 20 (AD 1500), and 10 (AD 1968). Photograph by Payson Sheets.

few chert chipped stone flakes. These artifacts, stored at the Museum of Natural History in Washington, D.C., have yet to be analyzed.

The second archaeological project in the Arenal area was a brief, unpublished, survey around the lake by Murray in 1974. A number of sites were found at or near the shore of the old lake, and most were Zoned Bichrome in date (Lange, personal communication, 1983).

The third project was conducted by Aguilar in 1977. It was the largest in the *cuenca* prior to the current project. He conducted numerous test excavations and a survey around the eastern end of the lake. His research was made urgent by the rising lake level, as the Sangregado Dam began to block the river. As bulldozers cut 20 m deep to extract fill for dam construction at the site known as El Tajo, some artifacts were encountered. Aguilar (1984) excavated ceramics, human bone, features, and other artifacts, and published the re-

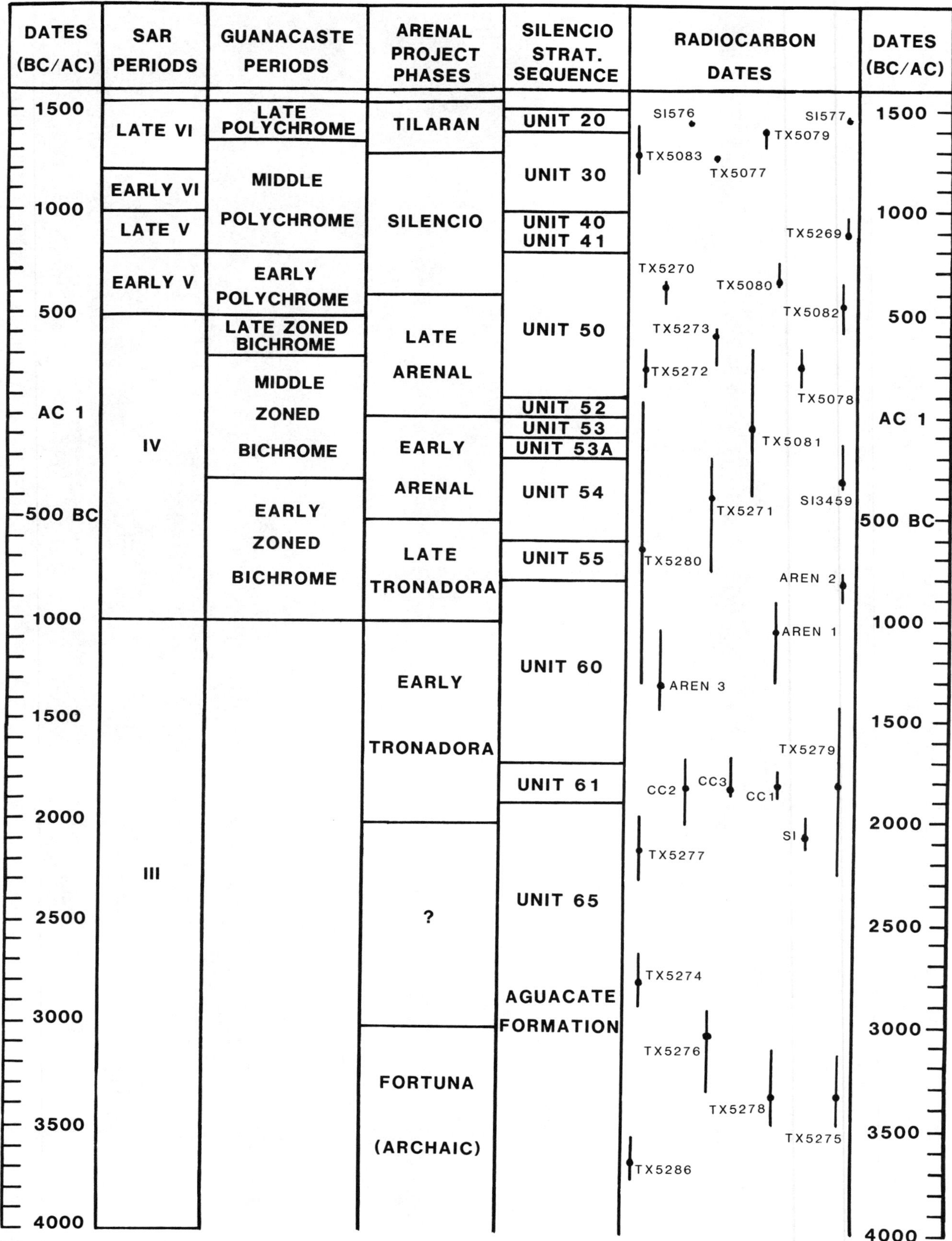

Figure 1-8.
Chronological chart relating calendar dates with periods and phases, the volcanological sequence, and all relevant radiocarbon dates from the research area. Chart by Brian McKee.

sults in preliminary form. A radiocarbon dating of wood from a hearth at the Tajo site yielded a date of 220 ± 65 BC, placing the deposits in the Zoned Bichrome Period. The site was of extraordinary importance, because vegetative preservation was excellent, owing to suddenness of burial by fine-grained tephra and sufficient tephra deposition on top of the preserved organic material. Melson observed casts of vegetation, including grasses, in and near the site. Unfortunately, the site is now inundated by the enlarged Lake Arenal.

Our project is the fourth to operate in the area. It began with a suggestion from Snarskis to me in 1980 that the Arenal area could provide the active volcanological framework within which to study tropical settlement and adaptation, similar to the research design in El Salvador (Sheets 1983). Melson and I visited the area in 1981 to collect samples and to study the feasibility of collaborative research. Drolet and I examined the large graveyard, now numbered G-150 (Fig. 1-4), on the Finca El Silencio in 1982, and decided it offered opportunities to study funerary practices "sandwiched" by volcanic ash layers. The results of the two preliminary visits are available (Sheets 1982–1983). The proposals we submitted to the National Science Foundation and the National Geographic Society were funded in 1983; fieldwork began early in 1984 and continued through 1987. Yet another field season, sponsored by NASA and Lockheed, occurred in 1991. We detected anomalies with remote sensing and excavated trenches to explore them. In the trenches we found clear evidence that the linear anomalies were human footpaths.

PROJECT OBJECTIVES AND METHODS

A major project objective was to determine the stratigraphic relationships between the various tephra layers and times of human use of the area. This necessitated a regional research design that required recording of strata from numerous localities, tephra and artifact sampling, and laboratory analyses. The results are presented in the chapters that follow.

Although we have not resolved all problems, we have established a regional tephra sequence (Chap. 2). That sequence, in part, is well related to the Tajo sequence, but some correspondences are not yet confirmed geochemically. Soils did form on top of the tephra layers, during periods of volcanic quiescence, and we found archaeological sites associated with those soils (dark layers in Fig. 1-7; Units 30, 50, 60, and 65 are dark soils formed on lighter-colored volcanic ash layers—Units 40, 55, and 61). Thus, human reuse of the volcanically hazardous area was the norm, with people remaining in the area following thinner ash falls, or reoccupying areas with thick ashfalls only when soil and vegetative recovery were sufficient.

Figure 1-8 presents, in condensed form, the Silencio volcanic unit sequence. Also presented are our best judgments, given present knowledge, of temporal relationships of these volcanic phenomena with cultural periods and ceramic phases.

Another project objective was to determine, insofar as possible, the subsistence strategies of the peoples of the Arenal area. One of the best approaches is direct recovery of carbonized organic remains, and Chapter 16 describes numerous specimens of cultigens. Pollen and phytolith samples were collected for analysis and provide additional subsistence data (see Chaps. 14 and 15). Use wear and other functional analyses of ceramic, ground stone, and chipped stone artifacts contribute important data toward subsistence reconstructions (Chaps. 10–12). Friedman and Gleason (1984) contributed invaluable information on diet, as the stable carbon isotope analysis of bone indicated a maximum of 12% of the diet during the Silencio Phase was from C-4 photosynthetic pathway plants. Because maize is the only known domesticated C-4 plant in prehistoric Costa Rica, and few nondomesticated C-4 plants were available, the consumption of maize must have been minimal.

Another project objective was to determine the variation in site locations, in chronology, and in site functions within the area. We conducted excavations in two funerary sites and in two habitation sites very close to the Continental Divide. We excavated funerary and habitation sites along the Lake Arenal shore. The survey of the present shore of Lake Arenal yielded excellent data on sites of various periods from the Formative to the Conquest (Chap. 3), along with some indications of earlier settlement. Most of the sites are habitations, and some are cemeteries. Two initially problematic large piled laja features near a large graveyard are described by Hoopes and Chenault (Chap. 7). They are now understood to have been repositories for storage of building stone for cemetery construction. They remained enigmatic until

TABLE 1-1
ARENAL PROJECT RADIOCARBON DATE CALIBRATIONS

Sample #	*Project Cat. #*	*Uncorrected Age (BP)*	*Intercepts (BC, AD)*	*1 Sigma Range*	*2 Sigma Range*
SI-577	N/A	400±30	AD 1460	AD 1445–1482	AD 1435–1619
SI-576	N/A	450±30	AD 1440	AD 1430–1449	AD 1416–1471
TX-5079	G-154-A2 #15	570±30	AD 1398	AD 1316–1407	AD 1298–1420
TX-5083	G-175-B7 #51	670±190	AD 1285	AD 1180–1430	AD 990–1640
TX-5077	G-150-C2 #2	740±50	AD 1270	AD 1252–1281	AD 1216–1295
TX-5269	G-164-A9 #87	1130±60	AD 894	AD 879–975	AD 780–1010
TX-5080	G-161-B4 #38	1340±70	AD 666	AD 642–758	AD 590–853
TX-5270	G-164-E18 #102	1410±80	AD 642	AD 567–669	AD 450–775
TX-5082	G-175-B1 #34, 43	1530±130	AD 544	AD 400–650	AD 230–758
TX-5273	G-164-B6 #84	1660±70	AD 398	AD 261–435	AD 230–550
TX-5078	G-150-B5 #4	1770±60	AD 244	AD 145–338	AD 110–410
TX-5272	G-164-A8 #85	1770±60	AD 244	AD 145–338	AD 110–410
TX-5081	G-163-C2 #31, 55	2030±300	43 BC	400 BC–AD 328	810 BC–AD 630
SI-3459	N/A	2170±65	331, *329*, 200 BC	368–120 BC	390–50 BC
TX-5271	G-164-B17 #98	2340±170	399 BC	770–200 BC	830 BC–AD 1
TX-5280	G-163-W35 #76	2470±560	757, 689, *651*, 648, 543 BC	1310 BC–AD 80	1950 BC–AD 660
Aren 2	N/A	2650±115	813 BC	910–780 BC	1050–422 BC
Aren 1	N/A	2895±145	1065 BC	1310–910 BC	1450–800 BC
Aren 3	N/A	3025±150	1305 BC	1440–1040 BC	1630–849 BC
CC-3	N/A	3460±70	1851, *1850*, 1761 BC	1886–1688 BC	1960–1620 BC
TX-5279	G-163-W18 #61	3480±320	1872, 1842, *1813*, 1807, 1777 BC	1897–1749 BC	1970–1694 BC
CC-1	N/A	3500±50	1877, 1834, *1824*, 1793, 1787 BC	2278–1430 BC	2860–1000 BC
CC-2	N/A	3510±120	1880, *1830*, 1829 BC	2027–1689 BC	2192–1530 BC
SI	G-163-I6 #13A	3675±50	2118, *2083*, 2041 BC	2139–1982 BC	2200–1930 BC
TX-5277	G-163-V9 #30	3730±100	2140 BC	2300–1986 BC	2460–1890 BC
TX-5274	G-163-I6 #13	4210±70	2883, *2796*, 2784 BC	2912–2667 BC	3014–2590 BC
TX-5276	G-163-L10 #27	4450±70	3096, *3053*, 3048 BC	3332–2929 BC	3360–2920 BC
TX-5278	G-163-I14 #37	4580±80	3351 BC	3493–3109 BC	3609–3040 BC
TX-5275	G-163-I6 #14	4600±70	3360 BC	3496–3147 BC	3609–3450 BC
TX-5286	AL-186-A2	4890±100	3675 BC	3780–3539 BC	3950–3301 BC

Note: N/A means not applicable.

the remote-sensing imagery detected a prehistoric footpath linking them with the cemetery, a feature that was confirmed by excavations (Chap. 9).

The analysis of artifacts from the project allows for a detailed reconstruction of variation through time and allows for the first detailed artifact sequence for the Cordillera in northwestern Costa Rica. The ceramics were analyzed by Hoopes (Chap. 10), the chipped stone artifacts by Sheets (Chap. 11), and the ground stone artifacts by Chenault (Chap. 12).

CHRONOLOGY AND RADIOCARBON DATING

In order to make all data available, radiocarbon dates are presented in this chapter in a number of ways, as can be seen on Table 1-1. The radiocarbon year estimate, as received from the laboratory, is presented in the column "Uncorrected Age (BP)." It is important to remember that these are radiocarbon years, not calendrical years, and thus it is improper to subtract radiocarbon years

TABLE 1-1
(continued)

Text Format	*Geological Context*	*Archaeological Context*	*Reference*
AD 1445 (1460) 1482	U. 20	N/A	Stuiver and Pearson 1986
AD 1430 (1440) 1449	U. 20	N/A	Stuiver and Pearson 1986
AD 1316 (1398) 1407	Pre–U. 20	Tilarán Ph. ceramics	Stuiver and Pearson 1986
AD 1180 (1285) 1430	?	Pit feature into U. 65	Stuiver and Pearson 1986
AD 1252 (1270) 1281	Post–U. 40, Pre–U. 20	Silencio Phase artifacts	Stuiver and Pearson 1986
AD 879 (894) 975	Pre–U. 41	Hearth and structures	Stuiver and Pearson 1986
AD 642 (666) 758	Post–50s, Pre–U. 41	Arenal Phase artifacts	Stuiver and Pearson 1986
AD 567 (642) 669	Post–U. 55, Pre–U. 41	Arenal Phase artifacts	Stuiver and Pearson 1986
AD 400 (544) 650	Post–U. 55, Pre–U. 41	Arenal Phase artifacts	Stuiver and Pearson 1986
AD 261 (398) 435	Post–U. 55, Pre–U. 41	Arenal Phase artifacts, cemetery	Stuiver and Pearson 1986
AD 145 (244) 338	Post–U. 55, Pre–U. 41	Middle Polychrome cer. early use of cemetery	Stuiver and Pearson 1986
AD 145 (244) 338	Post–U. 55, Pre–U. 41	Arenal Ph. artifacts, hearth between structures	Stuiver and Pearson 1986
400 (43 BC) AD 328	Post–U. 55, Pre–U. 41	Arenal Phase artifacts	Stuiver and Pearson 1986
368 (329) 120 BC	El Tajo U. 8	N/A	Stuiver and Pearson 1986
770 (399) 200 BC	Post–U. 55, Pre–U. 41	Arenal Phase artifacts, burial	Stuiver and Pearson 1986
1310 (651 BC) AD 80	Post–U. 55, Pre–U. 41	Arenal Phase artifacts, from tomb	Pearson and Stuiver 1986
910 (813) 780 BC	Arenal tephra near Q. La Palma	N/A	Pearson and Stuiver 1986
1310 (1065) 910 BC	Arenal tephra near Q. Guillermina	N/A	Pearson and Stuiver 1986
1440 (1305) 1040 BC	Arenal tephra E. of Sangregado Dam	N/A	Pearson and Stuiver 1986
1886 (1850) 1688 BC	Burned organics Base of Cerro Chato	N/A	Pearson and Stuiver 1986
1897 (1824) 1749 BC	U. 65, Pre–U. 61	Assoc. w/ house, Tronadora Phase artifacts	Pearson and Stuiver 1986
2278 (1813) 1430 BC	Burned branches on Cerro Chato	N/A	Pearson and Stuiver 1986
2027 (1830) 1689 BC	Burned branches on Cerro Chato	N/A	Pearson and Stuiver 1986
2139 (2083) 1982 BC	U. 65	Early occupation, lithics	Pearson and Stuiver 1986
2300 (2140) 1986 BC	U. 65	Tronadora Phase & earlier	Pearson and Stuiver 1986
2912 (2796) 2667 BC	Post–U. 65, Pre–U. 61	Early occupation, lithics	Pearson et al. 1986
3332 (3053) 2929 BC	Post–U. 65, Pre–U. 61	Tronadora Ph. artif. & architec.	Pearson et al. 1986
3493 (3351) 3109 BC	U. 65	Fortuna? and Tronadora phases	Pearson et al. 1986
3496 (3360) 3147 BC	U. 65	Early occupation, lithics	Pearson et al. 1986
3780 (3675) 3539 BC	U. 65	Fortuna Phase hearth, lithics	Pearson et al. 1986

Note: N/A means not applicable.

from AD 1950 and treat the result as if it were a date in the BC–AD calendrical system. Had atmospheric percentages of C-14 been constant in the past and present, it would be possible merely to subtract from AD 1950. Radiocarbon levels have varied, however, in history, in prehistory, and particularly in the past few decades with burning of fossil fuels and with atmospheric testing of nuclear weapons. We presented radiocarbon years for all dates, to facilitate comparisons with dates presented in other publications that are expressed in radiocarbon years. Those dates are presented in Table 1-1 in the column "Uncorrected Age (BP)" with their single standard deviations; this means that there is a 67% probability that the true date lies within this range. Because an objective of archaeology is to document and understand human societies within a calendrical framework, it is imperative that radiocarbon dates be calibrated, as accurately as possible, into calendrical dates.

The translation of radiocarbon years to calendrical years is based on studies of the content of organic samples that have precisely known ages, generally tree rings. A number of calibration systems have been devised; we are using the most recent and sophisticated system, as published in *Radiocarbon* in 1986. The column labeled "Intercepts (BC, AD)" presents the date calibrated using the computer program developed by Pearson and Stuiver (1986). In most cases, the radiocarbon year estimate crosses the calibration curve in one place, and thus there is a single intercept; however, the calibration curve, when inspected closely, often comprises a series of small oscillations, so some dates cross the calibration curve at three or even five intercepts. Where there are multiple intercepts, the central one is in italics. Fortunately, multiple intercepts are generally close to each other.

The column "1-Sigma Range" presents each date in the form of the single sigma (standard deviation) span of time, within which there is a 67% probability of the true event's being included. A doubling of the range would give a two-sigma span, and thus present a 95% probability of the true date's lying within that expanded range. It is unfortunate that, as archaeologists began to report radiocarbon dates, the convention became to emphasize the central date rather than the range, as the range is more true to the nature of a radiocarbon date than is a central, single figure. The "Reference" column is the specific source of the calibration program; the earliest dates are calibrated with the Pearson et al. (1986) program. The dates in the range from 2500 to 500 BC are calibrated with the Pearson and Stuiver (1986) program, and the dates more recent than 500 BC are calibrated with the Stuiver and Pearson (1986) program.

The "Text Format" column presents the calibrated date in the form suggested for the text of this volume, with an intercept date calibrated into the BC–AD system, along with a one-sigma range. The date in radiocarbon years is calculated with a one-sigma range that is equidistant on both sides of the mean; however, some people may be surprised that the proper calibration of radiocarbon years into a calendrical format results in a standard deviation that is not symmetrical. This is because the error decreases on one side of the date as it increases on the other side. Part of the reason is that the calibration from radiocarbon years to calendrical years involves a sloping zone that follows the calibration curve on the graph, and intersecting that one-sigma zone at an angle tends to elongate one side and shorten the other, thus resulting in an asymmetrical range.

The University of Texas Radiocarbon Laboratory calculated seven radiocarbon dates on samples submitted in 1984, and on thirteen in 1985. Those dates are accompanied by the three samples Melson submitted to the Smithsonian Lab. We present information on their artifactual and geological contexts to assist in placing them in a local, regional, and national archaeological context.

The oldest sample processed was Tx-5286, from an Archaic (Fortuna Phase) campsite numbered AL-186-A2, calibrated to 3780 (3675) 3539 BC. We found two hearths, considerable thermally fractured cooking stones, and lithic debitage in the Aguacate Formation. We found some possible Archaic lithic debitage and cooking stones at other sites, but not in "pure" deposits such as at this site. Thus, it appears that Archaic inhabitants were well established in the Arenal area at least by 3500 BC, and probably much earlier (we found a Clovis point at G-164), but with fairly low population densities when compared with Panama or Mesoamerica.

G-163-I6 yielded the next-oldest date, dendrocorrected to 3496 (3360) 3144 BC, number Tx-5275. It is from charcoal in the Aguacate Formation, underlying the earliest tephra for which we have knowledge (Unit 61; see Chap. 4). The charcoal sample was associated with two fragments of cooking stones, a small chalcedony percussion flake from biface manufacture, two debitage flakes (one petrified wood and one fine-grained dacite), and three unclassified stones. One of the debitage flakes terminated in a hinge fracture. The lab ran three radiocarbon samples from this one excavated lot, and all resulted in relatively early dates (central intercepts: 3360, 2796, and 2083 BC). We took samples not from a discrete living floor, but from a zone 5–10 cm deep into the top of the Aguacate Formation, the clay-laden tropical soil below the lowest volcanic ash layer from Arenal Volcano. Unfortunately, for dating purposes and for purposes of separating occupations, the Aguacate Formation, composed of gooey clay, is a very plastic horizon. Human utilization of its surface when moist would inevitably result in considerable mixing, and I believe we can see the evidence for that in dates spanning more than a millennium resulting from three samples of charcoal collected from the same depth within the same square meter. Unfortunately, the artifact sample associated with the charcoal samples is small, and direct association of the charcoal and the artifacts is not definitive.

Samples Tx-5278 and Tx-5276 yield two very

similar dates, dendro-corrected to 3493 (3351) 3109 and 3332 (3053) 2929 BC, respectively, both from the upper portion of the Aguacate Formation and both predating the Unit 61 emplacement. It is exceptionally important that both had ceramics associated with the charcoal. Lot I14 from G-163 had two sherds along with three fragments of cooking stones and an unidentified stone, a small sample of artifacts. In contrast, the G-163 lot L10 had sixty-seven sherds associated with it, and twenty-one lithic artifacts. Virtually all of the sherds that could be classified as to phase are from the Tronadora Phase. The lithics include five fragments of cooking stones, four general debitage flakes (two chalcedony, two fine-grained dacite), nine unclassified stones, one fine-grained dacite small percussion flake core, one cooking stone, and one rounded pebble. If the association of the artifacts with the charcoal is sound, this indicates the existence of a sophisticated ceramic and fairly elaborate lithic industry by 3000 BC in the Arenal area.

Another relatively early date, with a tight standard deviation, is Tx-5274, corrected to 2912 (2796) 2667 BC. The charcoal sample is from lot I6 at the G-163 site,, and is associated with an early occupation there. It was located in the upper portion of Unit 65, and antedates the fall of the Unit 61 tephra.

Date Tx-5277 is from G-163-V9, dating to 2300 (2140) 1986 BC, associated with a circular pole-and-thatch house with Tronadora Phase ceramics, cooking stones, and other features. It also antedates the Unit 61 eruption of Arenal Volcano, because we found the volcanic ash in situ overlying the floor of the house, the artifacts, and the charcoal. This apparently is one of the better dates documenting the emergence of sedentary village life and ceramics in northwestern Costa Rica, although some of the dates indicate that both ceramics and structures may have begun at the Tronadora Vieja site more than a millennium earlier.

Tx-5279 is from G-163-W18, dendro-calibrated to 1897 (1824) 1749 BC. It dates another circular house with the same kind of ceramics, artifacts, and other features as Tx-5277 and also antedates the Unit 61 emplacement. It is of less utility than Tx-5277 because of its large standard deviation, but it does tend to substantiate the validity of that date.

A later-phase occupation of the G-163 site (lot W35) yields a date of 1310 (651 BC) AD 80, Tx-5280, with a very large range. It is from a deep "trench" burial dug down into the Aguacate from Unit 54, and is associated with Arenal Phase ceramics. The range covered by the date covers the expected chronological territory, but its wide range limits its usefulness.

The Arenal Phase cemetery, G-164, lot B17, yields a date of 770 (399) 200 BC, Tx-5271, with a moderately large range. The date appears appropriate for the phase, but it seems to be a few centuries earlier than expected. Most of the one-sigma range falls within the Arenal Phase, but the artifacts we found at the cemetery are more typical of the Late Arenal Phase. The Tx-5272 date of AD 145 (244) 338 (G-164-A8) is closer to what we expected from that assemblage of ceramics, and it has a much tighter one-sigma range. It is a large sample of charcoal from a hearth located between two circular pole-and-thatch houses, associated with Arenal Phase ceramics. Stratigraphically, it postdates the Unit 55 eruption and predates the Unit 41 eruption.

We collected sample SI-3459 from the archaeological site of El Tajo, near the volcano, in the soil that had formed on top of Unit 8 in the Tajo sequence, which corresponds with Unit 55 in the Silencio sequence. It calibrates to 368 (329) 120 BC. As it is a site occupied after the soil formed on top of that unit, it more closely dates the emplacement of the next tephra layer, El Tajo Unit 7, which probably corresponds with Unit 53 in the Silencio series.

Date Tx-5081 (G-163-C2) is problematic in that the small sample size resulted in such a large one-sigma standard deviation that it is not very useful. It calibrates to 400 (43 BC) AD 328. The range does overlap both the Tronadora and the Arenal phases, and thus substantiates the proposed chronology in general terms, but it does not help resolve finer dating problems.

We collected date Tx-5078 to date the earlier end of the G-150 (lot B5) Silencio graveyard use, and it turned out to be earlier than expected, at AD 145 (244) 338. We collected it from an undisturbed grave, sealed by ash layers above (Unit 41) and below (Unit 55), and associated with a gold pendant. The dating of gold in northwestern Costa Rica this early, approximately the third century, is surprising, but it should be considered as a real possibility. On the other hand, it is possible that some earlier charcoal was mixed in the tomb fill; there is some ceramic evidence of at least a light use of the site in Arenal Phase times, and some charcoal from that earlier use could have become incorporated into the fill as the tomb was constructed. Thus, the artifact conceivably could be a few hundred years later than the calibrated date.

G-164-B6 yielded a sample that helps date the Arenal Phase large cemetery, at AD 261 (398) 435, and separates the earlier Unit 55 deposition and the later Unit 41 emplacement (Tx-5273). This is a very useful date, with a small standard deviation.

Date Tx-5082 is somewhat helpful, at AD 400 (544) 650, in that it dates late Arenal Phase artifacts and the Unit 50 soil at Site G-175-B1, and thus it antedates the Unit 41 eruption. The one-sigma range is too large to assist in fine-scale dating.

The large Arenal Phase cemetery, G-164-E18, yields a date of AD 567 (642) 669, labeled Tx-5270. It seems slightly late for the artifacts associated with it, but it is possible that such burial practices and the associated artifacts continued into the seventh century. The date is useful to separate the Units 55 and 41 eruptions chronologically, and it closely antedates the Unit 41 emplacement.

Date Tx-5080 is from charcoal associated with late Arenal Phase artifacts from the G-161-B4 site, and thus we expected it to be about AD 300–500. It is a bit more recent than anticipated, at AD 642 (666) 758. Thus, like Tx-5270, it suggests longer continuation of Zoned Bichrome traditions and sets a lower parameter for the Unit 41 emplacement.

The Tx-5269 sample yields a date of AD 879 (894) 975, from lot G-164-A9, a hearth between two circular houses, in the habitation area below the cemetery. The Tx-5272 sample is from a companion hearth between the same two houses, and the two hearths must have been used almost simultaneously. However, this date is too recent, according to the Late Arenal Phase artifacts found throughout the site, and I suspect the sample may have been contaminated by contemporary organic material in the lake water. The hearth had been disturbed by wave action.

Date Tx-5077 is from the later use of the high-status cemetery, G-150-C2, and is about the time expected, based on artifactual comparisons, at AD 1252 (1270) 1281. Given the fact that two rather thick ash layers, Units 41 and 40, separate the two times of graveyard use, one might expect a considerable time break between uses, allowing time for soil and vegetation recovery. And that might lead to the expectation that artifacts would show differences, based on a few centuries of culture change; however, artifact analyses indicate very little culture change. In Mesoamerica it would be unusual to find so little culture change over so many centuries, with the disruptions of two major explosive volcanic eruptions, but Arenal-area residents showed remarkable resiliency to volcanic perturbation and striking persistence of cultural traditions. And, some of the inhabitants who continued using the graveyard may have lived a considerable distance from it, farther outside the area severely affected by the ashfall, and thus have been minimally affected.

Date Tx-5083 is curious, at AD 1180 (1285) 1430, in that we collected it from an intrusive pit at site G-175-B7 that had Arenal Phase ceramics above and in it, yet it is surprisingly young. It does carry a moderately large standard deviation. We suspect sample contamination by inclusion of younger charcoal, but there was no field evidence of disturbance.

Date Tx-5079 chronologically fixes the latest occupation of the Silencio area, the Tilarán Phase, at AD 1316 (1398) 1407, based on remains at the habitation site G-154-A2. It postdates Units 41 and 40 and very closely predates the deposition of Unit 20, and thus makes an archaeological and volcanological contribution.

The SI-576 sample, at AD 1430 (1440) 1449, dates the emplacement of the Unit 20 tephra by dating the outer growth layers of a tree Melson found carbonized by that eruption near Arenal Volcano. Given the fact that a fire in a hearth burns contemporary and earlier growth rings of firewood, and thus generates a calibrated date somewhat earlier than the true age, this date and the Tx-5079 sample from a Tilarán Phase habitation buried by that ash appear exceptionally close. The last big eruption of Arenal Volcano is thus dated to the middle of the fifteenth century.

In summary, the radiocarbon dates with tight one-sigma ranges help in more precise dating of cultural and natural events in the Arenal area. Only one date (Tx-5083) is far beyond the anticipated range and is not useful.

THE ARCHAEOLOGICAL PHASES

The Arenal Project, based on considerable discussion, analyses, comparisons, and interpretations, has come up with what we feel is a relatively accurate and useful subdivision of the cultural sequence in the research area. It is composed of five phases, two of which are subdivided into facets. It begins with the Fortuna Phase, part of the Middle American Archaic Period. We have no quantitative evidence of when it began in the area, but the presence of the Clovis point may indicate that the area was inhabited as early as the tenth millennium BC. A rough guess of the Paleo-Indian—Archaic transition would be about 7000 BC. We created no named phase for the Paleo-Indian occupation of the basin, because the project did not excavate a chronometrically dated assemblage from the Paleo-Indian Period.

Defined conservatively, the Fortuna Phase, the local manifestation of the Archaic, ends at 2000 BC with the advent of sedentary villages, permanent structures, and ceramics. However, ceramics and postholes of structures are associated with two radiocarbon dates from the G-163 site that are between 3500 and 3000 BC. We have decided to draw the Archaic/Formative boundary at the conservative end of that range, at 3000 BC. One of the urgent future research priorities in the area is to understand human events in the millennium prior to 3000 BC, to research the changes from the Archaic into the Tronadora Phase.

The Tronadora Phase (2000–500 BC) saw the spread of small sedentary villages, based in part on maize agriculture. Unlike in Mesoamerica, Arenal-area residents avoided reliance on a maize staple by maintaining a diversified subsistence strategy using domesticated and wild species from the Tronadora through the Tilarán phases. Burials apparently were secondary, in small rectangular pits, within the villages. The chipped- and ground stone tools were simple and functional, but ceramics were surprisingly elaborate and sophisticated, showing affinities with early Formative pottery from northwestern South America and particularly with southern Mesoamerican pottery.

The Arenal Phase (500 BC–AD 600), the local expression of the Zoned Bichrome horizon, witnessed a peak in population density. Cemeteries were separated from households and were often constructed on ridges above villages. Domestic housing and lithic industries show little change, except that metates were becoming elaborated.

A population decline occurred during the Silencio Phase (AD 600–1300), as both the number and the size of sites decreased. Both chipped- and ground stone manufacture became slightly more elaborate, and polychrome ceramics began. Burials were primary, with bodies placed in cists made of flat-fracturing stone slabs. Cemeteries were at considerable distances from sources of stone and sources of bodies (i.e., villages). Remote-sensing imagery provided by NASA contains numerous linear anomalies, some of which have been confirmed as prehistoric footpaths linking cemeteries with villages, stone sources, stone storage areas, and springs.

Population continued to decline during the Tilarán Phase (AD 1300–1500). The strong cultural affiliation with Greater Nicoya that characterized the Arenal and Silencio phases was reversed, and the closest ties were with the east and the south. The settlement pattern became more dispersed, with hamlets widely scattered across the countryside. Decorative elaboration on pottery declined, as elaborate polychromes disappeared. Most pottery was monochrome, with occasional decoration by plastic surface manipulation and zoomorphic appliqués. The durability of ceramics was at its worst, evidently due to less care in manufacture.

AN ETHNOGRAPHIC ANALOG

It is often useful to use ethnography as a guide or stimulus for archaeological interpretation, so long as it is not used mechanistically. With that objective in mind, I suggest the use of Posey's ethnographic data (1983) on the Kayapó to stimulate interpretations of our project data. The following comes from Posey unless otherwise cited.

The Kayapó are an egalitarian tribal society living in the tropical rain forest of central Brazil. About 2,500 Kayapó live in a 2 million ha area, which is about 1.3 people per km^2. They inhabit nine sedentary villages, set in one of the most species-diverse environments in the world.

The Kayapó perceive their environment in terms of a series of ecological zones and subzones. The three principal zones are forest, mountains, and grasslands. Each of these is subdivided into an extensive series of categories, based on vegetation, soils, and other factors. The Kayapó are very sensitive to natural hazards and plant in a variety of areas to minimize risk. For instance, planting in the rich black alluvial soil can produce high yields, but it also can yield little or nothing when flooding occurs.

The Kayapó ecological classifications emphasize transitions between zones rather than demarcate clear, normative zones. Interestingly, they choose village sites deliberately in these transitional zones in order to take maximum advantage of zonal diversity. Also, the seasonal variation in nearby zones is important, because different zones provide varied plant and animal resources at different times in the annual round.

The number of wild plants used by the Kayapó is astounding. Posey estimates 250 plant species are used solely for their fruits, and this does not include plants used for their tubers, nuts, leaves, bark, or for medicinal purposes.

The Kayapó have an extensive inventory of cultivated plants, including manioc, maize, tobacco, beans, squash, cotton, pineapples, sweet potatoes, and papaya. They also have numerous domesticated medicinal plants.

A "vast network," consisting of thousands of kilometers of footpaths through the rain forest, links villages with hunting areas, current and previously worked gardens, and "natural resource islands." The last are natural openings in the forest canopy where some light penetrates to the ground. They are viewed as the natural equivalent to a garden plot, where people do the cutting to bring the level of photosynthesis closer to the ground. Both the natural resource islands and the active gardens are perceived as similar to abandoned gardens; the latter are still utilized for some species for many years after they have ceased being closely tended. The natural resource islands occur along trails and are considered "improved" natural forest. The Kayapó gather wild species of plants and deliberately plant them in the islands to provide food. Thus, when the men are on a hunting expedition, for 2 to 4 weeks, they carry very little food with them. They rely primarily on these pockets of improved forest. They also plant some semidomesticated species in forest fields, some at large distances from the village for use while hunting, while closer forest fields are used on day trips or are located at standard campsites. At least fifty-four species are planted in these forest fields. Posey uses the term "nomadic agriculture" to express the mobility and dispersed nature of their adaptation.

SUMMARY AND CONCLUSIONS

We conducted multidisciplinary research, involving archaeology, volcanology, pedology, remote sensing, and botany, in the Arenal area of northwestern Costa Rica from 1984 through 1987. We investigated habitation and funerary sites on the eastern and the western side of the Continental Divide. We found evidence of occupation of the area extending from the Paleo-Indian and Archaic periods through all the sedentary, ceramic-producing Formative phases to the Spanish Conquest. Village life was established by 2000 BC.

Certainly, the sophisticated ceramics and sedentism were important changes, yet other components of the presedentary life-style continued for 3,500 years to the Conquest. Prehistoric societies in the Arenal area avoided economies of dependency, and they maintained population densities lower than in other areas to the north and the south. We see both of these factors as major reasons for a remarkable record of continuity and cultural stability, in contrast with the instability of civilizations in Mesoamerica and the Andean areas. That stability was maintained in spite of at least nine large explosive eruptions of Arenal Volcano. These Arenal-area societies were more resilient to volcanic perturbation than were their more complex neighbors in Mesoamerica, as predicted by hazard theory.

Arenal-area prehistoric residents remained minimally agricultural, a factor that probably contributed to their superior recovery from volcanic-ecologic disasters, as well as contributing to the strong cultural continuity in the area. The most recent research employed digital and optical remote-sensing technology to find linear anomalies, which was followed by trenching the anomalies in the field to confirm or deny them as prehistoric footpaths.

This chapter describes the natural environment, presents the archaeological background for the research, the specific research objectives, and the results of research conducted in the area by project personnel during the past few years.

VOLUME ORGANIZATION

The order of presentation of the chapters in this volume is from general and regional to more specific. The regional volcanological sequence and the extensive lakeshore survey results are presented first. These are followed by a chapter on the earliest village yet found in Costa Rica, dating to about 2000 BC. The next two chapters focus on excavations into two funerary sites, one on the lakeshore and one on the Continental Divide. Then, information on the two laja features and two habitation sites in Finca El Silencio is presented, along with the detection of prehistoric footpaths by remote-sensing imagery and their verification by excavations. Detailed artifactual analyses follow the excavated site data. The final data chapters present results of pollen, phytolith, and macrobotanical analyses, which give information on cultigens and utilized wild plants. The last chapter presents the overview of research, setting it in the context of Intermediate Area research, and attempts to assess the contributions made, as well as the areas for future research.

ACKNOWLEDGMENTS

This research has benefited from the assistance of numerous institutions and individuals. The National Science Foundation (grants BNS8310599, 8419879, 8520829, and 8616312) and the National Geographic Society (grant 2728—83) provided funding, and their assistance is gratefully acknowledged. Sincerely appreciated are the publication subvention funds from the Committee on University Scholarly Publications of the University of Colorado, and from the Stennis Space Center of NASA. Other sources of funding include the Council on Research and Creative Work and the Institute of Behavioral Science of the University of Colorado. Gordon R. Willey at Harvard University graciously assisted John Hoopes's research. The Museo Nacional de Costa Rica has been exceedingly helpful, and I would particularly like to thank Lorena San Román, Marco Herrera, Lorena Aguilar, and Maritza Gutiérrez. The Comisión Nacional graciously granted permission for the project. ICE was helpful in granting permission for research on their property around Lake Arenal. The Anthropology Department of the Universidad de Costa Rica was of assistance in a number of ways. Michael Snarskis assisted the project in overcoming a variety of small and large problems and has contributed timely advice and general assistance. Fred Lange has always "been there" with sage counsel, enthusiasm, and his unique jokes.

Alonso Benavides, Associated Colleges of the Midwest, graciously provided a vehicle and housing during a key week. Patty and Robert Drolet also provided a vehicle and housing in the early days of the project, and their assistance is gratefully acknowledged. Tom Sever of NASA has contributed invaluable remotely sensed data along with sage interpretations and assistance in two seasons of field verification. Aida Blanca Vargas was very helpful in aiding the identification of archaeobotanical remains. Barbara and Earl Bolton donated over three months of volunteer work in the laboratory, in mapping and in drafting, and their commitment to the tedious tasks that helped keep the project running is certainly appreciated.

The landowners who graciously granted permission for surveys and excavations deserve vigorous acknowledgment. Clara Corneli, Luis and Gabriella Jiménez, and Yolanda Peraza are some of the finest people it has been my pleasure to know. It would be difficult to overstate the contribution made by the students on the project: Mark Chenault, John Bradley, Roberta Klausing-Bradley, Nancy Mahaney, Brian McKee, Marilynn Mueller, and John Hoopes. Meredith Matthews' contribution toward understanding utilized plant species was central to project success. Their dedication during difficult circumstances will forever be appreciated.

Certainly, there were numerous difficulties, including a serious automobile accident, a computer seized by Customs for weeks, a computer roasted by a large line surge, millions of ticks, numerous scorpions, inquisitive noxious snakes, deep mud, torrential rainstorms, and other unanticipated aspects of fieldwork. To all the people who have facilitated our research, a hearty *muchísimas gracias.*

I wish to express special gratitude to Brian McKee for his drawing of several maps in the survey chapter.

This chapter has benefited by critical readings by William Melson, David Wagner, and Brian McKee. Their assistance is greatly appreciated; they should not be held responsible for its shortcomings.

2

The Eruption of 1968 and Tephra Stratigraphy of Arenal Volcano

WILLIAM G. MELSON

INTRODUCTION

My 1984 article on volcanology (Melson 1984) concentrates primarily on the stratigraphic record of the prehistoric eruptions of Arenal. To provide background, some of that information is repeated here, but in this chapter, emphasis is shifted to the catastrophic eruptions of 1968, which provide a stratigraphic model for the interpretation of Arenal's prehistoric eruptions. The description of the 1968 eruption also is relevant to appreciating the impact on prehistoric Indian cultures of at least nine even more intense eruptions.

ARENAL VOLCANO

Arenal Volcano (10° 27.8′N, 84° 42.3′W) is a small stratovolcano (Figs. 2-1 and 2-2) in the Cordillera Central of Alajuela Province. To the west is a large graben, which was formerly filled by a natural marshy lake and which has now been flooded to create the reservoir of the Arenal hydroelectric project. Just to the southeast, and overlapping onto Arenal Volcano, is the presumably extinct, truncated volcano Cerro Chato (Fig. 2; see also Malavassi 1979).

In 1968 Arenal Volcano had the most violent eruption in Costa Rica's recorded history, resulting in a number of hot avalanches and base surges, impact field destruction (Fudali and Melson 1972), major devastation of arable land and rain forest, and about eighty-seven fatalities. The work reported here stems directly from studies of this eruption (Melson and Saenz 1968, 1973; Mi-

Figure 2-1.
Arenal (center) and Cerro Chato (lower right) volcanoes on March 16, 1961, prior to the 1968 catastrophic eruptions of Arenal. Photograph by William Melson.

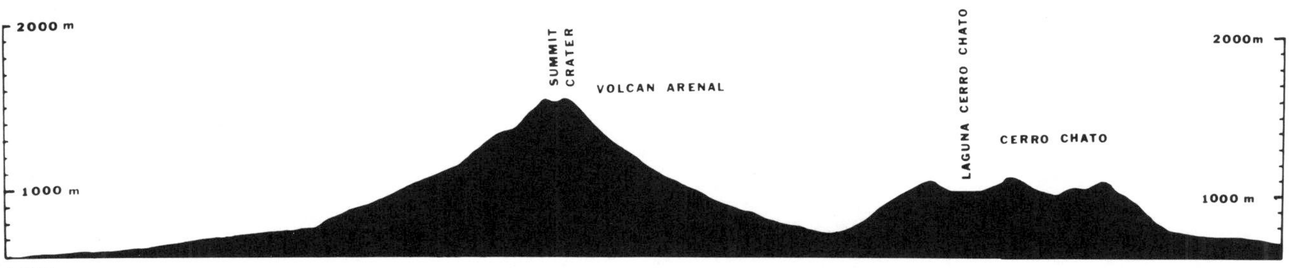

Figure 2-2.
Topographic profile of Arenal and Cerro Chato volcanoes. Vertical and horizontal scales are the same. Graph by William Melson.

nakami et al. 1969) and subsequent work that has led to the recognition of nine additional major explosive eruptions (Melson 1982, 1984; Borgia et al. 1988). It is possible that prehistoric sites were buried catastrophically, although none were uncovered in the present investigations. In the explosive eruptions of 1968, small farms were buried near Arenal, much closer to the volcano than where our excavations have so far been carried out.

As of July 1992 Arenal Volcano continued to erupt. The activity consisted of periodic lava flows, gas emissions, lava fountains, and weak-to-intense explosions, the last producing eruption columns that occasionally reached over 5,000 m above the summit crater and some accompanied by hot avalanches (nuees ardentes). An eruptive sequence with these components is termed "vulcanian" (Decker and Hadikusumo, 1961), and Arenal is important as one of a few volcanoes in the world having ongoing intense vulcanian eruptions punctuated by periods of less-intense explosions and accompanying lava flows, better termed "strombolian eruptions." A number of large nuees ardentes (Fig. 2-3), some reaching over 2 km from the summit crater, show that activity during 1989–1991 was intense on occasion.

REGIONAL GEOLOGIC SETTING

The active Costa Rican volcanoes are all major stratovolcanoes that are characterized by eruptions with considerable pyroclastic activity. Costa Rican volcanoes (Fig. 2-4) generally increase in both elevation and frequency of eruption moving from northwest (Orosi) to southeast (Turrialba). Arenal marks a dip in the elevation trend. Based on the dates of its prehistoric eruptions, it may be one of the youngest of the major Costa Rican volcanoes. Poas and Irazú have been the most active historically, but the 1968 eruption of Arenal was the most violent in Costa Rican history in terms of the loss of human life (Minakami et al. 1969; Melson and Saenz 1973; Saenz and Melson 1976). Studies initiated as a result of that eruption have revealed that Arenal and Turrialba have been the most active Costa Rican volcanoes in terms of cataclysmic eruptions over the past several thousand years (Melson et al. 1986).

Arenal is at the northwest end of a series of progressively older, closely spaced volcanic cones. Cerro Chato (Figs. 2-1 and 2-2) has been partially buried on the west by the growth of Arenal and is the next-to-youngest cone in this "micro-volcanic chain."

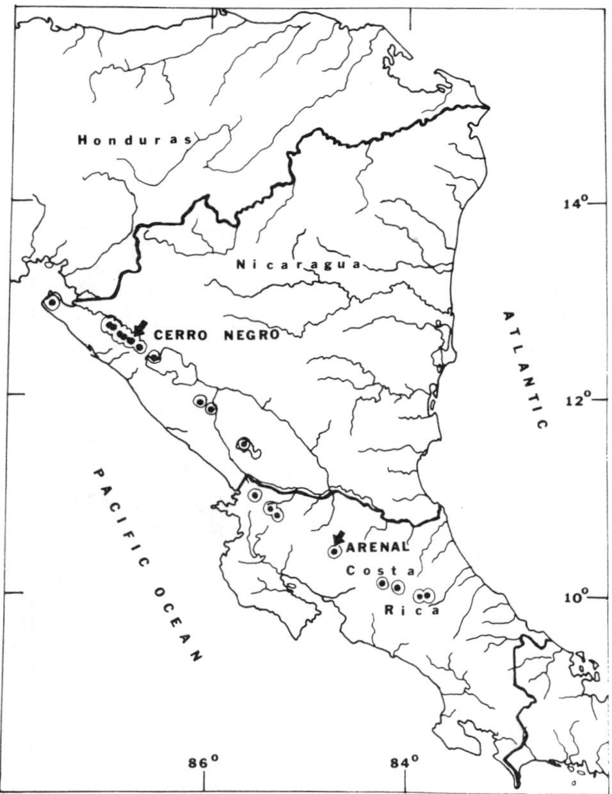

Figure 2-3.
Above: *Pyroclastic flow on west side of Arenal Volcano, July 13, 1987. Photograph by William Melson.*

Figure 2-4.
Left: *Location of Arenal Volcano. Cerro Negro, Nicaragua, which also erupted in 1968–1969 is labeled. Map by William Melson.*

Figure 2-5.
Facing page: *Arenal's three new explosive craters (*A, C, *and* D*), which opened between July 29 and 31, 1968.* B *represents the slope between them. Photographed August 5, 1968. Photograph by William Melson.*

CATASTROPHIC ERUPTIONS IN 1968

The following summary covers some of the dramatic events during the July 29–31, 1968, cataclysmic explosions of Arenal. The data come from interviews made by Rodrigo Saenz, Tom Simkin and me just after these explosions and from accounts published in the San José newspaper *La Nación* during and just after the disaster.

Yolanda Quesada provided a summary of her interviews with residents of Pueblo Nuevo concerning events before and during the initial explosions on the morning of July 29, 1968. In 1966, people at Pueblo Nuevo noticed that some stream waters draining from the volcano had become "sour, hot and tasted like Alka Seltzer." Weak earthquakes occurred for more than a week on one occasion. One small lake dried out after its temperature rose and it became milky. On Sunday, July 28, 1968, just before the first explosion, earthquakes began at about midnight. The first one in the initial series was the most intense. At about 4:00 AM, July 29, a still-stronger earthquake occurred, with "ground motion from east to west, and the other ones were from north to south and some were vertical." Before the explosion there were ground movements "from one side and then the other" and it was rainy and windy. Immediately before the eruption the rain stopped.

A minute before the first explosion people heard sounds like those of "three jet planes passing overhead." During the explosions, there were heavy rains and strong winds, and after the explosions it was stormy. The eruption itself sounded like the detonation of dynamite. Vapors from the eruption were rich in "sulfur acids" and children became nauseated.

A particularly valuable account of the initial explosion was provided by a Sr. Arraya, who lived near the Río Tabacón road crossing 5.5 km northwest of the volcano summit. He reported that intense earthquakes began at 10:58 PM, July 28. He remembered the time well because he had just heard it on the radio. The earthquakes increased in intensity until a few minutes before the climactic explosion of July 29. The earthquakes were so violent during the night that he and his wife moved from their house, which was on poles, to a house next door that was not on poles.

At about 7:00 AM, after the night of intense earthquakes, he and his wife left to visit their daughter and her family at Tabacón to see if they

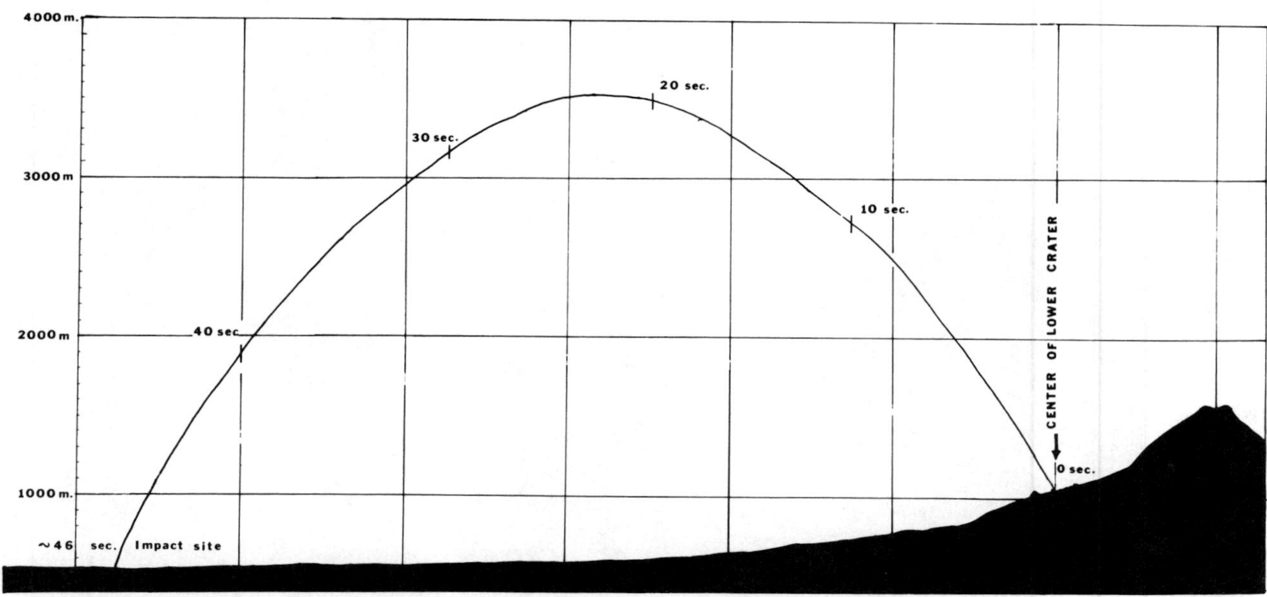

Figure 2-6.
Calculated trajectory of a block ejected from the lower crater onto Tabacón (impact site). Graph by William Melson.

Figure 2-7.
Impact crater field near Tabacón, August 5, 1968. Photograph by William Melson.

Figure 2-8.
Individual impact crater near Tabacón. Photograph by William Melson.

Figure 2-9.
Aerial view of impact field about 1.5 km south of Tabacón. Note black lahar deposits and the few trees that remain standing. Photograph by William Melson.

were all right. They never arrived. As they were walking, about 100 m from Tabacón, the first large explosion occurred. He first heard a noise he describes as a "tapping noise," then saw two dark, ground-hugging clouds moving down the volcano's lower flanks (the opening of the lowermost new crater, Crater A, Figs. 2-5 and 2-6) followed by the sound of a large explosion. Several clouds moved outward and he noted a vertical eruption column. He and his wife were quickly engulfed by an ash and steam cloud. It was warm, but not hot. Then, a "pressure wave" (shock wave) threw them to the ground when they were already covered by ashes. He said the pressure wave was like a strong wind and that the ground moved up and down violently. He neither heard nor saw impacting blocks (Figs. 2-5–2-9), but saw lightning in the eruption cloud. Also, a torrential rain started about 5 minutes after the ash cloud engulfed them. He smelled "sulfur" gas and found it hard to breathe. His wife's face turned brown as if she'd been sunburned. He thinks this was from a slight burn, one not severe enough to cause blistering. Also, his wife had a deep yellow conden-

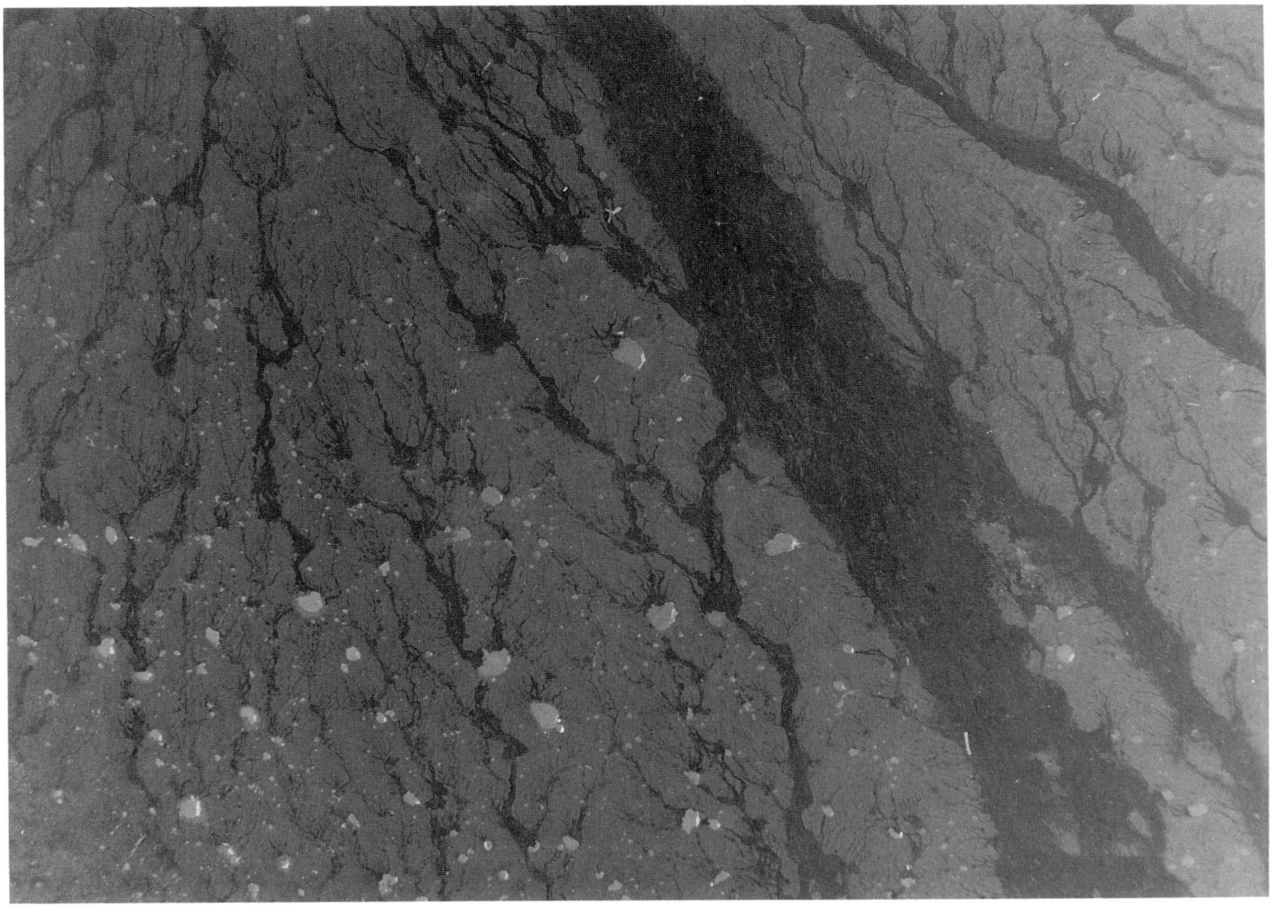

Figure 2-10.
Humans and animals were killed by a combination of hot ash, noxious gasses (mainly SO_2, H_2SO_4, and HCl), and impacting rock fragments. Photograph by William Melson.

Figure 2-11.
Collapsed corral just east of Pueblo Nuevo. Photograph by William Melson.

sation on her hair (iron chlorides or sulfur?). Burns on his bare arms occurred beneath patches of ash and were perhaps caused by both the high temperatures and the acid content of the ash. During this time, cattle around Tabacón were killed (Fig. 2-10).

The couple remained on the ground where they had been "hit" for about one hour and then headed back, that is, northward, to La Palma. Ash continued to fall for the entire hour they were on the ground and was still falling when they left. They had hoped to be rescued where they'd fallen, but were not. Four days later, while he was still in the hospital, he learned that their daughter, her husband, and their six children had been killed at Tabacón the same morning that he and his wife had been injured, presumably during the same explosion that knocked them to the ground. *La Nación* (July 30, p. 30) reported that the town of Tabacón had practically disappeared (located at impact site in Fig. 2-5).

A witness living near the Chiquito River reported that minutes before the first eruption "I could hear, along with other workers, a noise just like a fleet of big airplanes that filled the whole sky, cloudy, without sun, and much water. The eruption was followed by immense flames. The second eruption was the strongest. It came at 11:30 flinging a great quantity of burning lava."

Most of the estimated eighty-seven fatalities occurred in the explosions of July 29, and most *fincas* near the volcano were abandoned by that evening. By the next day, three thousand to four thousand people had been evacuated to Tilarán and Cañas. At Tronadora, about 20 km west of the summit, there was a "heavy rain of ashes" in the morning and, at the same time, there were "tremendous subterranean" rumblings (ibid., p. 28) and intermittently heavy rains for more than forty hours made the situation there even more difficult. No casualties occurred at Tronadora; all were restricted to within about 5 km of the summit. The total thickness of ashfall at Tronadora was about 4 cm.

In La Mansión on Nicoya, it was reported that the "hills . . . are white with ash. We do not know which volcano is erupting." From the air, it was reported that "it is incredible in the amount of territory that the eruptions are covering, some of which pass beyond Guanacaste and reach the Pacific by way of the Nicoya Peninsula." In Santa Cruz, 70 km west of Arenal, automobiles had to turn their lights on at 11:00 AM. Don Miguel Salquero, one of the editors of *La Nación*, re-

Figure 2-12.
View of devastated zone from the rim of the lowermost crater, August 1968. Photograph by William Melson.

ported that the eruption reminded him of the blind days of 1963 during the activity of Irazú, except that the affected area was more extensive and the ashfall heavier. In Liberia, 80 km WNW of Arenal, ashfall was so intense during the night of July 30 that visibility scarcely reached 10 m. By 5:30 PM, it was raining heavily and the city of Tilarán, 30 km to the west, had been almost totally evacuated. The traffic on the road between Tilarán and Cañas "looked like Central Avenue in San José" as people fled from Arenal.

Strong winds at ground level greatly aggravated rescue work in the devastated zone. During the afternoon of July 29, winds gusted to 50 km/per hour. Nonetheless, by the afternoon of July 30, sixty-five bodies had been recovered. "At three-thirty in the afternoon in the tiny cemetery of the destroyed town of Arenal (some buildings had collapsed from the weight of ash on their roofs but there were no casualties there), marked by a scenario gray with ashes, and of destruction and death, a small group of dirty and sweaty men led by the Bishop of Tilarán, Monsignor Román Arrieta, gave a Christian burial to thirty-six bodies of neighbors of the locality that Monday

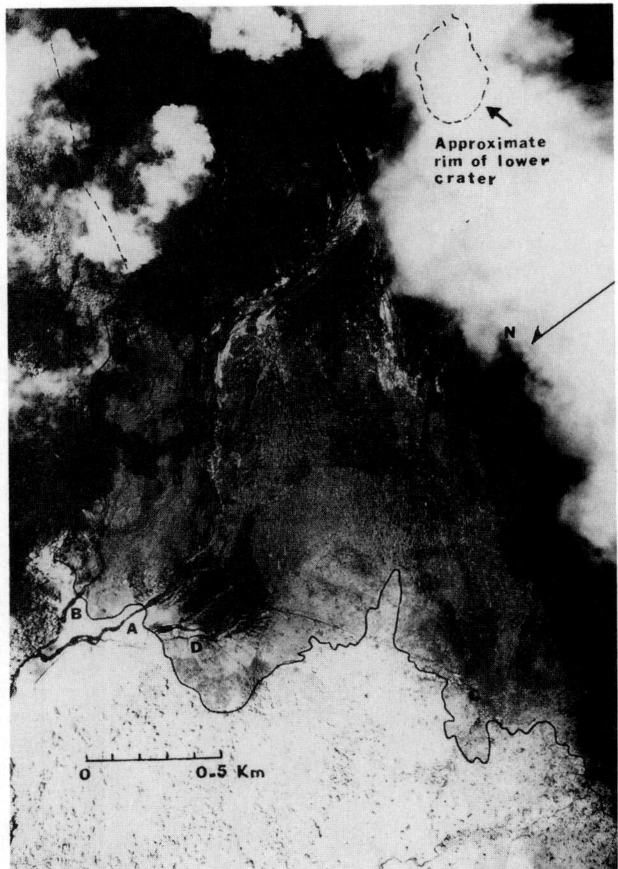

Figure 2-13.
Aerial view of the northwestern side of the devastated zone, mostly devastated by the July 31, 1968, hot avalanche and associated base surge. A: *Río Tabacón;* B: *Río Agua Caliente;* C: *town of Tabacón;* D: *site where jeeps were destroyed and eight men killed. Photograph by William Melson.*

morning had lost their lives calcined by the heat of the igneous rocks that crushed or asphyxiated them in the ashes that in millions of tons Arenal Volcano threw over them at mid-morning, Monday July 29. To the prayers and funeral responses of the bishop, the old volcano responded with a muffled and frightening roar, a volcano thought to be extinct but which had awakened suddenly to sow death and destruction on one of the richest agricultural and cattle areas of the country" (*La Nación*, July 31, p. 27) (Figs. 2-10, 2-11, and 2-12).

By July 30, observations near Arenal showed that the explosions had not come from the old summit crater but from one or more new explosion craters that had opened on the west side of the cone (Fig. 2-5). Calculations of likely trajectories for the impacting blocks that destroyed Tabacón indicate that it took only about 50 seconds from the time of the explosion(s) to the impact of the blocks (Fig. 2-6).

The initial eruption, at 7:30 AM, July 29, was followed by at least eight major explosions over the next 54 hours. The two most intense, based on the detection of infrasonic waves as far away as Boulder, Colorado, at the National Oceanic and Atmospheric Administration infrasonic station, were at 2:30 PM, July 30 and 1:10 PM, July 31. The latter explosion was the last cataclysmic one. In it, a hot avalanche moved down the Tabacón River and hot, ash-rich, hurricanelike winds on the margins leveled trees and killed eight men involved in rescue operations (Figs. 2-13 and 2-14). After this, there was a period of comparatively quiet ash emission from the new upper crater.

Starting on September 19, 1968, lava flows were emitted from the lower crater (Fig. 2-15). Figure 2-16 summarizes the eruptive phases and Figure 2-17 shows the area devastated during the explosions. All fatalities occurred within this zone. Neither fatalities nor destruction of buildings occurred in the region of our archaeological excavations, although inhabitants fled those areas because of the ashfall and the intense sound of the explosions. Most of the area between Tilarán and the Aguas Gatas River was reinhabited within two weeks after the end of the explosions. Figure 2-18 shows the airfall tephra thicknesses downwind from Arenal measured in March 1969, about 7 months after the explosions. The soil to the west of Aguas Gatas River was successfully replanted within one month of the eruptions as far east as the town of Arenal (Arenal Viejo, now beneath the reservoir), and pastures, grayed by the heavy ashfall, were again green.

Figure 2-14.
Surface of July 31, 1968, hot avalanche in the Tabacón River Valley. Photograph by William Melson.

On July 17, 1975, nearly 7 years after the cataclysmic explosions, a large explosion occurred, although far less intense than those of the initial phases. By this time, the activity had shifted to the uppermost active crater (Crater C, Fig. 2-17) and Crater A was buried beneath lava flows and no longer active. A fallback hot avalanche accompanied the explosion and moved down the Tabacón River and eventually reached the Arenal River. A hot bath and restaurant have been built on this avalanche at the La Fortuna-Sangregado Dam Road crossing of the Tabacón River, a most hazardous location indeed! The Tabacón River drainage basin is one of the most likely areas to again be devastated by hot avalanches should there be renewed large explosions.

ARENAL STRATIGRAPHIC MODEL

The 1968 eruptive cycle of Arenal provides a key to understanding the prehistoric eruptions. Near the volcano, the lowermost 1968 tephra consists of a basal coarse layer derived from the intense explosions of July 28–31, 1968. At distances greater than about 15 km, differentiation of these layers was not possible. On top of these coarse layers, fine ash layers were deposited during the waning pyroclastic phase. Beneath the 1968 explosive layers, a soil had developed on tephra deposited around AD 1500. Recent work by Chiesa (1987) indicates that this soil, on top of Unit 2, may be about 1,000 years old; however, many data from the archaeological excavations support the

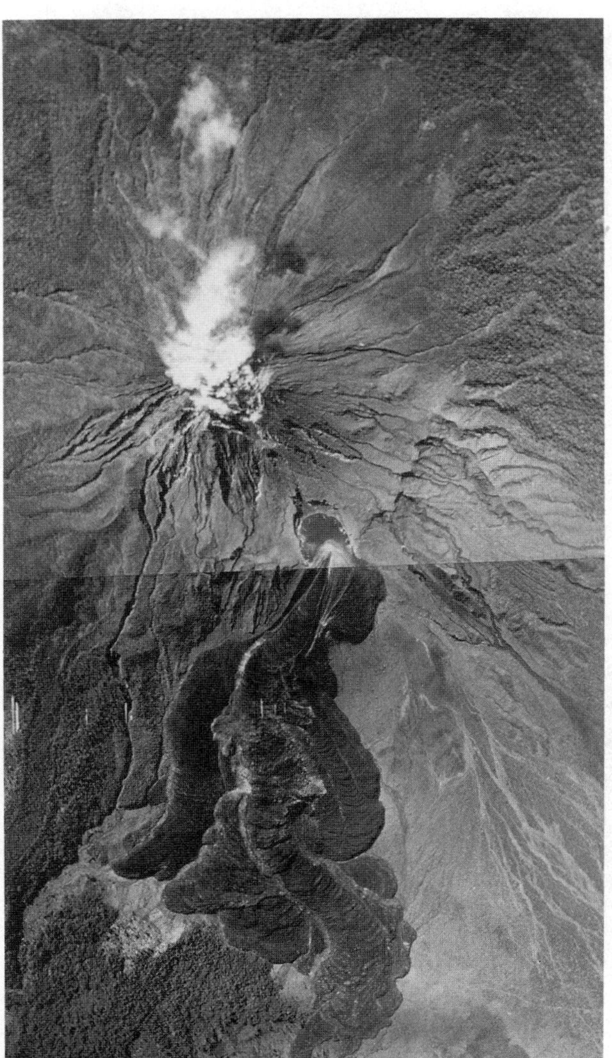

Figure 2-15.
Lava flows from the lower crater erupted between 1968 and 1971. Photograph by William Melson.

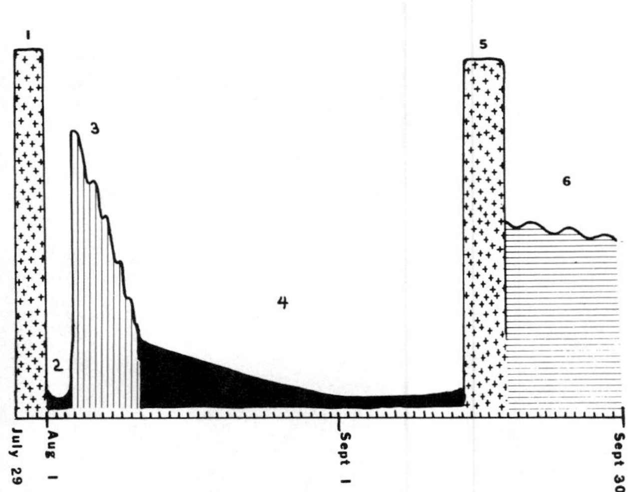

Figure 2-16.
Summary of the July 29–September 30, 1968, eruptive phases. 1: catastrophic explosions; 2: fumerolic phase; 3: renewed ash emission with frequent "jetplane–sounding whooshes"; 4: another fumerolic phase; 5: renewed but much less intense explosions of andesitic scoria from the lower crater, followed by 6: emission of lava flows from the lower crater. Graph by William Melson.

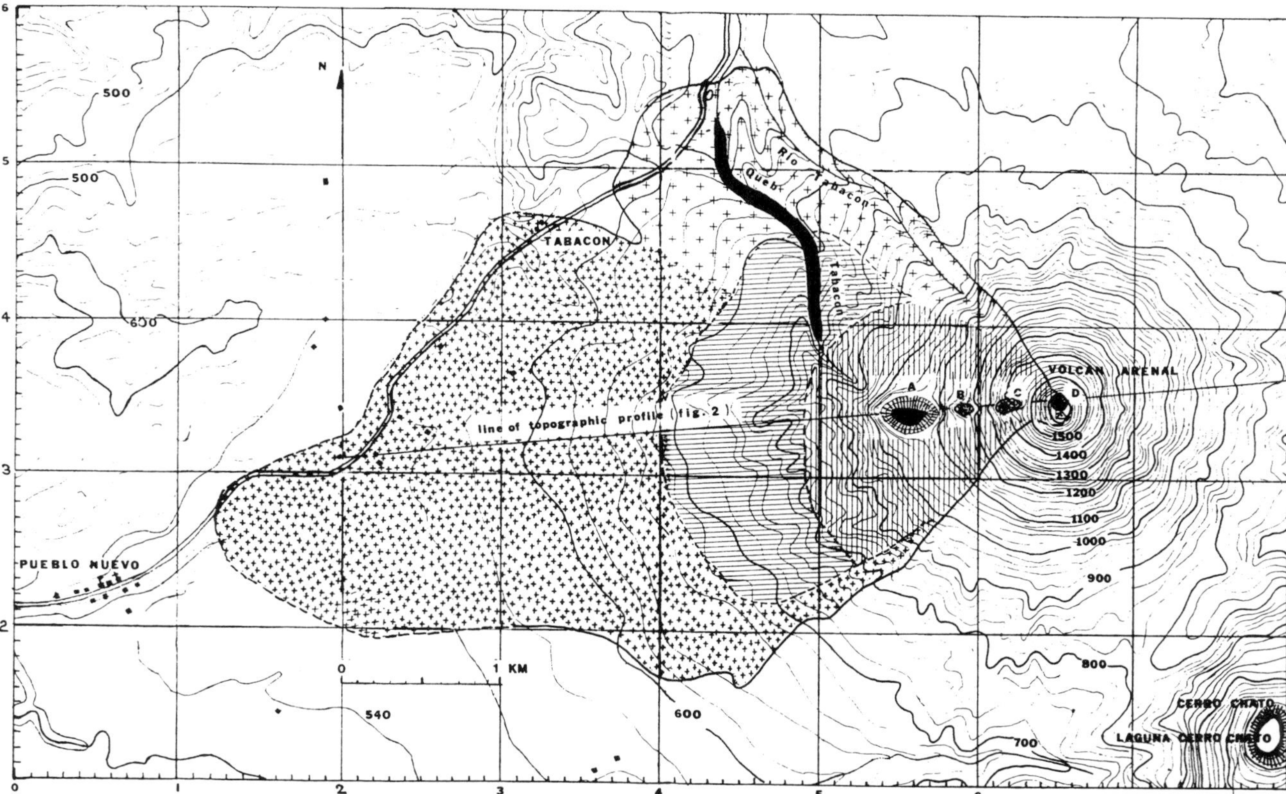

Figure 2-17.
Zone devastated by the explosions and hot avalanches of July 28–31, 1968. Map by William Melson.

ca. AD 1500 age. In our excavations we typically find similar coarse basal layers on earlier paleosols. Also, as in the 1968 eruption, the coarse layers are overlain by fine tephra (Fig. 2-19). Thus, we have inferred that each of Arenal's explosive eruptions began with violent ejection of coarse tephra, followed by finer layers, on which soil A horizons have formed. We have found that tephra that falls into tropical rain forests on flat areas is commonly well preserved. Rarely, minor erosional unconformities occur because erosion in such areas is minimal, even with high rainfall, because of the heavy vegetation cover. Falling trees, various burrowing animals, and the activities of people can cause small-scale disturbance of sections. We have found that tephra units are continuous over broad areas as long as individual tephra sets are thicker than about 50 cm to 100 cm. Where the units are thinner, bioturbation and other processes disturb and mix sets, making specific tephra set identifications difficult or impossible.

The major eruptions of Arenal involved Plinian ejections, which typically tapped compositionally zoned magma chambers that were more acidic at the top. This is particularly obvious for Unit 5 (Fig. 2-19), where a white dacitic basal pumice

Figure 2-18.
Downwind (to west) thickness of 1968 and Unit 2 tephra. Graph by William Melson.

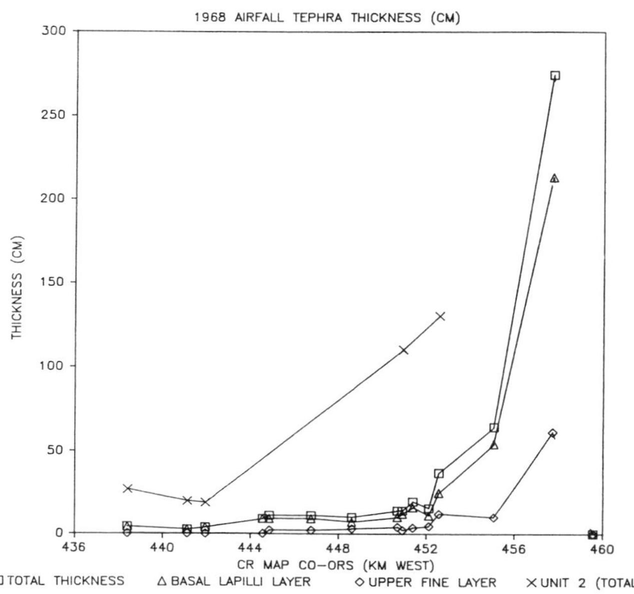

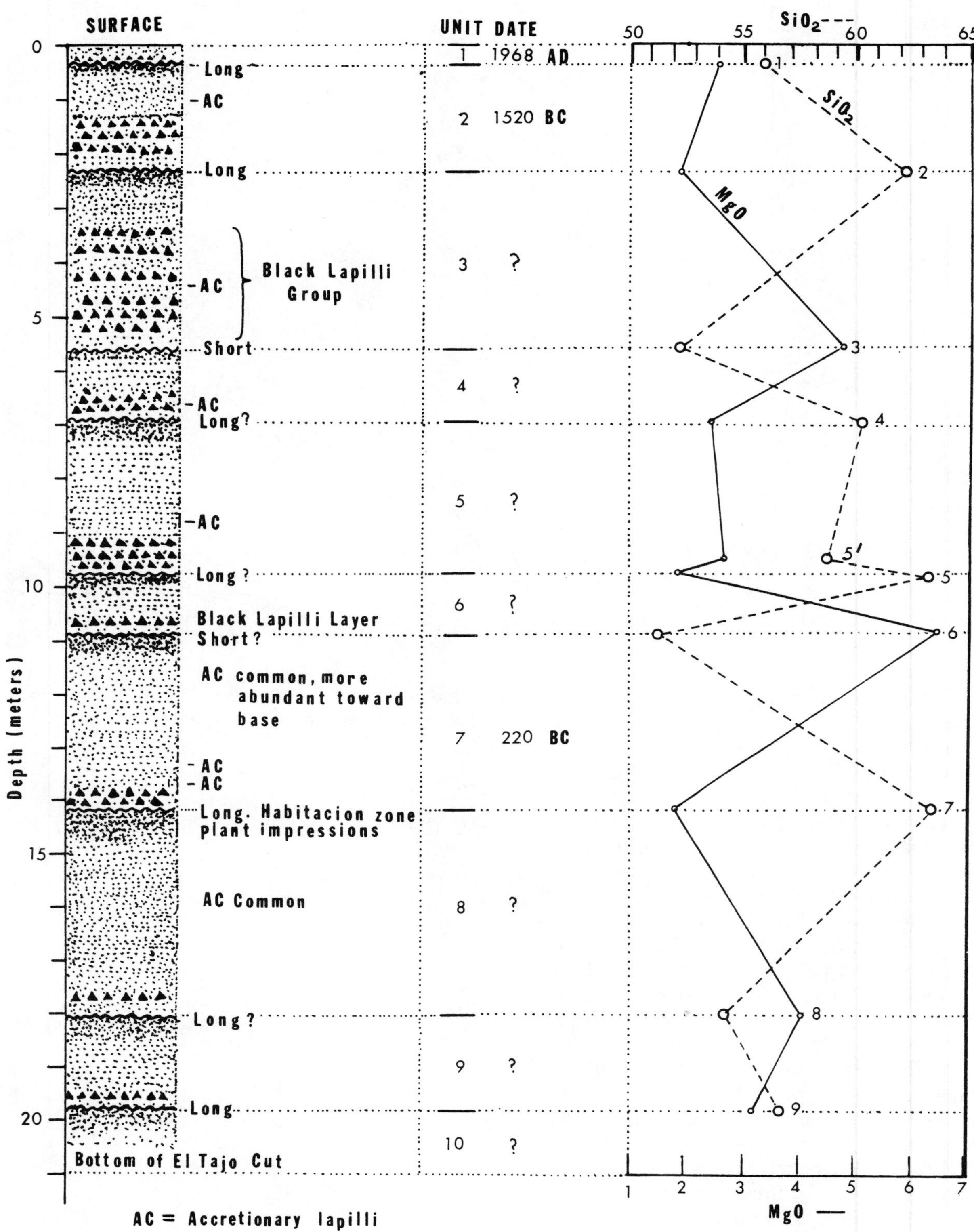

Figure 2-19.
El Tajo tephra sequence, Arenal Volcano. Indications of length of time between eruptions (long, short) are given at unit boundaries based on extent of paleosol development. Compositions of lapilli are from bulk analyses (Melson 1982). Chart by William Melson.

layer is immediately overlain by pumiceous basaltic andesite. We have found that even basic magmas were ejected in some of the Plinian events, a relatively rare phenomenon because of the usually low viscosities of basic magmas. We have found, however, that these basic magmas had high viscosities because of their highly phyric (crystalline) nature and highly acidic and thus viscous matrix glasses (Newhall and Melson 1983). Each eruption typically begins with violent explosions, which are recorded in the thick, downwind tephra section draped over the Lake Arenal region and extending to about 30 km west of Arenal.

Measurements of the thickness of each unit in many places reveal a nearly constant WNW (ca. 280°) trade wind direction during each eruption. The tephra apron for Unit 2, however, extends north and, rarely, winds have been observed at the level of the summit to blow eastward. There is no eastward-directed tephra apron, though. Indeed, the detailed knowledge we now have of Arenal's eruptive history provided a yardstick for comparisons with other Costa Rican volcanoes. Our present data indicate that Arenal's first major explosive eruption occurred around 1700 BC. It appears that Arenal has grown to its present form over the past 3,700 years.

ARENAL'S PREHISTORIC TEPHRA SEQUENCE

Previous work on the tephra sequence focused on deep cuts made within 10 km of Arenal Volcano during ICE's construction of the Sangregado earthfill dam. These rather spectacular exposures, some over 20 m into the sequence, are now either under the reservoir or heavily overgrown by vegetation. The record, nonetheless, can be made visible by clearing some of the deep road cuts between Castillo and the Caño Negro River along the south side of the reservoir.

The near-Arenal tephra sequence (Fig. 2-19) was examined in detail in 1977 at El Tajo (10° 45′N, 84° 76′W), a hilltop site about 7 km due west and downwind of Arenal's summit. Here, ICE excavated the south side of the hill to a depth of about 20 m and revealed a remarkably clear tephra sequence. Over nine major prehistoric explosive eruptions of Arenal were exposed, involving tephra ranging from dacite to basalt in bulk composition. Simultaneously with my work on the total tephra sequence, Carlos Aguilar of the Universidad de Costa Rica excavated prehistoric Indian remains uncovered deep within the sequence. The archaeological materials are now at the Universidad de Costa Rica in San José.

In 1969, George Metcalf and I excavated a site near La Palma to unravel some of the prehistoric eruptions of Arenal at the site of the former Arenal Volcanological Observatory. Here, the tephra sequence is poorly developed, as the site is north of the prevailing westerly wind direction. The archaeological materials recovered here are in the collection of the Smithsonian Institution and tentatively have been dated to between AD 1200 and 1400. A radiocarbon date of AD 1525 ± 10 was obtained on trees buried by a nearby pyroclastic flow assumed to be associated with this eruption (Melson and Saenz 1973). This date is assigned to the eruption of what is here termed Unit 2 and termed Unit 20 at Silencio, and which directly underlies the 1968 tephra. Chiesa (1987) presents evidence that Unit 2 may have been erupted about AD 1000. As he points out, the AD 1525 date is not based on carbon from the basal lapilli unit itself but from trees that were buried by a pyroclastic flow that I assume was associated with the Unit 2 eruptions. The archaeological data, however, strongly support the ca. AD 1500 age (Chap. 1).

The length of time between explosive eruptions is a critical parameter in both volcanological and archaeological interpretations. For the Unit 1 (1968) and Unit 2 (ca. 1525) eruptions, the break, or period of dormancy, is about 450 years. During this interval a well-developed humus-rich soil formed on the top of Unit 2. Similar soil development occurs at a number of other horizons at the Tajo site. These, plus the recognition of coarser material on top of each paleosol, allows recognition of nine major eruptive units. If we count Unit 10, which has only its upper portion exposed at El Tajo, as yet another major event, there were ten major explosive eruptions.

This is a minimum number of eruptions because (1) some units may have been removed by erosion, (2) the time between eruptions may have been too short for recognizable soil development, and (3) a significant, recognizable unit may not have been deposited here because of other-than-westerly wind directions during the eruption. The strong prevalence of westerly trade winds in recorded times and the absence of significant tephra sequences north, east, or south of the volcano makes this third factor unlikely. Factors 1 and 2 are more difficult to preclude. Erosional features are common along the tops of units. In places, at

El Tajo and in nearby road cuts, the soil zones can be traced to areas where they have been eroded or disturbed by uprooted trees, and entire units have been eroded away in places. Factor 2, a short time interval between eruptions, is simply not recognizable if it has occurred.

Given these caveats, the Tajo sequence is probably the most complete we have examined. Not only was the cut about 21 m deep, but its length was over 200 m. Thus, a unit that had been eroded at one place could be seen at another. The abundance of accretionary lapilli and the flat hilltop location preclude significant alluvial input or reworking of the Tajo site. With increasing distance from Arenal, complete tephra sequences become rare. Certain units though, such as Unit 2, were found in all sections that we have examined.

CHARACTERISTICS OF ERUPTIVE UNITS

The petrology of the coarse lapilli from each of the nine El Tajo units reveals considerable diversity (Fig. 2-19). This diversity, combined with the degree of soil development, the distribution of lapilli within a given unit, ceramic ages, total thickness, and individual thicknesses of the lapilli and fine zones, can allow correlations of given units throughout the Arenal tephra apron in undisturbed sections (Appendix 2-A). Unfortunately, undisturbed sections are rare, especially at distances of more than 10 km from Arenal's summit.

The bulk compositions of the lapilli range from dacite to basalt (Fig. 2-18). The appearance of these lapilli also ranges widely, as do the abundance and types of phenocrysts. With a hand lens or, preferably, a binocular microscope, many of the units can be distinguished during field investigations. The dacitic units, especially 2 and 7, contain light gray pumiceous lapilli and microphenocrysts of hornblende. These are thus readily distinguished from the dark-colored, phenocryst-rich basalt-to-andesite units. The soil on Unit 2 is rich in mafic minerals: olivine, hypersthene, and augite, minerals absent in the basal pumice layer. This minor mafic component in an otherwise dacitic unit is (1) a reflection of tapping of a zoned magma chamber, with eruption of a late-stage more mafic component, (2) an admixture of a minor, andesitic to basaltic tephra from a small eruption (or eruptions) that might have occurred before 1968 and after AD 1520, or (3) accidental fragments included with the essential and dominant dacitic pumice.

TEPHRA THICKNESS

The total thickness of Arenal's tephras in road cuts indicates that its axis of maximum thickness is along a line between Arenal's summit and Quebrada Grande, which is about 7.5 km southeast of Tilarán. This defines a line oriented about 8° south of west, near the historically typical downwind direction (Tosi 1980), as expected. Tilarán, Silencio, and El Tajo lie along a roughly east-west line at distances and total tephra sequence thicknesses of 28.5 km (.85 m), 23.5 km (2.5 m), and 7 km (20 m), respectively. Figure 2-18 shows the sharp drop in total tephra thicknesses near the volcano and the leveling off of the trend at greater distances.

The most voluminous of Arenal's eruptions are those recorded in the thickest tephra units, Units 3 and 8 (Fig. 2-18). Of these two, Unit 3 is particularly easy to recognize because of the dark color and multiple nature of its lapilli (many separate lapilli layers separated by finer tephra). The volumes of the airfall tephra from each eruption are estimated in Table 2-1. These are minimal because we do not know how much very fine tephra went far to the west and left no measurable record.

STRATIGRAPHIC CORRELATIONS

Each tephra set, or unit, was probably deposited over a short time interval, less than a year, and probably in a matter of days, if they were like the 1968 eruption, in which Unit 1 was deposited in less than 3 days. The ongoing periodic vulcanian and strombolian explosions after July 31, 1968, have added very little to the total 1968–1988 Arenal airfall thickness. Thus, each precisely identified unit gives a time line that has assisted immensely in the archaeological work; however, the more difficult aspect is correlation of the units of one excavation to another. The work of Knapp (Figs. 2-20*A* and *B*) and previous work permits tentative correlations between the Tajo section and those in the distal portion of Arenal's tephra apron.

Saenz and I measured a number of complete sections along the fresh road cuts near Castillo along the south side of the reservoir in 1978. We found that the ratios of thicknesses of each unit in these sections to their corresponding unit at El Tajo was about the same. If any unit were from Cerro Chato, we expected a greater thickness in these cuts than at El Tajo, as they are more di-

TABLE 2-1
ESTIMATED ERUPTION TIME (1), EL TAJO UNIT THICKNESS (2), VOLUME OF DOWNWIND TEPHRA APRON (3), PROBABLE SILENCIO UNIT CORRELATION (4), AND SAMPLE NUMBERS OF DATED SAMPLES (5)

Unit	*1*	*2 (cm)*	*3 (km³)*	*4*	*5*
1	AD 1968	30	0.024	10	
2	AD 1520*	200	0.16**	20	SI
3	AD 900***	330	0.26	30, 40, 41	TX-5269
4	?	130	0.10	41	
5	AD 300***	190	0.15	50	TX-5272, TX-5078
6		120	0.10	53, 53A	
7	220 BC	330	0.26	54	SI (uncorr.)
8		360	0.29	55	
9		180	0.14	60	
10	1800*** BC			61	TX-5297

Notes: Estimated total tephra apron is 1.48 km³.
* Chiesa (1987) suggests an age of about AD 1000 for Unit 2.
** Chiesa (1987) estimates the volume of Unit 2 to be 0.4 km³.
*** Possibly relevant dates from Sheets (Chap. 1).

rectly downwind from Chato than from Arenal. Thus, I continue to believe that the Arenal Project excavations reveal units deposited solely from eruptions of Arenal, with the first major Plininan event occurring about 3,800 years ago. Unit 61, the basal tephra set on the Aguacate Formation, probably corresponds to the little-known Unit 10 at El Tajo.

WEATHERING AND SOIL FORMATION

The long periods between many of the eruptions permitted considerable weathering and enrichment in humus. Some soil zones are particularly well developed on a regional scale. Some of the most striking occur on the tops of Units 2, 3, 6, 8, and 9. Weathering effects are most clearly visible and most rapidly developed in fine-grained tephras because of increased grain surface area. Humus enrichment, however, appears to be more directly related to length of exposure. Once a unit soil is buried, weathering is slowed, presumably because of less water infiltration and circulation, and less disintegration due to lower concentrations of organic acids.

Remarkably, lapilli at the base of even the oldest units (7, 8, and 9) are quite fresh. This is a necessary condition for our ability to infer the magma types of Arenal's explosive eruptions. The slower weathering of basal lapilli results partly from their larger grain size and the reduced surface area on which agents of chemical weathering can act. Weathering penetrating to a depth of 0.2 mm on the lapilli would have little effect, but similar penetration on finer tephra would lead to near-total alteration. This probably explains the greater weathering of the finer parts of most units. One exception to this tendency is the fine, gray, fresh-looking tephra of Unit 41 in the Silencio sequence. Its resistance to erosion may be due to partial cementation by minerals (gypsum?) released in volcanic emanations by the tephra immediately after deposition, a common phenomenon in the fine upper tephra from the 1968 eruption.

The units contain progressively less sand-sized lithic and mineral grains with depth (Figs. 2-20*A* and *B*). Joan Mishara, of the Smithsonian Conservation Analytical Lab, performed X-ray diffraction analyses on this sequence and found increasing amounts of kaolinite with depth. Both these trends reflect the effects of increasing weathering with age and parallel important chemical changes with depth and thus length of weathering.

All of Arenal's tephras contain more of the important plant nutrients potassium and phosphorous than the lateritic, highly leached soils (ultisols) at the top of the Aguacate Formation. Such soils usually are low in humus and organic carbon in the Tilarán region. The rich, black soils developed on some of the units probably reflect improved plant growth on the recent volcanic tephra with more available nutrients than in the Aguacate Formation. Figure 2-22 shows the variation of total potassium (reported as K_2O) and phosphorous (reported as P_2O_5) with depth in a 1.8 m deep excavation at G-163. The analyses of the G-163 and El Tajo lapilli were performed by Carr using

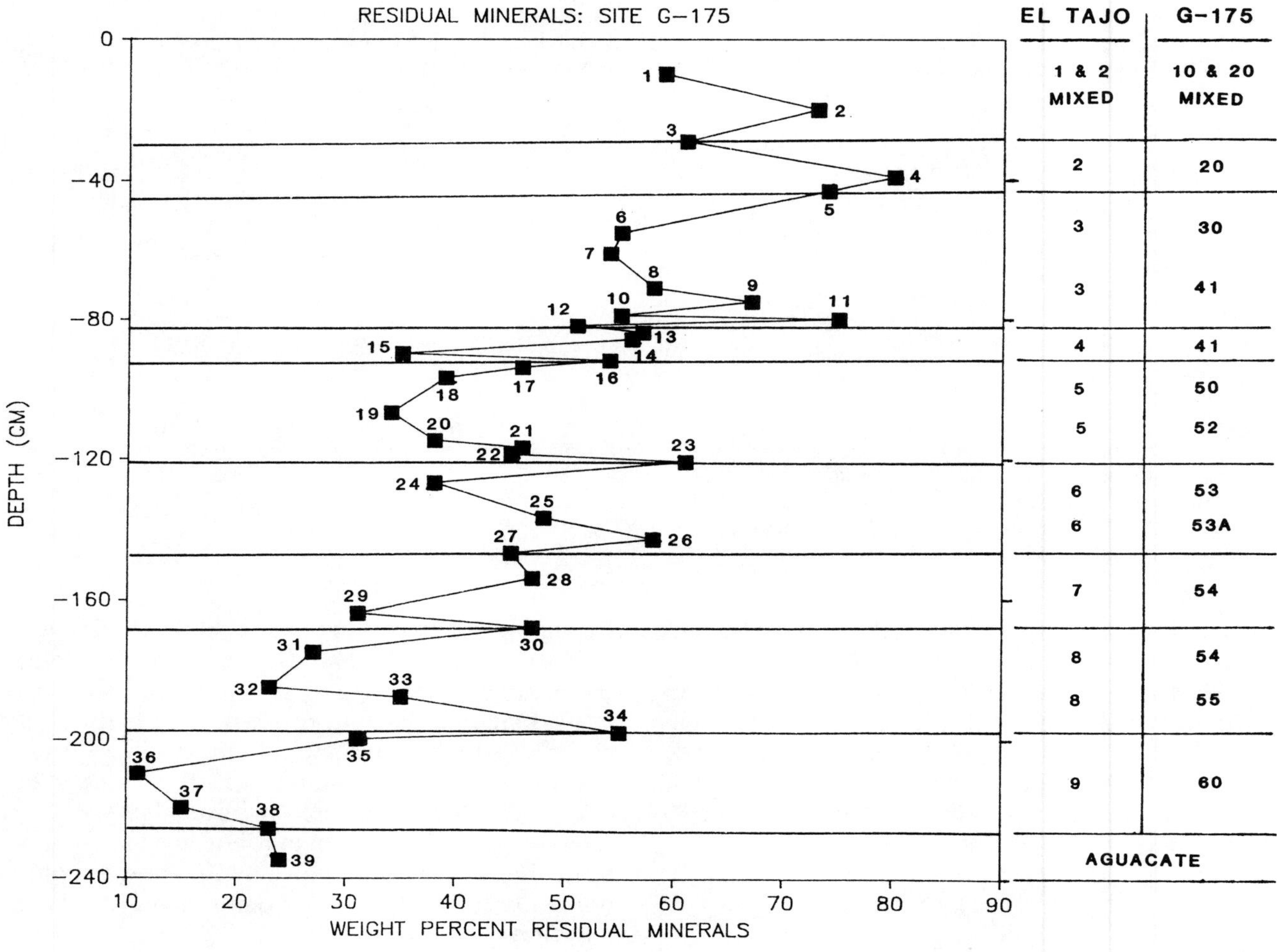

Figure 2-20.
*Correlations between site G-175 (Fig. 2-20*A*), G-163 (Fig. 2-20*B*), and El Tajo, and variation of weight percent residual lithic and mineral grains (sand-sized) with depth in washed and sieved bulk samples. Chart prepared with the assistance of Liz Knapp, personal communication to Payson Sheets, 1985.*

spark-source emission spectrography. The probable original range and distribution of these oxides is shown by a scaled-down El Tajo section; that is, the total 22 m El Tajo section has been scaled to about 130 cm, the depth to the probable Unit 9. This is a different sample at site G-163 than that sampled by Knapp (Fig. 2-20), where the basal Arenal sequence contact was believed to be at about 155 cm below the surface. The data for El Tajo Unit 4 in Figure 2-20*A* are from Carr and Walker (1987).

Reduction of K_2O with time during weathering is clear (Fig. 2-21*A*). Over the probable 3,700 years of weathering represented by the section at G-163, it has dropped from values around 0.5 to about 0.2 weight percent. A highly weathered exfoliated lava flow with residual exfoliated boulders that are fresh in their interiors (Fig. 2-22) provides a gauge of the extent of losses during longer weathering. We have analyzed both the weathered margin and the fresh interior of such a boulder

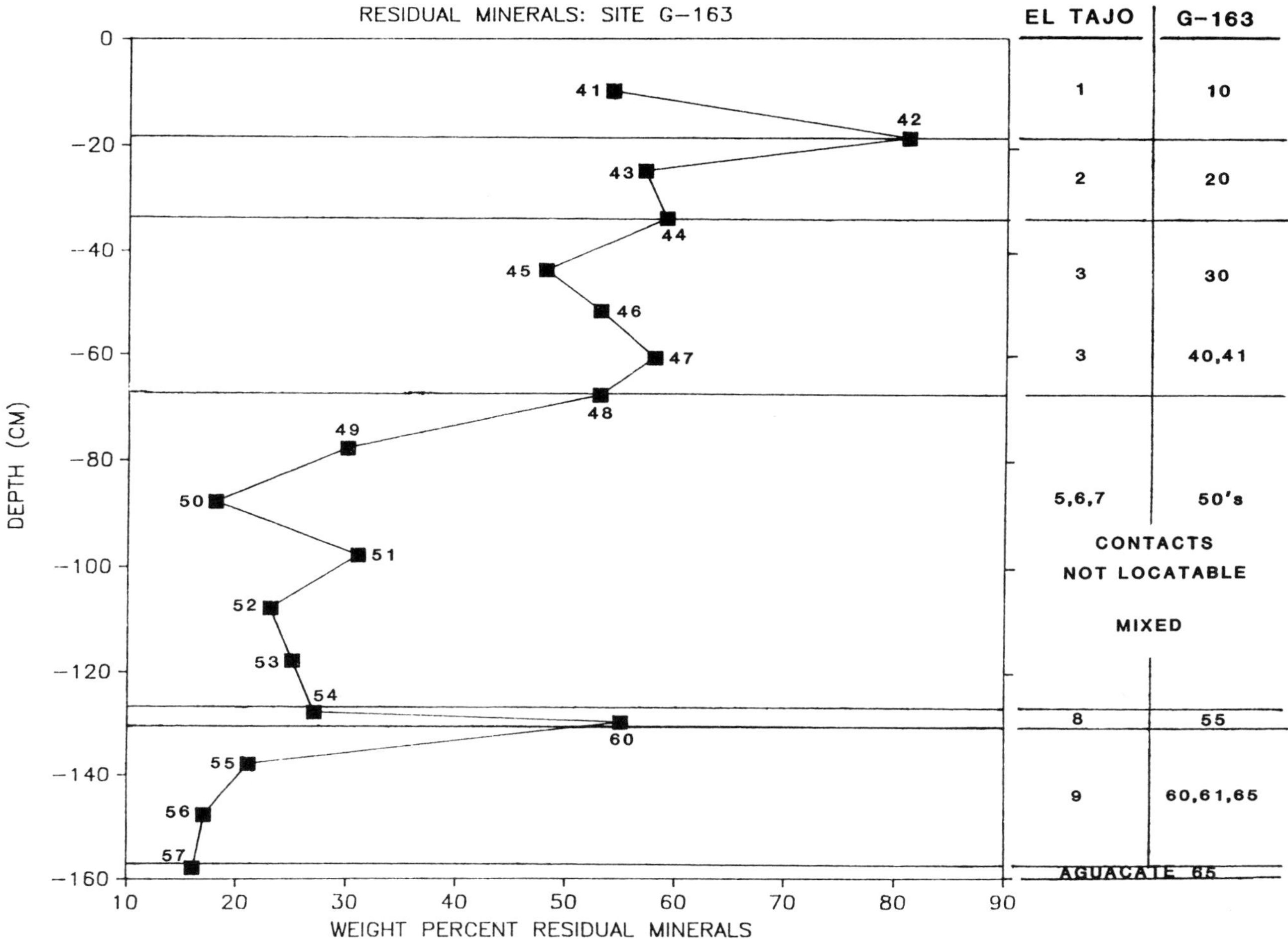

near Tilarán. We find that K_2O reaches 0.03% in the weathered exterior, starting from the fresh core value of 1.44%. Thus, the Aguacate Formation at site G-163 is still comparatively rich in K_2O compared with the ultisols developed outside of Arenal's tephra apron.

The rate of loss of K_2O appears to be most rapid during the initial stages of weathering of the tephra and then to decrease to a rate of 0.2 weight percent per 3,300 years (Fig. 2-21*A*), measured from the base of Unit 2 to the base of the Arenal sequence at G-163. Such estimated rates of oxide gains or losses during weathering provide a very rough gauge of the age of other weathered tephras and lavas in the same climatic regime. For example, this rate implies that the 1.41% K_2O lost from the lava flow mentioned earlier took about $(1.41 \div 0.2) \times 3{,}300$ years, or about 23,000 years (neglecting the original, rapid K_2O loss). This is a minimum estimate, because it seems likely that the extraction rate decreases as the K_2O content decreases. At site G-163, what we have termed the Aguacate Formation is still quite high in K_2O (0.20) and probably does not greatly predate the Arenal sequence (less than a few thousand years), and may well be part of a tephra sequence from Cerro Chato.

Phosphorous, another essential plant nutrient, also decreases with increased age (Fig. 2-21*B*). Its behavior in weathering depends on whether it is mainly contained in primary igneous apatite or in glass. In the former, loss appears to be slow. For the aforementioned boulder, in which apatite occurs, P_2O_5 dropped from 0.25% to 0.23% over the same time interval that K_2O dropped from 1.41% to 0.03%. At site G-163, where most of the P_2O_5 occurs in the glass matrix of tephra, the drop is much more rapid, from about 0.2% to 0.1% over about 3,700 years. In glass, phosphorous release is such that it becomes more readily available as a plant nutrient during weathering, whereas in apatite it remains largely unavailable.

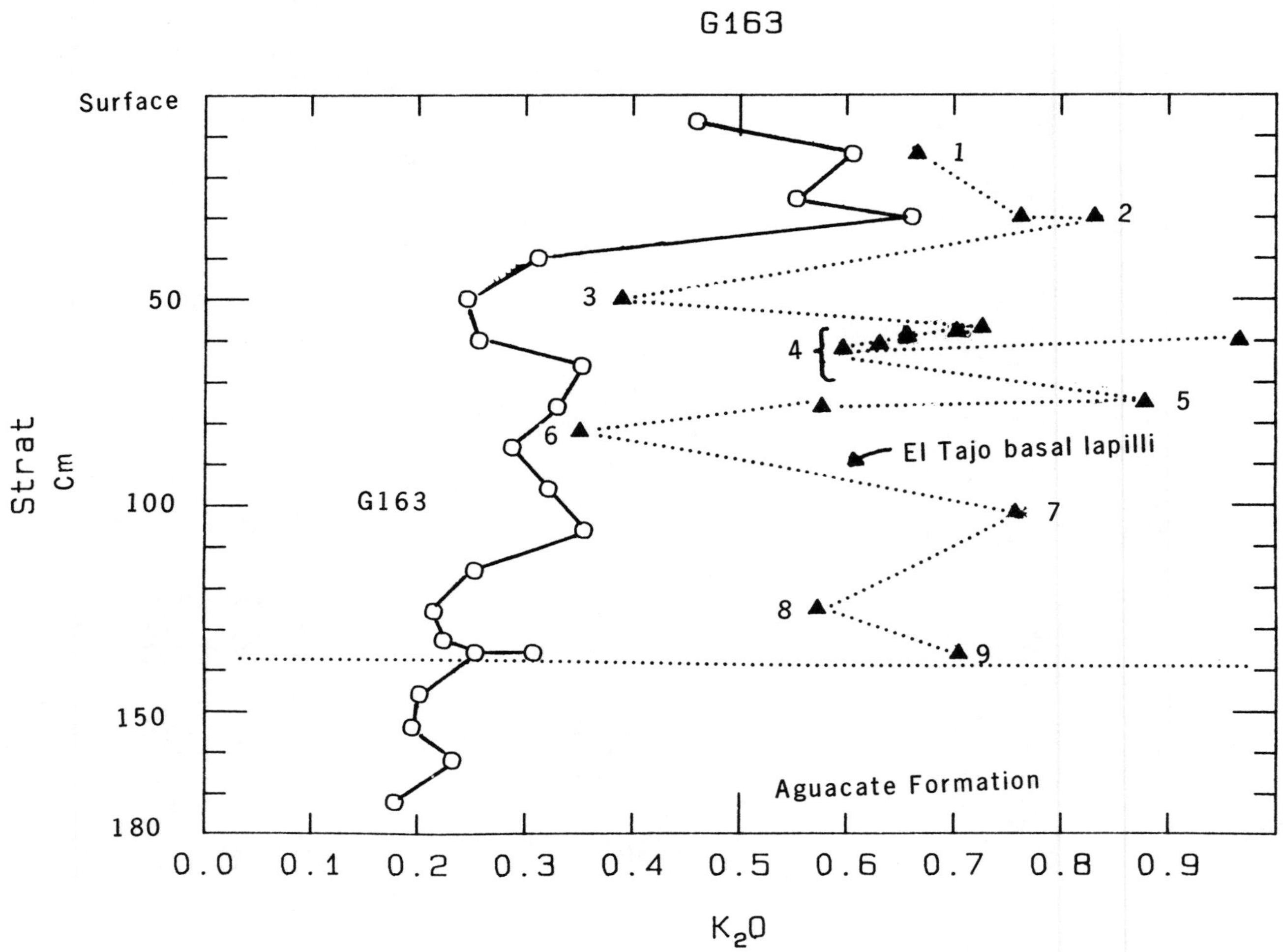

Figure 2-21A.
Variation of K_2O with depth at site G-163 (open circles and solid lines) compared with the proportionally scaled values from El Tajo (solid triangles and dotted lines). Chart by William Melson.

In summary, potassium and phosphorous both occur in high concentrations and are readily available as plant nutrients in the Arenal tephra apron. The rate of decrease of potassium with time appears to provide a crude but perhaps useful guide to weathered tephra and lava flow ages within the western Arenal region.

EROSION AND DISTURBANCES OF TEPHRA SECTIONS

The Arenal apron provides a close look at the properties of a tephra sequence that was deposited on the floor of a rain forest. Indeed, we interpret the rare preservation in places of even thin units, for example at Silencio, to the erosive protection of the floor of such rain forests. We can also see the increased erosion rates resulting from deforestation in the rapid erosion of much of the 1968 tephra.

All the tephra sections reveal evidence of some postdepositional changes. Such disturbances result from (1) erosion during periods of dormancy,

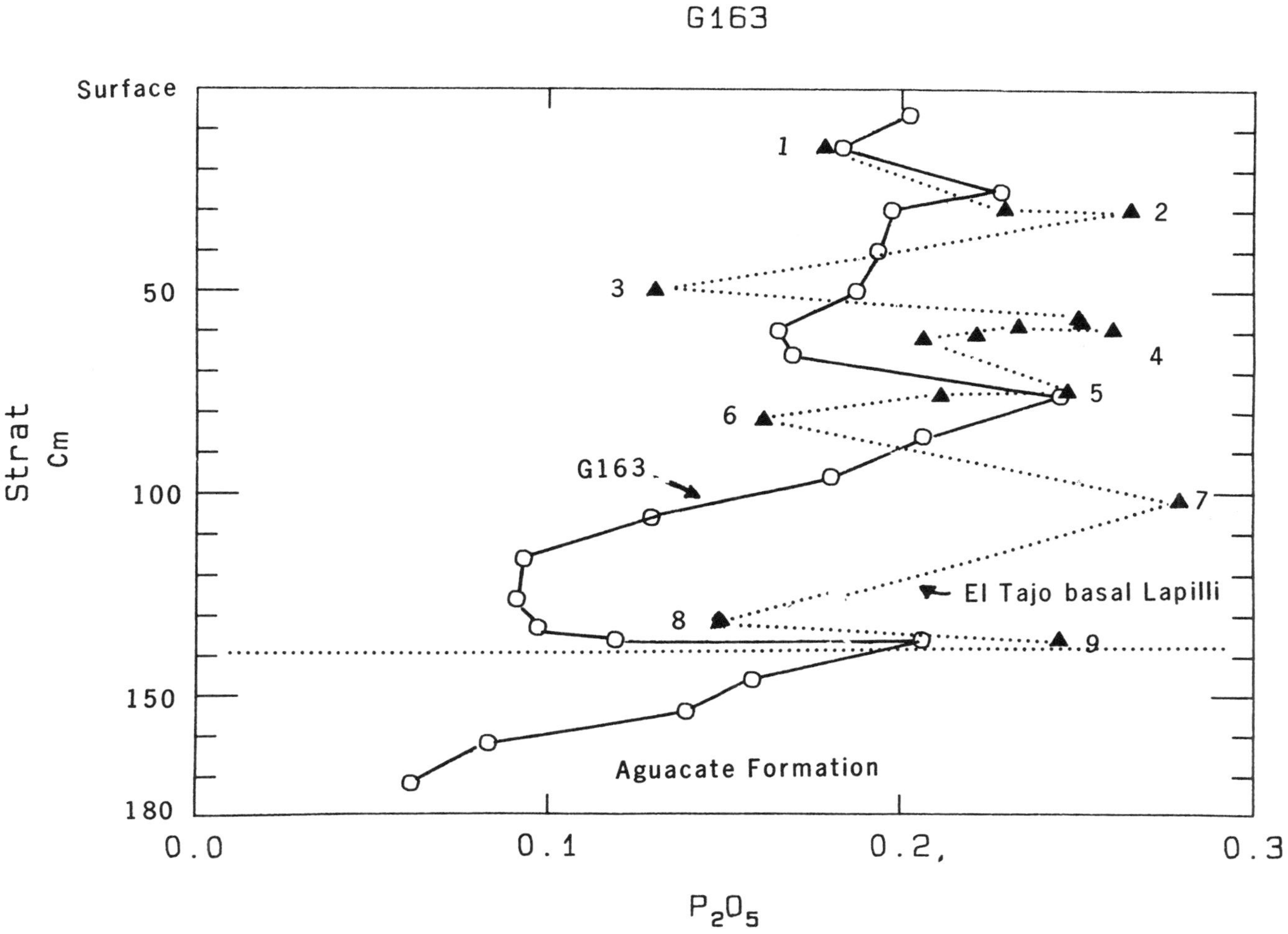

G163

Surface

Strat Cm

50
100
150
180

1 2 3 4 5 6 7 8 9

G163

El Tajo basal Lapilli

Aguacate Formation

0.0 0.1 0.2 0.3

P_2O_5

Figure 2-21B.
Variation of P_2O_5 with depth at site G-163 and El Tajo, same codes as in Figure 2-21A. Chart by William Melson.

Figure 2-22.
Weathered fragment of andesite in pre-Arenal lava flow in road cut about 3 km north of Tilarán. The weathered rind and fresh interior were analyzed for chemical compositional changes during weathering. Photograph by William Melson.

including landslides, (2) disturbance by plant roots and burrowing fauna, (3) uprooting of trees, and (4) human activity. In general, these effects are most dramatic near the distal parts of the apron, where the tephra sets are thinner. This partially explains the clearly visible stratigraphy of the thick units at El Tajo compared with the more difficult to interpret stratigraphy at, for example, Silencio.

A number of separate thin units in the Silencio and Tilarán regions have been homogenized by bioturbation. Such homogenization can produce mixed ceramic assemblages as well as mixed lapilli types. Radiocarbon dates on wood or charcoal fragments can, in theory, give a date related to any one of the mixed units and are of limited value compared with those clearly contained in a single eruptive unit. The "smoothing" out of the deceasing K_2O content with depth over original sharply changing values (Fig. 2-21*A*) certainly reflects in part mixing by bioturbation.

THE TILARÁN TEPHRA SEQUENCE

A series of tephra beds is exposed in road cuts near Tronadora and Tilarán, as well as on the road between Tilarán and Quebrada Grande. This series is in places a striking alternation of light- and dark-colored fine-grained paleosols. The distribution of these tephras indicates that they are in fact from Arenal and that they correlate with the basal units of the Tajo-Silencio sequences. The distinctive appearance of this series compared with the rest of the Arenal sequence has led to their being termed the Tilarán sequence. Part of this distinctive appearance is a result of the extraordinarily high carbon content in some of the black paleosols. Carbon reaches at least 5.6 weight percent in some of these according to analyses by Gene Jarosewich of the Department of Mineral Sciences, Smithsonian Institution. Tentatively, we correlate the typically light-colored basal layer and its upper dark soil zone with Unit 9 or Unit 10 at El Tajo (Basal Silencio U. 60?).

Unit 7 (ca. 220 BC) at El Tajo is also recognizable in some exposures of the Tilarán series by the occurrence of pumiceous dacite overlying a well-developed paleosol. Some of the clearest exposures of Unit 7 (Silencio U. 54) in the Tilarán series are in road cuts just outside of Quebrada Grande on the road to San Miguel. For ease of measurement, we have termed the basal, typically light-colored tephra "White 1" and its overlying dark-colored soil zone "Black 1." The following are tentative correlations with the Tajo sequence: "White 1–Black 1" refer to Unit 9; "White 2–Black 2," to Unit 8; and "White 3–Black 3," to Unit 7. We have found that in many exposures of the Tilarán series, one or more of these basal units have been either obscured by bioturbation or eroded before deposition of the next unit. Also, in the very distal exposures, the pumiceous dacite in the base of Unit 7 may be too fine-grained to be readily visible, and thus the correlations become more difficult if not impossible in the field.

The Tilarán series thins to only 20 cm 1.5 km NW of Guadalajara at the west end of the reservoir, a distance of 33 km WNW of Arenal's summit. Beyond this distance, the Tilarán series is represented by fine, dark tephra mixed with and not distinguishable from topsoil, and its integrity as a separate, measurable tephra series is lost.

The age of the basal Tilarán unit ("White 1 and Black 1") is critical in dating what is presumed to be the first major eruption of Arenal. Pottery in this unit and on the top of the Aguacate Formation here has been assigned to the Tronadora Phase, dating from 2000 to 500 BC. Carbonized wood from beneath this basal unit indicates an age closer to 1700 BC. The main cone of Arenal may have begun its growth around that time. This would suggest that Arenal has grown to its present form in about 3,700 years.

AIRFALL TEPHRA IN THE AGUACATE FORMATION

The Aguacate Formation as used here is a catchall term for all the usually reddish, highly weathered, clay-rich material beneath the less-weathered Arenal tephras. In places, the material beneath the tephras was derived from weathering of lava flows. Such derivation can be seen in road cuts a few kilometers SW of Tilarán on the Tilarán-Cañas road, and in a road cut just west of Piedras. Elsewhere, deeply weathered tephras and even paleosols can be seen. For example, a well-developed paleosol occurs within reddish clay about 3 m beneath the base of the Tilarán tephra series in excavations for the San Miguel soccer field, about 8 km southeast of Tilarán. These older tephras were deeply eroded before deposition of the much-younger Arenal series. Their volcanic source or sources remain uncertain but might well include Cerro Chato.

SUMMARY AND CONCLUSIONS

1. The 1968 explosive eruptions of Arenal, although volumetrically small compared to the at least nine prehistoric major Plinian eruptions, provide a model for interpreting both the stratigraphy and the likely environmental impacts of Arenal's prehistoric eruptions.

2. Arenal in July 1992 continued to have vulcanian and strombolian eruptions. It is unlikely that explosions in the near future will be as intense as the 1968 ones, and it is likely that soon Arenal will fall into a stage of dormancy for at least a few hundred years if we consider analogies with prehistoric eruptions. Nonetheless, near-volcano areas, like the Tabacón River, remain hazardous because of the possibility of hot avalanches like that of July 1975.

3. Arenal is both the youngest and the most active Costa Rican volcano in terms of frequency of Plinian eruptions over the past 3,700 years, and has grown to its current form during that time.

4. Although ashfall from the July 28–31, 1968, eruptions covered hundreds of square kilometers and reached over 110 km westward, long-term impact has been restricted to a relatively small area of about 10 km^2 on the west side of the volcano. Recovery of soil for agricultural use was rapid outside that zone, on the order of a few months.

5. Loss of life was large partly because the explosions occurred with only about 12 hours of premonitory earthquakes and other pre-eruption indicators, and because Arenal was not known to be an active volcano.

6. Arenal's eruptions have long periods of repose between them and begin mainly with cataclysmic Plinian eruptions, which wane to vulcanian and strombolian eruptions, producing much fine tephra. Thus, the tephra sets of each eruption consist of a basal lapilli layer from the explosive phase, which grades upward to a fine tephra layer deposited during the vulcanian phase. This upper fine layer develops into an organically-rich A-horizon between eruptions.

7. The prevailing trade winds cause a consistent westerly drift for the tephra from each eruption, and the buildup of a thick tephra apron to the west of Arenal.

8. Although correlations are difficult between the tephra units in thin stratigraphic sections because of bioturbation, erosional unconformities, and stratigraphic mixing, it has been possible to correlate most sections with the "type" section at El Tajo and between one another.

9. The weathering of the Arenal tephra apron appears to continue to provide K_2O and P_2O_5 as plant nutrients, whereas the ultisols outside of the apron contain little of these components. We have been able to roughly estimate the rate of K_2O extraction during weathering and to use this rate to infer the age of older tephra sequences. Using this approach and chemical analyses of a serial section from site G-163, we have determined that much of the Arenal tephra apron appears to be underlain by tephra from Cerro Chato.

ACKNOWLEDGMENTS

Special thanks go to Rodrigo Saenz, Jorge Barquero, and Erik Fernández of the Universidad Nacional for their many contributions to the fieldwork. Michael Carr, Rutgers University, kindly provided the chemical analyses used in the weathering studies. Payson Sheets, Marilynn Mueller, and John Hoopes provided much assistance and insightful discussion during and after the fieldwork. Elizabeth Knapp did essential lab- and fieldwork on the stratigraphic correlations. At the Smithsonian, Mair Moody supervised volunteers who assisted with determination of sand-sized fractions of weathered tephra; Debra Jérez assisted with many aspects of the lab studies; Joan Mishara assisted with X-ray diffraction studies; Eugene Jarosewich did bulk carbon determinations on some paleosols; and Victoria Funk, Department of Botany, contributed to many aspects of the field studies, as did my daughters, Mary and Amy Melson.

Finally, the ongoing persistence and commitment of Payson Sheets was essential in getting this work in print. He and Brian McKee assisted too with the editing of this manuscript. The early field studies (1968–1969) were funded by the National Geographic Society and Smithsonian research grants. More recent studies were funded by grants from the National Science Foundation and the National Geographic Society (Payson Sheets, P.I.), and from the Smithsonian Scholarly Studies Program.

Appendix 2-A

BRIEF DESCRIPTION AND DISCRIMINATING CHARACTERISTICS OF EACH ARENAL TEPHRA SET (FIGURE 2-19).

UNIT 1

Tephra deposited in 1968. Top of each section, and thinnest of the ten recognized tephra sets (Fig. 2-6). Light gray; coarse, lapilli-sized zone at base within about 10 km W of Arenal. Being rapidly eroded and commonly difficult to recognize except close to Arenal. Beyond about 10 km W of the volcano, it occurs as a sprinkling of sand-sized particles mixed with the soil on top of Unit 2. At the Silencio site, about 23 km W of Arenal, it occurs as scattered, sand-sized particles mixed with the topsoil. Its thinness and ongoing rapid erosion suggest that eruptions of such comparatively small volumes are not typically preserved in the Arenal tephra sequence even allowing for lower erosion rates in rain forests. Unit 1 corresponds to Unit 10 of the Silencio stratigraphic sequence (site G-151) and site G-163. In the western part of the devastated zone, about 6 km from the summit, a thin andesitic airfall unit is between Unit 1 and 2, suggesting the possibility of a small eruption between the times of Units 1 and 2, which is preserved only within 10 or fewer km of the cone.

UNIT 2

Unit 2 corresponds to Unit 20 of the Silencio stratigraphic sequence (site G-150) and of site G-163. Easily recognized and virtually ubiquitous unit extending to about 26 km W of Arenal. Thick, light-colored dacitic pumiceous lapilli unit at base. The unit ranges from 2 m thick at El Tajo to about 0.2 m at Silencio. In places, such as at site G-175, 16 km W of Arenal, near the Chiquito River, the basal unit consists of a thin, fine-grained layer on Unit 3, which grades up into a coarse lapilli layer, then another fine layer, and into yet another lapilli layer, suggesting two major explosive eruptions. These two separate basal lapilli layers are a typical feature of this unit. Ceramics are rare on the surface of Unit 2, suggesting a small population in the region after AD 1500. Dacitic pumice like that of Unit 2 occurs as a thin white layer at the base of Unit 5, which is otherwise composed of basaltic andesite, and makes up all the lapilli at the base of Unit 7, erupted around 220 BC. Each of these dacitic pumice layers contains light gray pumice containing rare but distinctive small black, elongated hornblende phenocrysts and are quite distinctive under the binocular microscope or a hand lens and are thus key unit markers. The paleosol on Unit 2 at the Tajo site contains fragments of basaltic andesite as well as single crystals of plagioclase, hypersthene, augite, and olivine (rare). Chiesa (1987) presents isopach data and uses new radiocarbon dates to suggest that the Unit was erupted about AD 1000.

UNIT 3

Distinctive features include numerous thin black basaltic lapilli layers throughout the lower two-thirds of its thickness, an upper, typically orangish brown soil zone grading in places to a humus-rich black soil, and thickness (about 40 cm even at Silencio). Silencio Units 30 and 40 correspond to the top fine portion and bottom lapilli-bearing portion, respectively, of Unit 3. Middle Polychrome ceramic assemblages buried in part before the deposition of Unit 3 suggest eruption after AD 900. Its eruption before AD 1520 (Unit 2) and its well-developed, quite weathered soil zone suggest eruption before about AD 1200, although this is a very crude estimate of its upper age limit. Middle Polychrome ceramics found near the top of Unit 3 suggest ages between AD 1000 and 1200. The numerous, distinct, black coarse lapilli layers separated by fine lapilli in much of Unit 3 probably reflect repeated violent explosive activity. Units 30 and 40 at G-163 also correlate with Unit 3.

UNIT 4

Thin andesitic unit, measuring about 1.3 m at El Tajo. Assuming that it thins at the same rate as Unit 2, its thickness at Silencio would be about 34 cm. So far, we have not been able to recognize Unit 4 clearly at sites G-175 or G-150 (Silencio). At site G-151 this unit correlates with Unit 41 of the Silencio sequence. At El Tajo, this unit has very poorly developed soil zone, suggesting a probable eruption date after around AD 800.

UNIT 5

Distinctive because of the thick, very fine, light gray tephra in the upper three-fourths of its thickness. It also contains a thin, white dacitic pumice layer at its base at El Tajo. Above the white pumiceous zone, the unit is andesite, not readily distinguishable from lapilli at the base of a number of other units. The fine gray tephra of the upper part of Unit 5 probably correlates with a thinner similar unit we have labeled Unit 41 in the Silencio sequence. Silencio Units 50 and 52 are probably the basal part of Unit 5. At site G-175 (Bradley et al. 1984), ceramics dating from AD 300 to 500 have been found beneath what we have tentatively identified as Unit 5. The unit correlates petrologically with Unit 52 at site G-151.

UNIT 6

Like Unit 5, this unit is quite thin, 1.2 m at El Tajo. It should be about 30 cm thick at Silencio. Petrologically, it is unique, containing plagioclase, hypersthene, augite, and olivine-phyric basalt lapilli. Binocular microscope inspection of millimeter- and larger-sized grains will allow its recognition where present. So far we have failed to recognize this unit with certainty at Silencio and nearby sites. Tentatively, though, we correlate it with Silencio Units 53 and 53A. Thus, its time of eruption remains uncertain.

UNIT 7

Thick and distinctive at El Tajo, and we have identified it at some sites near Silencio; distinctiveness centers on the hornblende-phyric dacitic pumice lapilli at its base. These are readily identifiable in sand-sized separates even in the far western Silencio region sites. Chronologically, this is a critical unit in that it was probably erupted about 220 BC. At El Tajo and in the Silencio area, it is typically underlain by a thick, humus-rich black soil zone of Unit 8, one of the most distinctive in the entire sequence. It is also a noteworthy unit because it marks Arenal's first eruption of dacitic magmas. Beneath, we find only basaltic andesite. Unit 7 appears to mark the beginning of frequent intense explosive eruptions. This is inferred from the coarser-grained character of this unit and of most of the units that overlie Units 8 and 9. Tentatively, we correlate Unit 7 with Silencio Unit 54.

UNIT 8

This is a thick basaltic andesite unit, composed mainly of fine tephra with but a thin basal layer of basaltic andesite lapilli. The habitation site excavated by Aguilar at El Tajo is in the well-developed black soil zone on the top of this unit. The date of this unit remains uncertain except that it is older than 220 BC. The extraordinarily well developed soil indicates it may be as old as 670 BC, assuming that, like Unit 2, such well-developed soil formation took about 450 years. Correlations of this unit with those of the Silencio sequence remain uncertain. Units below Unit 50 and, in places, even Units 60 and 65 may correlate with Unit 8. The Bichrome and other older ceramic assemblages from these units support such correlations. This unit appears to correlate with Units 55 and 55A, and possibly extends upward into Unit 54.

UNIT 9

This unit is similar to Unit 8, except that Unit 9 is thinner and has but a thin basal basaltic andesite lapilli zone at its base. At El Tajo, the soil zone on Unit 9 is less well developed than that on Unit 8, pointing to a probable short time span between its eruption and the eruption of Unit 8. A rough estimate based on this observation points to an approximate eruption date of about 900 BC. The ceramics that probably correlate with this unit in the Silencio region indicate a cultural age between 400 and 800 BC. This probably correlates with Silencio Unit 60.

UNIT 10

A thick, black, well-developed paleosol occurs at the base of the Tajo section, about 20 m beneath the surface. This has been termed Unit 10; however, excavation did not reach the base of this unit. The coarse (>24 mesh) portion of this paleosol contains basaltic andesite fragments, including phenocrysts of plagioclase, hypersthene, augite, and, rarely, olivine. This observation shows that this unit is not the top of the Aguacate Formation, which is distinctive in that it contains rare and deeply corroded lithic and mineral fragments. Unit 10 may correlate with some of the archaeological layers designated as Unit 61.

3

Archaeological Survey in the Arenal Basin

MARILYNN MUELLER

INTRODUCTION

Archaeological survey formed an integral part of the Proyecto Prehistórico Arenal research. The survey focused on settlement patterns, potential subsistence resources, and their relationship to volcanic activity. Both settlement patterns and subsistence strategies are problematic aspects of research in Costa Rican prehistory, due in part to poor preservation, the lack of large-scale, permanent architecture, and poor site visibility resulting from dense vegetation and, in some areas, volcanic overburden.

Archaeological survey in the Arenal basin (the watershed of the upper Arenal River) was designed to exploit the potential advantages of preservation resulting from sudden, catastrophic burial of sites by volcanic tephra as well as a regional stratigraphic sequence of alternating layers of tephra and soils formed from tephra. This sequence added temporal control to our study of the relationships between site locations, environmental variables, and the effects of volcanic activity. Survey was concentrated in three topographically and ecologically distinct areas: the modern shoreline of Lake Arenal, the Piedra River Valley northwest of the lake, and the middle Arenal River Valley north and east of Arenal Volcano. A brief subsurface survey using a posthole digger was also conducted in the mountainous zone southeast of the lake.

THE SURVEY AREA

The Arenal basin is a tectonic depression just east of the Continental Divide, between the Cordillera de Guanacaste and the Cordillera de Tilarán, in northwestern Costa Rica (Fig. 3-1). Arenal Volcano and Cerro Chato dominate the region both visually and geologically. Arenal Volcano is a conical stratovolcano, with a base 4 km in diameter rising to a peak elevation of 1,633 m. Cerro Chato, located SE of Arenal, is the collapsed caldera of an older, presumably extinct, volcano. These volcanoes are probably the youngest members of a regional volcanic cordillera that runs approximately 200 km from Orosi Volcano in the northwest to Irazú Volcano in the southeast (Tosi 1980).

Arenal Volcano has remained active since its last violent eruptive phase began in 1968 and must have played an important role in prehistoric adaptations in the region. Ten major prehistoric eruptions are known, the earliest dating to approximately 1800 BC (See Chap. 2). The alternating periods of repose and explosive eruptions that characterize Arenal's activity (Melson and Saenz 1973) have both ecological and social implications. The eruptions certainly affected the environment and resource base, and catastrophic eruptions may have directly affected the prehistoric residents of the region. One of the major goals of the project is to elucidate the relationships between such events and human occupation of the area.

Today the upper reaches of the basin (*cuenca*) are occupied by Lake Arenal. Prior to the construction of Sangregado Dam in 1980, this was a shallow, marshy lake. The dam doubled the size of the lake and raised the water level approximately 30 m, to 540 m above sea level.

Tectonic and seismic activity combined with

Figure 3-1.
Site G-169 in foreground, looking north across present-day Lake Arenal, with the northeastern shore of the lake visible in the background. The G-169 site is located on a ridge top overlooking the lake. Photograph by Payson Sheets.

erosion have played a major role in shaping landforms. Two faults related to the volcanic axis underlie the lake and a multitude of landslide scarps testify to the importance of seismic activity in the region.

Although hydrologically part of the Atlantic Watershed, Arenal basin exhibits the general east-west climatic gradient seen throughout northern Costa Rica. Within the basin, there is a pronounced climatic gradient from the western "Pacific regime," with distinct wet and dry seasons and relatively low rainfall, to the eastern "Atlantic regime," with more rainfall and less seasonality. Local variations can be dramatic, however, in part because of the geographic location of the basin in a tectonic depression between the two cordilleras where the two climatic regimes meet. Local conditions such as elevation, slope, temperature, exposure to winds, force of the wind, and solar radiation also contribute to this variability.

Topography, like climate, is characterized by a general west-east gradient with considerable local variation (Chap. 1, Fig. 1-3). Low, gently rolling hills in the west grade into mountainous terrain south of the lake and long steep-sided ridges paralleling the northern shore. To the east of Arenal Volcano and Cerro Chato lie the broad flat plains of San Carlos.

SURVEY STRATEGY AND METHODS

Survey methods were determined by first assessing the spatial distribution and density of cultural materials. Cultural materials were then assigned to one of four site classifications: (1) large sites: relatively dense concentrations of artifacts (over one hundred), usually spread over a fairly large area; (2) small sites: lesser concentrations of artifacts (thirty–one hundred) covering a smaller area; (3) sherd scatter: a light concentration of artifacts (usually fewer than thirty sherds); and (4) isolated finds (IF's): an isolated finished artifact or a very small number of diagnostic ceramics (fewer than ten) and any associated cultural material.

Recording and collecting procedures differed according to these classifications. The first step was to determine site dimensions. Locations were then plotted on 1:50,000 topographic maps and Lambert Projection coordinates recorded. A scaled sketch map of each site was drawn. Length and width of the site were determined by pacing. On-site measurements of slope were made with a Brunton compass. For sites with variable topography, several measurements were taken. Photos were taken and sites were recorded on site forms provided by the Museo Nacional.

Collection methods depended on site size. At all sites, special collections from artifact concentrations were designated lots A–3 through A–n. Examples of such collections would be concentrations of chipped stone, sherds from a single vessel, collections from stratigraphic profiles, or collections of artifacts found in situ. On small sites, all artifacts observed on the surface were collected. For large sites, areas of special collections were first designated. A 100% sample, lot A2, of a representative area of the site was then collected until approximately 1/2 L of artifacts had been obtained. Lot A2 was intended to be an unbiased collection and was usually made as a 1 m wide transect. Following this, a general surface collection, lot Al, was made. For large sites with high densities and numbers of artifacts, where it was not feasible to collect all diagnostic ceramics, we selected a wide variety. A grab sample thought to be representative of the range of variation of fire-cracked rocks and cooking stones was gathered, and their total numbers counted.

Isolated finds were plotted on topographic maps and collected. Notes were taken describing the extent and nature of the artifacts, and lot cards were filled out for each IF.

Notes were taken on sherd scatters and their locations plotted, but no collections were made. Although sherd scatters often included some lithics, no scatters of predominantly lithic artifacts were found.

Data on environmental variables expected to influence settlement patterns were also recorded. Field notes included information on topography, surrounding vegetation, and access to the site. Additional information on landforms and access to water was gathered from topographic maps that show former river courses and the old lake shoreline.

One of the advantages of working in a volcanically active region is a stratigraphic sequence that facilitates understanding of relationships between sites, settlement patterns, and environmental variables in a chronological context. The regional stratigraphic sequence is derived from tephra deposits from eruptions of Arenal and possibly Cerro Chato (Melson 1984). At El Tajo, a now-inundated site near the Caño Negro River at the east end of the former lake, the depth of the stratigraphic sequence exceeded 20 m (Melson

1982). The total thickness of these deposits measures as little as 20 cm in the Piedra River Valley, approximately 30 km from Arenal Volcano's summit. Underlying these recent volcanic strata is the Aguacate Formation, an ultisol derived from agglomerates, andesitic and basaltic lava flows, breccias, and tuffs of Miocene to Pliocene age (Castillo-Muñoz 1983).

Because the appearance of the strata changes with distance from the volcano, no single stratigraphic sequence could be employed throughout the survey area. Three sequences that have been correlated on the basis of visual, textural, and mineralogical characteristics provide stratigraphic control. The first stratigraphic sequence was established by Melson (1982) at El Tajo. Being the most complete sequence, it was the key to all correlations, but in most cases was not directly used for field designations. Field assessments of stratigraphic levels were based on the Silencio and Tilarán stratigraphic sequences (Melson 1984; Mueller 1984b). The Silencio sequence was defined on the basis of observations of road cuts and excavation units within a range of 25 km from the volcano. The Silencio sequence grades into the Tilarán sequence near Tronadora. Because of changing appearance, missing strata resulting from erosion, and mixing of stratigraphic units, establishing one-to-one correlations between the two sequences in the field is often difficult, and sometimes impossible.

Whereas the Aguacate Formation had previously been regarded as culturally sterile, evidence from both survey and excavation has invalidated this assumption. The Aguacate is readily recognizable in the field as a bright orange-to-red, highly weathered, clay-rich ultisol. Contrasts in color and composition between the Aguacate and overlying deposits allowed us to distinguish cultural features such as pits and postholes. Artifacts were also found in situ in the top of the Aguacate at several sites.

Field inspection was combined with microscopic analysis of soil and tephra samples in the field laboratory to correlate site strata with one another and with El Tajo sequence. Stratigraphic observations also provided a cross-check for ceramic dating of site components.

SURVEY OF THE LAKE ARENAL SHORELINE

Because of our interest in human ecology, we were interested in locating sites of all types, particularly habitations, which were largely undocumented in the Cordillera prior to this project. Another objective was to refine the regional stratigraphic sequence.

The shoreline survey offered unique opportunities. The shoreline crosscuts several ecological zones, allowing us to examine environmental variables and potential resources in relationship to settlement patterns. Shoreline erosion provided a window on the past by exposing sites in deeper stratigraphic levels (Fig. 3-2). Such sites would otherwise have been difficult to detect because of tephra burial and dense vegetative cover. In lower Central America, these conditions make it especially difficult to locate habitation sites. These sites often go unrecognized because they lack substantial architecture and artifact density is low and dispersed.

This phase of survey covered the shoreline of the lake and four small islands in the lake. The shoreline was traversed on foot by a team of one to three archaeologists and two or three local workers. The area surveyed was essentially a transect of the region at 540 m elevation. Width of the eroded shoreline varied from 10 m to 50 m.

Some areas were impassable on foot due to dense vegetation or marshy terrain. Such areas were most frequently encountered near the numerous *quebradas* (streams in steep V-shaped valleys) that drain into the lake. Much of the northern shore and eastern end of the lake are also inaccessible by foot. Other areas were traversed, but erosion was not sufficient to expose subsurface levels; therefore, the presence or absence of sites in these areas is not known. Approximately 58 km of the shoreline were either buried or inaccessible. Thus the actual length of shoreline surveyed was approximately 68 km, about one-half the perimeter of the lakeshore (Fig. 3-3).

At each site along the shoreline, the cut bank, or an eroded section of the shoreline, was cleaned and profiles were measured and drawn to record stratigraphy. Stratigraphic observations were compared with the regional sequences to determine strata in which artifacts were embedded and from which strata surface artifacts derived. The Silencio sequence (Melson 1984; Mueller 1984b) was used for sites along the lakeshore east of the Tronadora River. The Tilarán sequence (Melson 1984) was used at sites west of the Tronadora River.

Of the thirty-nine sites recorded during this phase of survey, thirty are located on the current lakeshore. Six sites are located on islands, only one of which (G-166) was an island prehistori-

Figure 3-2.
Site G-168, at the northern end of Lake Arenal, looking to the southwest. Note erosion of tephra-soil layers by wave action of the lake. The Continental Divide runs along the ridge top in the background. Photograph by Payson Sheets.

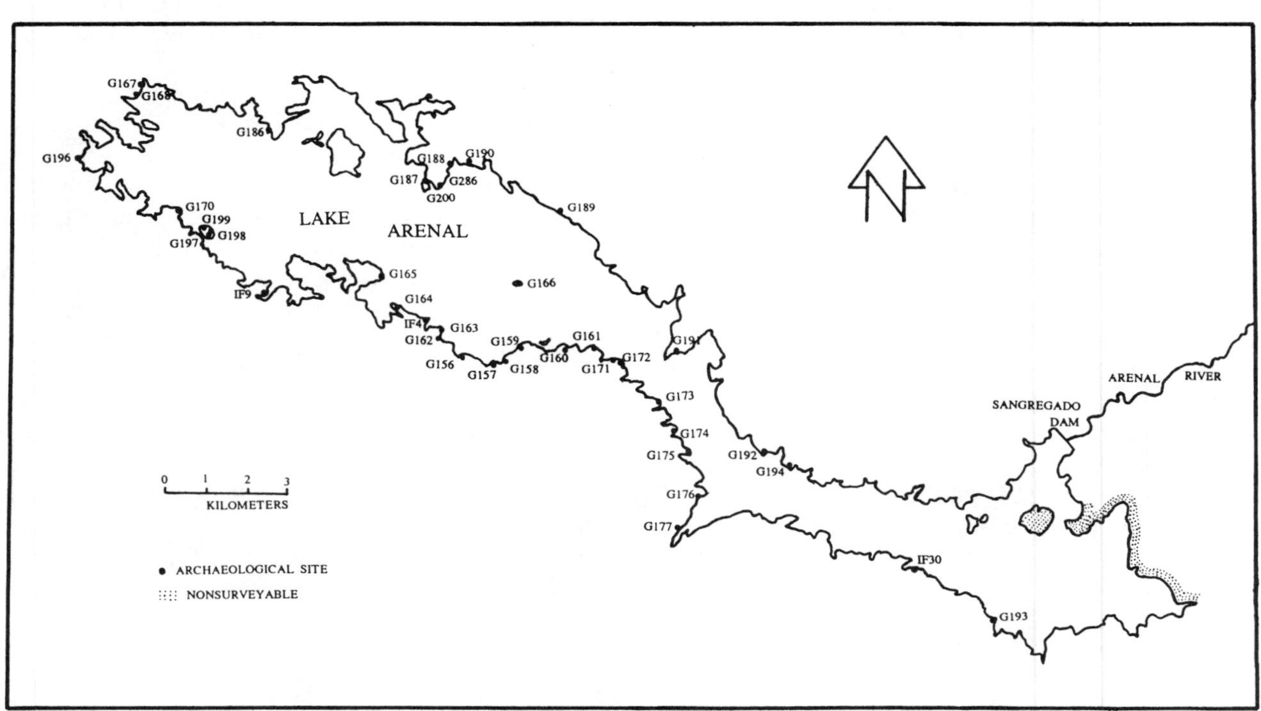

Figure 3-3.
Modern-day shoreline of Lake Arenal, showing the surveyable section and the approximate area of the non-surveyable section. Map by Brian McKee.

cally. Two (G-183 and G-195) are located in the surrounding area a short distance from the current shoreline. Four sites previously recorded by Aguilar (1984) were re-recorded: the island cemetery (G-166); one site on the northern shoreline (G-191); and two in the middle reaches of the former Arenal River Valley (G-176 and G-195).

Fifteen sherd scatters were recorded. No cultural materials were found in situ at any of these locations. Sherd scatters tend to be located in depositional rather than erosional environments and the location of the sites from which they are derived is difficult to determine. They may have been carried shoreward from inundated sites by wave action or transported laterally along the shoreline. They might also have been carried downslope by erosion.

Fifty-four isolated finds were also found and collected. Artifacts were observed in situ at eight IF locations (Fig. 3-3). Further research might well reveal that these are small sites.

SITE DISTRIBUTIONS AND ENVIRONMENTAL FACTORS

Statistical analyses were undertaken in order to elucidate the relationships between environmental factors and site locations. The following variables were included in the analyses: landforms (regional and site-specific), soil types, land use capacity, topographic subareas, Holdridge life zones, slope (regional and on-site), distance to nearest permanent water, distance to the old lakeshore, distance to the Arenal River, site area, and direction of exposure to waves (Mueller 1986).

Statistical analyses were limited to the thirty-five lakeshore sites where data were most complete and comparable and erosion allowed us to ascertain the presence or absence of sites. Statistics were calculated for all site locations, and for site locations by ceramic phase, to examine possible variations through time. Long-term trends were examined by considering each phase of occupation as a separate site, in effect weighting each case in terms of length of occupation. The rationale behind this is the concept of the settlement as a community with the option of continuing or abandoning the site (Chang 1968; Plog 1968).

The Kolmogorov-Smirnov one-sample test was used for ordinal data and the one-sample Chi-square for nominal data. Expected frequencies of sites for each category of a variable were weighted by the proportion of that category along the surveyable shoreline. For single-phase analyses, expected frequencies of topographic subareas and soils were too low for the use of Chi-square tests. It was therefore necessary to dichotomize these variables into a given category versus all other categories and to use binomial tests. The strength of association between variables was also examined. Details of the statistical analyses are available elsewhere (Mueller 1986).

Because of small sample size and problems inherent in the data base, the sample cannot be considered representative of the basin as a whole and interpretation is thus somewhat subjective. These problems stem from two basic sources: the recently enlarged lake and volcanic overburden. Enlargement of the lake has affected the sample by inundating sites below the 540 m level and through shoreline erosion. The most extensive areas of flat land, presumably those most attractive for both settlement and agriculture, have been removed from the sample. Approximately 25.72 km^2 of land around the old lakeshore and 38.89 km^2 of land in the Arenal River Valley were inundated. As mentioned earlier, volcanic overburden at the eastern end of the lake and lack of erosion in other areas has obscured site visibility along about half of the shoreline.

The amount of information lost through inundation is, of course, immeasurable. The proportion of a site that had been inundated was impossible to determine. In some areas, site size can be related to topographic features. In the *quebrada/* ridge zone between the Tronadora and the Chiquito rivers, artifact distribution often extends around the base of a ridge; the area of these sites can be estimated to include the entire landform. In other areas, however, no correlations can be drawn between landforms and site size. Comparisons drawn on the basis of the distribution of cultural materials along the shoreline thus may not be representative of actual site sizes or functions.

Exposed areas of sites do not appear to be a function of geological processes, however. The effects of wave-induced erosion on site size were examined, but no significant correlations were found between site area and either exposure to erosion or slope. Inundation of entire sites and the patchiness of eroded areas render any attempt to calculate distances between sites spurious. Lacking adequate information on the critical variables of site sizes, functions, and distances between sites, we were unable to use the settlement data as a basis for inferences regarding social organization.

Past fluctuations in the water level ranging from 480 m to 530 m in elevation (Tosi 1980) further complicate the situtation. Tosi (ibid.), basing his argument on geomorphological evidence, attributes the changes in water level to the appearance of the volcanoes to the east, and to Arenal in particular. This scenario has numerous implications for prehistoric settlement. Known early sedentary settlements (e.g., site G-163) predate Arenal's activity. Archaic and early ceramic sites might have been close to the ancient river valley preceding formation of the lake. If Tosi's reconstruction is accurate, then major fluctuations took place during the occupation sequence and some changes in population levels and site locations may relate to this. Much of the evidence which might be used to test this interpretation is no longer accessible because of inundation. Recent reconstructions of the history of the Arenal–Cerro Chato volcanic system tend to support the view that the prehistoric lake resulted from the early eruptions of Arenal Volcano (Borgia et al. 1988).

An alternative interpretation is based on the presence of Zoned Bichrome sites at the western end of the lake. These sites were discovered by Murray in 1979, when the lake was at the 512 m level (Lange, personal communication, 1984). It has been assumed that major fluctuations are therefore unlikely to have occurred during the last 3,000 years (Sheets 1984a). Precise site locations are unknown, however. Nor does the presence of sites at this elevation in a given period logically preclude later fluctuations in the water level. Nevertheless, because this is the only datable and mappable evidence on the relationship between sites and the old lake, the 512 m lake level has been adopted as a guideline for prehistoric conditions. In the following discussion, therefore, the terms "lake," "lakeshore," and "shoreline" refer to the prehistoric 512 m level rather than the 540 m survey level. Locations of sites in relationship to this lake level, former landforms, and river drainages are shown in Figures 3-4–3-7.

Results of statistical analyses underscore three fundamental aspects of the area: a high degree of local variability; the scarcity of flat land; and the obscuring effects of site inundation and volcanic overburden. Among the most important variables for sedentary communities were access to fresh water, topographic subareas, and regional landforms (Mueller 1986).

Water Resources

Most sites (75%) are within half a kilometer of running water. Only one site on the southern shore (G-170) and the island site G-166 (Fig. 3-8) are located closer to the lake than to a perennial source of running water. Along the northern shore, the trend is reversed; however, the 540 m contour of the survey is also farther from the old lake on the southern shore than it is on the northern shore. Sites on the northern shore are also separated from running water by a long ridge paralleling the shore. This may in part explain the lack of sites in the northwestern sector. Sites may be farther from the lake and closer to *quebradas,* where fresh water was available. Proximity to fresh water probably reflects the basic need for potable water for drinking, cooking, and washing as well as other daily domestic activities.

When the Sangregado Dam was constructed, Lake Arenal was a shallow lake overgrown with vegetation. Little study has been done of rates of eutrophication for tropical lakes (Tosi, personal communication, 1985), and hence it is difficult to tell whether the lake provided potable water at a given time in the past. Eutrophication can occur quite rapidly in tropical lakes once a critical threshhold of nutrients has been reached (Sheets, personal communication, 1986). Volcanism could have had rapid and long-lasting effects on the potability and productivity of the lake's waters. Aquatic species may be quite sensitive to chemical and temperature changes and to the increased turbidity and acidity of water resulting from volcanic input (Blong 1984:335–338). Volcanic activity may have altered the subsistence potential of the lake as well as the land, thereby affecting settlement patterns.

Assessing the nature and duration of the effects of particular eruptions on the lake's resources is a problem for future research. The hypothesis that the lake was not eutrophied during most of prehistory is viable and testable, however, and receives some support from the archaeological evidence (Sheets, personal communication, 1986). The island cemetery (G-166) was in use throughout the occupation sequence, implying open water and boats or rafts to reach it. The technology to construct the water-going craft necessary to exploit the resources of the lake was known throughout lower Central America in prehistory (Willey 1971; Lange 1978). The proximity of northern shore sites to the old lake may also

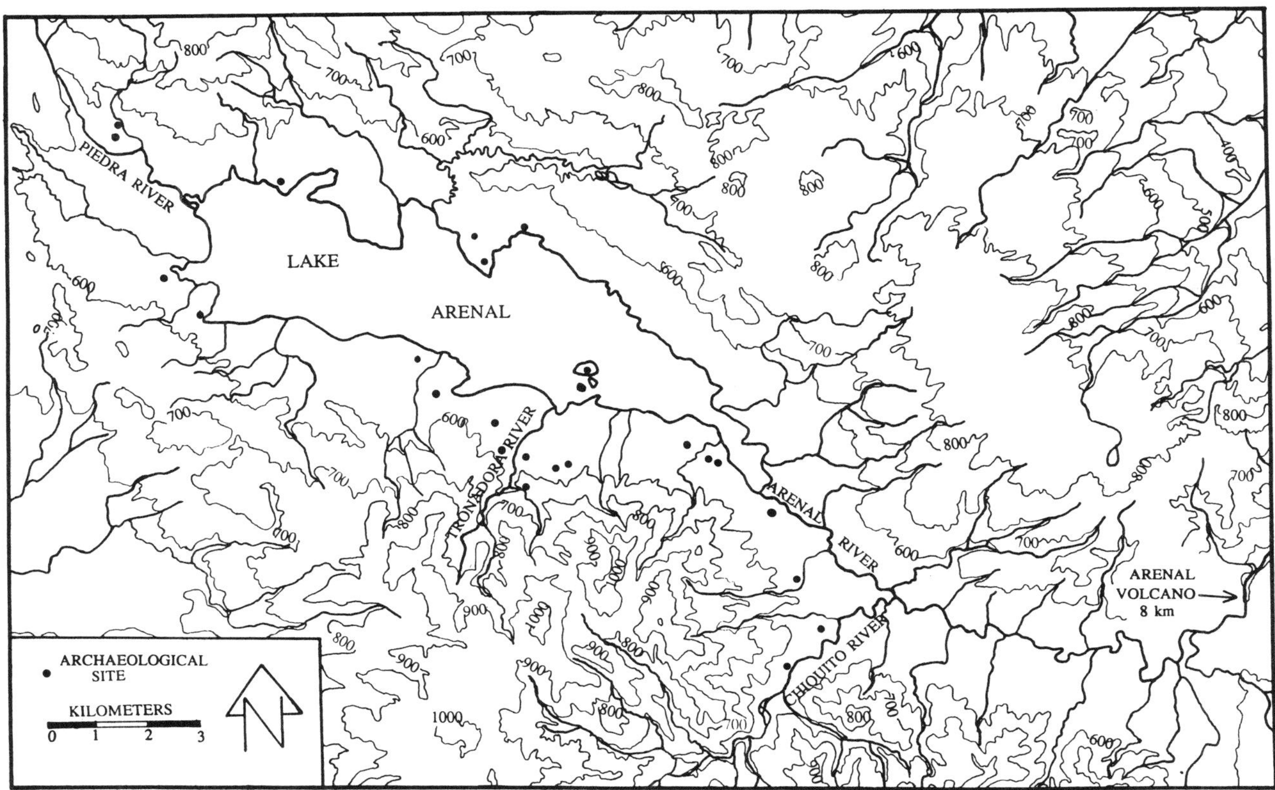

Figure 3-4.
Above: *Tronadora Phase sites (2000–500 BC). Map by Brian McKee.*

Figure 3-5.
Below: *Arenal Phase sites (500 BC–AD 600). Map by Brian McKee.*

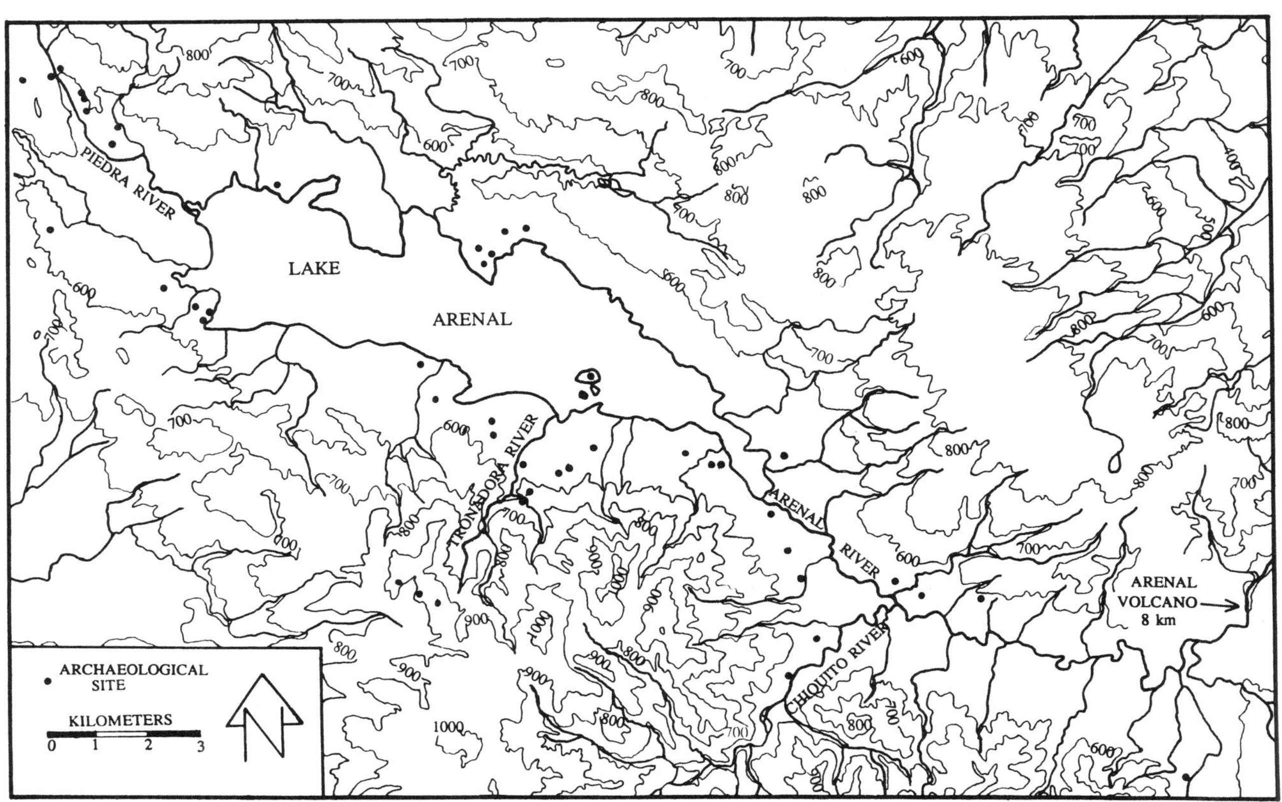

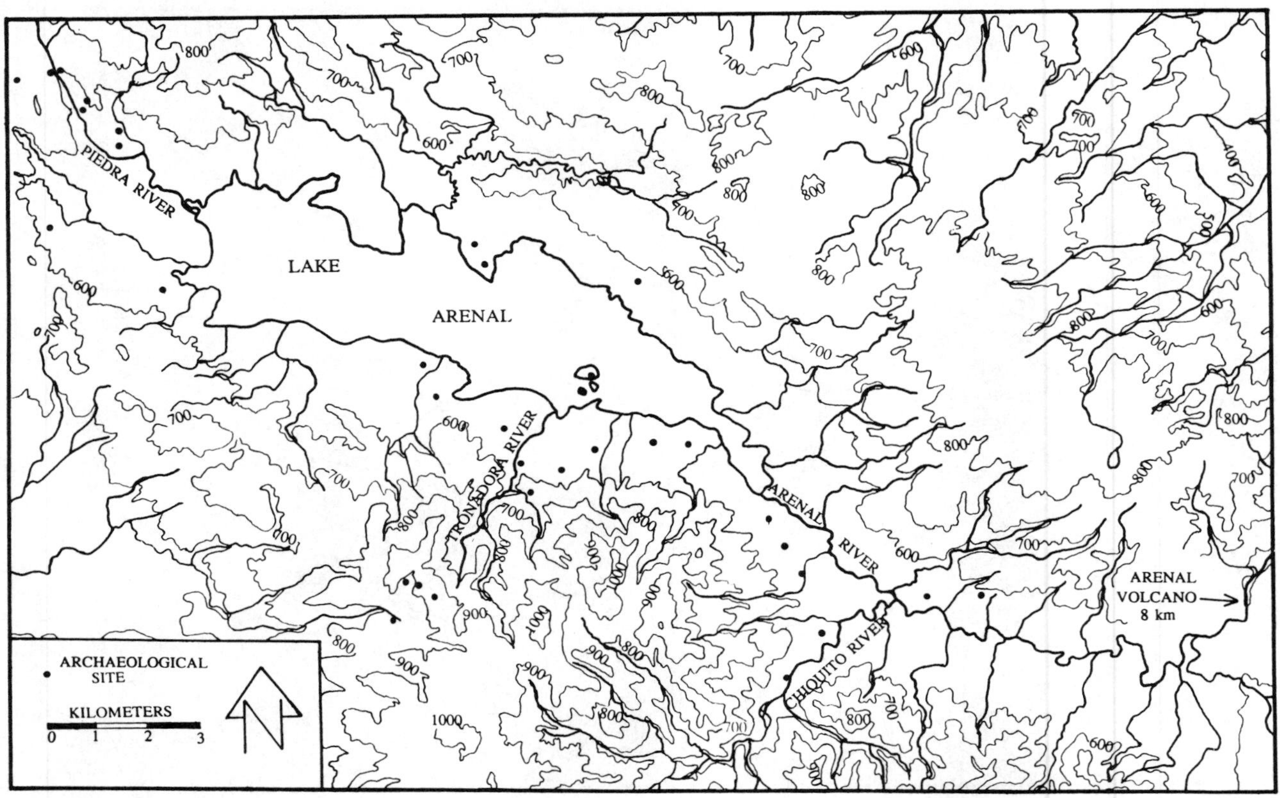

Figure 3-6.
Above: *Silencio Phase sites (AD 600–1300). Map by Brian McKee.*

Figure 3-7.
Below: *Tilarán Phase sites (AD 1300–1500). Map by Brian McKee.*

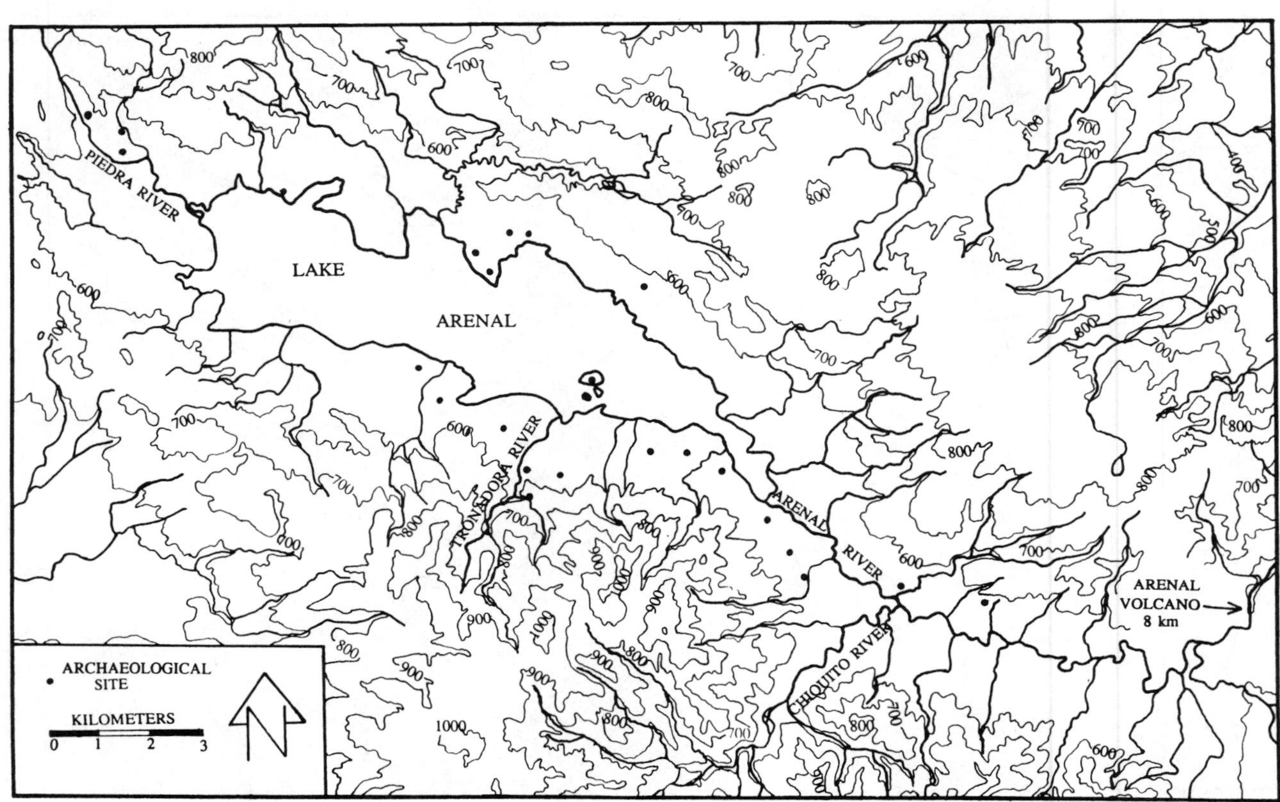

Figure 3-8.
The Island Cemetery, G-166, in May 1984, looking northeast. During much of the year, when the water level is higher, the site is completely under water. Photograph by Payson Sheets.

lend support to the hypothesis that the lake was open throughout the occupation sequence, since many of these sites were occupied during the Silencio and Tilarán phases.

If the lake were open, it may have been a focus of settlement due to the availability of relatively flat land, water, and opportunities for fishing and hunting waterfowl, as well as for gathering plant foods and molluscs along its margins. Thus it is highly probable that inundation has drastically affected the available sample of settlements.

Topographic Subareas

Topographic subareas were defined based on major physiographic characteristics and geographic location. Their boundaries are best summarized visually (Fig. 3-9). Despite their somewhat subjective nature, they did prove to be useful groupings for the examination of site locations.

Sites do not concentrate in areas most favorable, in terms of climate, soils, or topographic subareas, for agriculture. Rather, sites cluster around the base of the mountain massif southeast of the old lakeshore, particularly in the foothills between the mountains and the southeastern shore

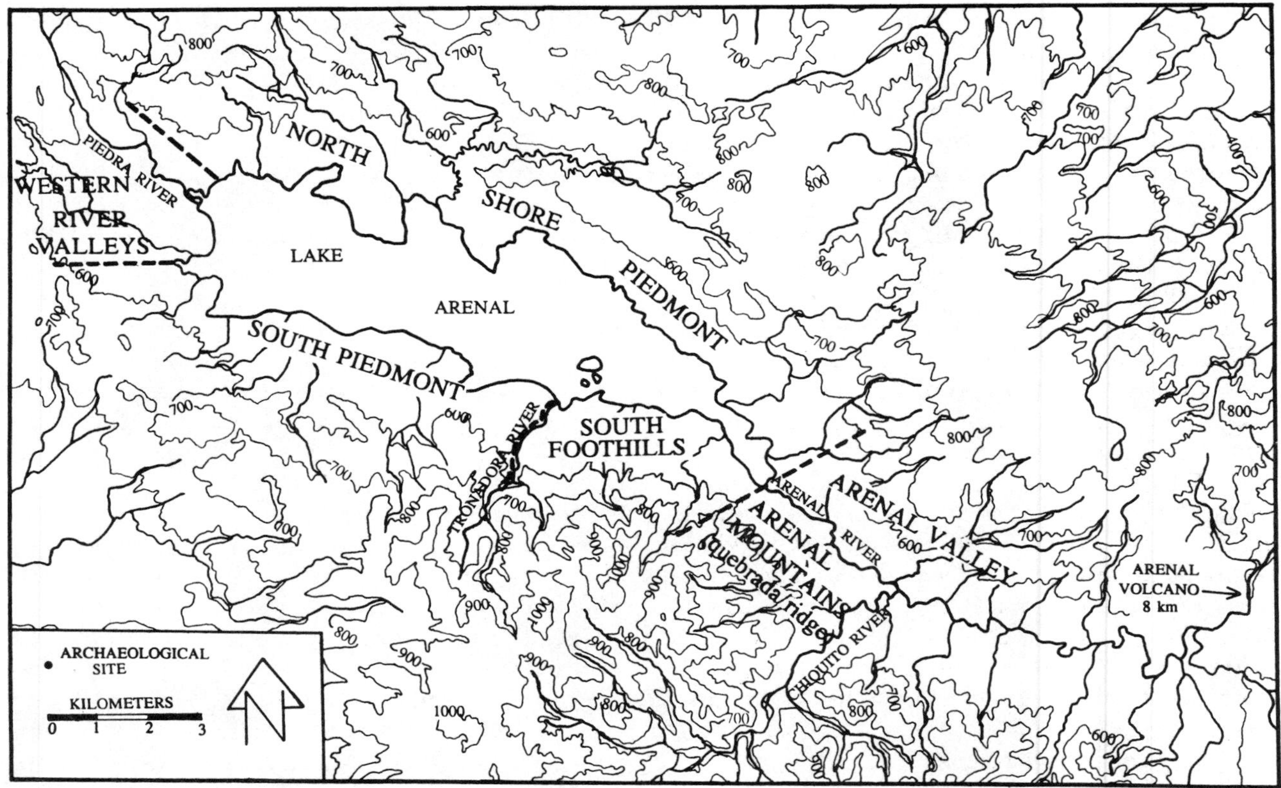

Figure 3-9.
*Topographic subareas in the Arenal basin: north shore piedmont, western river valleys, south shore piedmont, south shore foothills, Arenal Valley, Arenal Mountains (*quebrada*/ridge zone), and mountainous zone southeast of the old lakeshore. Map by Brian McKee.*

of the old lake. This pattern was established during the Tronadora Phase, beginning about 2000 BC, and persisted throughout the occupation sequence.

Although relief throughout this subarea is generally quite high, the average on-site slope at these sites (11°) is the lowest of any topographic subarea. The immediate juxtaposition of limited areas of relatively flat land suitable for habitation to steep slopes could have been a factor in the continued occupation of these sites. The steep slopes nearby would probably have been among the first areas to recover from the adverse effects of volcanic eruptions. Using the Paricutín eruptions as a model (Segerstrom 1950; Rees 1979), erosion of steep slopes would remove sufficient overburden to allow regeneration of vegetation. Weathering of remaining deposits and mixing with topsoil would promote soil enrichment, and thereby accelerate recovery and increase productivity.

These sites also had access to a wider variety of ecological zones than did settlements in other parts of the basin. They were close to valley bottomlands, a major river, the highlands, and the lake. The settlement data are thus in agreement with the macrobotanical, pollen, and phytolith studies that indicate a mixed subsistence base throughout prehistory (Matthews 1984; Chap. 16, this volume).

Eight more sites (not included in statistical analyses) were found at higher elevations, ranging from 600 m to 900 m, in the steeply dissected *quebrada*/ridge terrain to the west of the same mountain massif. This area is undersampled, however, with investigation limited to a brief post-hole survey, inspection of road cuts, and leads furnished by local informants.

Site density is conspicuously lower in the southern piedmont subarea at the western end of the lake. Here the relatively fertile soils, low relief, and drier climate would be expected to favor settlement and agriculture. This end of the historic lake was shallow and marshy (Tosi 1980). Given the low gradient, it is probable that these conditions can be projected back into prehistoric times. This need not necessarily be construed as detrimental to suitability for settlement, however. Although sites were farther from open water than those in some other subareas, marshland environments are exceptionally rich in flora and fauna. This richness, in proximity to both arable and forested land, would lead one to expect much higher site densities than those recorded during our survey.

Not only were fewer sites recorded in this area, but most were occupied during only one or two ceramic phases, whereas those bordering the mountains to the east were usually occupied for three or four phases. As this area is farther from the volcano, it seems unlikely that volcanic activity was a major factor; nor was there a paucity of sites in the nearby Piedra River Valley. We know from Murray's unpublished survey that some sites, now inundated, existed at this end of the lake. The apparent lack of sites may therefore be due to low site visibility.

The Arenal Valley also had fewer sites than expected, especially during the Silencio and Tilarán phases. Only two sites were occupied during the Silencio Phase and one during the Tilarán Phase. It should be kept in mind, however, that the amount of land inundated in this subarea was greater than in other parts of the basin.

Sites on the northern shore are distinctive in several respects. The terrain is steeper than in other parts of the survey area, and there is an inverse relationship between distance to the lake and distance to permanent water. Unlike other areas, these sites did not have access to large expanses of flat land. During the Tilarán Phase, this was the only subarea in which the number of sites appears to have increased.

Regional Landforms

As defined by Tosi (1980), landforms are morphological classifications derived from elevation, length and percent slope (first- and second-order slopes), relief, and, minimally, the nature of parent materials. The statistical significance of site location relative to regional landforms could be established only when considering each ceramic phase as a separate site.

Although landforms were expected to be important factors in site locations, analysis showed a trend the reverse of that anticipated. Rather than a concentration of sites in the flattest areas, as would be predicted by most settlement models, an unusually large number of sites were located on piedmont slopes, with regional variation between 6% and 12%, and local measurements between 0% and 20%. Statistical analysis appears to reflect a long-range trend resulting primarily from expansion of population into the highlands south of the lake during the Arenal and Silencio phases.

Slope

Slopes at sites along the lakeshore range from 6° to 23°. Most (70%) are between 10° and 20°. All sites are in areas that are flatter than the surrounding terrain. Statistical analysis, however, revealed no pattern relating on-site slope to settlement. This may be because most flatland is under water, or it may be a reflection of the scarcity of flatland around Lake Arenal. Both factors probably played a role. People probably took advantage of scattered benches and hilltops as population expanded into the highlands. This appears to have been the case in the area southeast of the lakeshore, where the lowest average on-site slope is found in an area of generally steep, rugged relief. Sites G-169, G-154 (Fig. 3-10), G-155, G-183, and G-150 are additional examples of sites in such locations.

Life Zones

The relationships between climatic variability, undisturbed vegetation, and land use potential within the Arenal basin can be explored with reference to data from meteorological stations and the Holdridge life zones, or "bioclimates." The primary vegetation in each life zone is determined by the seasonal variation and distribution of temperature and rainfall (Hartshorn 1983). Each life zone contains unique ecosystems with distinctive environmental conditions and associations of plants and animals.

Figure 3-10.
Site G-154 in lower center of photograph, overlooking the Santa Rosa River below. Rolling quebrada/*ridge topography is common on the Pacific side of the Continental Divide. The site was a small habitation in the centuries just prior to the Spanish Conquest. Photograph by Payson Sheets.*

All sites along the northern shore and those east of Quebrada Tronadorcita on the south shore are in the Premontane Wet Forest (*bosque muy húmedo premontano*) life zone. Pristine vegetation was a medium to tall semievergreen forest. This life zone exhibits wide variability. Mean annual rainfall near Site G-174 is 2,800 mm; there are no dry months and precipitation is distributed over 11 wet months and one month of excessive precipitation. Moving east and south to the Chiquito River, annual precipitation increases to 3,333 mm. Although there is one dry month, there are also 5 wet months and 6 months of excessive moisture (Tosi 1980).

Tosi (1980:1:29–33) has defined three provinces of soil and atmospheric humidity, which influence the biotic environment and hydrology of the Arenal area. The Tropical Premontane Wet Forest belongs to the perhumid province, which is highly productive for tropical forests, but limited for agriculture. During months of excessive rainfall, soils may become saturated, and anaerobic soil conditions may develop, making the soil difficult to work; open fields are subject to massive erosion, especially on steep slopes. The soils are generally low in fertility and very acid, except in exceptional cases, such as terrain with low slopes or alluvial soils (ibid.). Sites in the foothills along the south shore and in the Arenal Valley had access to alluvial soils. Crops that cannot tolerate a pronounced dry season are best adapted to this area, whereas crops such as maize, which require a dry season, are less so. Seasonal crops including maize, beans, tomatoes, and chiles are grown in these areas today, however, sometimes on amazingly steep slopes.

Although suitable for seasonal cultivation, the land on which sites near Tronadora or farther east are located is better suited to permanent or semipermanent cultigens such as tree crops (ibid.). When cultivated using methods that involve minimal soil reworking, maize and beans can be considered semipermanent crops (ibid.). Most Precolumbian agricultural practices, such as swidden agriculture, could be placed in this category. The practice of burning fields before planting, however, typical of maize agriculture in much of the New World, exposes the soils to potentially severe erosion (ibid.).

The southern shore west of Quebrada Tronadorcita is in the tropical moist forest, Premontane Transition (*bosque húmedo tropical, transición a premontano*) life zone. The original vegetation of this life zone was tall, multistoried semideciduous or evergreen forest (Hartshorn 1983).

The climatic gradient within the basin is apparent even within this life zone. Annual precipitation averages 2,233 to 2,440 mm at the western end of the lake, increasing to 2,600 mm at Tronadora. The western end of the lake has a dry season of 2 to 4 months, a wet season of 7 to 10 months, and at most 1 month of excessive rainfall. Farther east, sites near Tronadora receive slightly more rainfall but lack a real dry season. Eleven months of wet weather and one of excessive precipitation are characteristic of this area.

This life zone is in the humid province (ibid.), which offers almost ideal conditions for agriculture, with sufficient soil moisture even in the dry season. Compared to more humid bioclimates, such as the Tropical Premontane Wet Forest to the north and the east, soils here are less acid and more fertile and productive. The soils, long hours of sunshine, and relatively low humidity make the region well suited for cultigens with a short growing season. Fortunately, since the soil mantle in this zone is relatively thin, losses to runoff are relatively low.

Although, in theory, each life zone has a different resource potential, we found no statistically significant relationship between life zones and site locations. Given the high degree of local variability in the Arenal area, the life zones may be too broad to be useful. Many of the plants and animals of economic importance to prehistoric residents have extremely wide habitats, extending from southern Mesoamerica to northern South America, and crosscutting the boundaries of the life zones. Nor do life zones take into account soil characteristics, which interact with the biotic environment. Analyses of soil samples collected by the Proyecto Prehistórico Arenal and analyzed by the Facultad de Agricultura of the Universidad de Costa Rica do not support the general assumption that there are major differences in soil acidity between life zones; all were relatively neutral.

Soils

Although statistical analyses of soil types relative to site locations resulted in significant figures, this may be an instance in which statistical significance does not equal substantive significance. Projecting modern soils data into the past is somewhat dubious, especially in a tropical environment, where chemical weathering is extremely rapid; however, the soils classifications do take into account the entire profile and soil formation processes. Analysis of this variable was also predicated on the assumption that major climatic changes did not occur during the occupation sequence and therefore conditions of soil formation were relatively stable. It was thus intended to reflect only very broad trends. We found the greatest concentration of sites in the area of least-fertile soils, to the southeast of the lake. This phenomenon is thus attributed to the topographic subarea, which provided access to several different ecological zones, and supports the hypothesis that Arenal-area residents were not highly dependent on agriculture.

CERAMIC CHRONOLOGY AND STRATIGRAPHIC CORRELATIONS

All sites along the lakeshore are multicomponent sites. Tronadora Phase ceramics were the predominant component at two sites, G-162 and G-163. At both sites, sherds were observed in the first black soil above the Aguacate Formation.

At Arenal Phase sites in the eastern part of the survey area, artifacts were observed in situ in the Unit 50 Complex. At sites where the Tilarán stratigraphic sequence was used, artifacts were found in the top of the Aguacate Formation, Black 1, White 2, and/or Black 2. Arenal Phase ceramics predominated in only two cases in which artifacts were observed eroding from Unit 30 (Sites G-171 and G-176).

The presence of early ceramics in more recent strata has several possible explanations. Disturbance or reworking of soils at sites through cultural activities or natural processes may account for this at G-171. At G-176, erosion did not extend deeper than Unit 30. The site is located on the floodplain of the Chiquito River and some of the sherds could have been transported a considerable distance and deposited on the beach. This site corresponds to Aguilar's (1984) site 196 and our chronological placement agrees with his.

Silencio Phase ceramics were found both above (in Unit 30) and below Unit 41 (in the Unit 50 Complex). Artifacts at predominantly Tilarán Phase sites were consistently found in Unit 30.

East of the Chiquito River, erosion is too shallow to expose early sites. Occasional Arenal Phase sherds were noted, so it is possible that sites of this period are present but too deeply buried to be detected. Only one site (G-193) was found on the southern shore in this area. The erosional pattern here is extremely variable, however. The Aguacate Formation was exposed in only one location. In most eroded sections, the base of Unit 41 was discernible, and in some sections erosion cut into the upper part of the Unit 50 Complex. In other places erosion did not extend to the base of Unit 30. Thus the apparent lack of sites in this area may be due partly to volcanic overburden. Also, the current shoreline passes through steep hillsides, topographically unlikely locations for sites. Sites would more likely have been located in the valley of the Arenal River. On the higher ridge tops and hilltops only small sites, perhaps single-family dwellings, are likely to be found because there is little level ground.

Erosion is deep enough in most places in the Arenal River Valley to reveal sites occupied during the Silencio and the Tilarán phases, were they present. Only two sites were found dating to the Silencio Phase and only one dating to the Tilarán Phase. The absence of sites from the later phases supports the hypothesis of a population decline or a shift in settlements during the Silencio Phase. The thickness of tephra layers in this area is such that environmental disturbance may well have resulted in low population during much of Arenal Volcano's history. A thickness of over 1 m apiece for Units 40 and 41 is more than sufficient to have adversely affected wildlife, agriculture, and the lake. As little as 0.15 m of ash deposits can cause slight damage to trees and kill some shrubs and herbs; 0.5 m to 1.5 m can result in tree damage and heavy kill of shrubs and herbs (Rees 1979). Deposits of over 1.5 m compose a zone of total devastation. Given that Units 40 and 41 probably were deposited within a relatively short time and have been compacted, damage to vegetation in this area was no doubt severe and recovery would have been slow. Soils analysis supports this hypothesis, as it shows relatively low levels of major nutrients in the area near the Caño Negro River.

CHRONOLOGICAL AND DEMOGRAPHIC CHANGES

Data from preceramic occupations are limited. The occupation of the basin since the Paleo-Indian Period is suggested by the surface find of a Clovis point at site G-164. The Archaic Period is represented by a lithic workshop (AL-186) located close to sources of cryptocrystalline materials. The area surrounding the old lakeshore was also at least sparsely populated. At site G-163 an Archaic projectile point was found on the surface, and lithic debitage from the lowest excavation levels probably also dates to this period (Chap. 11). A similar range of materials was found on the surface at G-162.

The establishment of sedentary, ceramic-producing communities antedates the first eruptions of Arenal Volcano. Although many sites were established during this time (Fig. 3-4), only at sites G-163 and G-162 are Tronadora Phase ceramics predominant. A cluster of radiocarbon dates from G-163, supported by stratigraphic relationships, places the date of initial occupation at about 2000 BC, making these the earliest well-dated village communities yet excavated in Costa Rica (Chap. 4).

These dates are extremely important in placing Costa Rica in a regional perspective. Previous attempts to extend Costa Rican ceramic chronologies to even the beginning of the first millennium BC have been unsuccessful. These dates place the Tronadora Phase on a time horizon comparable to Early-Middle Formative Period developments in other parts of Central America.

Major occupation of the area occurred during the Arenal Phase (500 BC–AD 600). During that time, sites increased in size and frequency (Fig. 3-

5). The number of lakeshore sites increased from twenty-one to thirty-three and the quantity of cultural material is much higher. Arenal Phase ceramics predominate at twenty-seven of the thirty-five lakeshore sites, and at thirty-eight of the sixty-two sites recorded in the area. New sites were established beyond the lakeshore, in the highlands, the Piedra River Valley, and the middle reaches of the Arenal Valley.

While volcanic activity cannot be evoked as a primary causal agent in the original settlement of the area, it may have been an important factor in these later changes. Evidence of large-scale land clearing during the Arenal Phase (Chap. 14) may be related to population increase and apparent expansion beyond the lakeshore. By this time, some of the early volcanic deposits had weathered to form relatively fertile soils. If the formation of the lake is a result of Arenal's eruptions, which post-date early settlements in the area, improvements in the lake's productivity could also have contributed to the population growth during the Arenal Phase.

Along the lakeshore, there are conspicuously fewer sites with predominantly Silencio Phase (AD 600–1300) ceramics. Only two new sites (G-160 and G-189) were established and the total number of lakeshore sites dropped from thirty-three to twenty-one (Fig. 3-6). Silencio Phase ceramics are highest in percentage at only two sites, G-189, along the northern shore and G-174, a large habitation site in the *quebrada*/ridge zone of the Arenal Valley.

The paucity of Silencio Phase sites along the lakeshore and in the upper reaches of the Arenal Valley is offset by a dominance of Silencio Phase sites in other areas. The Piedra River Valley appears to have been densely populated at this time (see below). In addition, most of the sites in the highlands south of the lake are predominantly Silencio Phase. Thus, there may have been a population shift toward the west within the region in response to volcanic activity.

Highland sites include the G-150 cemetery (Chap. 6), and two sites (G-151 and G-152) that were apparently caches for the laja used in tomb construction at that cemetery (Chap. 7). In the Piedra River Valley, one large habitation site (G-180) and cemeteries with unique ground- and incised stone markers (G-181) (Chap. 12) or stone-faced masonry (G-184) date to the Silencio Phase. Two other possible elite cemeteries (AL-185 and AL-178) were located in the middle reaches of the Arenal River Valley. The nature of the grave goods, the presence of architecture at some cemeteries, new site types (the laja repositories), and the presence of a few large habitation sites may therefore point to changes in social organization rather than to population decline. On the other hand, there is little evidence that Silencio Phase habitation sites were more nucleated than the largest sites of the Arenal Phase. Further test excavations will be necessary to determine the degree of site nucleation during these two phases.

The Tilarán Phase (AD 1300–1500) appears to have been a period of instability within the area. Some sites increased in population, while others continued to decline, or were abandoned. Overall, the number of sites in the basin continued to decline (Fig. 3-7), but the rate was apparently slower than in other parts of the Cordillera and did not culminate in near-abandonment, as in other intermontane valleys (Finch 1982–1983; Norr 1982–1983; Ryder 1982–1983a,b). At only three sites along the lakeshore (G-160, G-161, G-188) and three beyond the shoreline (G-169, G-195, G-154) are Tilarán Phase ceramics the primary component. No new sites were established, but some previously abandoned sites on the northern shore were reoccupied (G-186, G-187, G-188, G-189, G-192). This is the only area where this phenomenon appears to have occurred. In other parts of the basin, sites were not reoccupied once abandoned. The distribution of sites closely resembles that of the Tronadora Phase.

THE PIEDRA AND ARENAL RIVER VALLEYS

Archaeological survey was extended into the valleys of the Piedra River to the west and the Arenal River to the east of Arenal Volcano to explore the effects of the environmental gradient within the basin on settlement patterns and to obtain comparative data on the effects of volcanic activity on soil development and fertility in relationship to settlement patterns.

THE PIEDRA RIVER VALLEY

The Piedra and the Sábalo rivers flow into the western end of Lake Arenal. This area is 30–33 km WNW of Arenal Volcano. Because the predominantly northeasterly winds carry most of the tephra to the southwest of Arenal Volcano, soil development in this area was less affected by volcanism than it was in areas to the east and closer to the volcano. Soils are shallow and relatively homogeneous.

The survey extended from the hilltops separating the two valleys to the hilltops approximately 1 km east of the Piedra River. While virtually all of this area was covered either on foot or horseback, the thick grass cover prohibited the recognition of sites in much of the area. Special attention was therefore given to road cuts, eroded areas, planted fields, paths, and other areas where the ground surface was exposed. Local residents also provided helpful information.

The river's headwaters rise in mountainous terrain to the northwest of the lake. In the middle and lower reaches of the valley, the alluvial plain is almost a kilometer wide. The lower valley is easily accessible from both the lakeshore to the east and the Sábalo River Valley to the west. The upper Sábalo River Valley forms a low pass in the Continental Divide, which may have provided a natural route for communication and trade with areas to the north and the west.

Eight sites were located in the Piedra River Valley, including G-167 and G-168, which were recorded as part of the lakeshore survey. These two sites may actually be part of one large site; today they are separated by the road around the lake. Six IF's were also recorded.

Although G-167/168 has a small Tronadora Phase occupation, the six sites upriver apparently were first occupied during the Arenal Phase. Although Arenal Phase ceramics predominate at most of these sites, occupation of the valley does not appear to have declined greatly during the Silencio Phase, in contrast with other parts of the basin. Changes in social organization, rather than population decline, are suggested by the nature of the sites and the artifact inventories. Site G-180 is a very large habitation site with high ceramic density and a preponderance of possibly special-purpose types. Cemetery G-181 yielded a sculpted stone that may have served as a grave marker and incised stones with hachured motifs similar to those found at El Silencio (G-150), a possible elite graveyard. Funerary architecture at Site G-184 includes a stone-faced mound surrounded by smaller possible graves, and linear stone features. Such features are not characteristic of the Arenal Phase and may indicate increasing social differentiation during the Silencio Phase. Only one site, G-180, remained occupied during the Tilarán Phase, and its population had dwindled.

Aguilar visited this area in his brief survey before the Sangregado Dam was built and reported "numerous and possibly large" settlements along the Piedra River, only one of which (Carmelo, a Late Zoned Bichrome cemetery) was recorded (1984:66). Another now-inundated site with two or three mounds of river cobbles is also mentioned. Ceramics were found along the roadway to El Jilguero, which runs northeast of the valley.

Aguilar postulates a substantial population in the Piedra River Valley. Our data seem to support this and could reflect a movement away from the lakeshore during the Silencio Phase. During that time, two major eruptions deposited Units 40 and 41, which were thick enough to have caused local environmental disruption in the eastern portion of the basin. Thus the increased population density in the Piedra River Valley might have been stimulated by volcanic activity, with some lakeside dwellers moving into the valley. The population decline during the Tilarán Phase cannot be correlated with volcanism, however.

The Piedra River Valley sites are in the Tropical Premontane Wet Forest life zone, as are the sites on the northern and southeastern lakeshore. Habitation sites are located on hill slopes or hilltops bordering the eastern floodplain (G-178, G-179, G-180), as well as on the floodplain itself (G-167/G-168). Of the three cemeteries, one (G-182) is on a high ridge straddling the divide between the Piedra and Sábalo river valleys, while the other two (G-181 and G-184) are on the floodplain. All of the sites on the floodplain are on slightly elevated ground, which, in the case of the cemeteries, was probably built up culturally. Site elevations vary from 540 m to 680 m.

ARENAL RIVER VALLEY

Prior to the construction of the dam, the Arenal River drained not only the ancient lake, but also a wide, flat valley with an extensive tributary system. The Arenal River flows northeastward into the San Carlos River, which in turn flows into the San Juan River and finally into the Atlantic Ocean. Ethnohistorical accounts relate that the San Juan was a major artery of communication and trade at the time of Spanish contact (Stone 1977:161–166), and it is possible that the Arenal River Valley residents participated in this trade.

There are three major physiographic regions in the Arenal Valley (Chacón 1982): the *quebrada/* ridge terrain to the west of the volcanoes; an area covered by lava flows, block avalanches, and lahars to the north of Arenal Volcano; and alluvial terraces in the lowlands to the east.

Nine sites discovered during the course of the lakeshore survey are located in the upper reaches of the Arenal River Valley. Aguilar (1984) surveyed this area in 1977–1978, and recorded seven sites that are now totally or partially inundated. Three of our sites correspond to his: our G-195 to his 192, our G-176 to his 196, our G-191 to his 197. Therefore, the total number of known sites in this section of the valley is thirteen. The majority of these sites were first settled during the Arenal Phase. The only predominantly Silencio Phase site (G-174) is a large habitation. Tilarán Phase ceramics predominate at two sites in this sector (G-173, a small habitation, and G-195, a large cemetery).

With the exception of G-176 and G-191, we did not include the sites reported by Aguilar in the statistical analysis because of imprecise or contradictory information on site locations and lack of quantified data on artifacts. Aguilar's sites seem to conform to the general pattern seen in other sites in the valley, however, in that they are closer to *quebradas* than to the Arenal River and situated on ridges, slopes, or hilltops above the floodplain.

Farther downstream to the east of the volcanoes, near the town of La Fortuna, are six sites on alluvial terraces and two on piedmont slopes. As in other parts of the basin, sites were located close to *quebradas*. The topography east of the volcano is markedly different from that surrounding Lake Arenal. Slopes are less than 5° (Chacón 1982) and relief is low. Site elevations range from 150 m to 300 m.

Sites to the west of the volcano are in the Tropical Premontane Wet Forest life zone. Those to the east are in the Tropical Wet Forest, the most species-rich life zone in Costa Rica (Hartshorn 1983). Mean annual precipitation varies from 4,200 mm near Sangregado Dam to over 6,300 mm near the volcano, with no dry season (Tosi 1980: table 33-7). Descending to the eastern lowlands, annual rainfall decreases, ranging from 3,600 mm to 4,500 mm, with at most 1 dry month. The main limitation of this area for agriculture is not soil fertility, but saturation due to high rainfall (Saenz, personal communication, 1985).

Three sites in the Fortuna area (AL-178, AL-182, and AL-185) are cemeteries. Other sites, with relatively low artifact densities, were found in plowed fields and are probably the dispersed remains of habitation sites. There is no established ceramic sequence for this area, but most sites are contemporary with the late Arenal and early Silencio phases of the Cordillera (Snarskis, personal communication, 1985). Two sites (AL-179 and AL-187) have earlier occupations contemporary with the Tronadora Phase.

COMPARISONS

For hunting and gathering peoples of the Archaic Period, the environment of the basin must have been rich in resources, and offered a wide variety of flora and fauna and raw materials for stone and wooden tools. Proximity to lithic sources seems to have been a factor in site location. The Archaic workshop (AL 186) is located close to the Venado Formation, the most likely source of cryptocrystalline materials. Similarly, the Turrialba site in the Atlantic Watershed of Costa Rica (Snarskis 1984a: 195) and Archaic sites in Panama (Weiland 1984: 43) are found close to sources of lithic raw materials.

Tronadora Phase settlement resembles the contemporary Atlantic Slope Middle Formative (800–300 BC) pattern, which suggests exploitation of both mountain slopes and lowlands (Findlow, Snarskis, and Martin 1979). The only other Cordilleran sites of comparable antiquity are the Naranjo River and Méndez burial mounds between Tenorio and Miravalles volcanoes northwest of the Arenal area (Norr 1982–1983). As in the Arenal and Atlantic areas, both sites are located at the juncture of the valley floor and the mountains. Although sample sizes from these areas (three from the Atlantic and two from the Cordillera) are clearly too small to allow the formation of more than tentative hypotheses, the similarities in location of early sites in each of these areas suggest a pattern to be considered and tested in future investigations.

The population increase in the Arenal basin during Late Period IV parallels developments throughout Costa Rica. In the Cordillera, population density appears to have been greatest during the Zoned Bichrome Period. Survey data showing a predominance of Zoned Bichrome sites comes from the Naranjo River/Bijagua Valley (ibid.), Hacienda Jericó on the western slopes of the Cordillera de Guanacaste (Finch 1982–1983), the Guayabo Valley on the southwestern slopes of Miravalles Volcano (Ryder 1982–1983a), and the San Dimas Valley (Lange and Murray 1972) in the far northwest of the country.

A shift in economic dependence from the lowlands to the highlands during the Zoned Bichrome Period in the Atlantic Watershed has been inferred from the location of sites at the confluences of small, narrow river drainages and major rivers (Findlow, Snarskis, and Martin 1979). In the Arenal area there are also more highland sites, but formerly established sites were maintained. The Arenal data thus suggest an expansion into areas beyond the lakeshore, rather than a movement from one area to another. Snarskis (1984a) posits a tendency for sites to aggregate on the rich alluvial bottomlands of the Atlantic slope, because of the demands of intensive maize agriculture and population increase. This trend seems to have begun as early as 1000–300 BC in western and central Panama (Cooke 1984; Cooke and Ranere 1984; Weiland 1984). If such a shift in settlement occurred in the upper reaches of the Arenal Valley, it is well hidden by the lake's waters. In addition, residents of the Arenal area apparently never relied strongly on intensive agriculture.

In the Atlantic Watershed, mortuary data indicate the development of social stratification and at least low-level chiefdoms during Period IV (Snarskis 1984a). Whether the degree of social differentiation seen at funerary sites in Greater Nicoya indicates that the chiefdom level of social complexity had been attained is currently debated (Lange, personal communication, 1986). In the Cordilleran regions mentioned earlier, social differentiation—but not necessarily a chiefdom—has been inferred from burial practices. In the Arenal area, burial practices at G-164, a Late Arenal Phase site, indicate there may have been some status differentiation (Chap. 5). We found few artifacts during the survey that might represent status differentiation, and the nature of the lakeshore sites precludes definitive statements. Thus in the Arenal area, this remains an open question.

After AD 500, there were dramatic changes in demography, subsistence, settlement patterns, and social organization throughout Costa Rica. The developmental pattern on the Pacific Coast and in the Atlantic Watershed contrasts sharply with that of the highlands.

On the Pacific Coast, population levels were relatively low during the Zoned Bichrome Period, with heaviest occupation during the Middle and Late Polychrome periods. The Middle Polychrome was the period of major occupation on the Santa Elena Peninsula, near Tamarindo Bay, and in Nosara Valley. At the Bay of Salinas the Late Polychrome was the most frequent component (Lange 1980b:91). In the Atlantic Watershed, dispersed villages located on alluvial terraces continued during Period V (Snarskis 1981a), but there seem to have been fewer sites (Snarskis 1984a). During Period VI numerous but relatively small, agglomerated villages were located on the fertile plains and valleys of east central Costa Rica (ibid.).

Most studies in the highlands suggest peak populations during the Zoned Bichrome Period followed by a decline in the Early Polychrome Period, from which there was no recovery. In the Naranjo River/Bijagua Valley, a substantial decrease in population seems to have occurred, with some sites approaching abandonment (Norr 1982–1983). At nearby Hacienda Jericó, the latest occupation is dated by scarce Early Polychome ceramics (Finch 1982–1983). One possible Middle Polychrome site was the only exception to an otherwise exclusively Zoned Bichrome Period occupation in the Guayabo Valley (Ryder 1982–1983a). A sharp decline in population that began in the Early Polychrome Period left the San Dimas Valley "virtually unoccupied" by Late Polychrome times (Lange and Murray 1972). In the Sábalo River Valley in the far northwest, however, Murray and Jess (1976:10) report Middle Polychrome occupations.

The available evidence from the Arenal basin allows several interpretations of events that occurred during the Silencio Phase, one of which is a population decline similar to that seen in other intermontane valleys; however, the decrease in population in the Arenal area appears to have been less drastic than in other parts of the Cordillera. Most previously established sites remained occupied. Other possible interpretations are a change in social organization and/or a shift in settlements within the area as a result of volcanic activity.

As in other areas of the Cordillera, the demographic decline that began during the Silencio Phase continued during the Tilarán Phase, but at a reduced rate. The nearly complete abandonment reported for other parts of the Cordillera (Lange and Murray 1972; Finch 1982–1983; Norr 1982–1983; Ryder 1982–1983a,b) did not occur here. Seventy-one percent of the sites established during the Tronadora Phase were still occupied during the Tilarán Phase.

Site hierarchies have been identified in the Atlantic Watershed during Periods V and VI. It has not been possible to establish site hierarchies in the Greater Nicoya subarea, however, and Lange

(1984b) suggests that the concept of areal hierarchies may be more appropriate. He also suggests an ecological basis for this difference between subareas, stressing the limitations on population density posed by the seasonally arid areas of Guanacaste (1971). The highlands are not subject to such seasonal severity. Yet studies in the Cordillera have defined no site hierarchies. In the Arenal area, because of the lack of adequate means of measuring even site sizes and distances between sites, it is difficult to determine whether the inability to define hierarchies is an artifact of sampling or a genuine reflection of prehistoric settlement.

The tendency for sites to be located on elevated ground near water, particularly on river terraces, is common throughout Central America (Lange 1971; Lange and Murray 1972; Linares and Sheets 1980; Creamer and Dawson 1982–1983; Norr 1982–1983; Ryder 1982–1983a,b; Black 1983; Drolet 1983, 1984a,b; Haberland 1983; Cooke and Ranere 1984). Compared with other parts of Central America, for example, the Zapotitán valley of El Salvador (Black 1983), slopes in the Arenal area are quite steep. Despite the fact that all sites were in areas that are relatively flat compared with the surrounding terrain, it is evident that common assumptions about the relationship between slope and site location are not applicable here and may not be applicable in other parts of the Cordillera. For example, many predictive models used in archaeological surveys—most of which have been developed and applied in temperate areas—use a criterion of less than 5% (3°). Using this criterion, all of the Arenal sites would have been missed. Our lowest on-site slope measurement was 7°.

The advantages of surveying the eroded shoreline become apparent when the ratio of known habitation to cemetery sites for the Arenal area is compared with that of other intermontane valleys. In the Arenal basin, habitation sites outnumber cemeteries by a ratio of 5 : 1. Most other highland surveys (Table 3-1) have probably recorded a disproportionately high number of cemeteries because of their high visibility compared with habitation sites. This may have contributed to underestimates of population densities. For example, if the ratio for the Arenal area could be extrapolated to the Naranjo/Bijagua Valley, the predicted number of habitation sites would be 150. Only 1 habitation and 5 sites of unknown type were recorded (Norr 1982–1983). The discovery of Zoned Bichrome cemeteries is especially likely because of their stone mound construction. For other time periods, however, when cemeteries were less prominent, this ratio may not be applicable. Hence, apparent demographic trends, such as the radical differences between the Zoned Bichrome and other time periods, in many highland areas have probably been in part a function of sampling bias and may have led to an exaggeration of the rate of population changes.

TABLE 3-1
FREQUENCIES OF HABITATION AND CEMETERY SITES IN THE CORDILLERAN REGION OF NORTHWESTERN COSTA RICA

Location	*Number of Habitations*	*Number of Cemeteries*	*Reference*
Sábalo River Valley	8	12	Murray and Jess (1976)
Upala	6	7	Creamer and Dawson (1982–1983)
Guayabo de Bagaces	2	17	Ryder (1982–1983a)
Hacienda Mojica	7	7	Ryder (1982–1983b)
Naranjo/Bijagua	6	29	Norr (1982–1983)
Hacienda Jericó	0	16	Finch (1982–1983)
Arenal basin	3	7	Aguilar (1984)
Arenal basin	50	12	This study

Note: All sites lacking evidence of funerary architecture are classified as habitation sites.

Cemeteries were often located on high ground, as in other areas of Costa Rica, especially the Atlantic Watershed; however, no simple one-to-one correlations between hilltops or ridges and site types can be made in the Arenal area, for many habitation sites were also located on high ground. Drolet's (1983, 1984a,b) Terraba Valley investigations also found both habitation sites and cemeteries on higher ground. Cemeteries located on river-banks were found in the Piedra River Valley and at Hacienda Mojica (Ryder 1982–1983b). Some of the sites on the floodplain of the San Dimas Valley also appear to have been cemeteries (Lange and Murray 1972). Both site types are also present on the alluvial plains of the Tempisque River Valley to the west of the Cordillera (Baudez 1967; Hoopes 1979). The high-altitude rule for cemeteries thus deserves a closer look in future work in the Cordillera, to determine what factors other than elevation might have been important in choosing their locations.

Most cemeteries in the Arenal area show evidence of domestic activity as well as funerary features. Site G-164, for example, has both cemetery and habitation areas, the former located on the ridge top and the latter below. At other sites, specific activity areas may not be as clearly demarcated as at G-164. The artifact inventory typically includes manos, metates, and cooking stones. Considerable postinterment activity has been suggested at G-150 (Chap. 6). The presence of domestic artifacts on the surface has also been noted at other funerary sites in the Cordillera (Lange and Murray 1972). Ethnographic evidence from the Cuna of Panama (Dillon 1984) and the Limón area on the Atlantic Coast of Costa Rica (Snarskis 1978) provides useful analogues.

The possibility that the lakeshore was a focus of prehistoric settlement in the northwest highlands cannot be dismissed. Rivers and lakes often foster dense concentrations of people. For example, the shores of Lake Nicaragua, with their fertile volcanic soils, appear to have been a center of population from Zoned Bichrome times onward (Abel-Vidor 1980, 1981; Healy 1980; Lange 1984a:49). The combination of fertile volcanic soils for subsistence farming, the lake for fishing, and ample resources for hunting and gathering presented an abundant setting (Healy 1980:332). The Arenal environment probably offered similar resources. Both areas maintained a varied subsistence base throughout their occupation, but the population trends are reversed. One major difference between the two areas that might account for differences in population levels is topography. The amount of flatland in the Isthmus of Rivas in Nicaragua is greater. Proximity to both oceanic and overland trade routes may also have been a factor in the greater population of the Rivas area.

SUMMARY AND CONCLUSIONS

The archaeological survey of the Lake Arenal shoreline provided the most representative sample of sites available from the highlands of northwestern Costa Rica because erosion cuts through the vegetative and volcanic overburden. Yet it was not without its problems, due to site inundation and the patchiness of exposed areas. These factors resulted in a lack of adequate data on site locations, sizes, and functions, and distances between sites. Critical factors in settlement "patterns" can therefore be only roughly estimated.

Individual site locations probably need no more elaborate explanation than that they reflect basic human needs for relatively flat, well-drained land for shelter and fresh water for daily domestic activities.

A clustering of sites southeast of the old lake, in an area that is not particularly favorable in terms of soils, topography, or climate, but that did provide access to more varied ecological zones than did other parts of the basin, persists throughout the occupation sequence. The settlement data are thus in agreement with macrobotanical, pollen, and phytolith analyses that indicate a mixed subsistence base. The juxtaposition of relatively flat land to steep slopes may also have been advantageous.

In general, trends in settlement location and demography during the Tronadora and Arenal phases parallel developments in other areas of Costa Rica, showing a rapid increase in population until about AD 500. Events during the Silencio and Tilarán phases are still unclear, but seem to depart from trends in other areas. Alternative hypotheses to be investigated in future research include (1) internal population decline; (2) changes in social organization; and (3) migration from the area stimulated by volcanic activity.

Despite environmental perturbations and fluctuating population, the Arenal area shows greater continuity and stability than other highland areas. The majority of Tronadora Phase sites remained viable communities. The Arenal region exhibits neither the drastic population decline seen in other intermontane valleys nor the radical shifts in site location brought about by agricultural intensification in Atlantic Costa Rica and Panama. One of the factors in that continuity may have been the diversity of the environment in terms of both subsistence and material resources. Relatively low population density and simpler, and therefore more resilient, societies also played an equal or perhaps even more important role (Sheets 1984c). Ethnographic studies show that tradition, a sedentary life-style, and the strength of the bond between the agriculturalist and the land reinforce maintenance of already established sites. Studies of the effects of Paricutín Volcano on nearby communities found that community solidarity and the rate of cultural change at the time of the eruption were also important factors in continued occupation versus abandonment (Nolan 1979).

Additional investigations beyond the basin and outside Arenal Volcano's tephra blanket will be required to determine the role of the lake's resources and volcanic soils as a possible focus for settlement.

ACKNOWLEDGMENTS

In addition to the NSF and NGS grants for the Proyecto Prehistórico Arenal, this research was supported by grants from the Natural Hazards section of the Institute for Behavioral Science and the Graduate Student Foundation Fund, both of the University of Colorado. These grants made possible the survey of the Piedra River Valley and exploratory reconnaisance in the Arenal River Valley. My thanks to my fellow field crew members not only for their contibutions to the survey and excavation, but also for their camaraderie. The chronological analysis of settlements obviously depends heavily on the ceramic analysis conducted by John Hoopes; Michael J. Snarskis also assisted in analysis of ceramics from the later phases of the survey, especially those from the Arenal Valley. Bill Melson shared his knowledge of the tephrachronology and mineralogy of Arenal Volcano; Liz Knapp and Lucy Foley also shared their knowledge of mineralogy and soils, respectively. Oldamar Comachos of ICE provided transportation to several islands in Lake Arenal. There were, of course, many landowners and local residents who provided invaluable information but whose names I shall never know. Joseph Tosi and Gary Hartshorn of the Tropical Science Center, San José, and Rodrigo Saenz of the Universidad Nacional offered thought-provoking ideas on some of the environmental factors. Above all, I shall always be indebted to Payson Sheets, principal investigator of the Proyecto Prehistórico Arenal, for the opportunity to work in Central America and, in this instance, for his patience and insightful comments in reading all-too-many versions of this manuscript.

Appendix 3-A

SELECTED SITE DESCRIPTIONS

At only two sites (AL-186 and G-185) was the artifact inventory primarily of chipped stone. Both are lithic workshops, but they represent opposite ends of the chronological spectrum.

SITE AL-186

This site was an Archaic campsite with a lithic workshop. The only ceramics found at the site were two small undiagnostic body sherds, presumably deposited much later, found on the surface.

Two hearths were located at the northwestern edge of the site, overlooking a very steep-sided *quebrada*. Each was roughly circular, with an 8 cm thick ash-laden layer overlying a slightly oxidized compacted gravel. Each contained abundant wood charcoal, fire-cracked rocks, and numerous flakes in and around the stained area. A radiocarbon date of 3780 (3675) 3539 BC was received for charcoal from one of these hearths.

The presence of a virtually complete stratigraphic section to the northwest of Arenal Volcano was also a surprise, considering that the dominant winds usually blow from the northeast. Those winds are seasonal, however, and this profile may indicate that some eruptions occurred during calmer months of the year (Hartshorn, personal communication, 1985). It may therefore be possible to employ the regional stratigraphic sequence in future investigations over a wider region than had been previously assumed. We located fire-cracked rock and charcoal in the profile at a depth of 3 m below the surface and 2.2 m below the base of Unit 41.

The chipped stone inventory includes numerous cores, debitage, and pieces of unworked raw material. The primary materials utilized were petrified wood and chalcedony, although some jasper, chert, and (rarely) volcanic materials were also worked. Most of this is probably local material. Petrified wood is found in several of the nearby *quebradas* and chalcedony may be derived from the nearby Venado Formation. Lithic artifacts from the lower excavation levels at Site G-163 are also predominantly cryptocrystalline materials (Chap. 11).

The site provides evidence of the early development of the informal, percussion core-flake industry, which dominated chipped stone production until the Conquest (Chap. 11). Bifacial trimming flakes make up a relatively large proportion of the assemblage, however. We found, in addition to chipped stone artifacts, an unusually large number (at least eighty-five) of cooking stones and fire-cracked rocks indicative of domestic activities.

SITE G-185

G-185 was a relatively large site, located in modern San Miguel, about 8 km SE of Tilarán. It has been largely destroyed by the bulldozer cut for the soccer field. The site is notable for both the amount of chipped stone and the variety of lithic materials used. Materials include chalcedony, jasper, chert, porphyry, and quartzite, as well as fine-grained volcanic rocks. General flakes make up the bulk of the artifact inventory, while evidence of bifacial reduction is limited to two large trimming flakes. The site indicates the continuation of a core-flake industry aimed primarily at the production of flakes for expedient use; this industry is typical throughout the occupation sequence in the Arenal basin (Chap. 11).

Although few diagostic ceramics were found, all of those classified date to the Tilarán Phase and were found near the top of Unit 30.

SITES G-197, G-198, AND G-199

These sites, along with IF 54, are located on what is now an island just off the southwestern shore of the lake. Prehistorically, they would have been on the slopes of a single tall hill and may have been part of one large site, probably a cemetery. Bocana Incised Bichrome is by far the predominant ceramic type at each of these sites. The ceramic assemblage includes two adornos—one avian and one mammal—of Bocana Incised Bichrome. Adornos are rare in this ceramic type (Lange 1984b). The sites also contained an unusually high frequency of chipped stone, compared with other sites on the south shore. Not only is the frequency high, but the materials are almost exclusively chalcedony and petrified wood. A fragment of an obsidian flake and several flakes exhibiting evidence of heat treatment were also found at this site. This is unusual for the area and the time period and in cemeteries. Volcanic materials predominate in most Arenal Phase collections and at cemeteries. G-199 has been badly looted and local residents report that many metates and jade pieces have been taken from this area. We found one small polished stone pendant fragment (Chap. 13) along with several flakes of cryptocrystalline materials at IF 54.

The many unusual artifacts found here indicate that this site may have been a cemetery, perhaps an elite graveyard. Also it is on an isolated and prominent landform. We found evidence of some domestic activity, represented by the high density of cooking stones and fire-cracked rock and one metate fragment, on the southern shore of the island. The presence of cores, hammerstones, and small bifacial trimming flakes points to on-site manufacture of chipped stone tools. A few possible postholes and medium-sized pits were found on the north side of the island, but no locational pattern was apparent.

SITE G-182

This cemetery is situated on a high ridge straddling the divide between the Piedra River and Sábalo River drainages. Tombs were constructed of river cobbles. Unlike most other cemeteries in the area, no laja or elongated marker stones or ground stone was noted. About half of the site has been looted; however, several whole or partially reconstructable vessels were recovered from an area near an old *huaquero* pit.

A large Mojica Incised vessel was found in the wall above a looter's pit (lot A2/1). Judging from its position and size (estimated diameter 60 cm), it may have been a burial urn. In Guanacaste, interment in burial urns was practiced during the late Zoned Bichrome Period. The burial urns are usually inverted and contain the bones of infants and, often, volcanic ash. The bottoms of vessels are often broken. The vessels are considerably smaller than that found at G-182 and are made of an undecorated gray ware. Although the ceramic types differ, the Piedra River vessel may be part of the same mortuary tradition (Lange, personal communication, 1986). Two identical miniature tripod vessels were found in the Aguacate Formation below and to the side of this vessel (one in the mouth of a medium-sized Los Hermanos Beige jar).

Above these vessels we found a 2–3 cm thick layer of medium-grained, light gray tephra. This does not appear to be a natural deposit and we found no such deposit elsewhere in the project area. It may have been deliberately placed here, perhaps to demarcate the area. Local lore, as usual, has it that many metates and even some jades have been taken from this cemetery, but the most interesting story recounts a "pavement of metates" at great depth below the surface.

SITE G-181

Site G-181 is a small cemetery on a low rise about 70 m in diameter on the western bank of the Piedra River. Most tombs were constructed of rounded river cobbles, but a fair number of laja slabs and elongated "headstones" were also found. Despite the extensive vandalism, unique ground- and incised stones were recovered from this site (Chap. 12). One is a tenoned stone carved with geometric designs, which may have functioned as a marker. It is made of a volcanic material that was imported (Melson, personal communication, 1985). A fragment of laja incised with multiple-line geometric and crosshatched designs was also found. It may have been broken off of a larger (90 cm long, 30 cm wide) similarly incised laja now in the possession of the head vaquero of Hacienda La Argentina. Both the latter piece and another complete incised laja are reported to have come from this cemetery. They have since been incorporated into the foundation of the fence around his house.

The cemetery was used most intensively during the Silencio Phase. Laja incised with similar hachured designs were found at the Silencio cemetery (G-150), and another was found at G-151, a late Arenal to early Silencio Phase laja repository associated with that cemetery (Chenault 1984b). It appears that this decoration may be diagnostic of the Late Arenal and Silencio phases.

SITE G-184

Site G-184 is a cemetery located on slightly elevated ground on the floodplain of the Piedra River and is notable for its architectural remains. It has two roughly circular burial areas, one mound approximately 50 m in diameter to the northwest and a small mound about 25 m in diameter to the south. Sherds found in the road cut through the hill to the east (about 50 m to 100 m from the burial areas), as well as about halfway up the hillside, may be from associated habitation areas.

Tombs are constructed primarily of rounded river cobbles. We also noted two pieces of laja and one four-sided stone column, which may have been a grave marker, in the northern burial area. Ceramics associated with tombs in this mound are Arenal Phase.

The small burial mound in the southeastern section of the site is at least partially artificially constructed. As many as five courses of stone facing cover the steeply sloped southern part of the mound, which is built up to about a meter above the floodplain. A curving line of eighteen large stones was exposed to the west of this mound and probably continues toward the east beneath the present ground surface. Small clusters of stones just east of the mound may represent individual graves. Most of the ceramics associated with this mound are polychromes dating to the Silencio Phase. Thus we may be seeing changes in mortuary practices between the Arenal and the Silencio phases.

SITE G-180

G-180 is a large habitation site overlooking the Piedra River floodplain. Its major occupation dates to the Silencio Phase. A large flat area atop a hill just east of the Piedra River showed the highest density of surface artifacts and appears to have been the focus of activity during this time. Several posthole tests in this area produced Belén Incised ceramics. Ceramics are also present on the Piedra River floodplain and a small hill to the south of this area, though the density is lower. Another concentration of sherds was found in situ in the top of the Aguacate Formation and the transitional zone just above it in the road cut at the base of a hill at the eastern boundary of the site, and on the surface of a low hill in the southeastern section of the site. Collections from these areas contain ceramics from the Arenal and the Silencio phases.

Hoopes (personal communication, 1985) has suggested that Belén Incised ceramics may have had a ceremonial function, but he also notes that our sample thus far is derived primarily from the G-150 cemetery. There is no surface evidence of a cemetery area at this site. It is possible that there is an undisturbed cemetery component, but this would be quite unusual, given the easy access to this site. There are some very low mounds and shallow depressions at the western edge of the bench where we found Belén Incised ceramics during posthole testing, but we discovered none of the stones typically used in cemetery construction. Belén ceramics may have served a more mundane, or at least different, function.

Sites G-178 and G-179 may be part of the Arenal Phase occupation of this site, as the distance between sites is small and boundaries somewhat arbitrary.

A prehistoric footpath connects G-180 with the nearby contemporaneous cemetery G-184 (Chap. 9).

SITE AL-178

AL-178 is a large site 6 km NE of Arenal Volcano. It extends over 500 m along a *finca* road. We do not know its exact dimensions for we could not examine the western section of the site. Although disturbed by the construction of *finca* buildings, AL-178 still has some extant architecture. The ceramic and ground stone artifact inventory displays an interesting mixture of Cordilleran and Atlantic characteristics.

We discovered a small stone-faced mound about 10 m in diameter and 1–2 m high in the corral. Numerous clusters of stone around its base are probably tombs. This arrangement is reminiscent of that at G-184. Just outside of the corral, we found remains of what appear to be corridor-type tombs, a continuous linear arrangement of tombs typical of the Bosque Phase on the Atlantic Watershed (100 BC–AD 500). One of the farmhands informed us that other tombs of this type had been found on the property. All visible construction was of river cobbles.

The majority of ceramics came from near a small *quebrada* to the north of the cemetery. A wide variety of types was present. The assemblage includes types such as Jiménez Polychrome, characteristic of the Cordillera, as well as Atlantic Watershed types such as Anita Fine Purple, Zoila Red Incised, and La Selva analogues. Others such as Mora and Asientillo are typical of Greater Nicoya. The majority, however, are Arenal Phase types commonly represented at other sites in the Arenal basin. The two major components are contemporary with the late Arenal and the early Silencio phases.

The ground stone inventory includes one metate fragment with a battered central section surrounded by a smoothed, well-worn area. It is similar to the basin metate from G-168 (Chap. 12), but the sections subjected to different modes of use are better differentiated. We also recovered a fragment of a small rimmed metate of the type usually associated with El Bosque Phase settlements of the Atlantic Watershed.

4

Tronadora Vieja: An Archaic and Early Formative Site in the Arenal Region

JOHN E. BRADLEY

INTRODUCTION

Excavations at Tronadora Vieja (G-163) encountered evidence of Archaic through Late Formative occupations. The test excavations of 1984 revealed two stratigraphically separated occupations dating to the Middle Formative Late Tronadora and Early Arenal phases and showed that significant architectural, artifactual, and botanical remains were present (Bradley et al. 1984). The more extensive excavations of 1985 uncovered earlier occupations dating to the Archaic and Early Formative periods. Occupations at the site date from the Fortuna Phase (pre-3500–3000 BC) through the Early Arenal Phase (500 BC–AD 1). The ceramic sequence extends from pre-2000 BC to AD 1 and is one of the longest continuous Formative sequences in Central America (Hoopes 1987).

Fortuna Phase deposits include two hearths and two lithic workshops (Chap. 12). Excavations located two Trondadora Phase structures as well as several associated subsidiary structures and other features predating the earliest eruption of Arenal Volcano at about 1800 BC. Postmolds and floors indicated two structures (probably houses), one subsidiary structure, and associated features in overlying levels. There were fewer features associated with the indications of Early Arenal Phase occupation. Two structures were excavated; one probably was a house. Structure floors from all phases were relatively devoid of artifacts. This may be the result of periodic cleaning, activities being conducted outside of the structures, or of site formation processes during and after the abandonment of the structures.

The objectives of this chapter are to describe the excavations at Tronadora Vieja, to examine changes in architecture, to study the cultural history of the region, and to relate the occupations to the regional volcanic stratigraphy. I shall make comparisons with Formative sites in Costa Rica, Panama, South America, and Mesoamerica. A more detailed treatment of the ceramics and chronology of Tronadora Vieja is provided by Hoopes (1987).

ENVIRONMENT AND GEOGRAPHY

Tronadora Vieja is located on the present shoreline of Lake Arenal, approximately 8 km NE of the Continental Divide, at 540 m elevation. The site is situated on a gently sloping bench at the base of an east-trending ridge above the relatively flat Arenal River Valley floor (Fig. 4-1). Portions of the site are now under water due to the construction of the Sangregado Dam and the subsequent 30 m rise in the lake's water level. Many sites have been found along the shoreline (Chap. 3), indicating that the prehistoric inhabitants of the region heavily utilized this and other benches that provided close access to the resources near the lake as well as good drainage during the rainy season. The eastern aspect of the site provides exposure to the morning sun and a clear overview of the river valley and lake.

The Arenal River channel was located approximately 5 km NE of the site prior to the construction of the dam, and the Tronadora River is located 0.6 km to the SE. Many springs are also present in areas surrounding the site. Cerro Chato and Arenal Volcano, which periodically buried the site with blankets of ash (Chap. 2) are both easily visible from the site.

EXCAVATION TECHNIQUES

Fieldwork was conducted at the site during 1984 and 1985. Investigations in 1984 included surface mapping and the excavation of five test units, Operations B–F, in areas near the shoreline, along the eroded cutbank. A charcoal sample associated with Tronadora Phase ceramics, lithic artifacts, and macrobotanical maize remains dates to 400 BC (43 BC) AD 328 (Tx-5081). This date, along with the presence of stratigraphically separated Tronadora and Arenal Phase occupations, prompted more extensive excavations in 1985.

We used a multistage excavation methodology during the 1985 season. We laid out a 10 m grid and probed the intersections of grid lines with a manual posthole digger, as in Dahlin (1980), to sterile clay. We recorded natural stratigraphy and the depth and frequency of cultural materials and drew a contour map of subsurface artifact density. We measured inorganic phosphate levels and mapped them for each of the identifiable soil strata using techniques developed by Eidt (1984).

Artifact densities and inorganic phosphate concentrations indicate that most cultural activity occurred in the relatively level central area, at depths greater than 80–90 cm. Because the upper strata were virtually sterile, we used a bulldozer to remove the upper 80–90 cm to the top of Unit 50 to facilitate excavations. We initiated seventeen 2 × 2 m excavation units, Operations G through Q, in areas with the highest artifact concentration, or highest inorganic phosphate levels. We utilized these criteria to increase our understanding of the natural and cultural stratigraphy and to expose as many structures and extramural areas as possible in order to understand changes through time. This purposive sampling design allowed us to make qualitative inferences about changes in the nature of occupation through time, but does not allow quantitative extrapolations to the site as a whole.

We excavated operations with shovels and trowels, using 10 cm arbitrary levels following the slope of the ground surface until natural or cultural stratigraphic changes were encountered. We initiated a new 10 cm level, designated a "lot" if it contained cultural material, when we encountered such changes. This enabled us to adjust excavation levels to the natural or cultural stratigraphy in 10 cm increments. During the 1985 field season, we determined that stratigraphic mixing was such that 10 cm levels did not provide significantly more information than 20 cm levels, which we instituted for the latter portion of the season. We mapped, profiled, and photographed all artifacts, features, living surfaces, and natural and cultural stratigraphic interfaces. We collected soil, macrobotanical, pollen, phytolith, carbon, flotation, tephra, and inorganic phosphate samples from features or activity areas of interest (Chaps. 14, 15, and 16).

The majority of the operations produced postmolds of structures and associated artifactual material at levels deeper than 90 cm. This indicates that early occupations occurred throughout the portions of the site we excavated. Operations ex-

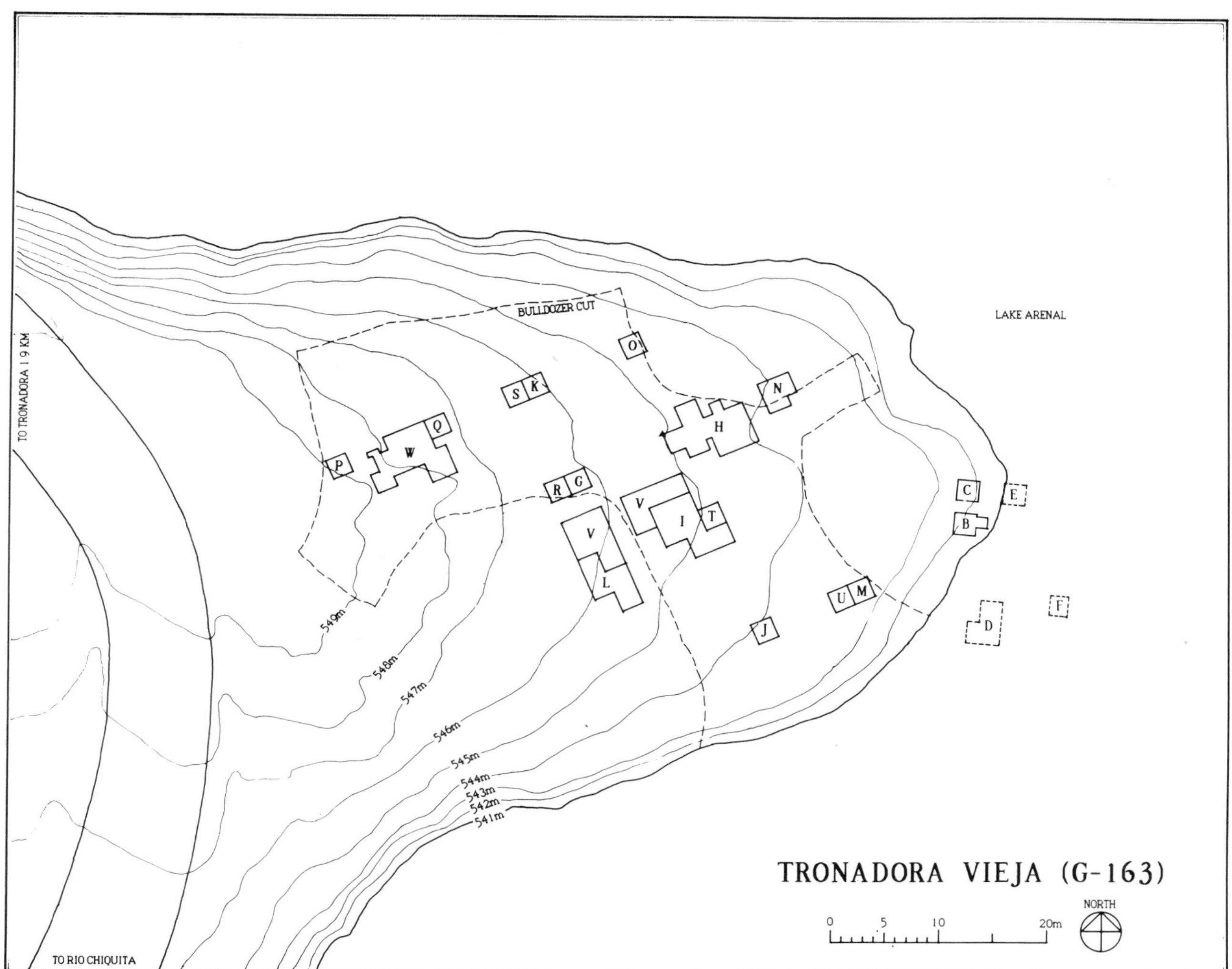

Figure 4-1.
G-163 site map. Map by John Bradley.

posing unusually good preservation of structural remains, artifact scatters, and macrobotanical remains were expanded laterally in order to define floor plans, associated features, and activity areas. Although we found no artifacts in Operation Q during posthole testing, excavation in this area of high inorganic phosphate levels produced the remains of Early Tronadora Phase and later structures.

STRATIGRAPHY

The stratigraphy of the Arenal region is discussed in detail elsewhere (Melson 1984; Mueller 1984b; Chaps. 1 and 2); only a brief overview of strata directly pertinent to Tronadora Vieja will be presented here. The periodic deposits of tephra from Arenal Volcano over the last 4,000 years dominated the stratigraphy. The explosive eruptions deposited layers of tephra, on which subsequent pedogenic processes have acted. The result is a series of alternating light (tephra) and dark (soil A horizon) layers, which are distinct in cross section.

We designated the earliest culture-bearing stratum Unit 65; it is known locally as the Aguacate Formation. This clay-rich, highly weathered soil derived from pre-Arenal volcanic deposits. Unit 64 is poorly preserved in most places, but appears to be the remnants of an A horizon at the top of the Aguacate Formation soil. It is thin and discontinuous, seldom greater than 10 cm in thickness, and at least partially anthropogenic. We found Fortuna and Early Tronadora Phase cultural materials within this unit.

Unit 61 is the lowest tephra layer from Arenal Volcano. It is a light, discontinuous ash layer and is somewhat compacted in places. The eruption that produced this unit dates to between 1900 and 1700 BC (Chap. 1). Unit 60 is a relatively thick (20 cm), organically rich A horizon developed from the Unit 61 tephra. It is continuous throughout the site and is associated with early and late Tronadora Phase occupations. Unit 55 is a beige tephra layer that is somewhat consolidated. It was deposited between 900 and 350 BC (Chap. 1), and is approximately 20 cm thick at the site. Problems in dating do not allow for finer resolution of the chronology of this unit. Unit 54 is a thin, weakly developed A horizon formed on Unit 55. The early Arenal Phase occupation occurred while this soil was forming. Unit 53 is a light gray tephra layer approximately 10 cm thick. Unit 50 is a well-developed A horizon, probably formed on the Unit 53 tephra. It varies from 15 cm to 20 cm in thickness at the site. Unit 53 and higher strata were devoid of cultural materials, and therefore were removed by power equipment.

RESULTS

FORTUNA PHASE (PRE-3500–3000 BC)

We found a stemmed Archaic projectile point (Chap. 11) during the shoreline survey in 1984, and substantial quantities of lithic debitage in Units 64 and 65, predating the earliest eruption of Arenal Volcano. Further excavations in 1985 confirmed the hypothesis that preceramic levels were present at the site. Two concentrations of carbonized wood from Operations V and I, near the center of the site, produced four radiocarbon dates ranging from 3500 to 2000 BC. The first, Tx-5275, dated to 3496 (3360) 3144 BC. The second (Tx-5278) yielded a date of 3493 (3351) 3109 BC. The third was Tx-5276, and dated to 3332 (3053) 2929 BC. The final date from these features was Tx-5274, 2912 (2796) 2667 BC. Detailed discussions of all radiocarbon dates and contexts are provided in Chapter 1. One biface, one biface fragment, four flaked cores, eight small biface trimming flakes, and additional debitage were also found in Operations V, I, M, and N. Together, these materials represent at least two hearths and associated core reduction and bifacial tool manufacturing areas (Chap. 12).

Unfortunately, the late Fortuna Phase and the early Tronadora Phase were not stratigraphically separated in the area around the hearths where the carbon samples were obtained. Therefore, it is not yet possible to determine with confidence when during the millennium from 3000–2000 BC the change between the Archaic and Formative periods occurred.

PRE–UNIT 61 TRONADORA PHASE OCCUPATIONS

Tronadora Vieja contains the most extensive Early Tronadora Phase remains of any site the Proyecto Prehistórico Arenal uncovered. Evidence of occupations clearly assignable to the time before the deposition of Unit 61 includes portions of two structure floors with postholes and other associated features, numerous artifacts, and isolated postholes in seven other operations. The dating of some of the deposits is somewhat problematic, but all of the structures were associated with ceramics.

Structure 1 (Operations Q and W)

The floor of Structure 1 (Fig. 4-2) corresponds to the top of soil Unit 64. The living surface was covered by an intact layer of tephra from Unit 61, separating it stratigraphically from later occupations. We excavated only the northern portion of the structure. A radiocarbon date of 1897 (1824) 1749 BC (Tx-5279) was obtained for carbon from the floor of this structure.

The structure is round and approximately 5.25 m in diameter. We uncovered seven postmolds (Fig. 4-2) of the perimeter, each 13–16 cm in di-

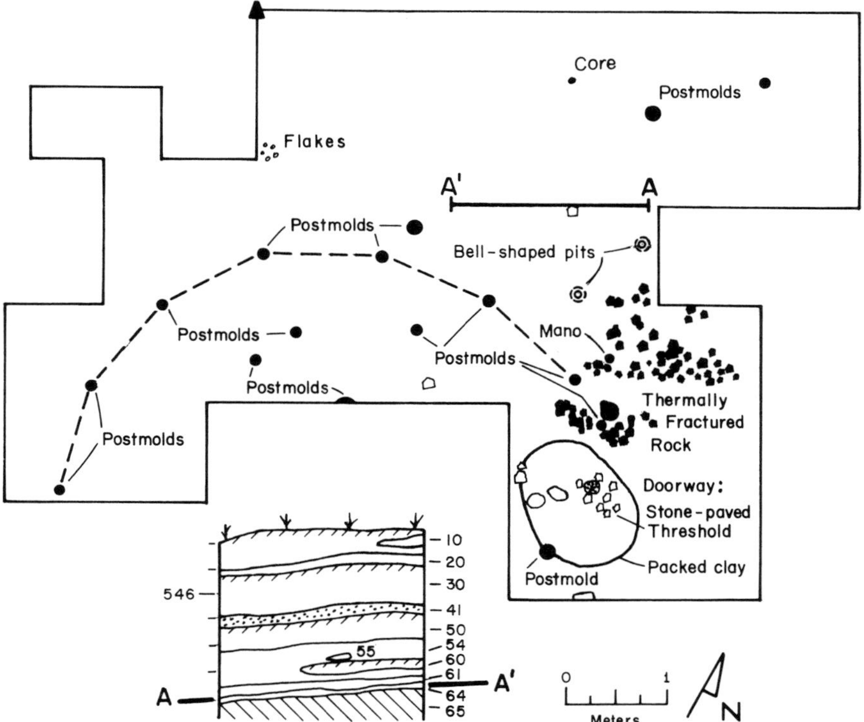

Figure 4-2.
Pre–Unit 61 Tronadora Phase Structure 1, Operations Q and W. Unit 64. Only the 2-by-2 meter area in the northern corner (upper-right corner) is operation Q; the remainder is Operation W. Map by John Bradley.

ameter and spaced approximately 1 m apart. A hard, compacted area, possibly a doorway, was defined on the northeast side of the structure, between two postmolds and facing the lake.

We found a stone- and pebble-paved surface (Feature 1, lot W30), approximately 40 × 50 cm in extent, in the possible doorway. There is ethnographic evidence for the use of stone-paved thresholds in low-lying wet areas of the Amazon. The feature contains two smaller features superimposed on one another. These consist of twelve small stones covering an area approximately 10 cm in diameter, overlain by about one hundred river pebbles covering a circular area 14 cm in diameter. The pebble feature is in the location that a postmold would be predicted, if we consider the radius of curvature of the structure and spacing of other postmolds. It may have served as a pad to support a post.

The upper portions of all postmolds were filled with intrusive tephra from Unit 61, indicating abandonment prior to the eruption. Each posthole had been prehistorically dug into the Aguacate Formation clay to a depth of 30 cm to 50 cm below the floor level. One postmold contained an unidentifiable body sherd, and one contained a flake and a fragment of carbonized wood.

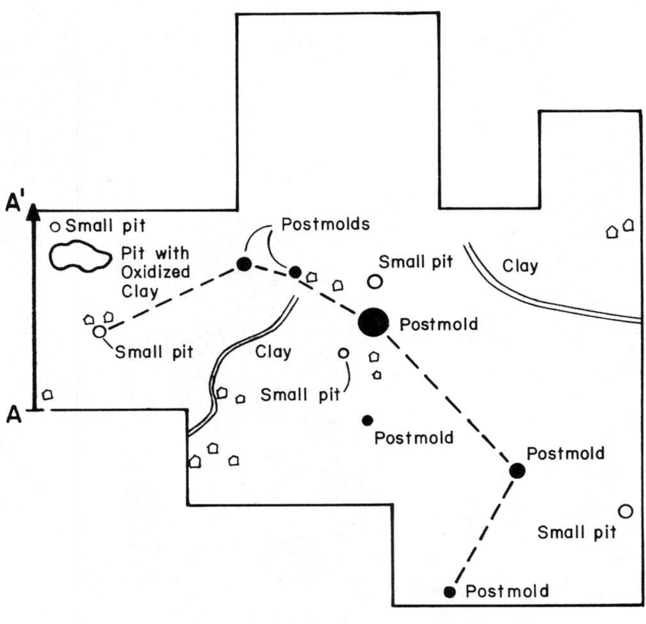

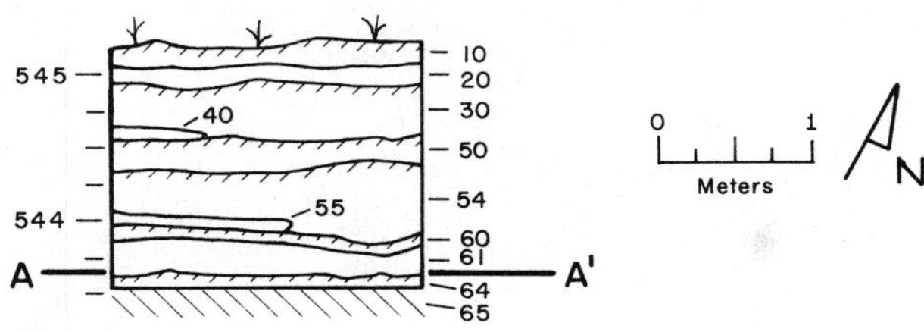

Figure 4-3.
Pre–Unit 61 Tronadora Phase Structure 2, Operation H. Unit 64. Map by John Bradley.

We found three additional postmolds in the interior of the structure, each approximately 12 cm in diameter and ranging from 9 cm to 16 cm deep. These posts may have functioned as additional roof supports, room dividers, or supports for elevated platforms for cooking, storage, or sleeping. They may also derive from an earlier structure. Two large and one small postmold north of the structure may indicate an additional structure.

Other features associated with Structure 1 include an amorphous concentration of ninety-nine cooking stones and fifty-seven thermally fractured rocks (Chap. 12) covering a 2 m x 2 m area just outside and north of the possible doorway, and two small pits located adjacent to that concentration. The pits have 10 cm diameter surface openings that widen to a 15 cm maximum diameter, and depths of 13 and 30 cm. A chalcedony core and flake, a mano, and six flat-lying sherds were also found to the north of the structure. Artifacts were extremely sparse inside the structure, and included a single flat-lying sherd and a piece of tabular stone.

Structure 2 (Operation H)

Structure 2 was located approximately 22 m east of Structure 1 in Operation H (Fig. 4-3). Its living surface is on the upper surface of Unit 64. The patterning of postmolds is less clear than for Structure 1, but the depth and spacing of posts are similar.

One pit, located to the west of the structure, is 25 cm × 50 cm in horizontal extent, 10 cm deep, and contains sherds and oxidized clay fragments. We found two smaller pits, 10 cm to 20 cm deep and 10 cm to 15 cm in diameter near the structure, one apparently inside and the other outside. Their function is unknown. We found an enigmatic curvilinear clay feature that traverses a 4 m length of the living surface outside of the structure. Dillon (1984) reports constructed clay drainage berms surrounding structures at Cuna cemeteries in Panama. Although the feature is not clearly aligned with any structure, it may have served a function related to drainage.

Four thermally fractured stones were found between two postmolds and may be discarded cooking stones that accumulated along the wall. We found four hoes stacked adjacent to one postmold; they were apparently cached unhafted (Chap. 11). We found no artifacts on the living surface.

Additional Operations

We found several postmolds in Operation V, approximately 16 m east of Structure 1. These may be the remnants of an additional early Tronadora Phase structure, although it is likely that they represent portions of more than one structure. There was no intact layer of Unit 61 tephra separating the Early Tronadora Phase from later activities in this area. Preserved Unit 61 tephra capping some of the postmolds indicates that at least some of them predate the Unit 61 eruption. Postmold diameter and depth are variable. We found a linear arrangement of stones to the north of the postmolds.

A feature, consisting of a compacted layer of the Unit 60 soil containing numerous sherds near its surface, was found 4 m to the southwest of the postmolds discussed earlier. It may indicate early or late Tronadora Phase activities. Stratigraphic Units 64, 61, and 60 are very mixed in this area and obscure definitive dating. One jasper core and one metate fragment were found on the surface of Unit 64, to the east and south of the possible structure, respectively. A sample of carbonized wood from the surface of Unit 64 dates to 2300 (2140) 1986 BC (Tx-5277), showing that activities occurred prior to the fall of the Unit 61 tephra.

We found evidence for construction predating the fall of Unit 61 tephra in six additional operations (K, M, N, P, S, and U). We found fifteen postmolds and three other features. In Operations K and S, a 2 m × 4 m excavation unit located 8 m NE of Structure 1, we found two large postmolds along with a compacted layer scattered with sherds and rock. One postmold contained a large stone and several sherds, and the other also contained sherds and was capped with Unit 61 tephra. We found eight postmolds associated with a living surface in Operations M and U, 18 m east of Structure no. 2. No pattern was apparent. Three of the postmolds contained cultural materials, including a large Tronadora Phase rim sherd. The sherd's position indicates that it may have been used to wedge a loose post. We found four small, shallow postmolds in Operation U, near a larger post. They may indicate wattle construction (small, closely spaced upright poles) in this area. We found concentrations of thermally cracked rocks to the east of the postmolds. Operation N contained two postmolds associated with a living surface, thermally cracked rocks, and two sherds, one diagnostic of the Tronadora Phase.

G 163 Area 4 (Op. Q & W) Unit 60

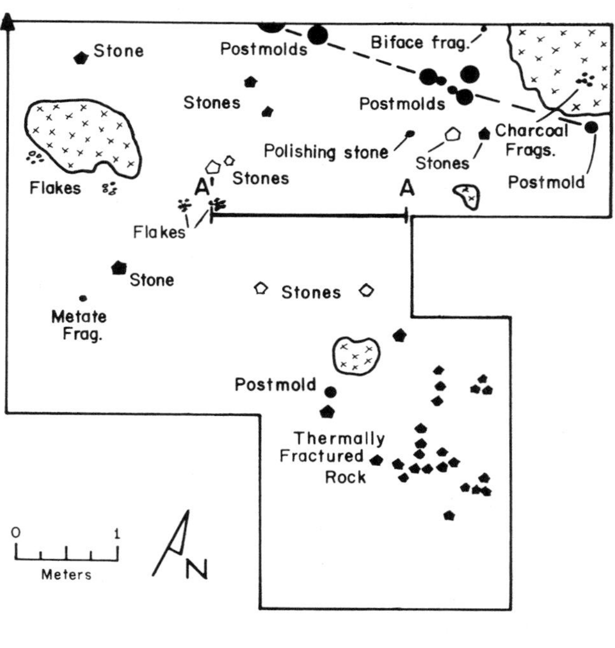

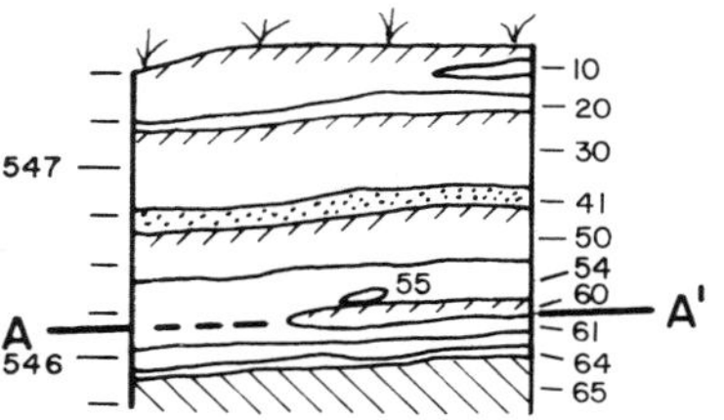

Figure 4-4.
Post–Unit 61 Tronadora Phase Structure 3, Operations Q and W. Unit 60. Map by John Bradley.

Operation P, 4 m west of Structure No. 1, contained five postmolds under a continuous layer of tephra Unit 61. There was a combination of smaller and larger postmolds similar to those found in Operation U. We found sherds diagnostic of the Tronadora Phase associated with these postmolds.

Numerous rectangular pits were found along the eroding shoreline. Two were accompanied by Tronadora Phase cylindrical vessels. Because of their size and similarities with known Costa Rican burials, they probably are the remnants of simple secondary burials.

POST–UNIT 61 TRONADORA PHASE OCCUPATIONS

Two structures and associated features and activity areas were found dating to the Tronadora Phase after the fall of Unit 61. Postmolds indicating one additional possible structure and several other features were also found dating to this time, as well as numerous artifacts.

Structure 3 (Operations Q and W)

Structure 3 (Fig. 4-4) was defined on the basis of a 3.5 m long row of eight postmolds running east-west through Operations Q and W. We inferred a wall from this linear arrangement. This wall occurs in the Unit 60 soil and was only partially excavated. The lack of other postmolds to the south and the heavy artifact concentration in this area suggest that the majority of the interior of the structure lies in the unexcavated area to the north. Six large postmolds (14–18 cm diameter, 10–16 cm deep) and two small postmolds (8 cm diameter, 10–12 cm deep) penetrate the intact Unit 61 tephra. These may be further evidence of wattle construction, as in earlier Tronadora Phase occupations in Operations U and P. Spacing of the posts is irregular, and one has an additional postmold 10 cm to the side. Within the 8 cm to 22 cm thick Unit 60 soil, we defined three relatively distinct, superimposed living surfaces. Postmolds were clearly definable only at the lowest of the three surfaces.

Two features are associated with this structure. The southwestern portion of Feature 1, a pit measuring approximately 1 m × 1 m, covers the northeast corner of Operation Q. It contains charcoal and a Tronadora Phase sherd. Feature 2 consists of a 1.5 m × 2 m scatter of thermally fractured debitage and cooking stones located 5 m south of Structure 3. We found a single carbonized maize kernel fragment in the feature. A portion of the feature overlaps a similar early Tronadora Phase feature (see discussion in Structure 1 Feature 2), and stones may have been borrowed from it.

Over fifty artifacts were found on the lower living surface, including more than twelve flat-lying sherds, a small knob-legged metate fragment, a small biface fragment, four flakes, and six diagnostic Tronadora Phase sherds of at least four varieties. Cooking stones, thermally fractured debitage, and other stones were also found on the lower living surface.

Structure 4 (Operations I and T)

Structure 4 is located in Operation I (Fig. 4-5). Unit 61 tephra preservation is poor in this area. We are uncertain whether the absence of tephra is due to erosion or to cultural disturbance, but there is no evidence of the latter. Six postmolds (12–15 cm in diameter, 10–30 cm deep) defined the structure. We have excavated only a small portion of the interior of the structure and the floor plan is unknown. One wall is at least 3 m long and straight to slightly curved. We have inferred inside (south) versus outside (north) of the structure from the curvature of the wall. Postmolds are evenly spaced at roughly 1 m intervals. Stones running east to west between two of the postmolds and extending to the southwest probably accumulated along the outside of the wall. Additional postmolds to the northeast of the structure may be the remnants of an ancillary or previous structure.

Several features are associated with the north and northeast sides of the structure. Lot T5 is an 80 cm × 60 cm concentration of cooking stones. Lot I5, located 1 m to the southeast of the cooking stones, consists of a 2-m-diameter scatter of thermally fractured rock. Located between the cooking stones and thermally fractured rock is a shallow, basin-shaped pit. The pit's contents, consisting of dark gray sediments possibly representing the remains of a hearth, were collected. Oxidized clay fragments, possibly the remnants of daub, are also scattered in this area.

A stone alignment, possibly acting as a wall foundation, lies along the exterior edge of the north side of the structure and includes cooking stones and thermally fractured rock. Beneath the thermally fractured cooking rock scatter and immediately outside the east wall of the structure is a compacted area adjacent to a postmold. This may be the remnants of a doorway. Sherds, rocks,

G 163 Area 2 (Op. I, T and V, Ext. 3&4) Unit 60

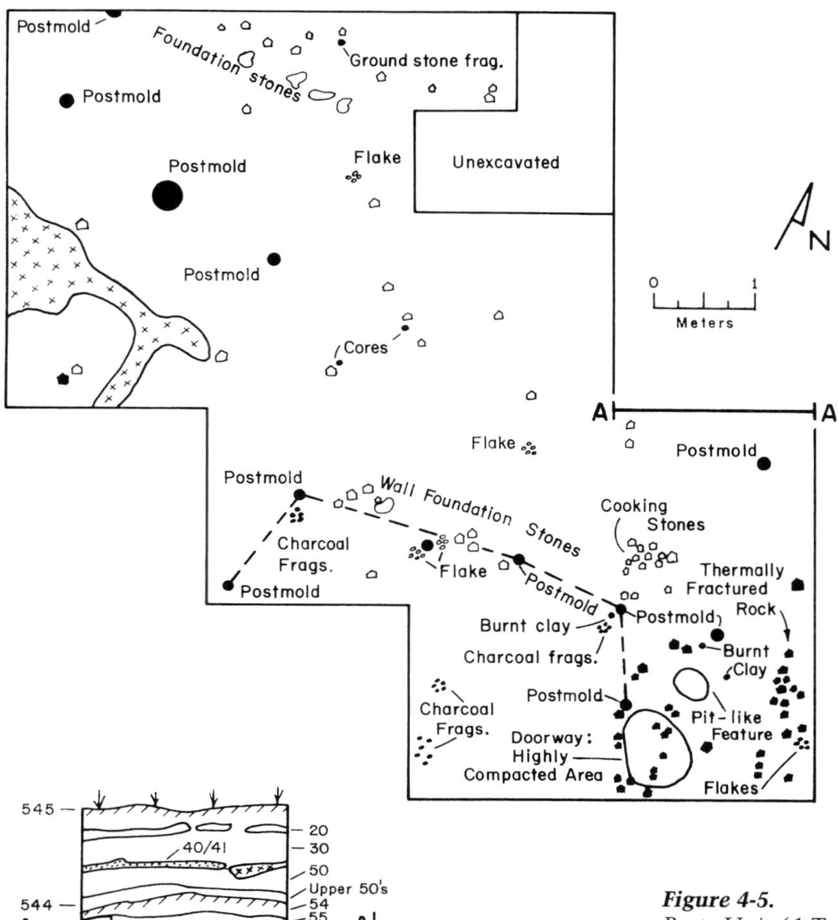

Figure 4-5.
Post–Unit 61 Tronadora Phase Structure 4, Operations I, T, and V. Unit 60. Map by John Bradley.

charcoal, and burned clay fragments are scattered just northeast of this compacted area, in contrast to the relatively clean interior floor to the southwest.

Additional artifacts associated with the structure include two flake cores, located 1.5 m to the northwest, a small bifacial trimming flake near the possible hearth, and lithic debitage north and east of the structure.

Additional Operations

We found four postmolds surrounding a 3 m × 4 m area (Fig. 4-6) that contains two small pit-like features in Operation L and Extension 1. Five small depressions are present between two of the posts. The posts may be associated with Structure 4, 4 m to the east, or may be from an independent structure. A shallow, linear depression 50 cm to 100 cm wide traverses the excavations for 2.5 m. The feature has eroded down to Unit 61 in places and may be the remnants of a footpath, although it could also be due to runoff from the roof (drip line) or natural drainage. Artifacts found on the surface in this area include rim sherds from a large jar, other Tronadora Phase sherds, general flakes, and stones.

We found a large irregularly shaped pit, which extends 110 cm into Unit 65, in Operations G and R. It may have been a borrow pit for clay. We found charcoal, sherds, and lithic artifacts within the pit. A large lump of Unit 65 clay had been excavated and redeposited near the top of the hole. A ground- and polished stone pendant fragment was apparently discarded in the pit, and some wood charcoal was also found in the pit. We found several postmolds just beyond the southwest side of the pit.

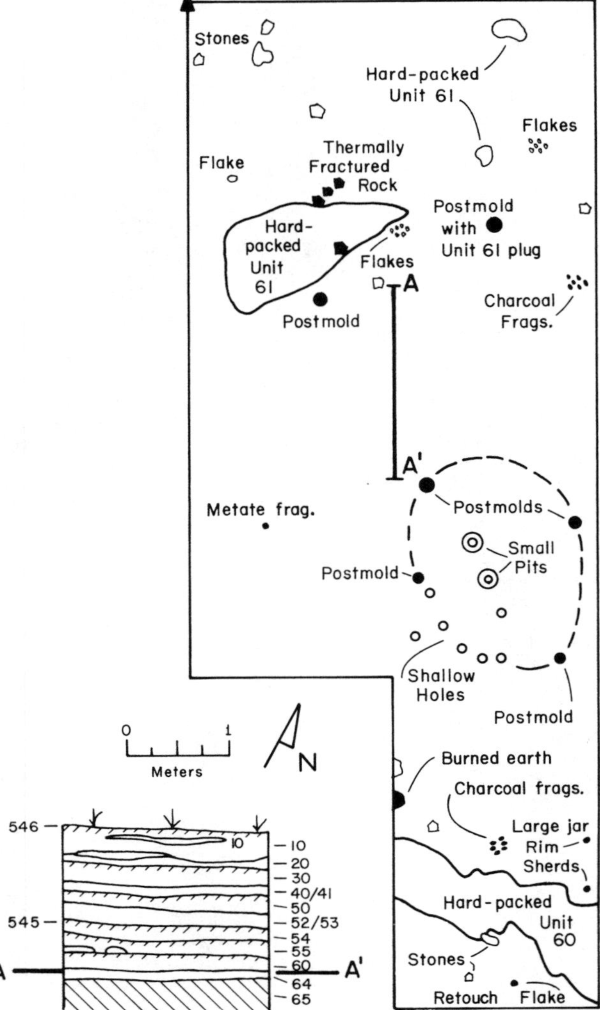

Figure 4-6.
Small structure and possible footpath or roof runoff erosion. Units 60/64. Map by John Bradley.

EARLY ARENAL PHASE
(500 BC–AD 1)

We found less evidence of Arenal Phase occupation than of the Tronadora Phase. This may be due to a decrease in the actual occupation of the site, or to changes in the distribution of structures through time and the limited excavations. We located one structure, one possible structure, and several additional features along with a moderate number of artifacts.

Structure 5 (Operation H)

The living surface of Structure 5 corresponds to soil Unit 54. We uncovered the southern portion of a prepared clay floor and five postmolds (Fig. 4-7). We found three additional postmolds to the west. The prepared clay floor is 3 cm to 5 cm thick and extends to the south and east beyond the postmolds. The Unit 54 soil is highly compacted in areas surrounding the structure to the south and west, possibly by foot traffic. The pattern of the postmolds suggests that the structure was slightly rounded and roughly rectangular. The majority of the interior of the structure is in unexcavated areas to the north and west. Postmolds are 18 cm to 24 cm in diameter and 10 cm to 35 cm deep. They are spaced at 80 cm to 100 cm intervals. The south wall was probably at least 3 m long.

We found four pits (Features 1–4), 8 cm to 36 cm in diameter and 10 cm to 20 cm deep, in or near the prepared clay floor. Feature 5, 2 m to the west, consists of two postmolds and may be either a part of the structure without a clay floor or an associated structure. Interior and exterior areas of Structure 5 were almost devoid of artifacts. We found one rock and sherd scatter near Features 3 and 5 and one small biface trimming flake on the living surface.

Additional Operations

We found evidence of a second possible Early Arenal Phase structure in Extension 1 of Operation W, where we found three definite and four possible postmolds. The postmolds are 12–16 cm in diameter, 8–20 cm deep, and spaced 75 to 125 cm apart. We found a total of twelve sherds in the area. Two of the three definite postmolds contained sherds or flakes in their fill, as did three of the four possible postmolds. Another shallow depression contained a sherd and a thermally frac-

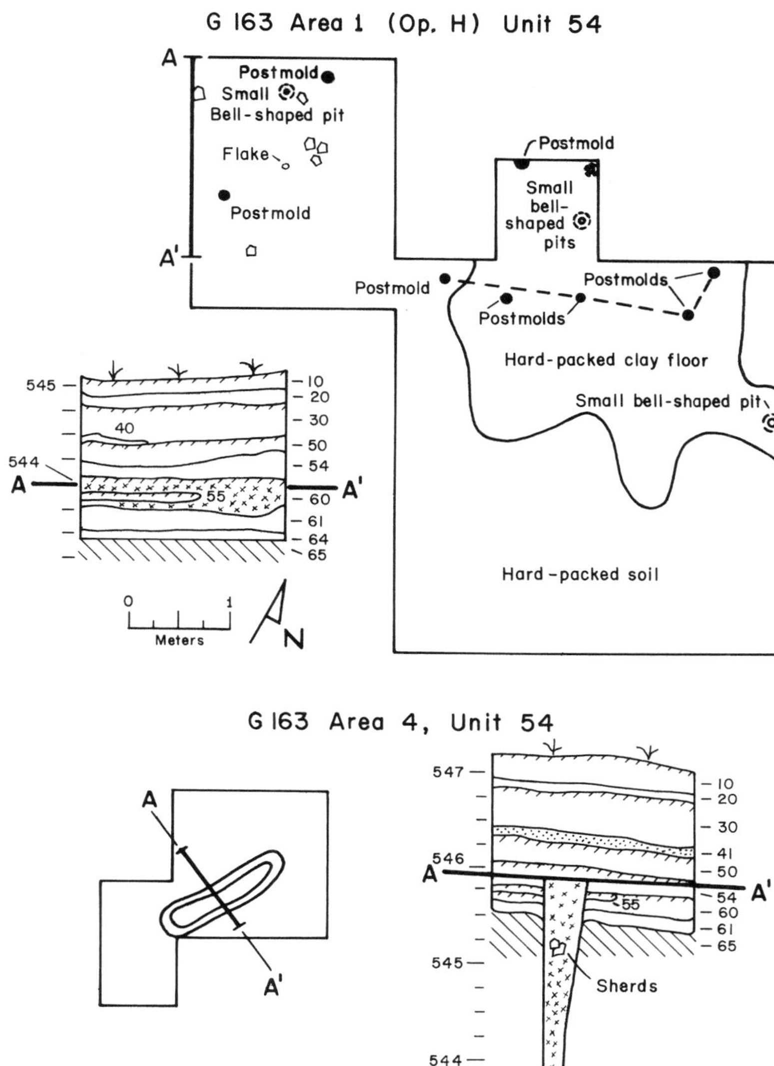

tured rock. Unit 54 is very soft in the area, probably due to bioturbation, and none of the objects were lying flat on the surface.

A feature that was excavated from Unit 54 into Unit 65 was found 4 m to the west of this area, in Operation W, Extension 3. The feature is a deep, trenchlike pit 30–40 cm wide, 1.4 m long, and over 2.0 m deep. The side walls are smooth and vertical. The pit contained Mojica Incised pottery fragments and carbonized *Zea mays* cob fragments just beneath the upper surface of Unit 65. Based on morphology and a small amount of white pastelike substance similar to highly decomposed bone encountered at the Silencio cemetery (G-150, Chap. 6) found at the bottom of the pit, it is believed to have been a burial. We found a similar feature, also dating to the Early Arenal Phase, during testing of G-175, a large Arenal Phase habitation site.

Figure 4-7.
Structure 5, Operation H. Unit 54. Trench tomb, Operation W. Unit 54. Map by John Bradley.

DISCUSSION

Although our knowledge of the occupation at Tronadora Vieja is still incomplete, we can make some preliminary assessments of the nature of the occupation. I shall briefly discuss the changes in habitation and architecture at Tronadora Vieja from the Fortuna Phase through the Early Arenal Phase and then examine Early Formative villages and architecture from neighboring areas of Mesoamerica and South America.

Based on the existence of hearths and lithic manufacturing areas in the central portion of the site, it was first occupied between 3500 and 2000 BC. Unfortunately, due to stratigraphic mixing, it is impossible to determine whether the dated carbon from the hearths is associated with Fortuna Phase or Early Tronadora Phase activities. Because there is no evidence unambiguously linking third millennium BC dates to structures or ceramics, Hoopes (Chap. 10) draws the dividing line between the Fortuna and the Tronadora phases at 2000 BC. Further excavations may find areas with only Early Tronadora Phase or only Fortuna Phase occupations and help resolve questions of chronology.

We excavated two structures and up to five other structures dating prior to the Unit 61 eruption of Arenal Volcano at the site. Structure 1 contained around 20 m^2 of interior roofed area, and Structure 2 may have been similar in size, based on information from the limited excavations. The structures are separated by about 20 m. Structure 1 is circular in plan, but the plan of Structure 2 is unknown. Other structures that were probably smaller are 4 m to 8 m from Structures 1 and 2 and may have served as special-purpose structures, possibly for storage, food processing, or cooking. Structure 1 may have had a stone-paved threshold, a feature still used in wet areas of the Amazon. The feature also may be a pad to support a post. Stone alignments found at the edges of two of the structures may be remnants of relatively crude foundations, or accumulations of trash outside of the structures. The floors of the structures followed the gently sloping natural ground surface of the time. Loose posts appear to have been wedged with stones or broken pot sherds. Closely spaced large and small postmolds suggest wattle construction. We have found only limited evidence of daub. This is not surprising, however, as daub rarely survives in wet climates without being burned.

Features found outside of the structures include hearths and small basin-shaped pits of unknown function. We also found several caches or discard piles of cooking stones and grinding stones. We discovered no definite burials or storage pits, but small rectangular pits found on the shoreline are likely the remnants of simple secondary burials. The large trenchlike pit located near Structure 5 may also be a burial.

The lack of artifacts inside of the structures and the presence of hearths on the outside indicate that most household activities, including food processing and preparation, may have occurred outside of the structures, although it is possible that cooking stones were heated outside of the structure and then transported in for cooking. We also found all grinding stones outside of the structures. Scatters of lithic debitage suggest outdoor manufacture and refurbishment of chipped stone tools, ethnographically a predominantly male activity.

The clean floors inside of the structures may be the result of intentional cleaning, a lack of activities inside, or of discard and site formation processes. Lange and Rydberg (1972) have shown that when a structure is abandoned, almost all useful items are removed by the inhabitants who are moving out or scavenged by neighbors. Prior to its burial by the Unit 61 tephra, the site may have been picked over many times for valuable and useful items.

Structures 3 and 4 are spaced approximately 25 m apart, but the roofed area and floor plans are not known. If we have accurately defined the extent of Structure 4, then it probably had an interior roofed area of roughly 20 m^2. The small structure found outside of Structure 4 may have been a special-purpose building. We found exterior activity areas for core reduction, tool manufacture, and possible food processing and preparation for the Late Tronadora Phase occupation.

Occupation during the Early Arenal Phase appears to have been lighter than before, at least in the limited area of the site that was excavated. Structure 5 had a prepared clay floor, the only one found at the site, and appears to be similar in size to the earlier structures. We found a second possible structure outside of Structure 5. The deep, trenchlike pit feature is one of the most interesting features found dating to this occupation. It may indicate, as do the shoreline features, that burials were associated with residences. We found very few in situ artifacts dating to this phase.

Roughly contemporary materials have been found in Panama and South America and in Mesoamerica. Later Formative structures have been found in Costa Rica and in Mesoamerica.

Evidence of very early Formative materials (ca. 3000–1000 BC) has been reported in littoral, estuarine, and riverine settings from Monagrillo in the Parita Bay of Pacific coastal Panama (Cooke 1984). Maize phytoliths, *tecomate*-like ceramics, and polished stone chopping and digging implements in shell mound and inland sites indicate a shift from a hunting-fishing-gathering economy to cultivation. Direct evidence of plant food in the diet (carbonized plant remains), food-processing artifacts, and housing remains are absent from the sites. Occupations from Puerto Hormiga (Reichel-Dolmatoff 1965a, b) in Caribbean coastal Colombia also date to approximately 3000 BC, and occupations at Barlovento are somewhat later (1550–1032 BC) (Reichel-Dolmatoff 1955). Carbonized maize and structural remains dating to before 2000 BC have been found on the Chanduy coast and Santa Elena Peninsula of Pacific coastal Ecuador at San Pablo (Zevallos et al. 1977).

The nearest roughly contemporary materials to the northwest of Arenal are from Chantuto, Pacific coastal Chiapas (Chantuto Phase—3000–2000 BC) (Voorhies 1976:6), and from Altamira, Guatemala (Barra Phase—1600–1500 BC) (Lowe 1971:57). Although sedentary or semisedentary villages apparently existed at Chantuto, on the coast of Belize (MacNeish et al. 1980), and at Puerto Márquez, Guerrero (Brush 1969) by 3000 BC or earlier, evidence of structures or living floors is sketchy, and no direct evidence of diet is available. Hammond's dating of 2000 BC for Swasey Phase pottery and structures at Cuello, Belize, is now in doubt (Andrews V and Hammond 1990).

Most Early Formative structures in Mexico and Central America date to later than 1500 BC. Some general similarities between the Early Tronadora Phase structures and these later structures include the size of the structures, the general arrangement and size of the roof support posts, the use of additional, slightly smaller posts to frame the doorway, and the wedging of loose posts. One possible difference is the lack of clay daub at G-163. Daub is a near-universal construction feature in Early Formative Mesoamerica (Vaillant 1930; MacNeish et al. 1967; Tolstoy and Fish 1975; Flannery 1976:20). So far, daub is relatively rare at Tronadora Vieja, but this may be a result of bad preservation in a wet climate. The absence of packed clay floors, except in the much later Early Arenal Phase structure, also sets Tronadora Vieja apart from Mesoamerican structures. However, prepared floors may not have survived in the wet climate of the Arenal area.

Several Mesoamerican Formative sites are of particular relevance to the discussion of Tronadora Vieja. Cuadros Phase (1000—850 BC) structures at Salinas la Blanca, on the Pacific Coast of Guatemala (Coe and Flannery 1967), have upright posts 10–15 cm in diameter spaced at 70 cm intervals. The structure measures at least 3 m across. Hearths and clay borrow pits were found near the structures. Middens are downhill from the structures on nearby slopes. As at Tronadora Vieja, there are few below-ground storage features. Moisture probably affected storage facilities (Linares and Ranere 1980; Cooke 1984). In the Valley of Oaxaca, Tierras Largas Phase (1400–1150 BC) structures are square, with wattle-and-daub walls often whitewashed with lime (Winter 1976). Doors are located on long walls and framed with stones. Floors were dampened, stamped, and covered with alluvial sand. Smaller, subsidiary structures were often located near the structure, as were bell-shaped storage pits.

Our understanding of Middle Formative ceramics in Costa Rica dating to after 1000 BC is improving. Sites from the Atlantic Watershed and Central Highlands include Chaparrón, La Montaña, and Turrialba (Snarskis 1981a). Ceramics that were utilized include raised-rim griddles similar to *budares* found in Brazil, Venezuela, and Colombia, suggesting the use of manioc. Formative materials from the Vidor site (Loma B Phase), on the Bay of Culebra on the Nicoya Peninsula, approximately 80 km west of Tronadora Vieja, date to between 800 and 300 BC.

SUMMARY AND CONCLUSIONS

Excavations at Tronadora Vieja in 1984 and 1985 uncovered evidence of occupations from the Archaic Fortuna Phase through the Early Formative and Late Tronadora and Early Arenal phases. We have excavated features and artifacts dating to all of these phases and have found evidence of architecture for the Tronadora and Arenal phases. Further work is needed to determine variability in construction techniques, and the household unit itself is still poorly understood.

The area of the site that has been exposed by erosion along the lakeshore is well under 2 ha. Even with relatively extensive areas eroded, the site would be defined as a small hamlet using criteria developed by Blanton (1972). The actual extent of the site and the total number of structures during each occupation is unknown. Although the number of excavated structurehold units decreases through time, the limited area excavated and differential preservation make any inferences regarding population changes on the site tenuous.

It appears that Tronadora and Arenal phase households utilized a single, relatively small (ca. 20 m^2) structure constructed of a framework of vertical support poles, likely with a thatched roof. The households sometimes utilized interior and exterior smaller structures in addition to the main structure for special purposes, possibly including food storage or processing. Hearths were outside of the structures, and burials appeared to have been outside of structures but within the hamlet. Direct evidence of food storage features is lacking, but the bell-shaped pits may have been used for this purpose.

Many questions remain regarding the occupations at Tronadora Vieja; however, the site offers some unique opportunities to study the prehistory of lower Central America. Future excavations should concentrate on finding areas with unmixed Fortuna Phase and early Tronadora Phase deposits to determine the date of transition from the Archaic to the Formative. Other questions concern the date of the introduction of maize to the site, and the variability of construction and structurehold units during the Formative. Tronadora Vieja has already contributed to the understanding of the Archaic/Formative transition in lower Central America, and further research can add to our understanding of this crucial period of cultural change.

5

Excavations at Sitio Bolívar: A Late Formative Village in the Arenal Basin

JOHN W. HOOPES
MARK L. CHENAULT

INTRODUCTION

Sitio Bolívar (G-164) is situated on a small point of land on the south shore of Lake Arenal.[1] It is 1.25 km NE of the modern town of Tronadora (ARENAL 1:50,000; UTM 276300 m N X 436500 m E) at a maximum altitude of 565 m above sea level (Fig. 5-1). The site extends northward below the present surface of the lake (540 m). It is named for Quebrada Bolívar, the small drainage 350 m to the west of the site. Sitio Bolívar is currently the property of ICE; however, the site is being farmed under agreements that include the planting of trees in order to control erosion. Modern agricultural activity on the property is intensive, with the principal crops being tomatoes, beans, *yuca* (sweet manioc), and corn.

The southern end of the site is marked by a stand of *yuca* and several citrus trees. The northern half includes corn- and beanfields, which are planted to the edge of the lakeshore. A heavily overgrown bulldozed road runs east-west across the site. Current access is via a small two-track road that leaves the main road 2.5 km east of Tronadora.

The site, as defined by the extent of subsurface features on the ridge top to the south and the lakeshore margin to the east, covers an area of approximately 2.5 ha. It is situated on a landform comprising small foothills in the Arenal Valley that are dissected by a number of small drainages and that has been largely denuded for pasture.

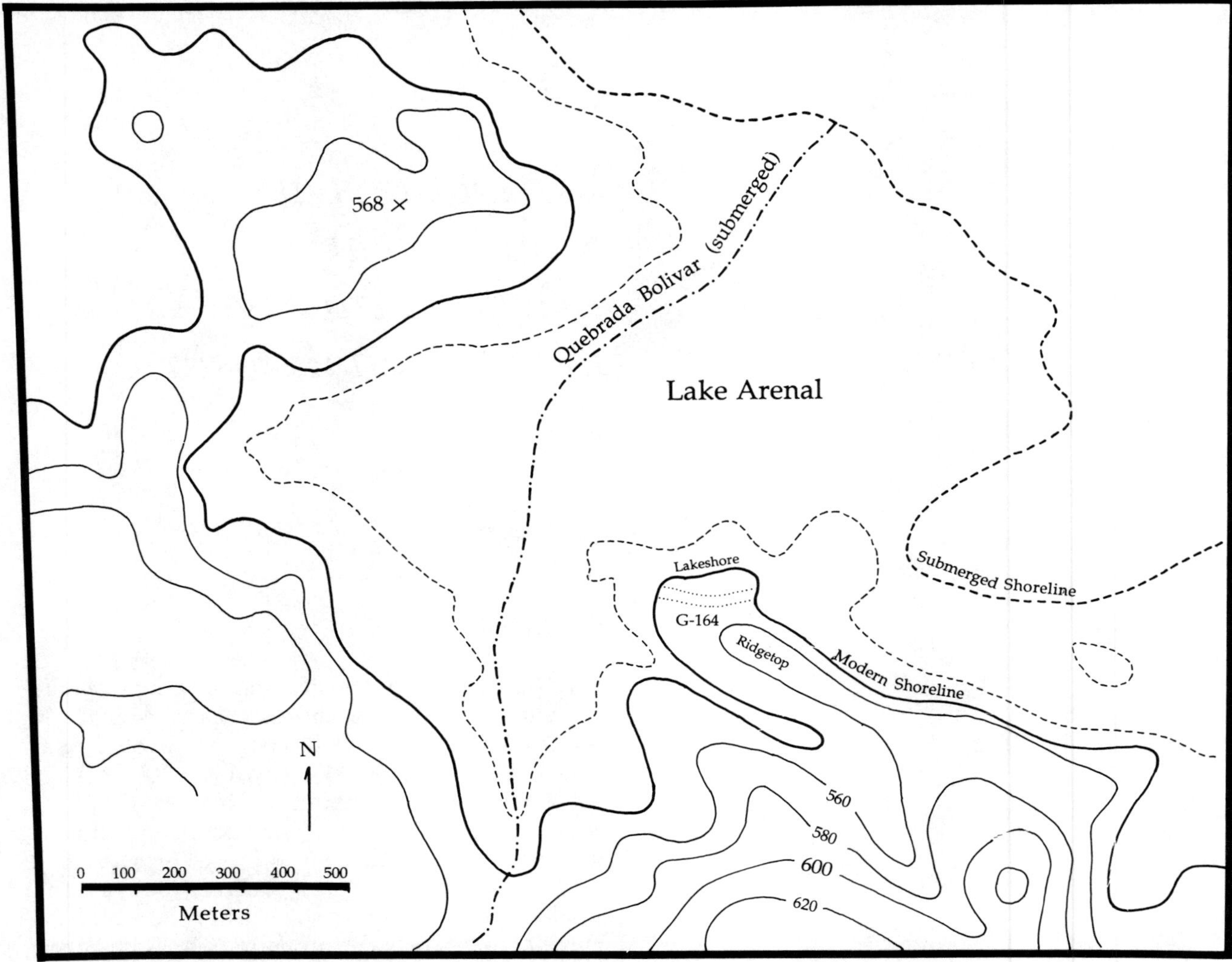

Figure 5-1.
Map indicating location of Sitio Bolívar (G-164) relative to the Quebrada Bolívar and the southern shore of Lake Arenal. Map by John Hoopes.

FIELD METHODS

RECONNAISSANCE

Hoopes, Matthews, and Sheets first recorded Sitio Bolívar at the end of March 1984, during a shoreline survey of Lake Arenal (Mueller 1984a; Chap. 3). A lowering of the lake during the dry season exposed deposits 10–30 m wide along the water's edge. Artifacts were scattered along 215 m of shoreline. Surface collection produced 271 diagnostic sherds, 23 chipped stone artifacts, eight ground stone artifacts, and one small fragment of a greenstone pendant. Approximately 140 fire-cracked cooking stones were recovered. These, together with a high proportion of monochrome ceramics, suggest the remains of domestic activities.

At the time of the initial reconnaissance, a local informant (Abel Gutiérrez) showed me a large number of round boulders in and around a looter's

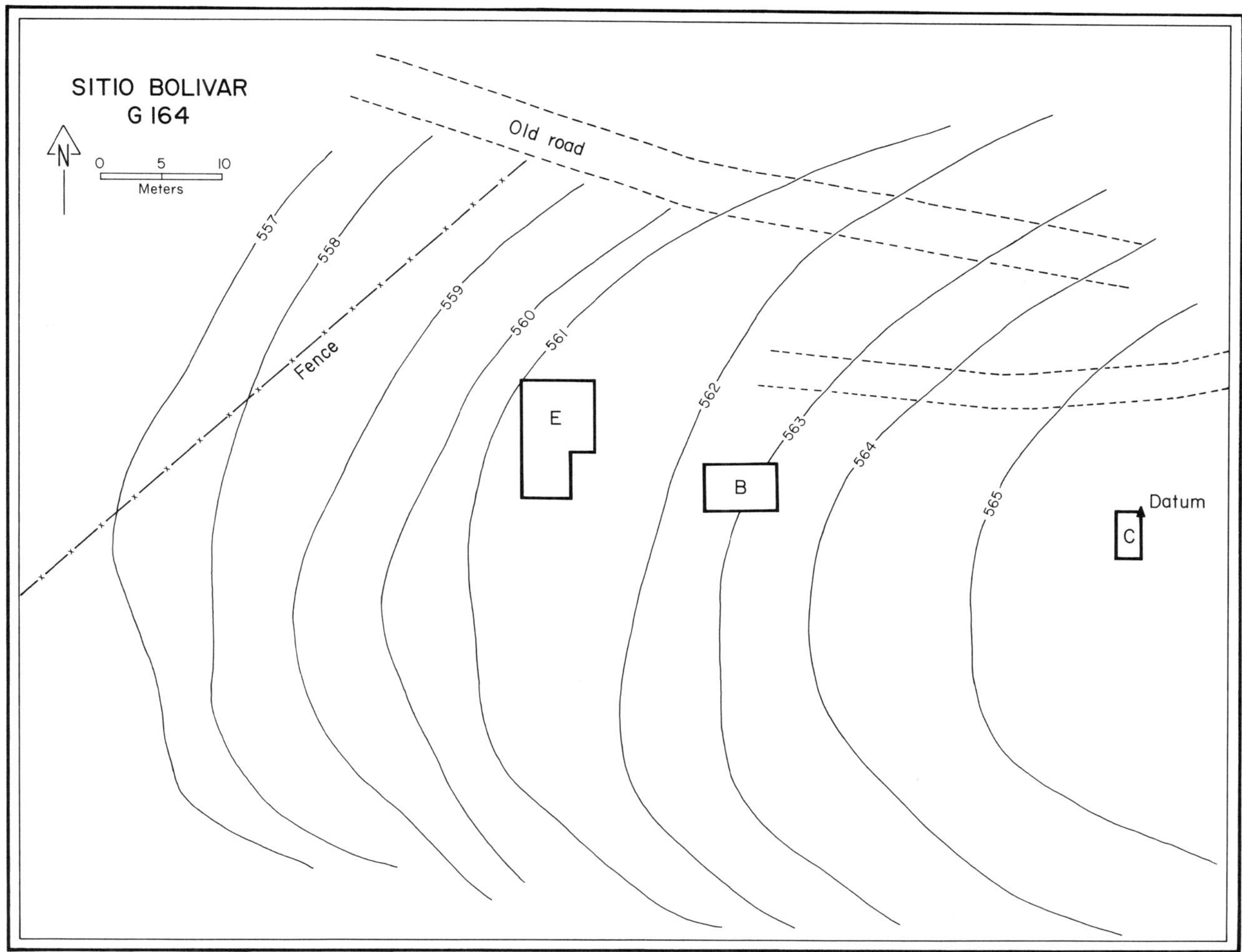

Figure 5-2.
Site map of the ridge top portion of Sitio Bolívar, indicating the relative locations of Operations B, C, and E. Map by John Hoopes.

pit near the top of the ridge overlooking the lakeshore. Their size and location suggested prehistoric burial features. The informant also mentioned that waves along the lake's edge had exposed whole vessels, subsequently removed by local collectors. Mueller, assessing the volcanic stratigraphy in the cut banks of the eroded lakeshore, noted a high density of artifacts embedded in layers below Unit 50.

SURVEY AND EXCAVATION

The specific goals of subsurface testing at the site were (1) to determine the nature of the disturbed stone features on the upper part of the site, and (2) to determine whether there was a functional difference between the features on the shoreline and those on top of the small knoll. Our working hypothesis was that the shoreline, with its high percentage of monochrome ceramics and large quantity of thermally fractured debitage, was a domestic activity area while the hilltop, with large stone features and evidence of looting, was mainly the locus of funerary activities.

We used a manually operated posthole digger to identify buried features and to determine the extent of artifact distribution, digging small holes every 10 m along two 70 m transects. Cultural materials appeared in nearly every posthole, indicating a continuous distribution of artifacts to the north and west of the site datum. Although some material was as shallow as 30 cm, we located the majority of artifacts between 90 and 110 cm below the present ground surface (Fig. 5-2).

TABLE 5-1
STRATIGRAPHIC UNITS IN OPERATION D

Depth	*Characteristics*
0–30 cm	Mixed, containing Units 10 and 20, corresponding to the modern cultivation zone
30–50 cm	Unit 30; dark gray, sandy, and friable
50–60 cm	Units 40/41. Yellow/gray sandy stratum
60–70 cm	Unit 50, dark gray to black soil
70–90 cm	Lighter horizon, Units 52/53
90–105 cm	Dark, clay-laden, with small white and yellowish particles. Unit 54, possibly mixed with eroded Unit 55
105–115 cm	Black, clay-laden. Probably Unit 60 and compressed lower strata, overlying the Aguacate Formation

LAKESHORE INVESTIGATIONS

Sheets and Mueller directed investigations along the modern lakeshore at the northern end of the site. They included excavation of a 2 m × 4 m test unit (Operation D; Fig. 5-3) and the cleaning and mapping of several features exposed by wave action.

OPERATION D

Operation D was placed next to in situ deposits in an eroded section of the lakeshore that had a particularly high density of surface artifacts. Given the domestic character of the lakeshore assemblage, we hoped that this operation would reveal intact domestic features and provide a stratigraphic cut with which we could determine the associations of cultural materials and tephra units.

Ceramic and lithic artifacts were present in Operation D, but we encountered no intact cultural features; however, the excavation did provide a continuous stratigraphic section from present ground surface to the sterile Aguacate Formation (Unit 65). The strata in this operation confirm the preservation of the regional tephra stratigraphy at this site. They are presented in Table 5-1.

In the southeastern corner of the operation, a light, fine, tephra-laden stratum approximately 15 cm thick was present as a small lens directly on top of Aguacate. It is probably Unit 61. The greatest artifact density was in the strata beneath Units 40/41, that is, in Units 50, 54, and 55. The greatest concentration of materials appeared in Unit 54—a light-colored stratum 10–15 cm thick.

The ceramic assemblage included types Charco Black-on-Red, Mojica Impressed (Corrida and Arrastrada varieties), Guinea Incised, Los Hermanos Beige and Los Hermanos Beige: Cervantes Variety—all of which date to the latter portion of the Late Arenal Phase (cal AD 300–600; Chap. 10). We found no ceramics from earlier or later phases and there was little apparent temporal variation within individual ceramic types.

LAKESHORE FEATURES

As noted earlier, the rise and fall of the lake between wet and dry seasons dissects Sitio Bolívar laterally at the water's edge. When the water level is low, the shoreline exposes a section of cultural deposits as much as 30 m wide. Although the erosion of softer strata is severe, harder strata such as the Aguacate Formation and portions of overlying tephra layers survive. In these we found several well-preserved archaeological features.

The lakeshore features consist of the following (in the order of their discovery):[2]

A6/1: A short, outflaring-necked, globular Los Hermanos Beige: Espinoza Variety *olla* (cooking pot). Its base was in Unit 65, but this vessel probably was deposited at the same time as Unit 54.

A6/2: A Los Hermanos Beige jar in a black stratum (Unit 60?) overlying Unit 65. Carbonized material on its interior indicates that it was used for cooking.

A8: A prehistoric firepit, demarcated by a circular depression 135 cm in diameter outlined by red, oxidized clay (Fig. 5-4). It contained 65 fragments of fire-cracked rock, 10 complete cooking stones, charcoal (C-14 sample Tx-5272), 14 sherds (one with charcoal on the interior), and lithic debris.

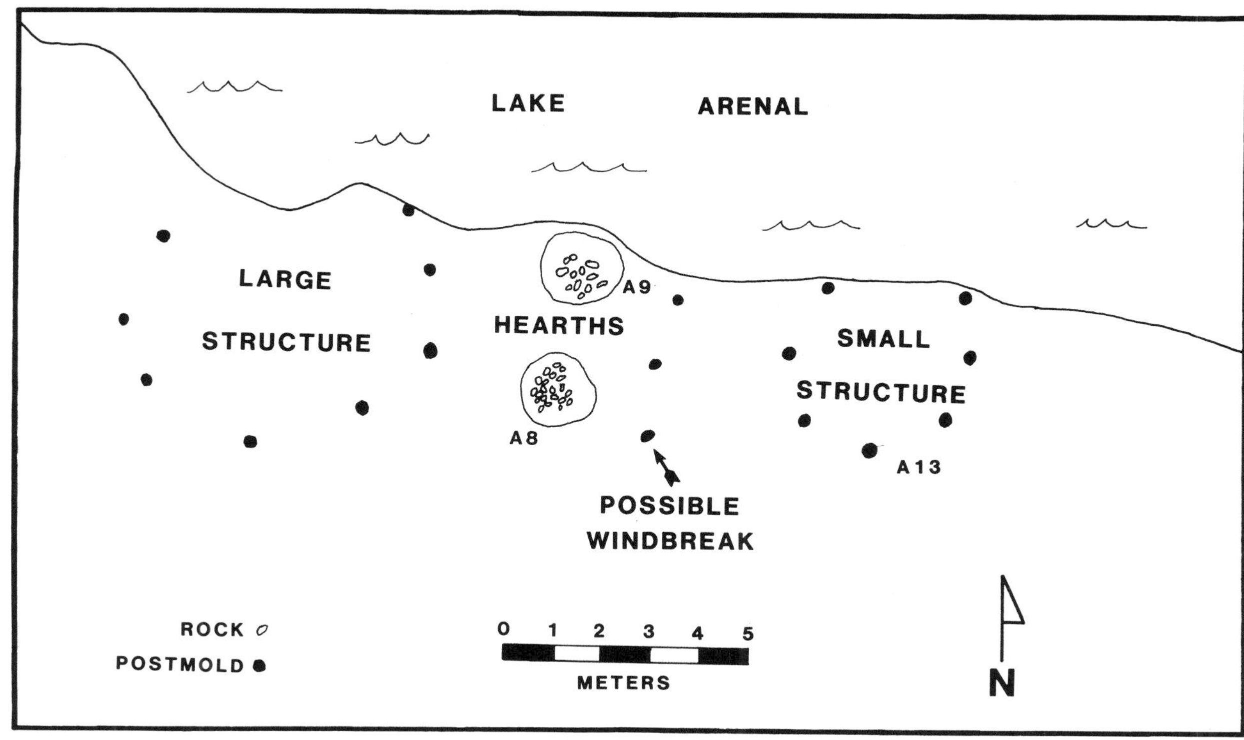

Figure 5-3.
Sketch map of the lakeshore portion of Sitio Bolívar, indicating features exposed by wave action. The map indicates the relative locations of two circular structures, with two large firepits between them. Three postholes near the hearths may represent traces of a windbreak. Map by Brian McKee.

Figure 5-4.
A firepit located between the circular domestic structures in Figure 5-3. Fire-cracked cooking stones are visible in a matrix of charcoal and burned clay at the base of the feature. A posthole of what may have been a windbreak is visible as a dark circle in the upper right corner. Photograph by Payson Sheets.

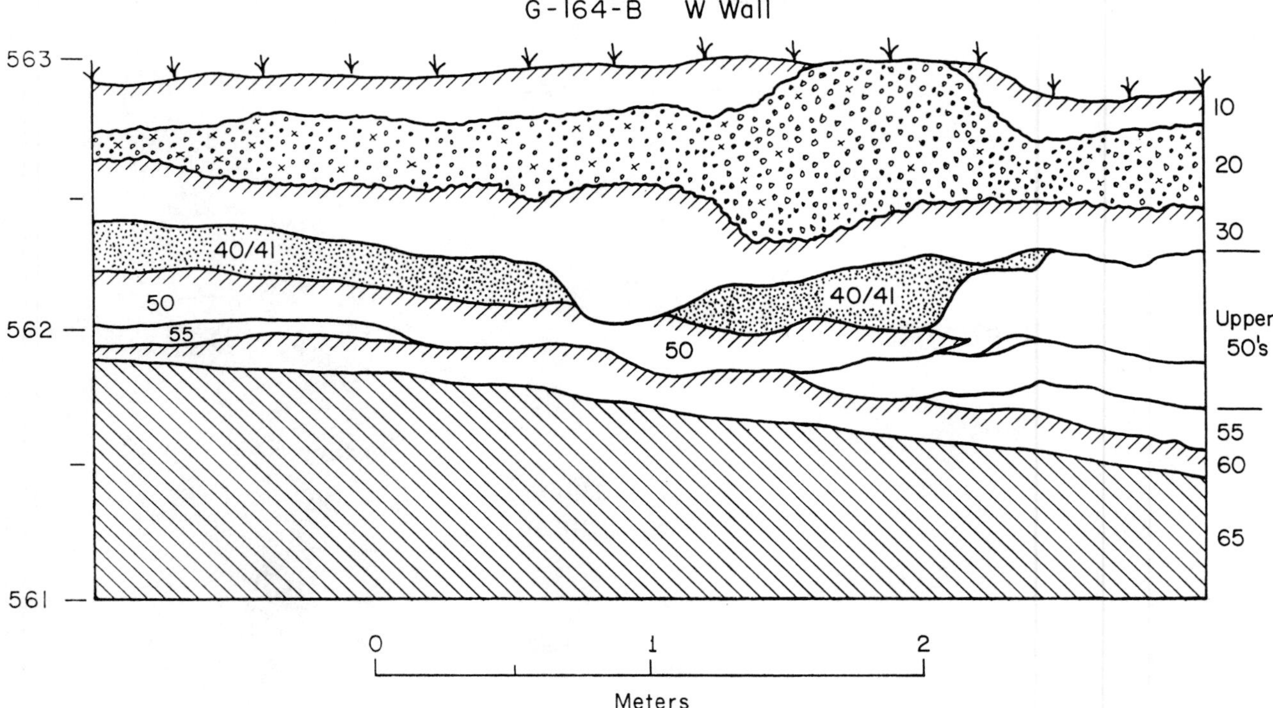

Figure 5-5.
Stratigraphic profile of the west wall of Operation B. Most of the mortuary activity was associated with strata below Unit 50. Drawing by John Hoopes.

Figure 5-6.
A midden feature in Operation B (G-164-B6). This feature probably represents the redeposition of broken vessels and other debris from previously utilized portions of the ridge top cemetery. Photograph by Payson Sheets.

A9: A second firepit, one meter NE of the first (Feature A8). Oval in shape, it measures 145 cm × 170 cm and contained 149 fragments of fire-cracked rock, large quantities of charcoal (C-14 sample Tx-5269), 29 sherds (including one jar neck fragment), and lithic debris (including one metate fragment). We found the artifacts on top of fine, hard black surface within the burned and oxidized margins of the feature. Differences in the amount of fire-cracked rock between A8 and A9 suggest that the latter had been cleaned after use.

A10: A probable firepit on the shoreline between Features A7 and A8. It measures approximately 45 cm in diameter and contained 17 fragments of fire-cracked rock, 4 small body sherds, and a small amount of flaked lithic debris. It was filled with a sandy, dark-gray tephra.

A11: A small firepit containing 7 fire-cracked rock fragments and 75 sherds, including rims from nine Los Hermanos Beige bowls, two Los Hermanos jars, a small carinated, complex-silhouette bowl of unidentified type, and a fragment of a gadrooned jar of Los Hermanos Beige: Espinoza Variety.

A12: Another probable firepit containing 1 complete cooking stone, 3 fragments of fire-cracked rock, and 19 sherds (including rims of a Los Hermanos Beige bowl and jar).

A13: The remains of a small structure, as indicated by a circular pattern of six postholes, spaced 120 cm to 135 cm apart. The feature had been partly eroded by wave action, leaving approximately 60% of the floor intact. Postholes vary from 36 cm to 45 cm in depth and 13 cm to 15 cm in diameter. One has a small "pocket" appended to one side, perhaps traces of an extra post. The enclosed area is about 3 m in diameter, for a total internal area of 7 m^2. Nothing remains of the living surface inside or outside of the feature, with the exception of a small, elevated patch of hard earth at the western end.

We identified a second round structure immediately to the west of A13. (We did not assign a lot number because we collected no material from it.) This feature is larger than the first and marked by eight postholes spaced from 1.30 m to 2.30 m apart. With the exception of the largest span, at the SW end of the feature, the average distance between them is about 1.5 m. The entrance was probably located on the southwestern side, which faces away from the prevailing winds. The postholes range from 14 cm to 19 cm in diameter. Although erosion had claimed the northern end of the feature, it is estimated that 60% to 70% of the total area is preserved. The structure has a reconstructed diameter of 5.5 m, for a total area of about 24 m^2. Unfortunately, all traces of the floor had eroded away.

A14: A small, roughly rectangular pit measuring about 140 cm × 110 cm, filled with a mixture of sand and Aguacate Formation clay. It contained 2 fragments of cooking stones and 188 sherds, including fragments of Mojica Impressed jars and both bowls and jars of Los Hermanos Beige.

We found several other features interpreted as postholes in the vicinity of the hearths and the circular structures; however, none demonstrate structural plans as clear as the aforementioned circular structures except for a small group of holes to the SW of the larger circle. This group was interpreted as the remains of a small windbreak built to shelter the two firepits (A8 and A9) from prevailing northeasterly winds.

INCIDENTAL LAKESHORE FINDS

We found a fluted Clovis-style point made of local chalcedony (Melson, personal communication to Sheets, 1985) under water 50 cm to 100 cm deep a short distance off the beach. This artifact greatly predates the major occupation of Sitio Bolívar (Chap. 11). We also found a fragment of a small greenstone pendant offshore (Chap. 12).

RIDGE TOP INVESTIGATIONS

OPERATION B

Operation B was located on the ridge top immediately to the south of the disturbed area of large stones noted on our initial survey of the site. The purpose of this operation was to discover whether any of the looted features remained intact and to expose a large enough horizontal area to judge their shape and size. At its maximum extent, Operation B provided a total exposure of 24 m^2.

Surface clearing revealed that large, rounded boulders visible on the surface had been moved by looters. Informants stated that the site had been looted within two years of our arrival; however, the presence of intact Unit 10 tephra above looted deposits clearly indicates that some looting had occurred prior to the 1968 eruption of the Arenal Volcano (Fig. 5-5). The informants also reported that no one had found anything at the location but large stones.

The upper 20 cm in Operation B were badly disturbed by agricultural activity and this "plow zone" was excavated quickly. Below this, excavation proceeded in 10 cm levels to a depth of 80 cm. Screens were not used; however, an attempt was made to collect all ceramic and lithic artifacts.

Stratigraphy

Modern disturbance, possibly as a result of deep-rooted *yucales* (manioc gardens), was evident to a depth of 50 cm throughout Operation B. Looting was heaviest in the eastern portion of the operation, where it reached depths of as much as 1 m. Unit 20 was present only in small patches throughout the operation. In the western half of the operation, patches of a harder matrix—possibly Units 40/41—were present at about 50 cm below the present ground surface. All strata above Unit 50, located approximately 60 cm to 80 cm below the surface, had been disturbed. Unit 50 itself was also somewhat disturbed, as indicated by the presence of Arenal Phase sherds in overlying levels—a context that is inconsistent with their stratigraphic position at other sites (Chap. 10).

Unit 50 overlies a large feature of ceramics, lithics, and other cultural debris (Fig. 5-6) associated with Unit 54—a light brown/orange stratum characterized by the presence of a large number of small white particles. This in turn overlies a hard, black matrix with a maximum thickness of 5 cm and traces Unit 55, a light yellow/orange, sandy tephra layer, which had probably been disturbed by cultural activity. When dry, the black matrix could only be removed with *macanas* (heavy hoes) and picks. Sherds embedded in it were identical to those of the feature above and probably do not represent an earlier occupation. This hard, black layer is situated directly on top of the Aguacate Formation substrate. It represents the partial erosion and compression of Unit 60 and underlying strata.

Features

Although several loose boulders that had been moved by looters were present on the surface, the broad, thick deposit of ceramics, chipped stone, and ground stone debris at 80 cm to 125 cm below the modern surface was the principal cultural feature in Operation B. This feature averaged 30 cm to 40 cm in thickness and covered an area of at least 16 m^2. It appeared to have been deposited within a short period of time and was excavated as a single lot (G-164-B6).[3] It was found to contain 9,856 sherds and 1,229 lithic artifacts, as well as a number of important botanical samples.

Initially, the feature appeared to consist of a relatively small number of vessels smashed at the same time. The large stones removed by looters suggest a large mortuary feature, and we assumed that the deposit of broken vessels represented a pile of ritually smashed offerings similar to features overlying Curridabat Phase burials at sites such as La Pesa Vieja (Snarskis, personal communication, 1984). Subsequent analysis, however, indicated that the assemblage was domestic in nature and consisted of hundreds of different vessels, few of which were complete.

The midden of sherds and lithic debris covered two small features. We have interpreted the first (G-164-B17) as either a hearth or a small burial pit, located at a depth of 110 cm below the present ground surface. It measures approximately 60 cm × 80 cm and was excavated into the Aguacate Formation to a depth of 20 cm. On the west it is enclosed by six large stones, one of which had fallen into the depression. In the southwestern corner is a small (6 cm rim diameter) Los Hermanos Beige outflaring-rim jar. Charcoal from the feature yielded a C-14 date of 770 (399) 200 cal BC (Tx-5271: 390 BC ± 170).

The second feature (G-164-B8) is a small pit excavated into the Aguacate Formation from a mixed, brown matrix. It is oriented roughly NE-SW and measures 115 cm × 65 cm with a maximum depth of 28 cm. The pit expands slightly below the surface from which it was excavated, undercutting the Aguacate matrix along its eastern edge. The only artifacts in it were the remains of a large, outflaring-rim Los Hermanos Beige jar, part of a large Mojica Impressed jar, and two large sherd disks (8 cm and 9 cm in diameter and 0.5 cm thick) from a single vessel of the same paste and thickness as the Hermanos jar. While it did not contain any trace of bone, its depth and shape, its location beneath a thick layer of broken pottery, its excavation into the Aguacate Formation substrate, and the associated artifacts suggest that it was a burial pit. The small size of the pit suggests that it was either a primary child burial or a secondary adult burial.

Artifacts

The painstaking matching of rim sherds of identical type, diameter, and thickness to estimate the minimum number of vessels represented by the assemblage indicates that at least 1,000 different vessels are represented by 1,492 diagnostic sherds from G-164-B6 alone. Over half of these are Los Hermanos Beige. The most common vessel forms are jars with outflaring, unthickened rims (205 vessels), outcurving-necked jars with exteriorly thickened rims (184 vessels), and open bowls with exteriorly thickened rims (122 vessels). Other important types are Mojica Impressed (99 vessels), Charco Black-on-Red (more than 50 vessels), Cervantes Incised-Punctate (27 vessels), and Guinea Incised (17 vessels). All of these are important types of the latter half of the Late Arenal Phase and suggest a date for the assemblage between cal AD 300–600. This time range, narrower than that for the Late Arenal Phase as a whole, is based on (1) a radiocarbon date from the feature of cal AD 261 (398) 435 (Tx-5273: AD 290 ± 70); (2) the close similarity between the ceramics from this assemblage and those of the Linear Decorated Period (AD 300–500) as proposed by Baudez (1967: 207); (3) the presence of a small amount of Carillo Polychrome, usually dated to the Early Polychrome Period (AD 500–800; see Chap. 10); and (4) the absence of any typical Silencio Phase types in the assemblage. The radiocarbon date was obtained from a consolidated sample of charcoal recovered from the matrix of the thick midden feature 125 cm below the present ground surface.

The assemblage suggests redeposited refuse rather than pottery broken in place. Sherd size is predominantly small to medium (less than 7.5 cm maximum dimension) and there were no fully reconstructable vessels. The nature of this midden is puzzling. The only complete ceramic artifact we found in Operation B is a crude, unslipped, miniature tripod bowl, only 2.2 cm high with a rim diameter of 3 cm. It was probably a child's toy. Not far from this was a perforated sherd disk spindle whorl, 7 cm in diameter. Both of these objects indicate domestic activities; however, sherds with carbonized residue—common in domestic deposits—were absent.

Ground stone artifacts (Chap. 12) support the interpretation of the feature as a household midden. Virtually all of the ground stone artifacts, including manos and metates, are broken or unfinished, and all fragments are small (maximum dimension less than 20 cm). The feature contained six metate fragments, five mano fragments, two small burnishing stones (used in the manufacture of ceramics), and one small, unidentified ground stone fragment. Also present was a small, tabular, unfinished ground stone pendant with two incomplete, biconical perforations.

Chipped stone examples include 56 percussion debitage flakes, 5 flake cores, and 1 percussion blade (Chap. 11). Cooking stones, of which we found 943 fragments and 17 whole examples, are the most abundant lithic category. In addition to these were 6 small, rounded pebbles and a total of 115 unclassified pieces. Chipped stone was mostly fine-grained dacite (49 pieces), with only 7 fragments of chalcedony and a few rare pieces of other materials. Only 2 hinge fractures were found in a total of 56 flakes—an indication of highly skilled knapping (Chap. 11). Sheets interprets this assemblage as clearly domestic in nature. He has suggested classification of this deposit as a "secondary midden," that is, a collection of waste material that was redeposited in a location different from that of its original disposal.

Botanical Remains

We recovered a small amount of carbonized, macrobotanical material from deposits in Operation B. Aida Blanco of the National Museum of Costa Rica identified these as two fragments of gourds (*cucurbitaceae*), two seeds of *nance* (*Byrsonima crassifolia*), four palm seeds (*Scheelia, Acrocomia*, or *Elais* sp.), and three kernels of maize (*Zea mays*). We identified an additional palm seed in a thin stratum between the large sherd feature and the surface of Aguacate (Chap. 16).

The presence of maize in this assemblage indicates its cultivation during the Late Arenal Phase; however, the presence of tree crops also indicates the concurrent gathering of wild foods. A combination of wild plant gathering and garden cultivation was probably characteristic of most indigenous Costa Rican subsistence economies.

Discussion

Ceramic analysis indicates that the pottery from the midden feature in Operation B represents waste material and broken vessels rather than ritual offerings broken in place. As with Operation E (see below), the presence of unfinished artifacts and small pieces of manos and metates, as well as a small amount of carbonized seeds, indicates that the midden's origin was ultimately domestic.

The presence of domestic debris, however, does not necessarily indicate the presence of dwellings. The ridge top portion of the site appears to have served as both a cemetery and a dumping ground

TABLE 5-2
STRATIGRAPHIC UNITS IN OPERATION C

A gray stratum with particles of Unit 20 lapilli
A brown stratum, possibly Unit 30
A black, uncompacted stratum, Unit 50
A brown compacted stratum, probably Unit 54
A brown stratum, Unit 64, mixed with Unit 61 tephra
The base stratum or Aguacate (Unit 65)

for broken pots and household artifacts. The midden feature probably represents a secondary deposition of this material—or perhaps midden material associated with burials (see below)—as a result of excavations for new tombs in a previously utilized section of the cemetery. This would explain the small sherd size and the large number of fragments from different vessels. Ceramic types present suggest that the contents of the feature accumulated over the space of two hundred or three hundred years. The lack of internal stratigraphy and soil development, however, suggests that the midden itself represents a short-term depositional event.

OPERATION C

Operation C was a 2 m × 2 m excavation unit with its northeast corner at the site datum. We placed it near the highest point of the site to explore the stratigraphy of the ridge top portion of the site and to identify funerary or domestic activities.

The stratigraphy for the operation consists of six strata, listed in Table 5-2. The upper 30 cm had been heavily disturbed by modern farming activities, and gray lapilli from Unit 20, which was not intact, were scattered throughout this level. Unit 50 and Upper 50s strata extend beneath the disturbed level to a depth of approximately 80 cm below the present ground surface.

The heaviest concentration of materials was in Unit 54, a stratum approximately 20 cm thick that contained both ceramics and lithics. We found a metate support and a mano fragment together at a depth of approximately 75 cm. In lower levels, we found five stones (each 10 cm to 15 cm in diameter) on the surface of Unit 61. We found a shallow, basin-shaped pit, 82 cm at its widest point and 11 cm deep, excavated into the Aguacate Formation in the northwest corner of the operation. We discovered broken pottery and chunks of Unit 61 tephra in the fill of the pit, but the feature's stratigraphic origin is unknown.

Artifacts

Lithic remains suggest that the assemblage from Operation C is primarily domestic in nature. The three pieces of ground stone include a bar mano fragment, a conical metate leg, and a grinding stone similar in morphology to artifacts from other parts of the site (Chap. 12). We also recovered a total of seventy-three pieces of thermally fractured rock and two complete cooking stones. We found all but four pieces of flaked stone debitage in the lower 30 cm, with the greatest concentration coming from directly above and within Unit 61 (Chap. 11). These levels also yielded a flake core, a hammerstone, and two small waterworn pebbles like those found in direct association with the remains of an early dwelling at Tronadora Vieja (Chap. 4). Other lithic artifacts include seven pieces of general percussion debitage and twenty-five unclassifiable items.

Botanical Remains

Botanical remains from Operation C consist of three fragments of either *Crescentia* or *Lagenaria* from Unit 54. We also recovered two samples of carbonized wood.

Discussion

This operation was useful for revealing the stratigraphic sequence in a relatively undisturbed portion of the ridge top. Its artifactual assemblage is suggestive of domestic activities such as food preparation and artifact manufacture; however, the artifacts are all fragmentary and were not found in association with any recognizable habitation features. They probably represent redeposited household debris from another portion of the site (as do the materials in Operation B).

OPERATION E

Operation E was begun as a 2 m × 2 m excavation unit with its southeastern corner located 45 m west and 10 m north of the site datum. It was later expanded to a total of 22 m^2. The purpose of the excavation was to investigate a concentration of large stones discovered during posthole testing.

Stratigraphy

Unlike the features in Operation B, those in Operation E had not been disturbed by looting. Natural strata that overlay the cultural features, above and including Unit 50, were intact (Fig. 5-7). In the first 2 m x 2 m square excavated in Operation E, we recognized Units 10, 20, 30, 40/41, 50, as well as a mixed, clay-laden brown stratum with yellow/orange flecks—probably Unit 54. This overlies Unit 64, which in turn overlies the Aguacate Formation (Unit 65).

The concentration of stones proved to be part of a large mortuary feature that consisted of burial pits outlined and covered by large boulders. These were in turn covered with a layer of ceramic and lithic artifacts (Fig. 5-8). This feature is located in the strata below Unit 50, in some places overlain by what appear to be Units 52 and 53 and in others overlain directly by Unit 50. In general, the strata below Units 52 and 53 are very mixed; however, portions of Unit 60 and Unit 61 are intact directly beneath the stone alignments. Upon excavation, it was evident that the stones had been placed around the perimeters of several burial pits excavated into underlying strata sometime during the formation of Unit 54.

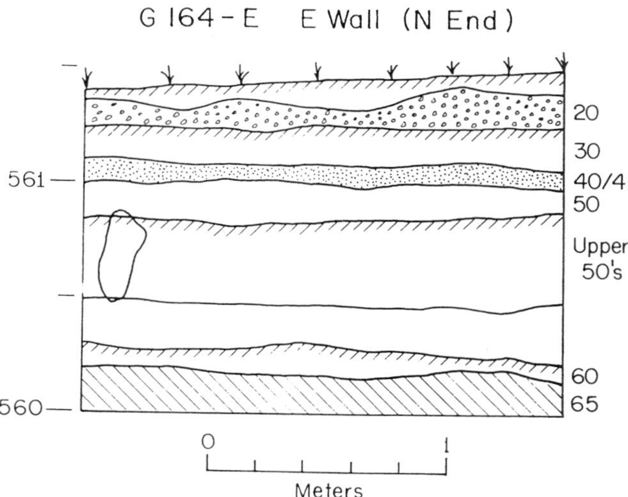

Figure 5-7.
Stratigraphic profile of the north end of the east wall of Operation E. Tephra layers represented by Units 40 and 41 are visible as light bands. Mortuary activity at the site ended prior to their deposition and was associated with strata below Unit 50. Drawing by John Hoopes.

Figure 5-8.
Dense artifact scatter above the layer of large rocks and boulders in Operation E. This feature represented the smashing of a large quantity of ceramic vessels and stone tools. Photograph by Payson Sheets.

Features

The principal cultural feature in Operation E consists of a layer of over two hundred large (30–50 cm maximum dimension), rounded boulders and cobbles overlain by a dense deposit of sherds, lithic debitage, and ground stone fragments. This deposit of tightly packed boulders probably appeared as a low stone mound, less than 1 m high and at least 8 m to 10 m in diameter, prior to its burial by later tephra deposits and the associated soil development. Although we were able to define the eastern, southern, and western edges of the feature through excavation, we could not determine whether the original plan was round, square, or amorphous. The northern edge of the feature continues beyond the limits of the excavation.

Most of the large stones that form this feature were not deposited with care. Many of the boulders fractured in place, probably from violent impacts as they were tossed on top of one another. Large, unmodified percussion flakes found throughout the layer of stones were produced as they were thrown together.

Stone Enclosures

Despite the haphazard appearance of most of the stones capping the feature, some of the large

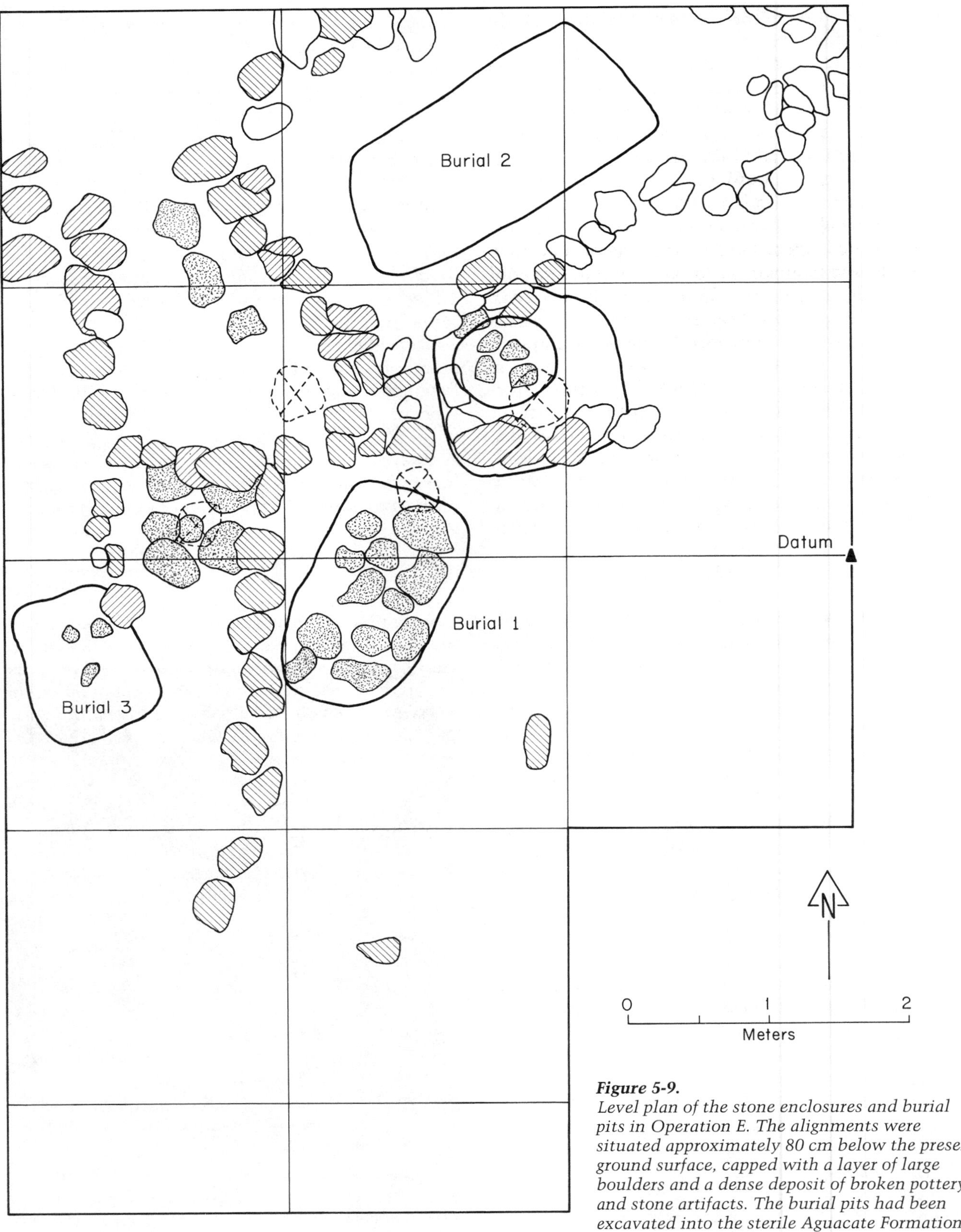

Figure 5-9.
Level plan of the stone enclosures and burial pits in Operation E. The alignments were situated approximately 80 cm below the present ground surface, capped with a layer of large boulders and a dense deposit of broken pottery and stone artifacts. The burial pits had been excavated into the sterile Aguacate Formation substrate. Map by John Hoopes.

stones in the deposit were found to be standing upright in linear arrangements (Fig. 5-9). In order to define these arrangements, all of the stones that were not upright or part of the alignments were removed after they had been mapped and photographed. This left four roughly rectangular stone enclosures.

We excavated the interior of each stone enclosure down to the sterile Aguacate Formation substrate. This revealed three roughly oval depressions that we have interpreted as burials on the basis of their similarity to features found elsewhere in the Cordillera (see below). In addition to there are two features whose functions are uncertain. One is a concentration of middle-sized (ca. 20–30 cm) stones in a roughly rectangular pattern at about 20–30 cm below the upper layer of the large stone feature in the southeastern enclosure. The other is a deep, circular pit, approximately 1.10 m deep and 74 cm in diameter, that contained several small sherds and three small (10–15 cm in diameter) stones. The latter is both deeper and narrower than the features interpreted as burials, but may nonetheless represent a vertical burial pit.

Burial 1

Burial 1, a rectangular pit 1.68 m long, 92 cm wide, and excavated to a depth of 15 cm to 25 cm into the Aguacate Formation, is situated directly beneath one stone enclosure. The only cultural materials we found in this feature are several sherds, one piece of heat-cracked rock, and a small bifacial flake. No skeletal material was present, and tests for the presence of bone collagen in soil samples were negative.

Burial 2

Burial 2 is another rectangular pit, 2.26 m long, 1.06 m wide, and excavated 32 cm into the Aguacate Formation. As with Burial 1, the sides of the pit correspond to the stone alignments above it, indicating that the alignments defined the boundaries of individual tombs. We found no evidence of bone or bone collagen in the feature, nor were there vessels or other grave goods.

Burial 3

Burial 3 is located near the western edge of the stone feature, roughly parallel to the alignment of stones that delineate the western edge of Burial 1. It is marked by a smaller (1.06 m long and 90 cm wide) and much shallower (2–3 cm into the Aguacate Formation) depression than the other features; however, it contained a single rounded-bit celt. We found two straight-bit celts near this pit at the base of the stone alignment delineating Burials 1 and 3. As with the other burials, we found no traces of bone in this feature.

Artifacts

Ceramics

We collected all of the sherds encountered during the excavation of Operation E; however, given the very large number of plain body sherds, we analyzed only the total of over three thousand sherds diagnostic as to vessel form or decoration. The vast majority of these appear to have come from whole vessels that were broken on the stones or otherwise deposited at the feature. Although we matched rim sherds and decorated pieces to the maximum extent possible in order to determine the minimum number of whole vessels represented by the assemblage, we reconstructed no whole vessels from the feature. The most common types present were Los Hermanos Beige, Charco Black-on-Red, Mojica Impressed: Corrida and Arrastrada varieties, Guinea Incised, an unnamed red monochrome, and Los Hermanos Beige: Cervantes Variety (Chap. 10). These help place the cultural features at the end of the Late Arenal Phase (cal AD 300–600). There were some differences in the frequencies of specific types between the assemblages in Operations B and E. For example, four types, Tamino Incised, Mojica Impressed: Laguna Variety, Tola Trichrome, and Carillo Polychrome, were represented in Operation B but not in Operation E. It should be noted, however, that the total number of sherds from these types is very small, making it difficult to draw any conclusions from their distribution.

Lithics

We recovered a total of 49 ground- and polished stone artifacts and fragments from Operation E (Chaps. 12 and 13). The twenty-three metate fragments include two plates with cylindrical supports, two cylindrical supports, and two conical supports. Other artifacts consist of fourteen mano fragments, three straight-bit celts and four celt fragments, a fragment of a slate mirror back, three grinding stones, and a nutting stone. With the exception of the three celts from Burial 3, all of the ground stone artifacts come from the dense deposit of artifacts on top of the stone feature.

The well-made bar mano fragments and pieces of undecorated metates are suggestive of a household assemblage, but the slate disk fragment suggests the presence of "elite" items. No ground stone fragments fit together, suggesting that they represent artifacts broken elsewhere and discarded on top of the mortuary feature. If the artifacts were broken during activity associated with the burials, they must have been widely scattered over unexcavated parts of the feature.

The 100% sample of lithic artifacts from Operation E include numerous cooking stones and pieces of heat-cracked rock (Chap. 11). We recovered these artifacts from hearths and other domestic assemblages at sites in the Arenal basin, and their presence suggests that a portion of the assemblage from Operation E consists of waste materials from domestic activities.

Interpretations

The concentration of ceramics in Operation E appears to have been the result of both on-site smashing of whole vessels and the disposal of previously broken ones (Chap. 10). The ground stone assemblage consists exclusively of broken fragments from incomplete artifacts, scattered widely across the feature. Flaked lithics represent a large quantity of domestic debitage, probably brought to the burial complex for disposal.

Botanical Remains

We found carbonized macrobotanical remains from Operation E in the material deposited on top of the layer of large stones. They consist of a carbonized fragment of an unidentified fruit and numerous samples of carbonized wood of unknown species. Unlike the sample from Operation B, which includes some remains of maize, Operation E yielded no direct evidence of this cultigen.

Discussion

We have interpreted the large stone feature in Operation E as a mortuary complex dating to the Late Arenal Phase. The nature of the feature suggests a special regard for those interred there. The transport of heavy stones from the streambed of a nearby *quebrada* indicates a substantial investment of energy—more than what is likely to have been undertaken by just one or two individuals. As noted earlier, however, the feature was not for the benefit of a single individual and the "compartmental" nature of the stone enclosures suggests that it does not represent a single episode of burial activity. Instead, the community or a single family may have utilized it at intervals. The deposition of materials over time was complex. As new burials were added, ceramic and lithic debris was either placed or redeposited between and within the tombs. Although sherds were found throughout the feature, however, the scatter of lithics and ceramics directly on top of the stones appears to represent a final dedicatory event. After all of the burials were in place, whether constructed all at once or by accretion, large stones and then a layer of vessels were thrown onto the feature and it was not used again.

INTRAREGIONAL COMPARISONS

The stone mortuary complex shares a number of important parallels with other contemporaneous sites in the Northwestern Cordillera region. Burial mounds constructed of river cobbles and rounded boulders have been recorded at Hacienda Jericó (Finch 1982–1983), Hacienda Mojica (Ryder 1982–1983a), Guayabo de Bagaces (Ryder 1982–1983b), and at Sitio Méndez in the Naranjo River/Bijagua Valley (Norr 1982–1983). In all of these locations, mounds appear both alone and in groups. They are frequently associated with petroglyphs. Human skeletal remains were found in burials within stone mounds at Guayabo de Bagaces and Sitio Méndez on the Naranjo River. At all of these sites, the principal occupations and mound construction took place during the mid- to late Zoned Bichrome Period, especially the last part (cal AD 300–600).

The most similar features were identified at Sitio Méndez, where one of six large mounds was trenched to reveal several burials (ibid.: 138–140). As in Operation E, a cluster of mortuary features built of large river cobbles was overlain by a deposit of crushed vessels. Ten burial pits surrounded by cobbles were identified. Four contained fragmentary skeletal remains of adults. As at Sitio Bolívar, burial offerings were rare. The only artifact recovered from any of the pits was a large jar of the type Mojica Impressed—also the most common decorated type in Sitio Bolívar assemblages.[4]

Similar features were excavated at Sitio Murillo, in the Guayabo de Bagaces region southwest of Miravalles Volcano (Ryder 1982–1983b). Large boulders and a layer of medium-sized (10–40 cm diameter) rocks formed a small, oval mound. Three "rock cluster features" built from combinations of columnar basalt pillars, thick stone slabs, thin lajas, and river cobbles within the mound were found to contain fragmentary skeletal remains. No grave goods were present. The ceramic assemblage at Sitio Murillo is similar to that from Sitio Bolívar, and Ryder suggests a date of around cal AD 300 (ibid.: 126).

Other similar features were excavated at El Carmen (or Hacienda Mojica; Ryder 1982–1983a: 106–110), a site with several stone burial mounds. Excavations exposed part of one mound, all of another, and the area between the two. A rich assemblage of seventy whole or nearly complete ceramic vessels was recovered from caches lacking skeletal remains. Burials were marked by alignments of large stones and two caches of ceramics were covered by large stones overlain in turn by a layer of sherds.

In one mound, six caches were associated with parallel lines of cobbles below a "cap" of large stones. Four of these yielded a total of seventeen ceramic vessels. Associated ceramics were Late Arenal Phase types, including two vessels of Carillo Polychrome from a cache and fragments of a Carillo bowl interpreted as a postburial offering, either placed or smashed in situ. A second set of stone alignments was associated with a rectangular tomb containing three simple metates, a mano, and half of a Las Palmas Red-on-Beige jar (an Early Arenal Phase type).[5]

Unlike Sitio Méndez, Mound 2 at El Carmen appears to have been built in stages. On the basis of the ceramics, Ryder (1982–1983a: 112) suggests that there were two or three principal phases of mound construction. The first, characterized by the tomb containing the Palmas Red-on-Beige vessel, is believed to represent the middle of the Zoned Bichrome Period (300 cal BC–cal AD 300). The second, given the appearance of Carillo Polychrome, probably dates to the latter half of the Late Arenal Phase, around cal AD 300–600.

Apart from the features at Sitio Bolívar, we did not identify large stone mounds in our own survey of the perimeter of Lake Arenal. It is possible that volcanic tephra and associated soil formation have buried or obscured stone mounds throughout much of the Arenal basin. Aguilar (1984: 82) reports a buried mound of river cobbles that was exposed by bulldozing at the site of Río Chiquito (G-176), where tephra deposits can be several meters deep. He estimates that the mound was approximately 40 m in diameter and 3 m high, comparable in size to examples at Hacienda Jericó, Hacienda Mojica (El Carmen), and Guayabo de Bagaces. Ceramic collections at the mound yielded late Zoned Bichrome types in association with Carillo Polychrome, as was noted at both El Carmen and Sitio Bolívar. Aguilar (ibid.: 81) also reports two or three heavily looted cobble mounds at Sitio Carmelo, near the Piedras River at the western end of the lake. The associated ceramics include Corrida and Arrastrada varieties of Mojica Impressed and help tie this site chronologically to Sitio Bolívar.

Ryder (1982–1983b: 127) notes that the wide variety of burial features from sites in and near the Cordillera de Guanacaste illustrates the complexity and diversity of mortuary practices in the region during the latter half of the Zoned Bichrome Period. While there is a wide diversity in the number and size of mound features, however, the use of stone burial features appears to have been a strong cultural tradition throughout the Cordillera around cal AD 300–500. Elements of mortuary features at Sitio Bolívar, such as cobble and boulder construction, thick deposits of sherds and broken vessels, burial pits marked by alignments of standing stones, and a relative paucity of burial offerings, are similar to those found in the larger mounds. These characteristics are also geographically distinct within the Cordillera. Stone burial mounds are not associated with Zoned Bichrome cemeteries in the Tempisque Valley (Baudez 1967), the Nicoya Peninsula (Guerrero 1982–1983), or the Pacific Coast of Guanacaste (Lange 1980b, 1984b). They are also unknown in the Rivas region of Nicaragua (Healy 1980).

The stone mounds at Sitio Bolívar have more parallels in the Atlantic Watershed region than they do in the west. El Bosque Phase (AD 0–500) burials are typically constructed of large river cobbles, and include a form known as the "corridor tomb," in which grave goods and burials are placed between long rows of cobbles (Snarskis 1978: 169, 1981a: 50) in a fashion similar to that noted at El Carmen (Ryder 1982–1983a: fig. 7.2).

Theories about the nature of social organization associated with Zoned Bichrome burial mounds are linked to the question of whether these features were built during a single construction effort or by accretion. Ryder proposes that the large mound at Sitio Murillo contains as many as one hundred tombs and was built in a single episode. Further, this might have required the direction of "an individual or group of special status" (1982–1983b:127). Norr, however, interprets the Sitio Méndez mound as "a continuous, family or community effort as individuals were added to the cemetery throughout the occupation of the site" (1982–1983:139).

To date, there is little evidence to support or refute either model. It is possible that both interpretations are correct, and that there was significant regional variation in social organization or mortuary practices in eastern Guanacaste during the Zoned Bichrome Period. In our view, the burials at Sitio Bolívar are probably best interpreted as an example of Norr's accretional model for mound construction.

All of the stone mortuary features that have been excavated contained multiple tombs, and none of them have been found to be particularly lavish in either their construction or the nature of burial offerings. In fact, despite *huaqueros'* (looters') reports of jades, ornamental metates, and elaborate ceramics from the mounds (Ryder 1982–1983b:124), very few artifacts of any kind have been recovered from these features in controlled excavations—with the exception of El Carmen. The "wealthiest" burials, such as those represented by Cache 1 at El Carmen (Ryder 1982–1983a:107), which contained fourteen ceramic vessels, or Cache 2, which contained two vessels of Carillo Polychrome in association with a large carved tripod metate and four other vessels, are not especially impressive as "chiefly" interments. While the use of basalt columns or large, volcanic lajas in tomb construction indicates the expenditure of a fair amount of energy, it is not beyond what one might expect from a single-family unit.

With the possible exception of the mound at Sitio Murillo, there is little evidence for centrally administrated construction in northwestern Costa Rica during the Zoned Bichrome Period. Burial patterns within the mounds themselves have not indicated the hierarchy one would expect for an elite-sponsored mortuary compound. The paucity of grave goods makes the internal chronology of burials in these features difficult to assess, and until we have further data it is probably wise to take a conservative stance on the value of stone mounds as evidence for political centralization. While we can see the beginnings of rank in the variable amounts of energy expended in tomb construction and in the accumulation of goods included in individual burials, evidence for powerful chiefs has yet to be found in these features.

DATING FEATURES AND ASSEMBLAGES

The features and assemblages at Sitio Bolívar have been dated by means of comparisons with material from similar sites in northwestern Costa Rica and new radiocarbon dates. The chronological placement of prehistoric activities at Sitio Bolívar is useful not only for reconstructing cultural development in the Arenal basin, but also for understanding patterns that characterize the Zoned Bichrome Period in both the Cordillera and the Greater Nicoya regions.

We obtained five radiocarbon dates from excavations in both the lakeshore and the ridge top portions of Sitio Bolívar. The earliest, 770 (399) 200 cal BC (Tx-5271: 390 BC ± 170), comes from a possible hearth at the base of deposits in Operation B. It suggests that Sitio Bolívar was utilized during the Early Arenal Phase, although few ceramics from this phase were present.[6] A second date of cal AD 261 (398) 435 (Tx-5273: AD 290 ± 70) from the sherd midden and a third of cal AD 567 (642) 669 (Tx-5270: AD 540 ± 80) from the matrix of the stone tomb features in Operation E date activities during the principal Late Arenal occupation of the site. A date of cal AD 145 (244) 338 (Tx-5272: 180 AD ± 60) was obtained from one of the two firepits (A8) on the lakeshore. The latter half of its range is consistent with the estimated dates for the principal occupation of Sitio Bolívar. The second firepit (A9) yielded a date of cal AD 879 (894) 975 (Tx-5269: AD 820 ± 50). It is several hundred years too late and does not overlap the date of the first firepit even with a two-sigma interval. We believe this second sample to have been contaminated.

On the basis of interpretations of a corpus of radiocarbon dates from related contexts and assemblages elsewhere in Costa Rica, the principal occupation of Sitio Bolívar is dated to cal AD 300–600, during which time both the mortuary features on the ridge top and the habitational features on the lakeshore are believed to have been constructed. At this time, the site was quite large relative to other sites in the Arenal basin. Both macrobotanical remains and ground stone artifacts such as manos and metates indicate the cultivation and processing of maize, but there is also evidence for a continued exploitation of tree crops such as palm fruits and *nance* (*Byrsonima crassifolia*). Long-distance contacts with areas to both the east and the west are suggested by Atlantic Watershed ceramics and greenstone pendants of imported materials. The association of a slate mirror back with mortuary features in Operation

E suggests the possibility of down-the-line trade from Mesoamerican cultures much farther to the north. These have also been found at the site of La Fortuna, just east of Arenal Volcano (Stone and Balser 1965), where they were associated with a ceramic assemblage very similar to that of Sitio Bolívar and dated to AD 300–500 (Baudez and Coe 1966).

The period of Sitio Bolívar's principal occupation coincides roughly with the Early Classic Period in the Maya Lowlands, during which time Classic Maya trade with the southeastern "periphery" was at its peak (Hoopes 1984b). Costa Rican contact with Mesoamerica at this time might have included a loose network for the procurement of jadeite from southern Guatemala (Lange and Bishop 1982–1983). Contact between Mesoamerican cultures and the Cordillera region, however, appears to have been confined to the exchange of small trinkets such as slate mirror backs and occasional incised jades. Neither the appearance of more elaborate burial architecture nor the level of sociopolitical complexity associated with its construction suggests strong cultural influence from Mesoamerica.

CONCLUSIONS

Sitio Bolívar is interpreted as the remains of a Late Arenal Phase village. Lakeshore and ridge top investigations indicate activities associated with both life and death in this community. The site appears to have been spatially organized with houses situated on a flat bench near a freshwater stream (now mostly inundated by the waters of Lake Arenal) and a cemetery on top of the ridge overlooking the site.

The features located on the shore of Lake Arenal at Sitio Bolívar are distinctly domestic in appearance. The circular patterns of postholes; the presence of firepits with charcoal, fire-cracked rock and large numbers of cooking stones; and the fact that vessels from this part of the site consist primarily of large jars for storage and cooking indicate that this portion of the site served as the locus for household activities, especially the preparation of food.

Unfortunately, given the narrow strip of shoreline and the problem of erosion since the lake's recent filling, we cannot infer numbers of dwellings or the size of the total habitation area. We do know, however, that structures were circular in plan and variable in size. We have estimated the internal areas of the two structures identified on the lakeshore at approximately 7 m^2 and 24 m^2. The larger one probably represents a family dwelling and the smaller one a special-function structure such as a sweat bath or a storage space. Most of the dwellings were probably located in a portion of the site that has been inundated by Lake Arenal. Water to the north of the exposed shoreline is fairly shallow, especially as one approaches the lagoon at the mouth of Quebrada Bolívar. This broad area of relatively flat ground would have been ideal for settlement. The habitational features that we were able to identify we interpret as the remains of the village that was served by the hilltop cemetery.

One of the most interesting characteristics of the lakeshore features is that they suggest the existence of round houses at Arenal Phase sites. This pattern indicates the continuation of a tradition established during the Tronadora Phase, as evidenced by the remains of structures at Tronadora Vieja (Chap. 4). At present, dwellings have not been reported from any other Zoned Bichrome sites in northwestern Costa Rica. The Sitio Bolívar structures, however, suggest that Late Arenal Phase architecture was distinct from contemporaneous El Bosque Phase structures in the Atlantic Watershed region. Snarskis (1984b) notes that El Bosque houses were rectangular, with foundations made of river cobbles. Citing a round/circular dichotomy between Mesoamerican and South American architectural traditions in the Formative Period, Snarskis attributes the rectangular shape of El Bosque houses to Mesoamerican influence that accompanied the introduction of intensive maize agriculture. He also notes a shift from rectangular to circular structures in the Atlantic Watershed/Central Highlands regions around AD 500. According to our evidence from the Arenal basin, the rectangular house form tradition did not extend to the Northwestern Cordillera region.

The contemporaneity of the occupation of the two areas of the site is clearly indicated by the associated ceramics. Although there is a higher percentage of decorated types in the ridge top cemetery, pottery from the lakeshore is identical to that associated with the mortuary features. As noted earlier, all of the features date to the latter part of the Late Arenal Phase, most likely between cal AD 300–600 (see also Chap. 10). Strata on which the major lakeshore occupation occurred had largely eroded away; however, it seems likely that the lakeshore features—like those elsewhere at the site—originated in Unit 54 and penetrated the Aguacate Formation.

We found no evidence of habitations during testing in the ridge top portion of Sitio Bolívar, which appears to have served a primarily mortuary function. The combination of both midden and mortuary features in this part of the site suggests that the ridge top was considered unsuitable for either dwellings or agriculture and was used for the disposal of both people and artifacts. The location of Zoned Bichrome cemeteries on the tops of hills and ridges is a common pattern in Guanacaste (Lange and Scheidenhelm 1972), and the choice of this type of setting for the cemetery at Sitio Bolívar is further evidence that Arenal Phase peoples were participating in cultural traditions characteristic of Greater Nicoya.

The feature in Operation B appears to represent a secondary deposition of material from surrounding burials, perhaps in conjunction with burials of individuals of lower social rank or with smaller families than those buried under the large stone features in Operation E. The group of enclosures of large river cobbles capped with heavy boulders in Operation E is interpreted as the remains of a funerary mound constructed by higher-ranking individuals or families.

The large quantities of broken ceramics and other artifacts found in association with these features are suggestive of the rites and ceremonies that may have accompanied Late Arenal Phase interments. Large feasts in conjunction with funerals are common to a number of cultures (Huntington and Metcalf 1979) and can include ritual vessel smashing. At La Ceiba, a site on the Tempisque River dating to the late Middle Polychrome Period (cal AD 800–1300), such activities are evidenced by a large complex of elongated clay ovens and huge quantities of faunal and floral remains in association with burials (Blanco et al. 1986:149). Unlike at La Ceiba, however, there is no evidence that the cooking of funeral feasts occurred on or near the burials at Sitio Bolívar.

It is possible that the artifacts on top of the mortuary features were the personal possessions of the interred. Smashing and depositing them on top of the burials would have removed the objects of the deceased from common use—the psychological equivalent of placing them in the grave. This could explain both the domestic nature of the artifact deposit and the paucity of offerings within the tombs themselves. As a practice similar to the burning of the house of a dead relative, the smashing and destruction of vessels would have helped to remove traces of the deceased's mortal existence from the community.

The destruction of objects that had been the property of the deceased has been reported from similar contexts. At the site of El Carmen (Hacienda Mojica), Ryder (1982–1983a:107) reports a contemporaneous burial cache of fourteen vessels, most of which had been ritually "killed" by punching holes in their bases. As noted earlier, deposits of broken pottery on mortuary features are common in the Northwestern Cordillera of Costa Rica.

An alternative explanation for this pattern is that cemeteries and tombs were considered appropriate locations for disposing of broken artifacts. Just as burial practices removed deceased individuals from the principal habitation areas, trash heaps and sherd middens would have removed broken vessels from paths and other areas in daily use. In addition, broken vessels served as both offerings to dead relatives and markers for grave locations. It seems likely that the features represent a cemetery that experienced relatively intensive use in a short amount of time, and that burial practices necessitated the frequent displacement of both soil and artifacts in and on it.

The features at Sitio Bolívar provide us with a glimpse of what village life was like in the Arenal basin at the end of the Late Formative Period. Late Zoned Bichrome society at the site appears to have had an economy based on both maize horticulture and the collection of wild foods. Social organization was probably organized along the lines of kinship, but evidence for centralized leadership is lacking. The similarities in ceramic styles and mortuary practices that Sitio Bolívar shares with other sites in both the Arenal basin and the Northwestern Cordillera region suggest participation in a more widespread, regional "culture," possibly maintained through intercommunity exchange networks and regional religious sodalities.

Understanding the nature of village life at sites like Sitio Bolívar is important for addressing problems concerning the nature of sociopolitical organization and the emergence of rank in lower Central America. At Sitio Bolívar, the only evidence for social ranking lies in the appearance of imported objects such as greenstone pendants and slate mirror backs and the differentiation between simple burials covered with sherds (Operation B) and more elaborate burials covered with both stones and sherds. Because evidence for chiefly individuals and centralized political authority is missing, it is difficult to substantiate an interpretation that Zoned Bichrome society was organized along the lines of chiefdoms (See Habicht-

Mauche et al. 1987; Hoopes 1988). There is clear artifactual evidence, however, that Arenal Phase peoples were actively participating in a network of communication (and probably exchange) that stretched westward into Greater Nicoya. This interaction, as well as the construction of stone burial mounds, was probably carried out in the context of a decentralized political organization. Understanding the nature of prehistoric society at villages like Sitio Bolívar can provide us with important insights into the emergence of ranking and complex *tribes*—as opposed to chiefdoms—in lower Central America.

NOTES

1. A detailed description of investigations at this site can also be found in Hoopes 1987:98–161.
2. Features are identified by individual lot numbers.
3. Although other material was grouped in separate lots, it is likely that *all* of it derives from this feature.
4. Norr (1982–1983:143) notes that ceramics from the stone "cap" of the Méndez mound were similar to collections from an unidentified stone burial mound near Arenal.
5. A large charcoal sample from this tomb yielded a date of 349 cal BC—cal AD 42 (UCLA-2167E: 160 BC ± 80; Ryder 1982–1983a:109). Its association with a vessel of Las Palmas Red-on-Beige makes this feature contemporaneous with the Early Arenal Phase, about 300 years earlier than the principal occupation at Sitio Bolívar.
6. This date is very close to that of a sample dated to 394–207 cal BC (UCLA-2163: 300 BC ± 60) from the base of a similar mound excavated by Norr (1982–1983:140) at Sitio Méndez.

6

The Silencio Site: An Early to Middle Polychrome Period Cemetery in the Arenal Region

JOHN E. BRADLEY

INTRODUCTION

The Silencio site, G-150, is a large Early and Middle Polychrome Period cemetery located on the Continental Divide between Tilarán and Lake Arenal in northwestern Costa Rica. It is situated on the top and northwest-facing slope of a large knoll covered by relatively undisturbed tropical rain forest (Fig. 6-1). Local residents have known the location of the cemetery for years and substantial looting has occurred in many areas. Sheets inspected the site in 1982 (Sheets 1982–1983) in response to complaints from the landowner regarding this looting. Initial inspection revealed that many areas remained intact and could provide valuable information regarding local mortuary practices. In addition, intact volcanic strata that could aid in the development of a local stratigraphic sequence existed in many areas. For these reasons, the site was a major focus of research conducted in 1984.

The 1984 excavations uncovered twelve undisturbed graves dating to two distinct times of interment. There was also evidence of extensive prehistoric landscaping involving earth and rock, and artifacts revealed considerable on-site domestic activity. Skeletal preservation was poor for all burials, but was sufficient to show that all were primary interments of adults in extended positions.

This chapter begins with a summary of the field techniques utilized during the 1984 investigations and a discussion of the stratigraphy and chronology of the Silencio site. A description of the burials and other evidence of prehistoric activity during each of the phases of interment and

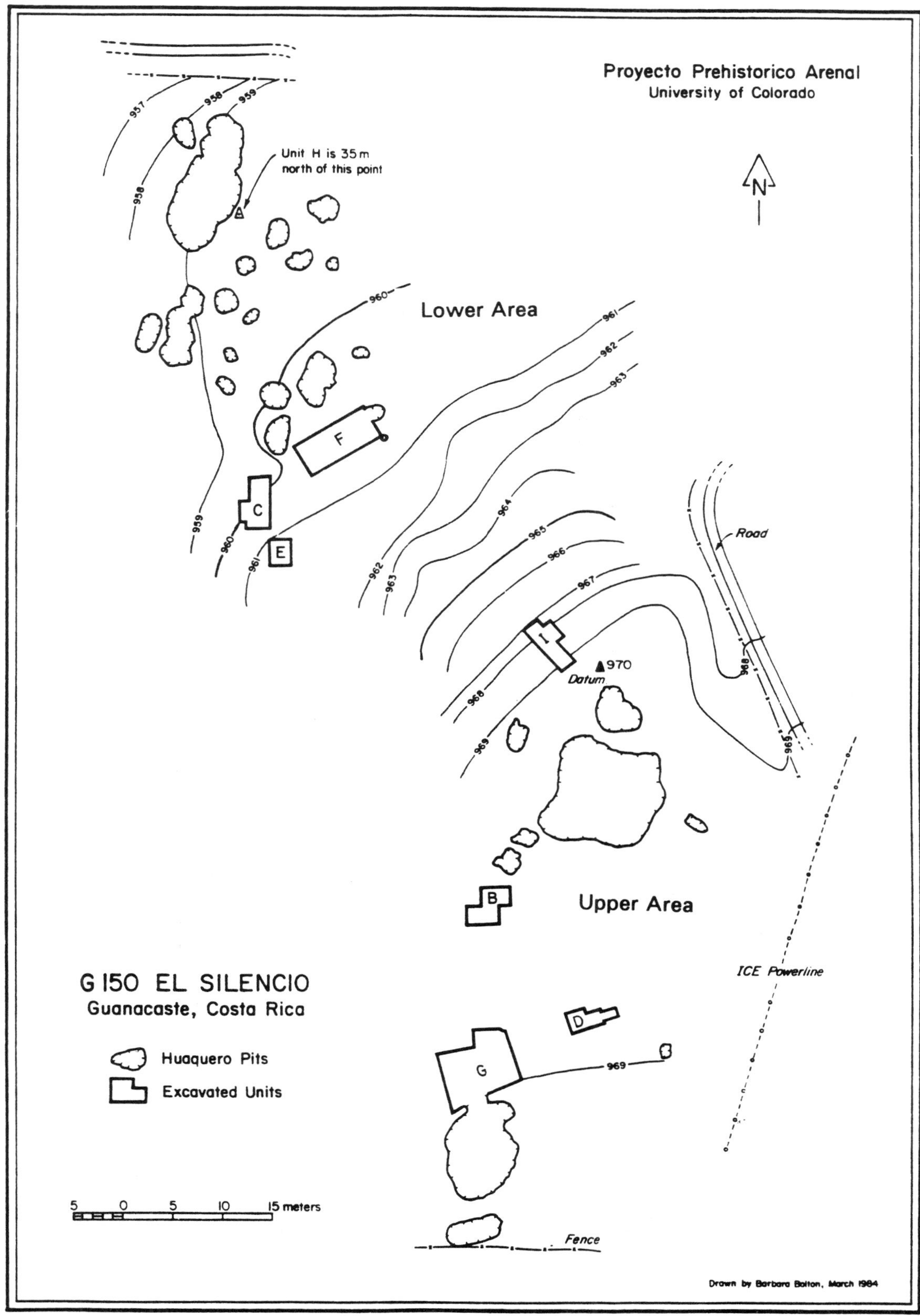

Figure 6-1.
G-150 site map. Map by Barbara Bolton.

a brief summary of stable carbon isotope analysis of bone collected at the site follow. I then compare the Silencio site with other funerary sites in Costa Rica and examine several indicators of the relative status of the individuals. I examine the Silencio Cemetery with reference to several ethnographic models in an attempt to explain various features of the site.

FIELD TECHNIQUES

We conducted field excavations at G-150 in 1984. The total area of the site is unknown, because of the dense vegetation cover, but evidence of burials can be found extending NW down the ridge at least 250 m from the excavated portion of the site. The clearing of dense secondary vegetation in the central part of the site revealed two relatively flat areas (designated upper and lower areas) divided by a slope approximately 25 m in length (Fig. 6-1). Much of the site had been disturbed by looting; at least twenty-five pits, up to 25 m long and 3 m deep, covered approximately 20% of the 2,000 m^2 area that was cleared and mapped. Large quantities of laja were present in back dirt piles from several looters' pits, indicating that looted stone cist graves probably were present in at least three of the pits. We found ceramic sherds diagnostic of the Early to Middle Polychrome periods (Silencio Phase, AD 600–1300) in back dirt piles and on the ground surface.

After we cleared vegetation from the central portion of the site, we drew a topographic map (Fig. 6-1) of this area. We then profiled several looters' pits for a preliminary understanding of the cultural and natural stratigraphy of the site.

The selection of areas for excavation was purposive and concentrated on four types of locations: large, flat undisturbed areas between looters' pits; areas in which in situ laja was exposed in looters' pits; areas in which the volcanic stratigraphy appeared to be undisturbed; and sloping areas exhibiting apparent cultural modification. The size of the excavation units varied between 2 m × 2 m and 4 m × 8 m. Data control was by the operation, lot, and item designation used by Sharer (1978) and modified by Sheets (1983).

Excavation was by natural or cultural stratigraphic levels where possible, and arbitrary 20 cm levels were used in cases in which natural or cultural levels were either not discernible or exceeded 20 cm in thickness. Sediments were screened through either 1/4- or 1/8-inch mesh hardware cloth in areas in which an abundance of lithic debitage or other artifactual material was encountered. Excavations were terminated when the sterile clay of Unit 65 was reached, usually about 160 cm below the present ground surface.

We collected samples of various materials to increase our understanding of the environment, the nature of the eruptions of Arenal Volcano, the diet of site inhabitants, lithic and ceramic technology, and site chronology. The results of the analyses can be found in Chapters 1, 2, 10, 11, 12, 13, 14, 15, and 16. Friedman and Gleason (1984) conducted stable carbon isotope analysis of bone recovered from the G-150 burials to determine the percentage of the diet consisting of maize.

STRATIGRAPHY AND CHRONOLOGY

The volcanic stratigraphy is described in detail in Chapters 1 and 2 and will therefore be summarized only briefly. Fifteen stratigraphic units, including seven deposits of volcanic tephra, were recognized at the site (Fig. 6-2).

Unit 65, locally called the Aguacate Formation, is the lowest-lying culture-bearing stratum. This clay-rich soil was derived from pre-Arenal volcanic tephra and rock. No evidence of unaltered Unit 61, the tephra from the earliest eruption of Arenal Volcano, has been found at the Silencio site, but Unit 60 soil, which is believed to have formed from Unit 61, is present and in some places is up to 20 cm thick. Unit 60 is a relatively well developed, organic-rich A horizon. Unit 55A is an orange sandy tephra, and Unit 55 is a clay-rich, orange-to-brown soil formed on top of it. Unit 53A is a fine, orange-to-brown tephra unit, and Unit 53 is a light brown A horizon formed on top of it. Unit 52 is a gray tephra, upon which the Unit 50 soil has formed. Unit 50 is a thick (up to 50 cm), relatively well developed, organic-rich A horizon.

Units 40 and 41 are two closely sequent tephra units that fell between AD 800 and 1000. Unit 41 is a fine-grained, light gray tephra unit, and Unit 40 is coarser and darker gray. Unit 30 is an orange-brown soil unit formed on Unit 40. Unit 20 is a coarse pumiceous tephra unit with a thick, well-developed A horizon overlying it, and Unit 10 is a thin, discontinuous light gray tephra layer from the 1968 eruption of Arenal Volcano not present at the spot of the Fig. 6-2 profile.

Excavations revealed two periods of burial activity and construction on the site. The first occurred before the fall of the Unit 40 and 41 tephras, around AD 800–1000. This activity evidently dated to the Late Arenal Phase and the first portion of the Silencio Phase. The second period postdated the eruptions and occurred during the latter half of the Silencio Phase. All of the burials in the upper area dated to the earlier burial period, and four of the six from the lower area may have dated to the earlier period. The majority of the construction activity at the site also dated to this period. Only two burials from the lower area clearly postdated the fall of Units 40 and 41.

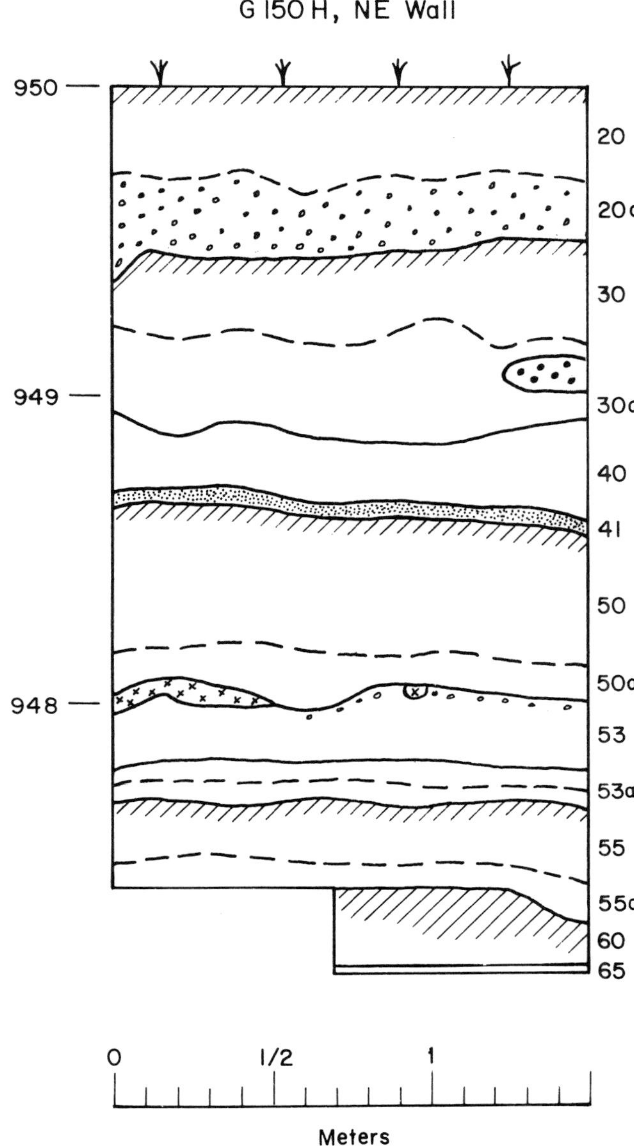

Figure 6-2.
Silencio stratigraphic sequence profile, Operation H. Unit 52 was preserved in two lenses between Units 53 and 50a, at the center and the left of the profile. Drawing by John Bradley.

RESULTS

The 1984 excavations located twelve undisturbed graves. Table 6-1 presents the burial types uncovered at the Silencio site. The excavations showed that many additional activities not immediately associated with the burials occurred on the site, and that apparently many living people spent considerable periods of time within the cemetery.

Much of the activity on the site occurred during the time period before the fall of tephra Units 40 and 41. There was some evidence of Late Arenal Phase use of the area, including sherds along footpaths at site G-151, and one Arenal Phase vessel found in Operation I, but all burials excavated dated to the Silencio Phase. Evidence of extensive construction activity dating to the Early Silencio Phase has been found in both the upper and the lower site areas.

UPPER-AREA BURIALS

We encountered six burials, three in Operation B and three in Operation D, in the uppermost flat area in the southeastern portion of the site. All were interred prior to the fall of Units 40 and 41 during the time of Unit 50 soil formation. Fill was a mixture of soil Units 60 and 65. Burials 1 through 3 were found in Operation B, a 14 m^2 unit. Burials 4, 5, and 15 were found in Operation D, a 9.75 m^2 excavation unit.

Burials 1 through 3 were in pits that were excavated during the development of soil Unit 50 and extended through Unit 60 into Unit 65.

Burial 1 (G-150-B5) was in a stone cist grave constructed of two vertical pieces of laja bridged by two horizontal laja slabs covering the head, shoulders, and chest of an adult. A vertical laja slab was placed at the head as a gravestone. The burial was oriented with the head to the north-

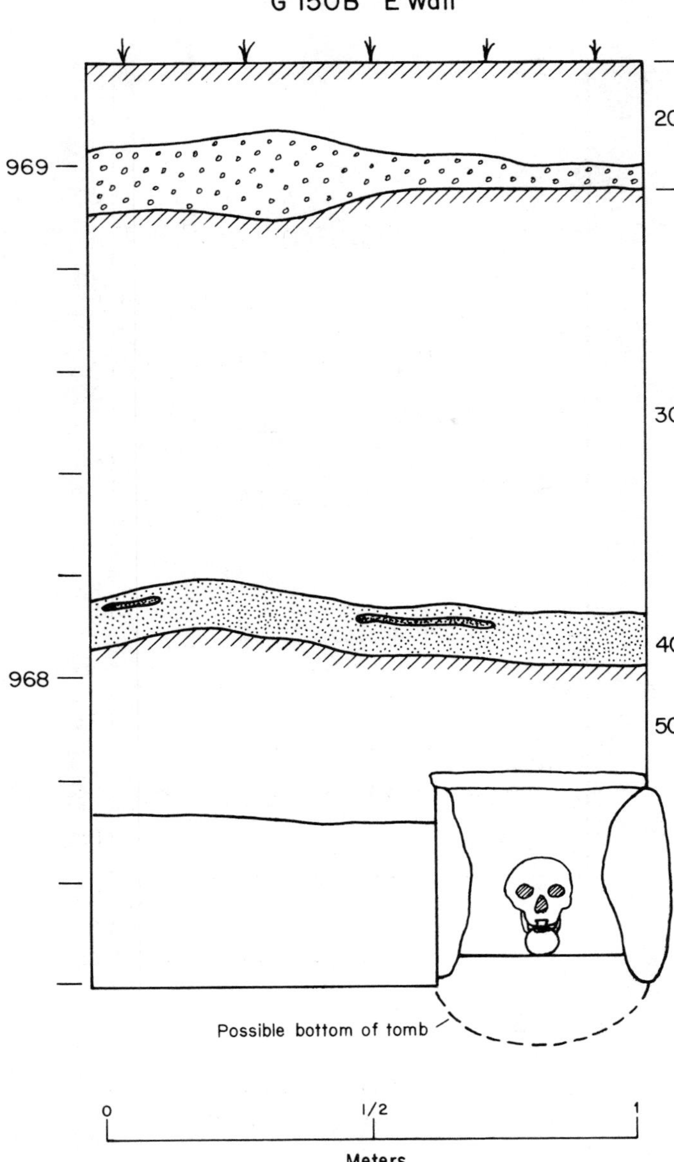

Figure 6-3.
Profile of Burial 3, Operation B. Drawing by John Bradley.

TABLE 6-1
BURIAL TYPES

Type	*Burial Numbers*	*Description*
I	12, 13, 14	Simple intrusion with no stone included in, on, or around the burial
II	8	Single vertical volcanic rock (laja) at the head of the skeleton in a tombstone position extending above the level of the skeleton
III	2, 9	One or more flat-lying laja slabs situated above the burial
IV	1, 3, 6, 7, 10, 11	Two vertical laja slabs on the side of the cranial portion of the skeleton, bridged by one or two flat-lying laja slabs
V	4, 5, 15	One or two vertical laja slabs on each side of the skeleton in two or more rows extending from the head to the pelvis or farther and bridged with one or more layers of laja extending over the entire length of the walled area

west. A gold avian pendant was found near the head (Chap. 13). Skeletal preservation was poor. Identifiable remains included portions of the cranium, the mandible, teeth, cervical vertebrae, clavicles, and femurs. The bones were damp and spongy when uncovered and turned to powder when they dried.

Burial 2 (G-150-B4) was located to the northeast of Burial 1. The upper portion of the body was covered by three horizontal laja slabs. The head was oriented to the north, and three miniature Cabuyal Polychrome vessels were found at the foot of the burial. No skeletal material was preserved, but a cranial-shaped discolored area was present at the head of the grave. A charcoal sample for radiocarbon dating (Tx-5078) was collected from this burial and was sealed above and below by Units 41 and 55. It was earlier than expected at AD 145 (244) 338. It is likely that the material backfilling the grave contained charcoal from an earlier occupation of the site.

Burial 3 (G-150-B12, Fig. 6-3) was located east of Burial 1. It was in a partial stone cist grave with the head and chest areas covered by a single horizontal laja slab capping two vertical laja slabs. The head was oriented to the east. A ceramic vessel and a broken tripod metate accompanied the burial.

Burials 4, 5, and 15 were found in Operation D. The burials were excavated into Unit 50, and covered by intact deposits of Units 40 and 41.

Burial 4 (G-150-D3, Fig. 6-4) was in a stone cist grave. It was constructed with a large number of laja slabs set up vertically to form a double wall around the body. The body was covered with a double layer of horizontal laja slabs. The length of the burial was over 1.9 m, and laja slabs encircled and covered the entire body. A carved metate (D3/1) formed part of the burial wall near the left side of the head (Chap. 12). The head was oriented to the northwest. Bone was poorly preserved, but identifiable portions included parts of the cranium, the mandible, cervical and thoracic vertebrae, ribs, one scapula, one humerus, one tibia, and the femurs.

Burial 5 (G-150-D6) is located east of Burial 4 in Operation D. It was in a stone cist grave with a single wall of vertical laja 1.41 m in length and was capped with a double layer of laja. The head was oriented to the west. No burial furniture was present, although a carbonized maize cupule was found. Bone preservation was poor; only fragments of the cranium, mandible, ribs, one humerus, the pelvis, the femurs, and tibia remained.

Burial 15 was in another stone cist grave, with a single vertical laja wall covered by a double layer of bridging laja. The head was at the eastern side of the grave. Two small Cabuyal Polychrome vessels were found near the right shoulder. Bone preservation was poor, with only a portion of the cranium and humerii recognizable.

Figure 6-4.
Burial 4, Operation D. Photograph by John Bradley.

OTHER UPPER-AREA FEATURES

A large stone feature was visible in a looters' pit at the western edge of the upper area (Fig. 6-5). Operation G, a 7 m × 7 m excavation unit, showed that the feature was a dry-laid laja wall over 1 m in height and up to 3 m wide. The base of the wall had been placed in a trench excavated into Unit 50, and was constructed prior to the fall of tephra Units 40 and 41. The lower portion of the wall appears to have functioned as a retaining wall to level off the western edge of the upper site area. The wall extended above the ground surface at the time of its construction and continued both north and south of Operation G along the western edge of the upper area. Heavy looting activities and large trees prevented the extension of excavations in these directions.

Figure 6-5.
Stone retaining wall, Operation G. Photograph by John Bradley.

Figure 6-6.
Laja steps connecting upper and lower site area, Operation I. Drawing by John Bradley.

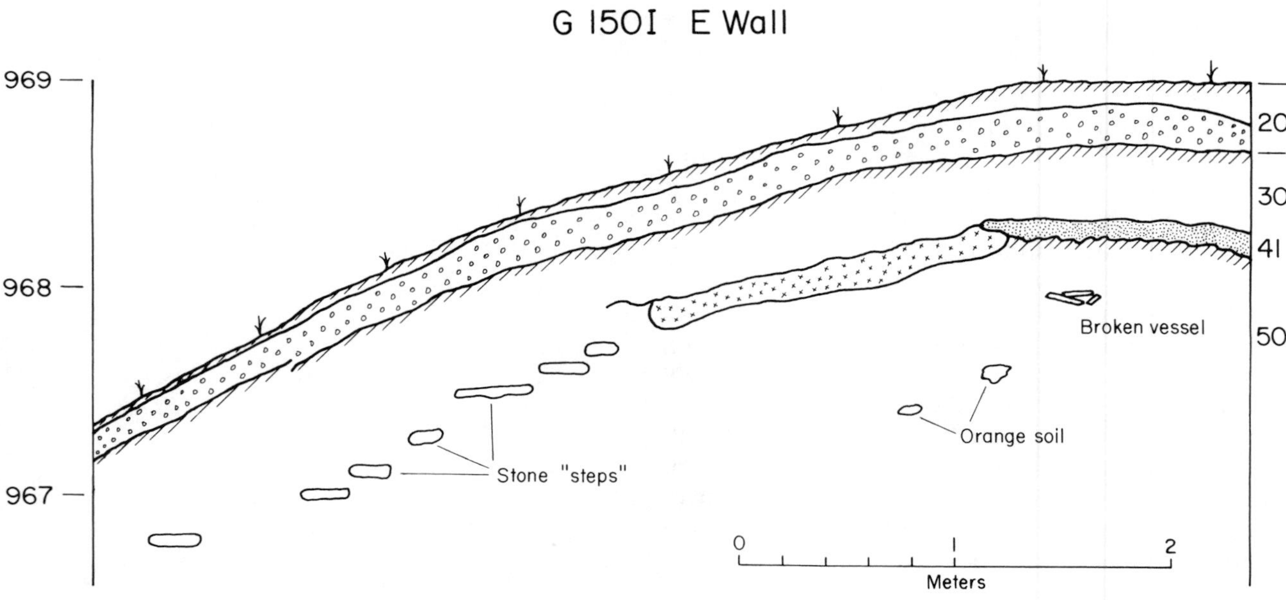

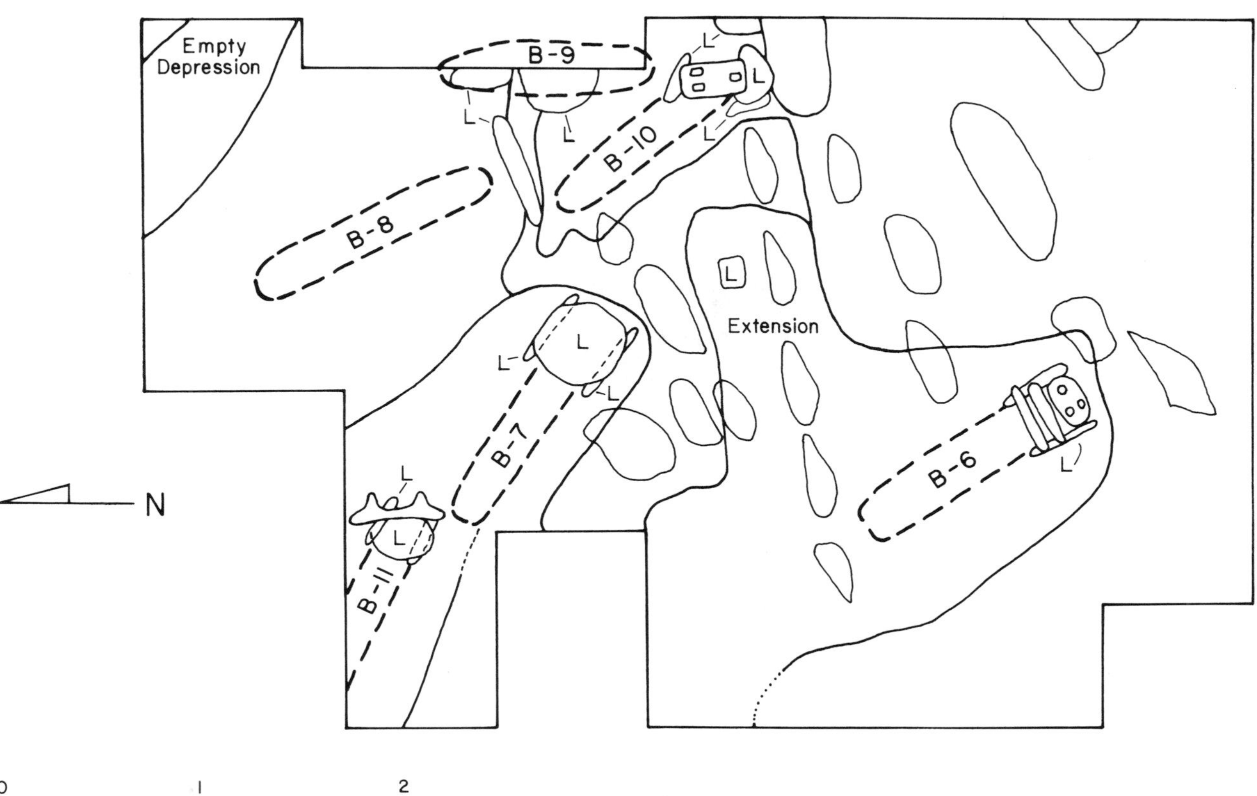

Figure 6-7.
Plan of burials in Operation C. Drawing by John Bradley.

Excavations in Operation J, the southernmost excavation unit, also indicated extensive landscaping activities. Stratigraphic Units 50 through 55 were removed from this area and placed inside of the laja retaining wall by the prehistoric inhabitants of the site to level the western edge of the upper area.

Operation I was a 3 m × 6 m excavation unit whose purpose was to determine the nature of the slope between the upper and the lower areas. Eight small, unshaped laja steps were found lying on top of the Unit 50 soil in this 3 m × 6 m excavation unit (Fig. 6-6). The steps were aligned in a direction slightly west of north. Intact deposits of tephra Units 40 and 41 were not present above the steps, but intact Unit 41 tephra in adjacent areas at approximately the same depth suggests that they were constructed prior to this eruption. Six broken ceramic vessels were found within soil Unit 50 in this area.

LOWER-AREA BURIALS

We found four burials dating to the Late Silencio Phase in the lower area. All four were closely spaced in Operation C. All were apparently excavated from the upper portion of Unit 50 through Units 55 and 60 and into Unit 65. Units 40 and 41, however, were not clear in this area, and it is possible that the burials postdate the fall of these tephra units. Burial 6 (G-150-C4) was a partial stone cist grave, with two vertical laja slabs at the sides of the head of the burial bridged by two horizontal laja. A small tripod metate (C4/1) was placed facing upward at the head of the grave, and may have served as an additional "capstone." We found forty-three sherds in the burial. The head was oriented to the southeast. A small area was excavated to the northeast of the main grave by the aboriginal site inhabitants, and a single unshaped laja slab was present in this extension.

Figure 6-8.
Excavated intrusions, Operation C. Photograph by John Bradley.

Burial 7 (Figs. 6-7 and 6-8) was constructed of two vertical laja slabs on the sides of the head capped by a single horizontal laja slab. Two greenstone beads, fifteen sherds, and two flakes were found in the burial pit, primarily in the cranial area. Bone preservation was extremely poor, with only a soft pocket of sediment about the size and shape of a cranium under the capstone. The head was oriented to the southwest.

Burial 10 (Figs. 6-7, 6-9, and 6-10) was constructed of two vertical laja slabs capped by two horizontal pieces of laja in a fashion similar to Burial 6. An inverted metate also covered the cranial area. The burial was oriented with the head to the southeast. A single greenstone bead, thirty-two sherds, and two flakes were present. Bone preservation was poor, with only portions of the mandible, maxilla, and two molars present under the collapsed laja.

Burial 11 was also constructed of two vertical laja slabs capped by two horizontal pieces of laja. The head was oriented to the southeast. We found a large tripod metate lying on edge above the laja and twelve sherds and five flakes within the burial. Bone preservation was poor, and no individual bones could be identified.

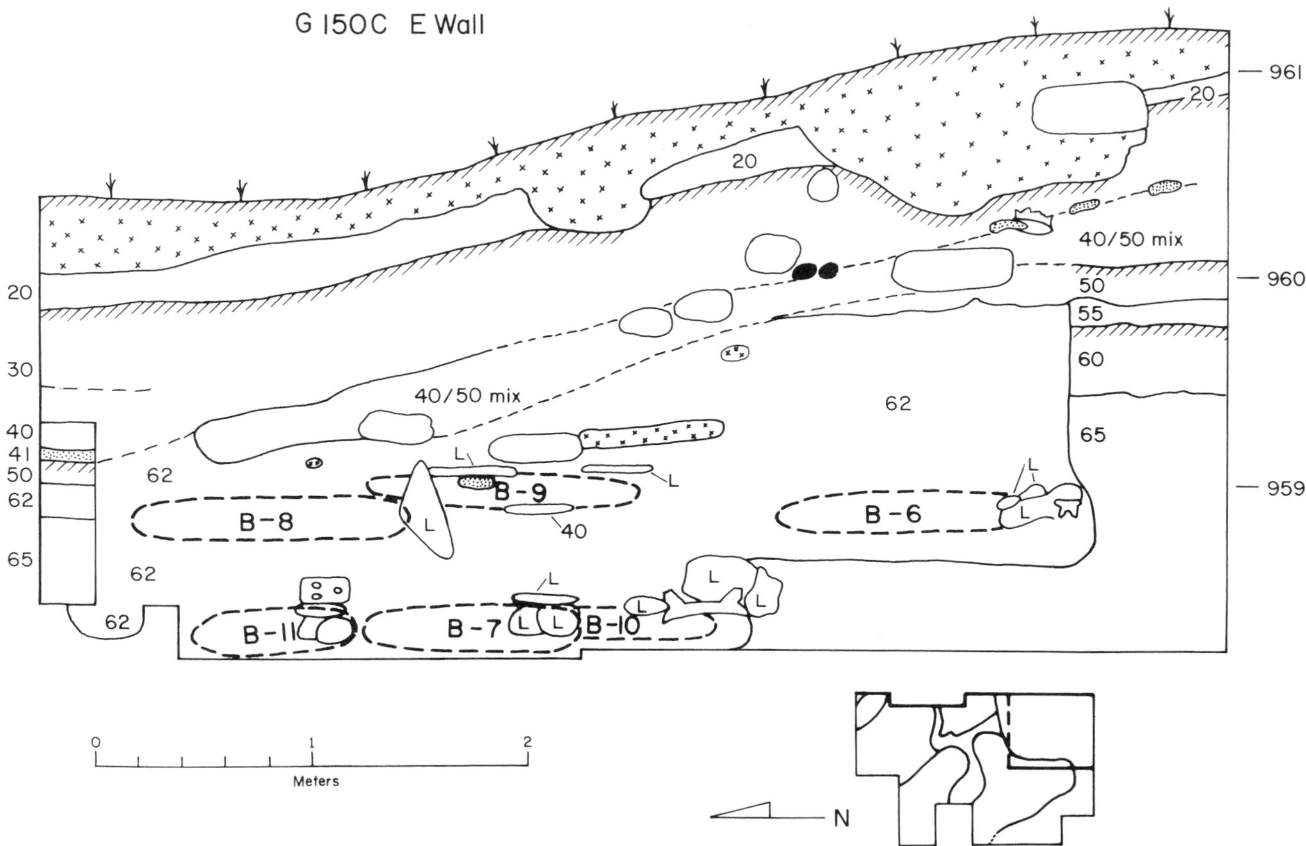

Figure 6-9.
East profile of Operation C, with burials and prehistoric ground surface artifacts superimposed on cobble-terraced surface. Drawing by John Bradley.

OTHER LOWER-AREA FEATURES

A large stone feature was present near Burials 6, 7, 10, and 11 in Operation C. This feature consisted of four parallel rows of slightly rounded river cobbles and laja aligned perpendicular to the slope. The stones rested on top of the Unit 40 tephra, approximately 1 m above the base of the burials. The lines of stones were located between the burials and may have served to mark grave locations in a fashion similar to the larger and more formal concentrations of stone found at the Arenal Phase Bolívar cemetery (Chap. 5). We found ceramic sherds and lithic debitage and cores between the rocks of this feature.

We found two other burials dating to the late Silencio Phase in the lower area, in Operation C. Both were located stratigraphically above tephra Units 40 and 41, in the lower area, in Operation C. Burials 8 and 9 were located adjacent to and northeast of Burials 6, 7, 10, and 11. They were different in form and content from the pre–Unit 40 burials. Both appeared expedient. Both were relatively shallow (ca. 50 cm below the prehistoric ground surface), and were placed on prepared beds of Unit 40 tephra and buried with the

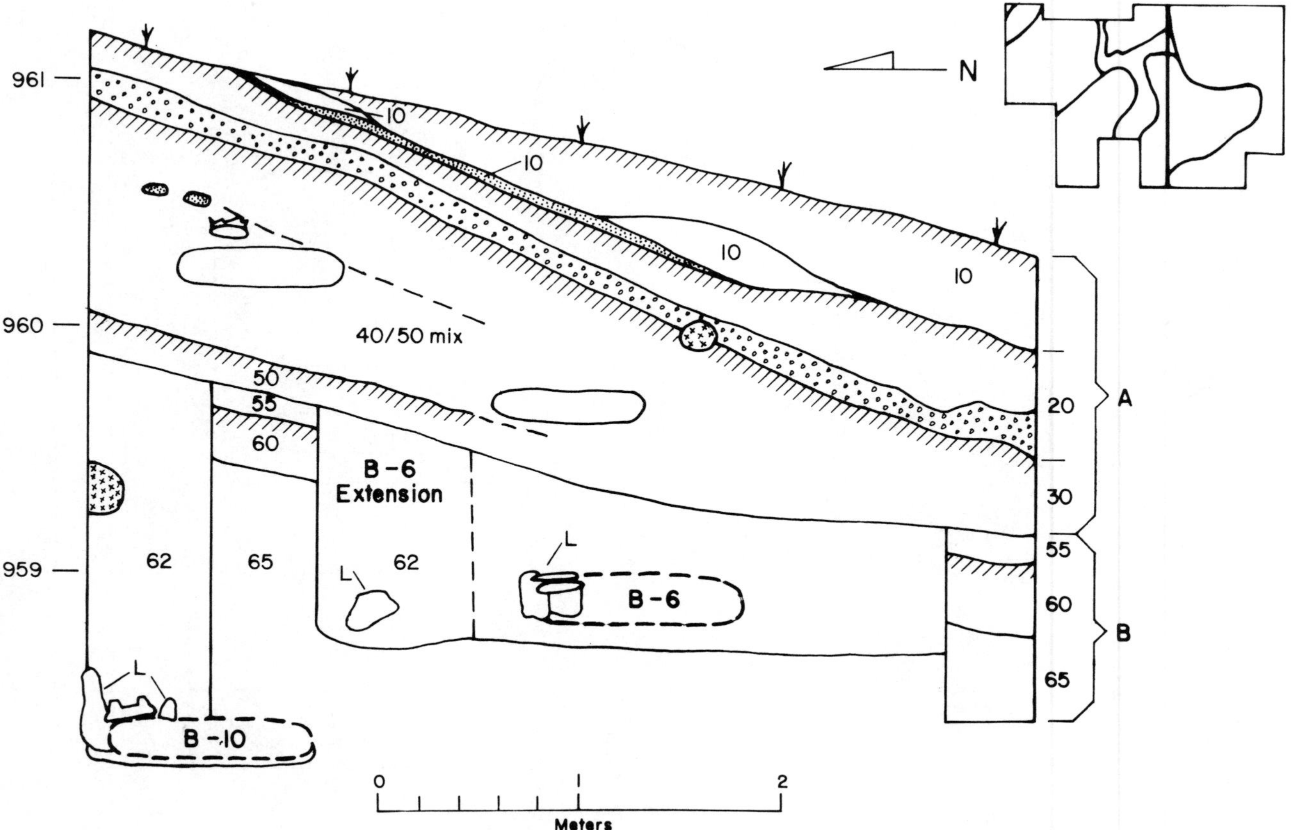

Figure 6-10.
South profile of Operation C, with nearby burials superimposed. Drawing by John Bradley.

same tephra. Burial 8 had a single upright laja slab at the head of the grave, in the position of a gravestone, but no other construction or artifacts were present. The head was to the southeast. Bone preservation was poor; four unidentifiable bone fragments from the upper body were present.

Burial 9 was similar to Burial 8 in most respects, but we found tephra from Unit 40 within the thoracic and pelvic cavities. The tephra may have been intentionally placed within these cavities before burial. We found a lump of clean Unit 41 tephra above the pelvic area, and it may have been intentionally placed in this position. Two flat-lying laja slabs were placed over the cranium and the pelvic area. We encountered no other grave goods. Seven bones were recognizable, including portions of the cranium and phalanges of the feet.

Based on the ceramic assemblage, substantial human activity occurred on the site following the fall of Units 40 and 41 (Hoopes, personal communication, 1991). Many sherds came from Unit 30 between these burials and from most areas of the site.

ADDITIONAL FEATURES AND ARTIFACTS

Both areas of the site had evidence of additional activities not directly associated with the burial. This evidence includes large quantities of chipped- and ground stone artifacts, cooking stones, and ceramics. This indicates that cooking, tool manufacture, and woodworking activities took place at the cemetery during both periods of use.

The range of chipped stone implements indicates many lithic manufacturing activities, including core/flake production, chipped stone celt manufacture, and biface manufacture/refurbishment (Chap. 11). Hammerstones, cores, flakes, celt flakes, and a biface fragment suggest these activities. None of the materials used in the manufacture of these tools occur naturally at the site. We inferred cooking from large quantities of complete and thermally fractured cooking stones (Chap. 11).

The overwhelming majority of ceramics found at the site are from the Silencio Phase (Chap. 10), although there was some evidence of occupation during the late Arenal Phase. We found utilitarian and decorated wares in roughly equal frequencies, indicating that many day-to-day activities were probably occurring at the site. We also found several metates at the site, but only one mano. The majority are undecorated, indicating that their function, prior to interment in the graves, was probably utilitarian (Chap. 12).

STABLE CARBON ISOTOPE ANALYSIS OF BONE

Friedman and Gleason of the USGS, Denver (1984) conducted analysis of the ratios of carbon 12 to carbon 13 in bone from the Silencio site to determine the percentage of maize in the diet. Stable carbon isotope analysis is a new technique in archaeology, but it shows promise for improving our understanding of the diets of human populations.

Plants that use a three-carbon photosynthetic pathway discriminate against the heavier C-13 when compared with plants that use a four-carbon pathway. Maize is the only known dietary staple in Precolumbian Costa Rica with a 4-carbon pathway (Norr, personal communication to Sheets, 1980). Therefore, the percentage of maize in the diet is represented in the C-13/C-12 ratio in bone collagen. We collected samples from Burials 1, 2, 3, 5, 8, 9, 10, and 15. Results show that less than 12% of the diet of the individuals buried here consisted of maize. This is a far lower percentage than consumed by past or present populations in Mesoamerica (Sheets, personal communication, 1991).

DISCUSSION

Comparison of the Silencio site with cemeteries from other parts of Costa Rica shows many similarities. In the Early and Middle Polychrome periods, cemeteries in the Greater Nicoya, the Central Highlands/Atlantic Watershed, and the Diquis subareas are found separated from habitation sites, in some cases by several hundred meters (Snarskis 1981a; Lange 1982–1983; Drolet 1984a). In all of these subareas, cemeteries have been found located on hilltops and river terraces. Some similarities in the construction of the graves appear to exist between the various subareas, particularly in the use of stone in construction.

The greatest similarities seem to be with the Atlantic Watershed/Central Highlands subarea. These similarities include large cemeteries located on hilltops, stone cist graves, and the use of stone in landscaping. In the Atlantic subarea, landscaping consists of large cobble-covered mounds (Snarskis 1984a), in contrast to the terracing operations observed at G-150. The grave construction of Burials 4, 5, and 15 (Type V, Table 6-1) at G-150 is similar to that observed for stone cist graves in the Central Highlands and the Atlantic Watershed (Snarskis 1984a), as well as in Diquis (Drolet 1984a). In the Atlantic Watershed, this burial type appears around AD 500—800 (Snarskis 1984a:221). Snarskis (ibid.) and Drolet (1984a) report alluvial cobbles surrounding or aligned with burials in these subareas.

Survey and excavations in the Guanacaste–San Carlos corridor, northwest of Silencio, found cemeteries separated from habitation sites following an Atlantic Watershed pattern of multiple burials within large cobble mounds (Lange 1982–1983, 1984b). Multiple burials in cobble mounds were also reported in the Naranjo River Valley (Norr 1982–1983), and at Guayabo de Bagaces (Ryder 1982–1983b).

Many researchers (see Hertz 1960; Saxe 1970) have noted the correlation between the status of the individual in life and the elaborateness of the facilities prepared for that individual after death. In addition, Hertz (1960) notes that persons suffering unusual deaths are often treated differently from those who die of natural causes. Binford (1971), following an ethnographic study of mortuary practices, proposes that two general components of social organization are symbolized in mortuary practices: the social persona of the individual, that is, "a composite of the social identities maintained in life and recognized as appropriate for consideration after death"; and "the composition and size of the social group recognizing status responsibilities to the deceased." The relevant characteristics include age, sex, relative rank within the social unit, societal affiliation, and the nature and location of death. Binford further proposes that the social persona and the social group of an individual determine discrimination in mortuary practices, which can be observed in the treatment of the body, the preparation of the burial facility, and the contribution of burial furniture. Tainter (1973, 1977, 1978) suggests that the degree of social disruption and the size of the group disrupted will positively correlate with the amount of energy or labor invested in mortuary activities for an individual. This correlation has also been noted by Dillon (1984) among the San Blas Cuna of Panama.

There are some clear differences in treatment of the individuals buried at the Silencio cemetery. These differences can be seen in the location and orientation of the graves, the nature of artifacts associated with the burials, the construction of the grave, and finally, in the labor investment involved in the transport of materials into the cemetery and the construction of the grave.

We defined five burial types based on differences in design and complexity of the burials (Table 6-1). Although Type I, consisting of a simple excavated pit with no stone construction, is not present at G-150, we have found it at other sites in the project area, and its absence here may be significant. In Table 6-2, the Silencio burials are presented in descending order of the total number of laja slabs present by phase and by area. The total number of laja slabs and artifacts found in each burial is reported as a relative measure of the labor contributed to each burial.

Comparison of the Silencio Phase burials by area shows that the average number of laja slabs is greater in the upper area. The total number of artifacts found in each burial is similar for the two areas, but we found decorated and nonutilitarian items only in the upper area. These include the gold pendant, miniature polychrome vessels, and decorated metates. We found no ceramic vessels in the lower area. Other differences in labor expended in the two areas include the construction of the laja retaining wall and the extensive earth moving in the upper area. The orientation of burials is also different in the two areas. Upper-area burials are oriented to the east, west, and northwest, while all burials in the lower area are oriented to the southeast.

In summary, burials from the upper area are more complex in construction, landscaping activities, and artifacts interred with the deceased and are more varied in orientation than those in the lower area. The lower area is more standardized in burial type, associated artifacts, and orientation. The individuals interred in this area appear to have been of a uniform status lower than that of individuals buried in the upper portion of the site. The lack of simple intrusive burials indicates that there might be a group of still-lower-status individuals buried elsewhere.

Two individuals were buried in the lower area shortly after the fall of tephra Units 40 and 41 (ca. AD 800–1000). Both were placed on prepared beds of Unit 40 tephra, and tephra from the same unit filled the body cavity of one of them. These burials do not fit the patterns observed for other burials at the site, but the sample size is insufficient to make inferences regarding the cause of these differences. The possibility of death by unusual circumstances cannot be ruled out.

We have postulated several possible functions for the Silencio cemetery. Much literature is available on the use of the dead to control critical resources. Saxe (1970) proposes that corporate groups used cemeteries to validate their control over critical resources. Chapman (1981) extends this hypothesis to the control of territory during times of critical resource shortage. Chapman states that formal disposal areas for the dead can provide a permanent claim for the use and control of those resources. Such an interpretation is more appropriate to cases in which critical resources are in short supply. It appears (Chap. 3) that land was never a critical resource in the Arenal area, as population density remained relatively low, even at its peak during the Arenal Phase. The resource base was rich and diverse at all times, and the inhabitants never intensified agriculture in the region. Flat, well-drained land that was suitable for agriculture might have been viewed as a critical resource, however. The topography is steep, and only a relatively small proportion of the land is suitable for flatland farming of maize.

Another possible function of the Silencio ceme-

TABLE 6-2
G-150 BURIALS IN DESCENDING ORDER OF LAJA COUNT BY STRATA AND AREA

Time	*Area*	*Burial # (Op., Lot)*	*Burial Type (# of Laja)*	*Artifact Type (#, Op., Lot)*	*Depth (m)*	*Orientation*	*Strati-graphic Unit*	*Total # Artifacts*
Pre–U.41	**Upper**	4 (D3)	V (20)	Decorated metate (1-D3/1)	2.39	East	50	21.0
		5 (D6)	V (8)	Maize cupule (1-D6)	2.00	West	50	9.0
		15 (D7)	V (7)	Nonutilitarian vessels (2-D7/1, /2)	2.40	East	50	9.0
		1 (B5)	V (5)	Gold pendant (1-B5/1)	2.48	Northwest	50	6.0
		2 (B4)	III (3)	Nonutilitarian vessels (3-B4/1, /2, /3)	1.97	East	50	6.0
		3 (B12)	IV (3)	Nonutilitarian vessel (1-B13/1)	1.75	East	50	4.0
		Average	(7.7)	(1.2)	(2.17)			(9.2)
Pre–U41	**Lower**	6 (C4)	IV (5)	Undecorated metate (1-C4/1)	2.60	Southeast	50	6.0
		10 (C8)	IV (4)	Undecorated metate and greenstone bead (2-C8/1, /2)	2.60	Southeast	50	6.0
		11 (C9)	IV (4)	Undecorated metate (1-C9/1)	2.35	South	50	5.0
		7 (C5)	IV (3)	Greenstone bead (2-C5/2)	2.50	Southeast	50	5.0
		Average	(3.75)	(1.5)	(2.51)			(5.5)
Post–U.41	**Lower**	9 (C7)	III (2)	Prepared U.41 bed	1.60	South	30	2.0
		8 (C6)	II (1)	Prepared U.40 bed	1.60	Southeast	30	1.0
		Average	(1.5)		(1.60)			(1.5)

tery could be to integrate the numerous villages surrounding Lake Arenal. The network of footpaths leading out from the cemetery (Chap. 9) indicates that the cemetery was probably utilized by several villages. The cemetery is located near a low pass over the Continental Divide, which served as a route of transportion between lowland Guanacaste and the Atlantic Watershed. It is possible that the paths predated the cemetery, and that the cemetery was constructed only after centuries of travel back and forth between these two widely different areas. The data are not yet available to test this hypothesis, but the blending of traits from both sides of the Continental Divide indicates that relatively large numbers of people were traveling over the Divide from at least Early Formative times onward, and the area around the Silencio site is one of the best routes. It is clear that there was a great deal of interaction between villages within the region, and the network of footpaths with the Silencio cemetery as one of its major nodes points to the importance of this cemetery as a factor in the integration.

The presence of many domestic artifacts and features at the site demands some explanation. Two possible, and not mutually exclusive, explanations exist. The first is that the landscaping and elaborate interment ritual required large numbers of people to spend considerable periods of time at the site. The extensive earth moving and rock work would have required many hundreds of person-days at the cemetery, and it is likely that workers constructed temporary shelters and needed to process large quantities of food.

The alternative explanation involves postinterment ritual. Lengthy *chichadas,* or drinking feasts, have been reported in Costa Rica as a part of funerary rituals (Bozzoli de Willie 1975), and have been postulated at archaeological sites in the Atlantic Watershed (Snarskis 1981a). An example of lengthy funerary rites that would be visible in the archaeological record are the "villages of the dead" of the San Blas Cuna (Dillon 1984). The Cuna construct huts over elaborate burial chambers in which high-status dead are entombed. At first glance, their cemeteries resemble living villages, with numerous thatched-roof huts. Friends and relatives of the dead visit them in the cemeteries, sometimes on a daily basis, and carry out normal domestic activities, including food preparation, eating, and drinking. It is interesting that the most elaborate huts are those most frequently visited. The Cuna also have extensive networks of trails cut in the rain forest to link the cemeteries with habitation sites and with one another (Dillon 1984).

SUMMARY AND CONCLUSIONS

Although many factors, including deep burial by volcanic tephra, thick vegetation cover, and extensive looting, made the excavation of the Silencio cemetery a difficult task, the site provided valuable information regarding burial practices during the Silencio Phase in the Arenal region. The distinctive tephra stratigraphy allowed for the separation of two different phases of burial at the site and aided in the preservation of the graves and indicators of extensive landscaping activities. Prior to the fall of tephra Units 40 and 41, the site was a large cemetery with high-status individuals buried on high ground above their lower-status contemporaries. Two individuals were found who were buried after these eruptions, and apparently the patterns of burial developed during the Late Arenal and Early Silencio phases were disrupted by the eruptions. The later burials bore little resemblance to their earlier counterparts. Examination of the effort expended in construction of the graves, the associated burial goods, and the orientation of the bodies indicates status differences within the cemetery.

In many ways, the burials are similar to others in Costa Rica. Stone cist graves such as several of those found at Silencio have been reported in the Atlantic Watershed and Central Highlands of Costa Rica, as well as in Diquis and the Guanacaste–San Carlos Corridor. Landscaping is reported from all of these areas as well, but generally consists of the construction of large mounds of river cobbles and laja slabs, rather than terraces with retaining walls, as at Silencio.

Comparisons with living populations have provided many potentially useful analogs for features found at Silencio. The presence of many artifacts indicative of domestic activities may be the result either of substantial time spent during landscaping and construction activities at the site or of substantial postinterment ritual and repeated visits to the grave sites. The cemetery may be located where it is in order to symbolize control of flat, arable land, a relatively scarce commodity in the Arenal region. The location, on the other hand, may be due to the site's location along a relatively easy route across the Continental Divide. The network of footpaths leading to and from the cemetery indicates that a variety of people from several habitation sites utilized the cemetery, and it may have served to integrate peoples through the region. The strategic location of the paths makes it seem likely that the route over the Divide predated the cemetery, which was placed in this location at a later date.

Appendix 6-A

THE PERAZA SITE BURIALS (G-155)

The Peraza site, a Tilarán Phase habitation with a small cemetery, is located 0.9 km northeast and downslope from the Silencio cemetery, adjacent to the Tronadora River. We found three burials during test excavations in 1984. Surface indications of prehistoric activity were limited to a few small depressions approximately 5 m in diameter and 30 cm deep. Short grass surrounds and covers the small knoll where the burials were encountered.

The investigations at G-155 proceeded in three stages: (1) examination of road cuts and other recent surface disturbances for cultural material and to determine the local stratigraphic sequence; (2) posthole testing of flat to gently sloped areas in search of subsurface materials; and (3) 2 m × 2 m test excavations.

Operation C, a 2 m × 2 m excavation unit placed over a circular depression that had produced subsurface material during posthole testing, revealed burials 12, 13, and 14 (G-155-C1 through G-155-C3). The burials are known only from the shapes of the empty intrusions and associated vessels (C/1 through C/3). Assuming the vessels were placed near the heads of the tombs, orientation was with the head to the southeast. A hard-packed floor at the base of G-155-C1 may be a prepared surface on which the burial was placed.

The Tilarán Phase burials from G-155 are more informative than their simple intrusions and single vessels might suggest. The absence of burial laja, as well as isolated nature of these burials, seems significant and suggests that few individuals (possibly only the immediate family) shared duty-status obligations to the individuals interred. Without more information on the range of mortuary variability at this time and in this area, however, little interpretation is possible.

7

Proyecto Prehistórico Arenal Excavations in the Santa Rosa River Valley

JOHN W. HOOPES
MARK L. CHENAULT

INTRODUCTION

The Santa Rosa River originates near the Continental Divide just south of the Finca El Silencio and drains westward toward Cañas and the Pacific Watershed of Guanacaste. While El Silencio (G-150) was the principal focus of excavations in the 1984 field season (Chap. 6), we also investigated four other sites in the Santa Rosa River drainage (Fig. 1-4; Fig. 9-1): Dos Armadillos (G-154), Neblina (G-151), Las Piedras (G-152), and El Jefe Suerte (G-153).[1]

The principal goal of these investigations was to identify habitation areas associated with the use of the hilltop cemetery at El Silencio. While none of the tested sites was a clear candidate for this interpretation,[2] each provided important clues to the nature of the prehistoric occupation of the Pacific Watershed east of Tilarán. Dos Armadillos proved to be the only site excavated with a significant Tilarán Phase component. Neblina, Las Piedras, and El Jefe Suerte all date to the Silencio Phase—principal period of use of the hilltop cemetery—and provide important information about local stratigraphy, lithic resource exploitation, and the possible functions of prehistoric footpaths that have been identified in the region (Chap. 9).

DOS ARMADILLOS (G-154)

This site is situated on the Finca El Silencio on a level terrace immediately south of the Santa Rosa River drainage (UTM 271,600 m N × 435,500 m

E on the Tilarán 1:50,000 quadrangle) at an altitude of approximately 850 m (Fig. 7-1). The site is located within the tephra blanket of Arenal Volcano at the top of a steep slope that drains northward into the Santa Rosa River. A small spring, located approximately 150 m SW of our excavations, would have been the nearest source of water after the river itself.

TESTING AND EXCAVATION

Clearing of an eroded cut near the Santa Rosa River streambed and excavations with a manual posthole digger confirmed the presence of a tephra sequence that could be correlated with the regional sequence and identified sherds at a relatively shallow depth. We selected two level

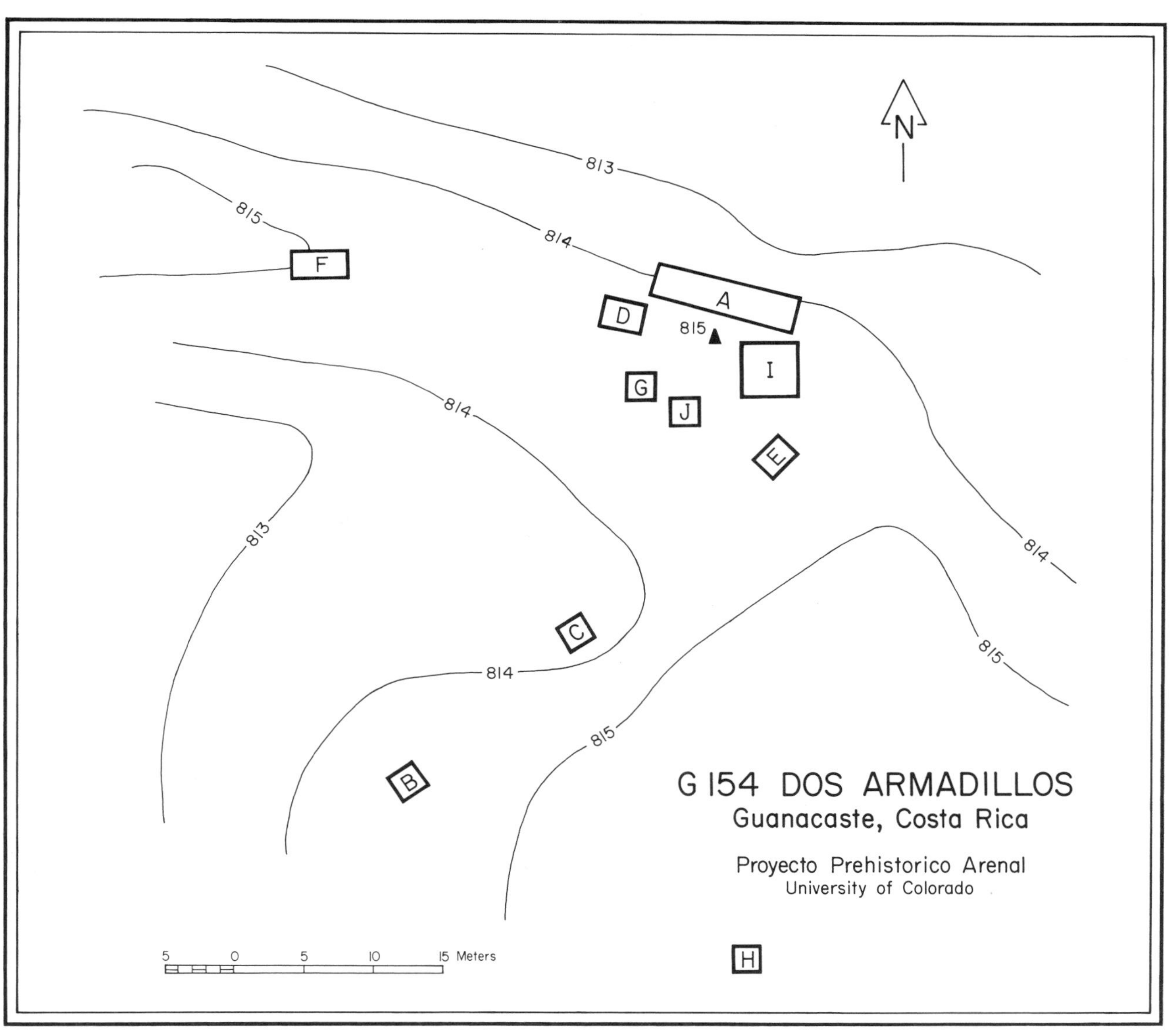

Figure 7-1.
Map of Dos Armadillos (G-154), showing the locations of Operations A through J. Map by Barbara Bolton.

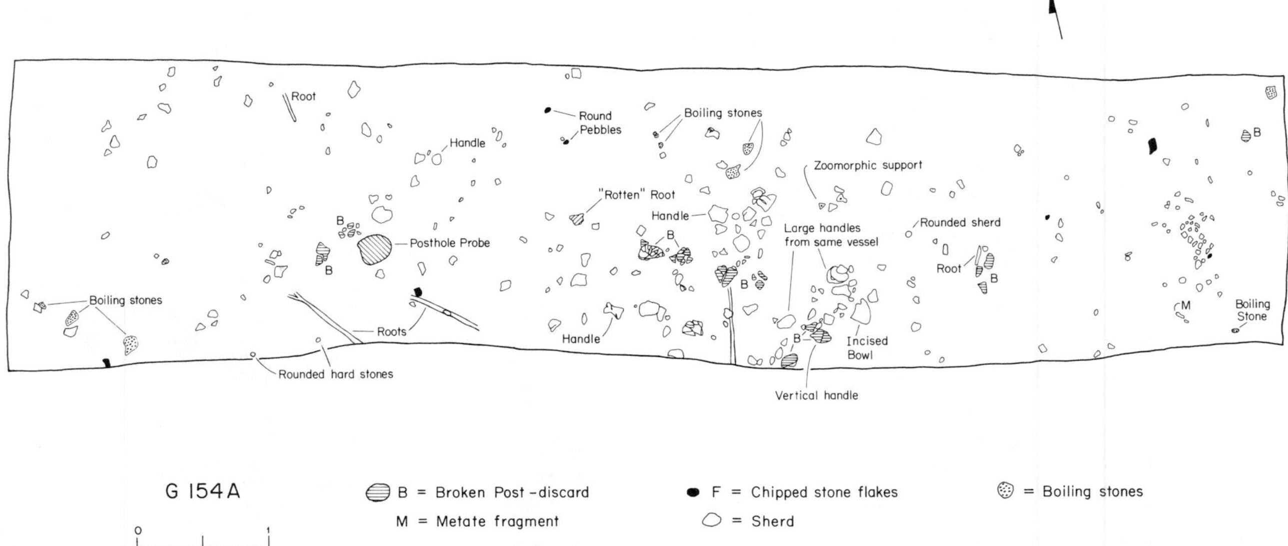

Figure 7-2.
Plan of Operation A at Dos Armadillos, illustrating the Tilarán Phase living surface. Figure by Barbara Bolton.

Figure 7-3.
The Tilarán Phase living surface at Dos Armadillos. Photograph by Payson Sheets.

benches for testing on the grounds that each was large enough to support a habitation at a convenient distance from a freshwater source.

We made fifteen soundings with the posthole digger. All were excavated to a depth of at least 150 cm below the modern surface, and three approached 2 m in depth. Of these, seven yielded cultural material, including small pieces of charcoal and monochrome sherds from Unit 30 at depths of 50 cm to 70 cm below the modern surface.

Excavations began with Operation A, on the northernmost side of the bench overlooking a steep slope down to the *quebrada*. We used Operations B, C, and H, each a 2 m × 2 m unit, to explore site stratigraphy and areas to the south. We used Operations D, E, F, G, and I to explore other portions of the habitation features identified in Operation A.

FEATURES

In Operation A, we identified an assemblage of ceramic and lithic artifacts in a horizontal deposit at the Unit 20/Unit 30 contact (Figs. 7-2 and 7-3). The relationship between the cultural materials and Unit 20 tephra—deposited as the result of a powerful volcanic explosion—immediately suggested the presence of a living surface sealed by an eruptive event. We exposed it by removing the modern surface (a grassy pasture at the time of excavation), the upper portion of the coarse, gray lapilli, and then the lower portion of Unit 20.

Natural processes had affected the distribution of artifacts in the deposit. Although a relatively uniform blanket of coarse tephra covered the feature, bioturbation was significant. The site was probably covered with dense, tropical vegetation for several hundred years between the site's abandonment and its relatively recent clearing for pasture. At the time of excavation, a number of roots of various sizes from a large strangler fig (*Ficus* sp.) and its host crisscrossed the feature. These trees, which were situated directly over the portion of the feature that appeared to have the greatest concentration of artifactual material, prevented the exposure of a larger contiguous area.

The relatively thin, horizontal distribution of the material, with all artifacts lying in a deposit with a maximum thickness of 15 cm, argues for its interpretation as a living surface and not as a midden deposit. Apart from one possible posthole, however, we could not discern any architectural features.

The living surface was approximately 35 cm below the modern surface. Excavation exposed 225 m^2 of the feature. The greatest concentration of material, a horizontal scatter of flakes, sherds, fragments of thermally fractured rock, and a metate fragment, was in Operation A. Several large sherds on the buried living floor had been broken in situ, probably from trampling. Screening with a 1/8-inch mesh yielded a large quantity of very small flakes of fine-grained basalt, chalcedony, and jasper and recovered a number of carbonized seeds, seed fragments, and other remains of fruits and cultigens.

CERAMICS

We collected 869 sherds from Operations A, D, E, F, and I, of which 786 (90%) were monochrome body sherds with no distinguishing characteristics of decoration or vessel shape. Of the remaining sherds, 81% (67) of those diagnostic as to type were either San Luis Coarse or Silencio Appliqué. Only 7 sherds from the assemblage were decorated with incisions, including 2 from a black-slipped, highly burnished, direct-rim hemispherical bowl of Tempisque Incised (cf. Creamer 1983:286–291, fig. 68). This vessel had been decorated with an incised frieze of triangles and dots immediately below the rim on the exterior. Creamer (ibid.:211) identifies the distribution of Tempisque Incised as characteristic of reciprocal exchange systems, and its presence at Dos Armadillos—where it may represent a trade vessel from the Gulf of Nicoya—suggests continuing relationships between the Arenal region and western Guanacaste in the Tilarán Phase.

A single sherd of Jiménez Polychrome was the only clear Silencio Phase sherd from the assemblage in Operation A. Ten Papagayo Polychrome sherds from Operation B suggest the presence of a Silencio Phase component in lower strata and suggest that the Jiménez sherd may have been intrusive from an earlier occupation. We also found four red-rimmed sherds of Tres Esquinas Beige, the most common monochrome type of the Silencio Phase, at the site. We discovered no sherds from the earlier Arenal or Tronadora phases at Dos Armadillos.

Vessels of a decidedly utilitarian nature dominated the ceramic assemblage. We collected sixteen large handles, handle fragments, or sherds with traces of handles from the feature in Operation A, including two pairs from the same vessels. Six more came from the same occupational level in Operations E, H, and I. Together, these represent the remains of at least eleven large storage vessels. Most of the handles were large and massive and shared modes of paste texture and surface finish with heavy-rim sherds and thick-walled body sherds from the assemblage. The most common forms were "butterfly" and "duck-tail" shapes of the type Silencio Appliqué (Chap. 10).

While the majority of sherds appear to have come from large storage or cooking vessels, a few smaller serving vessels were also present. These include beige-paste, unslipped tripods with zoomorphic supports, and black-slipped and polished carinated bowls. Ceramic artifacts from the occupational feature in Operation A also include a small sherd disk. The overall appearance of the ceramics from the occupational feature at Dos Armadillos is that of a late period (Tilarán Phase) domestic assemblage.

LITHICS

We recovered a total of 232 lithic artifacts (Chaps. 11 and 12), mainly from Operations A and I. Although the operations were very close to one another, significant differences in the assemblages may indicate separate activities on the same surface. The predominant lithic category for Operation A is "thermally fractured debitage." Out of 20 examples, there are 3 complete cooking stones. We recovered only one fragment of ground stone from the living surface in Operation A. This is a metate fragment and supports the identification of this feature as habitational. Operation A yielded a number of rounded stream rocks, presumably carried up from the Santa Rosa River. These were probably used in household activities (as pot rests, drying surfaces, or for pounding food or other materials), but bore no signs of use. Fifteen fragments of stone collected were classified as "other" (i.e., unclassified).

The assemblage from Operation I suggests the presence of a workshop for the maintenance of flaked stone tools. We recovered 193 fragments of flaked debitage—many of them quite small (less than 1 cm long and 1.5 mm thick) as a result of fine screening. Fine-grained basalt predominates, but the presence of chalcedony and jasper indicates procurement of high-quality material at some distance from the site. Sheets (1984b:162; Chap. 11) interprets the assemblage, which consists of 13 small bifacial trimming flakes, 2 flake cores, and 178 fragments of lithic debitage, as a workshop oriented toward the manufacture and resharpening of bifacial artifacts. The low percentage of hinge fractures (3%) indicates a relatively high degree of flaking proficiency. The multiple linear abrasions on platforms of chalcedony and dacite flakes may result from usage rather than manufacture. This abrasion probably resulted from use of a biface as a knife, and these flakes are wastage from resharpening, removed after use wear occurred.

It is unfortunate that time restrictions and the presence of a large tree prevented a greater exposure of the feature, but the evidence from the two nearly contiguous operations is highly suggestive of special activity areas within the horizontal deposit. In Operation A, thermally fractured rocks and a metate fragment suggest the preparation of food. In Operation I, the lithic debris indicates the maintenance of bifacial implements of imported, fine-grained stone.

BOTANICAL REMAINS

We collected a small but significant amount of carbonized, macrobotanical material in association with the living surface at Dos Armadillos. While we did not use flotation, the fine-mesh screening of deposits associated with the horizontal feature greatly enhanced our ability to recover small pieces. From Operation A came fragments of jícaro rind, fragments of *Zea mays* kernels, and indeterminate fruit remains. We recovered fragments of avocado seeds, palm fruits, and *Zea mays* kernels in Operation D. Operations I and J yielded more fragments of *Zea mays*, jícaro (*Crescentia* spp.), avocado, and other fruits associated with the same habitational level. We recovered fragments of charred wood from all operations, with the greatest quantity coming from Operation A.

The floral assemblage suggests a dependence on both tree crops and cultivated maize, a combination that is common to many indigenous groups of lower Central America (Smith 1980; Snarskis 1981a). The relationship of food type to artifactual remains is unclear, although metates were almost certainly used for the processing of maize. Unfortunately, we did not recover a single bone or other faunal remnant and can say little about other sources of protein utilized at the site.

The presence of jícaro shell is notable in light of the contemporary use of this gourd-like fruit for storage vessels—often elaborately decorated with carved designs—by the Guatuso Indians of northern Guanacaste and Alajuela provinces.

OTHER ARTIFACTS AND FEATURES

Once we had drawn and photographed the habitational feature, we collected all artifactual materials from the living surface and troweled all of Operation A to a depth of 20 cm below the feature. While Unit 30 extended to a depth of approximately 70 cm below the modern surface (ca. 40 cm below Unit 20), very few artifacts appeared below the sherd scatter. The only exception was a small polished stone celt located at the bottom of the stratum near the top of Unit 41, possibly a cached offering beneath the living surface. No other artifacts or features were associated with this item, and its relation to the habitational feature remains unclear.

DATING

A single C-14 date, cal AD 1316 (1398) 1407 (Tx-5079) was obtained from a large, aggregate sample of charcoal from the feature in Operation A. It was stratigraphically situated in the uppermost portion of Unit 30, less than 20 cm below the coarse Unit 20 tephra layer. Two dates obtained by Melson in 1968 from samples of trees charred by pyroclastic flows associated with Unit 20 provide an upper range for the possible occupation of Dos Armadillos: cal AD 1430 (1440) 1449 (SI-576) and cal AD 1445 (1460) 1482 (SI-577). These dates indicate that Unit 20 was probably deposited around cal AD 1450. The features and artifacts in Operation A do not appear to have been catastrophically buried, and the site was probably abandoned before the eruption. The habitational features probably date to between cal AD 1300 and 1450.

NEBLINA (G-151)

The Neblina site is situated on the Finca El Silencio, some 5 km east of Tilarán and 5 km south of Lake Arenal (UTM 272,700 m N x 435,700 m E on the Tilarán 1:50,000 quadrangle). It is located near the top of a ridge that faces the ridge top Silencio Phase cemetery (G-150), approximately 750 m to the southeast and on the opposite side of a north-south *quebrada* that drains into the Santa Rosa River. It was initially identified around 1970 by the landowner during the construction of a fence. Sheets recorded it in 1982, as did Hoopes in 1984. Hoopes noted the presence of large boulders outcropping from the hillside. Some of these appeared to have been dis-

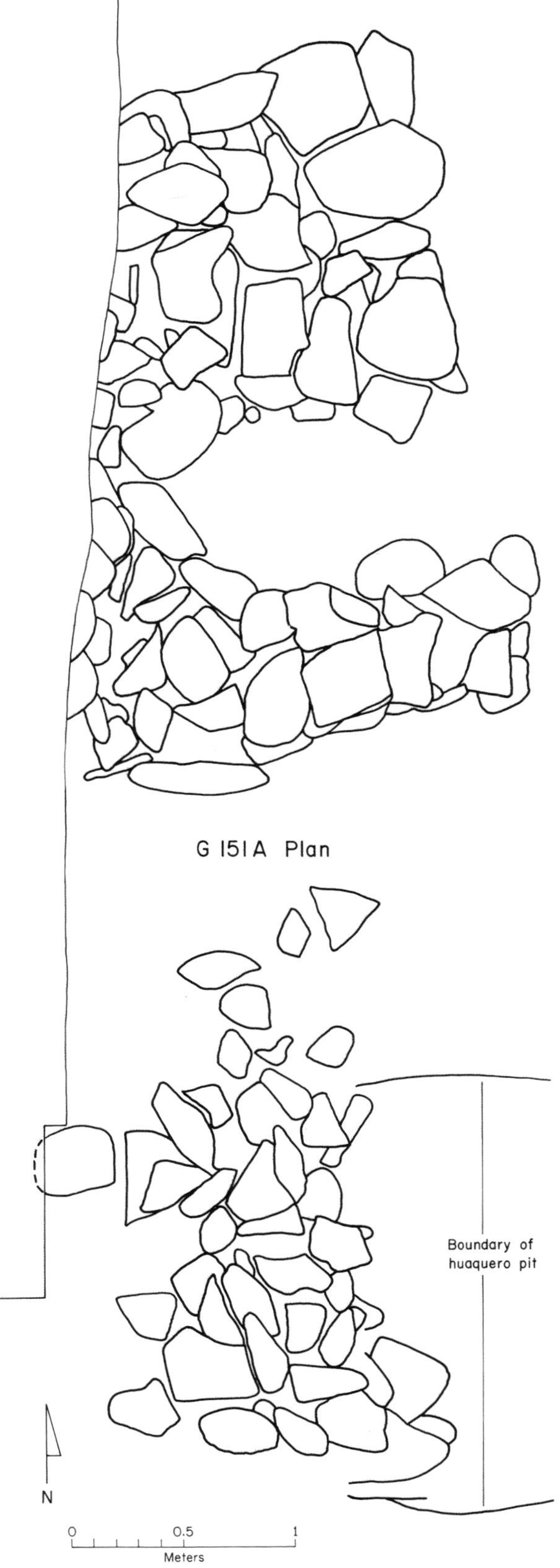

Figure 7-4.
Plan illustrating the form of the laja features at Neblina (G-151). Figure by Barbara Bolton.

Figure 7-5.
The laja features at Neblina. Note their stratigraphic position relative to Unit 20 (gray ash layer) and Unit 30. Photograph by Payson Sheets.

Figure 7-6.
Profile of the north wall of Operation A at Neblina, showing the relationship between the stone feature and the local stratigraphic sequence. The feature was exposed at the time of the Unit 41 ashfall (indicated by stippling). Figure by Barbara Bolton.

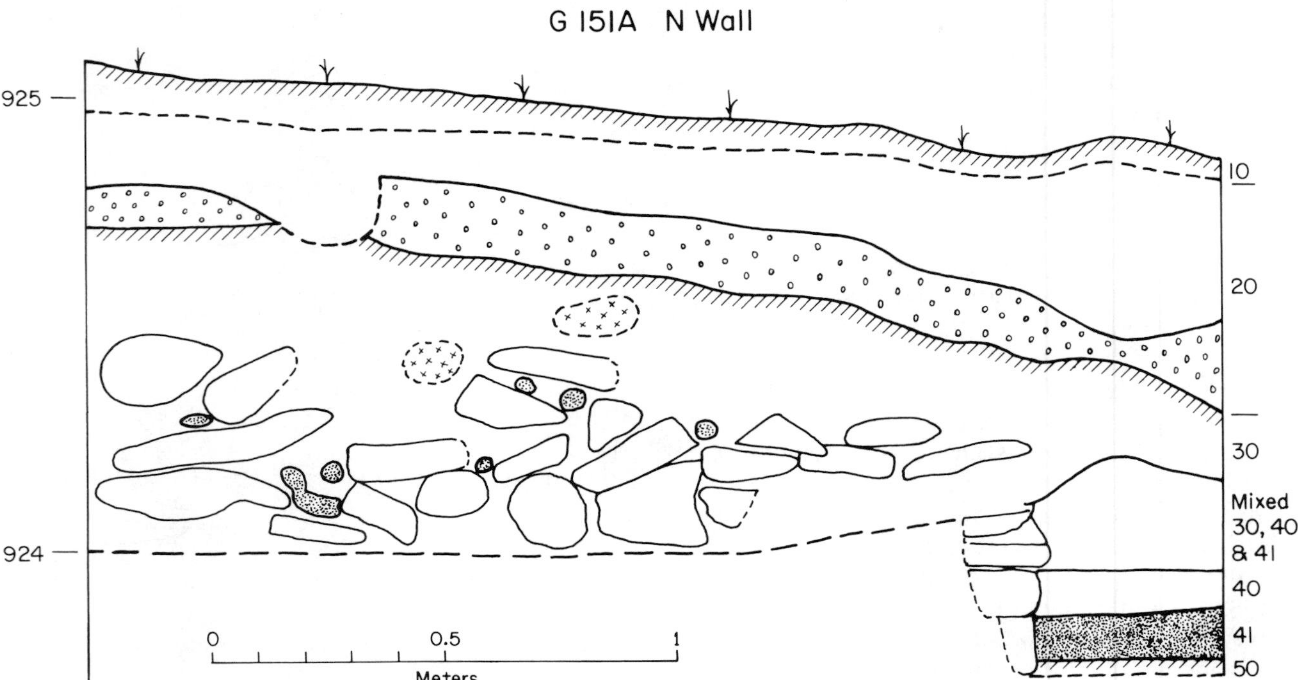

lodged by looting, and subsequent testing with a metal probe revealed extensive subsurface stone features.

Test excavation at Neblina (Fig. 7-4) was aimed at uncovering the stone features and determining local tephra stratigraphy. Horizontal exposure revealed a large concentration of laja piled together (Fig. 7-5). Individual lajas were 30 cm to 40 cm across and were stacked as many as three high in places. We cleared the limits of the stone feature on three sides, revealing it to be roughly rectangular in shape. It measured approximately 5.4 m long (east-west) and we estimate it to have been about 1.8 m wide (north-south). We did not determine the northern extent of the feature, but probing suggested that it did not continue for more than 30 cm to 40 cm beyond the excavated area. Probing revealed no further subsurface stone to the east, west, and south of the feature. Other excavation units on the ridge top to the east and west of the feature also failed to expose further subsurface stone.

The profile of the laja feature (Fig. 7-6) indicates its stratigraphic position. We were able to identify regional stratigraphic units that suggest that the lajas had been placed on Unit 50. They were subsequently buried by Unit 41 tephra, which occurs over and around the stones, but not beneath them, indicating that they were exposed when they fell.

As noted earlier, looting prior to our excavation of the site disturbed a portion of the stone feature. It also exposed a large, elongated laja with incised lines over part of its surface (Chap. 12). The stone was about 1 m long and weighed approximately 100 kg. It was lying at a 45° angle, the top extending into the undisturbed stratigraphy in the side of a modern pit. It is of the same material as the laja in the large, rectangular feature, but its position suggests that it may have been some type of upright marker. The incisions on the stone are fine and sharp-edged and appear to have been made with a pointed instrument such as an andesite or dacite flake edge. The identification of laja with similar incisions at the Silencio site (G-150) in the 1986 and 1987 seasons confirms their prehistoric nature.

We excavated a 2 m × 2 m excavation unit at the top of the ridge to the sterile surface of Aguacate. Despite its distance from Arenal Volcano, this unit provides one of the clearest stratigraphic sequences of regional tephra layers and associated soil strata (Fig. 7-7). We noted no cultural features in this unit, although it did yield Arenal Phase sherds from sub–Unit 50 strata.

LITHICS

Two different materials appear in the chipped stone assemblage at Neblina: dacite and phyric andesite. The dacite artifacts are large, thick flakes of the same type of material as a flaked stone celt from Las Piedras. Sheets (1984b; Chap. 11) has noted a full production sequence for the manufacture of flaked stone celts in the lithic assemblage from the site. The phyric andesite artifacts are smaller percussion flakes; these may represent laja breakage during placement, laja shaping, or the testing of raw material for lithic tool production.

We found no ground stone artifacts, thermally fractured rocks, or cooking stones at Neblina. Their absence, together with the general paucity of ceramics—especially from the Silencio Phase, which corresponds stratigraphically with the laja feature—suggests that domestic activities such as cooking and food storage did not occur at the site.

CERAMICS

We found only eight sherds in excavations at Neblina. Of these, five are Bocana Incised Bichrome, an Early Arenal Phase type dating to around 500 cal BC–cal AD 1. These include two hollow support fragments and a large body sherd burned on the interior. The remaining sherds consist of a long, tapering, solid support and two nondiagnostic body sherds. All are from stratigraphic levels below Unit 50 and predate the placement of the laja feature.

LAS PIEDRAS (G-152)

The Piedras site is situated approximately 500 m to the southeast of Neblina, on the opposite side of the small *quebrada* that drains into the Santa Rosa River (UTM 272,400 m N × 436,200 m E on the Tilarán 1:50,000 quadrangle). Las Piedras is located about 250 m to the northwest of El Silencio (G-150), downslope from the ridge top cemetery.

Las Piedras was initially discovered by workers on the Finca El Silencio, who identified a pile of large, subsurface stones as a possible prehistoric feature when they were erecting a fence. Exploratory digging at the time of the feature's discovery is reported to have yielded no artifacts besides a few sherds. Prior to testing, local informants identified the site as lying on an ancient stone road (*camino de piedra*), later identified in aerial photographs as a linear feature that originates at the ridge top site and crosses the drainage (Chap. 9). We selected Las Piedras for testing during the 1984 season on the basis of these descriptions and the presence of both large laja and sherds on the site's surface.

The principal feature at this site is another large assemblage of laja, amorphous in plan (Fig. 7-8). This feature is approximately 4 m long (north-south) and 3.75 m wide (east-west). The laja at this site is similar in size to that at Neblina, and its stratigraphic position—on top of Unit 50 with Unit 41 ash deposits on and around but not beneath them—is identical to that at Neblina. As at Neblina, stones were stacked three deep in parts of the feature. All of the lajas were horizontally placed with the exception of a row of upright stones at the downslope end (southwestern corner) of the feature. These may have been placed so as to prevent the pile of flat stones from sliding downhill or as a repository of special stones for tomb construction, kept separate from the slab laja.[3]

LITHICS

The flaked lithic collection from Las Piedras is more diverse than that from Neblina. It includes one chipped stone celt, one scraper, two hammerstones, two flake cores, and one percussion blade. An assemblage of dacite flakes representing debitage from all stages of the manufacturing sequence from cortex removal to edge trimming (Sheets 1984b: 162) indicates that flaked celt production occurred at this site as well.

We found no ground- or polished stone artifacts at Las Piedras; however, twenty-eight pieces of thermally fractured stone suggest that cooking activities may have occurred at the site.

CERAMICS

We collected 124 sherds at Las Piedras, most of which were nondiagnostic body sherds. They were situated in the same strata as the stones (Units 41 and 50). All diagnostic ceramics appear to date to the Silencio Phase. These consist of a variety of types, including Jiménez Polychrome (3), Palmares Incised (2), Carillo Polychrome (2 from same vessel), Mora Polychrome (3, identification tentative), and Tres Esquinas Beige (8). All of these types were common at the nearby El Silencio site (G-150) and strongly suggest that the two sites are contemporaneous and that activities at the sites were closely related.

EL JEFE SUERTE (G-153)

Site G-153 is located at UTM 272,400 m N × 435,700 m E on the Tilarán 1:50,000 topographic map, at an elevation of approximately 860 m. It is northeast of Dos Armadillos and is situated immediately downslope from Sitio Neblina (G-151), overlooking a small *quebrada* to the east. It is situated on the footpath that connects Neblina and El Silencio (Chap. 9), near the bottom of the valley between Neblina and Las Piedras. We found this site in the course of the regional posthole survey, when testing revealed fragments of an apparently whole vessel. We used two excavation units, Operations A and B, to explore stratigraphic and cultural features.

The principal aim of excavations at G-153 was to investigate the interfaces of Units 20 and 30 and of Units 41 and 50 for evidence of living surfaces that had been suddenly buried by volcanic ashfall. Unfortunately, these surfaces were absent or poorly preserved. Excavations in Operation A continued only as far as the interface between Unit 41 and Unit 50, with the exception of an area of disturbance where Units 40 and 41 had been penetrated by Unit 30 in the vicinity of a fragmented vessel of Tres Esquinas Beige (see below). Excavations in Operation B penetrated the uppermost part of Unit 50.

CERAMICS

Operation A, a 2 m × 4 m unit oriented east-west along the hill slope, yielded the remains of a single large vessel of the red-rimmed monochrome Silencio Phase–type Tres Esquinas Beige. This vessel was situated in the matrix of Unit 30 in a feature intrusive into Units 40 and 41. The only other sherds recovered from this operation were a single-rim fragment classified as the predominantly Arenal Phase–type Los Hermanos Beige, a large-rim sherd of Malekos Red, a Tilarán Phase utilitarian type, a hollow rattle vessel support, and seventeen monochrome body sherds, many of which were from coarse-paste, heavy vessels.

In Operation B, a 2 m × 2 m test pit, we found only ceramic materials within the matrix of Unit 50. Only three out of sixteen sherds were diagnostic as to type or form. These consist of one body sherd of Mojica Impressed and two rim sherds of the monochrome type Los Hermanos Beige, all characteristic of the Arenal Phase. Of the thirteen nondiagnostic body sherds from this operation, six are blackened and have burned material on the

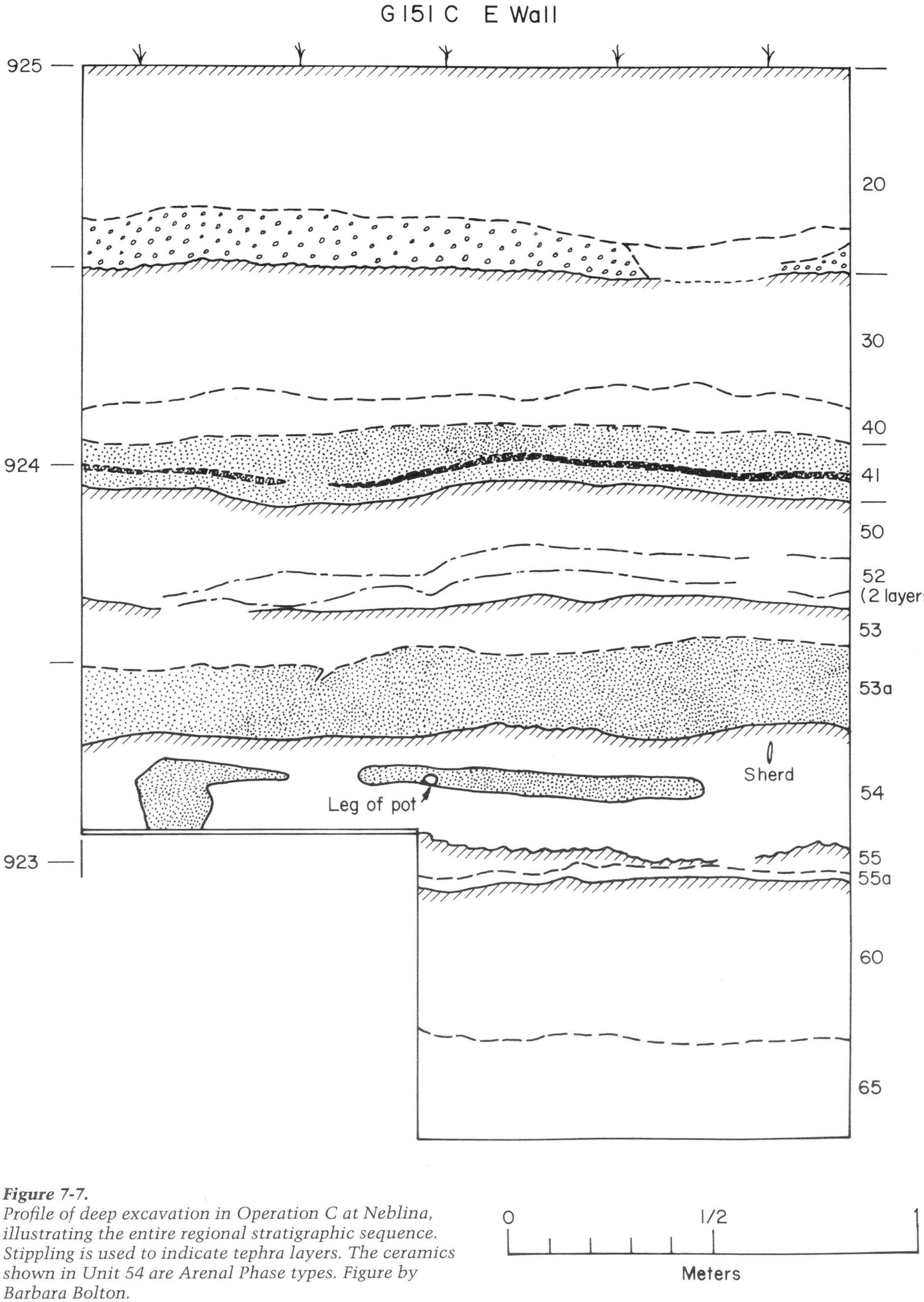

G151 C E Wall
925
924
923
20
30
40
41
50
52
(2 layers)
53
53a
54
55
55a
60
65
Sherd
Leg of pot
0
1/2
1
Meters

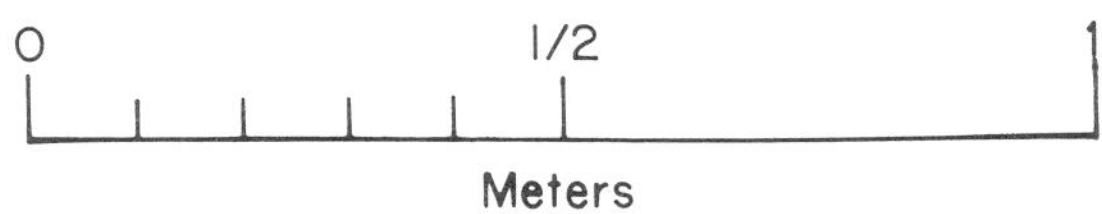

Figure 7-7.
Profile of deep excavation in Operation C at Neblina, illustrating the entire regional stratigraphic sequence. Stippling is used to indicate tephra layers. The ceramics shown in Unit 54 are Arenal Phase types. Figure by Barbara Bolton.

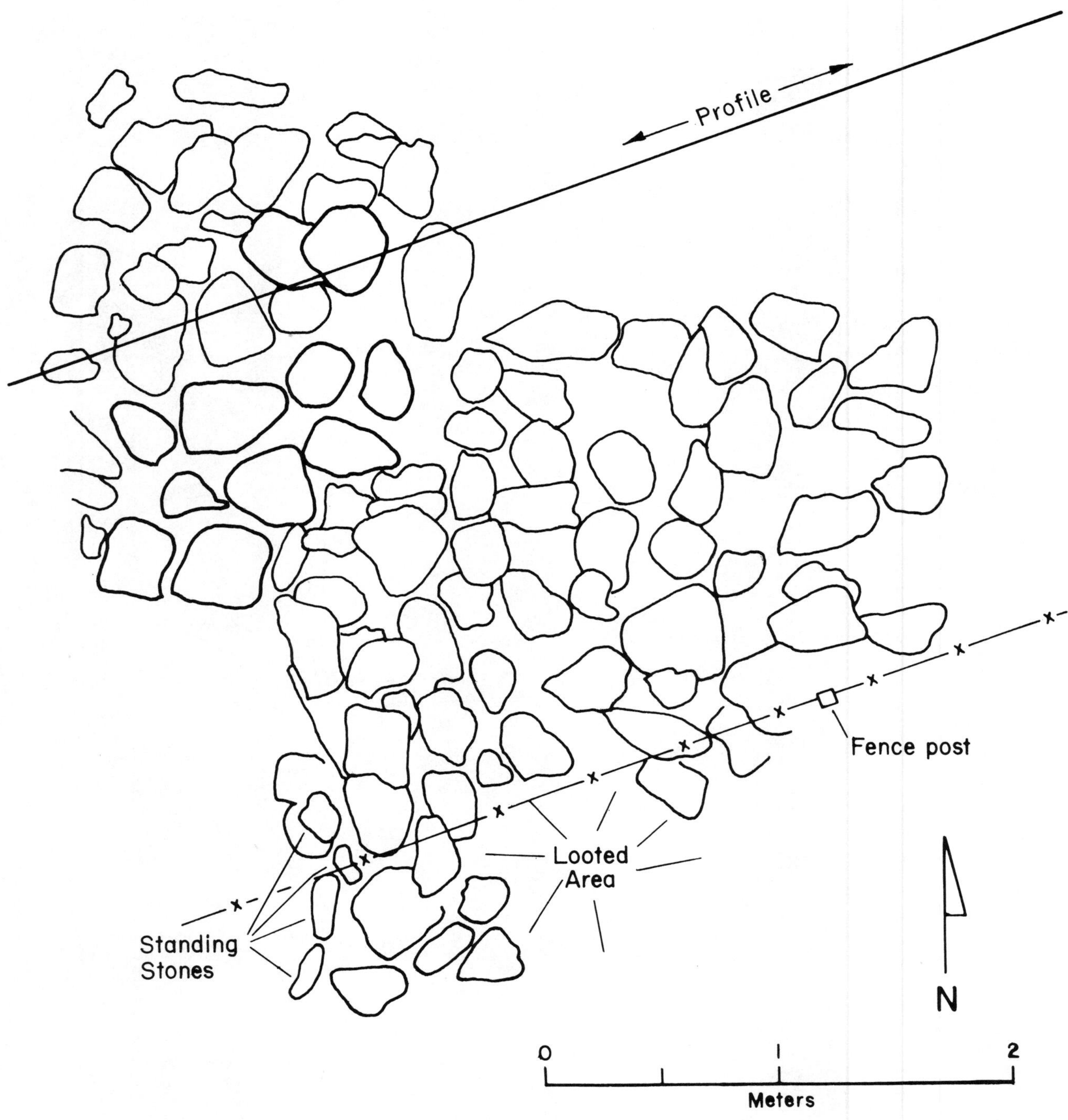

***Figure* 7-8.**
Plan illustrating the laja feature at Las Piedras (G-152). Although contours are not given, the feature slopes downward from west to east. Figure by Barbara Bolton.

interior, suggesting cooking activity. No other features were associated with this material.

LITHICS

Lithic remains were not abundant at G-153. We recovered ten fragments at the site, the majority from Operation A. These consist of one possible wedge, one flake, one flake core, five fragments of thermally fractured debitage, and two pieces classified as "other." The presence of fire-cracked cooking stones in association with charred sherds suggests domestic activities. Household manufacture of flakes is also indicated (Sheets, personal communication, 1984).

FLORAL REMAINS

We recovered macrobotanical remains only from Operation A at this site. These consist of small fragments of charred wood and indeterminate fruits (Chap. 16).

DISCUSSION

The Santa Rosa River sites provide important information on various activities that took place in the valley. Dos Armadillos and El Jefe Suerte yield evidence for domestic activities from the Tilarán and Silencio phases, respectively. Las Piedras and Neblina, representing caches of stone construction materials at strategic points on a prehistoric footpath, provide evidence for one of the functions of this Silencio Phase feature.

While we recovered ceramic, lithic, and floral assemblages similar to those of Dos Armadillos at other sites in the Arenal basin, the significance of this site lies in the unique context of the archaeological remains. Their stratigraphic location immediately below a layer of coarse lapilli (Unit 20) and their horizontal placement provide information on chronology and function. Although we recovered no architectural features to indicate either the shape or the orientation of an aboriginal structure, the high percentage of storage vessels and utilitarian wares, the abundance of flaked debris and thermally fractured stone, and the presence of maize and other vegetable foods indicate the presence of a small settlement on this bench overlooking the Santa Rosa River. The paucity of material recovered from postholes and excavations (such as Operations B, C, F, and H) elsewhere on the bench suggests that the occupied area was very restricted and may have been limited to an isolated family unit or a small hamlet rather than a village. Radiocarbon dates and ceramic comparisons place the occupation squarely in the Tilarán Phase.

Las Piedras, Neblina, and El Jefe Suerte are all located near the Silencio Phase ridge top cemetery (G-150) and are situated along the prehistoric footpath that runs from the cemetery northward toward Tilarán and beyond (Chap. 9). Excavations at these sites and elsewhere on the footpath indicate that the cultural features all date prior to the deposition of tephra marked by Units 40 and 41 in strata and that they can be associated with the Silencio Phase occupation of the region. Las Piedras and Neblina, both marked by large piles or caches of flat, volcanic lajas, are located at places on the footpath where there are marked changes in its direction and steepness. Each appears to have had a principal function as a repository for laja, probably carried into the area for use in the construction of box-shaped tombs and dry-stone walls at the ridge top site.

Evidence for cooking and tool manufacture at Las Piedras suggests that this site may have been a work area for the ridge top cemetery. Expedient flaked stone celts may have been produced here for clearing and maintenance of the larger site. Flaked celts would have been easier and faster to manufacture than polished stone celts and were probably used for cutting and clearing trees and underbrush or for removing smaller underbrush where a heavy, polished celt may have been less efficient. The presence of sherds of fancy polychrome types at Las Piedras suggests that these ceramics may not have had an exclusively funerary function, but may in fact have been vessels for everyday use. Other possible interpretations are that they represent sherds washed downhill from the cemetery to the stone repository by erosion, or that they represent the remains of vessels broken en route to the ridge top site, or that there are as-yet undetected Silencio Phase burials in the vicinity of the Piedras features.

As noted earlier, the features at El Jefe Suerte may represent traces of a domestic occupation contemporaneous with activities at Neblina, Las Piedras, and the Silencio cemetery (G-150). Although we identified no living surface, the nature of the remains in Operation A suggests the presence of a domestic occupation dating to the Silencio Phase. This occupation would have been contemporaneous with the use of the hilltop cemetery immediately to the east; however, it is difficult to interpret the modest remains from El Jefe Suerte as evidence for the Silencio Phase village that constructed the substantial mortuary features at El Silencio. This larger settlement remains to be identified.

A small number of Arenal Phase ceramics from Las Piedras and El Jefe Suerte confirm that portions of the Santa Rosa River drainage were occupied prior to cal AD 600. Together with a limited quantity of Arenal Phase sherds from El Silencio, they suggest a certain continuity in the utilization of these sites. The nature of the transition from the Arenal to the Silencio phases in the region remains poorly understood; however, the continued utilization of what were apparently small sites suggests that this transition may represent the results of external influence rather than population replacement. Sites like Sitio Bolívar (Chap. 5) demonstrate that large quantities of heavy stones were used for the construction of mortuary features in the period immediately preceding that of the laja features at Neblina, Las Piedras, and El Silencio. The adoption of polychrome ceramics in the Santa Rosa River Valley parallels their appearance in Greater Nicoya. As noted in Chapter 10, the Silencio Phase is marked by a combination of cultural characteristics indigenous to the volcanic Cordillera with an overlay of Middle Polychrome Period traits from Greater Nicoya to the west. Given their Arenal Phase antecedents, the stone features at Neblina and Las Piedras may be interpreted as examples of the former.

NOTES

1. Sites discussed in this chapter have also been described in a contribution to a preliminary report on the 1984 season of the Proyecto Prehistórico Arenal (Hoopes 1984b; Chenault 1984b).

2. Later research (Chap. 9) indicates that the villages that utilized the cemetery were in fact a few kilometers distant.

3. These stones are not laja, but long, narrow, and relatively flat river cobbles. Sheets suggests that they are headstones cached for use in tomb construction.

8

BRIAN R. MCKEE
THOMAS L. SEVER

Remote Sensing in the Arenal Region

INTRODUCTION

Remote sensing in the Arenal region began in the 1940s, 1950s, and 1960s, when Costa Rica's Instituto Geográfico took black and white 9 inch × 9 inch aerial photographs. More black and white aerial photographs were taken in the late 1970s and early 1980s in preparation for the construction of the Sangregado Dam. NASA has greatly expanded the remotely sensed data base recently with a variety of photographic and digital data acquired for the Arenal Prehistory Project. These include lasar profiler (Lidar), radar, Landsat Thematic Mapper (TM), and Multispectral Scanner (MSS), and Thermal Infrared Multispectral Scanner (TIMS) data, as well as color and color infrared photography. Through the use of these data, the Arenal Project has gained new insights into the regional environment, and discovered a network of prehistoric footpaths.

Remote sensing is the observation of phenomena at a distance. In the broadest sense, the human eye and most geophysical surveying techniques can be considered remote sensing. For the purposes of this chapter, however, we will utilize Sabins' definition (1987: 1): "remote sensing is commonly restricted to methods that employ electromagnetic energy (such as light, heat, and radio waves) as the means of detecting and measuring target characteristics." We will further restrict remote sensing to those devices that are not in direct contact with the ground surface.

This chapter begins with a discussion of some general principles of remote sensing. This is followed by a brief history of applications of remote

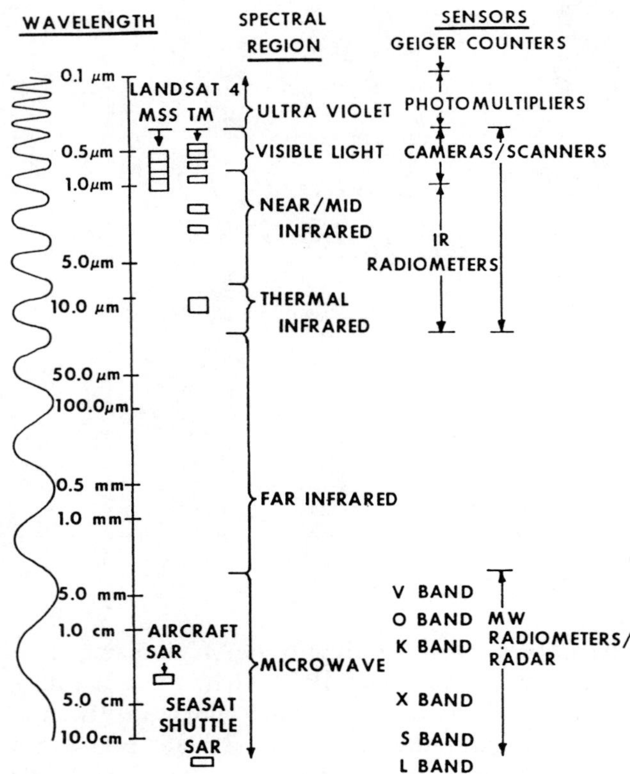

Figure 8-1.
Diagram of the electromagnetic spectrum. From Sever and Wiseman (1985: 10).

sensing in archaeology, and an examination of specific uses of remote sensing in the Arenal Project.

PRINCIPLES OF REMOTE SENSING

A basic familiarity with the principles and concepts of remote sensing is necessary to understand its applications. More detailed information is available in Sabins (1987), Jensen (1986), Siegel and Gillespie (1980), Ebert (1984), Lillesand and Kiefer (1979), and in the journal *Remote Sensing Environments*.

THE ELECTROMAGNETIC SPECTRUM

The human eye is sensitive to only a small portion of the electromagnetic spectrum. The eye (or a remote sensor) is sensitive to the interaction of light and the object that is observed. The eye and most sensors observe the reflection of sunlight from an object. In some cases, however, sensors record energy that has been absorbed by an object and is later emitted at a different wavelength. Active sensors, such as radar, provide the energy directly, rather than relying on the sun.

Electromagnetic energy consists of perpendicular interacting electric and magnetic fields, with the direction of propagation perpendicular to these fields. The electromagnetic spectrum includes a wide variety of energy, ranging from gamma rays, at the short end of the spectrum, through ultraviolet, visible, infrared light, and microwaves, to radio waves. The spectrum is divided into several regions or bands, based on wavelength (Fig. 8-1).

Gamma rays and X-rays, with wavelengths up to 3.0 nm, are completely absorbed by the upper atmosphere and are unavailable for remote sensing. Ultraviolet light has wavelengths between 3.0 nm and 0.4 μm, and only the longer portion of this band (0.3—0.4 μm) is transmitted by the atmosphere and can be detected by instruments. Atmospheric scattering is high in these wavelengths, leading to poor resolution.

Visible light occupies a narrow portion of the spectrum, between 0.4 μm and 0.7 μm. Many remote-sensing instruments utilize this portion of the spectrum, and the majority of remote-sensing applications are in the visible range.

The reflected infrared band, consisting of near- and mid-infrared regions, ranges from 0.7 μm to

3.0 μm. Many sensors use reflected infrared radiation (IR). Photographic infrared light occurs between 0.7 μm and 0.9 μm, within the near-infrared band. It is detectable using film or digital sensors and is the longest wavelength to which film is sensitive.

Thermal infrared radiation ranges from 3 μm to 14 μm. Several sensors operate in two portions of the thermal IR band, from 3 μm to 5 μm, and from 8 μm to 14 μm. The radiation between 5 μm and 8 μm is absorbed by the atmosphere, and thus is unavailable for remote sensing.

The microwave band, 0.1 cm to 30 cm, is widely used in remote sensing. The long wavelength of this band minimizes atmospheric effects. Microwaves penetrate clouds, fog, rain, and the ground surface under special conditions. Microwave sensors work in both passive and active modes. Active microwave sensors, which both transmit and receive energy pulses, are known as radar.

Radio waves, which have wavelengths greater than 30 cm, are seldom used in remote sensing.

THE USE OF FILM IN REMOTE SENSING

Photographic film is the oldest and most widely used recording medium in remote sensing. Photography is an analog technique, in which a light-sensitive chemical, through reactions with photons of light, is exposed and forms a latent image. The developing process transforms the latent image to an image visible to the human eye. Four different types of film are commonly used in remote sensing: black and white negative, color negative, color positive, and color infrared positive film.

Black and white negative film is the most commonly used medium in remote sensing. The simple technology, low cost, and excellent spatial resolution make this a very practical form of remote sensing. One band of data, roughly equivalent to that visible to the human eye, is recorded (Horder 1971).

Color photography works on the same basic principles as black and white photography. Instead of one layer of emulsion, however, there are three, sensitive to red, green, and blue (ibid.: 490–529). Combinations of these primary colors form the photographic image.

Color-infrared film (CIR) works much like color positive film. The only difference is that the colors to which the layers of emulsion are sensitive are shifted to slightly longer wavelengths. The blue layer of emulsion is exposed by green light, the green layer by red light, and the red layer by photo-infrared light. Healthy vegetation is highly reflective in the photo-infrared wavelengths and thus appears red in CIR photographs (Sabins 1987).

DIGITAL REMOTE SENSING

Much of modern remote sensing uses digital sensors rather than photographic film. Most digital sensors utilize reflected sunlight, as does photographic film. In digital remote sensing, the energy received by the sensor strikes a detector, which converts this energy into a voltage, which is then assigned a brightness value. This value is either stored on computer tape or, sometimes, in the case of satellites, broadcast to a receiving station on the earth. When acquiring digital data, a different detector, or array of detectors, is used for each band. The sensor records the scene as an array of small, square, discrete areas, known as pixels, rather than as a continuous image. The image consists of a two-dimensional array of pixels corresponding to the ground surface over which the sensor passed.

Digital Image Processing

Once data have been obtained in a digital format, they can be manipulated by a computer. The types of manipulations best performed by the computer deal primarily with differences in color or brightness of the image. The human eye and brain are superior for other types of analysis, notably those involving size, shape, and association (Jensen 1986). In digital image processing, the computer does not replace the human analyst, but is an aid that makes the final analysis by human observers more efficient and effective.

Digital image processing can be divided into three categories: image restoration, image enhancement, and information extraction. A fourth type of computer manipulation, geographical information systems (GIS), integrates digital imagery with independently derived information to increase the ease of interpretation. Image restoration corrects irregularities incurred in image acquisition. When an image is recorded, perturbations can occur in the platform (aircraft or satellite). Atmospheric irregularities also can affect the image. Through the computer, the analyst can correct for these problems (ibid.: 94–116).

Image enhancement makes interpretation and information extraction easier (ibid.: 117–176). The analyst can stretch the image to fill the full dynamic range of the computer. Unwanted speckling or "noise" can be eliminated from an image, and linear features or changes in the image can be enhanced.

Information extraction classifies an image into various categories that make interpretation easier (ibid.: 177–233). This classification is based on brightness values in the various bands. Computers also can be used to analyze texture and associations in images, but generally, humans are better at this type of analysis (ibid.: 6).

Advantages and Disadvantages of Digital Remote Sensing

Digital imagery has several major advantages over film; in particular digital data can be processed by a computer. All the manipulations described earlier can be conducted on digital imagery, none on film. Computers are also more consistent and less subjective than are humans, and allow repeatable results.

Another advantage of digital sensors is in increased spectral range. Photographic film is sensitive only to a relatively narrow portion of the electromagnetic spectrum. Digital sensors expand this range and can acquire images in near- and mid-infrared, thermal-infrared, and microwave portions of the spectrum, as well as in visible light.

The two major disadvantages of digital remote sensing are in spatial resolution and in cost. Spatial resolution is defined as "the minimum distance between two objects at which the images of the objects appear distinct and separate" (Sabins 1987: 8). The spatial resolution of film is superior to all digital sensors. This is an important concern for archaeologists, who often examine relatively small phenomena. Aerial photography is cheaper to obtain and process than even the lowest-priced digital imagery.

Digital Sensors

There are many remote sensors in operation. There are several cameras in use for aerial photography, but the standard of today is the 9 inch × 9 inch large-format aerial camera, with black and white negative, color negative, positive color transparency, or positive CIR transparency film. There is no such standard for digital images, however. A wider variety of wavelengths are recorded, and a wider variety of platforms are utilized. Satellite sensors have a fixed spatial resolution, as they orbit at a constant altitude, but the spatial resolution of airborne sensors varies with altitude. Typical pixel sizes for airborne sensors range from 3 m to 5 m. Table 8-1 does not include all, or even most, digital remote sensors in use today, but it does include those utilized by the Arenal Project, as well as a few others useful to archaeologists.

A BRIEF HISTORY OF REMOTE SENSING IN ARCHAEOLOGY

The first archaeological remote sensing occurred in 1891, when a British archaeologist photographed ruins in India with a camera attached to a crewless balloon (Deuel 1969). Capper's balloon-based photographs of Stonehenge (1907) were the first aerial photographs of an archaeological site to receive widespread attention. Between 1907 and World War I, several researchers used aerial photographs to study sites in the Middle East (Garnett 1938; Deuel 1969; Knightley and Simpson 1971; Ebert and Lyons 1983).

During World War I, photography from airplanes and balloons was utilized for intelligence and artillery purposes. After the war, archaeologists such as O. G. S. Crawford began to use airplane-based photography (Ebert 1984). Crawford (1923, 1924a, 1924b, 1929; Crawford and Keiller 1928) used his expertise in geography, cartography, and archaeology to study the direct and the indirect impacts of humans on the environment by examining topographic changes, crop marks, and soil changes.

Bushnell's photographs of Cahokia Mounds in Missouri in 1921 were the earliest American use of aerial photography in archaeology (Ebert 1984). U.S. Army photographs of the Gila and Salt River region of the Southwest in the late 1920s allowed Smithsonian researchers to study prehistoric Hohokam canals (Deuel 1969).

Charles Lindbergh was a key figure in the development of remote sensing in American archaeology. He took photographs of Tikal, Tulum, Chichén Itzá, and Chaco Canyon in the late 1920s (Lindbergh 1929; Kidder 1929, 1930a, 1930b; Ricketson and Kidder 1930). The Chaco photographs revealed several previously unknown Anasazi sites and provided the first record of the Chacoan roadway system, although it was not

TABLE 8-1
DIGITAL REMOTE SENSORS

Sensor	*Landsat MSS Bandwidth (micro-meters)*	*Landsat TM*	*Spot*	*TMS*	*Cams*	*Daedalus*	*TIMS*
Ch 1	N/A	0.45–0.52	0.50–0.59	0.45–0.52	0.45–0.52	0.38–0.42	8.2–8.6
Ch 2	N/A	0.52–0.60	0.61–0.68	0.52–0.60	0.52–0.60	0.42–0.45	8.6–9.0
Ch 3	N/A	0.63–0.69	0.79–0.89	0.63–0.69	0.60–0.63	0.45–0.50	9.0–9.4
Ch 4	0.5–0.6	0.76–0.90	N/A	0.76–0.90	0.63–0.69	0.50–0.55	9.4–10.2
Ch 5	0.6–0.7	1.55–1.75	N/A	1.55–1.75	0.69–0.76	0.55–0.60	10.2–11.2
Ch 6	0.7–0.8	10.4–12.5	N/A	10.4–12.5	0.76–0.90	0.60–0.65	11.2–12.2
Ch 7	0.8–1.1	2.08–2.35	N/A	2.08–2.35	1.55–1.75	0.65–0.69	N/A
Ch 8	10.4–12.6	N/A	N/A	N/A	2.08–2.35	0.70–0.79	N/A
Ch 9	N/A	N/A	N/A	N/A	10.50–12.50	0.80–0.89	N/A
Ch 10	N/A	N/A	N/A	N/A	N/A	0.92–1.10	N/A
Ch 11	N/A	N/A	N/A	N/A	N/A	8.00–13.50	N/A
Panchromatic	N/A	N/A	0.51–0.73	N/A	N/A	N/A	N/A
Ground resolution (M)	79 240 (band 8)	30 120 (band 6)	20 (multispectral) 10 (panchromatic)	varies with altitude	varies with altitude	varies with altitude	varies with altitude

Note: N/A means not applicable.

recognized in the photographs until 1971. Kidder utilized Lindbergh's photographs to study the relationship between settlement patterns and topographic features. He found Crawford's premise that changes in vegetation can be indicators of prehistoric human activities useful in these studies. During the 1930s, as aerial photography became a common tool of archaeologists, hundreds of flights were made to take photographs.

Color infrared photography (CIR) shows differences between healthy and stressed vegetation. CIR was first used in archaeological research in the 1950s to detect vegetation changes indicative of buried features in Normandy, France, and in Nova Scotia (Ediene 1956; Cameron 1958). Gumerman and Neely (1972) used CIR to study archaeological features and microenvironmental zones related to human occupation in the Tehuacán Valley.

Since World War II, the use of aerial photography, including black and white, true color, and color infrared, has expanded (Ebert 1984). In the 1970s and 1980s, new forms of remote sensing, including digital imagery, were developed and are slowly being adopted by archaeologists.

Digital image acquisition and processing were first developed by NASA in the mid-1960s for space and planetary exploration. Various satellite programs, including Landsat and SPOT, have provided digital coverage of most of the planet.

Archaeologists have been slow to adopt the new technology. Several archaeological and ethnographic applications of satellite technology were initiated in the 1970s, but many were not completed, and others had only limited success. Some of the problems were due to remote sensing's still being in the early stages of development, and there were software problems. Few anthropologists had adequate background and training to understand digital image analysis. The limited spatial resolution of satellite sensors also made certain types of analysis impossible.

Reining was one of the first to apply Landsat technology successfully to anthropology (1973, 1974a, 1974b). She combined Landsat imagery, aerial photography, sampling strategies and fieldwork to study human ecology on the Niger and Upper Volta and migration practices in West Africa. Fanale (1974) conducted similar work for the Dogon in Mali. Conant (1976; Conant and Cary 1977) used remote sensing to study cultural and human ecology in Kenya.

Archaeologists did not have the same success. Many features were too small to be observed in satellite imagery, and airborne sensors were prohibitively expensive. Most researchers lacked the skills to analyze data when available. The Chaco Canyon Remote-sensing Center was a notable exception. The Chaco Center was instrumental in encouraging optical and digital remote sensing.

The center applied modern analytical techniques, and carefully integrated ground truthing and survey with remote sensing. Its research, especially into the prehistoric Chacoan roadway system (Lyons and Avery 1977), laid a framework for future research.

Several other projects utilized digital data during the late 1970s and early 1980s. These included Lind's studies in the Mekong Delta, Vietnam (1981), the work of Shazly in Egypt (1983), and the research of Crumley (1983) and Madry (1983) in France. All of these researchers used satellite data for large-scale analysis and aerial photographs for site-specific analyses. Wagner (personal communication, 1989) has had considerable success in utilizing the Daedalus scanner in locating historic Spanish structures in Florida.

A conference held at the National Space Technology Laboratories in March of 1984 helped raise the awareness of archaeologists about remote sensing and explained the concerns and interests of archaeologists to the remote-sensing community (Sever and Wiseman 1985). Participants identified immediate applications of remote-sensing technology and raised concerns about possible misuse. The Arenal Project remote sensing, supported by NASA and NSF, was a direct outgrowth of this conference.

REMOTE SENSING IN THE ARENAL PROJECT

Based on the positive results of the conference, in 1983 NASA agreed to assist the Arenal Project with the acquisition and analysis of remotely sensed data. Under a three-year cooperative agreement, NASA conducted three overflights to obtain optical and digital remotely sensed data. Data were collected in several forms, including color and color-infrared aerial photography, data from a laser profiler (Lidar), TIMS, and L-band radar imagery. NASA also provided Landsat MSS and TM data for large-scale environmental analyses and has digitized maps showing topography, soils, landforms, and life zones. In addition, the Instituto Geográfico of Costa Rica provided black and white aerial photography. These photographs complement the recently acquired NASA data by providing time depth. The photos show areas now covered by the enlarged Lake Arenal (see Chap. 1) and illustrate changes that have occurred in the region over the last forty years, notably the effects of deforestation.

The Landsat images, particularly the TM, have proved useful in illustrating the climate of the area by documenting changes in vegetation. Environmental gradients are clearly visible as one moves from the dry Pacific side of the region, over the Continental Divide to the wetter Atlantic side, and to the extremely wet areas near Arenal Volcano. Environmental changes probably are related to variations in settlement patterns.

The most significant result of analysis of the remotely sensed data was the discovery of a network of prehistoric footpaths. These features are visible as linear anomalies. Ground examination and the excavation of trenches across them, identified them as footpaths, and this identification was confirmed by the rejection of alternate hypotheses (see Chap. 9). Evidence for the identification of footpaths includes their location relative to known prehistoric sites, their topographic position, associated artifacts, and their stratigraphy. The network of suspected and confirmed footpaths is shown in Chapter 9.

The footpaths were originally observed in color infrared photographs. Further analysis showed that they were also visible in true color photographs, black and white photographs, and the TIMS imagery. The color infrared photography has been the most useful in detecting the footpaths, as they are usually visible as vegetation changes across the landscape. The increased moisture content of the soil within the footpath traces leads to healthier vegetation. Healthy vegetation has a very strong signature in the photographic infrared band, and thus the paths show up as red lines or zones. The true color photographs also show the paths well, as do the black and white photographs. Analysis of the TIMS data is still in progress, but early indications are that this imagery will be useful in extending the footpath network.

To date, no known paths have been observed in the radar imagery. We had hoped that this imagery would reveal paths in the forested areas by showing changes in the elevation or composition of the forest canopy as it crosses the paths, but aside from the detection of a historic road leading to a bean field, the radar imagery has not been of great value. Numerous linear features are visible in the radar images, but the determination of the nature of these features has been complicated by two factors: (1) the radar is "seeing" phenomena invisible to the human eye; and (2) determining the location of the feature on the ground is hindered by the dense vegetation of the rain forest. This problem may be alleviated in future research by the use of the Global Positioning System (GPS). The GPS uses eighteen Navstar satellites in orbit around the earth. When GPS ground-based instruments are used, latitude, longitude, and elevation coordinates are displayed to an accuracy of a few centimeters. These tools can help locate features of interest in spite of dense vegetation.

The laser profiler can show topographic changes, but it is not an imaging system. The analyst cannot distinguish cultural from natural phenomena with this system. As it traverses the erosional trace of a path on the present landscape, it can detect paths as dips in the ground surface, but it also records dips caused by natural erosion and by modern cultural activity. Therefore, we are unable to tell whether the topographic lows that we see are prehistoric footpaths, modern footpaths, or natural features. It is further limited in that it is recording topography as a linear slice, while the photographic and radar instruments are recording two-dimensional areas within which linear anomalies are more readily apparent and can be traced relative to other features.

COMMENTS, SUMMARY, AND CONCLUSIONS

The technology of remote sensing is developing rapidly. Aerial photography has been in use since the late nineteenth century, but digital technology is still in its infancy. Many different sensors and computer processing techniques are in use.

Archaeologists have used remote-sensing technology since its inception and occasionally have been instrumental in the development of new interpretation techniques. Remote-sensing technology has repeatedly shown its value to archaeologists. Humans affect their environment, and these impacts are visible through a variety of means, including remote sensing. The development of digital remote sensing has provided valuable tools, but they must be used cautiously. A lack of awareness of the limitations of remote-sensing technology or inadequate time spent in field verification of hypotheses can lead to erroneous conclusions. Remote sensing is a powerful tool, but it will not replace ground survey and excavation techniques. Instead, it will improve the efficiency of more traditional methodologies and can, in some cases, serve as an independent source of data.

The use of optical and digital remotely sensed data has aided the Arenal Project in the study of environmental variation and in the identification and recognition of a network of prehistoric footpaths. Through a variety of analytical techniques dealing with the remotely sensed data, and field verification of these data, we have been able to find direct evidence of interaction between sites and between sites and sources of raw materials. Without remote sensing, it is virtually certain that these features would not have been recognized. Applied judiciously, these techniques, with ground verification, may be applicable to wider regions and can aid in our general understanding of prehistoric adaptation to the environment.

ACKNOWLEDGMENTS

This research would have been impossible without the help of many individuals and institutions. The assistance of the staff of the Earth Resources Laboratory of the Stennis Space Center of NASA is gratefully acknowledged. Chuck Wheeler, David Wagner, Mary Sullivan, and Payson Sheets read and commented on earlier versions of this chapter. Their suggestions improved the content and readability of the chapter and are appreciated. Alexander Goetz aided in general technical background and advice. We also drew heavily on the work of the other participants of the Proyecto Prehistórico Arenal, particularly the ceramics work of John Hoopes and the volcanological work of Bill Melson. The hospitality of Luis and Gabriella Jiménez is greatly appreciated, as is the support of Fran Mandel-Sheets. The dedicated work of our Costa Rican field crews made field confirmation of features possible. Finally, we would again like to thank Payson Sheets for his guidance and the unique opportunity to work on this project.

9

BRIAN R. MCKEE
THOMAS L. SEVER
PAYSON D. SHEETS

Prehistoric Footpaths in Costa Rica: Remote Sensing and Field Verification

INTRODUCTION

Remotely sensed imagery has revealed a network of prehistoric footpaths in the Arenal region. In this chapter we will examine how the footpaths were formed, and how they were detected, and interpret how they were used by the prehistoric inhabitants of the region.

Footpaths can be utilized as a window to a culture's religious, economic, political, and social organization. Human geographers have long analyzed paths, roads, and highways as networks of transport and communication (Haggett 1965), and archaeologists have studied systems of constructed roads, but they have discovered little evidence of prehistoric erosional footpaths. People use paths for a variety of reasons, including transportation, communication, and ritual; they leave a record of their presence and routes in the form of erosional footpaths. The study of the path networks and their integration of sites and resources is an application of behavioral archaeology, the use of prehistoric features to understand human behavior and activities. This research is primarily methodological, focusing on the recognition and confirmation of features as footpaths. Future research will attempt to expand the network, increase our knowledge of the processes involved in the formation of the footpaths, and improve our understanding of the uses and purposes of the paths.

Our focus is regional, extending from the very moist, nonseasonal eastern end of the research area, over the Continental Divide at 700 m to 1,000 m, to the more seasonal and drier Pacific

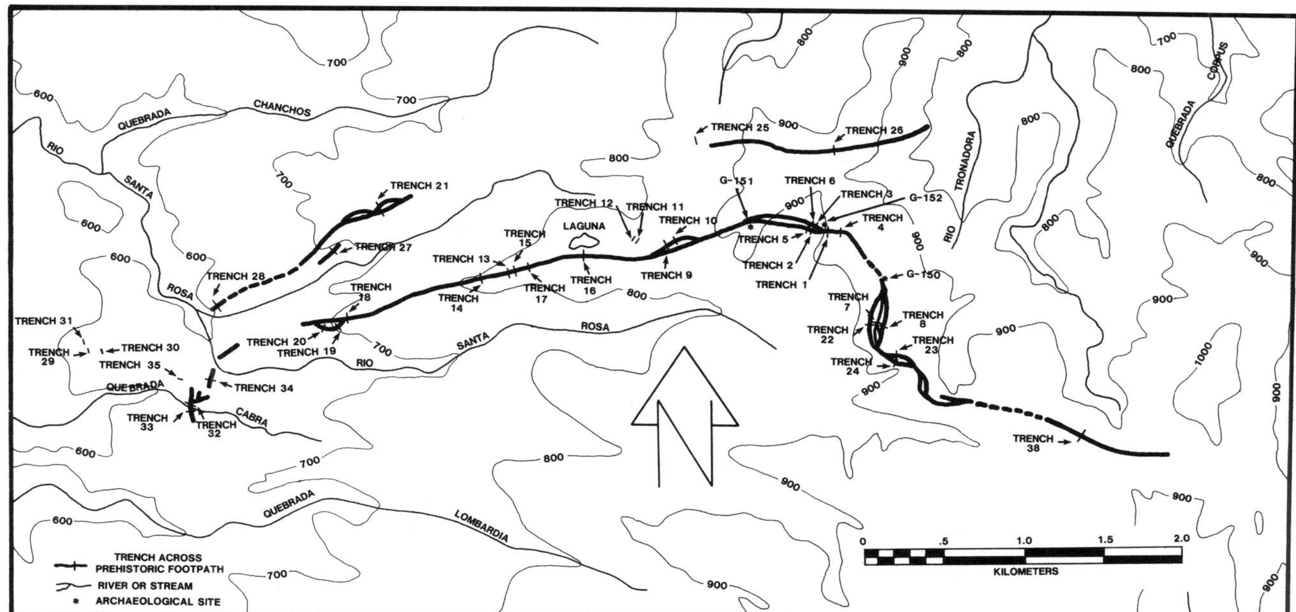

Figure 9-1.
Map of Silencio Phase footpaths in the Silencio/Tilarán area. Location of trenches across confirmed footpaths are shown. Numerous other anomalies have yet to be investigated; many may be prehistoric footpaths. Contour interval 100 m. Map by Brian McKee.

side (Chap. 1). We have detected linear anomalies and subsequently identified them as footpaths in all three areas. We have also detected footpaths and confirmed them in areas buried beneath up to 3 m of volcanic ash.

FOOTPATH DETECTION IN IMAGERY AND IN THE FIELD

During analysis of color-infrared prints in 1985, we observed a linear feature leading westward from the Silencio cemetery (G-150, Chap. 6). The feature made an obtuse bend around a repository of stone used in construction at the cemetery (G-152, Chap. 7), extended to a second stone repository (G-151, Chap. 7) on another ridge top, and continued westward from there.

The lines were considered to be probable footpaths or roads because of their relation to known loci of cultural activity and the crossing of several distinct geomorphic features. Three exploratory trenches excavated across the features demonstrated that they had existed prior to the fall of the Unit 20 tephra (i.e., they were formed before ca. 1500 AD), showing that they formed before European contact and were of prehistoric origin.

The most effective imagery in the detection of the footpaths has been the low-altitude color-infrared photography. The true color aerial photography and the conventional black and white photography have also been helpful (Chap. 8). The large-format black and white negatives provided

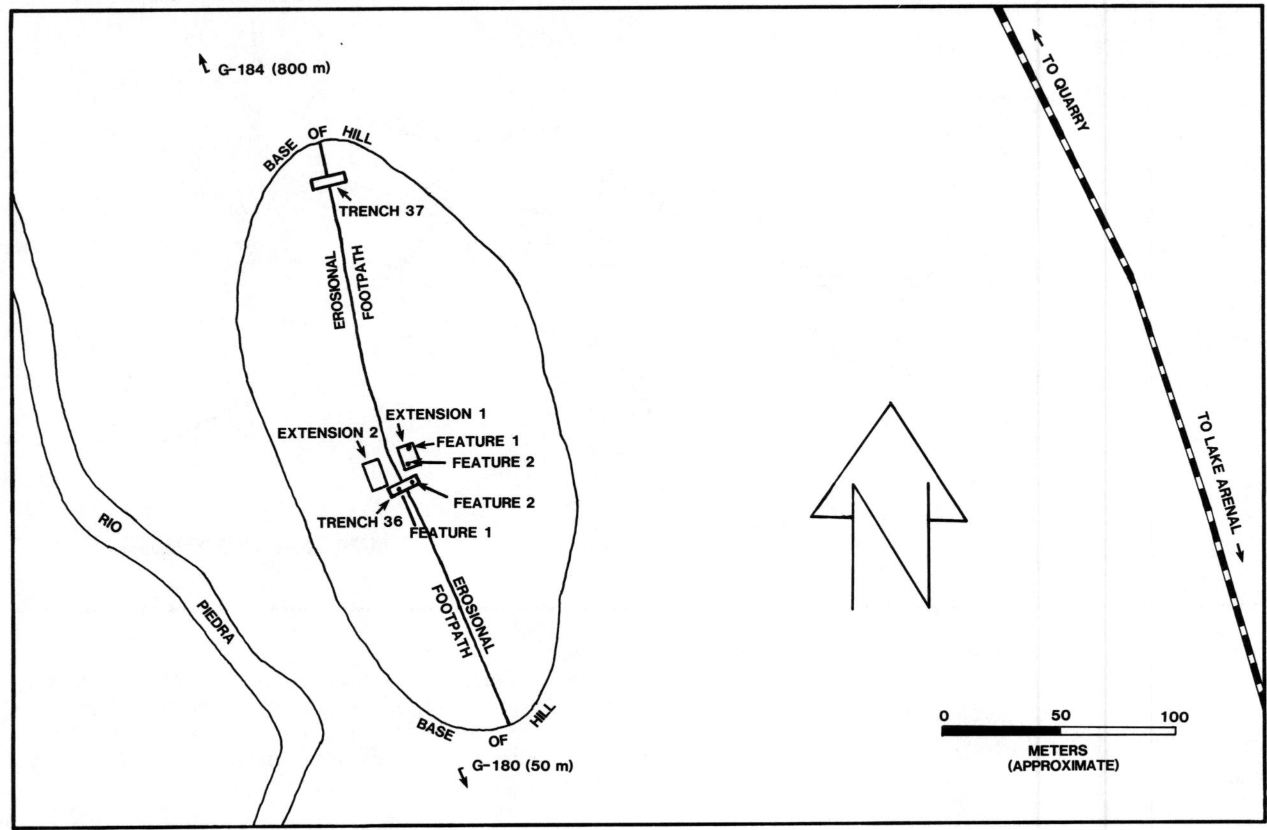

Figure 9-2.
Map of short Arenal Phase footpath crossing a hill northwest of Lake Arenal. Extent of hill, Trenches 36 and 37, and extensions 1 and 2 are illustrated. Map by Brian McKee.

by Costa Rica's Instituto Geográfico were especially useful when a quarter of a frame was enlarged to an approximately 1 m^2 print. The paths are visible as positive crop marks, where grasses grow better, in the photographs. This may be due to improved root matrix or to moisture retention in areas of the paths. The TIMS imagery clearly shows some known segments of footpaths, as well as other linear anomalies outside the area of known footpaths, but systematic analysis and ground-truthing of these data have yet to occur. We have had little success with radar or Lidar data (Chap. 8). Segments of linear anomalies that have been confirmed to be prehistoric footpaths are shown in Figure 9-1.

CONFIRMATION OF LINEAR FEATURES AS FOOTPATHS

Before examining in detail the processes responsible for the formation of the features, we must evaluate the evidence that they are prehistoric footpaths. Two possible alternatives exist: they are natural features, caused by erosion or faulting; or they are modern cultural features. Before they can be identified positively as prehistoric cultural features, these alternatives must be rejected.

The evidence comes from remote sensing, ground inspection, and excavation. This includes their topographic position, their relationships to sites and resources the prehistoric inhabitants of the region utilized, associated artifacts, and depositional and erosional phenomena recorded in the stratigraphy.

The topographic position of the footpaths can help distinguish them from modern roads. The paths tend to stay high, often along ridge tops, and follow relatively straight lines, frequently running directly across topographic highs and lows, rather than contouring around them, as do most modern roads. In one case (Fig. 9-2), a path between a village and a cemetery went directly over the top of a small hill, rather than around it. The paths' location on high ground may be explained by the extremely wet climate of the area; paths along topographically high routes are better drained than those along lower routes.

The topographic setting of the features also provides evidence for cultural origin. Ridge tops are areas of minimal water erosion, as there is a very limited catchment area upslope from which to draw water (Horton 1945). All water that causes erosion along ridge lines must come from immediately upslope, along the ridge line, or fall directly on the area that is eroded. Natural features caused by water erosion tend to be oriented along the steepest slope of the landform that they are draining, that is, perpendicular to the topographic contours, because this is the orientation along which water exerts the maximum erosional force (Ritter 1986). This direction is usually perpendicular to the trend of a ridge line.

The morphology of the features distinguishes them from faults. There are no scarps, and the geometry is not what would result from faulting. Other indicators of faulting, such as slickensides and alteration minerals, are absent, as is evidence of structural deformation in the area immediately surrounding the features.

The location of these features relative to archaeological sites and resources utilized by the prehistoric inhabitants of the region also indicates that they are footpaths. The first recognized path segments occur between a previously known cemetery (G-150) and a repository for stone (G-152) used at the cemetery, and between the cemetery and a spring. The locations led to their recognition as cultural features. The locations of the paths also help show that the features are not due to faulting. Faults generally do not connect villages with cemeteries, or sites with springs, stone sources, and stone repositories.

The association of artifacts with the features also indicates that they are prehistoric footpaths. We found ceramic and lithic artifacts in most trenches across features where other evidence indicated that they were footpaths. These artifacts were usually found along the path surface, or within the stratum of the first "infilling" after path abandonment. One footpath (Fig. 9-2) between a habitation site and a cemetery was associated with a large concentration of river cobbles and potsherds. The cobbles were transported to the top of a ridge and placed on the ground surface on either side of the footpath (Fig. 9-3). We found numerous potsherds, as well as several broken, but nearly complete, pots scattered over and among these rocks. This feature may be the remains of a pot-smashing ritual similar to those deduced from evidence at other sites during the project (Chap. 5). Snarskis (1981a) has interpreted smashed tripods found at Atlantic Watershed cemeteries as the remnants of *chichadas* (rowdy, drunken festivals), and the broken stones and pots may be reminiscent of similar rituals.

The final body of evidence to support the identification of these features as prehistoric footpaths uses the volcanic stratigraphy of the area (Fig. 9-4). Arenal Volcano, located about 20 km east of the study area, has erupted numerous times over the last 4,000 years, leaving a stratigraphic record of airfall deposits downwind (Chap. 2). Pedogenic processes have operated on the tephra, forming soils on most units. In general, the time for soil development was short, and only A horizons were distinguishable in the field. The soils were then buried by the next eruptive episode of the volcano. This process was repeated at least ten times. The only cases in which a dark soil layer would not be present above a tephra layer would occur when insufficient time elapsed between eruptive episodes for soil formation, or when erosion occurred between episodes. We have no evidence for the latter. The result of these processes is a series of alternating dark (A horizons) and light (unweathered tephra) "zebra stripe" strata.

In undisturbed areas, these layers are relatively flat and uniform (Fig. 9-5*a*). Where erosion occurs, however, some or all of the layers are removed. The paths formed as a result of natural erosional processes initiated by human behavior, rather than solely by natural means. Humans,

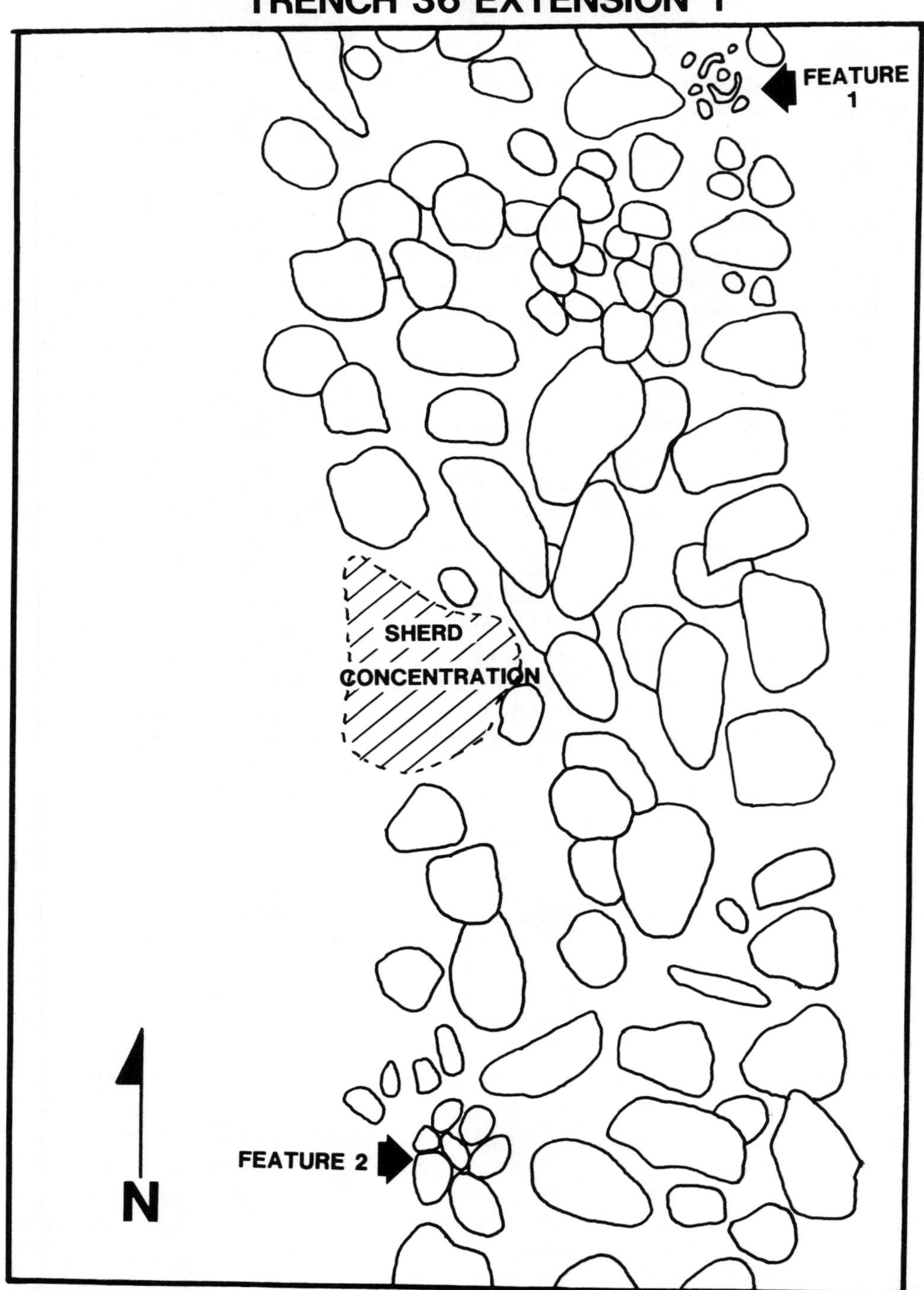

Figure 9-3.
Plan view Trench 36, extension 1, showing large rock feature constructed alongside the footpath, with smashed ceramic vessels. Feature 1 was a broken but nearly complete pot, and Feature 2 was a shallow pit, possibly a small grave. No bone or burial goods were found. Figure by Brian McKee.

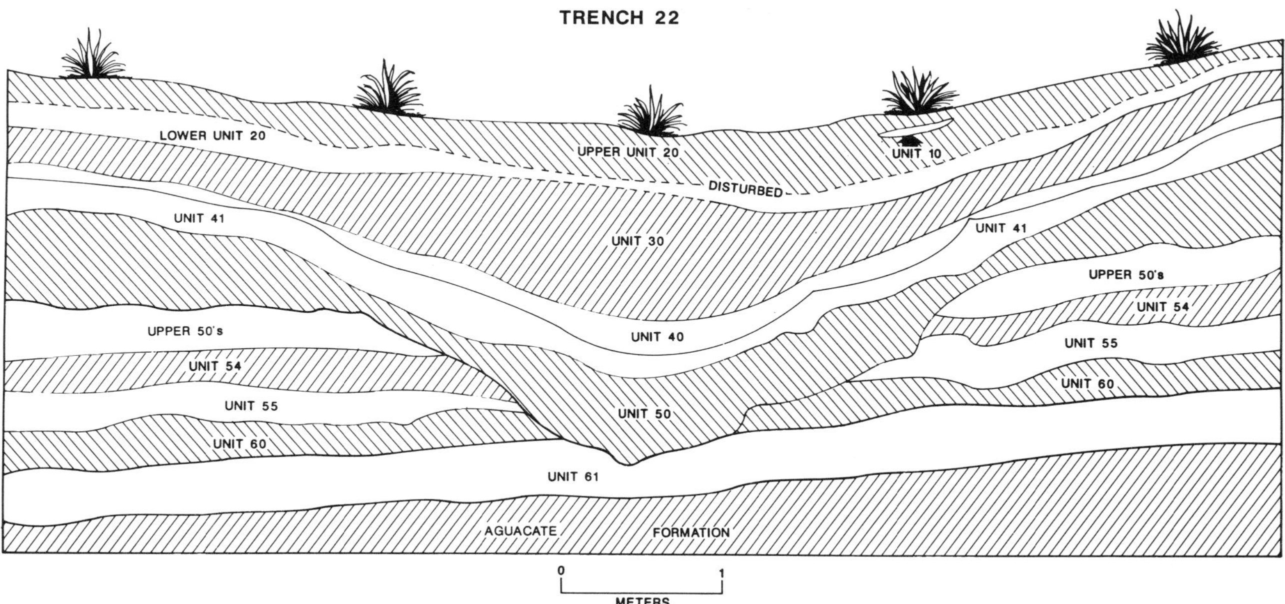

Figure 9-4.
Profile of Trench 22, 200 m south of the G-150 cemetery, on the path to the spring. The trench is located in the center of Figure 9-10. Note the uneroded stratigraphy at far right and left. The footpath eroded strata in the center of the drawing from the top of the Upper 50's layer. Use ceased during the time of Unit 50 soil formation; the eruption of Arenal Volcano that deposited Unit 41 postdates use of the path. The path at this location almost eroded down to the Aguacate Formation, the clay-rich soil that antedates the eruptions of Arenal Volcano. Drawing by Charlotte Timmons.

by walking over the ground surface and clearing vegetation, compacted the soil, retarded or killed vegetation, and initiated erosion. After the initial channel was established, natural processes continued the erosion. The original erosional cut associated with the footpath incision was probably narrow and U-shaped in cross section, and 30 cm to 70 cm wide, based on the widths of the bottoms of the paths. As erosion continued, the sides of the path also eroded, resulting in a several-meter-wide V-shaped erosional trace (Fig. 9-5*b*). The ground surface at the end of the footpath was the upper surface of this V. The next volcanic eruption following the abandonment of the path would then drape a layer of tephra across the path. Often, some infilling by eroding sediments from upslope would occur after abandonment, before tephra burial. The ground surface after the eruption would be roughly parallel to that before the eruption (Fig. 9-5*c*), with some slight topographic smoothing.

The burial process was repeated during subsequent eruptions. Some paths that were not deeply incised have been completely filled in and are thus invisible on the modern ground surface. More deeply incised paths have not been so obscured and can be traced on the present surface. Many of the paths can be seen in the remotely sensed imagery. The present ground surface is approximately parallel to that of the time of the footpath use, although in some cases as much as 2 m higher (Figs. 9-6 and 9-7).

HYPOTHETICAL PROFILE BEFORE PATH USE

UNIT 52
UNIT 53
UNIT 53A
UNIT 54
UNIT 55
UNIT 60
UNIT 61
AGUACATE FORMATION

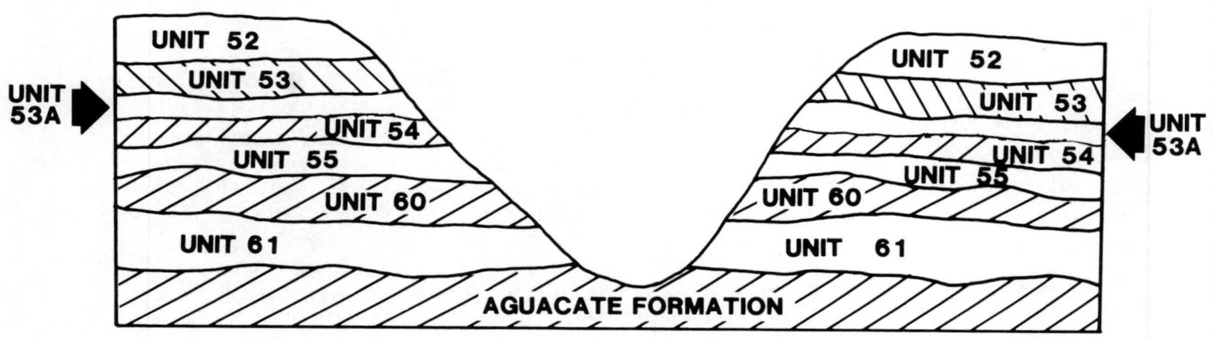

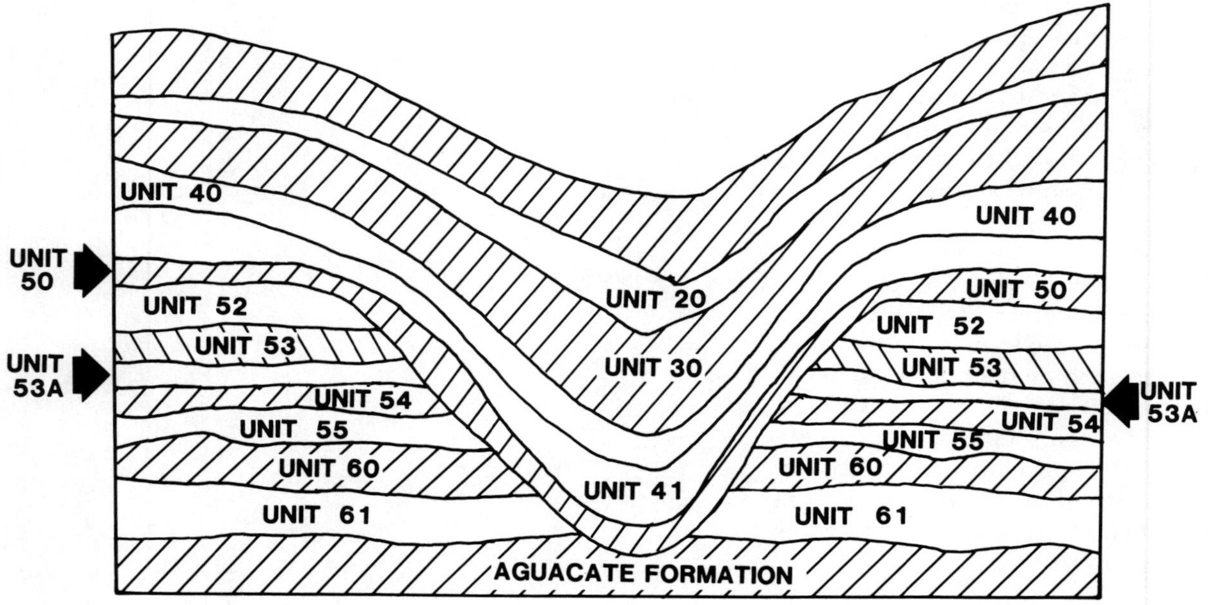

Figure 9-5.
a. *Hypothetical profile of volcanic strata before path use. Note the flat-lying, undisturbed strata.*
b. *Hypothetical profile of footpath at time of abandonment. Note the erosion of soil and tephra layers, and the* V*-shaped profile.*
c. *Hypothetical profile of footpath at present time. Note layers of tephra and soils draped across the erosional* V*. Drawings by Brian McKee.*

Figure 9-6.
Trench 38, showing the deep tephra burial in the area near the Chiquito River. Photograph by Payson Sheets.

Figure 9-7.
Profile of Trench 38. Note alternating soil and tephra layers and depth of burial in areas nearer the volcano. Figure by Brian McKee.

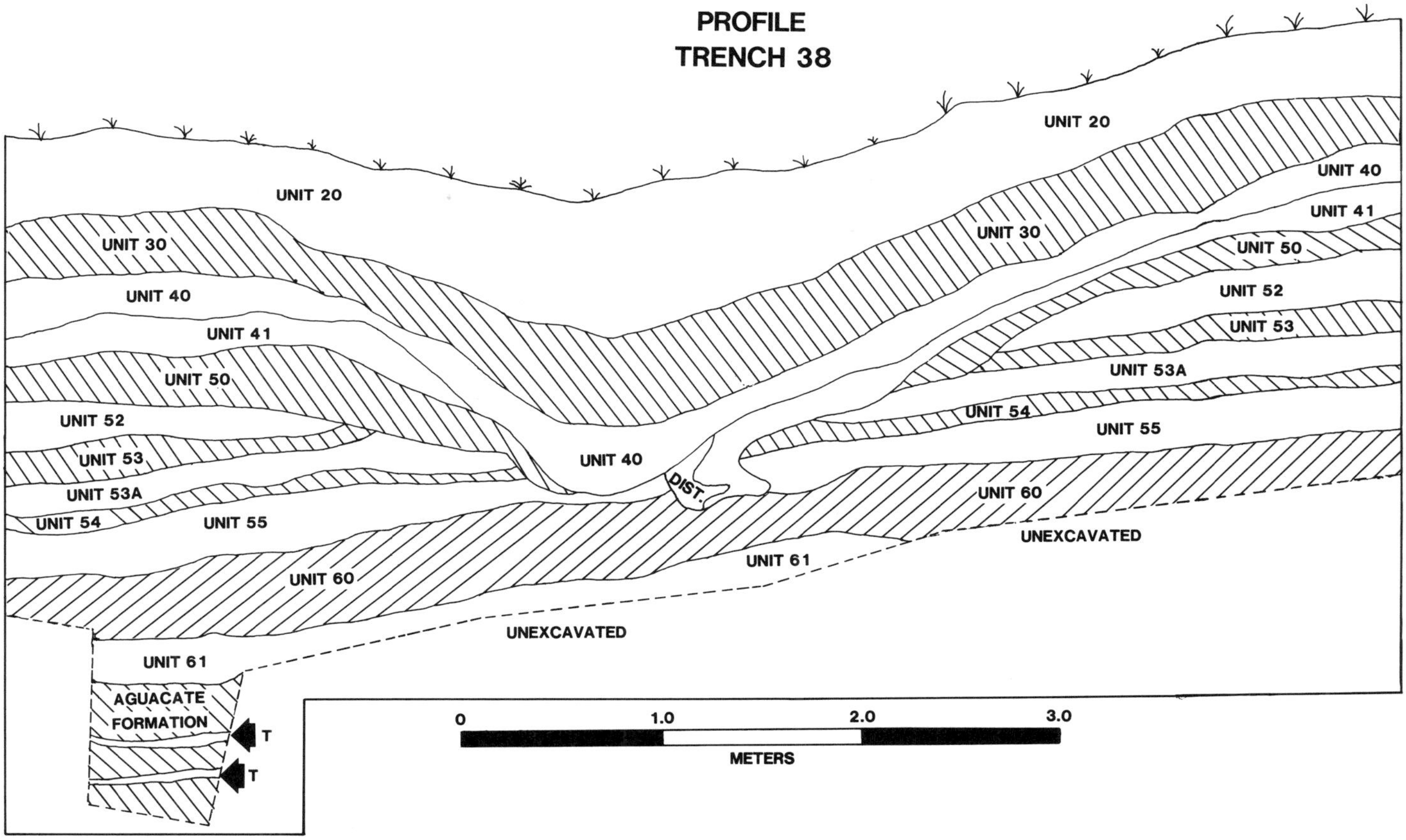

PROFILE
TRENCH 38
UNIT 20
UNIT 30
UNIT 40
UNIT 41
UNIT 50
UNIT 52
UNIT 53
UNIT 53A
UNIT 54
UNIT 55
UNIT 60
UNIT 61
DIST.
UNEXCAVATED
AGUACATE FORMATION
T
T
0
1.0
2.0
3.0
METERS

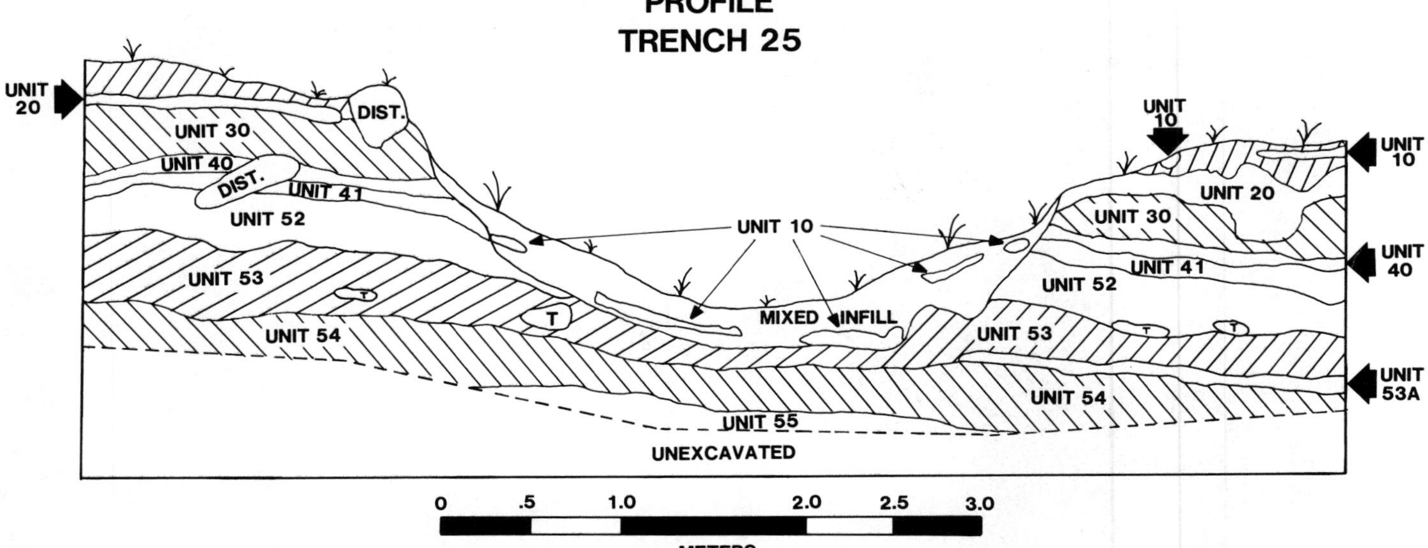

Figure 9-8.
Profile of Trench 25. Note that Unit 20 has been eroded away near the center of the profile, and that Unit 10 is relatively continuous across the full width. This trench was excavated across what proved to be the remnants of a historic road. Figure by Brian McKee.

Absolute dating of the eruptions allows us to use the stratigraphy as a chronological tool for dating footpath use. A lower bracketing date for the initiation of footpath use is provided by the date of the uppermost flat-lying tephra layer from which erosion began. An upper bracketing date for the end of path use is provided by the date of the first uneroded tephra layer draped across the footpath.

In three cases, the stratigraphy indicates that features are historic, rather than prehistoric. Trench 25 in particular is notable (Fig. 9-8). Erosion visible in cross section in the trench cut through stratigraphic Unit 20, which serves as a dividing line between prehistoric and historic times (Chap. 2). After excavation of the trench, informants stated that this feature had been a wagon road in the early decades of this century. The trench correlated Stratigraphic Unit 10 with the 1968 eruption of Arenal. The source of this unit was controversial (Borgia et al. 1988; Chaps. 1 and 2). Unit 10 draped across the erosional trace of the road, and because the 1968 Arenal eruption is the only eruption since the abandonment of this road, the hypothesis that this eruption was the source of the Unit 10 tephra is confirmed.

Two other trenches excavated in another area produced similar results. We observed two parallel linear features closely resembling confirmed footpaths in the CIR imagery at a location 1.4 km west of the G-150 graveyard. Excavations (Tr. 11 and 12) indicate that both features postdate the fall of the Unit 20 pumice, and thus must be historic. Interviews with local landowners divulged that it was a small road in use in the 1930s and 1940s, connecting Tilarán with the Finca El Silencio farmhouse.

PROCESSES OF FOOTPATH FORMATION

The erosional traces of the footpaths have formed because of different rates of erosion between the footpaths and adjacent areas, with surface water as the primary agent of erosion. Erosional processes are complex and will be summarized only briefly.

PROCESSES OF EROSION

Most of the theory utilized in this section comes from Horton's pioneering work (1945). Infiltration theory of surface runoff postulates that soil can absorb water at only a limited rate; this rate is its infiltration capacity. When the infiltration capacity of a soil is surpassed by the intensity of rainfall, overland flow occurs. Infiltration capacity depends on soil texture and structure, vegetal cover, biological structures, temperature, the initial moisture content of the soil, and the condition of the soil surface (ibid. 1945). Because of the variability of these factors, infiltration capacity can change widely across small distances, over time for a single area, and even during a single storm. Erosion of sediment particles too large to be carried downward through the soil profile can occur only during overland flow. In this study, we utilize four broad categories of variables involved in the erosion of the footpaths: climate, slope, soil properties, and vegetation cover.

Climatic variables are relatively independent and include the mean annual rainfall, the temporal distribution of rainfall, and the intensity of rainfall in a given storm. The mean annual rainfall of the region is exceptionally high, between 2,500 mm and 3,500 mm a year (Tosi 1980). Rainfall is lowest in the western portion of the study area and increases dramatically to the east. Only about half of the total precipitation is accounted for by evapotranspiration (ibid.); the rest must travel through the system underground (as throughflow), or on the surface (as overland flow or runoff). Temporal variation in rainfall is more important than is the total annual rainfall. The intensity of rainfall during a storm determines the amount of water that moves as throughflow and the amount that moves as overland flow. Because the rainfall in this region is seasonal, the quantity of water supplied at a given time varies from the amount expected based on the mean annual figure. The intensity of a storm also influences how much soil is detached by the direct impact of raindrops (rainsplash), which plays a major role in erosion of bare soil (Kirkby 1969). Rainfall in the Arenal region is intense and distributed unevenly in time, causing greater erosion than would otherwise be the case.

Slope also plays a role in the intensity of erosion. In a perfectly flat area, water does not flow, and thus erosion by overland flow cannot occur. Young and Mutcher (1969), in a study conducted in South Dakota, relate slope to erosion with the following equation:

$$E = -15.38 + .26R + 1.31S,$$

where E = sediment loss in tons/acre, R = runoff in ft^3, and S = % slope. Although the equation cannot be translated directly to an area with a different environment and soils, it does show that erosion is positively correlated to slope, and that in areas where other variables are equal, steeper slopes cause greater erosion.

Soil and sediment properties are important to both the infiltration capacity and the erodibility of sediments. Texture is probably the most easily understood variable. Coarser sediments have higher infiltration rates than finer ones (Carson and Kirkby 1972), largely because of their higher porosity. Coarse particles are less cohesive than are finer ones, however, because of lower total surface area and electrostatic properties, and are thus more easily detached by rainsplash. Therefore, although overland flow is less likely to occur in coarser-grained soils, when it does occur, erosion is more likely. The tephra-laden soils of the Arenal region consist primarily of sand-sized particles with high infiltration capacities and high erodibility. These soils rest on the Aguacate Formation, a clay-rich soil formed on Tertiary and Quaternary volcanic materials (Tosi 1980). The Aguacate Formation is highly impermeable, but it is also quite cohesive, because of the strong electrostatic bonds between clay particles. Overland flow is common on the Aguacate Formation, but the cohesiveness of the clay keeps total erosion lower than in tephra-derived soils.

There is a regional gradient in tephra particle size and depth. To the east, near the volcano, the particles are larger and the depth is greater. The greater tephra depth provides more easily erodible sediments near the volcano, and erosion should be deeper in this area. The grain size gradient also favors greater erosion near the volcano, as the coarser grains are less cohesive than the finer ones farther away; however, infiltration capacity is greater with increased grain size, indicating lower erosion.

Soil development also influences the erodibility of sediments. Open A horizons with a high organic content have a high infiltration capacity, while B horizons with concentrations of clays or carbonates have much lower infiltration capacities. Structural cracks along ped faces in soils also can increase infiltration capacity and lower the likelihood of erosion. The limited soil development in the Arenal area reduces the significance of this variable.

Vegetation plays a key role in both infiltration and erosion. According to Horton (1945:318), "Vegetal cover is the most important factor in relation to initial resistance to soil erosion." Kirkby (1969) states that overland flow is extremely rare in humid climates except where vegetation has been stripped. Vegetation increases infiltration in several ways. First, it keeps the soil open and increases porosity. Second, it increases the effective roughness of the ground surface and slows the flow of water, allowing more time for infiltration to occur. Vegetation also intercepts raindrops, and thus reduces their impact and rainsplash erosion. Increased infiltration capacity caused by vegetation also lowers overland flow by increasing the amount of water that moves as throughflow. Finally, the mat of organic debris and roots can bind soil together and further reduce erosion.

RELATIVE IMPORTANCE OF VARIABLES IN DEPTH OF FOOTPATH INCISION

A goal of the study is to determine the relative use of the different segments of footpaths. Several variables listed earlier are of particular relevance to this question. Precipitation varies throughout the study area and is conducive to high rates of erosion in areas stripped of vegetation. Depths of footpath incision are slightly higher in eastern portions of the study area, but other variables may play a greater role than precipitation.

Slope is more variable than climate. In theory, a footpath will be incised more deeply in steeper areas than in areas of less slope. Sediment properties also vary. The greater depth of the tephra blanket and the coarser particle size near the volcano should permit deeper erosion in portions of the paths near the volcano.

Statistical analyses were conducted, using SPSS-PC, to explore relationships between variables involved in footpath formation. We looked especially for correlation between the variables and the degree of erosion for each trench excavated. A goal of these tests was to determine the relative roles of the different variables in the depth of incision and if possible, to determine the relative use of the various portions of the paths. A Pearson product-moment correlation coefficient matrix was constructed, using slope, rainfall, and the depth of tephra present above the Aguacate Formation at each trench location, and the degree of erosion present at the same location. Correlations were low between all the variables and the width, depth, and eroded cross-sectional area.

There are a variety of possible explanations for this lack of correlation. First, we were able to control for only some of the variables involved in the erosional processes. We did not control many properties of the sediments, including texture, thickness of the A horizon, organic content, and soil permeability. We were also unable to take microenvironmental variation into account. Rainfall varies more than is recorded in Tosi's (1980) maps, and localized heavy storms, for which we have no record, probably played a major role in variations in erosion. Vegetation differences also may account for some differences in erosion. Some vegetation types are more resistant to trampling than are others. We have also assumed that the variables have remained constant through time. Although major changes are unlikely, it is possible that changes have occurred that could account for the lack of correlation. Finally, we were unable to control for the relative intensity and duration of path use. If a sufficiently large sample of trenches was examined from a segment of a path that received constant use, then we might be able to control for some of the environmental variables and extrapolate to other areas to examine the degree of use of the various footpath segments.

Unfortunately, we cannot yet separate the amount of footpath use from the other variables in our path analysis. There are clearly some variables that we have not controlled in examining the relative use of the different footpaths. According to Schiffer (1987:303), "the importance of identifying formation processes *before* behavioral or environmental inferences are attempted cannot be overemphasized. In far too many cases, the evidence used by an archaeologist owes many of its properties not to the past phenomena of interest, but to various formation processes." Until we have a greater understanding of the environmental factors involved in the formation of these paths, we cannot justify further inferences regarding the intensity and duration of path use.

BEHAVIOR INVOLVED IN FOOTPATH USE

The central questions of this study are behavioral. They include the identity of the people using the paths and the loads that they were transporting. We have some answers to these questions. We know that many live people and some dead people were moving along the paths, with the former carrying the latter for interment. People also carried large quantities of laja, flat-fracturing andesite used in construction of tombs and retaining walls at the cemetery. We have excavated two laja repositories (G-151 and G-152; see Chap. 7) between the cemetery and outcrops of andesite located farther to the west. Laja may have been transported most of the way to the cemetery as a secondary task while traveling to the cemetery for other purposes. The laja repositories were at least slightly organized internally. There was a tendency to separate flatter, larger slabs from smaller and more irregular slabs in both G-151 and G-152. Site G-152 had one section devoted solely to the elongated headstones, which were placed upright in a line. The headstones are long and cylindrical in shape, in contrast to the flat laja slabs, and were used for marking the heads of graves.

COMMENTS, SUMMARY, AND CONCLUSIONS

We have detected prehistoric footpaths as linear anomalies in a volcanically active tropical rain forest environment in northwestern Costa Rica. They were detected most successfully, to date, in the color, color-infrared (Fig. 9-9), and conventional black and white aerial photographs (Fig. 9-10), as well as in the TIMS imagery (Fig. 9-11). These media were most effective when enlarged to a scale such that features approximately 1 m wide could be seen. A variety of means have allowed the features to be confirmed as footpaths. The topographic positions, locations relative to known loci of prehistoric activity, associated artifacts, and stratigraphic profiles across the paths have all provided independent lines of evidence that these are indeed prehistoric footpaths. The ash layers from the eruptions of Arenal Volcano have been particularly useful in confirming their identification as footpaths and have assisted in dating path use and in determining the modes of path entrenchment and preservation. The combination of several lines of evidence provides a much stronger confirmation of the hypothesis that these features are prehistoric footpaths than any single line of evidence could produce.

Until recently, archaeologists have spent little time looking for ancient paths in imagery and on the ground. In spite of the obstacles presented by low population densities, a tropical moist environment, and frequent ashfalls, however, linear anomalies have been detected and confirmed as footpaths in the Arenal area of Costa Rica. Thus, the prospects of finding paths in other moist areas of the occupied New and Old worlds are good. We suggest that aerial photography, of a scale of approximately 1:10,000 to 1:30,000, be examined for any linear features linking known sites. This will need to be followed by on-the-ground inspection and testing to determine the processes of formation and preservation. Methods to separate prehistoric from modern and historic phenomena will need to be developed based on the formation processes involved in each region.

One of the previously unanswered questions of the project is how settlements were integrated during the Silencio Phase, a time when settlements were relatively large, but widely separated. The footpaths provide a partial answer to this question. Integration appears to have been based on ritual or ceremonial behavior. Multiple paths lead from the Silencio cemetery toward villages that buried their dead in that cemetery. The heavily used paths that lead to the spring, as well as the voluminous occupational trash left in the cemetery, argue strongly for long-duration ceremonies in the cemetery, likely directed toward ancestral and other spirits.

An unanticipated result of the footpath study was a direct contribution of data to help resolve one of the important research topics of the project, the degree of forest clearance in prehistoric times. We have made efforts to interpret the pollen, phytolith, and carbonized plant macrofossil record to understand the natural and cultural vegetation (Chaps. 14, 15, and 16). There are difficulties in interpreting these data sets, however, particularly when they are from samples taken from archaeological sites, which are by definition

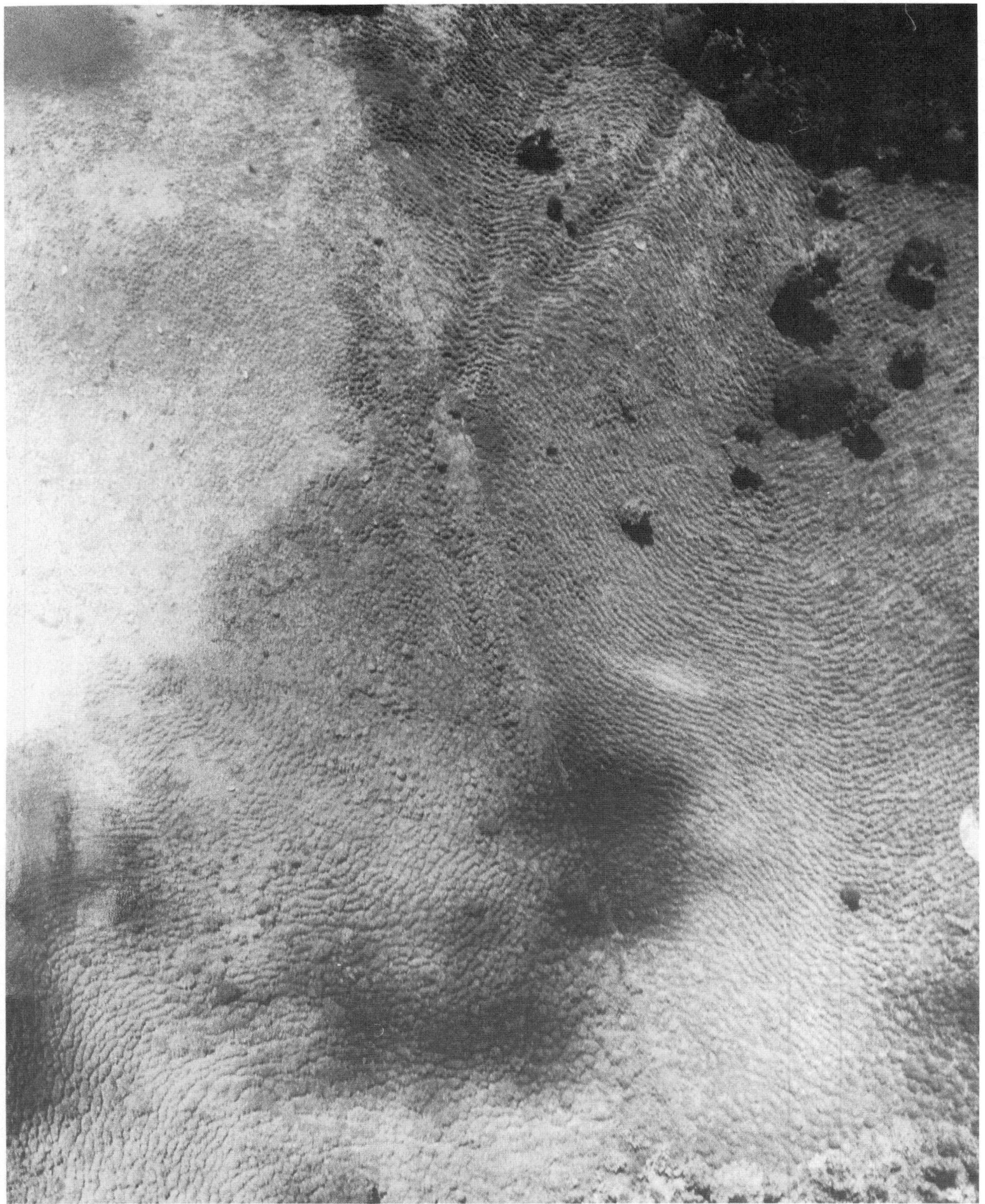

Figure 9-9.
Black and white print of low-altitude color-infrared aerial photograph showing a footpath near the Silencio cemetery. The straight line crossing the center of the photograph is a fence line, which the footpath intersects in the left-central portion of the photograph. As the footpath makes the bend, it divides in two as it heads downhill to cross a stream. The path with the sharper angle bend is earlier; later travelers used the path with the more obtuse angle bend. Photograph courtesy Thomas Sever and NASA.

Figure 9-10.
Black and white aerial photograph obtained from Costa Rica's Instituto Geografico showing areas near the Silencio cemetery. Note three lines indicating footpaths connecting the cemetery with a spring.

Figure 9-11.
Unprocessed TIMS imagery (Channel 4) of area surrounding Silencio cemetery. Note three parallel lines indicating footpaths between cemetery and spring. These are the same footpaths shown in Figure 9-10. All were confirmed with trenches. Photograph courtesy Thomas Sever and NASA.

disturbed localities. The contribution made by the path studies is based on the fact that the volcanic ash layers, particularly the Unit 55 tephra, will oxidize when exposed to significant solar radiation. Only one trench—Trench 7, between the graveyard and the spring—out of thirty-eight excavated so far, has encountered an oxidized tephra level. In all other cases, the forest canopy was sufficiently closed to inhibit oxidation of the tephra layers exposed by path use and erosion; this indicates a predominantly forested natural environment between sites. Within the village and the habitation sites, tephra layers are often oxidized, sometimes intensely. The most oxidized area found to date is the lower area of the G-150 cemetery, which must have been devoid of vegetation and exposed to direct solar radiation for a significant period.

It appears that the G-150 Silencio cemetery was more than a place to bury the dead (Chap. 6). There is extensive evidence of cooking, in the form of pottery vessels and especially cooking stones, in the cemetery. Stone tools, particularly expedient stone tools, were manufactured, used, and discarded in the graveyard. Palynological evidence indicates that some maize was grown near the graveyard. The forest was cut, particularly in the lower-status area. The footpaths leading in and out of the graveyard provide further evidence of extensive use of that graveyard. Based on the degree of erosion, it is likely that the traffic to and from the spring to the south of the cemetery was relatively heavy, indicating long stays in the graveyard, rather than rapid visits.

Similar footpath networks have been found in various parts of the world, linking settlements, agricultural fields, sources of water, and other resources. Jessup (1981) describes Apo Kayan settlements and fields in tropical Borneo. Jessup (personal communication, 1987) describes similar erosion and incision of major paths connecting those settlements and fields. There, erosion is accelerated by the efforts to keep the paths free of vegetation for a 2 m to 3 m wide swath, primarily so snakes can be seen from a distance. Sheets has seen numerous Guaymi Indian paths in western Panama, which are similarly incised into the tropical clay soils from 1/2 m to 1 1/2 m. The Guaymi also make an effort to keep the central path clear of grass and other weeds by machete swipes as they walk along the paths. Gross (personal communication, 1987) has observed similar footpath erosion and incision in moist tropical areas of the Brazilian Amazon. He has seen the process and the result in the Kayapó area in central Brazil, described by Posey (1983). Posey describes the deliberate siting of villages in ecological transition zones to maximize access to varied resources, and he describes their "vast network (thousands of kilometers) of trails interlacing villages, hunting grounds, gardens, old fields, and natural resource islands" (ibid. 241). Wendt (personal communication, 1986) has observed deeply eroded footpaths in tephra/soil strata on Mount Fuji, in some cases more than 3 m deep.

Footpath networks can provide a direct window on human transportation and communication in prehistory. Their discovery and interpretation in the Arenal area has been facilitated by the volcanic ash layers; efforts will be made over the next few years to modify the field and laboratory methodology to detect and confirm linear features as prehistoric footpaths outside of volcanically active areas, and in less-moist climates.

ACKNOWLEDGMENTS

This research has benefited from the assistance of a number of individuals and institutions. The Earth Resources Laboratory of NASA at the Stennis Space Center in Mississippi has conducted three overflights to acquire the data that provided the basis for the original observation of the footpaths. The staff of the laboratory has been extremely helpful in the acquisition and analysis of these data. Costa Rica's Instituto Geográfico has provided us with excellent black and white aerial photographs of the area, which have provided coverage and time depth otherwise unobtainable. Marilynn Mueller helped with field investigations in 1986. Chuck Wheeler, Ken Weber, and David Wagner all read early drafts of this chapter, and their sharp eyes and pencils are appreciated. The landowners of the area have graciously permitted us to conduct investigations on their property. Luis and Gabriella Jiménez, in addition to allowing our investigations on their property, have kindly offered the use of their house on several occasions. Finally, we would like to thank the Costa Rican field-workers, whose dedication and hard work have made much of this research possible.

10

Ceramic Analysis and Culture History in the Arenal Region

JOHN W. HOOPES

INTRODUCTION

The first attempt to formulate an archaeological chronology based on ceramics for the Greater Nicoya subarea was made by Coe and Baudez (1961, Baudez and Coe 1962). They suggested a succession of four major periods: the Zoned Bichrome, the Early Polychrome, the Middle Polychrome, and the Late Polychrome. Baudez (1967) presented the first detailed description of Greater Nicoya ceramic types. Lange (1971) made use of Baudez and Coe's periodization and Baudez' type descriptions in his research in the Sapoá River Valley. These also formed the basis for Healy's (1974, 1980) analysis of material from the Rivas region of Nicaragua, and Sweeney's (1975) analysis of ceramics from the Santa Elena Peninsula. It should be noted that, of these researchers, Healy made the greatest attempt to adhere to a well-defined type: variety methodology. He made explicit use of a classification that included taxonomic divisions by ware, group, and variety (as opposed to Baudez, whose categories often crosscut these divisions).

Parallels in cultural sequences and recognizable continuities in ceramic horizons from Rivas to the Gulf of Nicoya (Creamer 1983) have been important characteristics of the Greater Nicoya subarea (Lange 1984b). Ceramic sequences have played a key role in the interpretation of the region's prehistory, and their revision and fine-tuning have received a great deal of attention in recent years (Lange et al. 1984; Abel-Vidor et al. 1987). Principal concerns have been (1) "streamlining" lists of ceramic types and type descriptions in order to eliminate redundant categories (Abel-Vidor et al. 1987); (2) documenting regional variation and utilizing ethnohistoric documents (Abel-Vidor 1980, 1981, 1988) to define cultural and geographical subdivisions (e.g., northern and southern sectors) of Greater Nicoya; (3) using compositional analysis to investigate processes of pottery manufacture and distribution (Day 1984; Bishop et al. 1988; Healy 1988); and (4) strengthening chronological correlations (Abel-Vidor et al. 1987).

Although the basic outline of the Greater Nicoya sequence was available in the early 1960s, and an initial ceramic typology for the Atlantic Watershed was suggested in the latter part of that decade (Kennedy 1968), the working ceramic sequence for the Atlantic Watershed of Costa Rica did not appear in its current form until the late 1970s (Snarskis 1976, 1978). A great deal of research has focused on the Central Highlands and Atlantic Watershed regions of Costa Rica (see summaries by Snarskis 1981a, 1984a; Fonseca 1981), and many of the data are relevant to the Arenal area. Unfortunately, much less on ceramic classification has been published for this region than is available for Greater Nicoya.

The archaeology of the volcanic highlands and the Guatuso and San Carlos plains in the north-central portion of Costa Rica is less well known. Research conducted by Snarskis in central San Carlos (1978), by Aguilar in the Arenal area (1984), and by Norr in the Naranjo River Valley (1982–1983) suggests that these zones were occupied from as early as the Middle Formative Period up to the time of European contact. Evidence from the latter part of the sequence indicates that there were important contacts between these north-central regions of Costa Rica and both Greater Nicoya and the Atlantic Watershed; however, the nature of these contacts remains poorly defined.

Material collected during reconnaissance and excavation of sites in the Arenal region demonstrates that the Cordillera region was occupied as early as Paleo-Indian times (Chaps. 1 and 11). Lithics and ceramics suggest a continuous occupation of the region from the Archaic Period through the fifteenth century cal AD.[1] Ceramic analysis and stratigraphic excavations have revealed the existence of an Early Formative (ca. 2000 cal BC), pre–Zoned Bichrome complex associated with the remains of a small village—the earliest known settlement in Costa Rica to date. Pottery from all subsequent periods was recovered in both surface-collected and excavated lots from a variety of sites. The association of ceramic assemblages with dated volcanic stratigraphy has allowed the construction of a ceramic chronology for the Northwestern Cordillera (Hoopes 1984a), a culture area that includes the Arenal basin, the Cordillera de Tilarán, and the Cordillera de Guanacaste.

The Northwestern Cordillera ceramic sequence has important affinities with both the Greater Nicoya and the Atlantic Watershed sequences. It is also distinct in many ways. Its principal characteristics are (1) an Early to Middle Formative Phase whose ceramics bear strong similarities to Snarskis' (1978, 1984a) Chaparrón and La Montaña complexes as well as to other early Central American complexes; (2) an extensive Zoned Bichrome occupation sharing pottery types and a number of stylistic parallels with Greater Nicoya; (3) a late Zoned Bichrome/Early Polychrome transition with ties to both Greater Nicoya and the Atlantic Watershed regions; (4) Middle Polychrome assemblages dominated by local types and decorative modes, supplemented with imported polychromes from Greater Nicoya; and (5) a late occupation characterized by an absence of Nicoya-style polychromes and an emphasis on appliqué decoration, suggesting the existence of strong cultural ties with peoples to the east and south.

The sequence for the Northwestern Cordillera region will benefit from future refinement and further correlations with chronometric dates; however, the data presented here should provide a foundation for future research. While the present study may be interpreted as primarily cultural-historical, the construction and refinement of a working time-space framework is fundamental to further understanding of Costa Rican prehistory.

CERAMIC CHRONOLOGY IN THE ARENAL REGION

While a number of formal and decorative modes are specifically characteristic of pottery from the Northwestern Cordillera, the ceramics of the Arenal area are sufficiently similar to documented assemblages from Greater Nicoya and the Atlantic Watershed that cross-dating with published sequences (e.g., Baudez 1967; Snarskis 1978; Lange et al. 1984; Abel-Vidor et al. 1987; Chap. 1, Fig. 1-8) is possible. Six phases have been defined:

Tilarán (cal AD 1300–1500)—Late Prehistoric Period

Silencio (cal AD 600–1300)—Early/Middle Polychrome Period
Late Arenal (cal AD 0–600)—Late Zoned Bichrome Period
Early Arenal (500 cal BC–cal AD 0)—Early Zoned Bichrome Period
Late Tronadora (1000–500 cal BC)—Middle Formative Period
Early Tronadora (2000–1000 cal BC)—Early Formative Period

METHODOLOGY

We have based the ceramic sequence on the analysis of 12,629 sherds from 43 sites. Almost 75% of these come from stratigraphic excavations, with the remainder from surface collections. We examined ceramics from each of 431 excavation and survey lots individually and recorded information on sherd size, vessel part (rim, body, handle, support, etc.), ceramic type, and modes of decoration, manufacture, and vessel form. We entered data from index cards in the field on an electronic spreadsheet (Lotus 1-2-3) using a portable computer. Subsequent analysis was performed on an IBM-compatible personal computer. The spreadsheet contains tabulations of ceramic types, varieties, and modal combinations from each lot. When possible, each lot was assigned a number corresponding to its location in the various soil and tephra units of the Silencio stratigraphic sequence (e.g., 10, 20, 30, 50; Mueller 1984b; Chap. 2).

Using data base and statistical functions, we sorted and combined lots by site, operation, stratum, phase designation, and assemblage. Once data were tabulated, it was possible to manipulate large volumes of data quickly and easily. The computer allowed for the interpretation of thousands of potsherds by electronic rather than physical manipulation. This methodology was particularly useful in the field laboratory, where it was possible to evaluate ceramic frequencies during the course of fieldwork.[2]

The classification can be understood as a "modified type: variety" system. We adopted this system in the interests of compatibility with published descriptions of ceramics from Greater Nicoya (Baudez 1967; Lange 1971; Sweeney 1975; Healy 1980; Lange et al. 1984; Abel-Vidor et al. 1987). The method differs from the type: variety system commonly used in Mesoamerica (Smith, Willey, and Gifford 1960; Sabloff and Smith 1969) because it uses an abbreviated taxonomic hierarchy. To date, Healy (1980) has been the only researcher in Greater Nicoya to use "wares" and "groups" in a systematic fashion. In other references, the principal unit of classification is the "type" rather than the "group."

In lieu of detailed compositional information, I have been hesitant to postulate distinct "wares." The level of "group" is useful in the classification of ceramics that have identifiable characteristics of surface finish but do not carry sufficient information to allow identification at the level of "type." In general, most ceramics are well preserved and can be classified at the level of type. In our assemblages, the most useful "group" designation is one that would subsume Los Hermanos Beige and the varieties of Mojica Impressed, all of which share modes of form and surface finish. Because group designations have not been formulated as a taxonomic level in the classification of *all* of our ceramics, however, definitions at the group level are not included in the ceramic descriptions here. The most recent classification of Greater Nicoya ceramics (Lange and Bishop n.d.) does not utilize the group category, and the methodology we use here is designed to be compatible with the available comparative data.

A taxonomic level that *has* proved useful is that of "variety." Certain combinations of modes fell under existing type descriptions, but variation within these types was believed to be geographically or chronologically significant. In some cases, we have defined varieties to distinguish between these subcategories.

THE CERAMIC SAMPLE

The principal sites excavated during the 1984 season date to the Silencio and Tilarán phases. The Silencio cemetery (G-150), Las Piedras (G-152), Neblina (G-151), Dos Armadillos (G-154), and other sites yielded burial and domestic assemblages that helped correlate cultural occupations with the stratigraphic sequence from Arenal Volcano. Because Arenal's tephras were preserved as visible horizons, it was possible to use C-14 dates and stratified assemblages from individual sites to define an idealized regional stratigraphic sequence (Hoopes 1984a; Chap. 2). At El Silencio, whole vessels from burial offerings and sherds from burial and architectural fill provided information on Silencio Phase ceramics and interregional exchange. At Dos Armadillos, a horizontal deposit overlain by a well-preserved tephra layer provided a sealed and dated domestic assemblage from the Tilarán Phase.

The 1985 season provided the most important information on the Tronadora and Arenal phases. Tronadora Vieja (G-163) and Sitio Bolívar (G-164) each had primarily single-component surface assemblages (Tronadora and Arenal phases, respectively). Excavations at the two sites were extremely fruitful. Tronadora Vieja provided more than seven hundred diagnostic sherds, over 60% of them dating to the Tronadora Phase. Sitio Bolívar yielded an assemblage of almost six thousand diagnostic sherds in deposits pertaining almost exclusively to the latter half of the Arenal Phase. Domestic and mortuary features were identified at both sites, and the ceramic classes present indicated a wide variety of activities.

The ceramic assemblages represent a variety of cultural and depositional contexts as well as time periods. Given the location of the study area—on and near the Continental Divide and between the Cordillera de Guanacaste and the Cordillera de Tilarán—we expected a blending of culture traits. The ability to make extensive use of crossdating assisted our interpretations of sequences in the Northwestern Cordillera and facilitated an independent check on established sequences from neighboring regions. Ceramic analysis also provided important insights into interregional cultural change and interaction.

THE TRONADORA PHASE

The Early (2000–1000 cal BC) and Late (1000–500 cal BC) facets of the Tronadora Phase represent the earliest dated ceramic-producing culture in Costa Rica. They are characterized by the Tronadora Complex, an assemblage of compositional, formal, and stylistic modes (Hoopes 1985, 1987). The most common vessel forms are massive *"olla-tecomates"* (*tecomate*-like vessels with exteriorly bolstered rims); *tecomates* with comma-shaped rims; flat-bottomed vessels with cylindrical and "hyperboloid" profiles; and squat, necked jars. The pottery from this phase shares important modes with other early complexes from Costa Rica and Nicaragua as well as with those from Mesoamerica and northwestern South America. It is also distinctive, however, indicating that strong regional traditions of ceramic production were present in the Intermediate Area at least as early as the second millennium cal BC.

The Tronadora Complex stands out as a unified stylistic assemblage that is readily separated from assemblages of other phases in the Arenal region (Hoopes 1984a, 1985). It is similar to other early Costa Rican ceramic complexes, particularly Chaparrón, from the north-central San Carlos plains, and La Montaña, from near Turrialba (Fig. 10-1) (Snarskis 1978, 1984a). Norr's (1982–1983) Naranjo Phase ceramics from the Naranjo River and pottery from the site of La Pochota near Cañas (Odio 1989) are the most closely related, followed by Haberland's (1966) Dinarte ceramics from Ometepe Island in Nicaragua. Important affinities are also evident between Tronadora ceramics and pottery from Curré (Corrales 1985, 1989), in the Térraba–Coto Brús region. There are important similarities between Tronadora ceramics and those of Greater Nicoya, especially types Schettel Incised and Bocana Incised Bichrome of the Loma B Phase (Lange 1980a); however, direct comparisons show that Tronadora and Loma B are not identical. The later dates for Loma B assemblages and the presence of Bocana Incised Bicrome in Arenal Phase assemblages suggest that Loma B may have developed out of Tronadora Complex traditions (Hoopes 1987). In this respect, ceramics and associated C-14 dates from Tronadora Vieja provide the first evidence of stylistic traditions predating the Zoned Bichrome Period in northwestern Costa Rica. Tronadora ceramics also share a number of important modes with early ceramics from Guatemala, Nicaragua, Panama, and Colombia.

The type site of the Tronadora Complex is Tronadora Vieja (G-163; Hoopes 1987:43–97; Chap. 4), located during a reconnaissance of the southern perimeter of Lake Arenal in March 1984 (Bradley et al. 1984). Excavations at the site in 1985 demonstrated that, although some material from the later Arenal and Tilarán phases was present, the principal occupation of the site occurred during the Tronadora Phase.

TRONADORA PHASE DIAGNOSTIC MODES AND TYPES

Ceramic types as analytical units provide a convenient way of expressing frequently recurring sets of modes or attributes for purposes of interregional as well as intrasite comparisons. So far, with the exception of broad type classes such as the Atlantic Red-Filled Black Group or the Chaparrón Zoned Red on Brown Type (Snarskis 1978)—the latter of which might better be understood at the group level as well—Middle Formative Costa Rican ceramics have been analyzed and quantified only at the level of modes. To assist with the definition and identification of Tronadora ce-

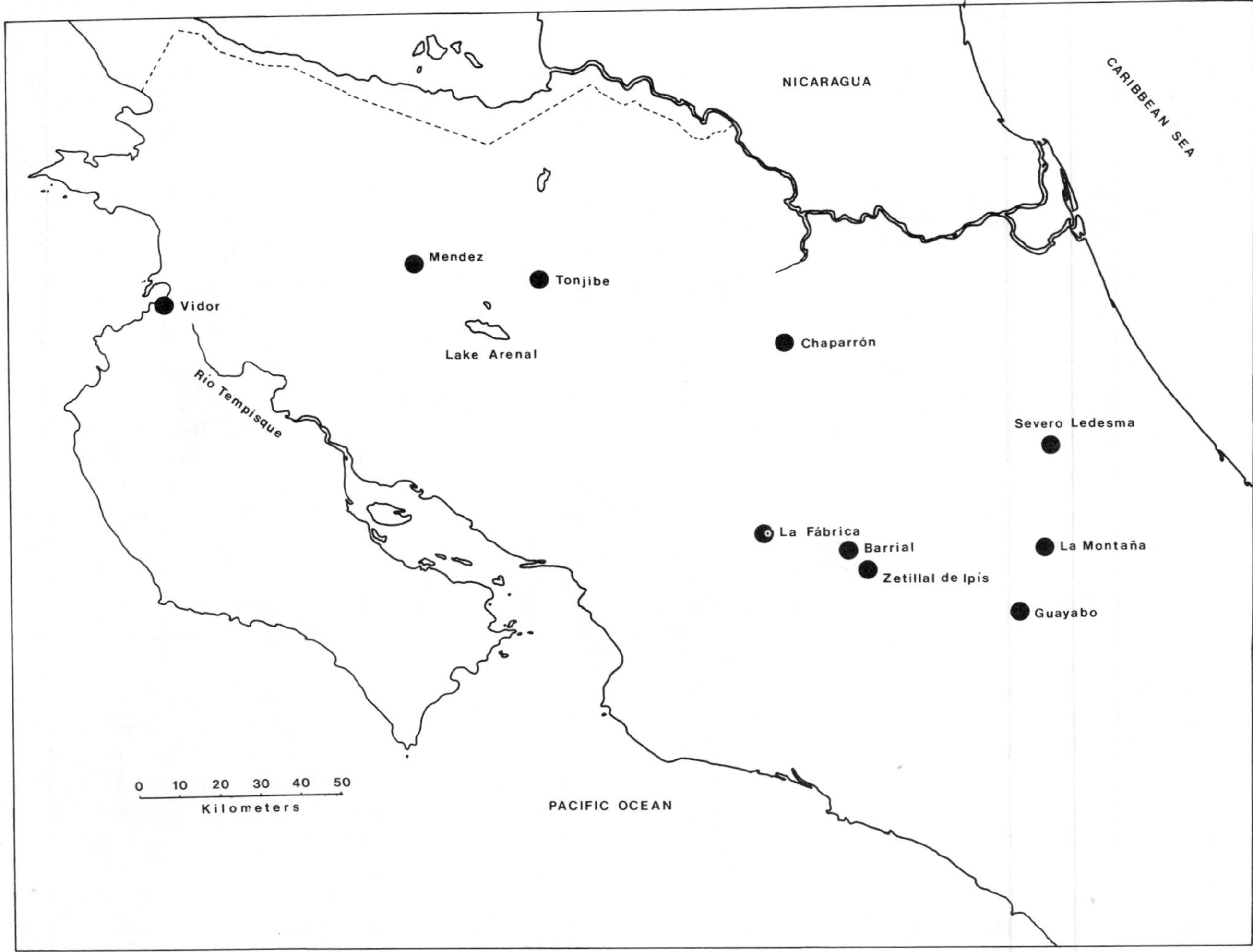

Figure 10-1.
Map of Costa Rica showing sites where Early and Middle Formative ceramics (Tronadora, Chaparrón, La Montaña, Barva, and Curré) have been reported. Map by John Hoopes.

ramics, I shall first discuss ceramic modes diagnostic of this phase; however, there are also certain sets of modes that may be labeled as specific ceramic types.

Diagnostic Modes of the Tronadora Phase

Most modes of the Tronadora Complex[3] are shared with those of Snarskis' (1978) Chaparrón and La Montaña complexes, as already noted (Hoopes 1984a). Excavations in 1985 yielded a collection of almost four hundred Tronadora sherds and provided stratigraphic data and C-14 dates to support their early placement. The chief diagnostic modes of the Tronadora Complex are as follows (alphanumeric designations refer to modes described in Snarskis [1978]).

Form

1. Large, incurving-rim, neckless jars (*olla-tecomates*) with exteriorly thickened, massive rounded or angular rims (R11).

2. Large, incurving-rim bowls or *tecomates*. Comma-shaped rims are thicker than vessel walls. These often have round-bottomed grooving along the lip and rim exterior (R6).

3. Squat, restricted-neck jars with exteriorly thickened rims. Decoration is usually found on the exterior neck, immediately beneath the rim.

4. Tall, hyperboloid or cylindrical vessels with flat bases. In the former, the walls gradually curve inward, and the base is always the widest part of the vessel (Snarskis 1978: fig. 25a).

Decoration

1. Round-bottomed groove incising, often used to outline horizontal bands of red paint (D10).

2. Round or oblique punctation in zones outlined with groove incising (D17), found beneath the rim on exteriors of both bowls and jars.

3. Red-painted strip appliqué emphasized by gouge incision, executed on the vessel body when the paste was soft. Strip appliqué can be linear and horizontal or can form curvilinear designs and figures. Unfortunately, the latter type has been found only in small fragments; full-design motifs are unknown.

4. Wavy shell-edge stamping (D18). This mode has two forms. The first is as a series of vertical impressions in a circumferential band around the vessel exterior, outlined with groove incising. The second is as a fine (sometimes barely visible) stamping or rocker stamping on an unslipped surface, used to fill large zones when the paste was soft and smooth.

5. Sharp-edged, multiple incisions, sometimes infilled with red ocher pigment. This mode recalls incision on Middle Formative ceramics from Mesoamerica and is closely related to Snarskis' Atlantic Red-Filled Black Group (ibid.: 76). One example from Tronadora Vieja has a curvilinear design, and the only rims known with this mode are direct and unthickened, probably from cylindrical bowls.

6. Plastic decorations including punctate, buttonlike appliqué or *pastillage* (ibid.: fig. 10jj), cord marking (ibid.: fig. 24x), and circular reed stamping (ibid.: fig. 24dd).

Paste

There appears to be a much greater variety of pastes in Tronadora materials than in either Chaparrón or La Montaña. Snarskis describes La Montaña paste, the most outstanding characteristic of which is the presence of gray particles, up to 1 mm in size, identified as a possible basalt temper (ibid.: 71). According to Snarskis, "virtually every Middle Formative sherd . . . whether from Turrialba, the Línea Vieja, the Central Valley or San Carlos, has possessed this grey-speckled paste" (ibid.).

This is not true for our collection. Most Tronadora Phase sherds are in fact "grey-speckled"; however, the gray-to-white specks are a weathered pumice rather than a basalt. There are a number of sherds in clear Tronadora style that do not have the characteristic Chaparrón and La Montaña paste. Variations include a fine-textured orange paste with few inclusions; a light brown paste with white inclusions, which are probably weathered plagioclase; and a fine-textured white paste. Tephra inclusions are ubiquitous in ceramics from *all* phases in the Cordillera de Tilarán.

Ceramic Types of the Tronadora Phase

Given the size of the assemblage from Tronadora Vieja, it has been possible to define preliminary type designations.[4] Large portions of whole vessels are known only for Zetillal Shell-Stamped.

Tonjibe Beige

This is the most common in Tronadora Phase assemblages (Figs. 10-2A–D, 10-3; Hoopes 1987: fig. 6.1). It is characterized by large *olla-tecomates* with thickly expanded rims (R11). The late Enrique Herra found sherds of this type at Palenque Tonjibe in San Rafael de Guatuso (Snarskis, personal communication, 1985). It is also known from Chaparrón and La Montaña assemblages (Snarskis 1978). Tonjibe Beige vessels were often massive, and their poorly fired thick rims frequently fracture into several small pieces. Rims are usually painted with a hard, glossy red paint on the lip. Well-preserved examples show a surface finish that is whitish-gray in color. Pastes contain a high proportion of gray-to-white particles, possibly pumice. The unusually large size, weight, and volume of these vessels (rim diameters range from 30 cm to 50 cm) suggest that they may have been used for brewing alcoholic beverages, such as *chicha*. Wide, thickened rims may have served as grips for lifting and moving these heavy vessels.

Tronadora Incised

This type is the second most common in Tronadora Phase assemblages (Figs. 10-2E–K, 10-4; Hoopes 1987:fig. 6.2, pl. 6.1:A-G). Similar ceram-

Figure 10-2.
Tronadora Phase: Tonjibe Beige rim sherds, A–D; Tronadora Incised rim sherds, E–K. Sherd widths: A, 10.3 cm; B, 9.2 cm; C, 5.6 cm; D, 4.5 cm; E, 6.6 cm; F, 5.9 cm; G, 7.3 cm; H, 3.9 cm; I, 4 cm; J, 5.5 cm; K, 6 cm. Photographs by John Hoopes.

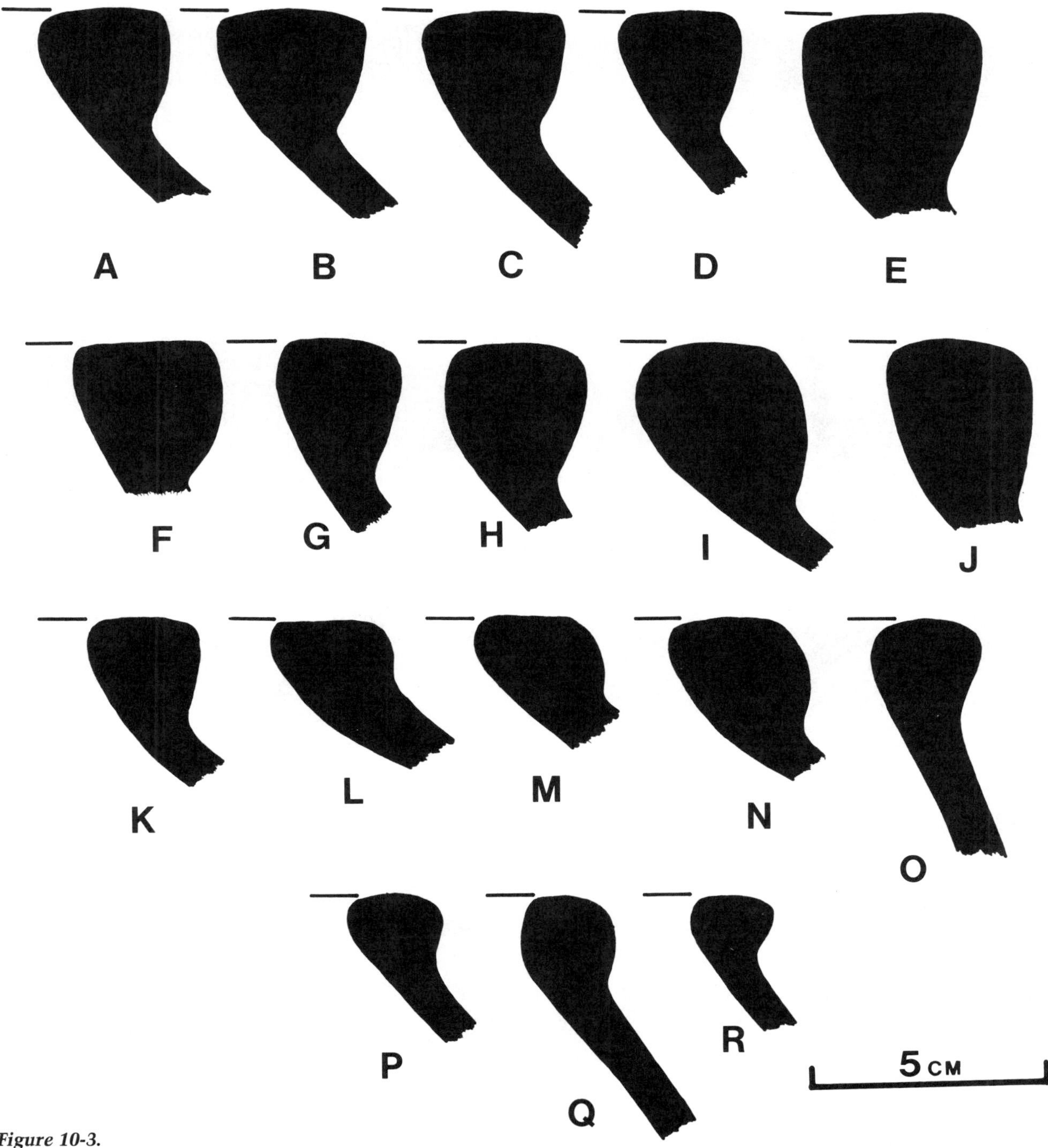

Figure 10-3.
Tonjibe Beige rim profiles. All are from Tronadora Vieja (G-163). Proveniences (by operation and lot): A (K4), B (I5), C (M1), D (V52), E (H23), F (P3), G (V8), H (H21), I (M6/1), J (M2), K (L2), L (T4), M (M2), N (L13), O (W18), P (P3), Q (R2), R (H4). Figures by John Hoopes.

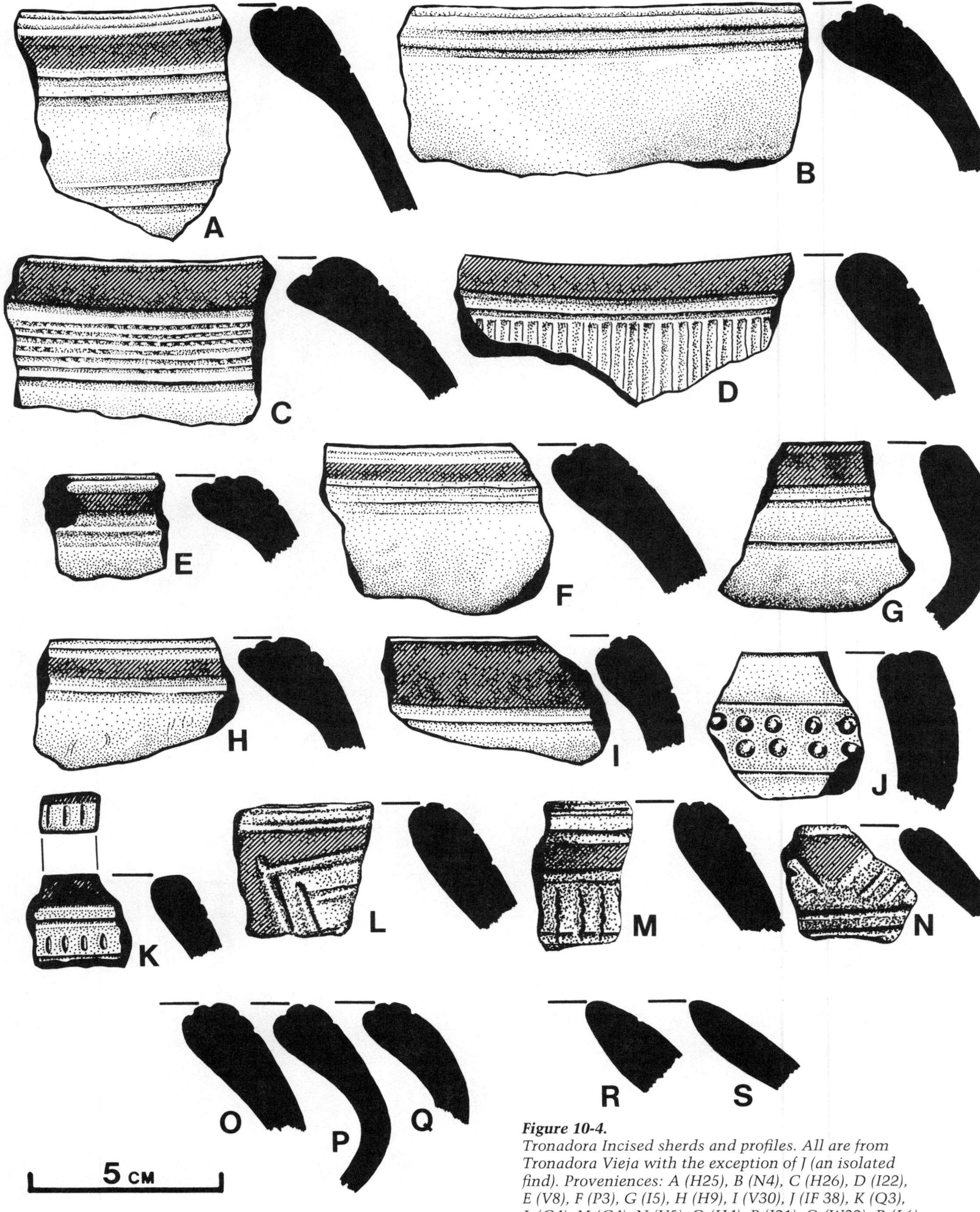

Figure 10-4.
Tronadora Incised sherds and profiles. All are from Tronadora Vieja with the exception of J (an isolated find). Proveniences: A (H25), B (N4), C (H26), D (I22), E (V8), F (P3), G (I5), H (H9), I (V30), J (IF 38), K (Q3), L (G4), M (G4), N (V5), O (H4), P (I21), Q (W32), R (L6), S (H6). Figures by John Hoopes.

ics from La Montaña and Chaparrón (cf. Snarskis 1978: fig. 12f–i; fig. 22a–f; fig. 23w) are identified as La Montaña Fugitive Red-on-Cream and Chaparrón Red-on-Brown. Tronadora Incised is characterized by *tecomates* and incurving-rim bowls expanded on the interior lip (R6), round-bottomed grooving (especially on the vessel lip), and red-painted bands delineated with grooving (D10). Surface finish is smooth and often white. Red paint, while frequently eroded, is bright and polished on well-preserved examples. Tronadora Incised has analogues in Ocós (Coe 1961) and early Zoned Bichrome assemblages (cf. Schettel Incised; Healy 1980:fig. 103), where grooved rims without the addition of red-painted zones appear.

Tigra Grooved-Punctate

This type is characterized by a combination of round or oblique punctations, delineated by horizontal lines of groove incision (Figs. 10-5, 10-6; Hoopes 1987:fig. 6.3, pl. 6.1:P–Z). Punctation is confined to the vessel neck or areas immediately beneath the rim on vessel exteriors. Vessel rims are painted red. Unlike the aforementioned types, Tigra Grooved-Punctate is not characterized by a single vessel form. Punctate decoration appears on both *tecomates* (Snarskis 1978: fig. 23s–u) and squat, necked jars. Sherds of this type appear in Chaparrón assemblages, but *not* in La Montaña. General similarities in incised and punctate decoration suggest that Tigra Grooved-Punctate may be an ancestor of the Catalina Phase–type Huila Zoned-Punctate (Baudez 1967), which belongs to the Greater Nicoya ceramic sphere.

Zetillal Shell-Stamped

The type vessel for Zetillal Shell-Stamped (Figs. 10-7, 10-8; Hoopes 1987:fig. 6.4, pl. 6.3:K, M–S) was found at the site of Zetillal de Ipis near San José (Snarskis 1978:69–70, fig. 25a). A second example—the only other complete vessel known—was excavated from the lakeshore at Tronadora Vieja. This type is characterized by the use of light shell-edge stamping on tall, hyperboloid vessels with outflaring, flat bases. These two modes almost always appear together. The distinctive stamping technique consists of a gentle marking of the soft clay surface, sometimes with a slight rocking motion. It is not found on any other vessel form. It is closely related to rocker stamping on Ocós sherds from the Pacific Coast of Guatemala (Coe 1961). Other decorative modes include horizontal and vertical groove incising. This usually appears around the neck and base, demarcating longitudinal zones. Appliqué pellets are occasionally present, as are deeper shell-edge stamping and punctation.

Snarskis notes, "The thick-walled basal angle and flat bottom are especially diagnostic, not appearing in any other period in the [Atlantic] regional sequence" (ibid.:70). Snarskis believes these vessels may have been pottery drums because of their elongated shape; however, their closed bases and the lack of any perforation would have inhibited resonance, making this function unlikely. Some of our examples have blackened interiors, suggesting they were used for cooking. The distinctive shape indicates a different function from the round bowls or *tecomates* in use at the same time. These may have been drinking vessels.

Tajo Gouge-Incised

This type (Fig. 10-9; Hoopes 1987:pl. 6.1:H–O) is defined by the use of red-painted strip appliqué the shape and texture of which are emphasized by a wide gouge incising, done when the paste was soft and pliable. There are two main classes of execution: (1) the use of simple red-painted appliqué strips in horizontal bands; and (2) the creation of unusual curvilinear patterns using gouge incision to emphasize contours and shapes. Pastes are usually a fine cream or white, sometimes with a reduced core, and the use of bright red paint on the raised appliqué design gives this ceramic a striking appearance.

Unfortunately, we could not identify a single rim sherd with the distinctive decoration. For this reason, vessel form is largely unknown. Most sherds indicate a globular shape, and the smoothness of their interior surfaces suggests bowls rather than closed jars. Tajo Gouge-Incised and Zetillal Shell-Stamped are the only Tronadora Phase ceramics decorated extensively on the vessel body rather than simply on the neck or rim, and there is little doubt that they both had specialized functions.

To date, this type is known only from the Arenal area. The curvilinear decoration on Tajo Gouge-Incised may be distantly related to carved designs on Olmec ceramics such as those from the San Lorenzo Phase (Coe and Diehl 1980), but a clear relationship cannot be established at present.

Figure 10-5.
Tronadora Phase: Tigra Grooved-Punctate. A–D: rim sherds; E–P: body sherds. Sherd widths: A, 5.3 cm, B, 4.3 cm; C, 4.2 cm; D, 4.1 cm; E, 4.1 cm; F, 4.3 cm; G, 4.7 cm; H, 5.1 cm; I, 3.2 cm; J, 3.4 cm; K, 3.5 cm; L, 3.5 cm; M, 3 cm; N, 2.8 cm; O, 2.8 cm; P, 2.7 cm. Photographs by John Hoopes.

Discussion

As noted earlier, the predominant vessel form of the Tronadora Complex is the bolstered-rim *olla-tecomate*. Tapering and comma-shaped rim profiles are also present. *Tecomates* are widespread throughout the Americas during the Formative Period, and the broad distribution of this form has stimulated much research on the early diffusion of culture and ideas in the Americas (J. Ford 1969; Myers 1978). *Tecomates* in the Tronadora assemblage suggest the participation of Costa Rican cultures in Formative patterns that appear throughout Nuclear America between 4000 and 1500 cal BC.

None of the sherds from Tronadora Vieja are as "primitive" or poor in quality as either Pox (Brush 1965) or Purrón (MacNeish et al. 1970) ceramics from Mexico, or the majority of Monagrillo ceramics from Panama (Willey and McGimsey 1954).

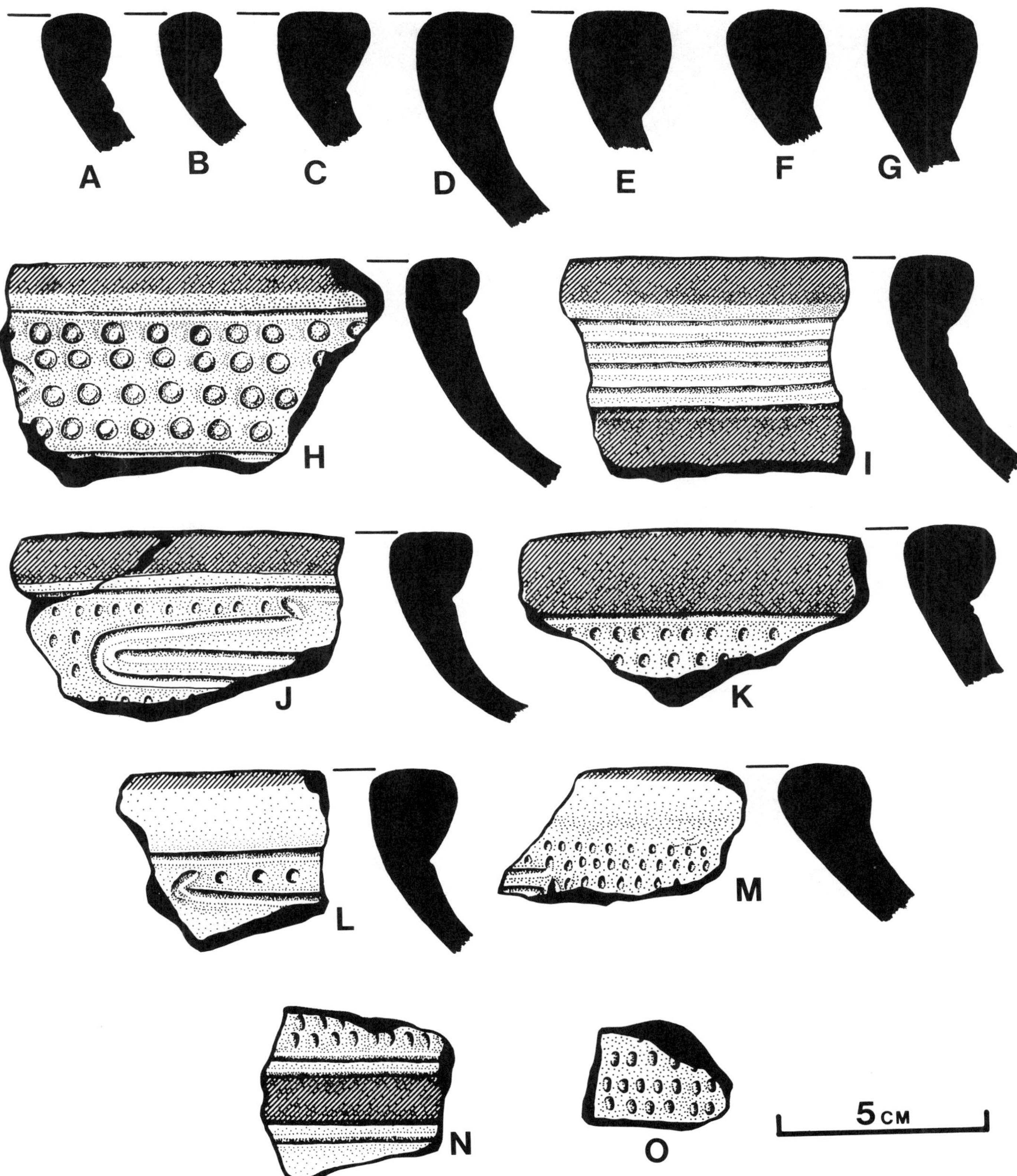

Figure 10-6.
Tigra Grooved-Punctate (A–G, J–O); reed-impressed jar (H); squat, groove-incised jar (I). All sherds are from Tronadora Vieja. Proveniences: A (L2), B (V8), C (H48), D (W18), E (L10), F (H3), G (P3), H (W3), I (W16), J (L2), K (I23), L (W16), M (W34), N (W18), O (L14). Figures by John Hoopes.

Figure 10-7.
Tronadora Phase: Zetillal Shell-Stamped. A–B: rim sherds; C–I: body sherds; K–L: base sherds. Sherd widths: A, 4.6 cm; B, 4.4 cm; C, 3.0 cm; D, 3.3 cm; E, 4.2 cm; F, 3.1 cm; G, 3.6 cm; H, 4.9 cm; I, 4.5 cm; J, cylindrical vessel fragment; K, 4.9 cm; L, 5.2 cm. Height of J, 21.5 cm. Photographs by John Hoopes.

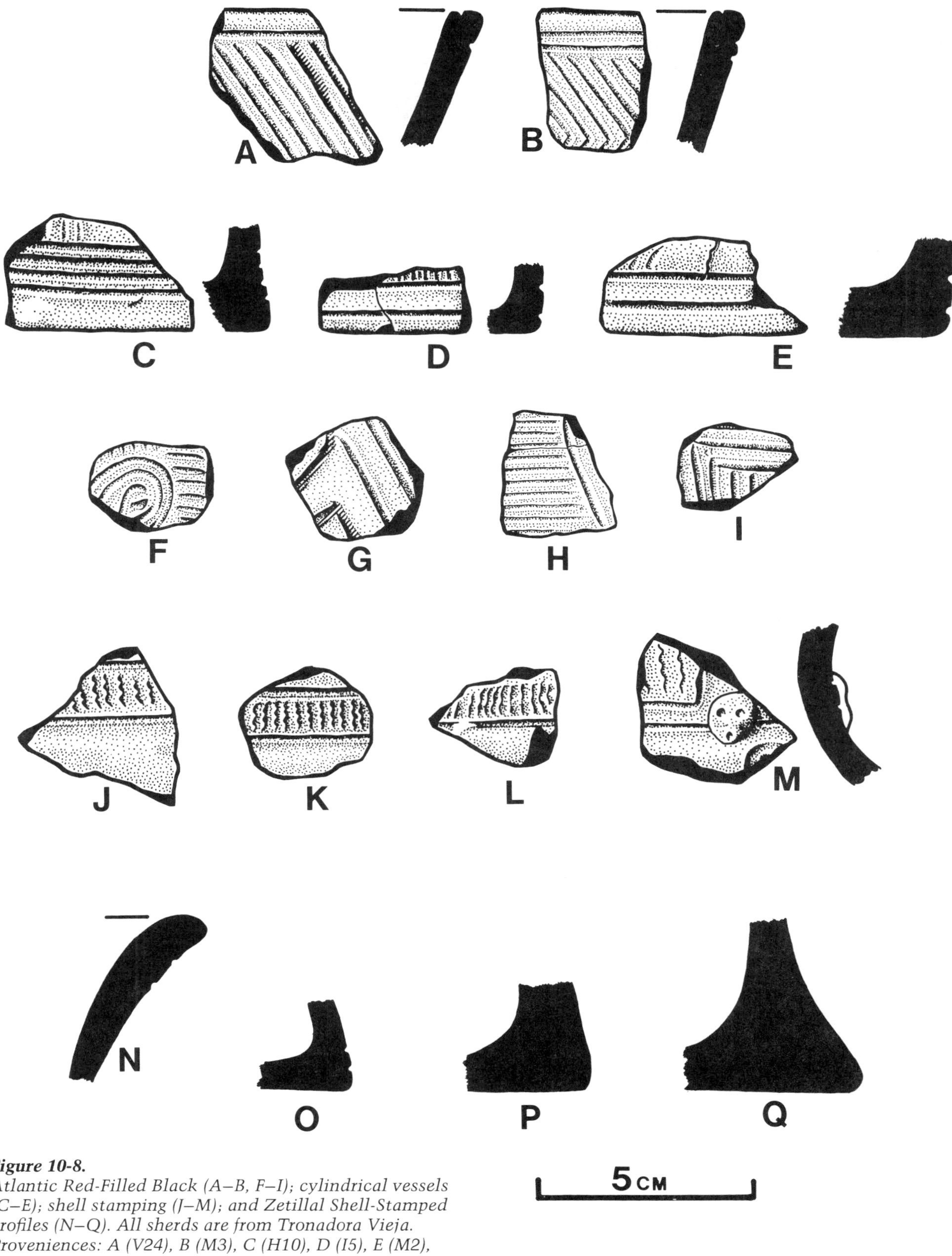

Figure 10-8.
Atlantic Red-Filled Black (A–B, F–I); cylindrical vessels (C–E); shell stamping (J–M); and Zetillal Shell-Stamped profiles (N–Q). All sherds are from Tronadora Vieja. Proveniences: A (V24), B (M3), C (H10), D (I5), E (M2), F (L14), G (I11), H (W7), I (V8), J (V8), K (W18), L (W28), M (W3), N (H5), O (Q3), P (I20), Q (W3). Figures by John Hoopes.

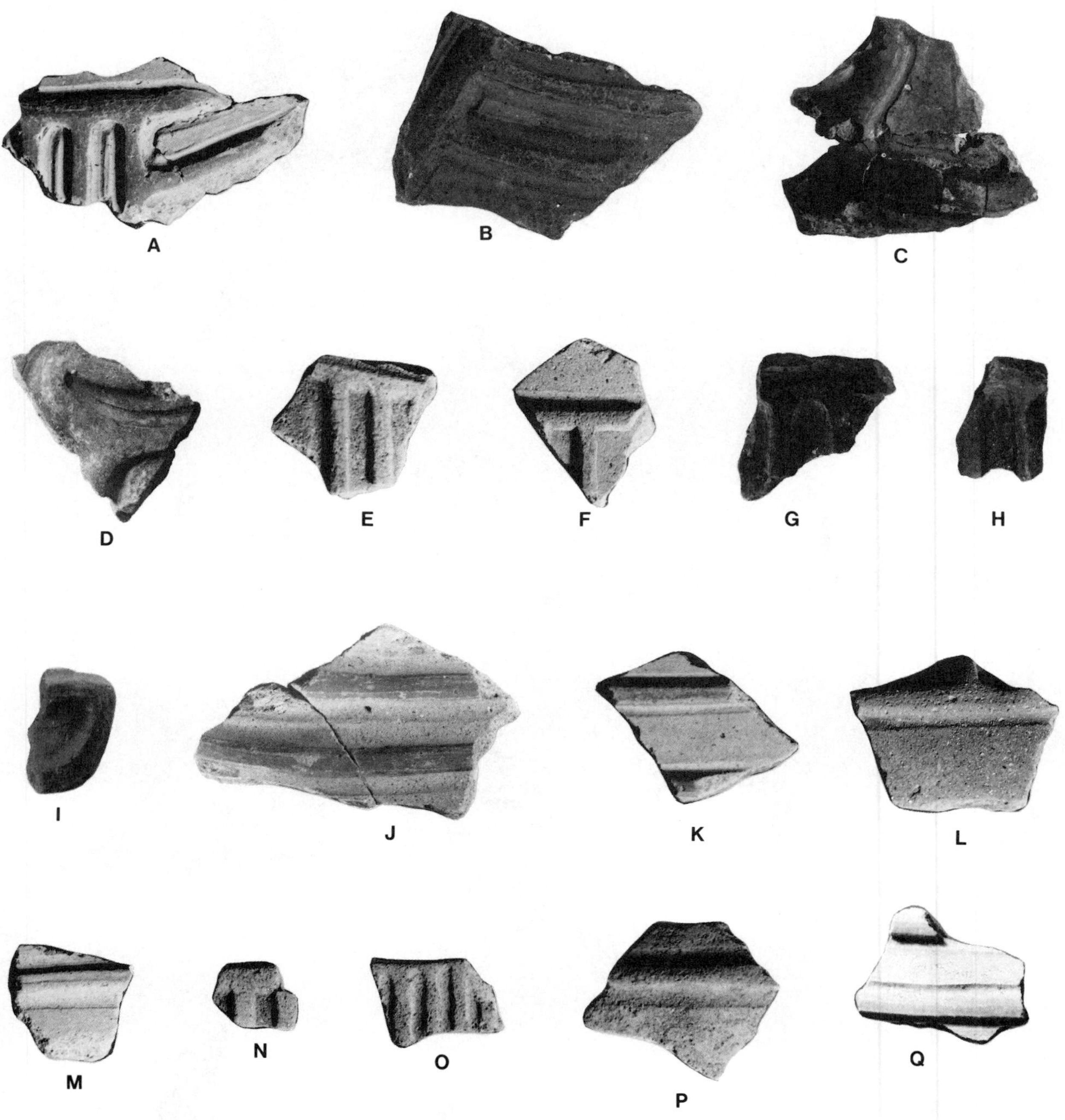

Figure 10-9.
Tronadora Phase: Tajo Gouge-Incised. A–Q: body sherds. Sherd widths: A, 7.5 cm; B, 7 cm; C, 6.2 cm; D, 4.4 cm; E, 3.8 cm; F, 3.5 cm; G, 3.2 cm; H, 2.0 cm; I, 1.8 cm; J, 7.0 cm; K, 5.0 cm; L, 5.2 cm; M, 3.1 cm; N, 2.1 cm; O, 3.2 cm; P, 4.7 cm; Q, 4.3 cm. Photographs by John Hoopes.

The assemblage gives the impression of a mature execution of the potter's craft rather than a weakly developed and incipient technology. Pastes are well fired and vessel forms demonstrate a high level of sophistication.

Important modes that Tronadora Phase ceramics share with other Early and Middle Formative assemblages include the use of round-bottomed grooving, heavy punctation, shell stamping (sometimes rocker stamping), and red zoning (Figs. 10-10, 10-11). In Panama, these appear on Monagrillo and Sarigua Phase ceramics (ibid.). In Mesoamerica, they are diagnostic of Barra and Ocós ceramics from the Pacific Coast of Guatemala and Chiapas (Green and Lowe 1967; Lowe 1975; Coe 1961), Ajalpan ceramics from the Tehuacán Valley (MacNeish et al. 1970), and other Early Formative assemblages (cf. Lowe 1978). Side-by-side comparisons of Tronadora ceramics and type collections of Panamanian and Guatemalan pottery indicate that the Costa Rican sherds are far more similar to Ocós ceramics than are any of the Panamanian examples. While some Ocós pottery, most notably the thin-walled, sharply-incurving "pumpkin" *tecomates*, has no parallels in the Tronadora assemblage, others are virtually identical. Among these are sherds with rocker-stamped and shell-stamped decoration, punctation, and groove incision, especially on vessel rims. Open bowls with bright red rims from both assemblages are close in form, color, and paste, although specular hematite—found on the Ocós ceramics—has not been identified on Tronadora pottery.

The small sample and apparent mixing in relevant stratigraphic deposits make it difficult to say with certainty which modes or types are characteristic of the Early versus the Late Tronadora Phase. At present, there is *no* stratigraphic evidence available to support the division of the Tronadora Phase modes into early and later facets. Their separation is based on broader comparisons with assemblages from other parts of Nuclear America (Hoopes 1987). Modes of form and decoration that are shared by Tronadora, Barra, and Ocós (as well as by early South American complexes such as Tesca, Canapote, Barlovento, and Machalilla) (Bischof 1972; Meggers et al. 1965) are characteristic of the Early Tronadora Phase (2000–1000 cal BC). Tonjibe Beige, Tronadora Incised, and Zetillal Shell-Stamped probably first appear during this period. The Late Tronadora Phase is characterized by modes that are transitional into Loma B Zoned Bichrome (Early Arenal) types. These include combinations of grooving and bichroming similar to Bocana Incised Bichrome. It is likely that Tronadora modes similar to "Olmec" or other Middle Formative ceramics, such as the unusual Tajo Gouge-Incised decoration and sherds infilled with ocher (Snarskis' "Atlantic Red-Filled Black" category), also date to the Late Tronadora Phase (1000–500 cal BC).

The two facets also assume a continuity between the Tronadora and the Arenal phases. Given a 1,500-year hiatus in the C-14 chronology, however, there is a strong possibility that Tronadora Vieja was not continuously occupied between the Tronadora and the Arenal phases. The persistence of round-bottomed grooving and punctation into the Arenal Phase blurs the transition between the Tronadora and the Arenal phases. Given an early date for Loma B ceramics, it is possible that the Arenal-type Bocana Incised Bichrome overlaps the Late Tronadora Phase. However, characteristics of Early Arenal ceramics that are *not* found in Tronadora include vessels with supports; a predominance of vertical, rather than horizontal, groove incision; red-painted zones and decoration that are not sharply zoned with incision; and multiple, "combed" incisions.

DATING THE TRONADORA PHASE

Eight C-14 dates are available from the Tronadora Vieja site, four of which pertain to the preceramic Fortuna Phase, and three of which are from ceramic-bearing contexts. (The correct association of the eighth date is unclear.) Two of the dates for Tronadora Phase ceramics are earlier by 1,000 years than any other dates for Costa Rican ceramics; however, they are similar to dates that have been obtained for comparable Early Formative ceramic complexes from Ecuador, Panama, Colombia, and Guatemala.

The earliest ceramic-producing inhabitants of Tronadora Vieja occupied the same living surface as preceding Archaic cultures. This was probably a thin, tropical-forest soil on top of Aguacate Formation clays. Tronadora Phase occupation continued through the initial eruptions of Arenal Volcano, which deposited large quantities of tephra in the Arenal area and contributed to the formation of fertile soils.

The earliest C-14 dates at Tronadora Vieja are associated with lithic artifacts and debitage embedded in the top of the Aguacate Formation. The dates range from 3609–3450 cal BC (Tx-5275) to 3014–2590 cal BC ± 310 (Tx-5274) and date the latter portion of the Fortuna Phase (the Archaic,

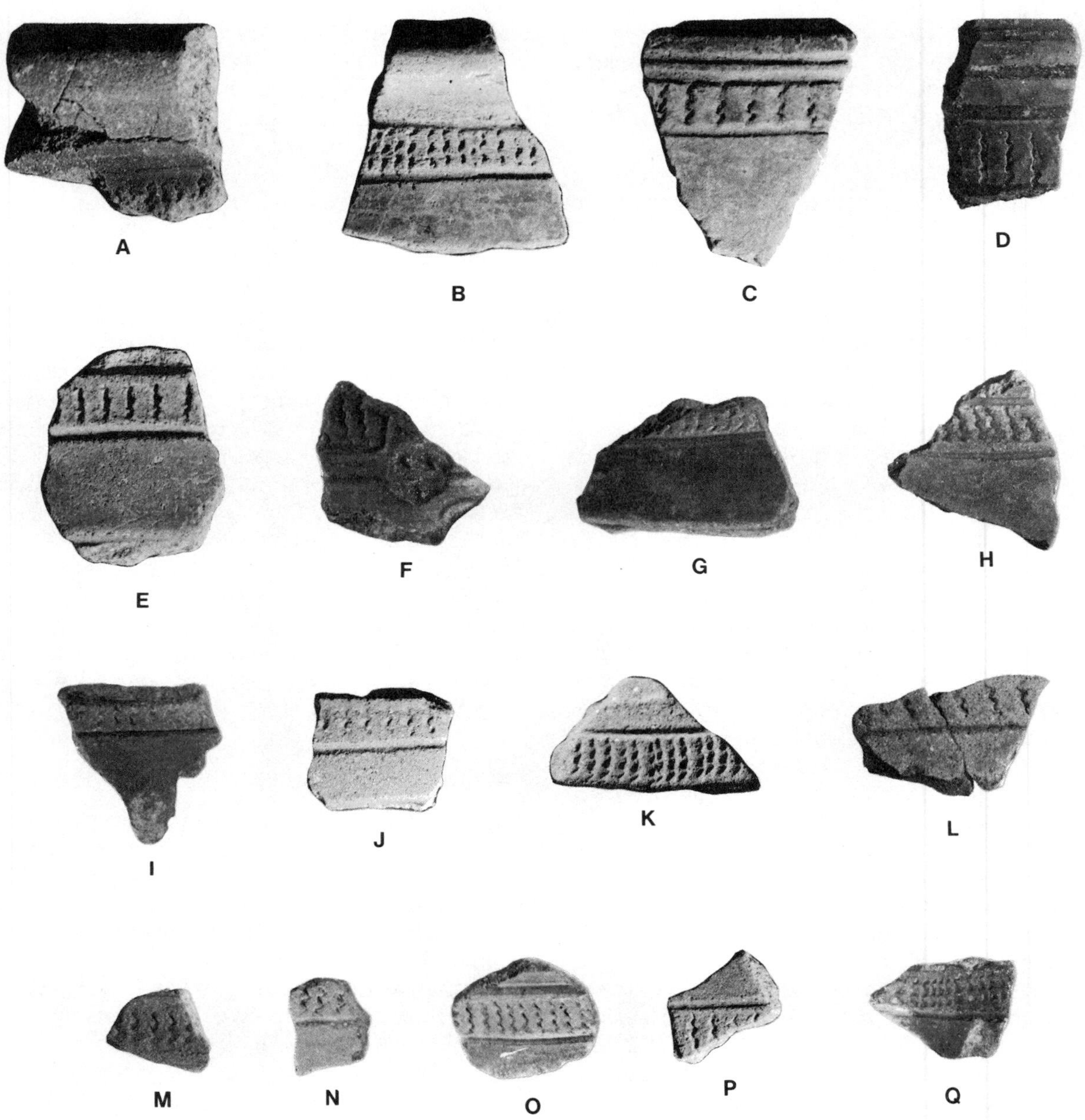

Figure 10-10.
Tronadora Phase: Unnamed Shell-Stamped. A–D: rim sherds; E–Q: body sherds. Sherd widths: A, 4.6 cm; B, 4.5 cm; C, 4.3 cm; D, 2.9 cm; E, 3.7 cm; F, 3.8 cm; G, 4.6 cm; H, 3.6 cm; I, 3.5 cm; J, 2.8 cm; K, 4.3 cm; L, 4.2 cm; M, 2.1 cm; N, 2.7 cm; O, 3.0 cm; P, 2.3 cm; Q, 3 cm. Photographs by John Hoopes.

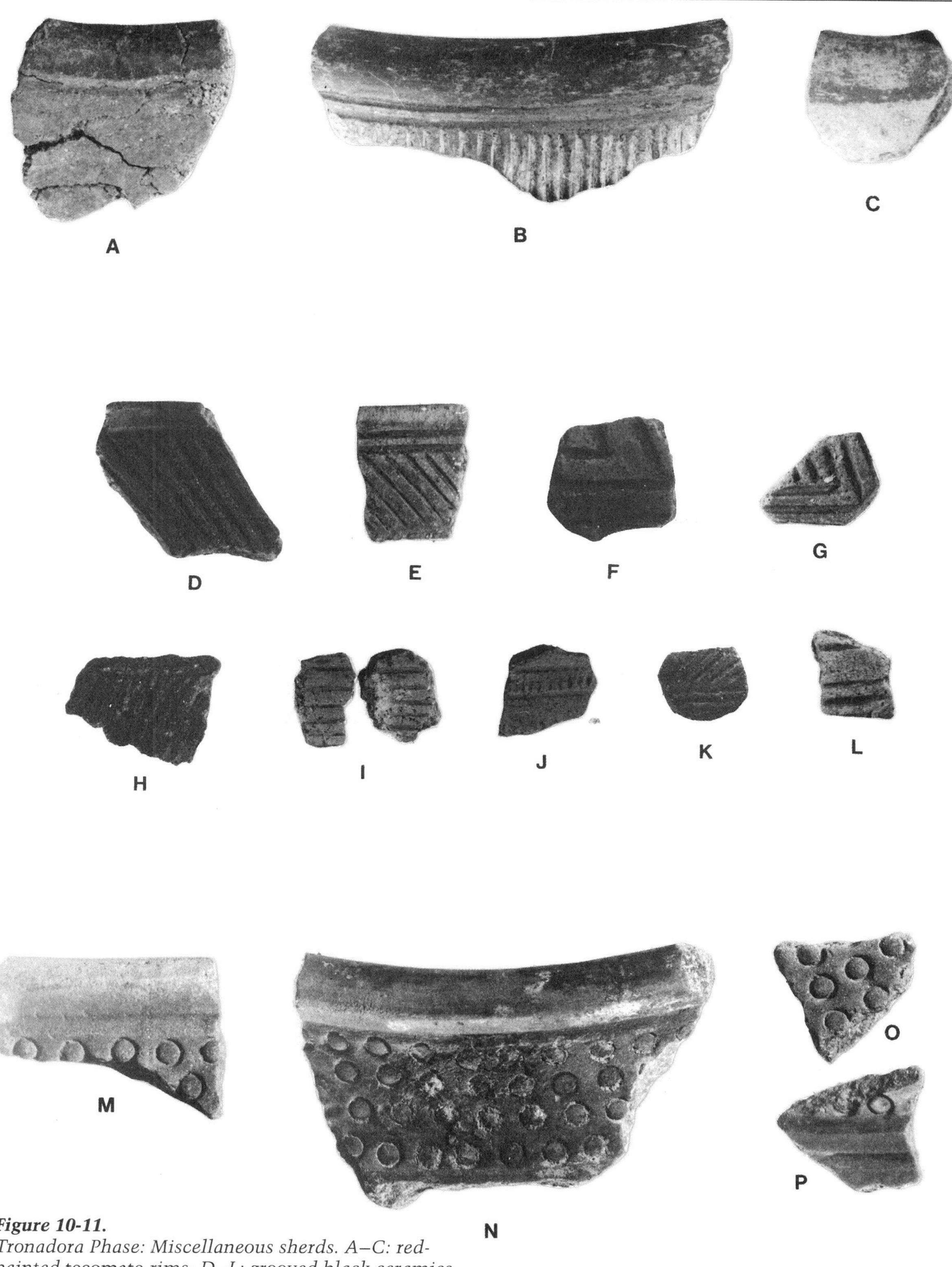

Figure 10-11.
Tronadora Phase: Miscellaneous sherds. A–C: red-painted tecomate *rims; D–L: grooved black ceramics with traces of red ocher (D and E are rims of cylindrical vessels); M–P: squat, necked jar fragments with reed impressions. Sherd widths: A, 5.0 cm; B, 9.5 cm; C, 3.3 cm; D, 4.0 cm; E, 2.5 cm; F, 3.0 cm; G, 2.7 cm; H, 3.7 cm; I, 3.2 cm; J, 2.5 cm; K, 2.0 cm; L, 2.0 cm; M, 5.3 cm; N, 9.3 cm; O, 3.2 cm; P, 3.2 cm. Photographs by John Hoopes.*

preceramic occupation).[5] The two dates for the beginning of the Tronadora Phase occupation of the site come from stratigraphic units immediately above the Aguacate. These are 2460–1890 cal BC (Tx-5277) and 1970–1694 cal BC (Tx-5279). The dendro-corrected 95% confidence interval of the first date completely overlaps that of the second, suggesting a date for the transition between the Fortuna Phase and the Tronadora Phase at about 2000 cal BC.

As noted earlier, Tronadora pottery is closely related to Snarskis' (1978, 1984a) Chaparrón and La Montaña complexes. Of the two, it is most similar to Chaparrón. Unfortunately, no dates are available for Chaparrón pottery. Snarskis (1978) did obtain a total of five dates for deposits with early ceramics at La Montaña, a site near Turrialba in the Atlantic Watershed region: 2271–1430 cal BC (UCLA-2113A: 3465 BP ± 160), 800–596 cal BC (UCLA-2113D,UCLA-2113N: 2500 BP ± 60), 800 cal BC-cal AD 52 (UCLA-2113B: 2275 BP ± 160), and 400–122 cal BC (UCLA-2113M: 2230 BP ± 60). The last two are thought to have been charcoal from a later period cemetery superimposed on the level containing La Montaña material. The earliest date was initially rejected as being too early (ibid.: 107); however, the Tronadora Vieja dates suggest it may not be.

At the Méndez site on the Naranjo River, northeast of the Arenal area but still in the Northwestern Cordillera, Norr (1982–1983) included ceramics similar to those from Chaparrón in her Naranjo Phase. It is defined as temporally equivalent to Lange's Loma B Phase at the Vidor site, and Norr dates it to 800–300 BC (uncorrected). Two dates are reported from Naranjo Phase deposits. The first, 2028–1645 cal BC (UCLA-2167A: 3500 BP ± 60), comes from sterile subsoil at the base of a large funerary structure. The second, 410–132 cal BC (UCLA-2163: 2250 BP ± 60), comes from ceramic-bearing deposits in the same feature. The earliest date was thought to be much too early for the ceramic occupation. The dating of the Loma B context at Vidor has also been controversial (Lange 1980a:35). There, in deep levels, sherds similar to those from Méndez and Tronadora Vieja were associated with a date of 1291–830 cal BC (UCLA-2177A: 2830 BP ± 80).

Inspection of a sample of Norr's ceramics revealed that several of the sherds from the lowest levels at Sitio Méndez were identical to Tronadora Complex sherds. The early date from this site (UCLA-2167A) is very similar to dates from Tronadora Vieja. Loma B ceramics are not identical to Tronadora sherds; however, they do bear important similarities. It now seems likely that the early dates from Méndez and Vidor are not aberrant and that they in fact date Early and Middle Formative horizons.

Haberland (1978:412) has suggested a date as early as 1200 BC (uncorrected) for Dinarte Phase ceramics from Ometepe Island, Nicaragua. This date is based on comparisons with material from the Guatemalan coast and the assertion that the succeeding Angeles Phase dates as early as 500 BC (uncorrected). The Dinarte ceramics are poorly illustrated (Haberland 1966); however, one of his examples appears to be a cylindrical vessel similar to Zetillal Shell-Stamped, and Haberland (personal communication, 1985) believes that Tronadora and Dinarte ceramics are likely one and the same. There is a close relationship between incised and zoned-incised decoration on Angeles Phase ceramics, and the type Bocana Incised Bichrome—a marker for the Loma B Phase—and Angeles may correspond to the Early Arenal Phase. The stratigraphic position of Angeles and Dinarte levels also parallels the relationships between Tronadora and Early Arenal pottery.

The principal culture-bearing strata at Tronadora Vieja are Units 50 and below. One-fourth, or 26%, of the entire assemblage of diagnostic Tronadora Phase ceramics, was found together with Arenal Phase pottery in levels below Unit 50 and above Unit 60. Of these, two in the upper 50's stratigraphic units were Tronadora types, a result of heavy mixing (probably due to a combination of bioturbation and cultural disturbance); however, the greatest concentration of Tronadora Phase sherds appeared in Units 60, 61, and 64. These correspond to El Tajo Units 9 and 10, and are derived from the earliest eruptive activity of the Arenal Volcano (Chap. 2). A small sample of Tronadora sherds was embedded in the surface of Aguacate (Unit 65), and may predate the deposition of Arenal tephras. Two C-14 samples from hearths in a well-developed soil layer on top of El Tajo Unit 8 at El Tajo (which appears to correspond to Silencio Sequence Units 55 and 55A) yielded dates of 390–50 cal BC (SI-3459) and 86 cal BC–cal AD 390 (I-10804: 1830 BP ± 80) (Aguilar 1984:74). According to Melson (1984), the amount of time needed for the formation of the soil from which the date was obtained suggests that the deposition of the Tajo Unit 8 tephra occurred several hundred years earlier, perhaps as early as 700 cal BC. All levels below Unit 55 at Tronadora Vieja (that is, Units 60, 61, and 64) would be older than this. At Tronadora Vieja, Units 60 and below yielded almost pure deposits of Tronadora ceramics.

The terminal date of the Tronadora Phase is based on conservative estimates for the deposition of Unit 55 and for the beginning of the Early Arenal Phase at around 500 cal BC. Neither of these events is well understood or well documented, and our absence of dates for the latter portion of the Tronadora Phase does not improve the situation. The two earliest dates associated with Arenal Phase material are 1950 cal BC—cal AD 660 (Tx-5280) and 830 cal BC—cal AD 1 (Tx-5271). The first has an excessive standard deviation. The second is associated with Late Arenal ceramics and has a large standard deviation. It is clear that the Tronadora/Arenal transition merits further investigation. As noted earlier, it is possible that there is an overlap of the Bocana Incised Bichrome type with Late Tronadora assemblages. Early Zoned Bichrome ceramics may well have evolved out of those of the Tronadora Phase, suggesting an important continuity of population in the region.

INTRASITE DISTRIBUTION OF TRONADORA PHASE CERAMICS

We found Tronadora Phase ceramics in the lower levels of all operations at Tronadora Vieja. The most interesting association of Tronadora ceramics and occupational features was in Operation W, where they were associated with the floor of an early house (Chap. 4).

In the nine excavation lots from Unit 60 and below in Operation W, 95% of the seventy-three diagnostic sherds recovered belong to the Tronadora Phase. The most common type is Tonjibe Beige, followed by Tigra Grooved-Punctate and Tajo Gouge-Incised. Small amounts of Tronadora Incised, Zetillal Shell-Stamped, and Atlantic Red-Filled Black were also present. Mode-groups include general groove incising, shell stamping, and reed stamping. Some reed-stamped jar fragments had a thick, black substance adhering to the exterior, decorated neck. Although this appeared to be charcoal, it did not burn when held over a flame. Its nature and purpose are unknown.

The assemblage of ceramics associated with the habitation features includes both decorated and undecorated vessels, with Tonjibe Beige present as well as both Tajo Gouge-Incised and Zetillal Shell-Stamped. Although the greatest number of sherds of Tajo Gouge-Incised appeared in Operation W, both this type and Zetillal Shell-Stamped occurred in similar quantities in Operations H, L and V. The proportions of other types and modal categories do not vary significantly over the site.

THE ARENAL PHASE

The Arenal Phase bears many similarities to the Greater Nicoya Zoned Bichrome horizon (Lange 1980a); however, it also has significant local characteristics.[6] Bocana Zoned Bichrome appears frequently in Arenal Phase surface assemblages; however, Rosales Zoned-Engraved, Tola Trichrome, and other marker types of Zoned Bichrome assemblages to the west are rare or absent.

The Arenal Phase is characterized more by the use of linear painting and stamped decoration than by zoned decoration. Las Palmas Red-on-Beige and Charco Black-on-Red are the two types most representative of the former; the different varieties of Mojica Impressed and the type Congo Impressed best represent the latter tradition.

The use of zoning (areas of color outlined with either incision or painting) is uncommon in Arenal Phase assemblages, except for Bocana Incised Bichrome. While zoned punctation and shell-stamping are common in the Tronadora Phase, these diminish in popularity. The only type with zoned punctation to appear during the Arenal Phase is Huila Zoned Punctate (cf. Baudez 1967: 59). This type is not very common in Tempisque Valley and Pacific Coast assemblages, and it is also rare in the Northwestern Cordillera.

ARENAL PHASE SITES

Of forty-three sites for which ceramics were analyzed during the 1984 and 1985 field seasons, twenty demonstrated a higher percentage of Arenal Phase ceramics than of any other phase. In addition to Tronadora Phase ceramics, we found a strong Arenal Phase component at Tronadora Vieja (G-163; Hoopes 1987:43–97; Chap. 4). At Sitio Bolívar (G-164; Hoopes 1987:98–161; Chap. 5) and Viboriana (G-175; Bradley et al. 1984:88–92) virtually all ceramics belonged to the Arenal Phase; however, the Arenal components at Tronadora Vieja, Viboriana, and La Isla (G-166; Hoopes 1987:323) were earlier than components at Sitio Bolívar.

Tronadora Vieja (G-163)

We recovered 177 Arenal Phase sherds from excavations at this site, of which 120 (68%) were located in 50's strata. Among the types represented (in the order of their importance) are Los Hermanos Beige; Los Hermanos Beige: Espinoza Variety; Mojica Impressed: Laguna Variety; Bocana Incised Bichrome; Las Palmas Red-on-Beige; Charco Black-on-Red; and Huila Zoned-Punctate. All of these appear in Zoned Bichrome assemblages throughout much of Greater Nicoya, and their presence suggests that the Arenal Phase was a time of strong cultural affinities between the Arenal area and regions to the west. One interesting difference between this assemblage and those of the Tempisque Valley is the presence in the Arenal region of Espinoza Red-Banded, a type defined by Healy (1980) in the Rivas region of Nicaragua (and defined for the Arenal region as Los Hermanos Beige: Espinoza Variety; Hoopes 1987: 415–420). This type suggests ties with the north as well, perhaps as part of a horizon extending along the volcanic cordillera, although its red decoration also has important parallels with El Bosque pottery from the Atlantic Watershed (Snarskis 1978).

Charco Black-on-Red sherds at Tronadora Vieja suggest that the Arenal Phase occupation extended through both Early and Late facets at this site; however, this sample of Charco differs from those of more typical Late Arenal assemblages. The black-painted decoration was executed in broad strokes rather than the narrow lines noted at Sitio Bolívar. This may be a characteristic of early examples of this type, but the sample was not large enough to clarify this point.

Sitio Bolívar (G-164)

What it lacked in longevity, the Arenal Phase occupation at Sitio Bolívar made up for in intensity. We recovered almost six thousand diagnostic sherds from relatively small excavations, providing us with a large assemblage that appears to have been restricted in time to the last 200 years of the Arenal Phase.

Los Hermanos Beige is the most important type at this site. Mojica Impressed (Corrida, Arrastrada, and Congo varieties) is second. Charco Black-on-Red, Los Hermanos Beige: Espinoza Variety, Guinea Incised, Los Hermanos Beige: Cervantes Variety, Zelaya Painted (Bichrome and Trichrome varieties), and unidentified trichrome sherds are also important types in the Sitio Bolívar assemblage. A number of early modes appear in this assemblage, most notably Usulután-type resist decoration and medial-flange bowls (both on Guinea Incised); however, all together the ceramics represent a clear assemblage of Linear Decorated types (cf. Baudez 1967). A few sherds of Carillo Polychrome confirm the dating of the assemblage to a time corresponding to the transition between late Zoned Bichrome and Early Polychrome periods in Greater Nicoya.

Viboriana (G-175) and La Isla (G-166)

Surface collections from these sites provided the best diagnostic assemblages for the Early facet of the Arenal Phase. Charco Black-on-Red and Guinea Incised, found in large numbers at Sitio Bolívar, are rare or absent while Bocana Incised Bichrome and Las Palmas Red-on-Beige are present. Excavations at Viboriana confirmed the stratigraphic position of Early Arenal sherds in the lower 50's strata; however, the excavated sample was not large enough for any stylistic changes over time to be determined.

ARENAL PHASE CERAMIC TYPES

Bocana Incised Bichrome

This type (Figs. 10-12A–E, 10-13J–K; Hoopes 1987: fig. 7.1:J–K, pl. 7.1:A–D) was first defined by Baudez (1967) for the Tempisque River. It was recorded by Sweeney (1975) and Lange (1976) at sites on the Pacific Coast of Guanacaste. Healy (1980) noted five sherds of Bocana Incised Bichrome in the Rivas region of Nicaragua. Bocana is the marker type for Early Arenal Phase assemblages in the Arenal area (Hoopes 1987:346–356). It is frequently associated with Las Palmas Red-on-Beige and Los Hermanos Beige: Espinoza Variety.

Bocana Incised Bichrome in the Arenal area is characterized by grooved, vertical incisions in combination with zoned red slipping on a beige, unslipped surface. Decorative technique ranges from wide, round-bottomed grooving to sharp-edged, deep incising. Incisions are usually found in multiple sets of three to four vertical lines, corresponding to Baudez' "combed variety" (1967:63: pl. 19) and Healy's "Bocana variety" (1980:91: fig. 26). Unlike on Tronadora Incised and other Tronadora Phase sherds with incised decoration, *verti-*

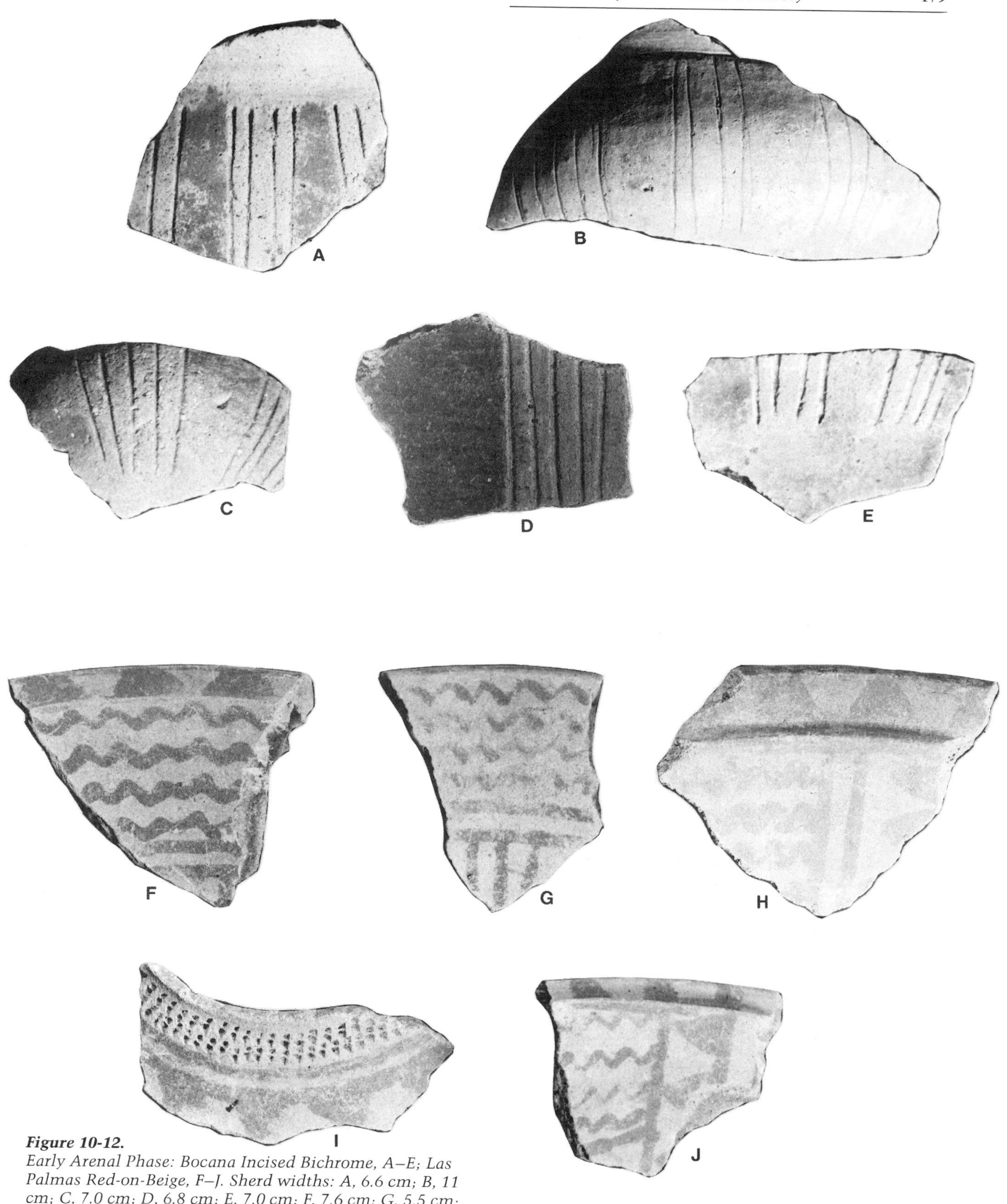

Figure 10-12.
Early Arenal Phase: Bocana Incised Bichrome, A–E; Las Palmas Red-on-Beige, F–J. Sherd widths: A, 6.6 cm; B, 11 cm; C, 7.0 cm; D, 6.8 cm; E, 7.0 cm; F, 7.6 cm; G, 5.5 cm; H, 8.0 cm; I, 8.0 cm; J, 6.0 cm. Photographs by John Hoopes.

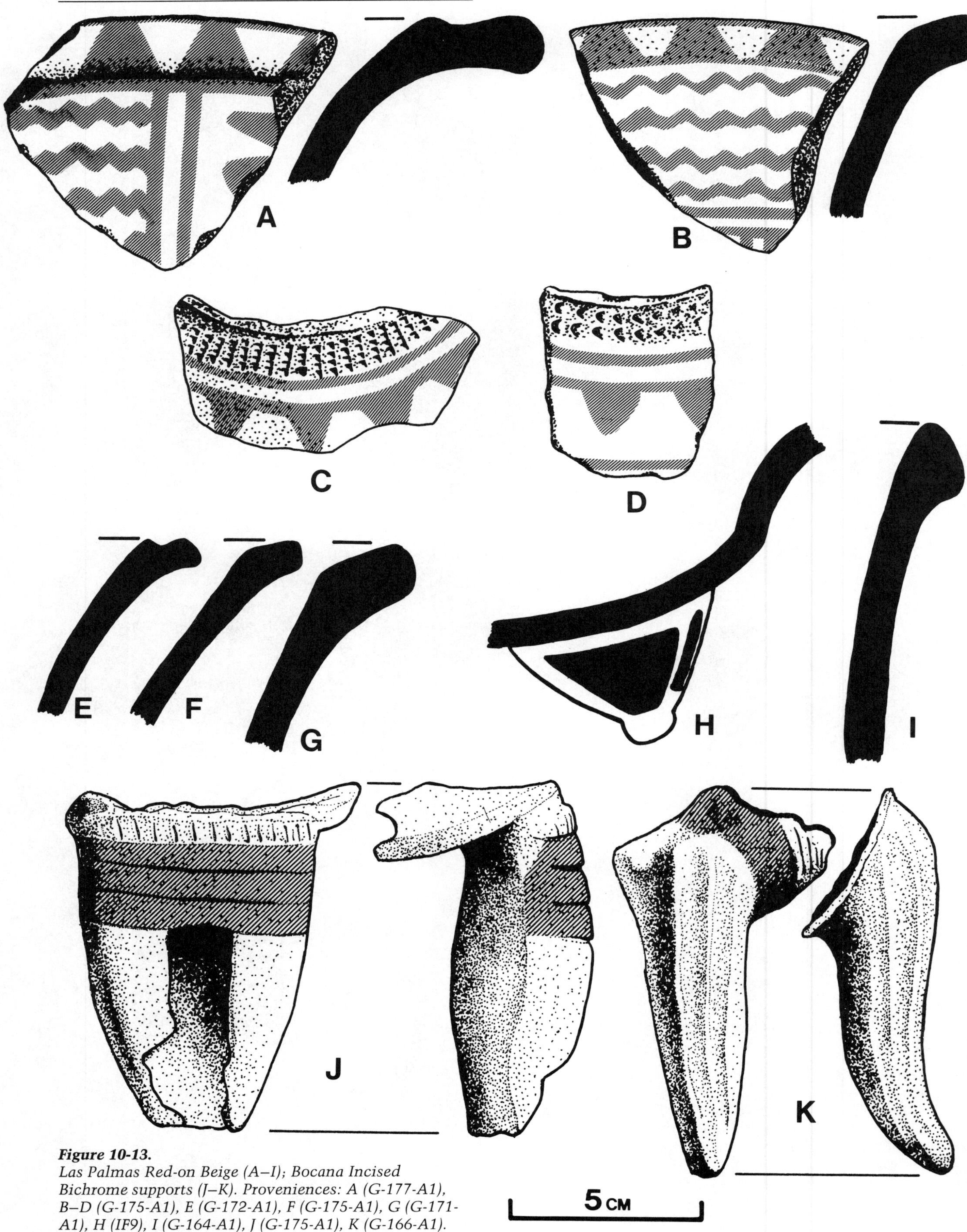

Figure 10-13.
Las Palmas Red-on Beige (A–I); Bocana Incised Bichrome supports (J–K). Proveniences: A (G-177-A1), B–D (G-175-A1), E (G-172-A1), F (G-175-A1), G (G-171-A1), H (IF9), I (G-164-A1), J (G-175-A1), K (G-166-A1). Figures by John Hoopes.

cal, rather than horizontal, incision predominates. Bocana Incised pastes differ from Tronadora Phase ones in that they include small crystals of black hornblende. These may be what Healy (ibid.: 92) tentatively identifies as "obsidian inclusions."

Rim sherds include simple and direct forms from incurving-rim bowls. As is true for other Arenal Phase types, however, it is likely that jar rim sherds without incision identified as Los Hermanos Beige may have come from Bocana Incised Bichrome vessels. We noted two distinctive support types. The first is a solid, elongated, curving support with longitudinal facets. The second is a hollow, rattle support, about 10 cm to 15 cm long, with vertical, rectangular slits on the exterior side. While not included in the type as defined by Baudez, these latter are decorated with the diagnostic incision and red bichroming found in Arenal assemblages. Examples from the Arenal area are identical to supports on vessels in the Museum of the Instituto Nacional de Seguros in San José and reported to have come from San Carlos in the Atlantic Watershed (Snarskis 1982: 88, upper right illustration—captions transposed). This latter support type was found associated with the early Loma B contexts at the Vidor site (Lange, personal communication, 1985).

Bocana Incised Bichrome is a diagnostic type of Lange's Loma B Phase at the Vidor site, and is considered a marker for the earliest Zoned Bichrome assemblages in Greater Nicoya. It is likely that Bocana Incised derives from incised types of the Tronadora Phase. Bocana Incised may well appear sometime during the Late Tronadora Phase. Until we can more clearly understand the transition between the Tronadora and Arenal Phases, however, Bocana Incised is interpreted as a marker type for the Early Arenal Phase.

Las Palmas Red-on-Beige

The use of multiple-brushed wavy lines of red ocher pigment is an important Arenal Phase mode, although it survives in later types such as Carillo Polychrome, Cabuyal Polychrome, and Jiménez Polychrome (Figs. 10-12F–J, 10-13A–I; Hoopes 1987:fig. 7.1:A-D, pl. 7.1:E–H). Its earliest appearance is on Las Palmas Red-on-Beige (Hoopes 1987:357–367), a type associated with Bocana Incised Bichrome. Baudez (1967: 89) reports that the most common vessel form of this type in his assemblages is the necked jar. Open, complex-silhouette bowls are much more common in our collections.

The principal decorative motifs of this type are wavy lines and solid triangles, executed in red paint on an unslipped surface. Bowls are decorated on the interior, with simple horizontal lines on the exterior. One example found has a hollow conical/mammiform rattle support. Jars are decorated exclusively on the exterior. A few examples in both the Arenal region and the Tempisque Valley collections bear Mojica-style impressions, indicating the contemporaneity of these two types.

Baudez (ibid.: 206) notes similarities between the wavy multiple brushing on Las Palmas Red-on-Beige and the decoration of Usulután ceramics of the Protoclassic Maya. Some of the hooked rim profiles on Las Palmas bowls (Fig. 10-3A) are also characteristic of Usulután and Iberia Orange ceramics of the Maya area. Healy (1980: 239–241) describes a type he calls "Usulután Resist" in the Rivas region of Nicaragua, which dates to the Avilés/San Jorge Zoned Bichrome Phases and may be related to Las Palmas. Despite its being a "resist" ware, diagnostic modes include "multiple brush produced straight and wavy lines . . . in orange or red . . . on a cream brown or orange base slip." His illustrated sherds (ibid.: figs. 110–111) are remarkably similar to Las Palmas sherds.

Mojica Impressed

The use of various implements to stamp rows of small marks on the necks and shoulders of unslipped vessels is a feature of Arenal Phase ceramics (Fig. 10-14; Hoopes 1984:fig. 2; 1987: 7.1:I–V). Baudez' type "Mojica à impressions de coquille" (1967: 57, pl. 16) is ubiquitous in both Early and Late Arenal Phase assemblages. Five varieties of Mojica Impressed have been defined on the basis of differences in impressed patterns (Hoopes 1987: 368–390). Because of their large size, Mojica vessels were probably used primarily for storage. The different varieties appear to have temporal significance. The Mojica Variety and Laguna Variety are both diagnostic of the Early Arenal Phase. The Corrida Variety, Arrastrada Variety, and Congo Variety are all diagnostic of Late Arenal.

Mojica Impressed: Mojica Variety

This variety (Hoopes 1984:fig. 2:E–H; 1987:pl. 7.1:I–L) bears small impressions in multiple rows and corresponds to examples of the type from the site of La Bocana (Baudez 1967:pl. 16A–C). On characteristic examples, the impressions resemble semicolons with an extra dot above. Individual impressions are deliberately placed and clearly defined. There is sometimes a slight "drag-and-jab" effect, but all marks are crisp and distinct. Interestingly, this type of decoration was noted on a few sherds of Las Palmas Red-on-Beige.

Mojica Impressed: Laguna Variety

This variety (Hoopes 1984:fig. 2:A–D; 1987:pl. 7.1:M–Q) is distinguished by single or double rows of impressions, usually made with instruments other than a shell. Fingernail and bar impressions fall into this category. Some sherds included in this variety appeared to have "pinched" or cord-marked decoration, reported by Snarskis (1978: 123) for Chaparrón pottery. The similarity between Mojica Impressed: Laguna Variety and certain Chaparrón ceramics and the former's appearance in earlier assemblages leads us to place this variety in the Early facet of the Arenal Phase. This variety may correspond to some examples classified as "Congo Punctate" by Baudez (1967:61).

Mojica Impressed: Corrida Variety

The Corrida Variety (Hoopes 1987:pl. 7.1:R–S) bears the same type of mark found on Mojica Impressed: Mojica Variety, but it has been drawn or jabbed more rapidly and less carefully, giving it a coarser appearance. The individual marks are still evident, but they run together. In general, the paste and surface finish of this variety appear to be coarser than that of the Mojica Variety.

Mojica Impressed: Arrastrada Variety

This fifth variety (Hoopes 1987:pl 7.1:T–V) is distinguished by decoration that is scraped rather than impressed. The pattern was made with the same multiple-point instrument used for Mojica Variety decorations (most likely the edge of a shell). Horizontal scraping has obliterated individual vertical marks, however, and the effect is that of a set of rough, contiguous horizontal channels (cf. Baudez 1967: pl. 16L).

Mojica Impressed: Congo Variety

This variety of Mojica derives its name from "Congo Punctate" (ibid.:61); however, the variety and the type do not completely overlap. Congo variety vessels are decorated with horizontal rows of triangular punctations on their shoulders (cf. ibid., pl. 18F), while Baudez' category includes a range of different decorations.

Discussion

Baudez illustrates examples of pottery corresponding to all five varieties of Mojica Impressed; however, he does not make any varietal distinctions or note temporal differences in the use of the different patterns. Data from the Arenal area indicate that Mojica Impressed decoration changed through time. Mojica Impressed: Mojica Variety and Mojica Impressed: Laguna Variety occur most frequently in survey lots with Bocana Incised Bichrome and Las Palmas Red-on-Beige, both diagnostic of the Early Arenal Phase. Las Palmas Red-on-Beige vessels will sometimes have impressions identical to those of Mojica Impressed: Mojica Variety. On the other hand, Mojica Impressed: Corrida Variety and Mojica Impressed: Arrastrada Variety appear in the large assemblage of Late Arenal ceramics from Sitio Bolívar, while Mojica and Laguna varieties were absent. In general, there was a tendency for the decoration on Mojica Impressed pottery to become hastier and less well executed over time. Mojica Impressed: Congo Variety was found in its most significant quantities at Sitio Bolívar, and it may belong in the Late Arenal Phase; however, the close similarity between some examples of this and the Laguna Variety suggest that the Congo Variety is not as clearly diagnostic as the other varieties.

Guinea Incised

This type, also defined by Baudez (1967:73), was best represented in assemblages from Sitio Bolívar (Fig. 10-15A–D; Hoopes 1987, pls. 7.2:A–F, 7.3). It is characteristic of the Late Arenal Phase (Hoopes 1987:391–402). In our assemblages, the surface finish of Guinea vessels is predominantly red and orange. Brown, beige, and tan examples are rare or absent. Virtually all Guinea Incised vessels are open, tripod bowls with large, hollow supports. Vessel profiles vary widely, with a predominance of basal angles and carinations. We noted some basal or medial flanges, often decorated with incision. We excavated a few examples of Guinea Incised vessels with Usulután-like resist decoration at Sitio Bolívar. Resist areas include parts of the incised panel on the vessel exterior and curvilinear designs on the interior surface of bowls. Both the use of resist decoration and the carinated, tripod bowl recall examples of

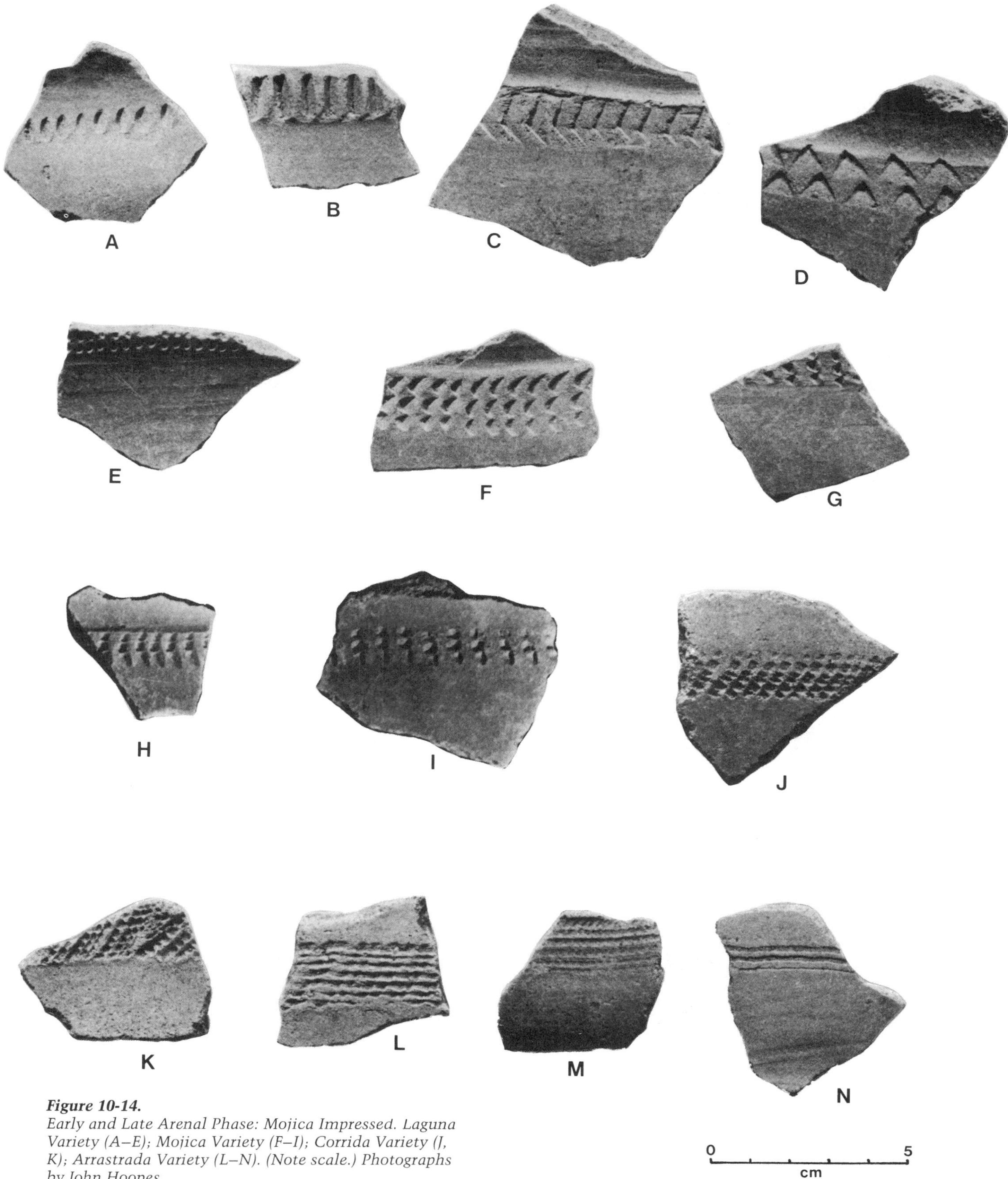

Figure 10-14.
Early and Late Arenal Phase: Mojica Impressed. Laguna Variety (A–E); Mojica Variety (F–I); Corrida Variety (J, K); Arrastrada Variety (L–N). (Note scale.) Photographs by John Hoopes.

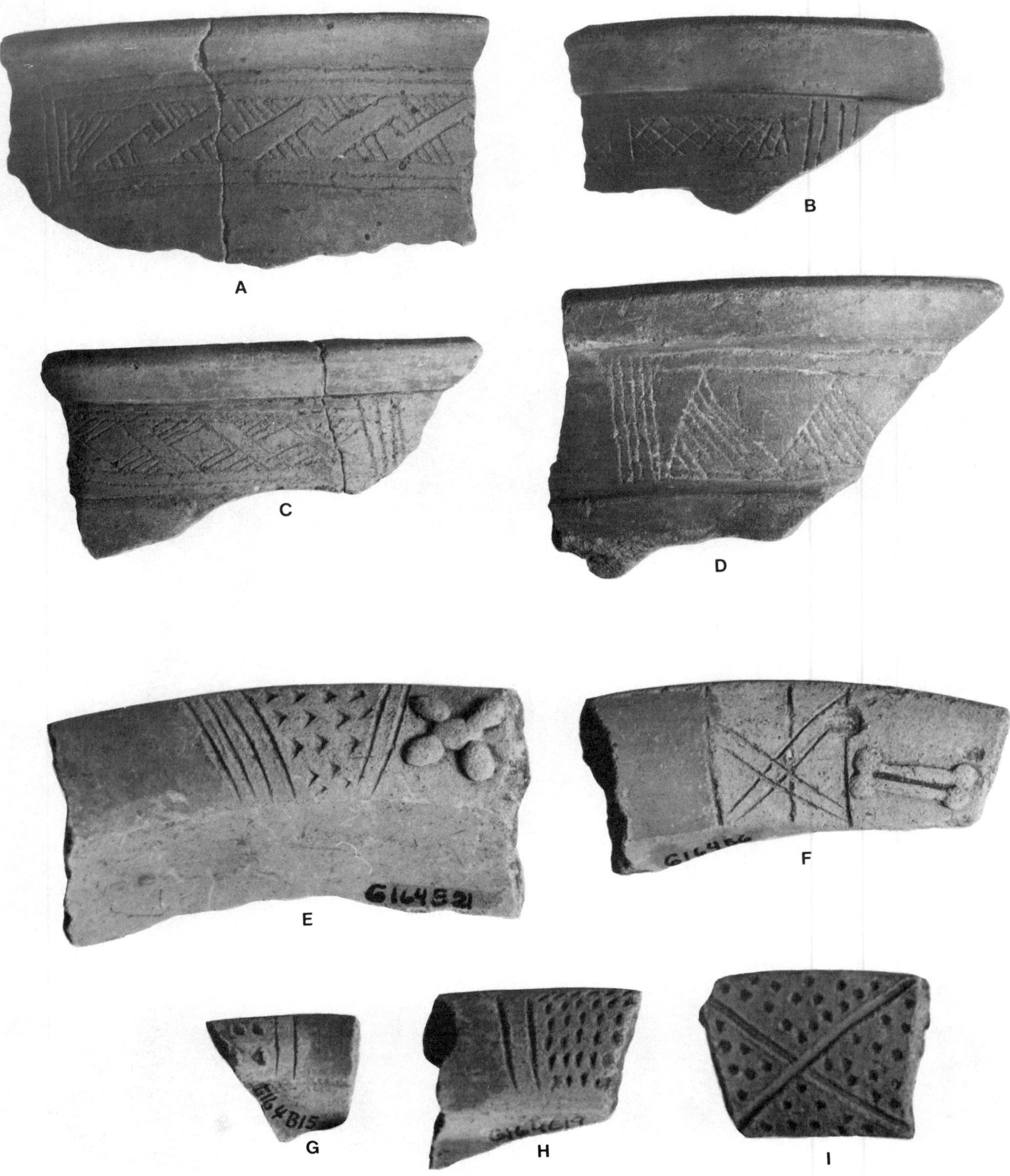

Figure 10-15.
Late Arenal Phase: Guinea Incised, A–D; Los Hermanos Beige: Cervantes Variety, E–I. Sherd widths: A, 12.0 cm; B, 9.5 cm; C, 11.5 cm; D, 11.5 cm; E, 12.0 cm; F, 11.0 cm; G, 4.0 cm; H, 5.5 cm; I, 6.0 cm. Photographs by John Hoopes.

Izalco Usulután from western El Salvador (Sharer 1978:39); however, the relationship is not close. Guinea Incised and analogous types are absent from contemporaneous assemblages in the Rivas region of Nicaragua (Healy 1980:313).

There is also a strong resemblance between some examples of Guinea Incised from the Cordilleran region and vessels of Snarskis' Zoila Red Group (1978:201–202) from the Atlantic Watershed region. Hollow, bulbous, rattle support forms (cf. Snarskis' modes S18 and S23; ibid.:figs 91–92) are common to both, as are the red surface color and geometric incision. Incision and engraving on open tripod bowls were common to both Greater Nicoya and the Atlantic Watershed regions of Costa Rica at around cal AD 500. These vessels appear to have been more important at inland sites than at coastal ones in Guanacaste.

Charco Black-on-Red

The definition of this type (Hoopes 1987:pl. 7.4:C–G) used here combines Baudez' Charco and Cobano Black-on-Red types (1967:83–87). Charco is the most common decorated type in assemblages from Sitio Bolívar. It is a rare type at Early Arenal Phase sites, however, and its representation is small when all Arenal Phase sites in our sample are considered (Hoopes 1987:421–426).

Charco is characterized by black line decoration on a red slip. The use of an overall red slip does not appear on Cordilleran ceramics until the Late Arenal Phase. Charco also signals the first use of fired black decoration on pottery in the region. On the great majority of Charco vessels from Sitio Bolívar, both slip and black paint tend to be soft and friable, in distinct contrast to the hard, often glossy finish typical of Early and Middle Polychrome vessels in Greater Nicoya. Decorative motifs on Charco echo those found on Las Palmas Red-on-Beige. These include multiple-brush wavy lines, triangular elements, and vertical and horizontal narrow lines. While most Las Palmas vessels are open bowls, Charco is represented more frequently by restricted-neck jars.

The temporal position of Charco Black-on-Red is not clear, either in the Tempisque Valley or the Northwestern Cordillera region. Baudez (1967:85) notes that Charco was common to both the Catalina and the Ciruelas phases, but found it more common in the latter, which corresponds to his "Linear Decorated" period (AD 300–500). Healy (1980:204) identifies Puerto Black-on-Red, from Rivas, as belonging to the San Jorge Phase. Both authors suggest that these black-on-red types appeared in the late Zoned Bichrome and diminished in frequency in the Early Polychrome Period. Charco is not typical of the Late Arenal Phase; however, a single vessel of this type was found beneath construction fill at the El Silencio cemetery, a site with an almost pure Silencio Phase ceramic component.

Los Hermanos Beige

Los Hermanos Beige (Fig. 10-16A–N; Hoopes 1987: fig. 7.2, pl. 7.2:G–O) is the most common type designation in Arenal Phase assemblages (Hoopes 1987:403–420); however, it also serves as a more-or-less catch-all term for red-rimmed beige jar and bowl fragments with characteristic profiles. Two partially reconstructed vessels and several large sherds indicate that rims designated as Los Hermanos Beige may have come from vessels of Mojica Impressed, Espinoza Red-Banded, Las Palmas Red-on-Beige, and even Bocana Incised Bichrome. Baudez (1967) places Los Hermanos Beige in the Ciruelas Phase (AD 300–500) of the Tempisque Valley. Red-rimmed beige vessels are also typical of his earlier Zoned Bichrome type, Monte Cristo Beige. It is not possible to distinguish Monte Cristo from Los Hermanos in our assemblages. Because of the wide application of this designation, we used "Los Hermanos" for vessels produced as early as the Late Tronadora Phase. Los Hermanos Beige is also the most abundant ceramic type at Sitio Bolívar, a Late Arenal site. The long duration of this type suggests a strong continuity in Northwestern Cordillera populations, and the tradition of red-rimmed storage vessels continues into the Silencio Phase.

Vessel forms range from incurving, direct-rim bowls to large, necked storage jars. In Late Arenal assemblages, the principal vessel forms are large, outcurving, exteriorly thickened rim jars; outflaring-rim jars; and open, thickened-rim bowls, usually with small solid conical supports (Baudez 1967: vessel groups I, II, and III).

Los Hermanos Beige: Espinoza Variety

This variety was not recognized by Baudez in the Tempisque Valley, nor has it been noted in assemblages from coastal Guanacaste (Fig. 10-17A–C). It was first defined by Norweb (1964:559) and later by Healy (1980), from ceramics excavated in the Rivas region of Nicaragua. The principal decorative modes are "Red painted and polished verti-

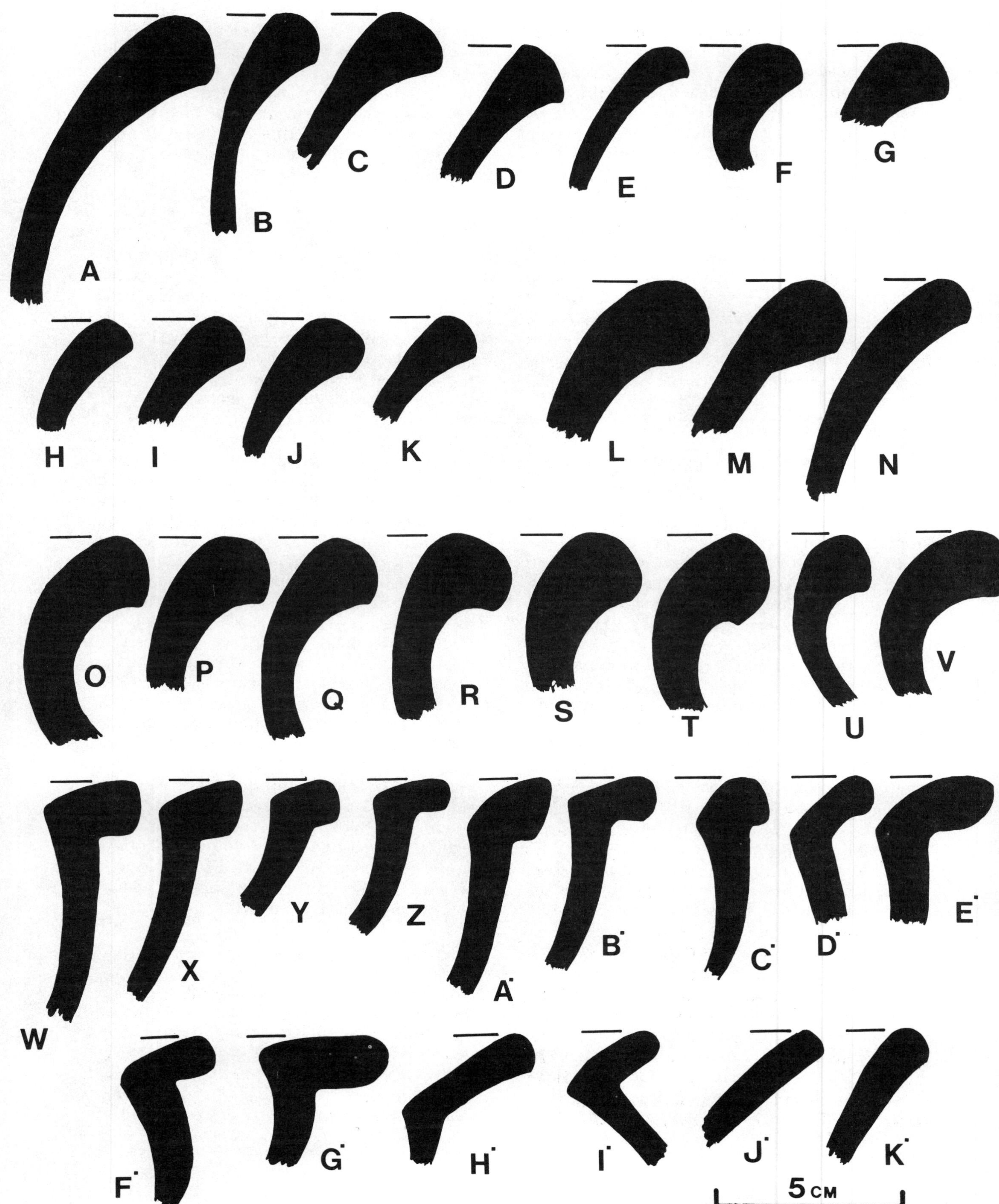
A
B
C
D
E
F
G
H
I
J
K
L
M
N
O
P
Q
R
S
T
U
V
W
X
Y
Z
A'
B'
C'
D'
E'
F'
G'
H'
I'
J'
K'
5 CM

Figure 10-16.
Left: *Los Hermanos Beige rim profiles. A–N: jar and bowl profiles from Tronadora Vieja; O–V: jar profiles from Sitio Bolívar; H′–I′: short-necked jars; J′–K′: direct-rim bowls. Figures by John Hoopes.*

Figure 10-17.
Above: *Late Arenal Phase: Los Hermanos Beige: Espinoza Variety: A–C; Huila Zoned-Punctate: D–E; unnamed incised, punctate, zoned-bichrome: F; Zelaya Bichrome: G–H; Carillo Polychrome: I–J. Sherd widths: A, 4.0 cm; B, 3.2 cm; C, 6.4 cm; D, 11.0 cm; E, 7.0 cm; F, 4.8 cm; G, 11.5 cm; H, 10.2 cm; I, 5.5 cm; J, 8.0 cm. Photographs by John Hoopes.*

cal bands . . . on a natural, buff colored base . . . on various-sized jars" (ibid.: 115). Unlike on the Nicaraguan examples, we did not note the use of appliqué on this type.

Espinoza Variety modes of vessel size and form are the same as Los Hermanos Beige (see foregoing). Decoration consists of red-painted rims and the use of broad strokes of red paint on vessel shoulders and sides. Strokes are usually vertical, appearing in sets of three or four linear elements; however, some examples show a rough, horizontal "wiping" of red paint on vessel walls. The latter are the most common at Sitio Bolívar. The decoration on examples of Espinoza Variety sherds and vessels from the Arenal area is usually rough, and vessel forms indicate that its principal function was probably for storage.

According to Healy (ibid.: 116), Espinoza Red-Banded dates primarily to the Zoned Bichrome period; however, the type continues through the Early and even into the Middle Polychrome periods (though clearly reduced in importance). Healy also suggests that Espinoza is homologous to Baudez' Matazana Red-on-Brown from the Tempisque Valley; however, I see Matazana as equivalent to Las Palmas Red-on-Beige and Espinoza as something different. Los Hermanos Beige: Espinoza Variety is characteristic of both Early and Late Arenal phases, with a marked deterioration in the quality of decoration over time.

Los Hermanos Beige: Cervantes Variety

Defined by Baudez (1967: 109) as the "Cervantes Incised-Punctate" type but assigned varietal status by consensus of the Greater Nicoya Ceramic Conference (Lange et al. 1984), this variety is characterized by the use of heavy incision, punctation, and (less frequently) appliqué to decorate the broad interior surfaces of open bowl rims (Fig. 10-15E–I; Hoopes 1987: pl. 7.2: G–O). While some punctation, especially triangular impressions, is reminiscent of Mojica Impressed, the incisions in Los Hermanos Beige: Cervantes Variety are usually coarse, made when the clay was wet and soft. Baudez places his type in both his Catalina and Ciruelas phases (ibid.). It is a principal diagnostic of our Late Arenal Phase.

Other Important Arenal Phase Types and Modes

In addition to Charco Black-on-Red, other decorated types that were first defined in Tempisque Valley assemblages (Baudez 1967) appear in Late Arenal contexts. These include sherds of Huila Zoned Punctate (Fig. 10-17D–E), Zelaya Painted: Bichrome Variety (Fig. 10-17G–H; Hoopes 1987: pl. 7.4B), Zelaya Painted: Trichrome Variety (ibid.: pl. 7.4A), and Carillo Polychrome (Fig. 10-17I–J). As noted earlier, they suggest that the Arenal region should be interpreted as an eastern extension of Greater Nicoya at this time.

A number of sherds from Sitio Bolívar are not typical of contemporaneous assemblages in Greater Nicoya and suggest communication between the Arenal region and other parts of Costa Rica (Fig. 10-18). Among these are rim sherds from wide-mouthed tripod bowls, unslipped on the exterior but coated with a thick maroon slip on the interior. These are tentatively identified as belonging to the Anita Fine Purple Group of the Selva Phase in the Atlantic Watershed and appear to have the same "powder-fine" paste noted at Línea Vieja sites (Snarskis 1978: 208–209). Both the paste and the purple slip found on these few sherds are different from those of local Arenal-area pottery. Snarskis traces Anita Fine Purple to southeastern Costa Rica and cites this as a trade ware in the Atlantic region. If this is correct, their presence at Arenal area sites indicates wide-ranging interregional interaction.

Other ceramics from Sitio Bolívar indicate contact with the Atlantic Watershed region. These include long, hollow conical supports with anthropomorphic adornos (cf. ibid.: fig. 90, S15); zoomorphic appliqué figures on vessel rims (ibid.: fig. 111, D23), and short vertical handles with appliqué (ibid.: fig. 100, H12). All of these are diagnostic of late El Bosque and La Selva assemblages from the Atlantic Watershed region. These modes were found in far lower quantities than those of the local Arenal Phase ceramic types. They may mark trade vessels from regions to the east of the Cordillera rather than local imitations of Atlantic Watershed ceramics. Atlantic-style sherds are far more common in the Arenal area than at contemporaneous sites to the west and their presence suggests a significant level of trade or exchange between the Cordilleran and Atlantic Watershed regions around cal AD 500.

DATING THE ARENAL PHASE

Lange (1980a) divides the Zoned Bichrome Period in Greater Nicoya into three phases on the basis of data from the Vidor site: Loma B (800–300 BC), Orso (300 BC–AD 300), and Mata de Uva (AD 300–500). The Loma B, or "Zoned Incised," Phase is marked by Bocana Incised Bichrome, Toya Zoned

Figure 10-18.
Late Arenal Phase: Miscellaneous sherds with modes suggestive of Atlantic Watershed influence. Adornos: A, E, G, K; appliqué: B–D, H; decorated support fragments: F, I, J; hollow supports: L, M. Sherd lengths: A, 4.0 cm; B, 5.2 cm; C, 4.8 cm; D, 3.6 cm; E, 4.7 cm; I, 12.0 cm; J, 9.5 cm; K, 14.5 cm; L, 10.5 cm; M, 11.5 cm. Sherd widths: F, 4.5 cm; G, 5.2 cm; H, 7.7 cm. Photographs by John Hoopes.

Incised, and ceramics common to Lothrop's "Palmar Ware" classification. The Orso Phase is characterized by the appearance of fine incised or engraved zoning as found on the marker type Rosales Zoned Engraved. According to Lange (ibid.: 40), Orso is contemporaneous with Catalina and Chombo in the Tempisque Valley and Santa Elena Peninsula, respectively, and corresponds to the Zoned Bichrome Period as initially defined by Coe and Baudez (1961). The Mata de Uva, or "Zoned Painted," Phase corresponds to the "Linear Decorated" Period (Baudez 1967: 194) and is signaled by the appearance of Tola Trichrome at coastal sites. Mata de Uva, and the ceramic traits associated with it, has been variously considered as the beginning of the Early Polychrome or the end of the Zoned Bichrome Period. I agree with the latter interpretation and see the "Zoned Painted" Phase as "a continuation, or termination, of Zoned Bichrome patterns" (Lange 1980a: 41).

The Arenal Phase is contemporaneous with all three of Lange's coastal phases, beginning with the appearance of Bocana Incised Bichrome and ending with linear painted and trichrome decoration. It therefore covers the "Zoned Bichrome Period" in its broadest conception. The beginning of the Arenal Phase (and the end of the Tronadora Phase) is placed at 500 cal BC on the basis of the available dates for La Montaña ceramics and conservative estimates for the beginning of the Zoned Bichrome Period. It should be noted, however, that the period from 1000 to 500 cal BC—during which time Early Arenal traits probably developed—is poorly defined in the Arenal area sequence.

The dates for the Arenal Phase are based as much on crossdating as on chronometric dates from project excavations. The early facet is marked by Bocana Incised Bichrome. Large, tapering hollow supports with rectangular apertures decorated with red paint zoned by deep incision are reportedly identical to a support associated with a date of 1291–830 cal BC (UCLA-2177A) from a large "oven" feature at the Vidor site (Lange 1980a: 35; Snarskis, personal communication, 1985). An example of one of these supports was excavated at Viboriana (G-175), where it was associated with sherds of Mojica Impressed and Las Palmas Red-on-Beige.

At Tronadora Vieja, levels with a predominance of Tronadora ceramics were overlain by those with Arenal types. This stratigraphic relationship has parallels at only two other sites in Greater Nicoya. At Los Angeles on Ometepe Island, Nicaragua, Dinarte ceramics were found beneath levels containing early Zoned Bichrome "Angeles Phase" pottery (Haberland 1966). These Angeles Phase ceramics were found below levels with Rosales Zoned Engraved and Schettel Incised, and they "seem to be connected with the Bocana Zoned Incised and Toya Zoned Incised of Baudez" (ibid.: 401). At Sitio Méndez, Norr (1982–1983) reports a mixture of Loma B– and Catalina–type ceramics from the lowest levels of a burial mound. The 410–132 cal BC (UCLA-2163) date from Méndez corresponds well with other Zoned Bichrome dates, as well as with the Early facet of the Arenal Phase. As noted earlier, the Méndez ceramics also include a number of Tronadora Complex sherds. It seems likely that Angeles ceramics correspond to Early Arenal and Lange's Loma B phases, Dinarte ceramics (as noted earlier) are equivalent to Tronadora, and that the lowermost levels at the Méndez site contain a mixture of Tronadora and Early Arenal types.

Our earliest C-14 dates for Arenal ceramics come from a trench tomb at Tronadora Vieja and the lowest excavation levels at Sitio Bolívar. The first, 1950 cal BC—cal AD 660 (Tx-5280) was associated with Mojica Impressed: Mojica Variety pottery. The second, 830 cal BC—cal AD 1 (Tx-5271) underlay a large Late Arenal component. Unfortunately, both of these dates are of limited value because of large standard deviations.

Rosales Zoned Engraved, the principal type of Lange's Orso Phase, is absent in our assemblages; however, other types diagnostic of Catalina and Chombo assemblages dating to the 300 cal BC—cal AD 300 range are present and imply an occupation of the Arenal area at this time. The C-14 dates from this time range come from three different sites. The earliest, 810 cal BC—cal AD 630 (Tx-5081) is from Tronadora Vieja. The very large confidence interval limits its utility, but the early limits of its range are consistent with the dating of associated Tronadora Phase ceramics. The next, cal AD 110–410 (Tx-5272), was recovered from shoreline deposits at Sitio Bolívar containing Late Arenal pottery. The third date came from the hilltop cemetery at El Silencio (G-150). It is identical to the second at cal AD 110–410 (Tx-5078), but was *not* directly associated with Arenal Phase ceramics (coming instead from a *Silencio* Phase context). Arenal ceramics from other contexts at this latter site suggest that it was in use at this time, but the date suggests that early deposits may have been disturbed by later activities.

The best C-14 dates for crossdating come from

Level 6 at Ortega (Baudez 1967: 205), which yielded an assemblage similar to that from the Upper 50's strata at Tronadora Vieja. Dates of 754—60 cal BC (GsY-100: 2195 BP ± 130—average of two dates) and cal AD 132–533 (Y-850: 1700 BP ± 70) were associated with types Bocana, Charco, Las Palmas, and Mojica. Coeval levels at Matapalo yielded a date of 390 cal BC–cal AD 598 (Y-810: 1870 BP ± 200). This suggests that the Arenal Phase occupation at Tronadora Vieja dates to the few centuries before and after the beginning of the Common Era.

With regard to the latest part of the Arenal Phase, it is significant that fragments of sherds that may be transitional into the Early Polychrome tradition appear in deposits at Sitio Bolívar. Four sherds from surface collections are tentatively identified as López Polychrome—the earliest of "Nicoya Polychrome" types—and four sherds in the large assemblage in Operation B are identified as an early variety of Carillo Polychrome. The presence of these types suggests an occupation dating to the latter part of the Arenal Phase and two C-14 dates from the site support this. The first, cal AD 450–775 (Tx-5270), is closest to estimates from crossdating ceramics. The second, cal AD 780–1010 (Tx-5269), was obtained from a hearth partly exposed by wave action on the lakeshore. It is later than expected, and may have been contaminated by more recent organic material. Early Zoned Bichrome types such as Bocana Incised Bichrome, Las Palmas Red-on-Beige, and certain varieties of Mojica Impressed (see foregoing) are rare or absent at this site, as are Tronadora ceramics. Tola Trichrome, the marker type for Lange's Mata de Uva Phase, is rare. A large number of other types of the "Zoned Painted" horizon are present, however, including Charco Black-on-Red, Guinea Incised, Cervantes Incised-Punctate, and Zelaya Bichrome. Baudez (1967) dates his "Linear Decorated" period from AD 300–500, and the Early Polychrome period is currently placed at roughly AD 500–800. Sitio Bolívar's ceramic assemblage is most closely related to the former, although the presence of a small number of later sherds suggests that it may have been transitional between the two.

Like the "Zoned Bichrome" period defined by Lange's three phases, the Arenal Phase has a duration of over 1,000 years. Given the nature of the Arenal assemblages and the absence of Rosales Zoned-Engraved, one of Lange's marker types for the period from 300 BC to AD 300, I am reluctant to subdivide the Arenal phase into more than two facets; however, patterns in assemblages from surface collections and excavations clearly indicate that some types were common early and others late. For this reason, the Arenal Phase has been provisionally divided into two roughly equal facets. The first of these, designated "Early Arenal," dates from approximately 500 cal BC to the beginning of the Common Era. The second, "Late Arenal," dates from cal AD 1 to 600. It is important to note that there is *not* a clear division between these facets. Rather, the period from cal 300 BC to cal AD 300 (what might be termed "Middle Arenal") is probably marked by characteristics of *both*, with a gradual transition from earlier to later characteristics.

The Early Arenal subphase is represented almost exclusively by surface collections, although we recovered a small amount of material in stratigraphic context at the sites of Tronadora Vieja (G-163) and Viboriana (G-175). The two principal Early Arenal surface assemblages come from Viboriana and La Isla (G-166). Late Arenal types are rare or absent at these sites. The most important types of the Early Arenal subphase are Bocana Incised Bichrome, Las Palmas Red-on-Beige, and Mojica Impressed: Laguna Variety. Of these, however, the latter two probably continue through the early centuries cal AD.

We recovered the principal Late Arenal assemblage at Sitio Bolívar (G-164). Definition of this subphase is complicated by the fact that the ceramics from this site are almost exclusively from the latter part of the subphase (cal AD 300–600). At Sitio Bolívar, the Late Arenal subphase is marked by a combination of Charco Black-on-Red, Guinea Incised, Los Hermanos Beige: Cervantes Variety, Zelaya Bichrome, and the Corrida and Arrastrada varieties of Mojica Impressed. It is important to note, however, that some of these types by themselves are not reliable chronological markers for the Late Arenal subphase. For example, Guinea Incised, Mojica Impressed, and Charco Black-on-Red all appear sometime during the Early Arenal subphase.

As with the early and late facets of the Tronadora Phase, it is important to realize that this division of the Arenal Phase is provisional. The recovery of more complete stratigraphic data and additional radiocarbon dates, especially from sites with both Early and Late Arenal components, will go a long way toward refining and improving our understanding of Arenal Phase chronology.

THE SILENCIO PHASE

The Silencio Phase is marked by the appearance of polychrome ceramics and has been defined primarily on the basis of comparisons between the Arenal basin ceramics and the well-documented sequences of western Greater Nicoya. It is estimated to date from cal AD 600–1300. As with the Arenal Phase, there are a significant number of similarities between Cordilleran assemblages and those from sites farther west at this time. Although vessels from the Atlantic Watershed region appear in Late Arenal contexts, however, trade vessels from Silencio contexts are exclusively from the west. Greater Nicoya techniques such as polychrome decoration and fine incision become dominant, and the presence of polychrome vessels from Greater Nicoya in burials suggests that there was a high level of contact between the two areas in the Silencio Phase.

In spite of contacts with the west, however, the Silencio Phase appears to have been a time of regional consolidation. There is an increase in the number of local ceramic types over those shared with Greater Nicoya. Stone cist burials, unknown in Greater Nicoya, appear in special cemeteries. Locally produced vessels show modes of both form and decoration that may be derived from Central Highland and Atlantic Watershed traditions, rather than from those of Greater Nicoya. The blend of ceramic traits noted in Cordilleran assemblages during the Silencio Phase may reflect the area's geographical location between two areas that were experiencing unprecedented growth in population and social complexity at this time.

The ceramic sample for the Silencio Phase comes primarily from excavations at the Silencio cemetery (G-150), an essentially single-component site. Relatively few sites from the lakeshore reconnaissance showed an abundance of Silencio Phase material (Chap. 3). At El Silencio, Silencio Phase pottery was distributed vertically through Units 30 and 50, which were separated by layers of tephra (Units 40 and 41). Unfortunately, the small size of the ceramic sample and the heavily disturbed nature of the site (with many deep burials, evidence of significant earth moving, and heavy looting) do not permit subdivisions of the Silencio Phase.

Ceramics diagnostic of the Early Polychrome Period (AD 500–800), as it is known in Greater Nicoya, are extremely rare in the Arenal area. With the exception of a few sherds of Carillo Polychrome from Sitio Bolívar (G-164), the two principal pottery types of this period, but farther to the west—Carrillo and Galo Polychromes—are practically absent in our samples. Decorative elements of both Carillo and Galo Polychrome are present in a local type—Jiménez Polychrome—identified at El Silencio.

At a general level, the ceramic assemblage from El Silencio is similar to Middle Polychrome (AD 800–1200) assemblages from La Guinea (Baudez 1967; Hoopes 1980), Vidor (Accola 1978), and La Ceiba (Blanco et al. 1986; Guerrero and Blanco 1987). Distinctive Middle Polychrome types such as Mora, Papagayo, Altiplano, Cabuyal Birmania, and Santa Marta (Fig. 10-19) are present in significant quantities, and both polychrome and incised decoration on local types indicate widespread stylistic trends at this time.

Typical Greater Nicoya polychromes may not have been manufactured in the Cordilleran region, however. Fancy Greater Nicoya polychromes appear only at the Silencio cemetery, in either burials (one of which contained five miniature Cabuyal polychrome vessels) or construction fill (Fig. 10-20). Moreover, the typical Greater Nicoya domestic types from Middle Polychrome assemblages such as Piches Red and Danta Beige are found only in small quantities. The dominant monochrome type is instead Tres Esquinas Beige, and the abundance of distinctive local polychrome vessels, which are not known from sites in western Greater Nicoya, implies that the high-quality polychromes may have arrived through trade or other special contacts.

As elsewhere in Greater Nicoya at this time, the Cordilleran region experienced an explosion of polychrome types during the Silencio Phase. With the exception of the local Jiménez Polychrome, all of the polychrome types at El Silencio are also found in Middle Polychrome assemblages in the Tempisque Valley (Baudez 1967) and the Pacific Coast of Guanacaste (Lange 1976). Many appear as trade items at sites in the Atlantic Watershed (Snarskis 1978:289–290) and Meseta Central (Snarskis and Blanco 1978).

A preliminary examination of the pastes of sherds of Mora and Papagayo polychromes from El Silencio suggests that they were not locally manufactured. The Mora examples have a compact, fine-textured paste devoid of the white flecks of tephra found in locally manufactured pottery. Papagayo sherds have a fine, orange-colored paste similar to that found in western Guanacaste and Rivas, Nicaragua. The relatively small numbers of these types in Silencio Phase assemblages sug-

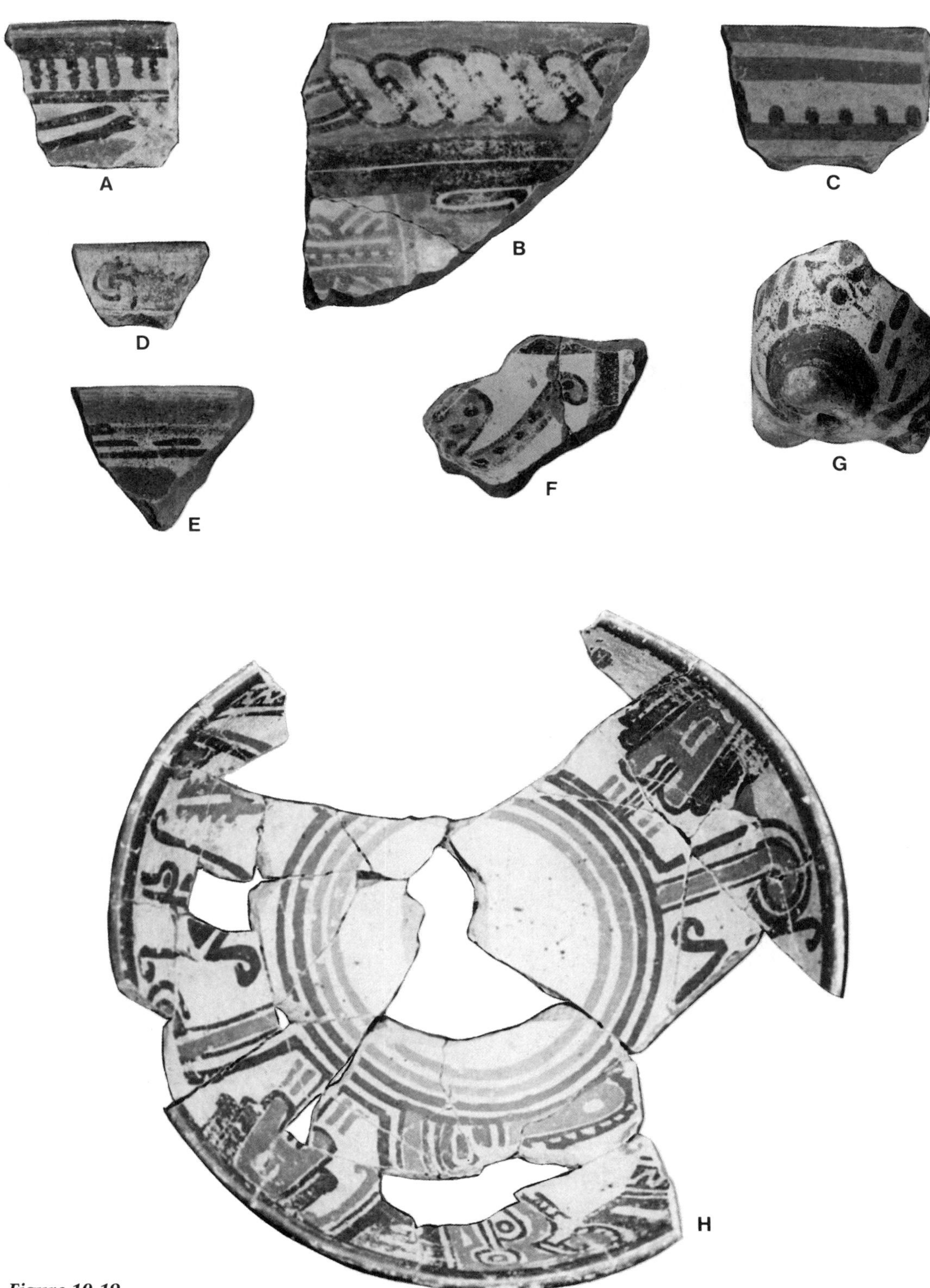

Figure 10-19.
Silencio Phase: Fancy polychromes. Birmania Polychrome: A; Papagayo Polychrome: B, C, E–G; Santa Marta Polychrome: D; Mora Polychrome (interior or ring-base bowl): H. Sherd widths: A, 4.2 cm; B, 8.5 cm; C, 5.0 cm; D, 3.5 cm; E, 4.5 cm; F, 5.5 cm; G, 4.5 cm. Diameter of H, 35 cm. Photographs by John Hoopes.

Figure 10-20.
Silencio Phase: Whole vessels from El Silencio cemetery. Cabuyal Polychrome: A, B; Jiménez Polychrome: C. Diameters: A, 6.0 cm; B, 6.5 cm; C, 26.0 cm. Photographs by John Hoopes.

gests that these fine-paste decorated wares were imported to the Cordilleran region from manufacturing centers in western or northern Greater Nicoya.

SILENCIO PHASE CERAMIC TYPES

Several decorative and formal modes have been noted that are distinctive to the Silencio Phase, and they have assisted in the definition of two local types and one local variety.

Jiménez Polychrome

Jiménez Polychrome is the principal diagnostic type of the Silencio Phase (Figs. 10-20C, 10-21; Hoopes 1984a: fig. 4). It combines decorative modes of the Early and Middle Polychrome periods of Greater Nicoya with formal modes that may have Atlantic origins. It is characterized by large, open bowls and restricted-neck jars with flattened or everted rims, and is decorated with painting in red and black on a cream or buff surface. Painting is also found on the upper, flattened surface of rims with a T-shaped cross section (Hoopes 1984a: fig. 4F). The lower half of the vessel is always slipped red, but the upper half bears a horizontal frieze of geometric motifs executed in broad strokes in combination with sets of horizontal wavy lines in red or black. Multiple brushing is also found on the broad lip surface of flattened-rim bowls. Vessel supports include small, solid conical feet and large, hollow mammiform rattle forms.

The use of broad-stroke geometric motifs in Jiménez Polychrome is similar in execution to motifs on Galo Polychrome (cf. Baudez 1967:pl. 38B; Lange 1976:fig. 7a), but the characteristic surface luster and both pear-shaped and cylindrical vessel forms of Galo are absent. Jiménez Polychrome is related to Cabuyal Polychrome in a fashion analogous to that between Galo and Carillo. That is, many decorative motifs are shared, but sufficient differences in the way they are combined—together with variables of paste, surface finish, and form—distinguish one from the other. Jiménez Polychrome shares the use of multiple brushing in red on a cream or white background with Cabuyal, and small sherds of the two are often difficult to distinguish. The modal repertoire of form and decoration for Cabuyal is substantially smaller than that for Jiménez Polychrome, and the former could in fact be classified as a variety of the latter (i.e., Jiménez Polychrome: Cabuyal Variety).

Jiménez Polychrome is placed earlier in the sequence than the AD 800 date assigned to the beginning of the Middle Polychrome Period in Greater Nicoya because of its affinities with both Galo Polychrome and Carillo Polychrome. Stratigraphically, Jiménez Polychrome was present in both Units 30 and 50; however, we found more than twice as many sherds in the upper than in the lower stratum.

Belén Incised

Jiménez Polychrome and Belén Incised (Hoopes 1984a:fig. 5) are the most important decorated Silencio Phase types. Incised vessels are as common as polychromes in Silencio Phase lots (313 Belén sherds and 325 Jiménez), and virtually all of the incised pottery falls into the newly defined Belén Incised: Ayotes Variety.

Belén Incised: Ayotes Variety

Incised decoration is the same as that defined for Belén Incised in the Tempisque Valley (Baudez 1967: 129). Principal motifs are cross-hatchured triangles and rectangles in a frieze on the upper vessel exterior. The Belén Incised: Ayotes Variety (Fig. 10-22) is characterized by a distinct T-shaped rim profile, which is shared with Jiménez Polychrome and Tres Esquinas Beige. Just as Jiménez Polychrome frequently bears decoration on the surface of flattened rims, Belén Incised: Ayotes Variety occasionally has incisions on the broad upper surface of the vessel lip. The most common vessel type is the open bowl, slightly incurving at the rim. Surfaces are slipped brown or left unslipped and burnished. Vessels are black to reddish brown in color. Infilling of incisions with white pigment is common. Pastes are fine but poorly oxidized and contain inclusions of tephra and ferric spherules.

Chronologically, Belén Incised enjoyed a later popularity than Jiménez Polychrome. We found more than three times as many Belén Incised sherds in Unit 30 than in Unit 50, whereas we found more than twice as many Jiménez Polychrome sherds in Unit 50 than appeared in Unit 30.

Tres Esquinas Beige

Another new type, Tres Esquinas Beige (Fig. 10-23; Hoopes 1984a:fig. 6:K–T), is the dominant domestic ceramic in Silencio Phase assemblages, al-

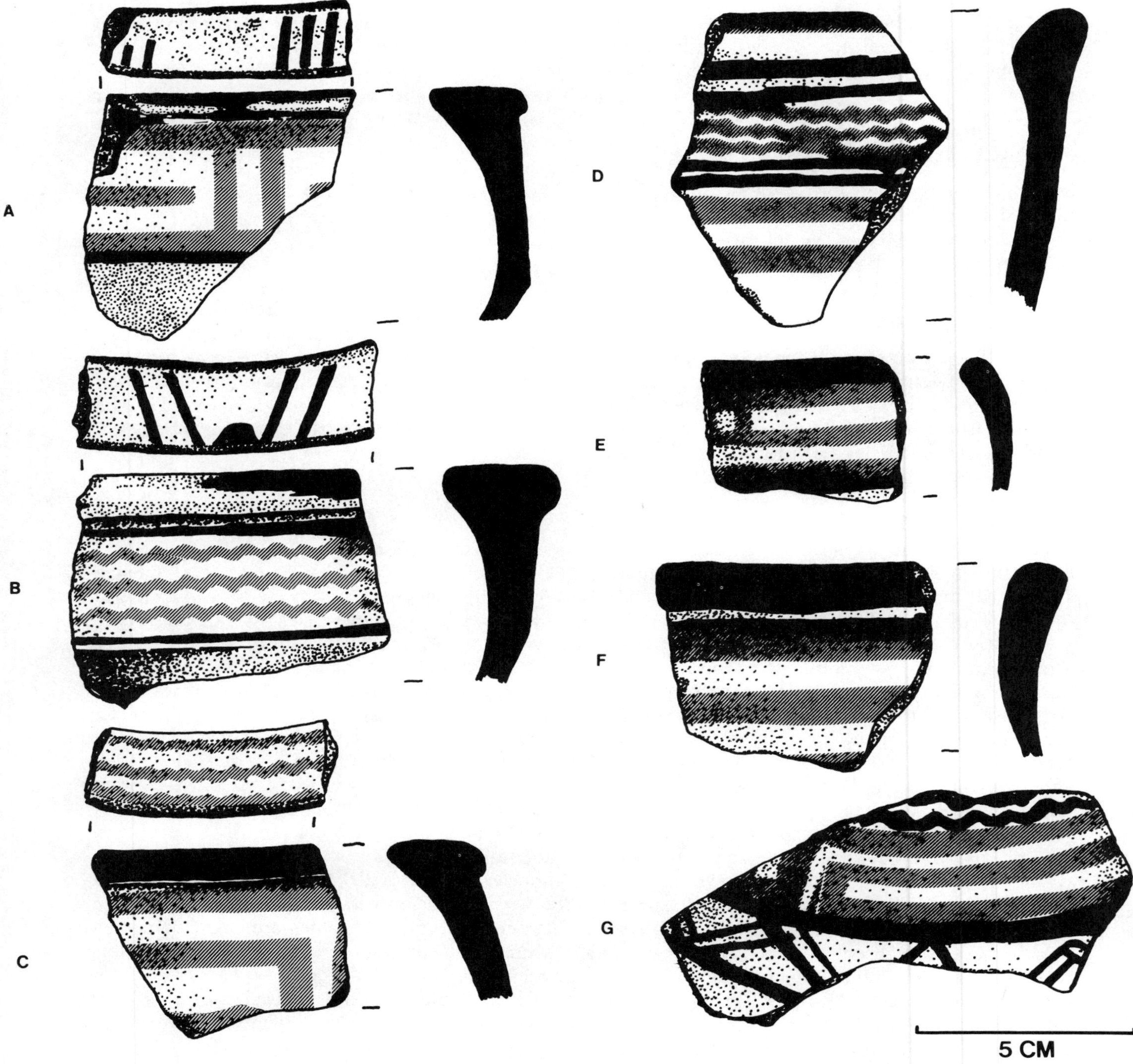

Figure 10-21.
Jiménez Polychrome. A–C: T-shaped bowl rims; D–F: open bowls; G: jar shoulder. Proveniences: A (G-150-B11), B (G-176-A1), C (G-150-G2), D (G-169-B4), E (G-150-C2), F (G-150-C2), G (G-150-C2). Figures by John Hoopes.

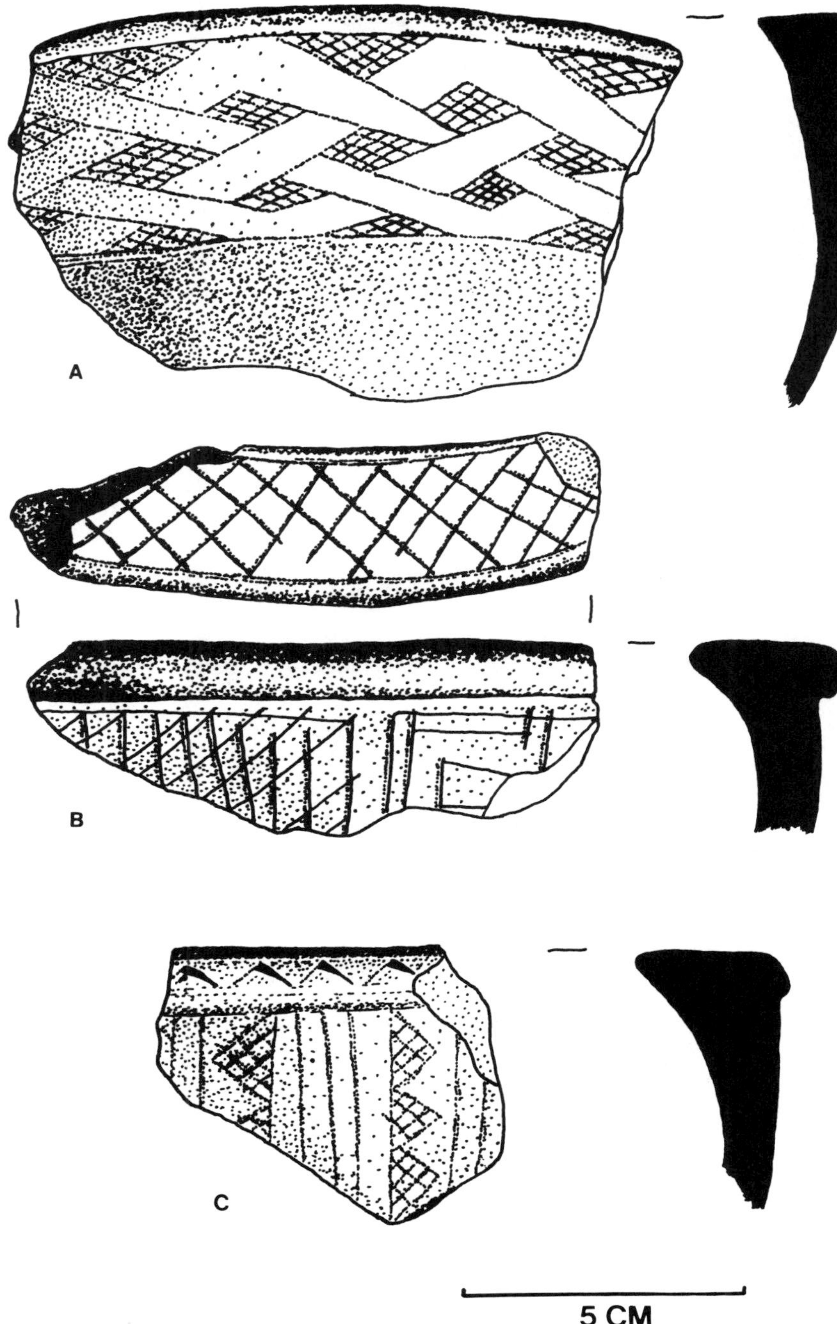

Figure 10-22.
Belén Incised: Ayotes Variety. A–C: T*-shaped bowl rims. Proveniences: A (G-150-B2), B (G-150-I2), C (G-150-G2). Figures by John Hoopes.*

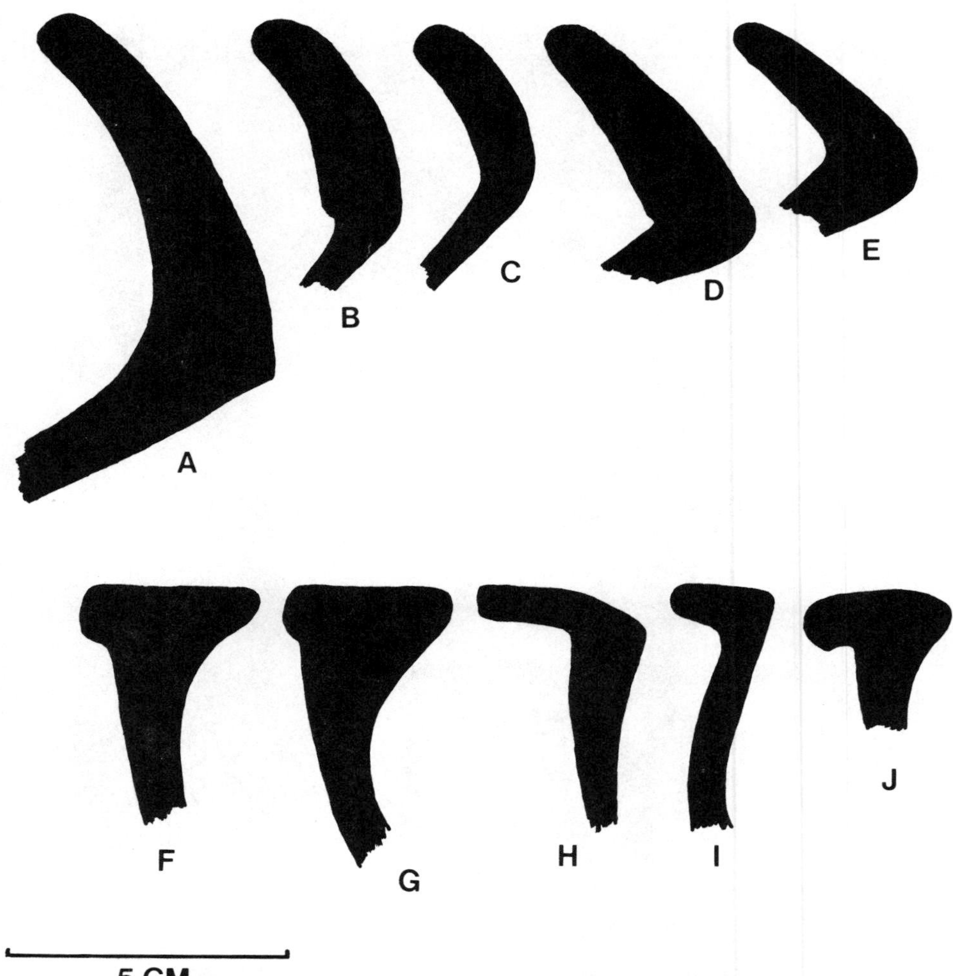

Figure 10-23.
Tres Esquinas Beige rim profiles. A–E: everted jar rims; F–G: T*-shaped bowl rims; H–J: horizontally everted jar rims. Proveniences: A–C, E, F, H–J (G-150-C2); D, G (G-176-A1). Figures by John Hoopes.*

though sherds of Piches Red, Malekos Red, and Danta Beige are also present in small quantities. Tres Esquinas Beige is closely related to the Hermanos Beige of the Arenal Phase, being characterized by red-slipped rims on buff-paste jars and bowls. As in the earlier type, the red slip extends to the interiors of jar rims and open bowls. The two types are distinguished on the basis of rim profiles. While Los Hermanos Beige jar rims are rounded and externally thickened, Tres Esquinas Beige rims are direct and unthickened. The early jars tend to have gently curving necks, while later types are more angular. In Tres Esquinas Beige, the rim/neck juncture is sometimes emphasized with a shallow groove. The most common Tres Esquinas bowl rim has the incurving, T-shaped profile, whereas Los Hermanos rims have a broad, outturned lip. In sum, although paste and decorative modes are virtually the same for some Arenal and Silencio Phase ceramics, rim forms are sufficiently different to allow for temporal distinctions.

DATING THE SILENCIO PHASE

The upper date for the Silencio Phase is based on a date of cal AD 1216–1295 (Tx-5077) for charcoal from a burial associated with a large assemblage of diagnostic ceramics at El Silencio. Previously, a terminal date of AD 1000 was suggested in the absence of C-14 assays (Hoopes 1984a). This suggestion was based primarily on the absence of a number of ceramic traits that distinguish the Middle Polychrome/Late Polychrome transition in Greater Nicoya. The small sample of Papagayo Polychrome consists entirely of early varieties, including a bowl fragment with a painted jaguar on the interior. The great majority of Mora Polychrome sherds are from varieties that Accola (1978) places in the Panamá Phase (AD 800–1000) of the Bay of Culebra. Asientillo Polychrome, a late Middle Polychrome type common in the Tempisque Valley, is another type that is not present. Late Polychrome white-slipped ceramics such as Vallejo, Mombacho, Pataky, and Madeira Polychrome are also completely absent from Cordilleran assemblages.

Decorative modes of Jiménez Polychrome, the dominant marker for the Silencio Phase, also suggest that the phase as defined may be weighted toward the earlier half of the Middle Polychrome Period. The principal decorative motif of both Jiménez Polychrome and Cabuyal Polychrome is wavy, multiple-brushed horizontal lines. Although this motif is not mentioned in the original type descriptions of either Carillo or Galo Polychrome (Baudez 1967:119,132), an examination of whole vessels from the collections of the Museo Nacional de Costa Rica and the Instituto Nacional de Seguros reveals that it occurs frequently on both. Multiple brushing is diagnostic of the Arenal Phase Las Palmas Red-on-Beige type, and it is also found on examples of Charco Black-on-Red from Sitio Bolívar. Its use on Silencio Phase pottery indicates a strong continuity in local ceramic traditions; however, multiple-brush decoration declines in usage sometime toward the middle of the Middle Polychrome Period across Greater Nicoya. This may also be true in the Northwestern Cordillera.

DISCUSSION

The dominance of red-rimmed ceramics and gradual transitions in ceramic styles over a space of more than 3,000 years argues strongly for a continuity in populations from the Tronadora through the Silencio phases. Domestic pottery is usually a more reliable indicator of ethnic identity than are decorated types, which are frequently imitated or traded. The relative scarcity in Arenal-area assemblages of the monochrome culinary wares that dominate Middle Polychrome assemblages in the Tempisque Valley suggests that the populations of the Arenal region had household traditions that were markedly distinct from those to the west. The use of rock-lined tombs in the Silencio Phase is a major divergence from Greater Nicoya patterns and indicates cultural affinities with the Central Highlands region. In ceramics, there is more evidence of stylistic regionalization in the Silencio Phase than in the preceding Arenal Phase. Ceramic patterns suggest that the local population had regular interchange with peoples of lowland Guanacaste, somewhat lesser interaction with the Atlantic region, and maintained distinct local traditions.

THE TILARÁN PHASE

There is evidence for a marked divergence in cultural patterns between the cultures of Greater Nicoya and those of the Cordilleran region in the Tilarán Phase (cal AD 1300–1500). There is some evidence for interaction with peoples of the Gulf of Nicoya, but local ceramic assemblages bear little resemblance to Late Polychrome assemblages from the Pacific Coast and the Tempisque Valley. None of the late painted types of Greater Nicoya, with the exception of Jicote Polychrome, are present in Tilarán Phase assemblages. Two sherds of Tempisque Incised hint at direct contacts between peoples of the Cordillera and the Gulf of Nicoya. In general, the phase is characterized by large, coarse ceramics with appliqué-decorated handles that are very similar to late prehistoric ceramics from the Gulf of Nicoya.

Silencio Appliqué, Malekos Red, and San Luis Coarse have been placed in the Tilarán Phase on the basis of clear stratigraphic associations. They were present in a large assemblage found immediately beneath a layer of coarse gray lapilli (Unit 20) at Dos Armadillos (G-154; Chap. 7). They also show a much stronger correlation with Unit 30 than with Unit 50, as does a small sample of Jicote Polychrome—a Late Polychrome type common in the Tempisque Valley.

In addition to the types described below, modes and modal combinations found in association with Tilarán Phase assemblages include unslipped zoo-

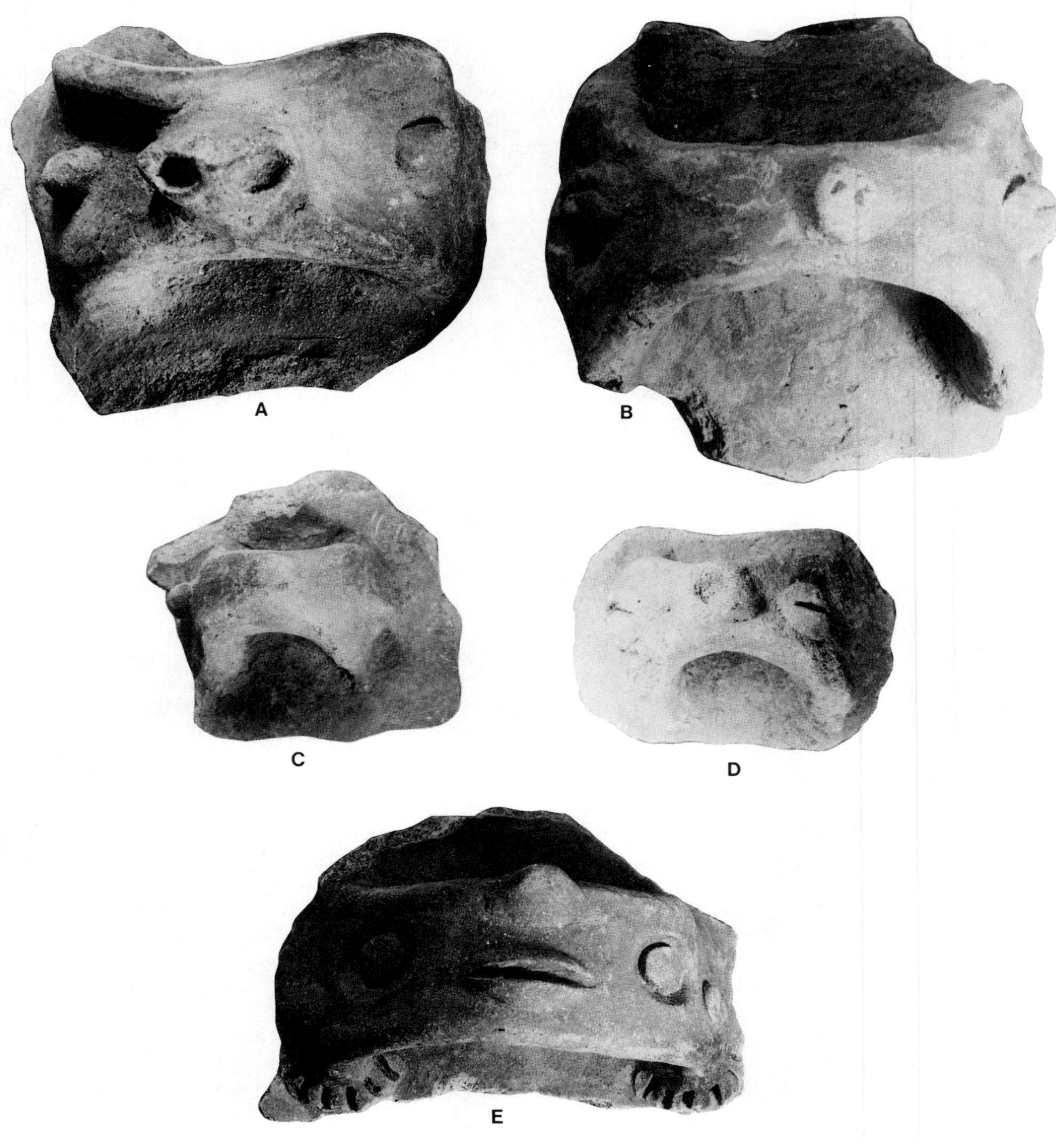

Figure 10-24.
Tilarán Phase: Silencio Appliqué handles. Sherd widths: A, 11.0 cm; B, 11.0 cm; C, 6.0 cm; D, 7.0 cm; E, 12.0 cm. Photographs by John Hoopes.

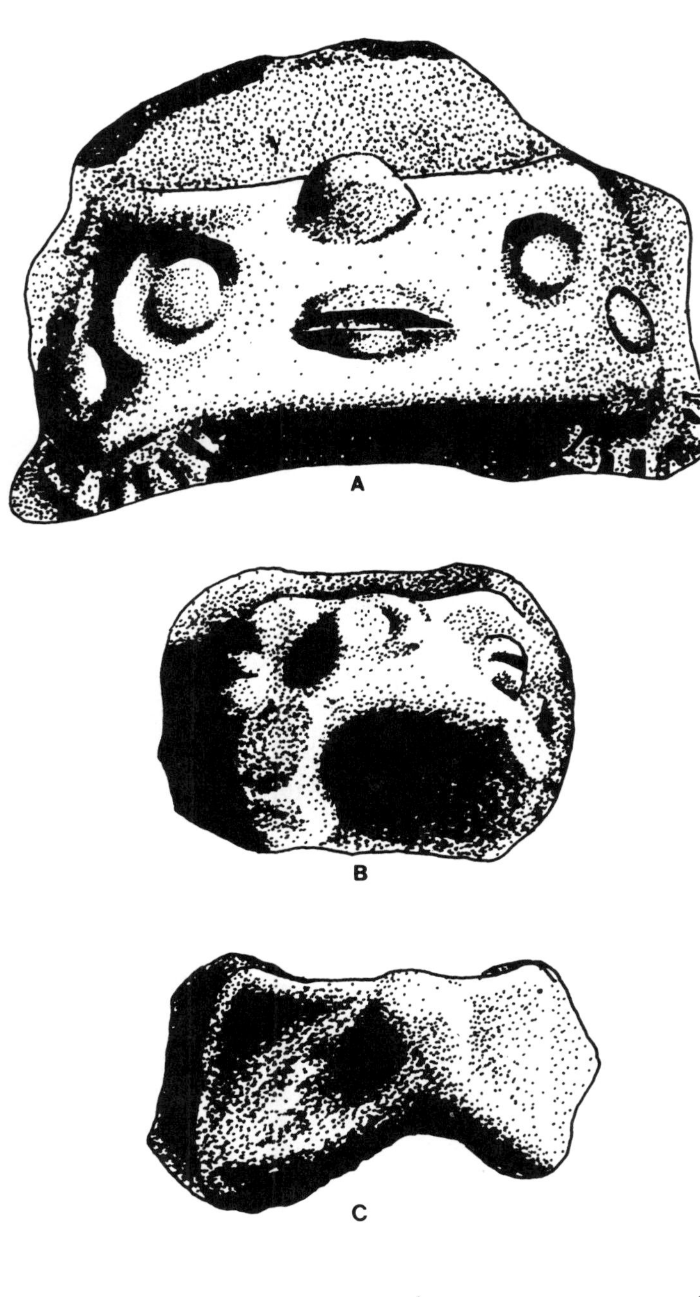

Figure 10-25.
Silencio Appliqué jar handles. Note differing degrees of stylized design from A to C. Proveniences: A (G-166-A1), B (G-154-A2), C (G-161-A1). Figures by John Hoopes.

morphic supports (coati heads are common); appliqué strips on vessel rims and body angles with triangular impressions (possibly related to Creamer's Gulf Incised and Princesa Incised rim modes [1983:313–317]); and carinated, outflaring-rim bowls.

Snarskis (personal communication, 1984) feels that Atlantic Watershed influence on the Arenal area increased during the Tilarán Phase, but it is difficult to identify specific ceramic types that the two regions have in common. At the level of modes, appliquéd strap handles, the use of appliqué on vessel shoulders and rims, and zoomorphic unslipped supports have a number of analogies in both the Stone Cist Period of the Atlantic Watershed (Snarskis 1978) and the late prehistoric period in the Gulf of Nicoya (Creamer 1983). The closest relationships appear to be with the latter. Dating of the Tilarán Phase is based on stratigraphy, tentative correlations with Snarskis' Stone Cist Period, Creamer's assemblages, and absolute C-14 chronology.

TILARÁN PHASE CERAMIC TYPES

Silencio Appliqué

Silencio Appliqué is the principal decorated type of the Tilarán Phase (Figs. 10-24, 10-25; Hoopes 1984a:fig. 7). It is a dark brown to reddish paste utilitarian ware with an often coarse, unslipped finish. Vessels are vertical-necked jars with direct or slightly everted rims. Appliqué appears on vessel necks, rims, and shoulders. One diagnostic mode is a decorated strap handle with a stylized face of appliqué buttons or modeled features. These handles are usually fairly crude. They are typically narrow in the middle and expanded at either end (Fig. 10-7).

Silencio Appliqué is very similar to Toro Appliqué, a type from sites near the mouth of the Tempisque River (Baudez 1967:168) and on islands in the Gulf of Nicoya (Creamer 1983:299–304, fig. 71), and may prove to be the same ceramic type. The representation of zoomorphic motifs (which Creamer identifies as bats and reptiles) on the two types is similar. As with Silencio Appliqué, Toro Appliqué has been identified only from vessel handles.

Malekos Red

The most common culinary type is Malekos Red, which shares outflaring-rim jar forms with Tres Esquinas Beige but differs in having a red finish. The distinctive color is achieved in two ways, either by the use of a thick red slip or by complete oxidation of the vessel exterior. Malekos Red bears many similarities to the Piches Red type of the Tempisque Valley, especially in wide-rimmed bowl forms and shoe-shaped vessels. Handles are usually round in cross section. Vessels of this type are often surprisingly large.

San Luis Coarse

A third utilitarian type of this phase has been termed San Luis Coarse (Fig. 10-26). It is distinguished principally by its crude execution. Vessels are principally thick-walled, vertical-necked jars that are unslipped and dark red, brown, or black. Both Malekos Red and San Luis Coarse share a number of characteristics with Gulf Plain, a type from islands in the Gulf of Nicoya (Creamer 1983:311–314), suggesting further affinities between late monochrome types of the Arenal area and Gulf of Nicoya regions.

Tempisque Incised

Two sherds from the site of Dos Armadillos (G-154) have been identified as Tempisque Incised (Fig. 10-27A and B), a type identified by Baudez from collections on Toro Island (1967:170) and by Creamer at sites on islands in the Gulf of Nicoya (1983:286–291). These are highly polished and decorated with narrow rim bands of zigzag incisions and dots (cf. Baudez 1967:pl. 47E; Creamer 1983:fig. 68). They may represent vessels brought or traded into the highlands by peoples from the Gulf.

DATING THE TILARÁN PHASE

A single C-14 date, cal AD 1298–1420 (Tx-5079), was associated with a Tilarán Phase assemblage at the site of Dos Armadillos. This sample came from the upper portion of Unit 30 in a deposit buried under a thick layer of Unit 20 tephra. Current estimates for the date of deposition of Unit 20 are based on the foregoing date and two others, cal AD 1416–1471 (SI-576) and cal AD 1435–1619 (SI-577), derived from samples of charred bark buried by a pyroclastic flow from Arenal Volcano. These suggest a date of approximately cal AD 1450 for Unit 20. The late dates for this phase are in agreement with estimates for the age of the ceramics from the Gulf of Nicoya mentioned earlier. No Tilarán Phase materials were identified in contexts that clearly postdated the deposition of Unit 20.

CERAMIC PHASE DISTRIBUTION

REGIONAL PATTERNS OF CERAMIC PHASES

Table 10-1 illustrates the distribution of ceramics from each of the four phases for the forty-three sites sampled during the 1984 and 1985 seasons. We identified Tronadora Phase pottery at 20 sites, and Arenal Phase ceramics were present at all but six. Only two sites, G-162 and G-163, yielded a predominance of sherds from the Tronadora Phase; however, a total of twenty sites proved to have a majority of ceramics from the Arenal Phase, with seven more having at least 25% of the ceramic assemblage in this phase. There were only three sites with strong Silencio Phase components, and five with predominantly Tilarán Phase components.

Of the forty-three sites sampled, few were strictly single-component sites. Almost all sites were occupied during two or more ceramic phases, and eleven had evidence of occupation during all four. This suggests that there was a strong continuity of site use throughout the study region, in some cases lasting as long as 3,000 years.

STRATIGRAPHIC RELATIONSHIPS OF CERAMIC PHASES

One of the principal aims of the ceramics analysis was to correlate the ceramic sequence with tephra layers from Arenal Volcano (Chap. 1, Fig. 1-8). In so doing, we were able to combine interpretations of volcanic and cultural stratigraphic units. Volcanic activity was responsible for the destruction of crops and habitations during violent eruptive intervals as well as for the creation of fertile, tephra-enriched soils. A recognizable sequence of volcanic strata was traceable throughout the study area. Although not all individual strata were visible at all sites, this sequence provided a unique opportunity for the calibration of stratigraphic deposits from a number of widely separated sites.

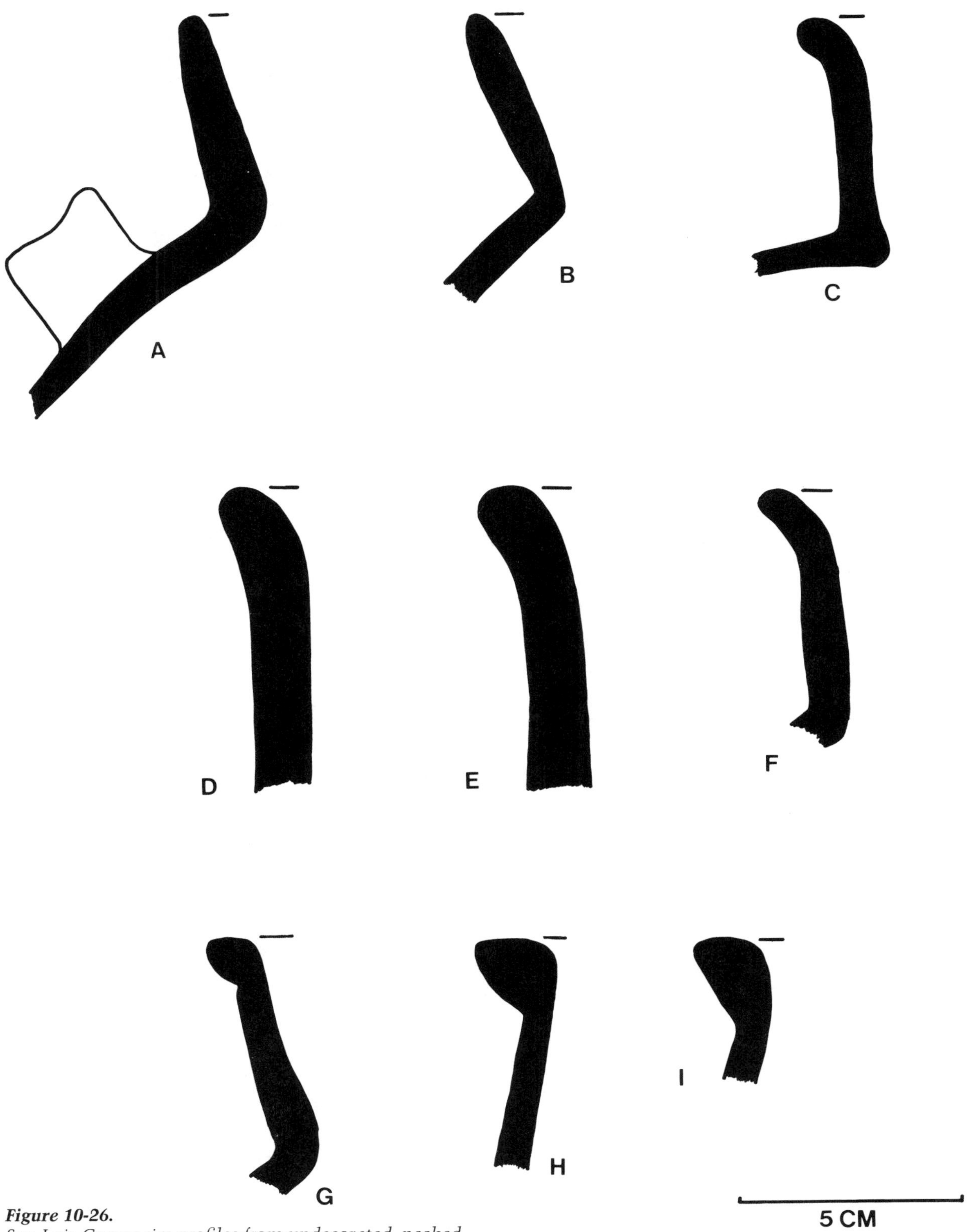

Figure 10-26.
San Luis Coarse rim profiles from undecorated, necked jars. A: jar rim and shoulder with strap handle; B: everted-rim jar; C–F: vertical jar necks and rims; G–I: exteriorly thickened jar rims. Proveniences: A (G-161-G1), B (G-161-D3), C (G-175-A1), D (G-154-A2), E (G-154-A1), F (G-161-A3), G (G-166-A2), H (G-154-A2), I (G-154-A2). Rim diameters: A (11 cm), B (14 cm), C (18 cm), D (38 cm), E (34 cm), F (12 cm), G (16 cm), H (22 cm), I (17 cm). Figures by John Hoopes.

Figure 10-27.
Tilarán Phase: Other decorated types. Tempisque Incised: A, B; tripod vessel with impression and appliqué: C. Sherd widths: A, 9.5 cm; B, 9.5 cm. Maximum width of C, 11.6 cm. Photographs by John Hoopes.

TABLE 10-1
CERAMIC PHASE REPRESENTATION FOR SITES RECORDED BY THE PROYECTO PREHISTÓRICO ARENAL

		Tronadora		*Arenal*		*Silencio*		*Tilarán*		*Unknown*	
Site	*Sample*	*No.*	*%*	*No.*	*%*	*No.*	*%*	*No.*	*%*	*No.*	*%*
Tronadora Phase Predominant											
G-162	24	16	66.7	3	12.5					5	20.8
G-163	836	474	56.7	210	25.1	1	0.1	16	1.9	135	16.1
Arenal Phase Predominant											
G-151	6			5	83.3					1	16.7
G-155	18			14	77.8			1	5.6	3	16.7
G-158	6	1	16.7	4	66.7					1	16.7
G-159	19			10	52.6	5	26.3			4	21.1
G-164	6,711	6	0.1	5,769	86.0	27	0.4	13	0.2	896	13.4
G-165	110	26	23.6	55	50.0	6	5.5	2	1.8	21	19.1
G-166	224	7	3.1	92	41.1	11	4.9	78	34.8	36	16.1
G-168	57	5	8.8	41	71.9	1	1.8	3	5.3	7	12.3
G-170	85	3	3.5	55	64.7	7	8.2			20	23.5
G-171	43	1	2.3	34	79.1					8	18.6
G-172	68	2	2.9	54	79.4					12	17.6
G-175	241	2	0.8	153	63.5	15	6.2	13	5.4	58	24.1
G-176	69	1	1.4	47	68.1	15	21.7			6	8.7
G-177	227	6	2.6	166	73.1	17	7.5	2	0.9	36	15.9
G-182	36			24	66.7	1	2.8			11	30.6
G-183	27			17	63.0					10	37.0
G-184	46			29	63.0	1	2.2			16	34.8
G-187	89	5	5.6	63	70.8			4	4.5	17	19.1
G-191	16			16	100.0						
G-192	12			8	66.7			2	16.7	2	16.7
Silencio Phase Predominant											
G-150	1,744			104	6.0	1,195	68.5	62	3.6	383	22.0
G-152	23					19	82.6			4	17.4
G-153	121			4	3.3	114	94.2	1	0.8	2	1.7
Tilarán Phase Predominant											
G-154	157					15	9.6	81	51.6	61	38.9
G-160	17					6	35.3	9	52.9	2	11.8
G-161	294	8	2.7	12	4.1	23	7.8	208	70.7	43	14.6
G-185	9							9	100.0		
G-188	22			2	9.1			17	77.3	3	13.6
Mixed Component Sites or Sites of Unknown Phase											
G-156	220	47	21.4	23	10.5	77	35.0	22	10.0	51	23.2
G-157	20	4	20.0	2	10.0	6	30.0	2	10.0	6	30.0
G-167	38	3	7.9	14	36.8	7	18.4	2	5.3	12	31.6
G-169	636	2	0.3	2	0.3	230	36.2	237	37.3	165	25.9
G-173	15			4	26.7	2	13.3	6	40.0	3	20.0
G-174	50			13	26.0	16	32.0	5	10.0	16	32.0
G-178	30	1	3.3	6	20.0	3	10.0			20	66.7
G-179	22			8	36.4	2	9.1			12	54.5
G-180	134			29	21.6	43	32.1	14	10.4	48	35.8
G-181	27			3	11.1	5	18.5			19	70.4
G-186	38			7	18.4			1	2.6	30	78.9
G-189	33					9	27.3	7	21.2	17	51.5
G-190	9			4	44.4			2	22.2	3	33.3
Total	12,629	620	4.9	7,106	56.3	1,879	14.9	819	6.5	2,205	17.5

Note: Total counts (where applicable) include sherds from both surface collections and excavations.

There was not a strong correlation between volcanic activity and cultural change in the Arenal region. No tephra horizons marked clear transitions from one cultural phase to another. Sealed deposits were rare with the exception of the Tilarán Phase assemblage at Dos Armadillos; however, it was possible to associate the ceramic sequence with regional volcanic stratigraphy.

We combined artifact lots of known stratigraphic affiliation for a regional sample of almost 9,000 diagnostic sherds with known stratigraphic provenience. We recovered close to 1,000 sherds from Unit 30, most of these from El Silencio and Dos Armadillos. We collected over 7,500 diagnostic sherds from 50s strata sampled at El Silencio, Sitio Bolívar, Tronadora Vieja, Viboriana, and other sites. We excavated over 350 diagnostic sherds from 60s horizons, virtually all from Tronadora Vieja. We recovered smaller numbers from Units 20 and 40/41, tephra horizons whose cultural contents were probably mixed from other strata.

The earliest Tronadora Phase occupation appears to have occurred just prior to the initial eruptive activity of Arenal Volcano, shortly after 2000 cal BC. This occupation continued throughout the deposition of the first tephras in the region. We identified some 74% of diagnostic ceramics recovered from Units 64, 61, and 60 as belonging to the Tronadora Phase, the remainder being either Arenal Phase or unclassified sherds. At Tronadora Vieja, we also found Tronadora Phase ceramics in the lower 50s horizons, although in small proportions relative to Arenal Phase ceramics. The frequency of Tronadora Phase ceramics is significantly greater in strata below Unit 55 than above it, but it is not clear whether this tephra horizon provided a "cap" to Tronadora Phase cultural deposits. It seems safe to say, however, that the 60s strata were formed during the Tronadora Phase.

Ceramic associations of 50s complex stratigraphic horizons above Unit 55 and below Units 40 and 41 are not as clear. Arenal Phase ceramics were plainly situated in 50s strata at both Tronadora Vieja and Sitio Bolívar. At Tronadora Vieja, the sample size from individual units within the 50s complex was not great enough to indicate ceramic change or the correlation of units with Early or Late Arenal assemblages.

At the Late Arenal site of Sitio Bolívar, the stratigraphic association of the ceramic assemblage was somewhat clearer. Unit 50 was visible as a separate stratum in profiles. The majority of artifacts were situated in Unit 54. Unit 60 was mostly disturbed through cultural activities such as burials. In most places this disturbance had penetrated down into the Aguacate clay (Unit 65).

While we found many artifacts in Unit 54, it appears that cultural activity at Sitio Bolívar occurred *on top of* this unit and not during its formation. The 390–50 cal BC (SI-3459) and 86 cal BC—cal AD 390 (I-10804) dates at El Tajo (Aguilar 1984:75) were reportedly obtained from a soil that had developed on top of Unit 8 (possibly Silencio Sequence Unit 55). These dates, which overlap from 86 to 50 cal BC, correspond well with estimated dates for the early facet of the Arenal Phase, and their stratigraphic position suggests a location in Unit 54. Given a period of about 500 years and the soil development that would have occurred during this time, an association of the cultural materials from Sitio Bolívar with Unit 53 seems more likely. There was a high degree of compression of strata beneath Unit 50 and above the cultural features, which made identification of stratigraphy difficult, but Arenal Phase materials appear to have been deposited sometime prior to the formation of Unit 50.

While the Upper 50s represent Arenal Phase deposits, Unit 50 dates to the first half of the Silencio Phase. We found a large number of Silencio Phase sherds in Unit 50 at El Silencio, where Units 40 and 41 sealed primary deposits in this horizon. Only a small Arenal Phase component was present. It should be noted that we found no Silencio Phase sherds at either Tronadora Vieja or Sitio Bolívar and that we found no excavated sites to have a significant amount of material from both the Silencio and the Arenal phases.

Just as the 50s complex appears to have been deposited and formed during both the Arenal and the Silencio phases, Unit 30 is almost equally divided between Silencio and Tilarán Phase materials. There was no dramatic change in the ceramic assemblage at El Silencio before and after the deposition of Units 40 and 41. The only type with any significant difference in frequency between the two strata is Belén Incised: Ayotes Variety, which is much more common in Unit 30 than in Unit 50.

The association of Tilarán Phase materials with the upper portion of Unit 30 was documented at Dos Armadillos, where we found a 100% Tilarán Phase assemblage in a deposit directly beneath the coarse lapilli of Unit 20. A single C-14 date of cal AD 1298–1420 (Tx-5079) for charcoal from an associated habitation feature is supported by a previous assay indicating Unit 20 was deposited prior to cal AD 1520 (Melson this volume).

SUMMARY AND CONCLUSIONS

Archaeological research in the Arenal area has produced one of the longest cultural sequences in lower Central America. It is especially noteworthy because of the early dates for the appearance of pottery. Arenal-area ceramics demonstrate a mixture of both Greater Nicoya and Atlantic Watershed characteristics; however, the region is not easily classified as belonging to either of these culture areas. Shifting affinities and strong local traditions indicate that the region had an important character of its own.

THE TRONADORA PHASE

The earliest pottery in the Arenal sequence is mixed with or superimposed on artifacts from the preceramic Fortuna Phase. This suggests that the preceramic/ceramic transition around 2000 cal BC was not accompanied by major changes in settlement pattern. Because Tronadora pottery does not appear to represent an incipient technology, it is unclear whether sites like Tronadora Vieja were reused or continuously occupied through the preceramic/ceramic transition. The appearance of a sophisticated ceramic complex in the area as early as 2000 cal BC suggests either an expansion of pottery-using populations into a region previously inhabited by preceramic societies or existing preceramic population's adoption of a developed ceramic technology. Our limited data on preceramic sites throws little light on either hypothesis. The Tronadora pottery is clearly related to both Chaparrón and La Montaña, but the available information is inadequate for determining which of the three has greatest antiquity. At present, the best explanation is that they represent a regional, Costa Rican development from a still poorly understood Formative substrate.

Although roughly contemporaneous, Tronadora is similar to the Panamanian complexes of Monagrillo and Sarigua only at the level of general modes (red rims, groove incision, shell stamping). Tronadora ceramics also have a general relationship with early ceramic complexes of northern Colombia, especially Barlovento (Reichel-Dolmatoff 1985), with regard to an emphasis on plastic decoration, especially round-bottomed groove incision, shell stamping, rocker stamping, and heavy punctation on large, incurving-rim bowls.

Like Chaparrón (Snarskis 1984a), Tronadora's closest affinities are to ceramics from southern Mesoamerica, especially in terms of rim forms, the use of red paint, and plastic decoration. In spite of some similarities between Tronadora and Ocós, however, there are significant differences. The bolstered rim (Tonjibe Beige) and tall, cylindrical vessel (Zetillal Shell-Stamped) are absent in Early Formative complexes outside of Costa Rica. Figurines, ubiquitous in Ocós and other early Mesoamerican assemblages, are completely absent in Tronadora. Furthermore, the earliest dates for Barra and Ocós (Lowe 1975), are *younger* than those for Tronadora. If there is a linear relationship between the Costa Rican and the Mesoamerican complexes, the influence is from south to north, not the reverse.

In Costa Rica, the inland valleys of the Northwestern Cordillera, the Central Highlands, and the northern plains may have had a head start over coastal regions with regard to the appearance of sedentism and ceramic technology (Fig. 10-1). Sherds related to Chaparrón and La Montaña have been reported from "Guácimo, Línea Vieja, Guayabo de Turrialba, Tatisco, near Cártago, Pavas, Barrial de Heredia, and four other sites within 30 kilometers of Chaparrón in San Carlos" (Snarskis 1984a:206). With the exception of a few sherds from Loma B levels at the Vidor site (Lange, personal communication, 1985), no Early Formative ceramic complex has been defined clearly in western Guanacaste. In a pattern markedly different from that in other parts of the "Intermediate Area," shellfishing and other coastal adaptations are not apparent until the Early Polychrome Period (Lange 1978). This suggests that the first sedentary communities in Costa Rica may have had inland-oriented economies.

The stratigraphic relation of Tronadora ceramics to the local tephra sequence is revealing in terms of cultural development. An initial hypothesis was that ceramics were brought into the region by incipient village agriculturalists who moved into the area to take advantage of fertile soils weathered from volcanic tephra. Pottery appeared *beneath* the first tephra layers in some excavation units, however, and sherds were embedded in the surface of the Aguacate Formation. The Arenal area was therefore occupied by ceramic-using cultures *before* significant eruptions around 2000 cal BC and before the appearance of deep, fertile soils. The fact that Tronadora pottery is found in the greatest quantities in Units 60 and 61 indicates that site use intensified with the deposition of fine tephras during explosive eruptions of Arenal Volcano.

THE ARENAL PHASE

A clear relationship between the Arenal area and Greater Nicoya is apparent with the appearance of Arenal Phase types, and the Arenal area should probably be considered as the easternmost extension of Greater Nicoya at this time. There is a dramatic increase in the number and size of sites in the Early Arenal Phase, indicating population growth. This may spur expansion westward into the Tempisque Valley and Pacific Coast regions. Specialized use of distinct landforms for cemeteries like La Isla (G-166) may signal the emergence of differential social status. Ceramic horizons linking the Arenal area with areas to the west suggest a certain amount of interaction throughout Guanacaste. However, significant regional differences in the appearance of types like Schettel Incised and Rosales Zoned-Engraved and in the use of jade and elaborate carved metates suggest that the cultures of highland and lowland Guanacaste were far from uniform.

While it is not clear that violent eruptions of Arenal Volcano disrupted the occupation of individual sites, the fact that few sites have both Early and Late Arenal components suggests that new sites may have been established in the early centuries cal AD. Although the number of sites appears to decrease in the Late Arenal Phase, evidence from Sitio Bolívar (G-164) indicates that the sites that *were* occupied were large and heavily utilized. An increased level of status differentiation in Late Arenal society is suggested by the effort expended in the construction of stone funerary structures, the presence of greenstone pendants, and the destruction of large quantities of ceramic vessels in cemeteries.

The Late Arenal Phase saw the continued use of ceramic types common to Greater Nicoya. The appearance of types and modes characteristic of the Atlantic Watershed, however, suggests that the region became a true "transition zone" around 300 cal BC. Central Highland contacts may have been an important influence at this time. Early Polychrome types, which dominate Greater Nicoya assemblages from AD 500 to 800, are virtually absent from Arenal assemblages, with the exception of a small number of polychrome sherds from Sitio Bolívar, probably acquired through trade. Sites with both Arenal and Silencio Phase components are rare, suggesting possible population displacement or consolidation.

THE SILENCIO PHASE

Silencio Phase ceramics appear in surface collections at only a small number of sites in the Arenal area. Except where cultural disturbance has occurred, they do not appear stratigraphically below Unit 50. The existence of special-use localities such as the Silencio cemetery suggests that regional integration and status differentiation, first apparent in the Late Arenal Phase, intensified with the Silencio Phase. Gold artifacts and carefully constructed stone tombs suggest the presence of high-status individuals. The appearance of fancy trade ceramics from Greater Nicoya indicates active interregional exchange.

It is possible that the rarity of Silencio Phase sites and the lack of continuity in occupation from the Late Arenal to the Silencio phases do not reflect a population decrease, but a more nucleated settlement pattern with an emphasis on defensible site locations. Populations may have been consolidated in larger villages with greater capacity for ceremonial and defensive activities, as evidenced by the large tombs and stone walls at El Silencio. This pattern would have been accompanied by the emergence of high-status community leaders and warriors and may have been a response to threats posed by expanding populations from the Central Highlands or western Greater Nicoya.

There is evidence that major volcanic eruptions affected both western Guanacaste (Accola 1978) and the Arenal area during the Middle Polychrome Period. In neither area, however, is there evidence that geological events had noticeable effects on nearby populations. Silencio Phase patterns continued more-or-less undisturbed through the deposition of Units 41 and 40, which blanketed the Arenal area with thick layers of fine volcanic tephra. The only changes in ceramic styles were from predominantly polychrome to predominantly incised decoration.

There is little sign of the Mesoamerican influence noted by Healy (1980) for the Middle and Late Polychrome periods of Rivas. Maya jades and incised slate disks have been found at La Fortuna (Stone and Balser 1965; Stone 1977), east of Arenal Volcano, but no evidence of any Mesoamerican artifacts was found in our excavations. Mesoamerican motifs were absent from all Silencio Phase ceramics, with the possible exception of Mora and Papagayo polychromes, which were probably imported from western Guanacaste.

THE TILARÁN PHASE

The final occupation of the Arenal area was characterized by a dispersal of local populations. Tilarán Phase sites are more numerous than those of the Silencio Phase; however, they are also smaller and less specialized. There is a dramatic change in ceramic styles between these phases. Polychrome pottery, which reached new heights in style and execution in western Guanacaste and Rivas at this time, is completely absent from Tilarán Phase sites. Local painting and incising traditions disappear, to be replaced by an emphasis on the use of modeling, appliqué, and adornos to decorate vessel handles and supports in a style similar to that found on islands in the Gulf of Nicoya (Creamer 1983:299–304). The rough, monochrome pottery of the Tilarán Phase is totally unlike the pottery of preceding phases.

The sharing of some ceramic characteristics between the Arenal area and the Gulf of Nicoya during the Tilarán Phase, together with the presence of possible pottery imports, indicates that contacts between highland and lowland Guanacaste continued during the centuries immediately prior to the arrival of the Spanish—and afterwards. The pattern recalls a statement by Castañeda, an early explorer who wrote of the mainland side of the Gulf of Nicoya that "the rest of the chiefs who live on the plain have few Indians, these people live by trade with those of the mountains, to whom they take . . . what those who live in the hills do not have" (cited and translated by author, from Peralta 1883:54).

Contact between the Gulf of Nicoya or the Tempisque Valley and the Arenal area during the Tilarán Phase is indicated by sherds of Tempisque Incised (Baudez 1967:170; Creamer 1983:286–291) from the occupational floor at Dos Armadillos and occasional sherds of Filadelfia Polychrome from surface collections on the shore of Lake Arenal. Similarities in appliqué decoration between Tilarán Phase ceramics and those from islands in the Gulf of Nicoya (cf. Creamer 1983:299–304) further suggest regular contact and possible ethnic continuity between the two regions.

As on the islands in the Gulf, the fancy polychrome ceramics that typify assemblages in western Greater Nicoya at this time are virtually unknown during the Tilarán Phase. These appear primarily in cemeteries, however, and no funerary sites have yet been identified from this time period.

CONCLUSION

The ceramic evidence from 2000 cal BC through cal AD 1500 indicates that the Arenal area had a dynamic and complex prehistory, characterized by fluctuating populations with changing regional affiliations yet noteworthy for its long-term stability. The region provides a good example of how cultural boundaries and population densities can change through time. While the Arenal area may be understood as a transition zone between Greater Nicoya and the Atlantic Watershed regions, it is hardly "marginal" or "peripheral" to cultural development in the two regions during the early part of the sequence. The Northwestern Cordillera played a significant role in the development of Formative economies in Costa Rica during the Tronadora and Arenal phases, and continued to support significant activity during the Silencio and Tilarán phases.

It has been suggested that the reason cultures in this part of Nuclear America never attained the sociopolitical complexity evident in Mesoamerica and the central Andes is that advanced systems of resource exchange and interregional resource exploitation were unneccesary. According to Willey (1984:376), "Redundancy of resources, from niche to niche, tends to stultify trade and trading control and, thereby, complex organizational development." The evidence from the Arenal area suggests that it was essentially self-sufficient and relatively independent from domination or exploitation by outside groups. Until the Tilarán Phase, there is no evidence for a significant amount of population movement into or out of the region. Sociopolitical change, even if part of a region-wide pattern, appears to have been largely autochthonous.

The Arenal area was one of a range of diverse ecological settings in Costa Rica whose cultures contributed jointly to prehistoric development in lower Central America. Its changing cultural manifestations are evidence for the complex ties that existed between cultures of prehistoric Costa Rica. It is necessary to understand the nature and chronology of culture change in order to address more complex issues pertaining to the adaptations of specific cultural systems. The present work emphasizes the importance of understanding regional culture history as a prelude to the formulation of models for culture change. It is hoped that this preliminary work will contribute to the establishment of a foundation for future research on the origins and configurations of lower Central American societies.

NOTES

1. All other dates in this volume are based on calibrated radiocarbon years—dates in real calendar time. These are used to indicate the actual duration of cultural activities in time and to allow for direct comparisons with calendar-based chronologies, such as are being constructed for literate Mesoamerica. In this chapter, however, both calibrated and uncalibrated dates are provided in order to facilitate comparisons with published sequences. Calibrated dates are reported with the prefix "cal" (for example, "1000 cal BC"), while uncalibrated dates do not have this prefix.

It is difficult to make direct comparisons between chronologies based on uncalibrated radiocarbon dates and those based on dates calibrated to real calendar years. For example, Baudez (1967:205) suggests a time span of 300 BC–AD 300 for the Catalina Phase in the Tempisque Valley, based in part on a highly problematic (see Hoopes 1987: 328–330) interpretation of radiocarbon assays. His dates are not radiocarbon assays themselves, however, but estimates based on a wide range of comparative data from Central and South America, of which radiocarbon assays are just a part. If we could convert his suggested phase dates to calendar years, they would be closer to 374 cal BC–cal AD 405—a time span about 30% longer in real time. Still, we cannot say whether this calibrated span accurately represents Baudez's interpretation. Although we can calibrate the individual radiocarbon assays he took into consideration, a direct calibration of his proposed chronology would be methodologically flawed. In order to evaluate new radiocarbon assays in the light of uncalibrated chronologies, it is therefore important to consider *both* uncalibrated and calibrated values.

2. A more detailed discussion of this methodology can be found in Hoopes 1987.

3. A more detailed discussion of these modes can be found in ibid.: 246–250.

4. See ibid. for additional information on Tronadora Phase ceramic types.

5. For the sake of accuracy, all radiocarbon dates in this chapter are presented with their calibrated, two-sigma confidence intervals (see Table 1-1). Dates not listed in Table 1-1 are accompanied in parentheses by laboratory reference numbers and uncalibrated BP dates with one-sigma confidence intervals (see Table 1-1).

6. For a more detailed description of these characteristics, see Hoopes 1987:320–433.

11

Chipped Stone Artifacts from the Cordillera de Tilarán

PAYSON D. SHEETS

INTRODUCTION

The principal objectives of this chapter are to describe and interpret the flaked lithic artifacts found in survey and excavation operations in the Cordillera de Tilarán during research conducted by the Proyecto Prehistórico Arenal in 1984 and 1985, and to explore pertinent theoretical issues. Two categories analyzed here—cooking stones, and thermally fractured debitage (the wastage created by the disintegration of the cooking stones by heat stress during use)—are not commonly reported in lithic sections of research reports in Middle America. Other, more conventional, categories are also presented, including bifaces, biface manufacturing and resharpening flakes, celts, celt flakes, and general lithic wastage.

The methods we used in analysis are not complicated. We subjected a sample of 600 lithic artifacts from the 1984 season's research to a preliminary analysis to explore the categories of lithics present and to see the range of variation within categories and within the entire collection. We designed these categories to be comparable to types already described from other Central American sites, insofar as possible. We subjected all lots, whether from survey or excavation, to a "lot readout," a detailed analysis and classification of each artifact into one of eighteen categories. Thus, each of the 8,755 lithic artifacts is tabulated by type and by excavated lot. We did this initially on paper, on large lot-readout forms prepared especially for Arenal-area lithics; however, when the eighteen types (along with six kinds of materials and hinge fracture frequencies) are all tabulated for 603 individual lots, the result is an unwieldy table containing 15,678 cells. Handling so many cells on paper is awkward at best, as they are difficult to conceptualize, sort, and manipulate. To facilitate data processing, we entered all lithic data into a microcomputer in the field using spreadsheet software for basic data processing. Later analyses employed a relational data base software package. We weighed, measured, described, and photographically recorded all retouched artifacts, and samples of the debitage.

CHIPPED STONE ARTIFACTS: TYPES

Table 11-1 presents the types of chipped stone artifacts sorted by site, and Table 11-2 presents the chipped stone debitage characteristics by site. Each type of chipped stone artifact is presented in this section by name, followed by the artifact frequency and the figure in which it is illustrated. The artifact count is presented with the frequency from 1984 and 1985, followed by the total. The usual archaeological practice is not to preserve data on the year of collection in this way, but there is a reason for doing so here. The 1984 season emphasized later materials in the sequence, particularly the Silencio Phase. In contrast, the 1985 research emphasized data from the earlier part of the sequence, particularly the Tronadora and Arenal phases. Therefore, the year of collection gives a rough chronological indication without a detailed provenience assessment. The detailed chronological assessment is presented later, in the typological presentation. Thus, the informal statement of "early" refers to the earlier Tronadora or Arenal phases, and "late" refers to the later Silencio or Tilarán phases. We performed a more rigorous chronological assessment of each type, using the relational software, by dating each lithic artifact by the types of ceramics associated with it. The blankets of volcanic ash (tephra), where they were preserved and identifiable, provided independent dating. Thus, the volcanic ash layer below provides the early end and the ash layer above provides the late end of the dating range for the "sandwiched" lithic artifact. Each type is then described and compared with similar specimens in Costa Rica and elsewhere in Central America.

Hence, we assessed each artifact type for chronology by two independent means: ceramic association and volcanic stratigraphy. The easiest way we found to explore the ceramic phase association of a lithic type is to use the software queries for the lot in which it is found. In the type descriptions that follow, a series of numbers are given, such as the 8-19-11-5 figures for thermally fractured debitage. These present the mean number of artifacts of that type per lot occurring in each of the sequent sedentary phases (Tronadora-Arenal-Silencio-Tilarán). Where there are four numbers, the Fortuna Phase is excluded, and where there are five numbers, it is included. More specifically, of the lots assigned to the Tronadora Phase that contain thermally fractured debitage, an average of eight of these artifacts are found per lot. Thus, this sequence indicates an increase and a decrease in relative frequencies, not in absolute numbers. This corrects for varying numbers of lots from different phases.

This chronological assessment is followed by an independent sorting by geological unit, beginning with the earliest. These figures are given in the percentage of lithics of that type relative to the total lithics from that unit, again divulging trends through time. As with the phase sorting, avoiding absolute amounts helps balance the sample. Otherwise, the few artifacts from the excavated components of Dos Armadillos, the small Tilarán Phase hamlet (G-154), would be largely swamped by the greater number of artifacts and excavated lots from the Silencio Phase, for instance. Table 11-3 presents the lithic types sorted by ceramic phases, and by habitation versus cemetery sites. Table 11-4 breaks debitage down into hinge fracture frequencies and materials, by ceramic phase and by site type.

THERMALLY FRACTURED DEBITAGE (669 + 3,371 = 4,040)

These are the fragments of stones fractured by the stresses generated by extreme temperature changes, not by applied percussion or pressure forces (Fig. 11-1). The fracture surfaces are rough and irregular. The surfaces lack the single point of force application that can be seen on chipped stone artifacts, and they lack the attributes of pressure or percussion flaking (bulbs, bulbar lips, radial fissures, gull wings, ripple marks, or specific terminations). Their outsides are often oxidized in a thin zone ranging from less than 1 mm to as much as 5 mm or even 10 mm. In general, we can distinguish these thermally fractured stones from the chemically eroded spalls and rinds on naturally weathering stones, as the latter

Figure 11-1.
Thermally fractured debitage from the Silencio site, G-150. On left, seven representative pieces (lot H4); on right, two very large pieces that fit (lot A1). All were heated and partially oxidized on the outside; fracturing was from rapid temperature changes, not from percussion. Photograph by Fran Mandel-Sheets.

are smoother and softer. Oxidation under natural conditions is minimal or nonexistent, at least to the eye. Distinguishing the two would have been more difficult without the dozens of kilometers of exposed Aguacate Formation along the lakeshore, as the abundance of thermally fractured debitage in known sites and the paucity between sites are important evidence of thermally fractured debitage's being cultural. Further, natural weathering affects the crystalline andesite differentially, attacking some components, such as the plagioclase feldspars, more rapidly and leaving a pitted surface. In contrast, the thermally fractured surfaces are fresher and rougher, created by an irregular "tearing apart" of the stone, fracturing through and around crystals. Another important ingredient assisting the recognition of these artifacts as cultural is their occurrence in sites within the tephra units, as they were transported through the air. Because they greatly exceed the grain size of the largest tephra particles, their

TABLE 11-1
TYPES OF CHIPPED STONE FROM THE PROYECTO PREHISTÓRICO ARENAL, TABULATED BY SITE NUMBER

Site	*THFRDEB*	*SMBIFFL*	*LBIFFL*	*CELTFL*	*GENDEBIT*	*UNCLASS*	*UTILFL*	*UNIFFL*	*BIFFL*
G-150	259	5	4	4	288	111	2	0	2
G-151	0	2	4	0	16	9	0	0	0
G-152	28	5	7	0	36	6	0	1	0
G-153	5	0	0	0	1	2	0	0	0
G-154	20	13	0	0	178	15	0	0	0
G-155	14	0	0	0	1	1	0	0	0
G-156	43	0	0	0	26	26	0	1	0
G-157	4	0	1	0	1	0	0	0	0
G-158	0	0	0	0	0	1	0	0	0
G-159	4	1	0	1	3	4	0	0	0
G-160	0	0	0	0	0	4	0	0	0
G-161	43	1	1	0	39	19	2	1	1
G-162	1	3	0	0	28	8	0	0	0
G-163	954	17	2	4	263	1,123	5	2	5
G-164	2,338	1	0	0	314	291	4	2	1
G-165	3	0	0	0	9	33	0	0	0
G-166	16	0	0	1	8	3	0	0	1
G-167	0	0	0	0	0	0	0	0	0
G-168	0	0	0	0	0	1	0	0	0
G-169	122	1	0	1	283	48	2	0	0
G-170	0	0	0	0	64	6	0	0	0
G-171	3	0	0	0	0	0	0	0	0
G-172	1	0	0	0	3	3	0	0	0
G-173	2	0	0	0	0	5	0	0	0
G-174	4	0	0	0	1	1	0	0	0
G-175	26	0	0	1	31	10	0	0	0
G-176	0	0	0	0	0	3	0	1	1
G-177	7	0	0	0	21	9	0	0	0
G-178	0	0	0	0	0	2	0	0	0
G-179	0	0	0	0	0	1	0	0	0
G-180	11	1	0	0	12	1	0	0	0
G-181	0	0	0	0	0	1	0	0	0
G-182	0	0	0	0	0	0	0	0	0
G-183	14	0	0	0	2	9	0	0	0
G-184	2	0	0	0	5	4	0	0	0
G-185	5	2	2	0	25	1	0	0	0
G-186	0	0	0	0	1	0	0	0	0
G-187	12	0	0	0	15	6	0	0	0
G-188	0	0	0	0	5	0	0	0	0
G-189	0	0	0	0	6	0	0	0	0
G-190	0	0	0	0	9	0	0	0	0
G-191	1	0	0	0	0	0	0	0	0
G-192	2	0	0	0	3	3	0	0	0
G-193	0	0	0	0	0	0	0	0	0
G-194	0	0	0	0	0	1	0	0	0
G-195	1	1	0	0	1	9	0	0	0
G-196	0	0	0	0	3	4	0	0	0
G-197	21	3	0	0	49	26	0	0	0
G-198	0	0	0	0	32	3	0	0	0
G-199	0	1	0	0	24	0	0	0	0
G-200	31	0	1	0	6	9	0	0	0
G-286	0	0	0	0	3	0	0	0	0
AL-178	0	0	0	0	1	2	0	0	0
AL-179	1	0	0	0	3	0	0	0	0
AL-180	0	0	0	0	1	1	0	0	0
AL-183	3	0	0	0	1	1	0	0	0
AL-184	0	0	0	0	1	0	0	0	0
AL-186	12	9	1	0	54	21	0	0	0
AL-187	0	0	0	0	2	0	0	0	0
Total	4,013	66	23	12	1,878	1,847	15	8	11

Notes: THFRDEB = thermally fractured debitage; SMBIFFL = small bifacial trimming flakes; LBIFFL = large bifacial flakes; GENDEBIT = general debitage; UTILFL = utilized flakes; UNIFFL = unifacially flaked; BIFFL = bifacially flaked; FLCORE = flake core; PERCBLD = percussion blades; CKSTNS = cooking stones.

TABLE 11-1
(continued)

WEDGES	*HAM-MERST*	*FLCORE*	*PERCBLD*	*CKSTNS*	*CELTBLNK*	*CELTS*	*PEBBLES*	*HOES*	*Total*
0	8	13	1	4	1	0	0	0	702
0	0	1	0	0	0	0	0	0	32
0	2	2	1	0	0	1	0	0	89
1	0	1	0	0	0	0	0	0	10
0	0	2	0	3	0	0	0	0	231
0	0	0	0	0	0	0	0	0	16
0	2	2	0	3	0	1	0	0	104
0	0	0	0	0	0	0	0	0	6
0	0	0	0	0	0	0	0	0	1
0	0	1	0	0	0	0	0	0	14
0	0	0	0	0	0	0	0	0	4
0	1	6	1	1	0	0	0	0	115
0	0	0	0	0	0	0	0	0	40
0	3	13	4	185	0	0	447	4	3,031
0	2	17	5	52	0	0	13	1	3,041
0	0	1	0	0	0	0	0	0	46
0	0	0	1	0	0	0	0	0	30
0	0	0	0	0	0	0	0	0	0
0	0	0	0	0	0	0	0	0	1
0	0	2	0	6	0	0	0	0	465
0	0	1	0	0	0	0	0	0	71
0	0	0	0	0	0	0	0	0	3
0	0	1	0	0	0	0	0	0	8
0	0	0	0	0	0	0	0	0	7
0	0	0	0	0	0	0	0	0	6
0	1	1	1	2	0	0	0	0	73
0	1	0	0	0	0	0	0	0	6
1	3	3	0	0	0	0	0	0	44
0	0	0	0	0	0	0	0	0	2
0	0	0	0	0	0	0	0	0	1
1	0	0	0	0	0	0	2	0	28
0	0	0	0	0	0	0	0	0	1
0	0	0	0	0	0	0	0	0	0
0	1	0	0	2	0	0	0	0	28
0	0	0	0	0	0	0	2	0	13
0	0	2	0	0	0	0	0	0	37
0	0	0	0	0	0	0	0	0	1
0	0	1	1	0	0	0	2	0	37
0	0	0	0	0	0	0	0	0	5
0	0	1	1	0	0	0	0	0	8
0	0	2	0	0	0	0	0	0	11
0	0	0	0	0	0	0	0	0	1
0	0	2	0	1	0	0	0	0	11
0	0	0	0	0	0	0	0	0	0
0	0	0	0	0	0	0	0	0	1
0	0	0	0	0	0	0	0	0	12
0	0	0	0	0	0	0	0	0	7
0	1	2	2	4	0	0	0	0	108
0	0	0	1	0	0	0	0	0	36
0	1	0	0	0	0	0	0	0	26
0	1	4	0	0	0	0	0	0	52
0	0	0	0	0	0	0	0	0	3
0	0	0	0	0	0	0	0	0	3
0	0	0	0	0	0	0	0	0	4
0	0	0	0	0	0	0	0	0	2
0	0	2	0	0	0	0	0	0	7
0	0	0	0	0	0	0	0	0	1
0	5	9	1	0	0	0	0	0	112
0	0	0	0	0	0	0	0	0	2
3	32	92	20	262	1	2	466	5	8,755

TABLE 11-2
BREAKDOWN OF GENERAL DEBITAGE BY HINGE FRACTURE FREQUENCY AND BY MATERIAL, PER SITE

Site	*GENDEBIT*	*HINGES*	*CHALC*	*PETWOOD*	*PORPH*	*RHYOL*	*JASPER*	*QTZITE*	*FGDACITE*
G-150	288	3	15	1	1	0	0	0	271
G-151	16	1	0	0	0	0	0	0	16
G-152	36	1	0	0	0	0	0	0	36
G-153	1	0	0	0	0	0	1	0	0
G-154	178	7	88	0	0	0	6	0	84
G-155	1	0	0	0	0	0	0	0	1
G-156	26	0	2	0	0	0	0	0	24
G-157	1	0	0	0	0	0	0	0	1
G-158	0	0	0	0	0	0	0	0	0
G-159	3	0	0	0	0	0	0	0	3
G-160	0	0	0	4	0	0	0	0	0
G-161	38	2	33	4	0	0	1	1	0
G-162	28	0	10	10	0	0	0	0	14
G-163	263	14	34	0	7	15	8	0	189
G-164	314	19	27	0	0	5	1	1	280
G-165	9	0	5	0	0	0	0	0	4
G-166	8	0	4	0	0	0	0	0	4
G-167	0	0	0	0	0	0	0	0	0
G-168	0	0	0	0	0	0	0	0	0
G-169	283	9	35	5	0	0	0	0	243
G-170	64	2	16	1	0	0	1	0	46
G-171	0	0	0	0	0	0	0	0	0
G-172	3	0	0	1	0	0	0	0	2
G-173	0	0	0	0	0	0	0	0	0
G-174	1	0	1	0	0	0	0	0	0
G-175	31	0	15	1	0	0	1	0	14
G-176	0	0	0	0	0	0	0	0	0
G-177	21	2	2	0	0	0	0	0	19
G-178	0	0	0	0	0	0	0	0	0
G-179	0	0	0	0	0	0	0	0	0
G-180	12	2	0	1	2	1	0	0	8
G-181	0	0	0	0	0	0	0	0	0
G-182	0	0	0	0	0	0	0	0	0
G-183	2	0	0	0	0	0	0	0	2
G-184	5	0	0	0	0	0	0	0	5
G-185	25	2	8	0	1	1	5	1	9
G-186	1	0	1	0	0	0	0	0	0
G-187	15	0	1	0	0	0	0	0	14
G-188	5	1	1	0	0	0	0	0	4
G-189	6	0	1	3	0	0	0	0	2
G-190	9	1	6	2	0	0	0	0	1
G-191	0	0	0	0	0	0	0	0	0
G-192	3	0	2	0	0	0	0	0	1
G-193	0	0	0	0	0	0	0	0	0
G-194	0	0	0	0	0	0	0	0	0
G-195	1	0	1	0	0	0	0	0	0
G-196	3	0	0	0	0	0	0	0	3
G-197	49	4	27	5	0	0	1	5	11
G-198	32	2	21	0	0	0	0	7	4
G-199	24	2	19	2	0	0	0	3	0
G-200	6	0	2	0	0	0	0	0	4
G-286	3	0	0	2	0	0	0	0	1
AL-178	1	0	0	0	0	0	0	0	1
AL-179	3	0	0	1	0	0	0	0	2
AL-180	1	0	0	0	0	0	0	0	1
AL-183	1	0	0	0	0	0	0	0	1
AL-184	1	0	0	0	0	0	0	0	1
AL-186	54	6	13	23	0	0	2	2	14
AL-187	2	0	0	1	0	0	0	0	1
Total	1,877	80	390	67	11	22	27	20	1,341

Notes: GENDEBIT = general debitage; CHALC = chalcedony; PETWOOD = petrified wood; PORPH = porphyry; RHYOL = rhyolite; QTZITE = quartzite; FGDACITE = fine-grained dacite.

presence in sites can derive only from human activities.

The material consistently used for these stones is a highly crystalline (phyric) andesite, not a very refractory rock (Melson, personal communication, 1984). Although it is not the ideal choice for resisting temperature stresses, it is the most common stone around, and thus it is eminently replaceable when it fractures.

Three different uses by which stone can become thermally fractured in aboriginal sites come to mind. One is the use of large stones to support vessels over fires; another is the use of parching stones in roasting; and the third is the use of heated stones to boil water. We can distinguish the stones, and sometimes the debitage, from these activities. Hearth stones are the large stones, perhaps 20 cm to 40 cm in diameter, that are still used in many traditional areas of Latin America to support cooking vessels over a fire, sometimes on an elevated cooking platform. Large size is the distinguishing feature of these stones, and much of the debitage resulting from hearth stone use consists of quite large spalls. Deep plunging fractures that carry through the entire hearth stone are rarer than with the two other types. Most of the surface heating takes place in an oxidizing rather than a reducing atmosphere, resulting in a red surface color. We excavated no hearth stones from in situ contexts during project research, but we found a number during surface survey.

The second way to heat and inadvertently fracture rocks is in roasting. Here, rocks are heated and then placed with nuts or other foods in protected (e.g., clay-lined) baskets or in pits. These rocks are much smaller, often 4 cm to 6 cm in diameter. Oxidation should predominate over reduction with these stones more than with other types, because they are exposed to the open atmosphere while they are hot for a longer time than are the other two types discussed here.

The third use of stones for cooking is stone boiling. Here, the stones are heated in a fire, removed (probably with wooden tongs), placed momentarily in an intermediate water bath to instantly steam clean the soot-blackened stone, and then placed in the water or stew. Vessels can be of wood, stone, waterproof basketry, or hide. Ceramic vessels could be used, but they are more fragile and could be broken by the stones. Stone boiling is an efficient technique in terms of the speed with which water can be boiled. The effects on the stones are more drastic than in the other two methods, however, because the temperature changes are much more rapid. Here, the fractures more often plunge through the stone in multiple directions, but potlidlike fracturing is common also. Oxidation is the predominant firing atmosphere preserved on the surface.

During an experiment I conducted in 1984, it became clear that the degree of weathering of the stone prior to heating is an important factor in the stone's longevity. I collected six phyric andesite stones from the Santa Rosa River near G-154. The stones were repeatedly heated in a fire and then placed in 3 L of water. The weathered andesite began fracturing after only two heat-cool cycles, whereas the relatively unweathered andesite was unfractured after ten cycles. The efficiency of stone boiling is demonstrated by the stones' ability to raise water temperature from 23.3°C (74°F) to 43.3°C (110°F) in 3 minutes. The more weathered stones began fragmenting both while being heated in the fire and while cooling in the water, and would suffice to boil only an estimated 50 L of water. The fresher stone, I estimate, could serve for at least one hundred heat-cool cycles. Thus, 2 kg of fresher stone could boil at least three hundred L of water. The most rapid boiling is achieved with two sets of rocks being heated in the fire while a third set is heating the water.

These figures allow for a very approximate calculation of the minimum volume boiled at a given site, based on a measurement of the weight of cooking stones found at a site. For instance, we collected 258 pieces of thermally fractured debitage from G-150. The mean weight per piece is 110 g. Multiplying 258 stones times 110 grams gives a weight of 28,380 grams. Because we collected slightly less than half of these thermally fractured debitage pieces in the field, we should double and round-off to 60 kg. This amount represents less than 1% of the total at the site, so the site total, figuring conservatively, is at least 60,000 kg of boiling stones. Because each kg of boiling stones can boil at least 150 liters of water, 60,000 kg of boiling stones could boil some 9 million liters of water. Because the cemetery was occupied for about 600 years, we can divide by 600 and get a figure of about 15,000 liters boiled per year. Of course, these figures should not be taken literally, because of the softness of the various estimates and working assumptions that used. The result does serve to give at least a general impression of the magnitude of that activity at this site, however. Cemetery use in the Arenal area was the antithesis of our quick visits to a grave on Memorial Day to drop off some flowers.

We found thermally fractured debitage in sites of all time periods from the Archaic to the Spanish Conquest, and at domestic and funerary sites. We found twelve specimens at AL-186, the Archaic lithic site with the corrected C-14 date of 3780 (3675) 3539 BC. Boiling stone technology is very appropriate for a hunting-and-gathering migratory life-style, as the stones are available throughout the area, and organic vessels (made of hide, basketry, gourd, or wood) are much more durable and transportable than are ceramic vessels.

The chronological assessment using the computer divulges a peak in thermally fractured debitage during the middle of the sequence. Following their beginnings in the Archaic, the average numbers in sedentary phase lots where they occur, by associated ceramic phase, is 8-19-11-5. Another chronological index is presented on Table 11-1, where the percentage of thermally fractured debitage of the total lithic assemblage is calculated for each phase, and the results are, in order and including the Fortuna phase as the first, 10-31-67-36-18. This means that 10% of the lithic artifacts of the Fortuna Phase are thermally fractured debitage; that percentage rises to 31 in the Tronadora Phase, to 67% in the Arenal Phase, and then begins to drop. Thus, thermally fractured debitage is most common in the Arenal Phase and diminishes toward the Conquest. The Unit chronology substantiates this, using dated volcanic ash-soil layers, with the percentage of thermally fractured debitage within the total lithics of that unit: U61: 37%, U60: 24%, U54: 78%, U50: 54%, and U30: 20%. I think it is of considerable significance that a cooking technique that is generally associated with preceramic migratory "Archaic" life-styles became more common with sedentism and the time of greatest population densities and construction efforts in the area. That increase in use is not simply because of an increase in population, as these figures are relative, or corrected, to be sensitive to proportional factors.

It is surprising that the cooking stone technology remained strong during the three millennia prior to the Conquest, when ceramic vessels were made in the area, particularly in light of the long time span of ceramics and their sophistication. This kind of cooking technology evidently was in use in the Arenal area for 5,000 years prior to the Conquest, an impressive continuity. In the samples excavated in 1984, cemetaries had higher frequencies of thermally fractured stone relative to the total lithics than did habitation sites, 35% to 26%, respectively. This was an unexpected result, and it seems sufficiently consistent (Table 11-1) to represent a real phenomenon. Perhaps stone boiling was preferable to cooking with a fire under a ceramic vessel at the cemeteries, given the distance of cemeteries from settlements. They may have favored durable and lighter organic cooking vessels over ceramic vessels. In contrast, there may have been more emphasis on cooking in pottery vessels in the habitation sites because of the permanency of their occupation, given a lesser need to move vessels and thus a reduced risk of breakage.

Fire-cracked rocks are not unusual in Costa Rican habitation or funerary sites, but they have yet to be studied systematically as a potential indicator of a food-processing system that appears to be chronologically and spatially widespread. Snarskis (1984a) found large amounts of fire-cracked rocks associated with abundant charcoal in the early La Montaña site in the northern Atlantic Watershed, with radiocarbon dates during the first two millennia BC. Some funerary sites have fire-cracked rock in direct association with cooking features and graves. For instance, La Ceiba (lowland Guanacaste, Middle Polychrome) had fire-cracked rock in carefully-constructed elongated clay hearths that overlaid individual burials. Although the Silencio site lacks La Ceiba's direct association of burial and cooking features, both sites have abundant evidence of cooking, evidently as a part of funerary rituals.

COOKING STONES (19 + 244 = 263)

We selected eleven cooking stones from 1984 operations and fifteen from 1985 operations for typological analysis (Fig. 11-2). These are the complete versions of the thermally fractured debitage. They were previously called "Boiling Stones" (Sheets 1984b), but that term is now considered too restrictive, given the possibility that a few of these stones may have been used for roasting, or as hearth stones to support vessels during cooking, or that some stones were used for heating liquids to less than the boiling point. The majority of these stones probably were used in boiling, however. The 1984 sample averages 382 g and ranges from 60 g to 1,560 g. The average diameter is 6 cm. The 1985 sample, from earlier contexts, tends to be larger, with an average mass of 545 g and an average diameter of 7.4 cm (respective ranges: 81–1,560 g and 4.4–10.8 cm). This apparently indicates a decrease in mean size of cooking

Figure 11-2.
Cooking stones. All are oxidized on the surface, but had fractured slightly or not at all. Top: G-164-B6 and G-164-A8. Bottom: G-153-N4, G-163-I11, and G-163-I11. Photograph by Fran Mandel-Sheets.

stones through time, but this assumption is based on a very small sample. The metric data combining both years' research are 471 g mean mass and 6.8 cm mean diameter. The stones are rounded to oval in shape. Three have some thermal fracturing, and they may have been discarded for that reason; however, some were useful for other purposes after they no longer were used for cooking. For example, five of the postholes at G-163-A7 had fractured cooking stones wedged down into their edges (Chap. 4). The strong NE trade winds that buffet the area from November through March probably loosened many a post.

Cooking stones were used during all periods in funerary and habitation sites. All have some oxidation on their exteriors, ranging from a very thin and discontinuous zone to a thick (8 mm) and continuous zone. The boiling stone experiment discussed earlier produced more reduction (soot blackening) than oxidation, but I believe this is due to a cramped and slow fire, and that a more open and vigorous fire would result in more oxidation. Only a small fraction of the cooking stones found on survey or during excavations were collected, but the number observed was recorded. For instance, we collected three boiling stones out of fifty-six observed at G-156.

When broken down by phase, the relative frequencies of cooking stones are 7-3-1-1. When examined by percentage of the lithics of a given phase, and including the Fortuna Phase, the pattern is 4-7.6-1.9-.06-.08, indicating an increase and then a general decline in use. The data by Unit and percentage are 61: 25, 60: 2, 54: 2, 50:1, and 30:1. Thus, all windows on chronology indicate a relatively great use of cooking stones in the Tronadora Phase, with somewhat less use in the preceding and succeeding phases. The data are in agreement with the thermally fractured debitage pattern in showing a diminution in the last two phases; however, the thermally fractured debitage peaked in relative frequencies in the Arenal Phase, whereas the whole specimens are more common in Tronadora Phase lots. Because of larger sample sizes, I think the thermally fractured figures are more reliable. Cooking stone data are also less reliable because they are very heavy, they are ubiquitous, they show little variation within the category, and so they were often noted in the field and only a few were collected. For instance, we counted over eighty-five in the field at the AL-186 site, but we brought back only five to the laboratory for tabulation and analysis. If all were collected from sites discovered during survey, the sheer weight would have decreased survey efficiency. Thus, we made the effort in the field to collect a sample that was representative of the artifacts exposed at the site, as some sites had a few hundred cooking stones exposed. Hence, cooking stones are the most underrepresented category on Tables 11-1 and 11-2.

The large number of whole and fragmentary thermally altered cooking stones in these sedentary, pottery-producing sites is surprising. Stone boiling is common among migratory hunter-gatherers, or sedentary nonagricultural peoples (e.g., California Indians), but it is not commonly noted in the literature of sedentary agricultural societies; however, stone boiling in sedentary Middle American societies may not be as rare as the archaeological record indicates. These stones are mundane in appearance and could easily be discounted as nonartifactual. The volcanic ash strata assisted our recognizing these as at least minimally artifactual, in that rocks of that size in a tephra-derived soil must have been hauled in. The largest grain size of tephra at site G-163, for instance, is about 5mm, so a sizeable rock in a soil formed from tephra (controlling for erosion and redeposition) would have to be brought in. Closer examination indicated that they were thermally fractured and that they were abundant from the Archaic to the Conquest.

LARGE BIFACIAL TRIMMING FLAKES (19 + 6 = 25)

The length measurement that separates large from small bifacial trimming flakes is 4.0 cm. The category "Large Bifacial Trimming Flakes" (Fig. 11-3) subdivides into two varieties: those associated with the fine bifacial flaking done during the Archaic and into the early Tronadora Phase, and those associated with celt manufacture. The large flakes from celt manufacture are found in all phases from Tronadora through Tilarán. The flakes that derive from fine bifacial flaking tend to be thinner and generally are of very fine-grained materials such as high-quality chalcedony, whereas the celt-associated flakes are thicker and are of tougher materials such as dense, nonvesicular andesite or dacite. Because of the different chronological emphases of the two field seasons, most of the celt-associated flakes derive from 1984 research, whereas most of the early fine bifacial flakes were found during 1985 research.

Of the nineteen celt-associated flakes we collected in 1984, we chose eight large bifacial trimming flakes as a grab sample for more detailed analysis. They average 119 g and range from 10 g to 440 g. All are of a fine-grained dacite or andesite and all bear multiple flake scars on their dorsal surfaces. This is a deliberately conservative category, in that only the specimens that clearly were bifacial wastage are included. I agree with Ranere (Linares and Ranere 1980) that bifacial manufacture yields few flakes that are clearly diagnostic of that technique. Thus, the low frequency of this type should not be interpreted as indicating a paucity of bifacial manufacture in the Cordillera. Most of these flakes bear some cortex.

Celt-associated flakes come from a wide range of contexts. Fully 58% of the specimens derive from the relatively small excavations at sites G-151 and G-152, the laja repositories associated with the large Silencio graveyard. Another 21% come from that graveyard, indicating that a high

Figure 11-3.
Large bifacial trimming flakes. Top: All G-152-A2 ventral sides, with platforms at top. Bottom: G-152-C2, G-150-C2, and G-152-A2, ventral sides, with platforms at top. Photograph by Fran Mandel-Sheets.

proportion of the chipped stone celt manufacture and use is cemetery-associated. It is not surprising that the sole flaked andesite celt was found at G-152. Chipped stone axes are easier to make than are ground stone axes, but their edges are more fragile and thus they are more easily damaged during use; thus, there is a trade-off between manufacturing ease and durability. The preferences were clearly toward manufacturing ease in the G-150-151-152 funerary complex.

The large celt-associated bifacial trimming flakes are found in all ceramic periods, with the bulk (79%) deriving from Late Period V or Period VI (Silencio Phase) contexts. So many derive from relatively late contexts primarily because of the emphasis placed on excavations of the high-status Silencio Phase cemetery and associated stone storage areas during 1984. The oxidized tephra layers, particularly Unit 55, in the cemetery likely were from forest clearing, which probably was achieved with celts.

Figure 11-4.
Celt flakes; all dorsal views, with platforms at top. Top: G-159-A1, G-166-A3, and G-175-A1. Bottom: G-150-C2, G-150-C2, G-150-I2, G-150-I1. Their loci indicate celt use and damage, or resharpening. Photograph by Fran Mandel-Sheets.

Both of the specimens from G-163, excavated in 1985, are relatively small. One is early (Unit 60 or 61, in the Tronadora Phase), while the larger is associated with the Arenal Phase occupation of the site. Their average lengths and thicknesses are 7.2 cm and 1.7 cm, respectively, with ranges from 5.6 cm to 11 cm and from 0.6 cm to 3 cm. The smaller dates to the early Tronadora Phase.

The provenience of the others from the 1985 survey is instructive: G-185, G-200, and AL-186. The last is a confirmed Archaic site, and the other two may well have Archaic components. These consistently are of fine materials, either fine-grained chalcedony or petrified wood, and thus they contrast strongly with the dacite-dominated bifacial flaking directed toward celt manufacture of the later ceramic horizons. Cooke (1984:268) states that pressure flaking and bifacially flaked projectile points had dropped out of lithic assemblages in Panama by 5000 BC. According to our evidence, fine bifacial flaking used to manufacture projectile points and knives continued in Costa Rica from Paleo-Indian through Archaic times to at least 3000 BC. Bifacial flaking during Paleo-Indian and Archaic times was impressively well controlled, with the detachment of thin, expanding flakes during the finishing stages of manufacture. I see no evidence of pressure flaking after the Paleo-Indian Period, but the percussion flaking of the Archaic was far from sloppy. Bifacial percussion flaking never dropped out of the Costa Rican technological repertoire, as it was used during all the ceramic phases for the manufacture of celt preforms. It reemerged for the making of "projectile points" during the latter part of the first millennium AD in the form of the "Silencio Points" (see below), but the more irregular percussion flakes removed during their manufacture contrast with the more regular debitage flakes from earlier biface manufacture.

In summary, bifacial flaking of projectile points and knives in the Arenal area began in Paleo-Indian times, continued through the Archaic, and possibly into the beginnings of the Tronadora Phase. It may have ceased during the Tronadora and Arenal phases, as we have no examples of fine bifacial flaking from those phases, but sample sizes are small for all phases. Fine bifacial flaking evidently reemerged during the Silencio Phase and continued to the Conquest. Bifacial flaking of celts began after the Archaic, in the Tronadora Phase, and continued to the Conquest.

SMALL BIFACIAL TRIMMING FLAKES (32 + 33 = 65)

Small bifacial trimming flakes, by definition, have lengths less than 4 cm. The average weight of a sample of twenty-two we chose for analysis is 2.8 g, but that obscures some significant variation. The mean mass of 1984 flakes is 3.7 g, yet the mean mass of 1985 flakes is only 1.25 g. This is explained by the fact that most of the 1984 sample derives from the final shaping of celt blanks, and thus are larger, but the 1985 sample is dominated by the small, fine flakes involved in Archaic bifacial flaking. Ten of the thirteen small bifacial flakes found at G-163 came from the lowest strata and probably are associated with the early cluster of radiocarbon dates at about 3000 BC. They almost certainly date to 3500–2000 BC. The three found in upper layers may not necessarily indicate fine bifacial flaking at that time (in the Upper 50's stratigraphic units, or associated with Arenal Phase ceramics). It is possible that they were moved upward in the strata by human activities. Anthroturbation in thinly stratified sites always causes some anachronisms. The mean length, width, and thickness of these earlier flakes are 1.5 cm, 2.2 cm, and 0.5 cm, respectively. We took the length measurements along the fracture surface in the direction of applied force. That the mean width is greater than the mean length is a quantitative measure of the broad, expanding nature of these early flakes. This contrasts with the very thick flakes from celt preforming and the elongated flakes from manufacture of the Silencio Phase stemmed bifaces.

The 1984 sample is composed of small bifacial trimming flakes from the manufacture of late bifaces, such as the stemmed bifaces from the Silencio Phase, with a few flakes probably deriving from celt blank shaping. As a whole, they are larger than the Archaic and Tronadora Phase small bifacial wastage, and their average length is 1.8 cm. They range from 0.9 cm to 3.9 cm. They clearly represent the later stages of biface manufacture. All have multiple flake scars on their dorsal surfaces. Dacite and chalcedony dominated, with an occasional flake of jasper or other microcrystalline silicate.

The frequencies of small bifacial trimming flakes that could be attributed to a phase are as follows: Fortuna, nine; Tronadora, five; Arenal, six; Silencio, eleven; and Tilarán, nine (percentages of each: 8-0.3-0.2-1.2-1.2). The frequencies are rather evenly distributed through the ceramic phases following the peak during the Archaic, yet the percentages show an increase in the last two phases. Using the tephra unit series to assess chronology independently also indicates a rather uniform distribution, with somewhat higher frequencies in the Unit 50 and 30 soils.

Heat treatment was performed rarely in the Cordillera. One small chalcedony flake, from G-154-I (Tilarán Phase), bears evidence of heat treatment, as do three flakes from G-197 (probably Arenal Phase). The evidence is the markedly increased luster on the ventral surface, compared to the flake scars on the dorsal surface.

Three sites account for half of the small bifacial trimming flakes. Site G-154 had thirteen, and twelve came from the G-151/G-152/G-153 funerary-associated complex; Archaic site AL-186 had eight.

CELT FLAKES (8 + 6 = 14)

These are the flakes that derived from celt resharpening or from celt abuse (Fig. 11-4). Thus, some were deliberately and some were accidentally removed from the bits of celts. Celt resharpening flakes are direct evidence of the locus of celt maintenance. Celt abuse flakes identify the loci of celt use, where wood was being cut. In composite, they average 7.4 g in weight, 3.6 cm in length, and 0.9 cm in thickness. The materials match those Chenault (Chap. 12) describes for celts, as would be expected, with the exception of two somewhat phyric andesite flakes from G-163-H10.

Fortunately, resharpening and abuse flakes can often be distinguished. Known celt resharpening flakes (Sheets et al. 1980) tend to be thin and often carry a small portion of the rounded or damaged bit end with them as their platforms. On the other hand, celt misuse can detach a large part of the bit, or a corner of the bit. Some celt resharpening flakes are quite large, however, such as the pair of flakes from G-163-I24, which clearly were detached in an ambitious celt resharpening effort.

The celt resharpening flakes that we identified in 1984 collections are small, thin, and weigh less than 2 g each. Most are incomplete; average length probably is over 3 cm. It is significant that five derive from the G-150 graveyard. The large graveyard witnessed considerable ground stone celt use, as well as the expedient chipped stone celt manufacture and use, probably when a ground stone celt was not available. The others were found in habitation sites from all phases.

All of the celt flakes recovered in 1985 research are of the celt-resharpening variety; we found no celt abuse flakes. These flakes provide earlier evidence of celt maintenance than does the 1984 collection. Two derive from the Arenal Phase and four from the Tronadora Phase. We have found none prior to the Tronadora Phase, that is, in Archaic contexts. These six flakes are larger than the later (Silencio Phase) resharpening flakes, as these average 9 g in weight. All come from the G-163 village, whereas most of the later flakes come from the G-150 cemetery. Although samples are small, it appears that the dominant locus for celt maintenance shifted from the village early in the sedentary sequence to the cemetery later.

Two celt-resharpening flakes from G-163-I24 fit together. The first of the two to be removed was struck from the side of the celt's bit end and neatly removed 1.5 cm of the bit. There is no evidence of bit damage on this flake; presumably, the damaged portion was farther inward. Prior to its removal, the lateral edge of the celt had been battered strongly, as evidenced by a welter of tiny step and hinge fractures, apparently to set up platforms for flake removals. The extensive preparation prior to removing flakes in this area of the celt and the large amount of resharpening that was being done are surprising. The celt must have been deeply damaged to warrant such an effort. Two flakes (G-163-V57 and V30) are identical in material and are from the same stratum; they probably come from the same artifact, but they do not fit together. Both were removed by lateral blows, one at the poll end and one probably from the center of the celt. Both have some postremoval edge nicking, probably from secondary use as cutting implements.

The three celt-abuse flakes are longer (average 3.8 cm), thicker (average 1 cm), and heavier (average 13 g) than the celt-resharpening flakes. One removed the entire corner of the bit. Another removed much of the bit's central portion. The third carries no platform, because the flake snapped laterally. It appears, based on dorsal morphology, to have been flaked from the bit. All three were surface finds and are not well dated. One probably is late Period IV, and the others probably are late Period IV or V.

The frequencies of celt flakes by phase, in order, are 4, 3, 2, and 1; an apparent diminution through time is corrected by the percentage figures on Table 11-1, which indicate a consistent and small percentage, with a drop during the Arenal Phase.

POLISHED FLAKES (5 + 0 = 5)

We tabulated these five stones on the lot readouts as general flakes, because they are wastage in chipped stone implement manufacture (Fig. 11-5). Four are chalcedony and one is petrified wood. Instead of being discarded as lithic wastage, they were polished on all surfaces, as if subjected to lapidary polishing. Their distribution is not indicative of a special artifact category that was associated with burials, chiefs, or other unique status or location. We found them in graveyard and village contexts. The two from G-150 are very small; they average only 1 cm in length. It is possible that they were used in shamanistic activities, but we have no direct evidence supporting such use.

The three larger polished flakes all come from the Joluvi site (two from G-162-G2 and one from B4). They average 2.2 cm in length. Chronologically, two of the polished flakes are from the Silencio Phase, and three from the Tilarán Phase.

GENERAL DEBITAGE (1,101 + 794 = 1,895)

General debitage is the lithic analog to "undiagnostic body sherds" in ceramics (Fig. 11-6). These are the miscellaneous wastage of a variety of percussion manufacturing procedures, including biface manufacture, uniface manufacture, core-flake technology, and perhaps others. A few of these flakes probably derive from misuse of chipped stone celts, unifaces, fragmenting hammerstones, and wedges. It is clear, however, that the majority derive from the informal percussion manufacture of cutting flakes, with some also deriving from biface and celt manufacture.

Many of these flakes were employed as utility cutting tools in a variety of cutting, piercing, shaving, and scraping tasks, but such uses resulted in minimal edge abrasion. They are made of very tough and generally grainy raw materials that retain signs of only the most extreme of use wear. It is probable, however, that a sophisticated use wear study, employing microscopy in the range of 40 to 200 power (with dark field and light field illumination), some scanning electron microscopy, and experimentally induced wear on replicated tools would yield important insights. It would take a major study to generate substantial results in the use of northwestern Costa Rican chipped stone artifacts. Such an effort was beyond the scope of this study; here we tabulated under "Utilized Flakes" only the flakes that exhibited unequivocal evidence of wear and those whose depositional context was sufficiently clear to indicate that the abrasion derived from use (and not from postabandonment damage, etc.).

The general flakes from G-150-C2 are used here as an illustrative sample. They are from the Silencio Phase cemetery. For purposes of comparison, a description of Tilarán Phase general debitage is presented below in the section "Aspects of the Collection." A description of earlier phase debitage immediately follows this discussion. Some of these flakes are complete, but many are shattered. They are not thermally fractured, but, rather, they clearly result from controlled fracturing. They average 7.5 g in weight and have mean lengths, widths, and thicknesses of 3 cm, 2.8 cm,

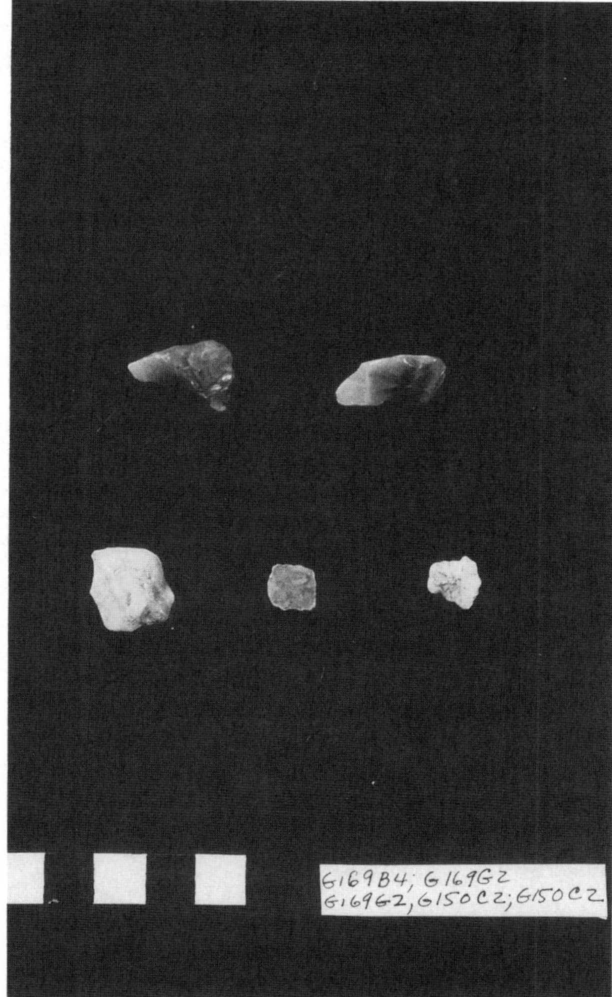

Figure 11-5.
Polished flakes. Top: G-169-B4, G-169-G2. Bottom: G-169-E2, G-150-C2 (two). Photograph by Fran Mandel-Sheets.

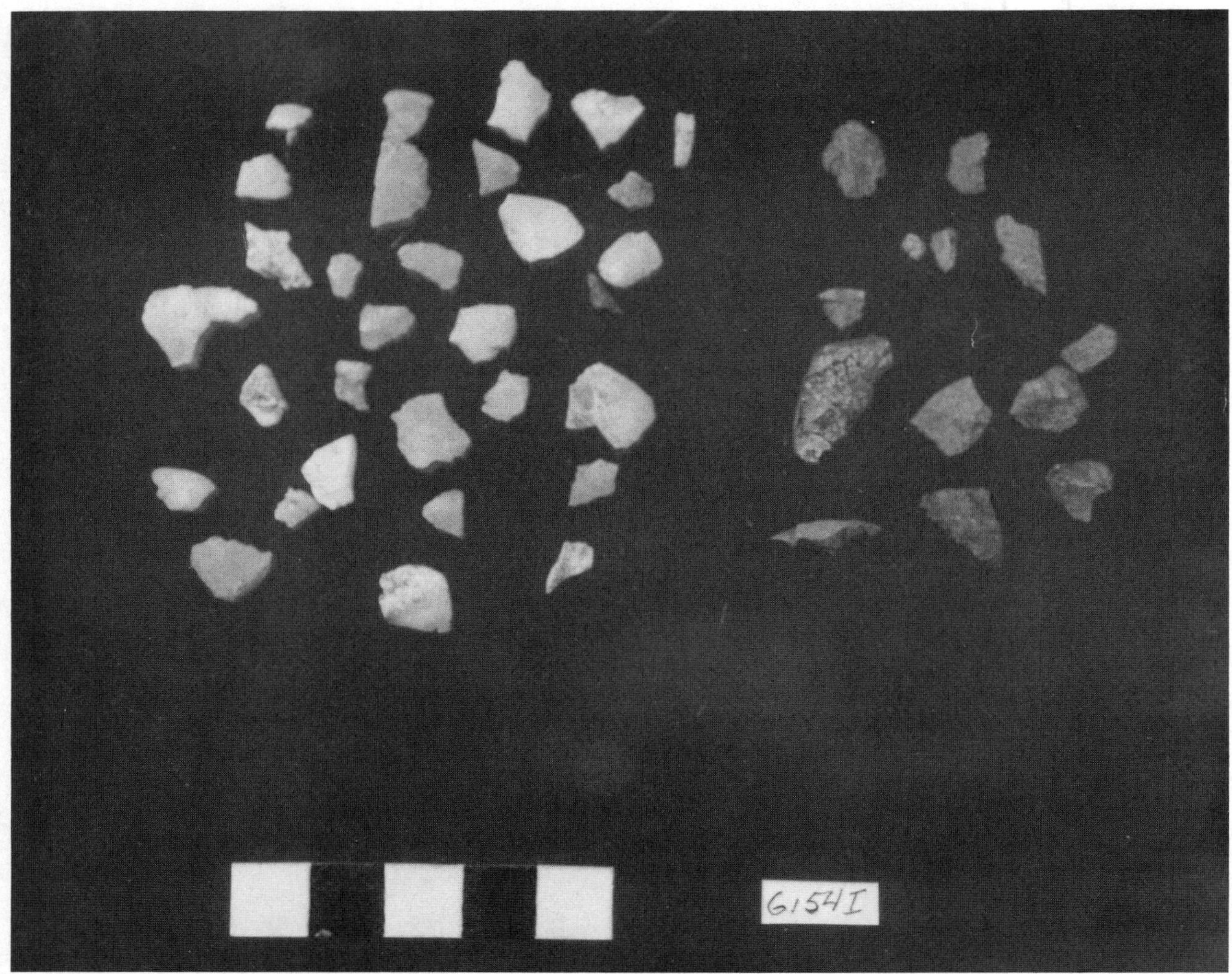

Figure 11-6.
Bifacial flakes, the debitage deriving from biface manufacture, from the workshop at the Dos Armadillos site (G-154, Operation I), from the Tilarán Phase. Fine chalcedony flakes on left, fine-grained dacite flakes on right. Photograph by Fran Mandel-Sheets.

TABLE 11-3
METRIC DATA, SAMPLE OF FORTY-FOUR DEBITAGE FLAKES, G-163-B6

Characteristic	*Mean*	*Minimum*	*Maximum*
Weight (g)	34.9	0.8	281.0
Length (cm)	4.4	1.1	8.4
Width (cm)	4.1	1.4	4.6
Thickness (cm)	1.4	0.4	4.0

TABLE 11-4
METRIC DATA, SAMPLE OF THIRTY-TWO DEBITAGE FLAKES, G-163

Characteristic	*Mean*	*Minimum*	*Maximum*
Weight (g)	7.2	0.3	83.0
Length (cm)	2.8	1.8	9.1
Width (cm)	2.5	1.1	6.5
Thickness (cm)	0.7	0.3	2.2

and 0.7 cm, respectively. These flakes are technologically representative of the entire collection, but they are not representative in terms of materials. The general flakes from other sites have much higher percentages of chalcedony and other microcrystalline silicates. Fully 93% of these flakes are dacite and only 7% are microcrystalline silicates, whereas most other sites have one-third to over one-half microcrystalline materials.

There are alternative explanations for this difference, including deliberate selection or differing availability. If the explanation is deliberate selection, people may have been deciding on materials appropriate for specific uses. The tougher yet duller edge of dacite flakes would be more appropriate for harsher uses or more resistant substances. On the other hand, the abundance of dacite implements at the graveyard could reflect easier access. Based on our finding of debitage and some expediency tools there, the piles of cached building stone at sites G-152 and 151 were evidently used as quick sources of andesite or dacite for flaking. In contrast to my initial interpretation (Sheets 1984b), I now think the more likely of these alternatives is availability. Such large amounts of dacite were only a few hundred meters away, and I suspect that short trips were made there to obtain materials for rapid tool manufacture when needed. Only 2% of the debitage had hinge fractures, which is here interpreted as highly skilled manufacture, as controlled fracture is more difficult in dacite than in microcrystalline materials.

We chose randomly two samples of earlier debitage to compare with the Silencio Phase debitage: a sample from an Arenal Phase site and a sample from a Tronadora Phase site. The Arenal Phase sample is taken from G-164-B6, in the lower-status area of the Zoned Bichrome cemetery. It is not, however, a purely funerary assemblage, because of the large amount of habitational trash that was hauled in and spread over that area of the site. In fact, with the exception of some very large percussion flakes, it is better considered an Arenal Phase domestic assemblage. Most of the flakes are fine-grained dacite, with 20% being more granular. Those more phyric flakes are mega-percussion flakes created by the violent smashing of rocks on top of the graveyard. Most still have stream cobble cortex on their dorsal surfaces. They are very large; most are between 70 g and 300 g in weight. The sweepstakes winner for the largest rock-smashing flake is a phyric dacite flake from G-164-E13; it measures 14 cm × 12 cm × 6.2 cm and weighs 1,289 g. Despite the very grainy material, the blow was sufficiently powerful to impart radial fissures. Its platform had crushed, and it partially hinged at its termination. Data on the Arenal Phase debitage from G-163-B6 are presented in Table 11-3.

We examined a randomly selected sample of thirty-two flakes from the G-163 site. It dates predominantly from the Tronadora Phase, with some flakes probably deriving from the Archaic occupation. These phases are difficult to separate stratigraphically, because both are on the Aguacate Formation. And the flakes from different phases are difficult to separate stylistically, as they are not markedly distinctive in either period, other than an apparent predominance of finer-grained materials being preferred earlier, and a tendency to produce smaller, thinner flaking debitage earlier. Measurements are summarized in Table 11-4.

Chronologically, it is significant that the relative proportion of general debitage to the lithics per phase changes notably. Beginning with the Fortuna Phase, the percentages are as follows: 46, 9, 14, 45, and 62. In the Archaic, general debitage accounts for almost half of the lithics, but the proportion drops to only 9% in the Early Formative. This is in large part due to the decrease in fine bifacial flaking. During the sedentary, neolithic phases, the percentage rises steadily to more than half of the lithics at the time of the Conquest. Such a steady rise in percentages has to take place at the expense of some other artifact category, and that apparently is thermally fractured debitage, which drops significantly during the Silencio and Tilarán phases, and Unclassified, which drops after the Tronadora Phase.

UNCLASSIFIED
(363 + 1,494 = 1,857)

This is a residual category, that is, what is left over after all the other artifacts have been assigned to other categories. An advantage of doing archaeology in a volcanically active area, where periodic eruptions deposit airfall volcanic ash over the countryside, is the greater ease of identifying human-transported stones. At distances of 15 km to 30 km from Arenal Volcano, the zone in which we conducted the bulk of our excavations, the largest particles that arrived through the air are only a few millimeters in diameter. And, because Arenal has been active only during the past three millennia, weathering differences are quite striking between freshly deposited rock versus the weathered rock from the Aguacate Formation.

Chronologically, these unclassified artifacts occur throughout the sequence with no significant variation in size, in material, or in perceived functions. The only differentiation by time is an increase in frequency from the Fortuna to the Tronadora phases, and a decrease in their frequency from the Tronadora and Arenal phases to the later two phases.

UTILIZED FLAKES (6 + 9 = 15)

It is tempting, in a lithic collection, to pick out large numbers of flakes with tiny nicks removed from their edges, and call them utilized flakes (Fig. 11-7, Table 11-5). However, flakes on the surface of an occupied site are subject to edge damage after discard by trampling, soil compaction, and a variety of other causes. Thus, these are very conservatively classified; only those flakes that clearly have edge attrition from use are included.

The frequency breakdown by project year (6+9) indicates that utilized flakes are more common in earlier lots. This is substantiated by a detailed listing of frequency by phase: 4-4-3-1. The same pattern was divulged by checking stratigraphic contexts.

Use wear varies somewhat chronologically. In the earlier sample (1985), the most common type of wear (found on five of the nine specimens) is a combination of use flaking and battering of the edge, evidently in hard chopping. Not surprisingly, these are the largest of the group; their mean weight is 224 g. All are fine-grained andesite. All but one are large percussion flakes; the exception is a wedge-shaped piece of andesite that weathered naturally to have a rounded back and a surprisingly sharp edge. All seem to have been hand-held, and probably all were used for woodworking, as evidenced by the use wear.

We surmise, based on the fine feathered-edge microflaking that resulted from use, that the three smaller flakes collected in 1985 were used for cutting. Also, all three had some grinding and microscopic polishing from use, particularly on more prominent parts of the edge. These probably were woodworking tools, but they also could have been used as utility tools for cutting hides, vines, roots, tubers, and a plethora of other substances.

Three of the 1,984 flakes exhibit fine polishing along an edge, two by motion parallel to the edge and one with a motion perpendicular to the edge. One has dull attritional wear from motion parallel to the edge, and one has tiny but systematically removed flakes along the distal end of the flake. The amount of heavy woodworking seems reduced in this later collection. Two of these flakes come from the Silencio graveyard, two from the G-161 habitation site, and two from G-169. Utilized flakes are more common in habitation sites than in graveyards.

UNIFACIALLY FLAKED IMPLEMENTS (6 + 4 = 10)

These implements must meet two criteria to be included here: steep unifacial retouching (generally between 50° and 90°) and some evidence of use wear (Fig. 11-8, Table 11-6). In all cases in which we determined directionality of use, it was perpendicular to the line of the prepared edge, probably making the designation "scraper" appropriate for these implements.

Chronologically, these scrapers extend from Zoned Bichrome times to the Conquest, with a clear peak in the Arenal Phase. The detailed frequency breakdown by phase is 0-5-1-1. Although they were not a particularly common implement at any time, it does seem curious that we found none in excavated contexts at the Tronadora Phase G-163 site. They were found exclusively in habitation sites and at G-152, a laja repository. None are from graveyards. The two found at G-164 might initially seem to be an exception, but they both come from Operation A5, a habitation portion of the site. A lot of lithic and ceramic artifacts were hauled from the habitation area to the lower-status zone (Operation B) of the G-164 cemetery. No scrapers were taken from the village to the cemetery, however, and this may reflect deliberate selection. Scrapers may have been regarded as a mundane artifact, not suitable for use or deposition at graveyards.

Another curious aspect of their distribution in the Arenal basin is that they are most commonly found in pairs, although this may be coincidence in a small sample. We found two in the Arenal Phase habitation residues at G-164, two at IF 28, and two on the surface at G-163, possibly deriving from the later occupation of that site associated with the Upper 50's soil. Thus, more than half of the collection represents pairs. These are split evenly by material, with half of dacite and half of andesite.

Figure 11-7.
Utilized flakes. Top: G-163-W18, G-164-E21. Bottom: G-163-H3, G-163-V55, G-163-I13, G-163-J5. Photograph by Fran Mandel-Sheets.

TABLE 11-5
MEAN DATA FOR UTILIZED FLAKES

Sample Year	*Diameter (cm)*	*Thickness (cm)*	*Weight (g) and Range*
1984	6.2	2.2	114, 3.1–542
1985	5.0	1.7	144, 4.2–680

Notes: The 1984 sample is from Silencio and Tilarán phases; the 1985 sample is from Tronadora and Arenal phases.

TABLE 11-6
MEAN DATA FOR UNIFACIALLY FLAKED IMPLEMENTS (SCRAPERS)

Sample Year	*Diameter (cm)*	*Thickness (cm)*	*Weight (g)*
1984	6.2	2.2	114
1985	6.4	2.2	105

Figure 11-8.
Unifacially flaked implements (scrapers). Top: both G-163-A1. Bottom: G-152-A1, G-176-A1, and G-156-A1. Photograph by Fran Mandel-Sheets.

BIFACIALLY FLAKED IMPLEMENTS (6 + 5 = 11)

Bifacial flaking for the purposes of making celt blanks has a very different history and chronology than bifacial flaking for the manufacture of projectile points and knives (Figs. 11-9, 11-10). Celts that were ground in their manufacture are discussed in Chapter 12; celts that were chipped only are included in this chapter. Bifacial flaking for celt manufacture continued during all sedentary phases from Tronadora through Tilarán. Bifacial flaking of projectile points and knives was done in the Arenal basin from Paleo-Indian times through the Archaic, but it declined or disappeared during the Tronadora and Arenal phases. When it picked up again, in the Silencio Phase, it was rougher percussion flaking to make the stemmed, rounded based bifaces (e.g., Fig. 11-10C). It continued through the Tilarán Phase to the Conquest, as evidenced by the G-154 bifacial workshop excavated in 1984. I base these chronological observations on changes in bifacial flaking on implements and debitage.

This section is organized chronologically, beginning with the Paleo-Indian Clovis point, following with the Archaic "Fortuna" point, and finishing with the later Silencio points and various unidentified biface fragments. The term "point" refers to morphology and does not imply use as a projectile point.

The Clovis-Style Point

The Clovis-like point is made of local chalcedony, honey-colored, of moderate-to-good flaking quality (Figs. 11-9, 11-10). We found it on the Aguacate Formation along the present shore of the lake, in Site G-164 (lot A5). It measures 8.0 cm × 3.2 cm × 0.8 cm and weighs 24.0 g. The maker of the point encountered a zone of rougher material, indicated by stippling on the dorsal view (left of Fig. 11-10) of the point. Dorsal and ventral refer to the sides of the blank from which the point was made. The blank was greatly modified from its original shape; the point of force application was from the "10 o'clock" position relative to the finished point. Approximately one-half of the original ventral surface of the blank is preserved on the finished implement, between the edge flaking and above the flute (see right of Fig. 11-10). In this, the Arenal Clovis point is comparable to the Hartman point, probably from Guanacaste (Swauger and Mayer-Oakes 1952). The artisan probably

Figure 11-9.
Bifacially flaked artifacts. From left to right: Clovis point from G-164-A5; Fortuna point from G-163-A1; Silencio points from G-150-C2, G-166-A2, and G-150-B2. Photograph by Fran Mandel-Sheets.

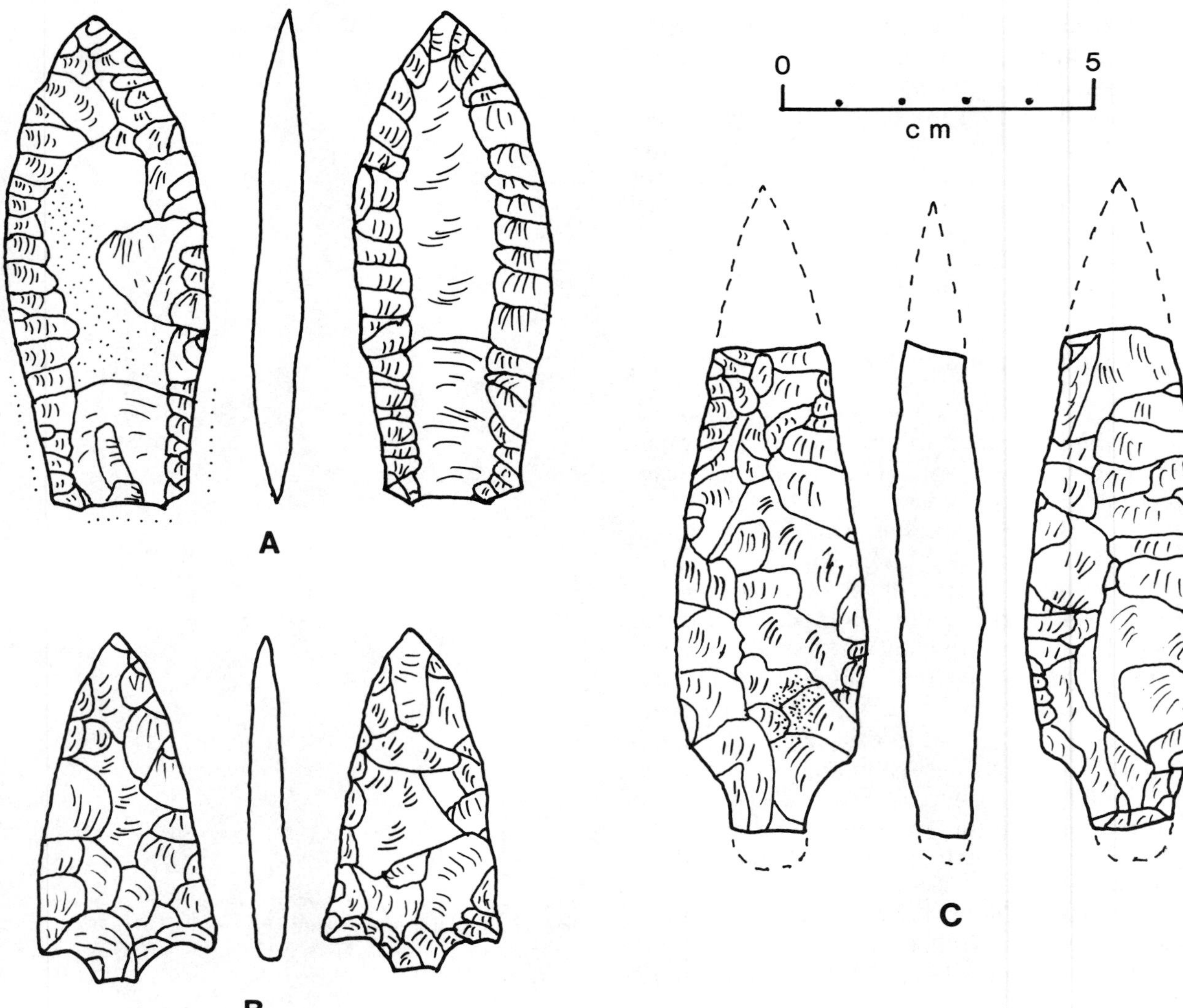

Figure 11-10.
Bifacially flaked artifacts. A: Clovis Point. B: Fortuna Point. C: Silencio Point. Proveniences provided in Figure 11-9. Drawings by Payson Sheets.

did not know of the coarser zone of chalcedony lurking within the blank, but the problem was handled with consummate skill.

Virtually all of the thinning and most of the shaping (i.e., flaking for outline) was done on the dorsal side of the blank. Flakes were removed from all margins, beginning with broad, thin expanding flakes. The dorsal thinning encountered the 2 cm × 3 cm zone of granularity during flaking from both edges. Two flakes came close to terminating in hinge fractures at the juncture of the fine and the coarser chalcedony, but, fortunately, the fracture path was sufficiently well controlled to terminate shallowly at that interface, and thus avoided a deep hinge fracture. Then, the fluting, somewhat longer on the ventral side than the dorsal, was done on both faces. That was followed by the final shaping and sharpening flaking, almost certainly by pressure, along the sides and the tip. These are highly controlled short and narrow flakes, which left a very regular outline to the biface.

The final manufacturing stage was basal faceting and grinding. The "ears," or projecting basal lateral portions, were removed, almost certainly by pressure flaking, by detaching a short invasive flake from each corner of the base. One was removed from the ventral surface, and the other from the dorsal surface. The result in each case was a small facet almost perpendicular to the face of the point. Then, 1.2 cm of the concave base and 2.4 cm of the proximal portion of each side were carefully and extensively ground. Striations visible under 100× magnification with an optical microscope indicate, not surprisingly, that the grinding motion was parallel to the edge. That the faceting occurred before the grinding is evidenced by the grinding's slightly overlapping onto the corners of the facets. The order of faceting and then grinding indicates that this was a deliberate faceting; it did not occur inadvertently during handling.

We examined both edges of the Arenal point under 10× to 100× by optical microscopy to see if we could observe evidence of use wear or abrasion in manufacture. Some very slight abrasion was found along one edge (the left edge of the ventral view, Fig. 11-10*A*, right-hand side). If it was use wear, it would indicate use as a knife, and a preference of one edge over the other. The use wear traces were not extensive, and the possibility remains that some of the abrasion may have been done to strengthen platforms prior to the final flaking. Most of the striations observed were parallel to the edge, but the fact that some of the tiny striations were transverse to the edge tends to indicate use wear, rather than manufacture. Thus, I feel that this biface was used, at least somewhat, as a knife. It is possible that it was made and hafted as a lance or dart point, and occasionally used as a knife when needed.

There is only slight evidence for reflaking or resharpening of this point. In contrast, the Hartman point appears to me to have been resharpened a number of times, leaving a stubby appearance, with the proximal hafting area seemingly oversized relative to the distal point portion. If this is correct, it probably would indicate that a functional characterization as a knife would be more appropriate than as a projectile point for both Hartman and Arenal specimens.

Specific comparisons with the Hartman point (Swauger and Mayer-Oakes 1952) are appropriate here. The Arenal specimen is longer, but they are of identical widths (3.2 cm). The Arenal point is thicker: 0.8 cm versus 0.5 cm. The Hartman point is fluted on only one side and is made of a "dull black flint," which looks like a dark, fine-grained chert to me. Swauger and Mayer-Oaks were unsure if the proximal end grinding was deliberate or was from "successive rehaftings," but the latter seems unlikely. Other than these differences, the two points are very similar in outline, flaking style, technology, and other characteristics.

Turrialba, the multicomponent quarry and workshop site located about 140 km ESE of Arenal, has yielded a number of Clovis-like fluted points (Snarskis 1979). The specimens illustrated by Snarskis (ibid.: 128–129) in his figures 2D and E and 3B are very similar to the Arenal artifact.

The Fortuna Point (Archaic)

We found a complete bifacially flaked point on the Aguacate Formation surface at G-163 (lot A1), and it apparently dates to the Archaic. It is made of dacite and is highly weathered, to the point of obscuring many flake scars. The phenocrysts, almost certainly of feldspar, have weathered out, leaving a pockmarked surface, indicating greater age than other dacite implements in the collection with uneroded phenocrysts found in Tronadora through Tilarán phase contexts. We found a few flakes with phenocrysts similarly weathered away in deeper lots at G-163, and it is likely that they are of roughly equivalent age. Thus, it appears that there was an Archaic (Fortuna Phase) occupation at G-163, but it was very slight compared with the Tronadora Phase occupation there. The point is deeply and broadly corner-notched, with a flat-bottomed, short stem. The stem is slightly asymmetric. It measures 5.5 cm × 2.9 cm × 0.6 cm.

Dacite is one of the most obdurate of materials available for flaking in the area. In spite of that, the flaking is well controlled, and only one flake is step-fractured. The result is a very thin biface, an Archaic characteristic in Costa Rica (Snarskis, personal communication, 1984). Other specimens of probable Archaic age with similar stems and broad notching and flaking are in Museo Nacional de Costa Rica collections. It would be typologically erroneous to classify this specimen, with or without the similar specimens in the Museo Nacional, with a named type from a long distance away. Hester (1986:412) notes the misuse of Texas projectile point typology in Central Mexico and the Maya area, wherein Texas point type names are applied to Mesoamerican specimens in spite of major chronological and geographic disjunctures (and, I would add, cultural and linguistic boundaries). Because of these considerations, and based on the finding of the point at the site near stratigraphically sealed and technologically identical debitage, along with well-dated charcoal, I feel that there is sufficient information to name the type and date it to the late Archaic. It is here christened a "Fortuna point."

The Fortuna point is most similar to what MacNeish calls "Shumla-like" points from Belize. These belong to the Melinda Phase, "guess-dated" by him to approximately 4000 to 3000 BC (personal communication, 1985). These points are quite similar to the Shumla type from Tehuacán, where they date from the Coxcatlán to the Santa María Phase, or about 5000 to 200 BC (MacNeish et al. 1967:68).

The Silencio Point

As mentioned earlier, bifacial flaking of projectile points and knives resumed after the time of Christ in the Cordilleran region, judging from our small sample (but the bifacial flaking of celt blanks never ceased). The most distinctive implement of this era is the Silencio point, a stemmed, rounded-base biface with a thick cross section. We found one percussion-flaked example, made of black, fine-grained dacite, at the island cemetery (G-166, lot A2). We found two smaller fragments of the same type at G-150, in lots B2 and C2. Private collections in the area commonly contain these implements from graves apparently dating to the Silencio Phase. Complete specimens in private collections range in length from 10 cm to 15 cm. Estimated lengths of project specimens, when they were complete, are 13 cm; thicknesses are 1.3 cm, and widths are 2.9 cm and 3 cm. These characteristically are thick, with accentuated midlines. They are very similar to the late stemmed, rounded base bifaces from Nicaragua (Late Classic–Postclassic) and somewhat like the Late Classic and Postclassic specimens from the Maya area (Sheets 1978, 1983:206). It is possible that they represent a sloping horizon marker, earlier in the northwest. It is also possible that they were a part of the southeastward migrations of the Pipil and Nicarao from Central Mexico into Central America during the Late Classic and Postclassic. They are similar to the tanged points from the Stone Cist Period in the Atlantic area, which date to AD 1000 to 1500 (Snarskis 1978:270).

The type is chronologically and contextually tight; that is, all come from graveyards and all probably are from Period V. Flaking is fairly good, but is not the highly controlled, flat, patterned flaking of Paleo-Indian or Archaic periods. Each face has two to five step or hinge fractures, which contributes to the prominent medial ridge. These are much thicker than Archaic or Paleo-Indian bifaces. They may have been projectile points or, more likely, hafted knives.

A few comments specific to individual examples of these stemmed, round-based bifaces are needed. The G-166 specimen displays apparent haft wear (the stippled area in Fig. 11-10*C*); however, this seems somewhat high on the specimen for haft wear. The haft may have extended farther than on many stemmed bifaces from other areas of the Americas. It is about 3 cm from the extrapolated proximal end. Slight polishing wear is visible on the ridges formed between intersecting flake scars on both sides of the proximal end of the biface, which substantiates the haft wear interpretation. It appears that the haft may have been more open on one side, allowing for dirt to act as an abrasive at one locality. The biface may have been resharpened a few times; the flake scars are highly variable in morphology and possibly in percussion implements used. A very slight degree of abrasive wear is visible under magnification (20–40×) along both edges of the blade portion, probably indicating use as a hafted knife. That wear is not visible to the unaided eye.

The G-150-B2 specimen is more consistently flaked than the foregoing. There is no evidence of haft wear or use wear. It has the appearance of having been freshly made, very likely as a burial offering.

We found six bifacially flaked projectile points or knives that are not identifiable to type. They are described here only briefly. Two are tiny fragments about which little can be said because of their size. One is from G-161-A3 and one comes from G-176-A1. Both small fragments appear to have broken in manufacture. One is rhyolite and one is chalcedony.

Certainly the most finely made of the typologically unidentified bifaces is a tip of a jasper biface from G-163-V34. It weighs only 0.8 g. It derives from a deep level, stratigraphic Unit 65, the Aguacate Formation. Flaking is very well done. It probably dates to the Fortuna Phase. Because one face is finished better than the other, it appears likely that it broke during manufacture.

Also found in a deep level (Unit 61–64) at the Tronadora Vieja site (G-163-Q4) is a bifacially flaked specimen of the metamorphic stone often used for celts. This almost certainly is a portion of a celt broken early in the manufacturing sequence. It probably broke while being made. One side is fairly well shaped and thinned, but little was done on the other (ventral) surface. Curiously, a slight amount of grinding was done in a small area where two flake scars intersect. It is possible that someone was checking to see how grinding might proceed, but the implement did not get to the grinding stage because of percussion errors.

The two other biface fragments that are not typologically identifiable derive from G-163-V11 and L14. Both of these date to the Tronadora Phase, and both are of fine-grained dacite. Both have percussion flakes removed from both sides, hence they are included in this section on bifaces; however, they might have been shaped for use as wedges. Neither is sufficiently complete for us to be certain, but both exhibit the pounding and edge battering characteristic of wedges (see below). If this interpretation is correct, they fractured badly during use and were discarded. They measure 6.2 cm × 5 cm × 2 cm and 7.8 cm × 4.3 cm × 2.6 cm, respectively, and they weigh 57 g and 90 g. The estimated weights of these artifacts when complete are 150 g to 200 g.

WEDGES (2 + 1 = 3)

Three wedges were found during survey, from G-153, from G-177, and from G-180 (Fig. 11-11 and Table 11-7).

Wedges are a distinctive type of bifacially flaked implement. They are stubby and thick because they need to withstand the stresses of being pounded into wood. They become battered at the poll end and are subject to considerable proximal end damage and to severing or fracturing where there are imperfections in the material. It is unfortunate that we recovered none in excavations because they would have contributed chronological information. By looking at associated ceramics, however, one wedge can be assigned to the Arenal Phase and one to the Silencio Phase. The other comes from site G-180, where those two phases are found in approximately equal amounts. All three are intermediate in size between Ranere's large and small wedges (Linares and Ranere 1980:322–327). The Panamanian wedges exhibit much heavier use wear than do these.

TABLE 11-7
METRIC DATA OF WEDGES

Specimen	*Length (cm)*	*Thickness (cm)*	*Weight (g)*	*Material*
G-153	6.5	2.8	110	Fine-grained andesite
G-177	6.5	2.0	80	Medium-grained andesite
G-180	4.1	2.5	59	Impure chalcedony

Figure 11-11.
Wedges. Top: G-150-E2, G-177-A1. Bottom: G-180-A9, G-153-A1. Photograph by Fran Mandel-Sheets.

Figure 11-12.
Flake cores. Left: G-150-G1. Right: G-175-A1 (both). Photograph by Fran Mandel-Sheets.

CELT BLANK (1 + 0 = 1)

We found the basal portion of a chipped stone celt blank, broken by end shock during manufacture and discarded, at G-150-E2. It measures 7 cm × 5.5 cm × 2.5 cm. Most of the cortex was removed from one surface, and all from the other. The material is a fine-grained dacite. It apparently is a failed attempt at expedient manufacture of a chipped stone celt.

HAMMERSTONES (18 + 14 = 32)

These average 194 g (range: 42 g–832 g) and have a mean diameter of 5.6 cm, with a range from 3.6 cm to 7.5 cm. Materials are andesite, dacite, and chalcedony (in descending order of frequency). All exhibit the pecking/battering and the welter of overlapping Hertzian cones from percussion impacts during chipped stone manufacture or from pecking ground stone implements during manufacture, for roughening, or other uses.

Ten come from the G-150/G-151/G-152 Silencio Phase funerary complex, and others come from habitation sites around the lake. Two come from the Arenal Phase cemetery (G-164) and we found one in the associated habitation area just north of that cemetery. We found five at the Archaic site AL-186, and one at G-163. Although we found hammerstones in deposits from all phases, they are most common during the Archaic and during later times, particularly in Period V. Although samples are small, their chronological placements can be seen on Tables 11-1 and 11-2.

We found an interesting irregularly shaped hammerstone at G-183. It is somewhat pyramidal in shape, and use battering is found on all four corners. As contemporary lithic knappers know, an irregularly shaped hammerstone can be very useful, especially for fine percussion flaking, or for working irregularly shaped bifaces or flake cores. This specimen measures 15.5 cm × 8.7 cm × 6.5 cm and weighs 832 g.

It is somewhat surprising that we did not find more hammerstones. Granted, bifacial flaking was not a lithic obsession with Arenal-area residents, but there certainly was a lot of percussion lithic manufacture of flakes from cores and many celt blanks were preformed. And there was a lot of pecking of ground stone artifacts (see Chap. 12). The use of hardwood, bone, or antler percussors could be a partial explanation, but even extensive use of perishable percussors does not seem to be a satisfactory explanation. Part of the problem may be the rapid rate of weathering in the hot and moist Arenal area; a hammerstone that was exposed to the elements for long could lose evidence of its use fairly rapidly. We found and identified numerous hammerstones at the Archaic AL-186 site, however, dating to the fourth millennium BC.

FLAKE CORES (43 + 54 = 97)

Core-flake technology is the most widespread type of chipped stone technology in the area (Fig. 11-12). It begins with our earliest sites, and continues to our latest. It is found in both funerary and habitation sites. It is an informal, cottage industry showing considerable variation in raw materials, skill, and in core shaping and reduction. It is an expedient technology, in that flakes were made when and where they were needed, they were used, and then they were discarded.

The classification here is conservative, so that only items from which a number of flakes have been removed or items for which the objective was the usable flake rather than a shaped implement are included in this rubric. Therefore, it is virtually certain that a few flake cores from which very few flakes were removed were not recognized as cores. The advantage of conservative classification, however, is a high degree of confidence that core reduction occurred in cases in which cores are tabulated. One result of a conservative classification is a heightened ratio of flakes to cores. Overall, the project collected 1,895 flakes (general debitage), which, when divided by the 97 cores, yields a 20:1 flake:core ratio. At first glance this seems very high, but most of the items tabulated under general debitage are broken into three or more pieces. Taking that into account would yield a ratio of about seven flakes per core, which is within the realm of possibility, based on core size and the number of flake scars on the cores. Given the conservative classification of flake cores, the actual mean number of flakes removed per core probably is between 4 and 6.

The cores average 202 g in weight, 5 cm in diameter, and 3.5 cm in thickness. Diameter and thickness ranges are 3.3 cm to 14 cm, and 2 cm to 6.6 cm. Their shapes are highly variable. As one would expect, the dacite:microcrystalline material ratios match the materials in general debitage. Here, 28% are chalcedony, 3% are jasper, 1% a somewhat phyric andesite, with the rest dacite.

We found three megacores of a slightly crystalline andesite at the Zoned Bichrome cemetery, G-164-E19. They average 1,775 g in weight and have average diameters of 12 cm and heights of 6.4 cm. Flakes produced would have been neither very sharp nor very tough, compared with dacite or chalcedony flakes. All come from the same funerary lot and evidently represent a cemetery ritual resulting in particularly forceful percussion flake manufacture.

Some cores are unidirectional, some are bidirectional, and some are multidirectional. Approximately half of the flake cores in this category are unidirectional, but for reasons explained earlier, the sample is biased toward the more easily recognizable unidirectional cores. Unidirectional cores probably represent less than one-third of the region's cores. Some are conical, some are discoidal, and many are irregular. There is no formal manufacturing stage of core shaping, as exists in other areas. Cores are shaped only insofar as it aids the next flake removal.

Chronologically, the frequency of cores for each of the five phases is 9-5-28-13-8. All of the Fortuna Phase cores come from the AL-186 site, where flake cores represent 8% of all the artifacts collected. It appears that the Tronadora Phase witnessed a decline in percussion core-flake manufacture, and this is substantiated by the products of that activity tabulated under General Debitage. Core-flake manufacture picked up considerably in the Arenal Phase, however, to decline again in the Silencio and Tilarán phases. This is substantiated by unit associations, as flake cores are rare in Units 65–60, but are more common in Units 54 and 50, and become rarer still in Unit 30.

PERCUSSION BLADES (9 + 13 = 22)

Percussion blades (Fig. 11-13) are defined as percussion flakes that are more than twice as long as they are wide, with relatively straight, parallel sides. The percussion blades in the Arenal area are not the product of an organized blade industry. Rather, they appear to be incidental or fortuitous by-products of core-flake technology.

The percussion blades average 69 g and have mean lengths of 8.5 cm, widths of 3.4 cm, and thicknesses of 1.4 cm. Lengths range from 3.2 cm to 18 cm. The smallest is a chalcedony microblade. Ten are dacite, eight are andesite, and the following materials are represented by one specimen each: andesite porphyry, jasper, chalcedony, and petrified wood. The porphyry blade was finely retouched along its outside margin, probably to sharpen and strengthen the edge. No others were retouched or show use wear.

Chronologically, percussion blades' frequencies per phase are 1-2-7-1-1. Stratigraphic evidence also indicates a peak in percussion blade frequency at about the same time, in Units 54 and 50. Thus, the Arenal Phase contains most of the percussion blades made during the sequence. Also, there seems to be an increase in the average size of these blades during the Arenal Phase, and then a decrease to the Conquest. However, I think this is best accounted for by the tremendous amount of rock smashing that was done in Arenal Phase graveyards (e.g., G-164), with resultant mega-flakes, among which were some elongated flakes with parallel edges that were detached from rocks with prominent ridges. Those are here tabulated as percussion blades, even though I feel that few were deliberately manufactured at the G-164 cemetery. Distributionally, there is little clear patterning, other than that smaller specimens tend to be found at habitation sites.

CHIPPED STONE CELTS (2 + 0 = 2)

Chipped stone celts (Fig. 11-14) share the early shaping stage of percussion flaking, and they probably were used for many of the same cutting and chopping tasks as were ground stone celts. Evidently, chipped stone celts did not require the flaking precision that ground stone celts required, and that may explain why they are not very well shaped. In contrast, a preform for a ground stone celt that is poorly shaped requires a great amount of additional effort in pecking and grinding to achieve a working implement. Both of the specimens in Figure 11-14 date to the Silencio Phase; the sample is inadequate to sustain much interpretation of chronological trends or patterns.

We found a dacite chipped stone celt at G-152 (a lithic repository), along with much lithic wastage, which indicates that chipped stone celt manufacture occurred there. It is missing only 2 or 3 cm of its poll end. Thus, its original length would have been 12 or 13 cm. Its width is 6.6 cm, and its thickness is 2 cm. It weighs 151 g. Interestingly, it is lightly ground along both sides and at the bit end, in a narrow zone 1 mm to 2 mm wide. The grinding clearly resulted from manufacture, not from use. Grinding's effect on the bit end would be to dull the edge somewhat, but it would have strengthened the edge considerably. The reason for grinding both edges is not known. A possibility would be to decrease haft wear, but if so, then why grind uniformly along the entire side? It was used after the bit was ground, as use had detached a few flakes, leaving only about one-third of the bit length with the ground surface.

A double-bitted, waisted axe was found at G-156. It is missing portions of both bits and appears to have been broken in manufacture. It is of andesite and weighs 282 g. It is 20 cm long, 6.6 cm wide, and 2.7 cm thick. It was not carefully made, as hinge fractures abound, and the "waisting," or medial constriction, is composed of a welter of small hinge and step fractures. A flaw in the material, a hidden natural fissure, was encountered at one end and probably contributed to its premature abandonment. Similarly shaped specimens are very common in Atlantic Costa Rica during the first millennium AD. Snarskis (1978:153)

Figure 11-13.
Percussion blades. G-150-A, IF13, G-152-A4, S6, G-175-A1, G-163-A1. These appear to be fortuitous, and not the product of a blade industry. Item S6 is of petrified wood. Photograph by Fran Mandel-Sheets.

reports large numbers of them, of fine dark shale, chipped and then usually ground, from cemeteries and from some habitation sites. Shale is such a weak material and would be very poor for percussive cutting, so I wonder if these could be slate (metamorphosed shale). Stone (1977: 148) reports a similar specimen from the Línea Vieja, Early Period A (300 BC—AD 1). I prefer Snarskis's later dating, largely because of the association of these axes with the thick, stemmed bifaces (ibid.: fig. 189), which we have securely dated to the Silencio Phase, the latter portion of the first millennium.

PEBBLES (0 + 466 = 466)

These rocks are artifacts only in the sense that they have been selected from numerous other rocks in streams and transported to sites. They were selected carefully for size, for having a moderate to high degree of stream rounding, and for a

Figure 11-14.
Chipped stone celts. G-156-A1, G-152-A2. Photograph by Fran Mandel-Sheets.

lack of weathering. About 90% are phyric andesite and the remainder are dacite. We measured a sample of seventy-eight pebbles, yielding a mean weight of 4.2 g and a mean diameter of 1.6 cm (range 1.2 cm to 2.1 cm). At first glance, they look like miniature cooking stones, because of their being stream-worn, being of the most common rock material available, and being relatively unweathered. None show any evidence of heating and rapid cooling, however, in contrast with cooking stones. Also, their small size would make use as cooking stones very inefficient.

So, what are they? Functionally, they could have been slingstones, gaming pieces, used as an architectural feature, for counting or other transactions, or perhaps they functioned in some yet-unimagined way or ways. They do seem small for slingstones, but they would have served well as gaming or counting stones. In at least one case, they apparently were laid into the floor of the entryway of an early Tronadora Phase house (G-163-

W30; see Chap. 4). Almost all of the specimens (447, or 96%) were found at site G-163. The extraordinarily high proportion found at a single site makes one wonder if some idiosyncratic factor could be at work here, or simply the use of stones in games or set into floors, a use that was not shared by other villages.

There is a subcategory of pebbles, here called "small pebbles." These are of a softer stone, darker, nonphyric, and are more thoroughly smoothed, yet with a wider range of shapes than the other pebbles. We found a total of twenty, all from G-163, Units 60 and 61, indicating that they date to the Tronadora Phase. They average 1.4 g in weight (range 0.4 g to 3.9 g) and have mean diameters of 1.7 cm (range: 0.7 cm to 2.4 cm). They apparently were selected for their variety of shapes, their greater smoothing, and for the material. Use as gaming or counting stones seems possible, but other functions should be considered.

We recorded no pebbles during the 1984 season. We first recognized them early in the 1985 season, during excavations at the early G-163 site. We found very few at the Arenal Phase G-164 site. Were they present in the 1984 collections but simply not recognized, or are they unique to the Tronadora Phase? Had they been present in lots being excavated in 1984, they would have been collected, as they are larger than any components of airfall tephra. With this problem in mind, we reanalyzed a number of lots from 1984 research (including G-154, G-161, G-153, G-157, G-174, G-172, and G-177), but we found no pebbles. Thus, it appears that they may be temporally specific, being almost entirely restricted to the Tronadora Phase. It should be pointed out that we recognized these with the benefit of excavations of structures within tephra units. It is unlikely that they would have been recognized as artifacts in surface survey collections or in excavations in sites located beyond volcanically active areas.

HOES (0 + 6 = 6)

All of these hoes were made from naturally eroded, fortuitously shaped pieces of dacite or andesite (Fig. 11-15, Table 11-8). Each received some lateral percussion shaping to regularize the outline and create shallow notches for hafting. Five of the six are from Tronadora Phase contexts at G-163, and one is from the surface of G-164, and thus probably is Arenal Phase. Thus, chronologically, one can conclude that these are relatively common in the Tronadora Phase, and also are found in the Arenal Phase. Small sample size does not allow for firm conclusions about their existence or nonexistence in later phases.

We found four hoes stacked on top of each other in a small depression on the side of a posthole in lot G-163-H41. They were not hafted when they were stacked in the cache. The nature of flaking for haft notching is easily recognizable: a few steep flakes and some edge battering result in a shallow, dulled notch. The location of the notching is variable. Two are notched so that the weight is equally distributed on either side of the haft. The other two have three-quarters of the weight on the bit end of the haft. (This is true for the two specimens we found outside the cache as well.) We do not know if this has functional significance.

The edges are quite fragile and would have had to have been used with caution. Edge angles are acute, from 20° to 25°. The actual working edges are blunted, however, so that if the measurement of edge angle were taken from the most distal point to the faces 1 cm back from the edge, one gets an angle of about 50°. That certainly would have improved their durability, as a less-acute edge will absorb the shock of percussive impact better without fracturing; however, they still would have had to be used with gentle strokes. Some of the edge blunting was deliberate, by removal of short (1/2 to 1 cm) flakes, but most seems to have been from use. If the hoes were used in the soil contemporary with them, that is, the soil developed on Unit 61 (Arenal's earliest eruption layer), then some abrasion would be expected from contact with tephra particles. It is likely that digging and hoeing would occasionally penetrate into the underlying Aguacate Formation and thus occasionally contact rocks, resulting in edge damage. Also, an inadvertent contact with a tree root would result in damage to these relatively fragile edges.

I briefly describe the hoes individually, in order of their presentation in Table 11-8. The first one has at least four flakes removed from the poll end for shaping. The haft notching is from both faces and includes battering to smooth the flaked surface. Some haft wear has further smoothed the notches.

The second hoe has the most irregular surface. It sports some fine abrasive wear 3 cm from the bit, with striae perpendicular to the edge, further supporting its functional identification as a hoe. The poll end is completely unmodified. Only

TABLE 11-8
METRIC DATA FOR HOES

Catalog No.	*Weight (g)*	*Length (cm)*	*Width (cm)*	*Thickness (cm)*	*Material*
G-163-H41/1	510	15.2	10.5	3.0	Dacite
G-163-H41/2	409	14.4	9.9	2.3	Dacite
G-163-H41/3	293	14.1	10.2	2.0	Andesite
G-163-H41/4	Incomplete	Incomplete	8.8	1.5	Dacite
G-163-I5B	Incomplete	Incomplete	6.4	2.3	Andesite
G-164-A5	588	13.2	9.2	3.7	Dacite
Average	450	14.2	9.1	2.5	

Figure 11-15.
Hoes. G-163-H41/1 and G-163-H41/2. Both were found in a pocket adjacent to a posthole, against the wall of a structure, and were cached unhafted. Photograph by Fran Mandel-Sheets.

fourteen flake scars can be counted on the entire specimen. Notching is short, only extending 3 cm on a side, in contrast to the 6-cm-long notches on the first hoe.

The third hoe has a triangular shape, the most uniform bit, and the least wear of the six. Curiously, it has two sets of hafting grooves, one near the poll end and one closer to the middle. The more distal pair of notches exhibit a slight degree of haft wear. Interestingly, a third set of haft notches was started closer to the middle, but a percussion blow severed the implement into two pieces. Why it was kept, and placed in the cache, is unknown.

The fourth hoe is the thinnest of all, and it is incomplete. It is missing the bit end, but its poll end is the most well shaped of the group. Haft wear is the most extensive of the G-163 hoes and has thoroughly smoothed the notch.

The I5B specimen from G-163 is a small fragment of the bit end. It shows abrasive and flaking edge damage and has a narrower bit than the others.

The G-164-A5 specimen is larger than the others, but in other aspects such as manufacture, material, and probable use, it is the same. At least three-quarters of each face is cortex, although the edge has been retouched all the way around. At least fifty-six flake scars are recognizable. The haft wear is the most well developed of all the hoes. Haft notching is identical to that of all the G-163 specimens, but is more carefully done, over 3 cm in length, and notch depth is 5 mm. Other than the notching, the lateral flaking generally results in feather edge terminations. In two places, fine abrasive wear (composed of small striations and abrasion perpendicular to the bit edge) has survived postabandonment weathering.

ASPECTS OF THE COLLECTION

Some aspects of the collection deserve special mention. An exclusively typological analysis of artifacts subsumes or eliminates topical and modal factors, so this section is intended to resolve that problem.

We encountered lithic workshops at a few sites, and some of these were described earlier, including workshops for the manufacture of dacite chipped stone celts and andesite general utility flakes. As with most lithic collections, some types have a sufficiently large number of specimens, from known contexts, so that we can date them well and study their distributions and associations. Some types, however, are represented by very few specimens, thus placing limitations on chronological or functional interpretations.

OBSIDIAN FLAKES

In striking contrast with sites in Mesoamerica and the northern part of the Intermediate Area, obsidian is extremely rare in the Arenal area. We found only two tiny obsidian flakes, out of a total of 8,755 lithic artifacts, for an extremely low percentage of 0.02. We found one tiny (5 mm × 4 mm × 2 mm) obsidian flake in Burial 1 at the Silencio graveyard, G-150-B5. It was close to, and perhaps associated with, the gold pendant. It is a fragment of a small percussion or pressure flake. It is very poor quality obsidian, and it would be difficult to make a usable artifact, even a simple cutting flake, from that kind of obsidian. It has a large pumiceous inclusion in the middle, but the rest is a smoky transparent obsidian.

The other obsidian artifact is a small percussion flake fragment found at G-197-A2, a site on the southwestern shore of present Lake Arenal, about 4 km northwest of Tronadora. The flake is 9 mm long, 7 mm wide, and 3 mm thick, with a roughly triangular cross section. It contains a relatively large xenolith of dark gray material on its dorsal ridge. It has three dorsal flake scars. It could be part of a bifacial thinning flake, but it is too fragmentary to be certain. The quality of material is only slightly better than the flake from G-150. These two flakes may be from a local Costa Rican obsidian source of poor quality and yet to be reported, or they may have come from the sources of small nodular obsidian located east of Lake Managua in Nicaragua. It seems unlikely that they are from known sources farther to the northwest in Mesoamerica, or farther to the southeast in the Andes.

BIFACIAL WORKSHOP AT G-154

Fine screening of Operation I, at the Tilarán Phase G-154 habitation site, with 1/8-in. mesh, yielded 185 small flakes of dacite and chalcedony. Most flakes are less than 1 cm long, and less than 1.5 mm thick. Although only 13 can unequivocally be identified as bifacial trimming flakes (Fig. 11-6), it is clear that the primary, if not the sole, objective was manufacture and maintenance of bifaces. Most of the chalcedony flakes evidently are from the initial manufacture, but 5

TABLE 11-9
TYPES OF CHIPPED STONE ARTIFACTS, SORTED BY PHASE AND BY TYPE OF SITE (HABITATION VERSUS CEMETERY)

Phase	*Thermally Fractured Debitage*	*Small Biface Flakes*	*Large Biface Flakes*	*Celt Flakes*	*General Debitage*	*Un-classified*	*Uni-facially Flaked*	*Bifacially Flaked*
Tilarán	84	9	0	1	294	64	1	1
% of total	(17.7)	(1.9)		(0.2)	(62.0)	(13.5)	(0.2)	(0.2)
Silencio	338	11	12	2	423	116	1	2
% of total	(36.0)	(1.2)	(1.3)	(0.2)	(45.0)	(12.3)	(0.1)	(0.2)
Arenal	2,375	6	0	3	494	501	5	3
% of total	(66.8)	(0.2)		(0.1)	(13.9)	(14.1)	(0.1)	(0.1)
Tronadora	559	5	1	4	168	671	0	2
% of total	(31.1)	(0.3)	(0.1)	(0.2)	(9.3)	(37.3)		(0.1)
Fortuna	12	9	1	0	54	21	0	0
% of total	(10.3)	(7.7)	(0.9)		(46.2)	(17.9)		
Total	3,368	40	14	10	1,433	1,373	7	8
% of total	(48.9)	(0.6)	(0.2)	(0.1)	(20.8)	(19.9)	(0.1)	(0.1)
Habitation sites	1,343	41	7	9	1,143	1,378	5	7
% of total	(28.7)	(0.9)	(0.1)	(0.2)	(24.4)	(29.5)	(0.1)	(0.1)
Cemeteries	2,624	7	4	5	619	429	2	4
% of total	(68.6)	(0.2)	(0.1)	(0.1)	(16.2)	(11.2)	(0.1)	(0.1)

have platforms taken from used bifacial knives, and thus were detached to resharpen the implement. The evidence is the manufacturing abrasion that each carries on its platform; the flake's removal left a sharpened edge. Four of the black dacite flakes likewise carry an abraded platform and indicate maintenance activities. Thus the main activity was manufacture of dacite and chalcedony knives, but some effort was also devoted to resharpening.

MIXED WORKSHOP AT G-185

Both the bifacial workshop at G-154 and the core-flake and bifacial workshop at G-185 date to Period VI (the Tilarán Phase). This small workshop, located 8 km southeast of Tilarán, yielded thirty-five lithic artifacts and sixteen sherds. All of the diagnostic sherds date to the Tilarán Phase; stratigraphic corroboration of this late dating is provided by all in situ artifacts deriving from the upper portion of Unit 30. The lithic collection includes five thermally fractured cooking stones, two large bifacial thinning flakes, twenty-five debitage flakes (including two with hinge fractures), two flake cores, and one unclassified stone. One significant aspect of the collection, substantiated at other sites, is that three of the characteristics of the Archaic Fortuna Phase—stone boiling, core-flake technology, and bifacial manufacture—were still being practiced in the research area, after some 5,500 years, up to the Spanish Conquest.

The range of material variation is great, with dacite, chalcedony, and jasper common, and quartzite, porphyry, and rhyolite rare.

BIFACIAL WORKSHOPS AT G-151 and G-152

We found two bifacial workshops that appear very similar to each other at these laja repositories to the west of the Silencio graveyard (G-150). Both of these repositories are directly linked with the graveyard by means of the footpaths discovered in the remote-sensing imagery and confirmed by excavations (Chap. 9). The workshops are composed almost entirely of flakes of dark dacite. These flakes represent the full manufacturing sequence from cortex removal and early shaping to final edge trimming. We found insufficient ceramics in either repository to date them adequately. We found only five diagnostic ceramics in G-151, and they were Arenal Phase, contemporary with the beginnings of cemetery use. We discovered only twenty diagnostic sherds in G-152, and they were Silencio Phase. More important for linking the sites and establishing chronology, however, are the footpaths that directly relate the sites and the tephra burial layers that establish the temporal framework. The sherds indicate that the G-151 repository was begun before the closer G-152 repository was established. It is probable that both were in use during the Silencio Phase use of the large cemetery.

TABLE 11-9
(*continued*)

Wedges	*Hammer-stones*	*Flake Cores*	*Percussion Blades*	*Cooking Stones*	*Celt Blanks*	*Chipped Celts*	*Utilized Flakes*	*Pebbles*	*Hoes*	*Total*
0	1 (0.2)	8 (1.7)	1 (0.2)	4 (0.8)	0	0	1 (0.2)	5 (1.1)	0	474
1 (0.1)	10 (1.1)	13 (1.4)	1 (0.1)	6 (0.6)	1 (0.1)	0	3 (0.3)	0	0	940
1 (0)	9 (0.3)	28 (0.8)	7 (0.2)	68 (1.9)	0	0	4 (0.1)	49 (1.4)	1 (0)	3,554
0	1 (0.1)	5 (0.3)	2 (0.1)	137 (7.6)	0	0	4 (0.2)	239 (13.3)	0	1,798
0	5 (4.3)	9 (7.7)	1 (0.9)	5 (4.3)	0	0	0	0	0	117
2 (0)	26 (0.4)	63 (0.9)	12 (0.2)	220 (3.2)	1 (0)	2 (0)	12 (0.2)	293 (4.3)	1 (0)	6,885
3 (0.1)	14 (0.2)	48 (1.0)	11 (0.2)	205 (4.4)	0	1 (0)	9 (0.2)	451 (9.6)	4 (0.1)	4,679
0	11 (0.3)	30 (0.8)	7 (0.2)	58 (1.5)	1 (0)	0	6 (0.2)	15 (0.4)	1 (0)	3,823

G-169 SITE ASSEMBLAGE

The Joluvi site is unusual for its concentration of lithics and for the lack of much variation within it. Although we excavated only five 2 × 2 m test pits in this fairly large site, we recovered 484 lithic artifacts. This is the second-highest site total; G-150 had more lithic artifacts, but that is in part because much more volume was excavated there. Six cooking stones and 141 pieces of thermally fractured debitage indicate great amounts of cooking at the Joluvi site. A small flake from a ground stone celt shows possession of celts by inhabitants of the site. A bifacial trimming flake does indicate bifacial manufacture at the site, but what is notable is how little was done there compared to flake manufacture.

The predominant lithic activity was core-flake manufacture. The total for general flakes, 276, is large, and production is largely composed of flakes manufactured for domestic use. The hinge fracture rate, 3.3%, is high relative to many sites in the basin, and is additional evidence for household, not specialist, production. The percentage of microcrystalline materials, 13, is quite low. The manufacturers evidently favored the immediately available andesite and dacite over the rarer chalcedony or other microcrystalline materials that would have required more effort to obtain, either by longer-distance travel or through an exchange system. Also notable for their absence in such a large collection are unifacial implements, bifacial implements, and chipped stone celts. The site lithics give the impression of a mundane, domestic, local cutting flake assemblage with few frills.

LITHICS: CHRONOLOGY

Using stratigraphy and associated ceramics, we compared the dated lithics from all time spans. Ceramically based time spans are the phases; stratigraphically based time spans are the sequent Units. Fortunately, we found that the chronological tables based on ceramic phases and volcanic units were very similar, so only the tables based on phases are presented here, as Tables 11-9–11-12. The time spans correspond to the four ceramic phases plus the Fortuna Phase. A total of 6,885 chipped stone artifacts were so used. We excluded the lithic artifacts that came from mixed lots or multicomponent sites without clear separations. We prepared lithic tables for each component with a spreadsheet and then compared. We used the relational software for more detailed sortings. Because each phase has a different total number of artifacts, we use the percentages of each type within its total per phase, instead of the raw frequencies, for comparison.

The percentages of thermally fractured debitage vary through time, with a steady rise to the Arenal Phase and then a decline to the Conquest. We found bifacial flaking of celts in all ceramic phases, and it increases somewhat through time.

TABLE 11-10
GENERAL DEBITAGE PER PHASE AND SITE TYPE, BROKEN DOWN INTO HINGE FRACTURE FREQUENCIES AND MATERIAL FREQUENCIES

Phase	*General Debitage*	*Hinge Fractures*	*Chalcedony*	*Petrified Wood*	*Porphyry*
Tilarán	294	8	120	3	0
% of category total		(2.7)	(40.8)	(1.0)	
Silencio	423	11	30	2	0
% of category total		(2.6)	(7.1)	(0.5)	
Arenal	494	27	63	5	0
% of category total		(5.5)	(12.8)	(1.0)	
Tronadora	168	4	33	9	5
% of category total		(2.4)	(19.6)	(5.4)	(3.0)
Fortuna	54	6	13	23	0
% of category total		(11.1)	(24.1)	(42.6)	
Total	1,433	56	259	42	5
% of category total		(3.9)	(18.1)	(2.9)	(0.3)
Habitations	1,143	50	330	41	10
% of category total		(4.4)	(28.8)	(3.6)	(0.9)
Cemeteries	619	22	47	1	1
% of category total		(3.6)	(7.6)	(0.2)	(0.2)

The evidence lies in the relative frequencies of implements and debitage. Bifacial flaking of projectile points or knives was done in the Archaic and the Tronadora phases, but evidently not in the Arenal Phase; it was resumed in the Silencio and the Tilarán phases. The increase in general flakes in the Tilarán Phase is at least partially explained by an increase in bifacial flaking, because bifacial technology has a much higher ratio of wastage to implements than does core-flake or unifacial manufacture. Flake cores are common in Fortuna Phase lots, but drop in Tronadora Phase lots, and then steadily increase in percentages of lithics in later phases.

Hinge fracture percentages, computed as a percentage of general flakes, do show variation through time. The highest percentages are in the Fortuna and the Arenal phases, with other phases being slightly above 2%. The 11% figure seems very high for the Fortuna phase, but it is on a small sample. It is surprising that the cemeteries have slightly lower hinge fracture percentages than do the habitations.

A high degree of variation in materials is notable through time. Chalcedony starts fairly high and drops through time, but rises dramatically in the Tilarán Phase. The drop in the Silencio Phase may or may not indicate a societywide decline in chalcedony use. It does indicate that very little chalcedony was used in cemeteries during that phase. Until Silencio Phase habitations are explored, we will not know how much chalcedony was used in everyday activities. The rise in chalcedony use to 41% during the Tilarán Phase is also notable, and in part derives from the fine-screened bifacial workshop at the G-154 habitation site. Chalcedony edges are sharper and seem to have been favored at habitation sites for some uses. Cemetery needs for cutting edges apparently were met more satisfactorily by more granular materials, particularly dacite.

THE FORTUNA PHASE: THE ARCHAIC IN THE CORDILLERA

Finding Archaic remains during the research of the Proyecto Prehistórico Arenal was a fortunate, although unforeseen result of survey and excavations. Two sites (AL-186 and G-163) are particularly notable for yielding artifacts and features of the Archaic Period; they are locally designated the Fortuna Phase.

Data from the Archaic in Central America are rare and, as a result, it is a poorly dated and poorly understood time period. Participants at the School for American Research (SAR) Advanced Seminar agree on 8000 and 4000 BC as the time boundaries for the Archaic (Lange and Stone 1984), but recognize that these dates are little more than rough estimates. The most reliable Fortuna Phase radiocarbon date is from AL-186, at 3780 (3675) 3539 BC. It is a single-component site stratigraphically well separated from other cultural and natural horizons, and contamination

TABLE 11-10
(continued)

Rhyolite	*Jasper*	*Quartzite*	*Fine-Grained Dacite*
0	5	1	165
	(1.7)	(0.3)	(56.1)
0	2	0	389
	(0.5)		(91.2)
13	3	1	409
(2.6)	(0.6)	(0.2)	(82.8)
2	3	0	116
(1.2)	(1.8)		(69.0)
0	2	2	14
	(3.7)	(3.7)	(25.9)
15	15	4	1,093
(1.0)	(1.0)	(0.2)	(76.3)
17	24	17	704
(1.5)	(2.1)	(1.5)	(61.6)
5	1	1	563
(0.8)	(0.2)	(0.2)	(90.9)

or mixing of that charcoal is unlikely. This date is followed by a series of dates from the lowest levels of the G-163 site. It appears that the Archaic life-style lasted for perhaps a millennium longer in the Arenal area than envisioned by the SAR symposium participants.

That series of C-14 dates from the lowest levels of the G-163 site, using the intercepts of calibrated dates, falls between 3400 and 1800 BC, or, the one-sigma ranges extend from 3500 to 1750 BC. Only the more recent dates, around 2000 BC, are stratigraphically separated from the earlier dates by the emplacement of the Unit 61 tephra from the earliest eruption of Arenal Volcano. As mentioned in Chapter 1, there are difficulties in separating the small Archaic occupation of G-163 from the beginnings of the Tronadora Phase occupation that occurred on the same Aguacate Formation surface. Drawing the Archaic-Tronadora Phase boundary at 3300 BC does divide the earlier C-14 date that has lithics and no ceramics from the earliest two ceramic-associated dates (3351 and 3053 BC intercepts). Until more research is done, our best estimate of the Archaic-Formative transition is that it occurred sometime between 3300 and 2000 BC in the Arenal area, and we will conservatively use the 2000 BC date.

The AL-186 site is a campsite on the top of a small hill overlooking a stream just north of the Arenal basin. The site is buried by an unusually complete stratigraphic sequence of Arenal tephra layers. It was exposed at 3 m below the present ground surface by earth-moving equipment during road construction. The presence of two hearths, along with abundant charcoal and wood ash and a tremendous number of cooking stones, clearly indicates that it was a campsite. We collected and tabulated twelve pieces of thermally fractured debitage, with over eighty-five cooking stones field-identified and counted but not collected. These constitute the earliest dated evidence of stone cooking technology in the Cordillera. The hearths are approximately circular, and their use resulted in a slight oxidation of the clay surface.

While camped at AL-186, the Fortuna Phase residents engaged in manufacture of bifacially flaked implements. Some of the small biface trimming flakes may have been detached for purposes of resharpening, but the presence of a large bifacial trimming flake is evidence of primary manufacture. All biface trimming flakes are thin, expanding flakes, in contrast to the thicker and narrower bifacial flakes characteristic of the Silencio Phase. Also while camped there, residents made a lot of utility flakes from informally shaped cores. We found nine flake cores—a very high proportion of a Cordilleran lithic assemblage when compared with later sites. Also unusual for their abundance were hammerstones, surely used in core-flake and bifacial technology.

The fifty-four general flakes recovered derive from core-flake and from bifacial manufacture. The materials breakdown is different from that of

TABLE 11-11
TYPES OF CHIPPED STONE ARTIFACTS, SORTED BY PHASE AND SITE TYPE WITHIN EACH PHASE WHEN POSSIBLE

Phase	*Site Type*	*Thermally Fractured Debitage*	*Small Biface Flakes*	*Large Biface Flakes*	*Celt Flakes*	*General Debitage*	*Un-classified*	*Uni-facially Flaked*	*Bifacially Flaked*
Tilarán	Habitations	84	9	0	1	294	64	1	1
		(17.7)	(1.9)		(0.2)	(62.0)	(13.5)	(0.2)	(0.2)
Silencio	Habitations	104	1	1	0	158	32	1	0
		(33.9)	(0.3)	(0.3)		(51.5)	(10.4)	(0.3)	
	Cemeteries	206	5	4	2	217	78	0	2
		(37.6)	(0.9)	(0.7)	(0.4)	(39.6)	(14.2)		(0.4)
Arenal	Habitations	174	5	0	2	185	212	3	2
		(26.4)	(0.8)		(0.3)	(28.0)	(32.1)	(0.5)	(0.3)
	Cemeteries	2,201	1	0	1	314	289	2	1
		(75.9)	(0)		(0)	(10.8)	(10.0)	(0.1)	(0)
Tronadora	Habitations	559	5	2	4	168	671	0	2
		(31.1)	(0.3)	(0.1)	(0.2)	(9.3)	(37.3)		(0.1)

TABLE 11-12
GENERAL DEBITAGE BROKEN DOWN INTO HINGE FRACTURE FREQUENCIES AND MATERIAL TYPE FREQUENCIES, TABULATED FOR EACH PHASE AND SITE TYPE WHEN POSSIBLE

Phase	*Site Type*	*General Debitage*	*Hinge Fractures*	*Chalcedony*	*Petrified Wood*
Tilarán	Habitations	294	8	120	3
% of category total			(2.7)	(40.8)	(1.0)
Silencio	Habitations	158	7	16	2
% of category total			(4.4)	(10.1)	(1.3)
	Cemeteries	217	3	14	0
			(1.4)	(6.5)	
Arenal	Habitations	185	8	36	5
% of category total			(4.3)	(19.5)	(2.7)
	Cemeteries	314	19	27	0
			(6.0)	(8.6)	
Tronadora	Habitations	168	4	33	9
% of category total			(2.4)	(19.6)	(5.4)

later sites, but it should be noted that AL-186 is close to the Venado source of petrified wood. The Venado source is 15 km east of the present town of Arenal. The materials are 43% petrified wood, 24% chalcedony, 26% fine-grained dacite, and 4% each for jasper and quartzite. It is important to note that core-flake manufacture using dacite, a volcanic (extrusive) rock, was relatively rare in the Archaic, compared with later phases; however, it is also important to note that continuity with shifting emphasis, rather than dramatic qualitative changes, is what characterizes most of the Archaic-Formative transition. What was a minor characteristic of the Fortuna Phase came to dominate core-flake manufacture during later phases.

We tabulated six hinge fractures among the fifty-four general flakes. This is an 11% hinge fracture rate, which is intolerably high in controlled bifacial manufacture. I suspect, but cannot prove, that most of the hinge fractures occurred in the more informal core-flake industry, where a hinge can be corrected more easily, it can be ignored (rendering a section of the core inoperable), or it can result in core abandonment and use of a substitute core. Also, much of the petrified wood has structural imperfections, and these increase the hinge fracture rate.

The Fortuna point found on the Aguacate surface at G-163 probably dates to some time between 4000 and 3000 BC. Thus, bifacial manufacture continued longer in Costa Rica than in

TABLE 11-11
(*continued*)

Wedges	*Hammer-stones*	*Flake Cores*	*Percussion Blades*	*Cooking Stones*	*Celt Blanks*	*Chipped Celts*	*Utilized Flakes*	*Pebbles*	*Hoes*	*Total*
0	1 (0.2)	8 (1.7)	1 (0.2)	4 (0.9)	0	0	1 (0.2)	5 (1.1)	0	474
1 (0.3)	1 (0.3)	2 (0.7)	0	4 (1.3)	0	1 (0.3)	1 (0.3)	0	0	307
0	7 (1.3)	9 (1.6)	1 (0.2)	2 (0.4)	1 (0.2)	0	2 (0.4)	0	0	548
1 (0.2)	7 (1.1)	13 (2.0)	3 (0.5)	16 (2.4)	0	0	16 (2.4)	37 (6.6)	0	660
0	2 (0.1)	15 (0.5)	5 (0.2)	52 (1.8)	0	0	52 (1.8)	12 (0.4)	1 (0)	2,900
0	1 (0.1)	5 (0.3)	2 (0.1)	137 (7.6)	0	0	137 (7.6)	239 (13.3)	0	1,798

TABLE 11-12
(*continued*)

Porphyry	*Rhyolite*	*Jasper*	*Quartzite*	*Fine-Grained Dacite*
0	0	5 (1.7)	1 (0.3)	165 (56.1)
0	0	2 (1.3)	0	138 (87.3)
0	0	0	0	203 (93.6)
0	8 (4.3)	2 (1.1)	0	134 (72.4)
0	5 (1.6)	1 (0.3)	1 (0.3)	280 (89.2)
5 (3.0)	2 (1.2)	3 (1.8)	0	116 (69.1)

Panama, where biface manufacture ceased at about 5000 BC (Cooke 1984:268). The phenocrysts have fully weathered out of its surface, indicating a greater age than the Tronadora and later phase dacitic implements. We found a few dacite flakes at AL-186 that had phenocrysts eroded to the same degree as the Fortuna point, probably indicating that they were manufactured at about the same time.

Some of the small biface thinning flakes and the general debitage found in Units 65 and 61 probably also derive from this earliest occupation of the Tronadora Vieja site. The fine-grained microcrystalline flakes (chalcedony, jasper, and petrified wood), which are relatively thin and wide and expand from the platform, are particularly likely candidates for the Fortuna Phase. Cooking stones and thermally fractured debitage are found in the lowest levels (Units 65 and 61), and it is virtually certain that many derive from the Fortuna Phase occupation.

ARCHAIC LITHIC COMPARISONS

Comparisons are made here with Archaic artifacts collected in Mexico, Belize, Panama, and Colombia. It is clear that little is known about Archaic artifacts and lifeways in Central America, but the beginnings of a data base and comparative framework do exist.

The Tehuacán Project in South-Central Mexico obtained considerable information on the Archaic

(MacNeish et al. 1967). The Coxcatlán Phase (4800–3500 BC) exhibits a diet of only about 15% from domesticated sources. The tanged projectile points of the Coxcatlán, Almagre, and Shumla types (ibid.: 65–69) bear a general resemblance to the Fortuna point, but none can be considered typologically identical. The Abejas Phase (3500–2300 BC), with about 30% of the diet from domesticated sources, witnesses a continuation of the Coxcatlán and Shumla points. A few pithouses are evidence of increasing sedentism. Unfortunately, due to the strongly typological nature of the Tehuacán report, assemblage comparisons are not possible. Thus, broader comparisons of core-flake, core-blade, bifacial, and cooking stone technologies are not possible.

MacNeish's recent work on the Archaic in Belize provides some comparisons (Zeitlin 1984). The very early date for obsidian (6000 BC) is astounding and indicates a much greater mobility of early Belizeans than contemporaneous Costa Ricans, or probably later prehistoric Costa Ricans, for that matter. The direct line distance to the closest in situ obsidian sources is 375 km, and even the alluvial gravels of the Ulua River, which contain obsidian, are some 200 km distant. The Belize Complex (5000–4000 BC) contains societies still intensifying a coastal broad-spectrum adaptation. The Melinda Complex (4000–3000 BC), not as well known, shows more utilization of littoral animal and plant resources and has basal notched points similar to Shumla points, and these bear some resemblance to the Fortuna point. Here, similarities between the Costa Rican and the Belizean points are sufficiently great that they appear to have been a part of a generalized shared tradition of cutting implement manufacture.

The Progreso Complex (3000–2000 BC) is the end of the Archaic, and sites show a greater preference for riverine, deltaic access. Evidently, people were turning toward agricultural production, and manos-metates, picks, and adzes characterize the assemblages. Such artifacts continue into the subsequent settled agricultural phases.

The area closest to the Cordillera where sufficient Archaic data exist to allow for comparisons is Central Panama (Cooke 1984), located some 500 km to the east. Cooke notes the gradual changes from Paleo-Indian into Archaic times, which contrasts with the dramatic changes that occurred about 5000 BC. His Period IIA (Preceramic A, or Early Archaic) runs from 8000 to 5000 BC and is characterized by bifacially flaked tools and evidence for hunting and fishing, with the best data coming from the Cueva de los Vampiros near the Parita Bay coast. In contrast, Period IIB (Preceramic B, or later Archaic, from 5000 to 3000 BC) has no bifacial flaking whatsoever. Tools were made by rough percussion flaking, and some crude grinding stones were found along with many edge-ground cobbles. Small scraping and boring tools were numerous and variable. The emphasis is on adaptation to coastal resources, particularly shellfish, crabs, and palm fruits. Cooke's suggestion that Isthmus inhabitants had adapted to a variety of tropical habitats early is supported by the marked differences in Late Archaic adaptations and artifact inventories in the Cordillera de Tilarán and in Central Panama. About the only things they shared were the use of an informal percussion technology to generate cutting edges, and possibly a strong emphasis on exploitation of palms. In spite of different survey techniques and areas covered, it is clear that the coastal area of Central Panama was more densely occupied during the Archaic than was the much moister and higher Cordilleran area in Costa Rica. Why that was so is a very important and yet-unanswered question.

The similarities between Cordilleran lithics and those of sites farther southeast become rather general. Bray (1984) summarizes Colombian prehistoric societies and finds he can define a general Isthmian Interaction Sphere extending from Yucatán to central Colombia. Within it he notes the longevity of cultures, and the Arenal area data strongly support his argument.

During the Paleo-Indian Period of Colombia, the Abrian industries were found in high elevation sites (ca. 2,600 m) near the upper forest-*páramo* (high grassland) boundary (ibid.). The sites include mastodon kills as well as rock shelters, and deer are the most common animal exploited. The products of Abrian industries are generally very small, with unifacial percussion retouching only. It is apparently basically a core-flake technology, with prepared striking platforms uncommon. This technology continues into the early Holocene, and is only vaguely similar to the Fortuna Phase of the Arenal area. The Abrian industries differ in that the irregular scraper is the most common implement, and both cores and flakes were used for tool blanks. The Abrian assemblages are devoid of bifacial implements and bifacial debitage in terminal Pleistocene and Holocene times. Thus, the loss of bifacial flaking apparently occurred early in some parts of Colombia, and perhaps had spread to central Panama by 5000 BC, but that did not include northern Costa Rica.

LITHICS BY SITE TYPE

We prepared spreadsheet tables for the lithics from cemeteries versus the lithics from habitation sites, and later converted these to relational software. (They are summarized in Tables 11-11 and 11-12). The most striking result is that there is considerable overlap. There is not a crisp demarcation, at least in most categories, between habitation and graveyard assemblages. It appears that the graveyards were turned into temporary residences for sufficiently extended periods to introduce a lot of habitation-oriented lithic artifacts.

We can see some differences. The percentage of thermally fractured debitage is much higher at cemeteries (68%) than at habitations (29%). This may be due to the difficulty of transporting bulky ceramic cooking vessels for many kilometers. It may have been easier to use organic containers for stone cooking at the graveyard. Ceramic vessels are found in large numbers at cemeteries, however, in some cases, deliberately smashed as part of post-interment rituals, in some cases as burial furniture, and in some cases as broken utilitarian vessels. General flakes are more common in habitations than in cemeteries, probably reflecting a greater need to cut various substances. Both bifacial flakes and implements are more common in habitations than in cemeteries.

Cemeteries contain slightly fewer hinge fractures than do habitations, perhaps because of greater care in manufacture. This lower frequency occurs in spite of the rarity of chalcedony (5%) and other microcrystalline rocks in the graveyards. The habitation sites have a relative abundance of chalcedony (29%), petrified wood, and jasper. The chalcedony is available locally, and there is a good source of petrified wood near Venado (Tosi 1980:2–129). Evidently, the range of needs was greater in habitations, from needing the sharper but more fragile edges of chalcedony and the other microcrystallines, to the tougher but duller edges on fractured andesite and dacite. Graveyards apparently witnessed a lot of woodworking, as evidenced by celts, celt flakes, and some wear on dacite flakes. This probably included tree and branch cutting and trimming, firewood cutting, digging stick manufacture and maintenance, temporary shelter construction and maintenance, and vine cutting and land clearance.

We found wedges, hoes, and the small rounded pebbles exclusively (or almost exclusively in the case of hoes and pebbles) in habitation sites, for reasons that are not hard to discern. The hoes are almost certainly horticultural implements, and one would expect most of them to be found in villages. The only hoe found at a cemetery may have been used to dig graves. It could indicate some tillage in or near cemeteries, however, somewhat like the adaptive spread across the landscape of the Kayapó (Chap. 1). One would expect most woodworking to occur in the villages, and the finding of wedges only in the villages substantiates that expectation.

Sorting lithics by phase and site type (habitations versus cemeteries) yields some interesting results. There are no Tronadora Phase cemeteries separate from villages, apparently because people were buried within the village, and burials apparently were associated closely with the household. We have no data on Tilarán Phase burial practices. The percentage of thermally fractured debitage in Arenal to Silencio Phase cemeteries drops from 76% to 38%. This is mirrored in a general drop in thermally fractured debitage in habitations through the four sedentary phases, from 31% to 26% to 38% to 18%.

A contrary trend is visible with general debitage; it increases consistently through the sedentary phases in habitations. It begins at 9% in the Trondadora Phase and increases to 28%, then to 52%, with a peak at 62% in the Tilarán Phase. The reason is not clear, although there is a relative increase in core-flake manufacture and an increase in bifacial manufacture in the later two sedentary phases. There is a similar but slower increase of general debitage from Arenal to Silencio phase cemeteries.

Chalcedony use in the sedentary phases is relatively stable through the first three sedentary phases (19%, 19%, 10%) but rises to 41% during the Tilarán Phase. We do not know the reason for that rapid increase, but it could be explained by some factor such as the discovery of a closer source of chalcedony. In contrast, the use of petrified wood, so common in the Archaic, dropped steadily during the sedentary phases.

CONCLUSIONS

We collected and analyzed a total of 8,755 lithic artifacts during the 1984 and 1985 field seasons of the Proyecto Prehistórico Arenal. Of these, 6,885 are well enough dated to be useful in chronological sorting in Tables 11-3 and 11-4. We found very few artifacts during the 1986 and 1987 seasons, while trenching linear anomalies detected with remote-sensing technology. These are presented in Chapter 9. We found chipped stone artifacts from all periods, from Paleo-Indian and Archaic periods through all ceramic phases up to the Conquest. We found a surprisingly large number of cooking stones, for a sedentary, ceramic-producing society. In fact, the most common stone artifact type in the area is thermally fractured debitage from cooking stone disintegration. A core-flake industry is the dominant component of the chipped stone tool manufacture, followed by bifacial manufacture of celts and knives. The core-flake industry, which is the primary way of making cutting edges, developed by 4000 BC and remained largely unchanged during the prehistoric occupation of the Cordillera. We found only a few categories of chipped stone implements to be sensitive temporal indicators. As with ceramics, lithics can be assessed for external relationships. If we use the Clovis point as evidence, during the Paleo-Indian Period, affiliations were to the northwest, with upper Central America, Mexico, and the rest of North America more than they were with lower Central America and South America. That northwestern orientation continues in the Archaic, where lithic similarities are greater with Belize and Mexico than they are with Panama and Colombia, in spite of the latter two countries' greater proximity to Costa Rica. It is during the succeeding four ceramic phases that the Arenal area largely turns inward and exhibits little outside influence. Only the Silencio point shows some outside affiliation, as it could be a part of the Pipil-Nicarao migrations from Mesoamerica into the Intermediate area. Other than that, the lithic industry, dominated by core-flake technology to manufacture utility cutting tools within the household, remains largely unchanged, self-sufficient, and successfully isolated.

To summarize outside relationships, the only times when the Arenal-area residents were participating in a widespread lithic tradition was during the Paleo-Indian and Archaic periods, and the orientation of that contact is toward Mesoamerica and North America. From the Formative to the Spanish Conquest the lithic industry is internally oriented, with few exceptions. When those exceptions occur, they too are derived from the northwest, and not from South America.

The most striking aspect of the entire lithic industry is its conservatism; the lithic component of a successful adaptive strategy was developed early and remained largely unchanged for four millennia. The efficient utilization of locally available resources allowed Arenal-area residents to avoid economies of dependency, in contrast to other societies in Mesoamerica and the Andean area. That probably was a major contributor to a stable adaptation over many centuries, in spite of occasional volcanic disasters. Chipped stone tool manufacture is dominated by core-flake technology from its inception during the Archaic or earlier, and it continues virtually unchanged until about AD 1500. Simple core-flake percussion manufacture using local materials is securely dated in the Arenal area to about 4000 BC, but it is not known how far back into the Archaic or possibly the Paleo-Indian Period it goes.

One way of viewing this conservatism is stasis, that they became stuck in their own narrow lithic ways and refused to change and to keep up with their neighbors to the north or south. However, I prefer the interpretation that a successful means of generating cutting edges, for various uses in adapting to a tropical rain forest environment, was achieved early and continued. There was no need to change a technological system that was so successful. It was a simple system, evidently performed within each household, and by varying raw materials, edge angles, shapes, and lengths, varied cutting needs readily were met. Artifacts requiring highly skilled manufacture were not needed, allowing the household to maintain self-sufficiency and avoid the economic and social compromises that derive from reliance on a centralized economy. Certainly, they avoided reliance on long-distance-traded obsidian, in contrast to most societies in Nicaragua, El Salvador, Guatemala, Honduras, and Mexico. I suggest that their avoidance of an economy of dependancy is better viewed as a positive achievement, not as a "lack of progress."

Of interest is the high frequency of thermally fractured stones, along with occasional complete cooking stones, throughout the entire sequence from the Archaic to the Conquest. This is a holdover from preceramic times, when stone boiling was a primary cooking technique, if not the primary technique. Although the ratio of cooking stones to all other artifacts drops from the Archaic to the Formative and later periods, the use of cooking stones is remarkably persistent in spite of the manufacture of ceramic cooking vessels after the third millennium BC. A factor encouraging the continued use of cooking stones is the burial of people in distant cemeteries. As people traveled to cemeteries for extended rituals and visits, they may have found stone boiling preferable to carrying heavy and fragile ceramic vessels over slippery trails. Habitation sites during all neolithic phases (Tronadora through Tilarán), however, have cooking stones in complete and fractured condition, so it is clear that this technology was performed in Archaic campsites as well as in sedentary villages until the Spanish Conquest. This kind of cooking technology would be easy to overlook, were it not for the periodic deposits of volcanic ash from Arenal Volcano. Soils derived from ash have particles no larger than those that traveled through the air from the volcano, so rocks larger than these particles must have been transported by people. It is hoped that archaeologists working in other sites of the Intermediate area can find cooking stones, and their temporal and geographic range can be studied.

Celts continued from the Tronadora through the Tilarán phases, and probably are associated with forest clearance and obtaining wood for house construction and wooden artifacts. Evidence for the continuity of celt manufacture from the Tronadora through the Tilarán phases is found in the implements and in the debitage. We found two types of celt flakes, those deriving from celt resharpening and those unfortunately detached by celt abuse.

The small, highly polished flakes are enigmatic. They were deliberately polished, but for what purpose? It is possible that they were used in rituals, or they could have been used in games, or possibly as practice or experimentation for polishing hard greenstones.

The category of "general debitage" includes most of the utility flakes made for the variety of cutting functions needed to live in a tropical rain forest using a broad-spectrum adaptation. Certainly, many were used for various tasks, but the specific uses remain unknown. Part of the problem is the intensity of weathering in the hot, moist tropics; another difficulty in recognizing use wear is that Arenal-area residents were using very obdurate materials that record only extreme or extended use wear. All artifacts tabulated under "utilized flakes" had clear evidence of use, but many of the general debitage flakes must have been used as well.

Almost one-fourth of the collection is tabulated under the "unclassified" category. Again, the volcanic ash layers and soils of sites in those layers were instrumental in identifying stones that needed human transport, but that showed no clear evidence of being worked or used. These stones were brought in by people, probably for a wide variety of uses (wedging posts of houses, controlling erosion, gaming, etc.), and most of these would not be recognized as being imported if these sites had not received aeolian deposition.

Unifacially flaked artifacts ("scrapers"), wedges, and hammerstones are notably rare in the Arenal area, when compared to Nicaragua and Mesoamerica, or to Colombia. Their percentages would increase greatly if the collection did not include so much thermally fractured debitage, general debitage, and unclassified items. However, their absolute frequencies seem lower than one would expect, for reasons that are not clear.

Flake cores are quite common, and the approximate ratio of one core to seven flakes is reasonable. We found relatively few hinge fractures in the core-flake industry, making it notable for its efficiency in use of materials as well as in time and effort expended.

We found some percussion blades, but clearly they were not a part of a structured blade-making industry such as was found in Mesoamerica. The hundreds of small, rounded pebbles found in the Tronadora Vieja site are a puzzle, but some were used as a doorway tread. As with thermally fractured stones, these probably would not have been recognized were it not for the accretional landscape of volcanic ash deposits. These were collected from stream or lakeshore deposits, selected for roundness and uniform size, and brought into the village. Hoes almost certainly were used for moving soil. It is likely that they are horticultural implements, and they may have been used to quarry clay and dig graves.

We found a number of workshops specialized in bifacial manufacture, dating to a variety of phases. Very little deliberate thermal treatment was done.

An important contribution to the prehistory of the area is the Archaic assemblage of lithics from site AL-186. The most common artifact is the cooking stone. We found these in great numbers associated with the two hearths. Bifacial manufacture was done at the campsite, as evidenced by the hammerstones and the bifacial trimming flakes. The percussion manufacture of utility cutting flakes from irregular cores made of local materials was established by 4000 BC and continued to be the primary means of making cutting edges in the Arenal area for the next 5,500 years, an impressive record of continuity and success.

In summary, the almost nine thousand lithic artifacts discovered by the Proyecto Prehistórico Arenal facilitated a successful adaptation to a tropical rain forest environment over many millennia. It was a broad-spectrum adaptation; although maize was known before 2000 BC, it never became a staple crop, and the diet continued to focus on wild species. Stone boiling was devised in the Archaic if not earlier, and remained as a major cooking technique in spite of the sophistication of ceramics in the area from about 3000 BC to the Conquest. The main means of producing utility cutting flakes was by percussion removal from informal cores made of locally available materials. Apparently, the household was the primary locus of production and consumption of lithic implements.

Bifacial manufacture of projectile points and knives began in the area in Paleo-Indian times and continued through the Archaic. After a lapse in the two millennia before Christ, it was resumed in the Silencio and Tilarán phases. Bifacial manufacture of blanks for ground stone celts was done from the Tronadora Phase to the Conquest with no lapse.

By utilizing locally available materials, and manufacturing within the household or village, settlement self-sufficiency was maintained. Economies of dependency were avoided, in contrast to so many villages in the northern Intermediate area or Mesoamerica that came under the economic and political domination of expanding states. This, I suggest, is a major reason why social stability is such a deep-seated characteristic of the Arenal area. Long-term social stability was not characteristic of so many other areas of Middle America.

ACKNOWLEDGMENTS

I want to thank David Wagner for reading this chapter, assisting with data processing, and helping with the text. Brian McKee assisted by improving the readability of numerous sections and helped the manuscript through various metamorphoses. His sharp eye and even sharper blue pencil are greatly appreciated—as is his ability for doing various sorts with the relational software.

12

Precolumbian Ground, Polished, and Incised Stone Artifacts from the Cordillera de Tilarán

MARK L. CHENAULT

INTRODUCTION

Roof combs do not stand, Tikal-like, above the canopy of the Costa Rican rain forest. Nor do stone-walled ballcourts stretch through Costa Rican archaeological sites. Great cities, with canals and pyramids and thousands of inhabitants, did not greet the sixteenth-century Spanish when they reached Costa Rica. But what the small country of Costa Rica lacks in prehistoric architecture it compensates for in artifacts; the Precolumbian Costa Ricans excelled in the production of intricately carved stone sculpture and ground stone tools. Some of the metates found throughout Costa Rica, for example, are among the most elaborate and interesting artifacts in the New World.

This chapter describes and compares the 224 ground, polished, and incised artifacts recovered during survey and excavation in the 1984 and 1985 field seasons of the Proyecto Prehistórico Arenal. We also analyzed fifteen ground- and 6 polished stone artifacts from the Jiménez family collection. The pieces from the Jiménez collection are all from the Silencio cemetery (G-150), but cannot be assigned to specific contexts. The project collection is from a variety of site types, and is probably representative of the range and variety of morphological types of prehistoric ground stone artifacts in the Cordillera de Tilarán region.

Terminology used in this chapter follows Hummer (1983). The term "ground stone" refers to all artifacts for which grinding was the final technique used in their manufacture. Polished stone artifacts are those for which polishing was the final production technique. We divided the ground stone artifacts into types based on morphology and use. Morphology is the initial criterion for categorization; however, the morphological designation has to be supported by the use wear evident on each artifact. The most recent use is the ultimate criterion for classification. For example, a broken metate leg reused as a mano is categorized as a mano.

We performed analyses in the field laboratory. We examined artifacts for use wear under a 10× to 70× stereo microscope, or a 10× hand lens, in the case of items too large to fit under the microscope. We subjectively recorded the degree of production grinding in three levels: (1) fine, (2) moderate, and (3) rough. We described the raw material for the ground stone artifacts as either nonvesicular or vesicular. We listed the average size of the vesicles as (1) small (less than 2 mm in diameter); (2) medium (2 mm to 3 mm in diameter); or (3) large (greater than 3 mm in diameter). We subjectively recorded use wear as heavy, moderate, or light.

A stone's vesicularity affects its suitability for shaping. For example, stone with large vesicles is unsuitable for the production of elaborate metates such as those found in Guanacaste. Decorated metates in the Arenal area were also carved from nonvesicular stone; however, vesicular stone may have been preferred as a grinding surface. As a metate is worn through use, vesicular stone retains a rougher grinding surface that does not require pecking for sharpening.

The majority of ground stone artifacts in the project assemblage are made of plagioclase-phyric basaltic andesite (Melson, personal communication, 1984). Most of the polished stone artifacts consist of hydrothermally altered plagioclase-phyric andesite. We recorded the weight, length, width, and thickness, or height, for each item. Averages of those data are presented in Table 12-1.

GROUNDSTONE

TENONED STONES

Tenoned Stone Platform (1 Complete Specimen)

We found a large, decorated, tenoned stone platform at Site G-181 during survey (Fig. 12-1). To my knowledge, this type of artifact has not been previously reported in Costa Rica. Although the artifact is broken, we recovered four pieces representing at least 90% of the object.

The platform portion of the object is rectangular with a flat upper surface. The platform is 30 cm long, 24 cm wide, and 11 cm thick. A shallow pecked design is present on all four sides and consists of one set of concentric diamonds between two sets of concentric rectangles. The upper portion of the tenon carries a design very similar to that on the sides of the platform. The remainder of the tenon is shaped but undecorated and not well smoothed. The height of the entire object is 44 cm.

The top of the platform exhibits very little evidence of grinding; what is present is probably a result of manufacture. There is, however, some evidence of pecking and battering on the surface. The battering suggests the preparation of some item—perhaps food, pigment, or other substance. The lack of grinding indicates that corn was not prepared on the surface. It is also possible that the pecking scars are a result of production. The stone has small vesicles and was quarried from a volcanic deposit (Melson, pers. comm., 1985).

Site G-181, where we found the tenoned stone platform, is a cemetery utilized during the Arenal and Silencio phases. The cemetery context for the stone platform and its uniqueness and elaborateness suggest that it had a ceremonial rather than a utilitarian function.

Possible analogs for the tenoned stone artifact are the carved stone "seats" from Guanacaste and Nicoya (Snarskis 1981b, catalog numbers 99 and 100). These, however, are rounded in plan view, have projecting zoomorphic faces, and are not tenoned. Although the morphology of our tenoned stone object differs greatly from that of the stone seats, it is conceivable that it was a seat rather than a platform. The tenon could have been placed in the ground to hold the object upright.

Stone (1972) reports tenoned stone sculpture from Guanacaste-Nicoya, and Squier (1860) illustrates numerous stone statues supported by tenoned bases at Zapatero in Nicaragua. These monumental pieces are zoomorphic and anthropomorphic sculptures. The tenons are mainly quadrilateral, with only a few appearing to be cylindrical like the tenon on the Arenal artifact. Tenoned stone heads have been found in the Atlantic Watershed region (Mason 1945; Snarskis 1978, 1981a; Graham 1981). Columnar sculptures from Nicaragua and Nacascolo, Costa Rica, are illustrated by Richardson (1940: fig. 39). Nothing, however, with a flat platformlike surface, such as the Arenal specimen, has been reported.

TABLE 12-1
METRIC DATA FOR COMPLETE GROUND- AND POLISHED STONE ARTIFACTS

Artifact	*Length (cm)*	*Width (cm)*	*Height (cm)*	*Weight (g)*
Metates				
Rectangular decorated	33.5	22.5	13.5	7,450.00
Rectangular tripod with zoomorphic head	39.5	22.2	15.0	667.00
Rectangular tripod	49.0	26.1	19.6	11,575.00
Rectangular tripod with cylindrical legs	29.5	22.0	14.0	No data
Ovoid tripod	50.5	29.8	17.0	12,300.00
Ovoid with knob legs	45.5	28.0	9.5	No data
Ovoid nonlegged	29.0	20.0	8.5	6,700.00
Oval tripod	29.5	20.7	9.0	6,250.00
Basin	21.0	29.0	9.5	No data
Unshaped boulder	32.0	26.0	13.0	13,500.00
Manos				
Bar	23.45	5.9	4.6	1,308.25
Ovoid	14.93	8.25	4.05	764.80
Oval	9.5	7.15	4.3	440.00
Loaf-shaped	12.15	6.62	4.75	747.22
Grinding stone	5.15	4.7	3.45	135.90
Burnishing stone	3.3	3.0	2.9	36.00
Nutting stone	11.5	6.1	5.4	255.00
Tenoned stone	30.0	24.0	44.0	No data
Celts				
Flaring-bit	5.9	5.2	3.3	145.00
Straight-bit	7.6	3.8	2.4	138.90
Rounded-bit	7.2	3.2	1.9	66.70

Note: Measurements are the average of the items in each category.

Tenoned Stone Artifact (1 Fragment)

We recovered a portion of a tenoned stone artifact from the surface at the Silencio funerary site (G-150). It consists of a large cylindrical tenon (20 cm long and 20 cm in diameter), and a broken, irregular upper section. This artifact may have been a tenoned platform like the one described earlier, but we did not recover enough of the upper portion to identify it positively. The tenon is shorter and broader than that of the platform described earlier.

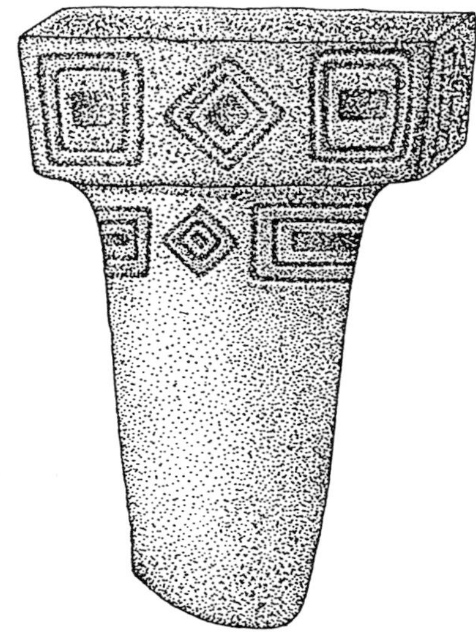

Figure 12-1.
Drawing depicting the probable appearance of the complete tenoned stone platform. Drawing by Mark Chenault.

METATES

We recovered ten whole metates and eighty-six metate fragments during excavation and survey. We also analyzed nine whole metates from the Jiménez collection, all of which were found at site G-150. We devised ten types, based on differences in plan view and leg shape, for this study. Figure 12-2 depicts these types.

Figure 12-2.
The metate types from the Cordillera de Tilarán (drawings by Nick Lang): a, *rectangular decorated tripod metate;* b, *rectangular tripod metate with zoomorphic head;* c, *rectangular tripod metate;* d, *rectangular tripod metate with cylindrical legs;* e, *ovoid tripod metate;* f, *ovoid metate with knob legs;* g, *ovoid nonlegged metate;* h, *oval tripod metate;* i, *basin metate;* j, *unshaped boulder metate.*

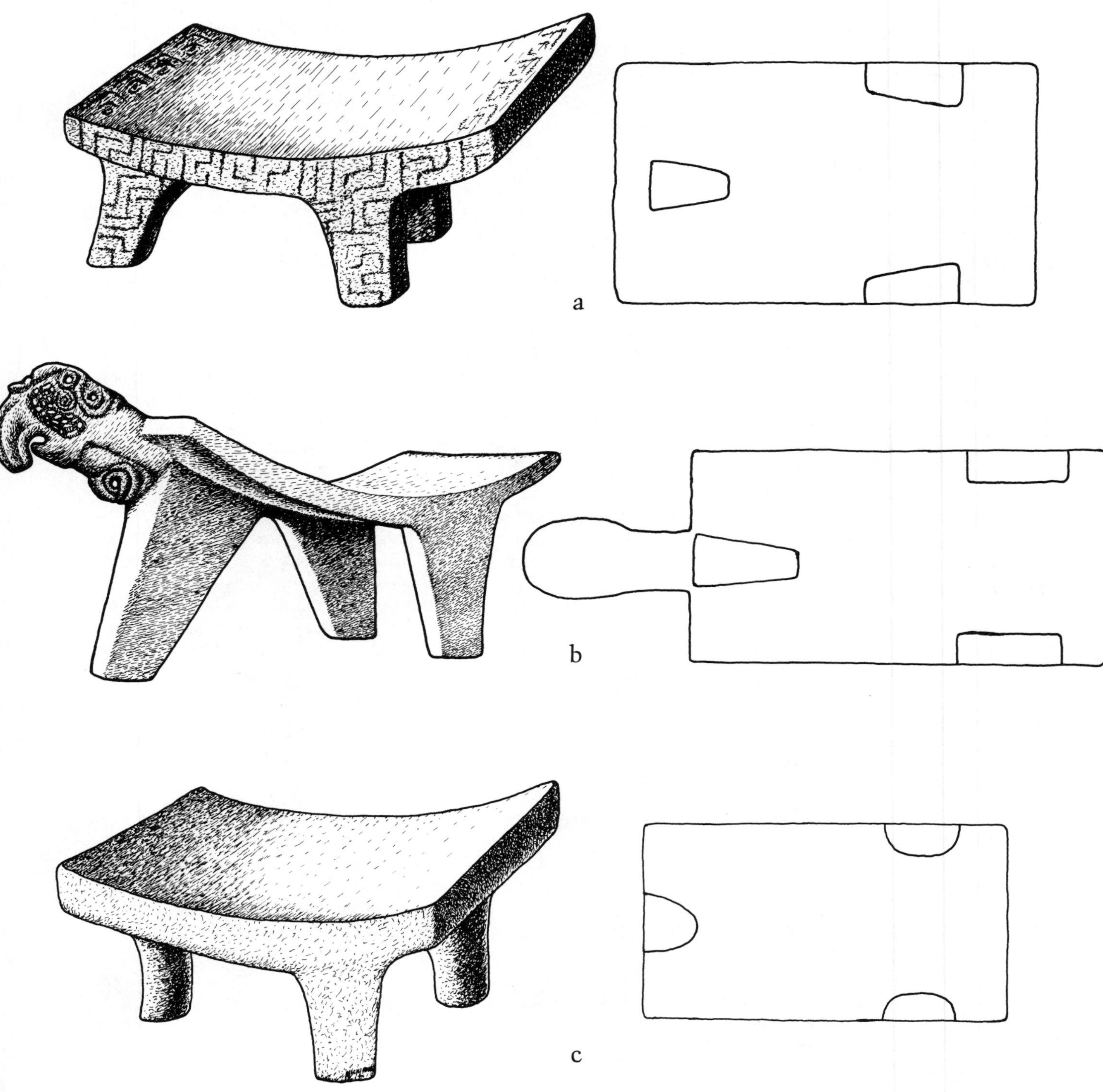

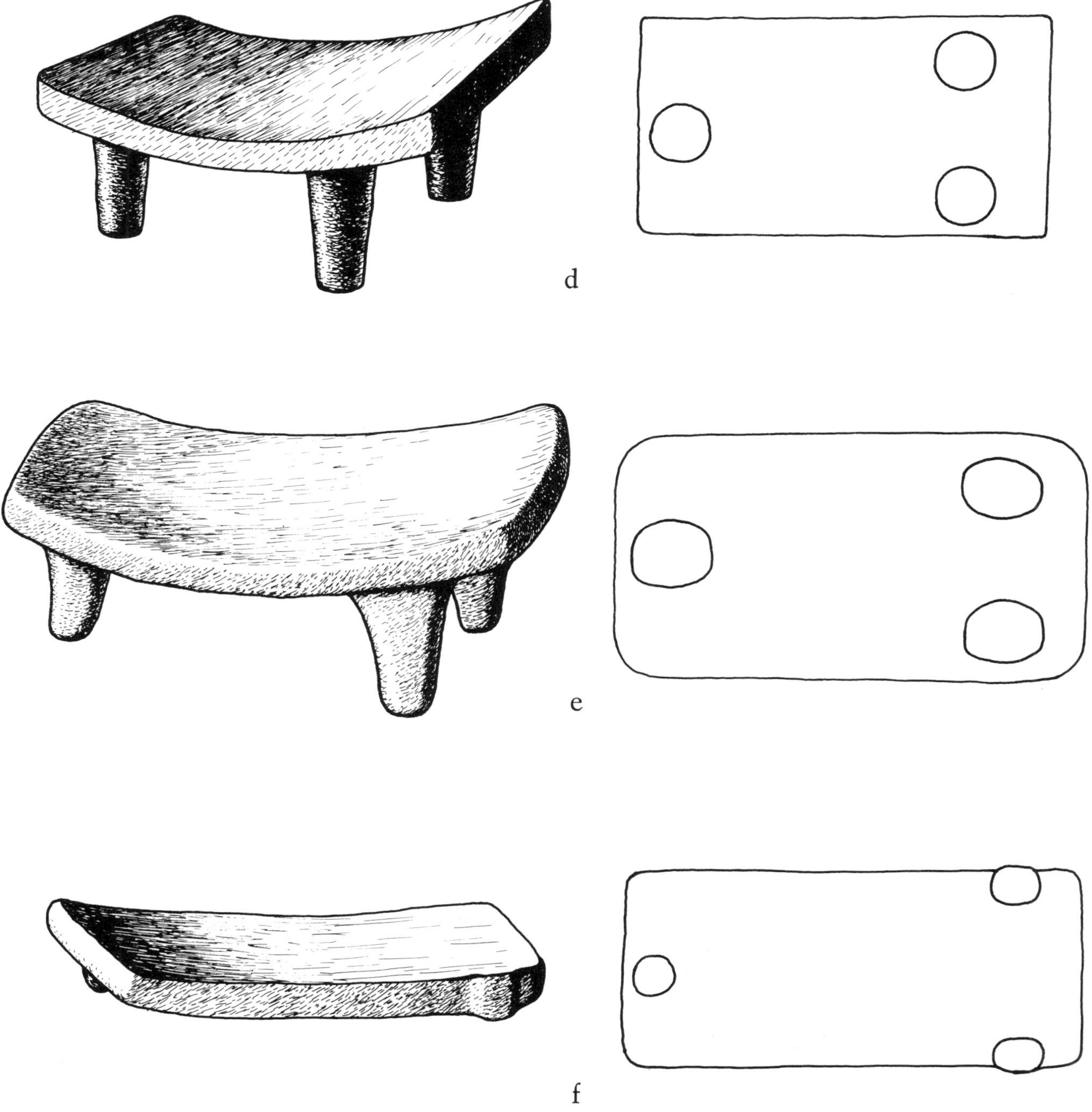
d
e
f

g
h
i
j

Rectangular Decorated Metate (1 Complete Specimen)

This category encompasses those metates with pecked or incised surface decorations. We recovered only one specimen of this type (Fig. 12-2*a*). We found it at the Silencio cemetery associated with Silencio Phase ceramics. It is a tripod metate with pecked geometric designs on its edges, on the outside of the back legs, and on both sides of the front leg (Fig. 12-3). Another type of geometric decoration occurs on the underside of the metate. This design was formed with incised lines rather than pecked. The metate exhibits heavy grinding use wear. This is evident in the truncation of grains on the grinding surface and the partial obliteration of the bands of geometric design that occur on the grinding surface. The metate is made of nonvesicular stone. It is bowed in the middle of the grinding surface. Its legs are trapezoidal in cross section, and the bottoms of the legs are smoothed, apparently from movement while grinding. The back legs are flush with the sides of the metate.

Tripod metates with geometric decoration are commonly found in the Guanacaste-Nicoya area from Late Period IV to Early Period V (ca. AD 300–700). The Silencio Phase date of the Arenal Project specimen fits in with these dates. Elaborate decorated metates are illustrated by Snarskis (1981b: catalog numbers 73 and 74) and by Graham (1981:pl. 49 and 50).

Rectangular Tripod Metate with Zoomorphic Heads (3 Complete Specimens)

All of these metates are from G-150 and are in the Jiménez collection (Fig. 12-2*b*). Two have jaguar heads extending from the single-legged end of the metate (Fig. 12-4). Both are made of a stone with small vesicles and exhibit fine workmanship. The grinding plates of these metates are bowed. The single front legs are triangular in cross section with slightly concave sides, and the two back legs are somewhat L-shaped in cross section. The plane of the grinding surface continues across the tops of the zoomorphic heads, some of which display evidence of use grinding. The eyes and other facial features were produced through pecking. These metates are similar to others from lowland Guanacaste, although not as elaborate as that illustrated by Graham (1981:pl. 49). Unlike many of the more elaborate metates, the legs on the metates from the Silencio cemetery are not decorated.

The third metate in this category has a protruding head, which is either highly stylized or unfinished. It appears to be an avian representation with a downturned beak; however, no eyes or other facial features are present. It is made of a nonvesicular volcanic stone, probably a basaltic andesite. This metate also underwent heavy use grinding. A metate of similar shape, also with a stylized projection, from Guanacaste is illustrated by Stone (1977:fig. 131). The heads on all three of the metates in this category extend only 5 cm to 6 cm from the body. Striations on all three indicate unidirectional or, as termed by Hummer (1983), reciprocal use grinding parallel to the long axis.

We found a carved stone head of a bird at the Silencio cemetery (Fig. 12-5). It is probably from a rectangular tripod metate with zoomorphic head. The head is made of a stone with small vesicles. The eyes protrude, as do apparent topknots. There is a geometric pattern in low relief on the back of the neck. The head is probably a continuation of the plane of the metate grinding surface, although grinding is not heavy across the neck or top of the head. It appears to have been reworked and smoothed at the point where it broke away from the metate.

Rectangular Tripod Metates (7 Complete Specimens and 3 Fragments)

These metates are angular, blocky and massive, lack decoration, and have thick, wide legs D-shaped in cross section (Fig. 12-2*c*). The rear legs are flush with the sides of the metates. The metates are made of nonvesicular stone and appear to have been pecked to shape and roughly ground. We found all examples of this type at the Silencio cemetery. Rectangular tripod metates exhibit little use grinding. These metates may have been produced for interment as mortuary offerings.

Rectangular Tripod Metate with Cylindrical Legs (1 Complete Specimen and 3 Fragments)

The Jiménez collection contains one example of this type (Fig. 12-2*d*). It is a fairly small metate (29.5 cm long, 22 cm wide, and 14 cm high) with thick, cylindrical legs. Although the body is

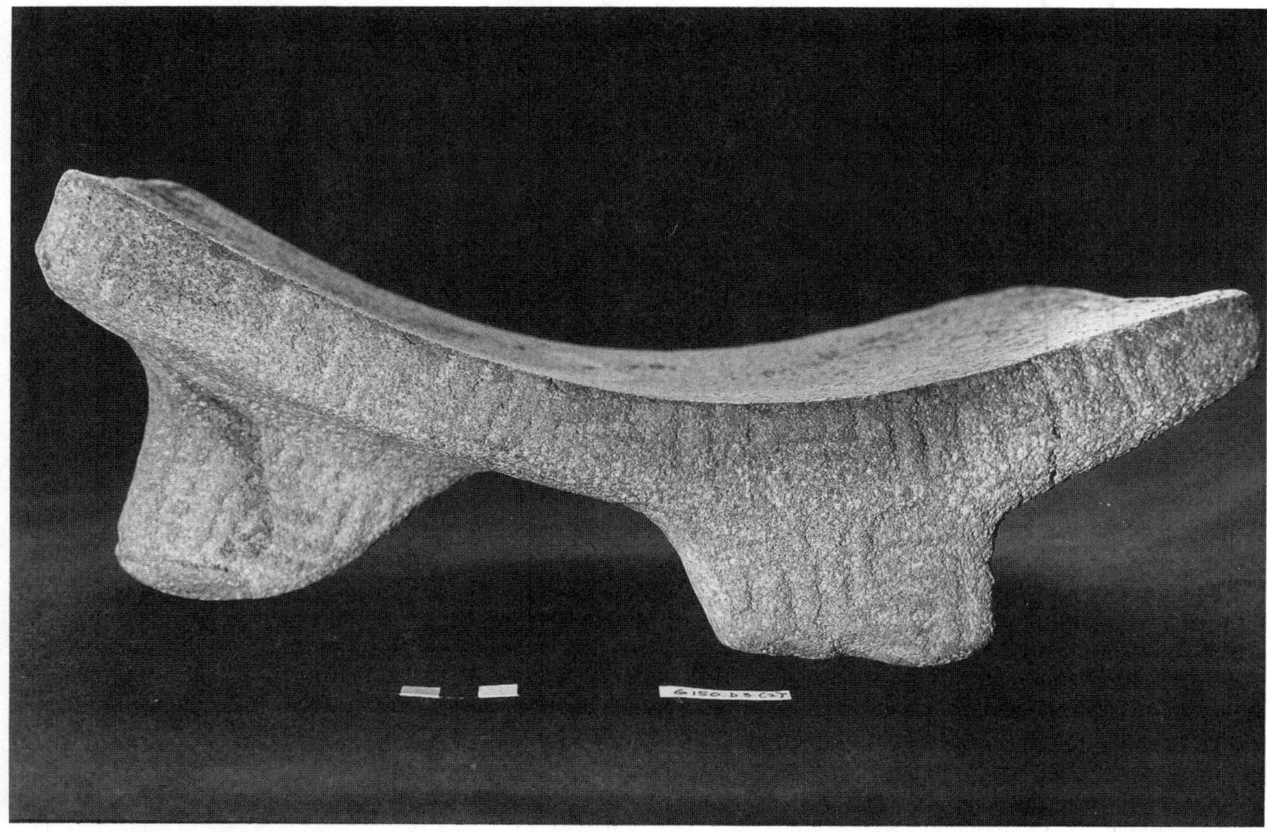

Figure 12-3.
Rectangular decorated metate from site G-150. Photograph by Fran Mandel-Sheets.

thick, the metate is not as blocky as the rectangular tripod metates. This specimen underwent fairly heavy use grinding and has some evidence of pecking to roughen the grinding surface. It is made from nonvesicular stone. The edges are not well defined, and, in general, this metate does not appear to have been produced with great care.

Project personnel recovered a large portion of a rectangular tripod metate with cylindrical legs (approximately the back two-thirds). This metate appears to be better made than the example just described, as are two other fragments from the corners of metates.

Ovoid Tripod Metate (1 Complete Specimen and 1 Fragment)

This type of metate is ovoid in plan view (Fig. 12-2*e*). The edges are rounded, and there is no surface decoration. These metates are made of vesicular volcanic stone, sometimes with large vesicles. The whole example (Fig. 12-6) has legs that are oval or slightly D-shaped in cross section. They are inset from the edges of the metate. It is large (50.5 cm in length), but not as blocky and massive as the

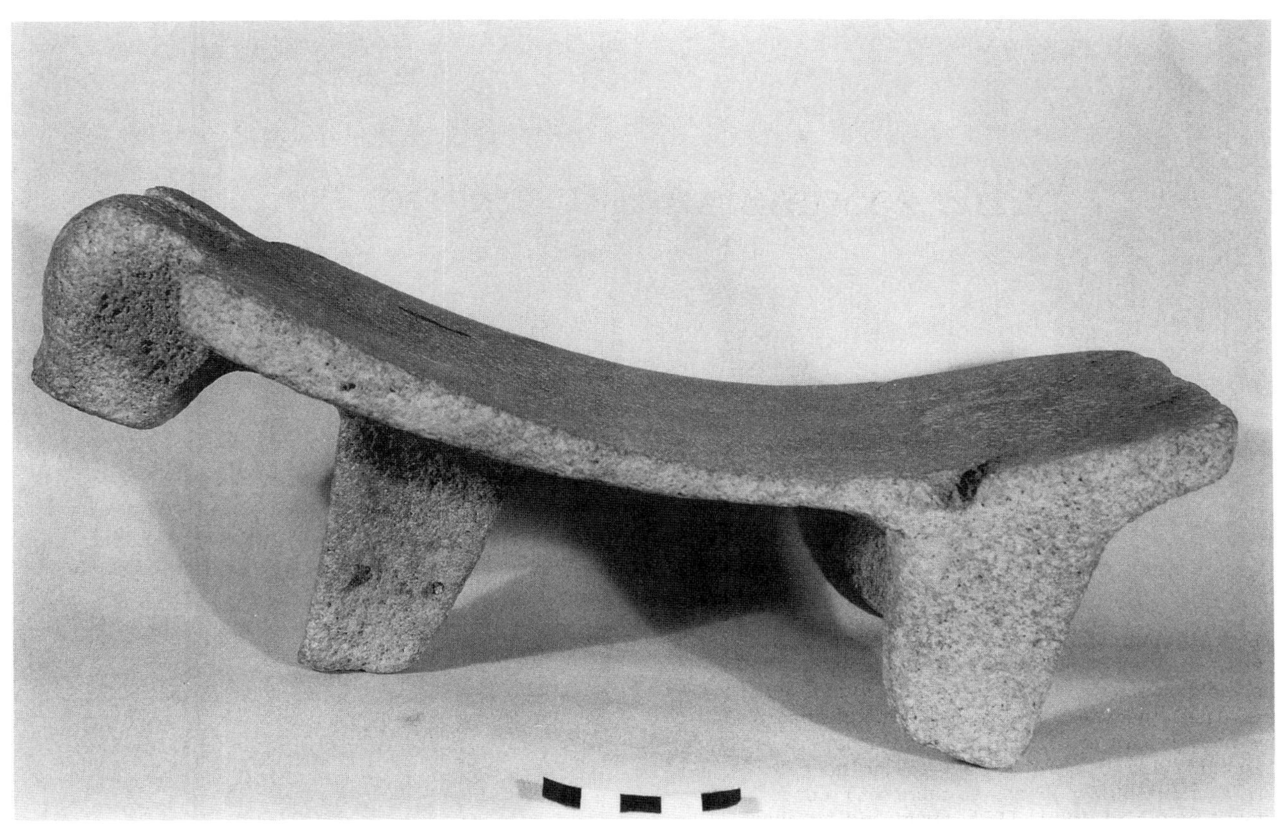

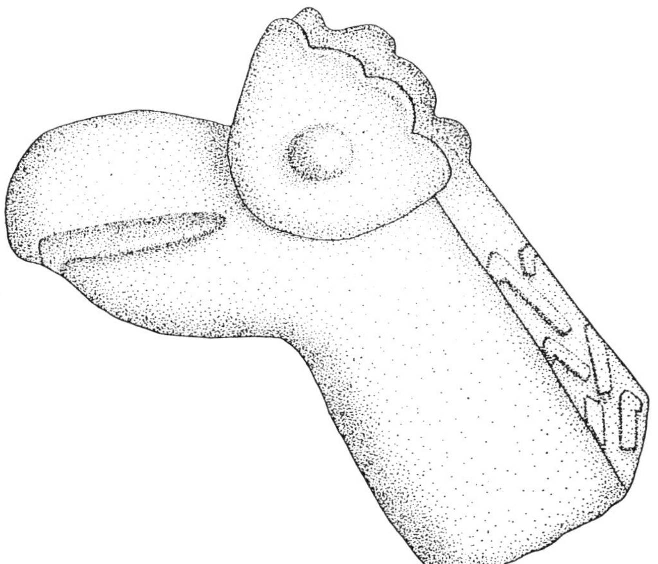

Figure 12-4.
Rectangular tripod metate with zoomorphic head (jaguar) from G-150. Photograph by Fran Mandel-Sheets.

Figure 12-5.
Drawing of a carved stone bird head from a rectangular tripod metate with zoomorphic head, from G-150. Drawing by Mark Chenault.

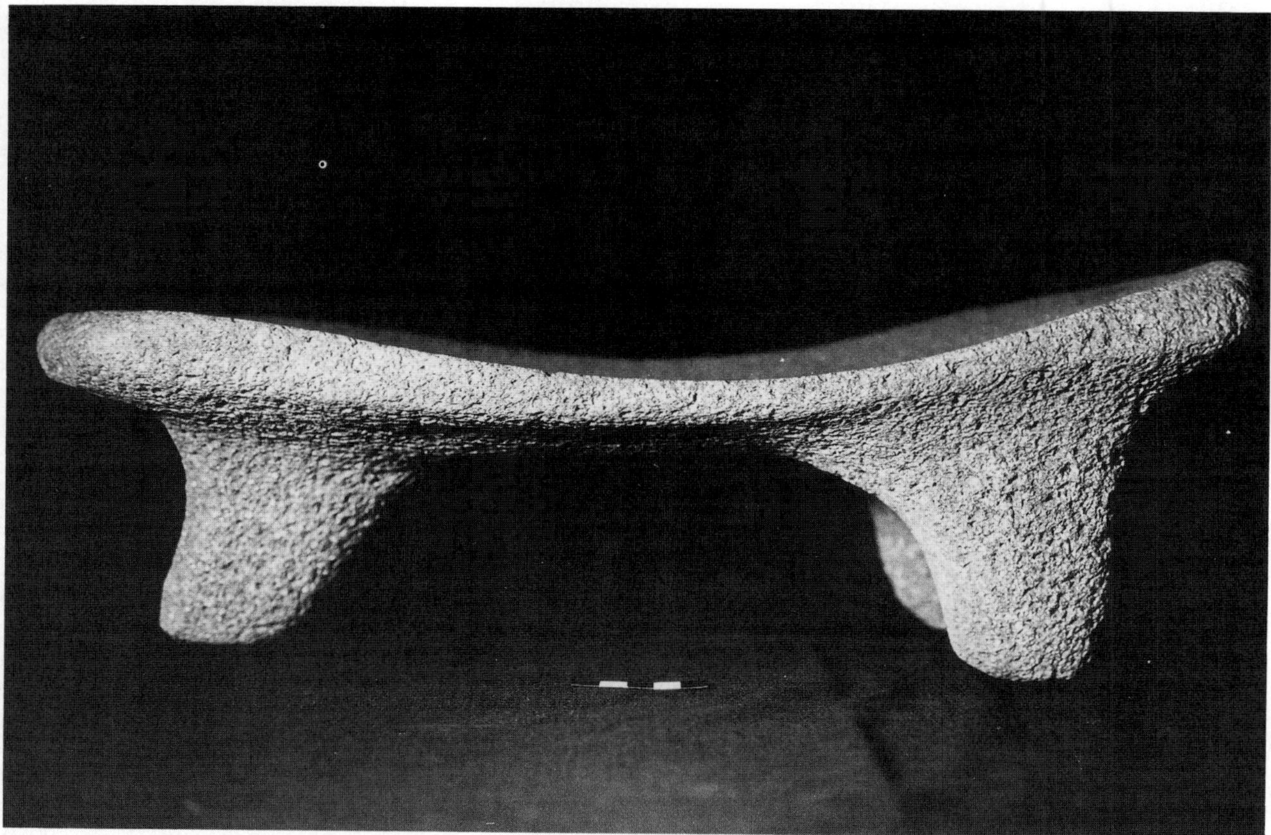

Figure 12-6.
Ovoid tripod metate, from site G-150. Photograph by Fran Mandel-Sheets.

rectangular tripod metates described earlier. The complete specimen exhibits heavy use grinding. It shows truncation of grains and polish on the grinding surface. Striations running parallel to the long axis indicate a back-and-forth grinding motion. The bases of the legs are also ground smooth from movement of the metate during grinding and have striations parallel to the long axis of the metate. The fragment was not as heavily used.

Ovoid Metate with Knob Legs (1 Complete Specimen)

One specimen from the Jiménez collection is representative of this type (Fig. 12-2*f*). The metate is long (45.5 cm), but has short knoblike legs. The front leg is square in cross section, and the back legs are circular. The grinding surface is flat and covers the entire top of the metate. The artifact, though squat and heavy, is well shaped on both its rounded edges and underside. It was heavily used, although no striations are evident. The stone from which the artifact was made is markedly vesicular.

Ovoid Nonlegged Metate (1 Complete Specimen and 1 Fragment)

Metates in this category are shaped, but lack legs and decoration (Fig. 12-2*g*). They are plano-convex in cross section, with flat grinding surfaces and round undersides. They are made from moderately vesicular stone and exhibit fairly heavy use grinding with truncation of particles and parallel use striations.

Oval Tripod Metate (1 Complete Specimen and 3 Fragments)

This type is small with a rounded underside (Fig. 12-2*h*). The three legs are small, inset, and knoblike. These metates are made from volcanic stone ranging from non-vesicular to moderately vesicular and are undecorated. The whole metate shows moderate use grinding, with striations running parallel to the long axis of the grinding surface; the fragments exhibit lesser amounts of use. Small, oval tripod metates are also found in the Atlantic Watershed (Snarskis 1978) and Diquis (Drolet, personal communication, 1984).

Basin Metate (2 Nearly Complete Specimens)

This type of metate is made from large, minimally shaped pieces of volcanic stone (Fig. 12-2*i*). They were used with a circular rather than a back-and-forth grinding motion, in contrast to most other metates produced by the prehistoric Costa Ricans. This motion, probably with a one-handed mano, formed a basin in the center of the metate rather than a flat or troughed grinding surface. Evidence of battering at the bottom of the basin indicates that crushing or pounding was also performed with these stone tools. Both metates are surface finds and are extensively weathered. That weathering may account for the lack of visible striations in the grinding basins.

We do not know the prehistoric use of these metates. They may have been used for grinding a substance other than maize, or represent a different method of preparing corn. I am unaware of metates of this type from elsewhere in Costa Rica. Sheets, Rosenthal, and Ranere (1980) report similar grinding implements from western Panama.

Unshaped Boulder Metate (1 Whole Specimen)

We recovered the one example of this type (Fig. 12-2*j*) during surface collection of Site G-175. Production of this type of metate would consist merely of taking a boulder—in this case, of nonvesicular stone—and pecking a flat surface on one side for use as a grinding platform. However, even this might have been unnecessary; use grinding alone may have formed the flat surface. No striations are evident on this specimen. The function of this metate is unknown.

Metate Fragments (74 Specimens)

Seventy-four metate fragments are too incomplete to be placed into the formal categories described earlier. One is from a circular or oval decorated metate of unknown type. Another small fragment may be from a rectangular tripod metate with zoomorphic head. There is the remainder of a broken projection on the edge of the metate, which may be an animal head protruding from the front of the metate. We found three metate fragments with cylindrical legs and five corner fragments from rectangular metates without evidence of legs. We also recovered three cylindrical metate legs, three conical legs, one D-shaped leg, and one knob leg. Two fragments from the grinding plates of metates are very thin and appear to have been well made. One fragment retains a D-shaped leg, the other has a leg that is L-shaped in cross section. Though the legs differ, the thinness and fine artisanship of the fragments suggest that they are from similar metate types.

We could specify fifty-four metate fragments as to type. Most of these fragments appear to be from shaped metates, and most exhibit some degree of use grinding. Six have striations, all of which are parallel and unidirectional.

MANOS

The Proyecto Prehistórico Arenal recovered thirty-nine manos and mano fragments. We also analyzed four whole manos from the Jiménez collection, found at the Silencio cemetery. We devised seven categories to classify the manos. Figure 12-7 depicts these types.

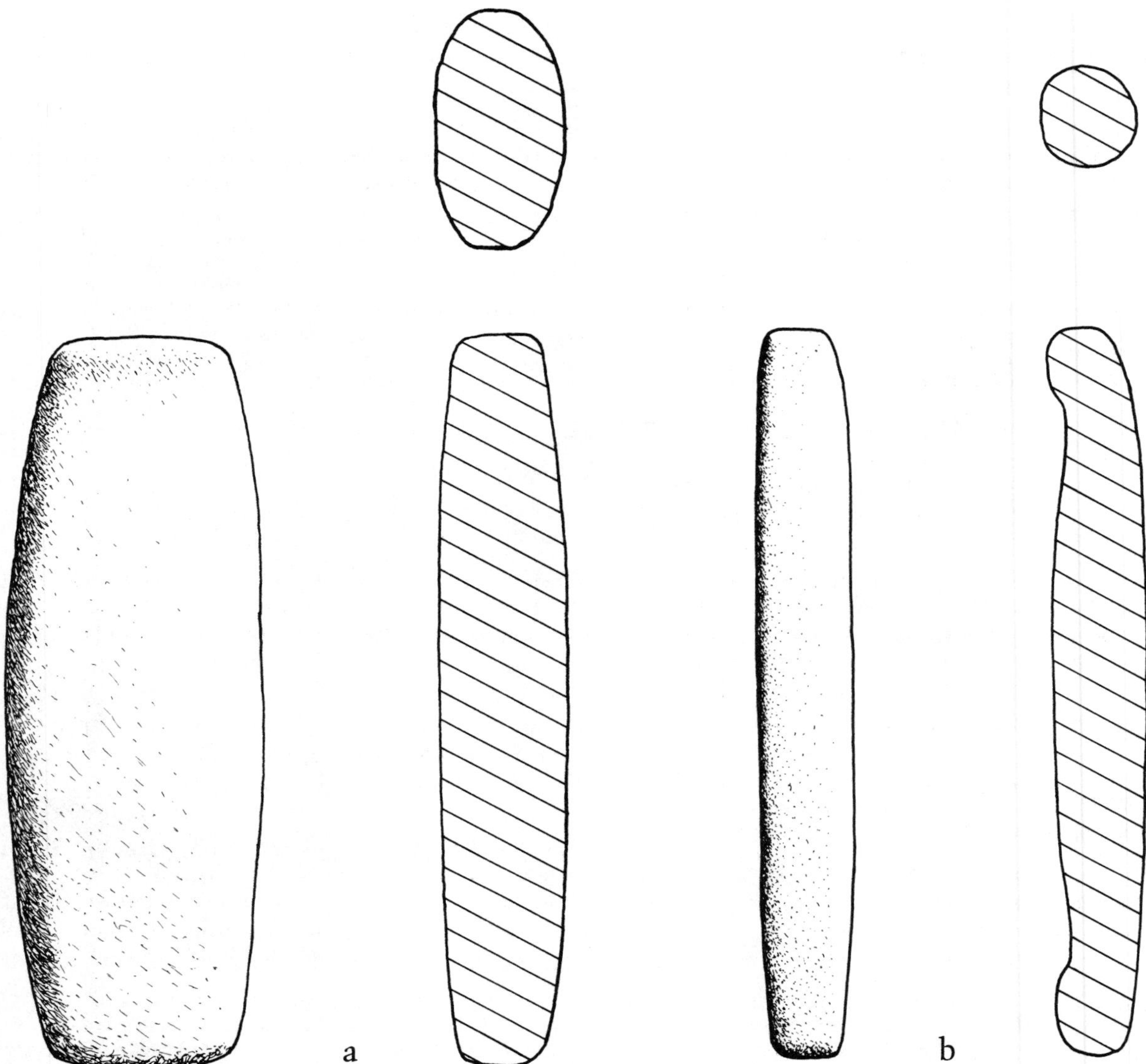

Figure 12-7.
Mano types from the Cordillera de Tilarán (drawings by Nick Lang): a, *bar mano;* b, *overhanging bar mano;* c, *concave bar mano;* d, *ovoid mano;* e, *oval mano;* f, *loaf-shaped mano;* g, *rectangular mano.*

Bar Manos (20 Fragments)

Bar manos are long and were meant for use with two hands (Fig. 12-7*a*). They vary from oval to nearly circular in cross section. All specimens of this type are fragmentary, so we do not know their average lengths. The manos are made of stone ranging from nonvesicular to moderately vesicular. The ends of the manos are pecked flat, as are, to a lesser extent, the edges. The majority of the bar manos exhibit use grinding on two sides and several have use striations. One has striations running diagonal to the long axis, rather than perpendicular, as is the case with other project manos. Einhaus (1980: fig. 15/9) discusses bar manos from La Pitahaya, Panama.

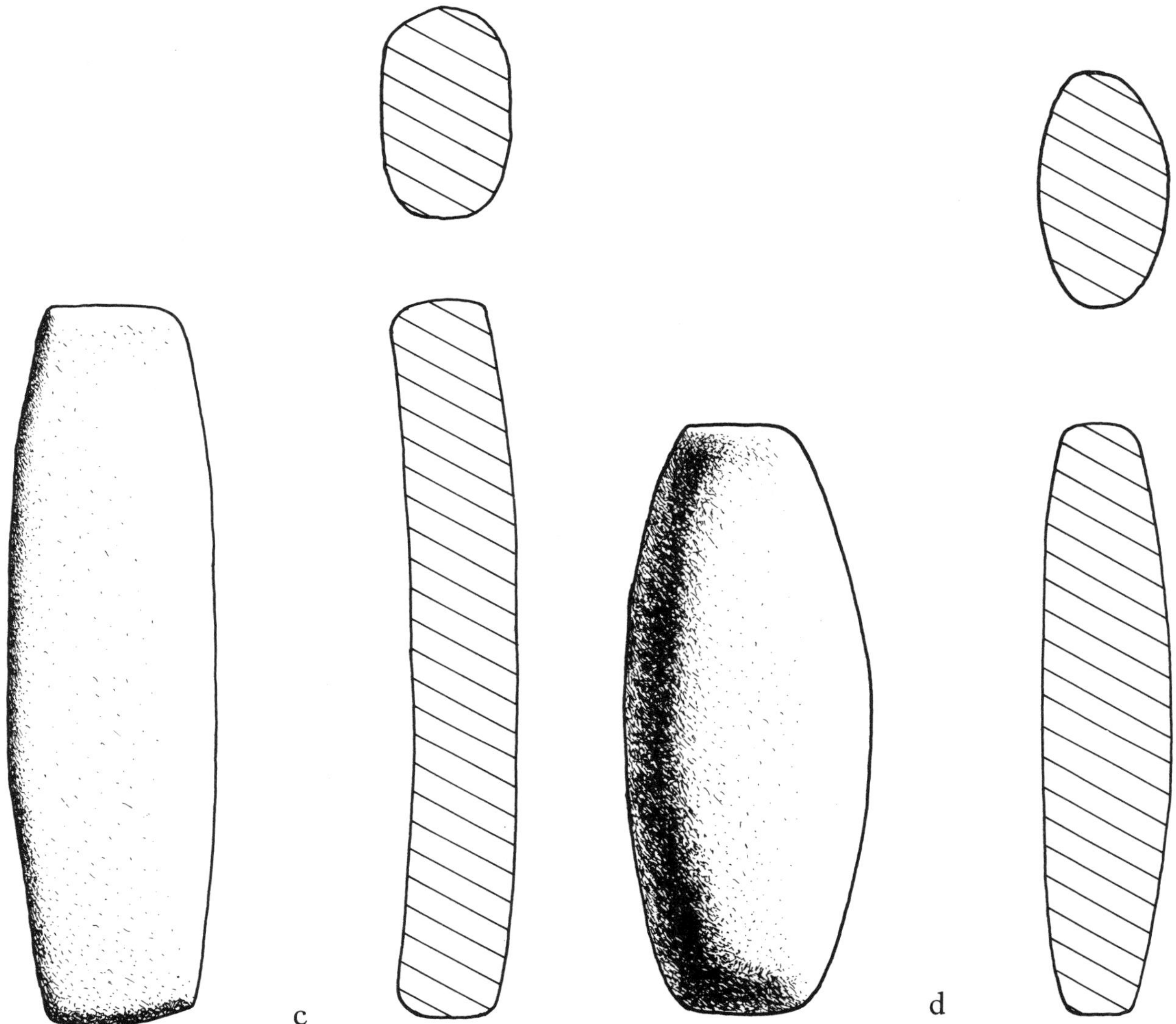

Overhanging Bar Mano (1 Whole Specimen and 1 Fragment)

One complete, overhanging bar mano is included from the Jiménez collection (Fig. 12-7*b*). The specimen is very long (38 cm) and was certainly used with two hands. The ends of the mano overhang the sides of the metate, which caused facets to form near the ends. A side view of the mano reveals that the middle section is convex, while the end sections are slightly concave. This shape would match a metate on which the entire surface was used, resulting in a shallow trough. The mano is biconvex in cross section. Both sides exhibit heavy use, one side more than the other. Numerous use striations are evident perpendicular to the long axis. The striations indicate a unidirectional or reciprocal grinding motion. Some rocking is indicated by the rounded grinding surfaces. If the mano was not rocked, a biplano, or plano-convex cross section would have resulted. Project personnel recovered one additional fragment of this type of mano. Graham (1981) illustrates elaborate, overhanging bar manos. This type of mano is characteristic of the Guanacaste-Nicoya area (ibid.).

Concave Bar Mano (2 Fragments)

We recovered two fragments of bar manos with concave grinding surfaces (long axis) (Fig. 12-7*c*). These apparently were used on metates with

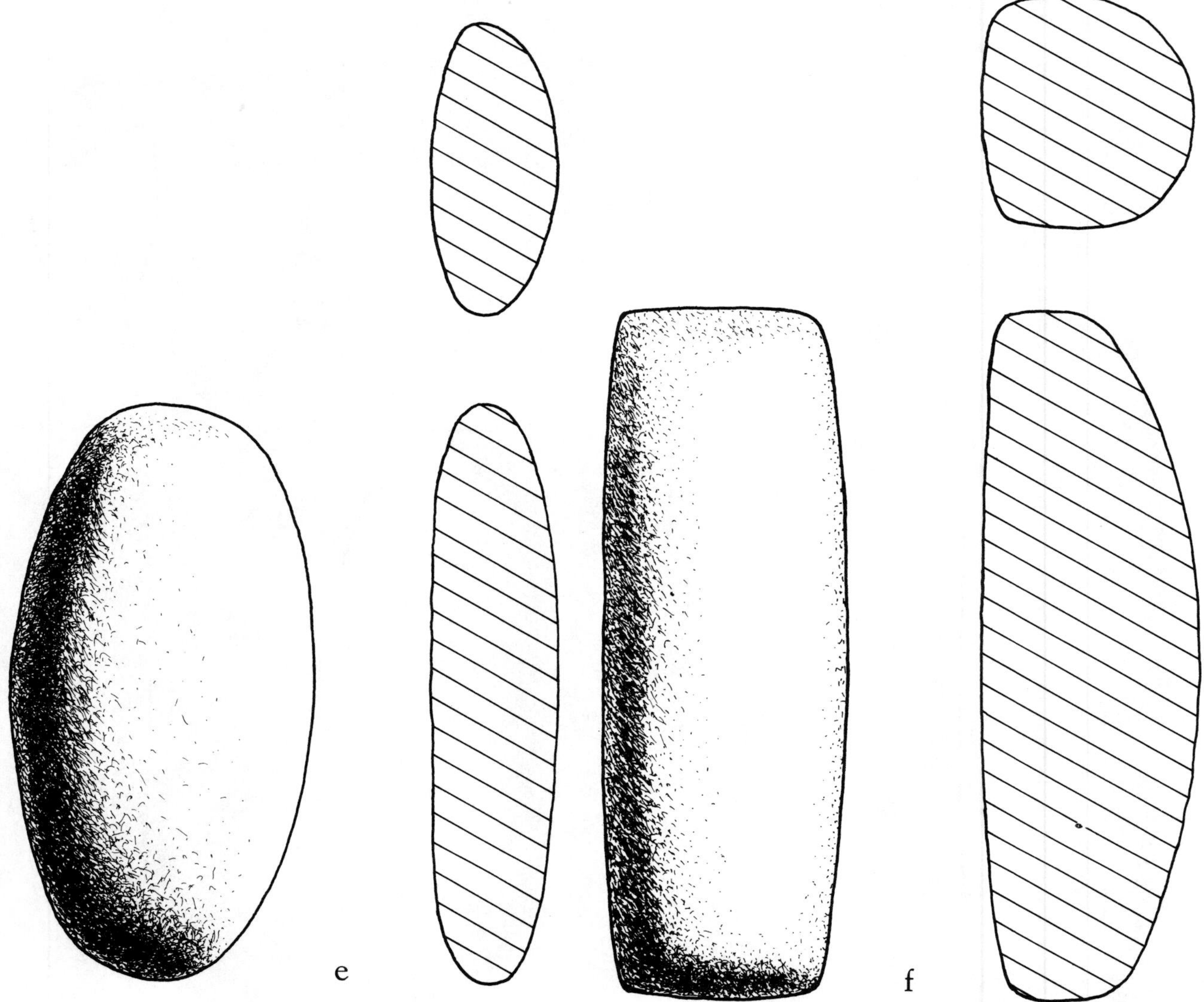

slightly convex grinding surfaces. We also found two edge fragments from metates that may have had that characteristic. These manos are biconvex in cross section and are made from nonvesicular to moderately vesicular volcanic stone. The two fragments show evidence of use grinding.

Ovoid Mano (2 Whole Specimens and 2 Fragments)

These manos are ovoid in plan view and biconvex in cross section (Fig. 12-7*d*). Both sides were used for grinding, and striations are perpendicular to the long axis. The ends of the manos are pecked flat and smoothed. The manos are made of nonvesicular stone. The Jiménez family found one ovoid mano at the Silencio cemetery. It is similar to the other manos in this category in plan view, but is biconvex in cross section rather than oval. Einhaus (1980:455) illustrates what she terms ovoid handstones, which actually range from ovoid to oval in plan view.

Oval Mano (4 Fragments)

This type is oval in both plan view and cross section (Fig. 12-7*e*). They are made from volcanic stone, which varies from nonvesicular to slightly vesicular, and are not extensively shaped. They can have one or two grinding surfaces. The four mano fragments show evidence of grinding, but do not have use striations. One mano fragment has extensive battering on one end. The grinding surfaces and battering suggest the use of these manos for both milling and crushing. It is likely that this type was used with basin metates.

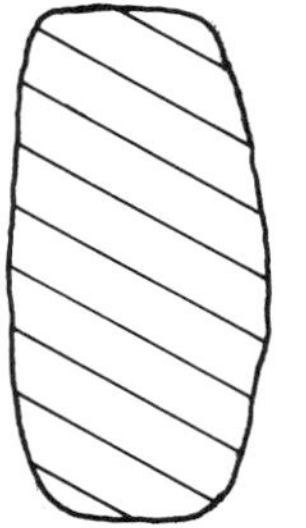

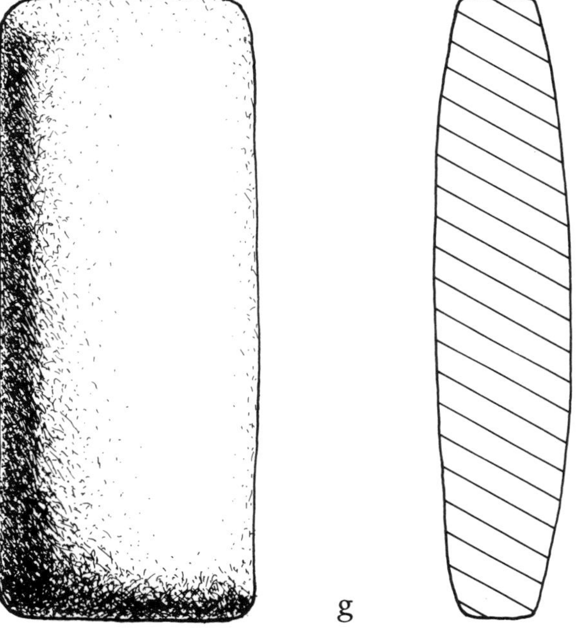

Loaf-shaped Mano (2 Whole Specimens and 6 Fragments)

Loaf-shaped manos have plano-convex cross sections and, as their name suggests, are shaped like a short loaf of French bread (Fig. 12-7*f*). Two whole manos of this type, one small (9.2 cm long) and one larger (23 cm long), come from the Jiménez collection. The smaller is of nonvesicular stone; the larger is of a stone with small vesicles. The small mano shows little use wear, while the large mano shows heavy use on two sides. Striations running perpendicular to the long axis occur on both sides. Those loaf-shaped manos that display use on both sides may have been dual-function grinding tools. A rocking motion was used with the convex side and a flat, back-and-forth motion was used on the other side.

Rectangular Mano (1 Fragment)

This mano fragment is rectangular in plan view and slightly biconvex in cross section (Fig. 12-7*g*). The mano is well shaped and is made of nonvesicular volcanic stone. It is highly weathered and shows little sign of use and no striations.

Mano Fragments (3 Specimens)

The Arenal Project recovered three mano fragments, which are too fragmentary to allow further classification.

GRINDING STONES

Grinding stones are pebbles or stones too small to be considered manos. These objects may have been used to grind pigment or other substances, or to burnish or polish other ground stone artifacts or ceramics.

Cobble Grinding Stones (4 Whole Specimens)

These are unshaped river cobbles with one faceted surface. They were used with one hand and possibly in a circular grinding motion, although we observed no striations indicating direction of grinding. According to Snarskis (personal communication, 1984), stones similar to these may have been used to grind paint pigments. Artifacts of this type have been found associated with such pigments.

Discoidal Grinding Stone (2 Complete Specimens)

These grinding stones are small (less than 4 cm in diameter). They are circular in plan view and slightly biconcave in cross section. Both have two slightly used grinding surfaces. Their function is unknown.

Burnishing Stones (1 Complete Specimen and 1 Fragment)

The one burnishing stone and fragment of a burnishing stone we found were probably utilized in smoothing or polishing ceramics. These stones are small (the complete item is 3.3 cm long), unshaped pebbles. Each has a faceted grinding surface, with no striations evident.

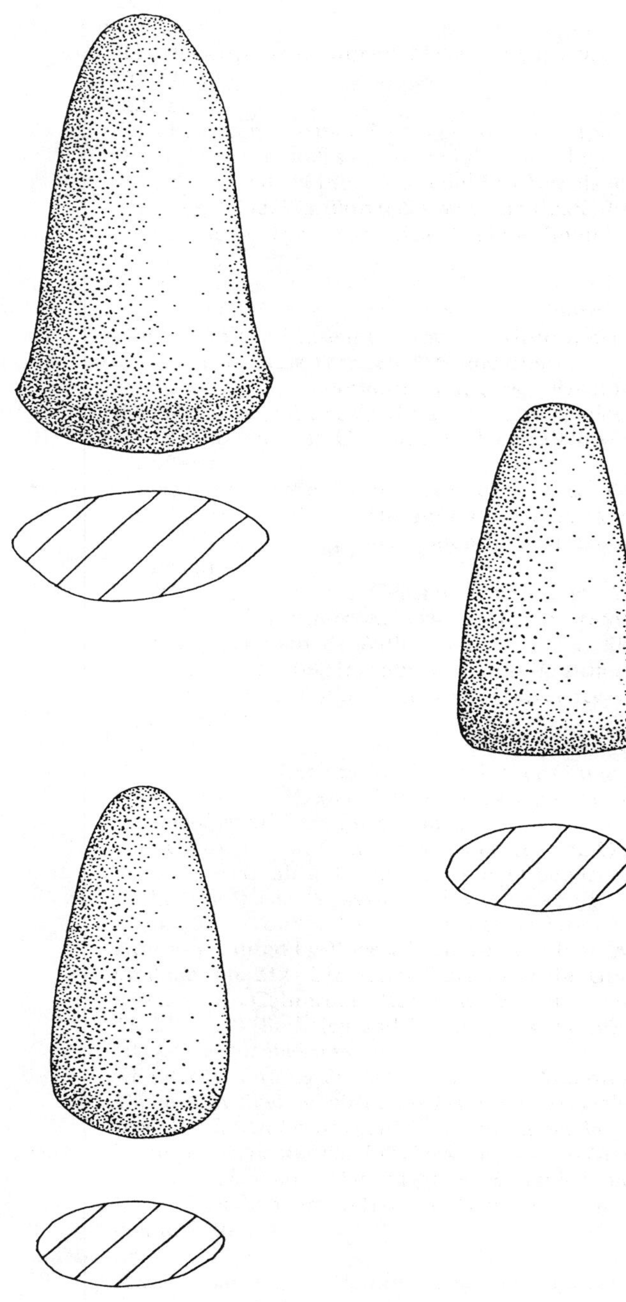

Figure 12-8.
Celt types for the Cordillera de Tilarán. Clockwise from upper left: flaring-bit celt, straight-bit celt, and rounded bit celt. Drawing by Mark Chenault.

NUTTING STONE

This rectangular "brick-shaped" stone with small circular pecked depressions was probably used for cracking nuts. It has two circular depressions on each of three sides. On the fourth side there is only one depression and what appears to be the start of a second. If this item is a nutting stone, we do not know why depressions would be needed on all sides, as only one side could be used at a given time. A very slight amount of grinding is evident on one side of the stone. The stone is nonvesicular andesite. Nutting stones are illustrated by Lange (1980a: fig. 4, B and C). Similar artifacts, though of a softer stone (siltstone), have been found in Panama (Einhaus 1980). An andesite boulder with five small, shallow depressions is described as a nutting stone by Sheets, Rosenthal, and Ranere (1980).

MISCELLANEOUS FRAGMENTS

There are four ground stone fragments that, due to their small size, we could not categorize. One piece appears to be from a carved artifact and has a small groove running across it. The remaining three fragments have ground surfaces, but no other diagnostic features.

POLISHED STONE

CELTS

We analyzed seven stone celts and twenty-seven celt fragments collected by the Arenal Project. We also studied two whole celts and three celt fragments from the Silencio cemetery and now in the Jiménez collection. Melson (personal communication, 1984) has identified the raw material of most of the tools as slightly hydrothermally altered plagioclase-phyric andesite. This is a dense and hard nonvesicular volcanic rock. Figure 12-8 is a drawing of the three celt types from the Arenal basin.

Flaring-Bit Celt (5 Fragments)

These celts have bits that flare outward at the edges. None of the fragments has an intact poll. Use striations are not evident on any of the specimens. Two of the celts have small flakes removed from the bit, apparently during use. On several of the celts, production or sharpening striations are present. These are short parallel lines that occur across the bit of the celt, perpendicular to the long axis of the tool. These striations occur only at the bit end.

Straight-Bit Celts (5 Whole and 6 Fragments)

The Proyecto Prehistórico Arenal found three complete specimens and studied two from the Jiménez collection. This type of celt has edges that do not flare or become round at the edge of the bit. Instead, the edges and the bits almost form right angles. In some specimens the edges are ground, forming a flat, faceted surface. A straight bit celt from the Guanacaste region is illustrated by Bernstein (1980: fig. 5).

One of the project celts of this type is small (7.7 cm long) and well made, with a poll section that is not as well smoothed as the bit section. The poll is pointed and shows some signs of battering. No use striations are evident on the bit. Another celt is rough, with flake scars over most of its surface; only the bit section is well ground. The poll is pointed and battered. A third celt is short (8.1 cm), but wide and thick (5.1 cm wide, 4.2 cm thick). Its shortened form suggests that it may have been broken and reworked. The poll appears to be very battered. The edges and most of the surface of the celt are rough. Only the bit is ground smooth.

Two small celts (5.2 cm long and 5.8 cm long) come from the Jiménez collection. These celts are well polished over most of their surfaces and exhibit fine production striations. On one, the production striations run in all directions; however, short use striations occur on the bit, parallel to the long axis of the celt. On the other, the production striations occur perpendicular to the long axis. No use striations are evident.

Rounded-Bit Celts (2 Whole and 4 Fragments)

A fragment of a rounded-bit celt is illustrated by Bernstein (1980: fig. 7, item on the right). This type of celt has a bit with rounded edges (Fig. 12-9). One of the whole specimens has a somewhat rounded poll, the other has a pointed poll. The polls on both of these celts are battered. The celt with the pointed poll is polished on only about one-fourth of its surface (the bit portion). The remainder was left rough, perhaps to facilitate in hafting the tool, or perhaps to decrease time spent in manufacture. A small (7.2 cm long), rounded-bit celt is part of the Jiménez collection. It has a pointed poll that shows signs of battering. The celt is rough over most of its surface, and is ground smooth on only a portion of one side.

Celt Fragments

Two celts lacking bits are part of the Jiménez collection. The bit on one celt appears to have broken off, probably a result of use damage. The other celt displays evidence of resharpening. It appears that most of the surface of the celt was roughened by pecking, with only the bit section on one side retaining a portion of the former polished surface. The bit was then apparently flaked to prepare a platform for further flake removal. A flake was successfully removed from the polished side of the celt. The other side, however, appears to have been damaged during the resharpening process. We also recovered the midsection and two highly weathered fragments of celts. One of the weathered fragments appears to have been reused as a hammerstone after breakage.

CHISEL

We recovered a small ground and polished chisel fragment from site G-169. We found the fragment in Stratigraphic Unit 30, indicating that it probably dates to the Silencio Phase, although we found some Tilarán Phase materials in Unit 30 at this site as well. The chisel fragment measures 2.9 cm long, 2.0 cm wide, and 1.8 cm thick. It weighs 15 g. The bit end appears to have been heavily used. Chisels are not as wide as celts, but, like celts, are biconvex in cross section (Einhaus 1980).

SLATE MIRROR BACK

We found a small fragment of what is probably a slate mirror back (Snarskis, personal communication, 1985) at Site G-164. The fragment is 4.9 cm long, 2.1 cm wide and 0.4 cm thick. By projecting the curved edge, however, we have determined that the complete artifact would have been a disk 14 cm in diameter. It probably dates to the Arenal Phase. One side of the fragment is ground flat and polished. The edge of the disk is ground and beveled. The edge is also smoothed to a polished surface. The other side, which would have supported the mirror pieces, is ground, but not polished. Grinding striations are visible running diagonal to the long axis.

Figure 12-9.
Rounded bit celts from G-169, G-174, and IF-17. Photograph by Fran Mandel-Sheets.

Slate mirror backs occur in many areas of the New World, ranging from the southwestern United States to Peru (Stone and Balser 1965), with numerous slate-backed pyrite mirrors having been found in Mesoamerica (Adams 1977) and in lower Central America (Stone 1977). Prehistoric mirrors in the New World have been described by several authors including Nordenskiöld (1926), Mason (1927); Kidder et al. (1946), and Strauss (n.d.). Slate-backed pyrite mirrors consist of disks of slate, although other forms such as rectangles can occur (Mason 1927), with mosaics of pyrite glued to them using some type of organic glue. The cut and polished pieces of pyrite form a highly reflective surface. Some of the mirror backs are polished but lack carved designs, as is the case for the Arenal mirror back fragment, whereas others are highly decorated. Other types of mirrors also occur in Mesoamerica, such as the concave pyrite mirrors of the Olmec (Carlson 1981; Heizer and Gullberg 1981), and Aztec obsidian mirrors (Pasztory 1983).

Stone and Balser (1965) discovered twelve slate disks at the site of La Fortuna and seven slate disks at Guácimo in Costa Rica. These disks are all believed to have been mirror backs, many retaining traces of the gum used to glue the mirror pieces in place. Three of the disks are highly decorated, one with human figures, including a ball player, another with an abstract design, and the third with incised Maya hieroglyphs (ibid.: figs. 15, 21, and 22). The hieroglyphs were apparently used for decoration only, as they do not make grammatical sense. The disks are believed to have been manufactured in the Mesoamerican region, possibly in the Petén, around AD 500. The slate disks were all found in mortuary contexts with associated grave goods of reworked jades, gold objects, and incised pottery (ibid.).

INCISED STONE

We recovered six large volcanic stones with incised lines from several sites in the Arenal basin. We found these stones in cemeteries, although we found none in completely undisturbed stratigraphic context. Because of this, and because the incised lines usually do not extend deeper than the weathered outer portion of the stone, we at first doubted their antiquity (Chenault 1984a). However, several of these objects have more recently been recovered from additional sites. One of these stones—a very large piece (more than a meter in length and 30 cm to 50 cm in width and thickness)—was found in a large looters' pit at site G-151 with one end extending into the undisturbed stratigraphy. Because of this evidence, we now believe that these objects are prehistoric.

The stones are incised with shallow lines forming geometric patterns (Fig. 12-10). Their function is unknown, but they may have served as markers to define site boundaries or areas within a site. In addition to the large incised stone from Site G-151, we recovered three smaller stones and one large piece from Site G-150, and one at Site G-181.

TEMPORAL DISTRIBUTION OF GROUND, POLISHED, AND INCISED STONE

Based on stratigraphic context and association with ceramic materials, we postulated the following temporal distribution for the ground, polished, and incised stone artifacts from the Arenal basin. We do not include materials found on the modern ground surface in the temporal analysis.

TRONADORA PHASE

Very few ground stone or polished stone artifacts were recovered from deposits that date to the Tronadora Phase. Six of the eleven ground and polished stone artifacts from Site G-163 were surface finds. Ceramic analysis indicates a major Tronadora Phase and significant Arenal Phase occupation of the site. We found a small amount of Silencio and Tilarán Phase ceramics in the upper levels at the site. We found one metate fragment, with a knob leg, associated with Tronadora and Arenal Phase ceramics. We discovered one small knob leg from a metate in Unit 60 and associated with Tronadora Phase ceramics. It is impossible to tell, due to the fragmentary nature of the pieces, if they are from the same metate type. The remaining pieces from G-163, with stratigraphic context, are too fragmentary to allow placement in the typology and, therefore, provide little interpretive data.

ARENAL PHASE

The ground and polished stone collection is much more substantial for the Arenal Phase. We recovered no whole metates during excavation of Arenal Phase sites; however, we found numerous fragments of deliberately broken items at Site G-164. The predominant metate type found in association with Arenal Phase ceramics is the ovoid tripod type. Metates dating to the Arenal Phase are thin with rounded edges and cylindrical or conical legs. Vesicular to moderately vesicular stone is the predominant raw material. Many of the metate fragments exhibit heavy use grinding. None are decorated.

The majority of manos in use during the Arenal Phase were bar manos, including the overhanging and concave varieties. Most are made of stone with small vesicles, and many show extensive use wear. All of the manos recovered are fragmentary. The breakage of these stone artifacts may be a result of postinterment practices during the Arenal Phase. Nearly all of the ground stone recovered in Arenal context was found at Site G-164 (Chap. 5), where human burial practices appear to have involved the breakage of artifacts on top of rock mound tombs.

We found numerous celts associated with Arenal Phase ceramics at G-164. We recovered both straight-bit and flaring-bit celts. Most of the celts found at G-164 are complete and were found in graves, not on top of the stone mounds. We found the slate mirror back near the top of the stone mound at G-164.

SILENCIO PHASE

The majority of the ground stone artifacts collected by the Arenal Project were found during excavation of Site G-150. Occupation of the site dates primarily to the Silencio Phase, with only very minor amounts of earlier and later phase ceramics (Chap. 6). The large, tenoned stone platform found at Site G-181 also apparently dates to the Silencio Phase. Although both Arenal and Silencio Phase ceramics are found at G-181, the blocky nature of the object and its relative elaborateness indicate that it most likely dates to the Silencio Phase. It appears that Costa Rican ground stone had a tendency to become more angular and blocky later in time (Snarskis, personal communication, 1985). The other tenoned stone item recovered by the project was found at the Silencio cemetery (G-150), but was a surface find.

Metates made during the Silencio Phase take many forms, including the following types: rectangular decorated, rectangular tripod with zoomorphic heads, rectangular tripod, rectangular tripod with cylindrical legs, ovoid tripod, ovoid with knob legs, and oval tripod metates. Although oval tripod metates appear to occur in all areas of Costa Rica during several time periods, the only whole item project personnel recovered is clearly associated with Silencio Phase ceramics. One whole ovoid tripod metate was found in a Silencio Phase burial at Site G-150. It appears to be somewhat anachronistic in that context, since ovoid tripod metates are the predominant type during the earlier Arenal Phase. The legs of the metate do show some tendency toward angularity, however; in fact, the front leg is roughly D-shaped, a trait found on rectangular tripod metates. The blocky, angular, and heavy rectangular tripod metates are definitely dated to the Silencio Phase. The D-shaped front leg of the ovoid tripod metate found at the Silencio site suggests that this type may be transitional between the Arenal and Silencio phases. It may also have been curated for some time before it became a grave offering.

Manos made in the Silencio Phase are very similar to those in use during the preceding phase, and are mostly bar manos. This interpretation, however, could be biased because of the small sample size.

Rounded-bit and flaring-bit celts are found with Silencio Phase occupation. We have not unearthed rounded-bit celts at earlier sites, and straight-bit celts do not seem to occur at Silencio Phase sites.

TILARÁN PHASE

The Arenal project found no identifiable ground, polished, or incised stone artifacts dating to the Tilarán Phase.

SUBSISTENCE

It is difficult to determine the function of many of the prehistoric stone artifacts found in the Arenal basin. The stone tools have lain buried in the acidic rain forest soil for centuries, or were eroded out onto the surface and weathered by the elements. Most traces of the vegetal materials the tools were used to process have long since disappeared. Yet, through ethnographic analogy, we can suggest uses for many of the ground, polished, and incised stone artifacts.

Most of the ethnographic data are concerned with subsistence. These data show that tripod, volcanic-stone metates are ubiquitous in Mexico and much of Central America. Modern Indian groups throughout the region use metates and manos to grind many substances.

While the Arenal Project found some remains of corn (*Zea mays*), the amount was quite small (Chaps. 13, 14, and 15). This is partly a result of poor preservation. Evidence from bone collagen tests indicates that the percentage of maize in the aboriginal diet was under 12 (Friedman and Gleason 1984; Chap. 6).

In addition to maize, we discovered several other types of seeds, which might have been ground with manos and metates, at sites in the Arenal area (Chap. 16). These include one bean (*Phaseolus vulgaris*) found at Site G-150, and a fragment of a bean recovered from G-169. There is ethnographic evidence that indicates that beans are sometimes ground, usually after being cooked. We recovered palm nuts, both of pejibaye (*Bactris gasipaes*) and of unidentified species, from Sites G-154, G-163, and G-164 (Chap. 16). Nutting stones are believed to have been used, with a hand-held stone, to crack open the hard shells of the nuts.

Figure 12-10.
An example of an incised laja from site G-150. Photograph by Fran Mandel-Sheets.

One of the most important stone tool types to the ancient Costa Ricans must have been the celt. In the tropical environment of the Arenal area, celts would have been used extensively in clearing away the thick vegetation for agriculture and habitation. They were also used in cutting wood for fuel, housing, implements, and other uses.

CEREMONY

The location of many of the ground and polished stone artifacts in human burials indicates their possible function as ceremonial objects. We recovered the majority of whole metates and celts from cemetery sites. This may be due to sampling error, but the inclusion of these tools as burial offerings removes them from a purely subsistence context.

We also recovered the tenoned stone objects and the incised stones from cemetery sites. Their nature as highly decorated objects with little use wear, together with their provenience, indicates their nonsubsistence role.

It is not clear whether many of the artifacts were used in both subsistence and in ceremony. Many of the metates are highly decorated, but some also exhibit a high degree of use wear. Simpler metates are also often found with burials, and sometimes show heavy use.

Manos and grinding stones do not appear to have been used as burial offerings. Most of the manos are surface finds, and we recovered metates from burials without finding corresponding, or indeed any, manos. We found some manos, however, in the deposit of broken cultural materials overlying the stone burial mound at Site G-164 (Chap. 5).

Mirrors and slate mirror backs were almost certainly high-status objects in Precolumbian society. Carlson (1981), in discussing Olmec mirrors, suggests that they may have functioned as symbols to "capture" the power and light of the sun, to create fire and smoke, or they may have been used in shamanistic healing practices (as indicated by Mesoamerican ethnographic analogy) and functioned as symbols of elite status. A similar function can be suggested for the Costa Rican mirror backs, as stated by Stone and Balser (1965: 321): "There is little doubt that iron-pyrite mirrors backed by slate plaques were coveted articles of trade even in a land so remote from their point of manufacture as lower Central America. It is possible that at one time they might have been used as heirlooms. It seems clear that they were highly esteemed and perhaps served as ceremonial objects or as symbols of rank."

The slate mirror-back fragment from Site G-164 probably also served a ceremonial function. Its inclusion with the assemblage of broken objects covering the stone burial mound indicates that it was part of the ceremony associated with the interment of the dead. Prior to its inclusion as a grave offering, the complete slate disk was probably a high-status item, as were similar objects occurring throughout Mexico and Central America.

SUMMARY AND CONCLUSIONS

The sample of ground and polished stone tools from the Arenal Project is relatively small, yet it provides some information concerning subsistence, ritual, and chronology. The majority of artifacts recovered are metates or metate fragments. This is probably due to sampling error. Most of our excavations occurred at cemetery sites, where metates were common burial furniture, especially during the Silencio Phase. Their inclusion in burials indicates that they were considered important, even perhaps in the afterlife.

Metates were no doubt used by the ancient Costa Ricans to grind many different materials in addition to maize. Recent studies have examined ethnographically some of the variety of products that are processed using manos and metates (e.g., Southward 1982). Replicating ground stone tools and using them to process a variety of materials can help to determine the causes of use wear on archaeological, ground stone specimens (Cater n.d.); however, no experimental work has been done to replicate the use wear on the Arenal metates.

The metates recovered from the Arenal area vary a great deal in appearance, from unmodified boulders and plain tripod metates, to those with carved decoration and animal heads. It is clear from the artistic treatment of many of the metates that they were not thought of as purely utilitarian objects. Instead, many were used as a medium of artistic expression and may have had ritual or ceremonial significance. In any case, they were valued enough to have been placed in the graves of the deceased.

The Arenal metates have some use as relative chronological markers. Metates with smoother, more delicate lines and rounded edges preceded the blockier, heavier pieces with sharper edges. Along with the evolutionary trend toward blockiness, however, went a tendency toward more extensive and finer surface decoration. Also, some of the heaviness and squareness of the later pieces seem to have, at times, been alleviated by creating openwork in areas such as legs.

The majority of manos found by the Arenal Project are bar-shaped. During the excavation of the Arenal Phase, we found manos in ritual context in their placement, often in broken form, over the stone burial mound at Site G-164. They were not interred with human remains in this phase or in the later Silencio Phase, when metates without manos were commonly placed in graves. Whatever the ritual importance of metates, it did not apparently require the presence of manos in the Silencio Phase. The Arenal manos, though often well shaped, are not decorated.

There appears to be little chronological change evident in the manos from the Arenal basin. This, as stated earlier, is perhaps a result of the small and uneven sample; we recovered very few manos from contexts dating to other than the Arenal Phase.

We suppose that the manos, especially the two-handed bar types, were used in conjunction with metates. Again, experimental work has not been done to try to replicate the use wear found on the Arenal manos. The wear evident on the vast majority of those manos, however, indicates that they were used in grinding against another stone. This stone-against-stone grinding is indicated by the truncation of grains found on the grinding surfaces of most of the manos. Striations, when present, usually indicate a reciprocal grinding motion.

Other ground stone artifacts include small grinding stones and one apparent nutting stone. Data are too incomplete to tell if these items changed significantly through time; therefore, little can be said about their role in subsistence. They appear to have had utilitarian functions as, for example, ceramic smoothing stones and anvils for the cracking of hard substances.

Nonutilitarian uses can be suggested for the large tenoned stone objects and for the incised laja. While their uses are unknown, their provenience in cemetery sites, their high degree of surface decoration, and their lack of use wear indicate that their function was ritual. The complete tenoned piece may have been an altar or chair/throne, and the incised stones may have been markers of some kind.

Polished stone recovered from the Arenal basin consists of a number of celts, one apparent chisel fragment, and one fragment of a slate mirror back. In a tropical environment, celts would have been important tools in clearing land and for obtaining wood for building materials. The celt must have been so important in subsistence that it also took on some ritual importance, as indicated by the occurrence of many celts in the context of human burials. This ritual significance may have also resulted from the difficulty in manufacturing celts, many of them being of hard and dense greenstone, and because the greenstone had to be obtained from the distant Santa Elena Peninsula. Celts exhibit a change in form through time, with the straight-bit and flaring-bit celts associated with Arenal Phase ceramics and the rounded-bit celts with the Silencio Phase materials.

As a collection, the ground and polished stone artifacts from the Arenal basin show a general trend through time toward blockier and heavier pieces with, however, an increasing emphasis on finer surface decoration and perhaps increased use of the zoomorphic head motif. The sample of artifacts from stratigraphic contexts and the data on use wear analysis are too incomplete to allow for determination of changes in subsistence practices through time based on ground stone analysis. What is apparent, however, is that the prehistoric Costa Ricans were not satisfied with purely functional objects, but instead imbued many of their ground and polished stone tools with artistic grace.

ACKNOWLEDGMENTS

I would first like to thank Payson Sheets for giving me the opportunity to work in Central America. One's job does not often provide a vista of rolling green hills, tropical rain forest, and a smoking volcano across the waters of a highland lake. I would also like to thank William Melson, Michael Snarskis, Frederick Lange, and Robert Drolet for their help and advice in the preparation of this chapter. Figures 12-2 and 12-7 were drawn by Nick Lang, and his help and services are greatly appreciated. I drew the remaining illustrations. A thank you to Fran Mandel-Sheets for the photographs of the artifacts, and to the Jiménez family of the Finca Silencio for the loan of their ground stone collection. Thank you to Marilynn Mueller and Brian McKee for editing of this chapter. A special thank you is extended to Earl and Barbara Bolton. And finally, thanks to the crew of the Proyecto Prehistórico Arenal for the laughs and the rum.

MARILYNN MUELLER
MARK L. CHENAULT

13

Prehistoric Jewelry from the Arenal Basin

INTRODUCTION

Nearly all human cultures have carved precious stone and produced items of personal adornment. The prehistoric Costa Ricans were no exception. In fact, the small country of Costa Rica is famous for its numerous jadeite and greenstone pendants, and for its gold and copper alloy ornaments. The abundance of gold artifacts gave Costa Rica its name when Europeans first arrived early in the sixteenth century.

Although it does not appear to have been a center for the production or use of gold or greenstone, the Arenal area shares culture traits with the rest of the region, including artifacts in these two media. During the 1984 and 1985 seasons of the Proyecto Prehistórico Arenal, we recovered several pendants and beads through excavation and site survey. These artifacts consist of three greenstone pendant fragments, one siltstone pendant, one gold pendant, and six stone beads. The portion of this chapter dealing with the stone jewelry was written by Chenault; that related to the gold pendant was written by Mueller.

We did not find direct evidence for greenstone or metal ornament production in the Arenal area. The evidence more likely indicates long-distance trade. According to Melson (personal communication, 1984–1985), the closest source for the raw materials for most of the stone artifacts discussed in this chapter was the Santa Elena Peninsula. There was, either through exchange or travel, contact between the people of the Arenal basin and the people of the Pacific Coast of the Guanacaste-Nicoya region. This contact, the exchange of information, and the sharing of cultural characteristics and styles is expressed by the ground stone and polished stone (Chap. 12) and greenstone artifacts collected by the Arenal Project.

In contrast, the gold pendant bespeaks influence from the south. Metallurgy arose in South America and diffused through Colombia and Panama into the southern portion of Costa Rica (Snarskis 1981a; Bray 1981). Gold is found along the Chiquito River near Lake Arenal and is mined there today. It is therefore possible, but unlikely, that the small gold avian pendant was produced in the Arenal basin.

GREENSTONE

The Arenal-area pendants can be categorized based on the typology for Costa Rican jade and greenstone artifacts devised by Chenault (1986). While not of jadeite, the greenstone pendants were probably produced with techniques similar to those employed by prehistoric Central Americans in the carving of jadeite figures. Comprehensive descriptions of jade-working technology are provided by Foshag (1957), Easby (1968), and Chenault (1988). A brief description of the techniques employed in the manufacture of each of the greenstone pendants recovered by the Arenal Project will be provided.

BOSSED BAR PENDANT

Bar pendants consist of long, tabular pieces of stone drilled conically or biconically, allowing them to be suspended horizontally (Chenault 1986). The boss refers to a raised area, usually circular or roughly circular, which is often a decorative element on bar pendants. Bossed bar pendants have been illustrated and referred to as jade pendants by Easby (1981: pl. 79).

We recovered one bossed bar pendant fragment at Site G-163 (Fig. 13-1). We found it in the fill of a large, amorphous pit that extended from the upper 50 stratigraphic units into the Aguacate Formation in Operation G (Chap. 4). The pendant is associated with Tronadora Phase artifacts.

The fragment is 5.6 cm long, 3 cm wide, and 1.1 cm thick; it weighs 28.5 g. It is olive gray 5Y 4/1, following the Munsell color system (Goddard Rock Color Chart, 1948). The material is a metabasite (Melson, personal communication, 1985). The pendant was formed by abrading the stone with a saw and abrasive powder. Because this item is made from a fairly soft stone, pecking and grinding may also have been used in its production. Pecking and grinding were not extensively used in jadeite production, due to the hardness of that material (Foshag 1957; Easby 1968). Two biconical holes were drilled through the object for suspension. The artifact was probably polished with a wooden tool and fine abrasive powder. The fragment shows evidence of regrinding in the area of breakage. Figure 13-1 suggests the probable size and shape of the complete pendant.

We found the pendant fragment in a probable burial pit. Site G-163 was a domestic habitation site (Chap. 4), although we found burials within the site. If the pendant is not from a funerary context, then it may have been undergoing reworking in a domestic locality.

WINGED BAR PENDANT

Winged bar pendants often display a zoomorphic figure, usually bat or avian, with outspread wings; however, plain or stylized winged objects also occur. The latter type has an area in the center of the pendant that is spatially demarcated with raised bands or other dividing elements. Winged greenstone and jade pendants are described and illustrated by Easby (1968, 1981) and Balser (1974).

We surface-collected a fragment of a winged bar pendant (Fig. 13-2) at Site G-164, which dates primarily to the Arenal Phase (Chap. 5). The pendant is made of serpentinite, an amphibole (tremolite-actinolite), and serpentine (Melson, personal communication, 1984). The fragment appears to be about one-half of the original pendant. It had a carved figure in the center, probably a bat. Winged bar pendants with bat figures are illustrated by Easby (1981: pl. 85 and 86). The fragment is 2.7 cm long, 1.8 cm wide, and 0.4 cm thick; it weighs 15 g. The pendant was probably roughly shaped through pecking and grinding. The figure in the center of the pendant was carved using a combination of incising and grinding or sawing (see Chenault 1988). An abrasive material would not have been needed to work the soft stone of which this pendant is composed.

HALF-CELT AVIAN PENDANT

Pendants in this category were very common in Precolumbian Costa Rica. The pendants were made from whole celts that were cut in half longitudinally, probably using a hardwood saw and

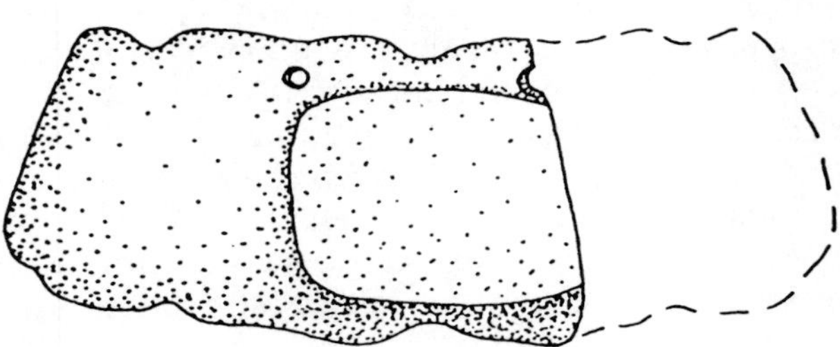

Figure 13-1.
Bossed bar pendant fragment. Actual size. Drawing by Mark Chenault.

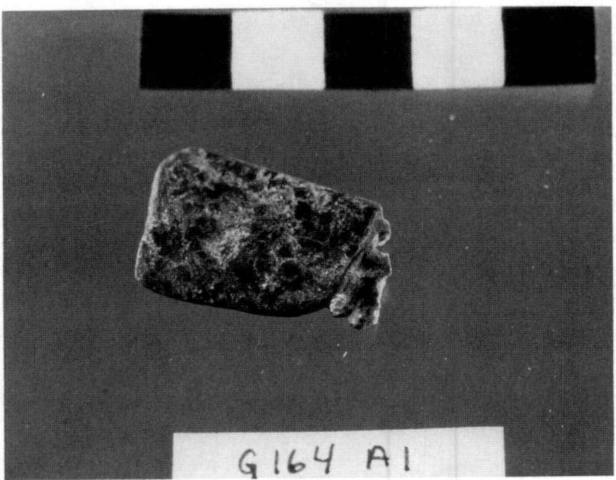

Figure 13-2.
Winged bar pendant fragment. Scale in cm. Photograph by Fran Mandel-Sheets.

abrasive powder. The celt was cut before decoration was added to either half. Saw cuts were started from both edges of a whole celt, and an uncut portion was left in the middle. The halves were then snapped apart, leaving a rough septum on both pieces. In many cases, the septum was abraded or ground smooth or, sometimes, completely removed. Avian characteristics, such as beaks, wings, and feathers, decorate the upper portion (poll) of the pendants, while the lower portion (the celt blade or bit end) remains blank. The objects were almost always biconically drilled for suspension as pendants. This type of pendant, or similar types, are illustrated by Easby (1968, 1981), Balser (1974), and Chenault (1986).

We found a half-celt avian greenstone pendant fragment on the surface at Site G-164 (Fig. 13-3). The site dates predominantly to the Arenal Phase (Chap. 5). This pendant fragment is 4.3 cm long, 3.2 cm wide, and 1.2 cm thick; it weighs 20.1 g. Though mottled, the material is mainly greenish black 5 G 2/1 (Goddard Rock Color Chart 1948). The pendant is made from hydrothermally altered gabbro (Melson, personal communication, 1985).

The half-celt was decorated with incised lines cut with a hard sharp stone. The eyes on the original pendant probably consisted of conical holes. The complete pendant probably had a horizontal, biconical suspension hole, and the pendant broke in or near that structurally weakened area. The area of breakage shows clear evidence of regrinding or reabrading. It appears that, after the pendant broke, biconical suspension holes were drilled from the back of the pendant, through the eyes. Because it was made of a relatively soft stone, abrading with a wooden tool and a hard abrasive material may not have been required, and grinding would have sufficed. The entire surface of the item exhibits striations both perpendicular and parallel to the long axis of the greenstone fragment. This indicates that the object was in the process of being reground or reabraded. The septum on the back of the fragment also shows evidence of smoothing. Thus, it appears that the pendant fragment was in the process of being completely reformed. Figure 13-4 shows the probable size and shape of the entire pendant.

MISCELLANEOUS: PENDANT

This category encompasses all of the greenstone items that do not fit into any of the formal categories and have no counterparts with which to form a separate type (Chenault 1986). The fourth pendant described in this chapter is best placed in this miscellaneous category, as pendants of this simple form have not been observed by Chenault in Costa Rican greenstone collections. It is tabular, pear-shaped (Fig. 13-5), and made of pale yellowish brown (10 YR 6/2, Goddard Rock Color Chart 1948) siltstone. The object is 5.2 cm long, 3 cm wide, 1 cm thick, and weighs 23.3 g. We recovered it from Operation B at Site G-164 from the Unit 54 stratum (Chap. 5). Ceramics associated with that stratum date to the Arenal Phase.

Due to the softness of the stone, grinding was probably the only technique required to shape this pendant. The surface of the item is covered with striations running parallel to its long axis, indicating grinding. Two conical holes occur on each side of one end of the object. It appears that it was being drilled biconically in two places, for suspension, but this had not been completed. This is the only evidence for stone ornament production in the Arenal area.

BEADS

We excavated three greenstone beads (Fig. 13-6) from a human burial at G-150, the El Silencio cemetery (Chap. 6), in a tomb predating the Unit 41 tephra fall. These beads therefore date to the end of the Arenal Phase or to the first part of the Silencio Phase. The beads are tubular and were drilled biconically. The ends of the beads are smooth and slightly rounded. Fine striations running parallel to the long axis are evident under magnification on one bead.

We recovered three beads made of an unidentified, soft black stone (Fig. 13-7) from Site G-154, in the Unit 30 level. We found these beads in association with Tilarán Phase ceramics. The beads are disk-shaped and appear to have been produced by cutting sections off of a longer tube. Unlike the beads from G-150, these disk-shaped beads are not ground smooth on the ends. The sides of the beads do, however, show evidence of production through grinding. Metric data for all six beads are presented in Table 13-1.

Figure 13-3.
Half-celt avian pendant fragment. Scale in cm. Photograph by Fran Mandel-Sheets.

Figure 13-4.
The probable shape and size of the complete half-celt avian pendant. Actual size. Drawing by Mark Chenault.

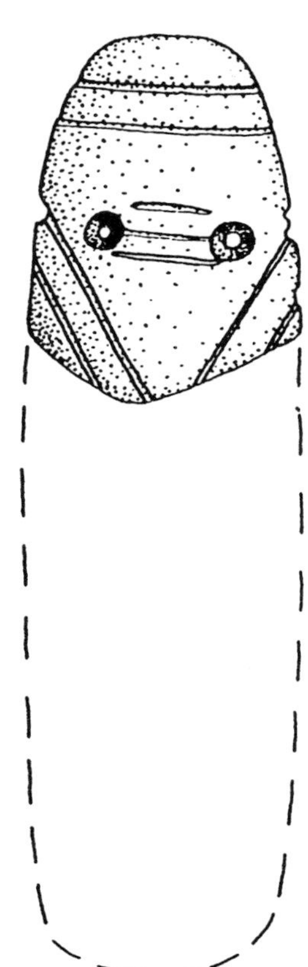

Figure 13-5.
Pear-shaped stone pendant. Photograph by Fran Mandel-Sheets.

Figure 13-6.
Greenstone beads form site G-150. Scale in cm. Photograph by Fran Mandel-Sheets.

TABLE 13-1
METRIC DATA FOR BEADS

Site	*Operation and Lot*	*Length (cm)*	*Diameter (cm)*
G-150	C-5/2	.5	.4
	C-5/2	.5	.4
	C-8/2	.6	.4
G-154	IC-2	.5	.5
	IC-2	.3	.4
	A-2	.3	.4

INTERPRETATION

The small sample size does not allow detailed interpretations of lapidary work in the Arenal basin; however, some patterns are apparent. For example, the three greenstone pendants are broken, and each shows signs of reworking. This reworking suggests that the materials from which the objects are made were highly valued, and that damaged pieces were reworked rather than thrown away. This is likely because the raw materials were from sources as far away as the Nicoya and Santa Elena peninsulas. This indicates that the inhabitants of the Arenal region either journeyed to the sources to obtain materials directly, or participated in long-distance trade for raw or finished materials. If the latter is true, then the self-sufficiency evident in other aspects of Arenal society (Chaps. 1, 17) was not complete.

Another apparent pattern is the predominance of greenstone use during Zoned Bichrome times. This is also the case elsewhere in Costa Rica (Snarskis 1981b). It appears that carving techniques used in greenstone production were the same as those used elsewhere in the country. There is no proof that the objects were produced in the Arenal area; however, the ability to work the materials is apparent in the signs of reworking and in the unfinished nature of the tear-drop-shaped stone pendant.

We found all provenienced greenstone artifacts in mortuary contexts; although we found the bossed bar pendant at a habitation site (G-163), we

Figure 13-7.
Black stone beads from site G-154. Scale in cm. Photograph by Fran Mandel-Sheets.

Figure 13-8.
Gold pendant from chest area of Burial 1 at the Silencio Cemetery (G-150-B5). Scale at bottom is in cm. It dates to about the middle of the first millennium AD. *Photograph by Fran Mandel-Sheets.*

found it in a pit that may have contained a human burial. This suggests that the pendants may not have been undergoing recarving, but that the broken areas had been ground smooth and the pieces used as they were, or interred shortly after as grave offerings.

GOLD PENDANT

We found one small gold avian pendant (Fig. 13-8) in a soil sample in Burial 1 at site G-150, El Silencio (Chap. 6). The burial was in a rock-lined tomb in lot B5. The occupant of the tomb was not accompanied by other grave goods. The pendant measures 1.2 cm in height, with a wing span of 1.5 cm, and a maximum body thickness of 0.12 cm. On the basis of density, it is estimated by Mueller and a goldsmith in San José to be of solid 22K gold.

The pendant was produced by lost-wax casting and was probably cast as a single piece. It appears to have been fashioned from six separate pieces of wax, which were joined by wax welds or pressure before casting (Chenault and Mueller 1984: fig. 2). No evidence remains of the sprue that conducted the molten metal into the mold.

After casting, the rough edges along the wings were removed with a coarse file or abrasive to give a smooth outline, but these edges were not finely finished. The surface of the body was smoothed and polished with a very fine abrasive, used principally with a vertical motion but occasionally obliquely. Finishing of the front was much finer than of the back. The high polish on the inside of the jump ring, grooves worn into the back of the head, and wear polish on the lower edge leave no doubt that this piece was worn, rather than made specifically for a burial.

As Bray (1978, 1981), observes, the Isthmus (including Colombia, Panama, and Costa Rica) forms a single metalworking "province" in terms of style and preference for lost-wax casting and copper-gold alloys. Within the Isthmus, objects were widely traded in Precolumbian times. Thus, it is not surprising that, stylistically, the pendant seems to be something of a hybrid. In size, shape of the tail, beak, and eyes, it resembles some of the small solid gold "eagles" found almost exclusively in the Atlantic Watershed and Central Highlands of Costa Rica and dated to Late Period V–Period VI (AD 800–1550) (Snarskis 1981b: figs. 185, 186). According to Snarskis, they were probably made there. Stylistically, those Snarskis illustrates would fall into Aguilar's (1972:34–37) Guapiles and Línea Vieja types, which he claims are highly localized styles. The El Silencio specimen differs from these in shape of wings and lacks the body bulge. The arch of the wings suggests more southern associations, such as with the Diquis subarea or the Veraguas region of Panama (Lothrop 1950, 1963). It differs from both of these types in that it is simpler in design, with the body, wings, and tail making up a single flat element. It also lacks the strongly hooked beak and claws typical of the Veraguas style. Pendants with similar bases and arched wings, but usually more elaborate, have also been found in the Diquis region (Ferrero 1981: pl. 26b, 27b; Snarskis 1981b: fig. 266). Dates range from AD 700 to 1500. The El Silencio pendant most closely resembles, in both style and material, the *aguilitas* (little eagles) of the Atlantic Watershed and Central Highlands. It was likely produced in one of those areas, possibly the Línea Vieja region, which was an early center of metalworking (Bray 1981). It may have been traded into the Arenal region via the Arenal River Valley.

There is little question that metallurgy developed in South America and moved northward. It is generally believed to have reached Costa Rica between AD 500–700. While not abundant, there is archaeological evidence of imports and local copies of Colombian and Panamanian forms as early as AD 500–800 in the Atlantic Watershed region (ibid.; Snarskis 1985). Due to the scarcity of gold objects found in Guanacaste, and their close stylistic resemblances to the gold artifacts of the Línea Vieja and Diquis areas, it is thought that metallurgy may have arrived late in Greater Nicoya (Ferrero 1981). Prior to the uncovering of the El Silencio pendant, no dated archaeological specimen older than AD 1000 had been found in northwestern Costa Rica (Bray 1981).

Metal objects from controlled archaeological investigations are rare in any part of the Isthmus, and well-dated pieces are even scarcer. Two other specimens that are very similar stylistically to the Silencio piece have come from excavated contexts in Costa Rica. A virtually identical piece was recovered from Barrial de Heredia (Snarskis, personal communication, 1985). It was found beneath a large quadrangular structure and is dated to about AD 900, based on evidence provided by Guanacaste-Nicoya polychrome vessels and three radiocarbon dates from tombs beneath the same structure (Snarskis 1985: 9–11). A single tumbaga (gold-copper alloy) specimen was found in a tomb on San Lucas Island in the Gulf of Nicoya and has been dated to the Late Polychrome, or Period VI (AD 1300–1500) (Creamer 1983). Although this example is stylistically similar, its workmanship is inferior to that of the El Silencio pendant. The late dates of these two pieces, compared to that of El Silencio, may indicate continuity of the style over at least several centuries, or possibly the curation of gold.

It has generally been assumed that goldwork in Costa Rica evolved from simple to more complex forms (Aguilar 1972; Ferrero 1981; Bray 1984). Aguilar (1972), in a stylistic analysis of materials in the Banco de Oro, San José, proposes such a chronological sequence. If accurate, the seriation would place the El Silencio pendant early in the sequence because of the triangular shape of the tail and lack of embellishment of other features. This scheme is based on poorly provenienced and undated specimens, however. The history of art is replete with examples of evolution in the reverse direction. This, together with the foregoing evidence of simple forms from late archaeological contexts, suggests that such chronologies should be applied only with caution and close attention to contextual data. An additional problem for dating archaeological metals is that, because of their durability and value, the time of manufacture need not coincide with time of use or discard.

Dating of the pendant from El Silencio is somewhat problematic. The corrected radiocarbon date from a large charcoal sample from the tomb in which it was found is AD 145 (244) 338. The tomb definitely predates the fall of tephra Unit 41, which was found intact above it. This unit has been tentatively correlated with the top of Unit 5 from the Tajo sequence, or possibly Unit 4 (Melson, this volume). The eruption that deposited this unit is estimated to have occurred about AD 800. Only Silencio Phase ceramics were associated with this burial (Hoopes, personal communication, 1985). The AD 244 intercept seems early in comparison with both dated goldwork from other parts of Costa Rica and stratigraphic and ceramic evidence. The carbon sample is from tomb fill, which may have incorporated earlier material. Therefore, the dating may not be reliable. Given the simplicity of the design of the pendant, the general time frame for metalwork in Costa Rica, stylistic similarities, and stratigraphic relationships, it can be tentatively dated to the middle of the first millennium AD.

In lower Central America, gold is often taken as the hallmark of chiefly status and long-distance trade in luxury goods; however, the discovery of a mold for lost-wax casting in Guanacaste (Lange and Accola 1979) documents at least some local manufacture in northwestern Costa Rica. The mold is believed to date to the Late Polychrome Period (AD 1200–1500).

It is possible that the Arenal gold pendant was manufactured locally. Gold and copper both occur in small quantities in the Cordillera de Guanacaste (ibid.; Lange 1984b), but we do not know whether these resources were exploited prehistorically. Gold has been mined at the Chiquito

River, 5 km from the Silencio cemetery, for almost a century, and this source may have been exploited prehistorically. There is no direct evidence for this, however, and geologists now working there do not consider it likely. All known aboriginal gold was native gold (i.e., free metal in the form of flakes or nuggets); that mined today is found in quartz veins and in hydrothermally deposited clays. We do not know whether native gold was ever available at the Chiquito River in sufficient quantities for aboriginal use. Gold is also found in the Líbano area southwest of Lake Arenal.

The avian motif makes up a large percentage of Precolumbian goldwork in Costa Rica. The significance attributed to this form in lower Central America has ranged from that of a general symbol of status and power to more specific representations of psychic or physical long-distance journeys to exotic places imbued with power (Helms 1979), or the god Sibu embodied in a *zopilote* (buzzard) (Meléndez 1984). More recently, Snarskis (1985) has suggested that they represent birds drying their feathers after a damp night or rainfall. The latter two interpretations are not, however, of symbolic meaning, but of pictorial representation. They serve as a reminder, however, that Precolumbian metalwork has an aesthetic element, as well as a possible symbolic meaning, that these are decorative items to be worn, and that the source of artistic forms—and symbols—is as often the mundane world as it is the exotic "other world."

SUMMARY AND CONCLUSIONS

Like most peoples, the Arenal-area residents tended to value exotic items. Although most of the jewelry from this area was recovered from mortuary contexts, the majority was also apparently worn rather than produced solely for burial offerings. Whether the possession of such items indicates status differences is uncertain. Using ethnographic analogues and its location in a possibly elite section of the El Silencio graveyard, we can surmise that the gold pendant more likely is an indicator of status.

The materials, manufacturing techniques, and stylistic elements of the jewelry from the Proyecto Prehistórico Arenal confirm the contact of the area with both Greater Nicoya and the Atlantic Watershed regions from a very early date. The greenstone artifacts point to connections with Greater Nicoya, while the gold points toward the Atlantic. As in other parts of Costa Rica, the Zoned Bichrome Period (Arenal Phase) seems to have been the predominant time of greenstone use. Dating of manufacture and use of the gold pendant is problematic, but it is tentatively estimated at the middle of the first millennium AD. This is an early date for metalwork in Costa Rica.

Greenstone was worked using the same methods employed for carving jade, although no jadeite artifacts were found. We found ornaments of a wide variety of materials and forms, including pendants of metabasite, sepentinite, hydrothermally altered gabbro, and siltstone, and beads of greenstone and an unidentified black stone. These raw materials probably could not be obtained locally, but the sample is too small to determine the means of their procurement from the Nicoya or Santa Elena peninsulas. Likewise, material for the gold pendant seems unlikely to have come from the Arenal area.

The ground- and polished stone jewelry shows some signs of reworking and possible local production, but the manufacture of the gold pendant within the area is not likely. It was more likely an import from the Atlantic Watershed region, perhaps from the Línea Vieja area, a known center for the production of gold.

14

Phytolith Records from the Proyecto Prehistórico Arenal

DOLORES R. PIPERNO

INTRODUCTION

Some plants absorb soluble silica from groundwater and transfer it from their roots into their aerial organs. It polymerizes there to form solid deposits within and around plant cells. When the plant decays, very durable and faithful replicas of living cells are left behind in soils. These silicified cells are called phytoliths.

The analysis of phytoliths has only recently been systematically applied to reconstructions of prehistoric economies and environments. Comparative collections of tropical plants have only recently been initiated, and we know that some plants do not produce phytoliths. Some contribute shapes that are repeated in unrelated species; however, a large number of wild and domesticated species form diagnostic phytoliths, contributing a reliable and informative paleobotanical record (Pearsall 1989, Piperno 1984, 1985a, b, c, 1988; Bozarth 1986). Although phytoliths are subject to some horizontal and vertical movement in soils after deposition, taphonomic studies have shown that they are no more mobile than pollen grains (Piperno 1985b, c, 1988).

For this study, we analyzed thirty samples from seven sites. They were from deposits in two graveyards, G-150 and G-155, and five habitation sites, G-154, G-161, G-163, G-164, and G-175. The habitation sites span most of the range of occupation thus far uncovered in the Arenal area, from approximately 2000 BC to AD 1500. Table 14-1 summarizes the samples analyzed, their associated cultural periods, and phytolith content.

EXTRACTION TECHNIQUES

We recovered phytoliths from archaeological deposits through laboratory separation techniques involving soil particle size separation and chemical flotation. We deflocculated soil samples by repeated stirring in a 5% solution of sodium bicarbonate. We then wet-sieved them through a 270-mesh screen to separate the sand fraction, the portion greater than 50 μm in diameter. The next step was the removal of clay, the soil fraction less than 5 μm in diameter. This was accomplished by gravity sedimentation.

Next, we divided the remaining silt fraction into fine (5–20μm) and coarse (20–50 μm) fractions by gravity sedimentation. We then placed between 1 g and 1.5 g of each silt fraction and the sand fraction in a test tube. We removed carbonates by a 10% solution of hydrochloric acid, followed by washing with water. We destroyed organic material by adding concentrated nitric acid and heating the samples.

We then added a heavy liquid solution of specific gravity 2.3 comprised of cadmium iodide and potassium iodide to the samples. We removed, washed, dried, and mounted the floating phytolith fraction on slides in Permount, after mixing and centrifuging. The phytolith content of the samples ranged from abundant to absent. Table 14-1 lists the relative quantities of phytoliths in each sample.

PHYTOLITH PRODUCTION AND TAXONOMY

Maize (*Zea mays*) and squash (*Cucurbita* spp.) are the only domesticates expected to have been present in the study area that have currently recognizable phytoliths. The maize identification procedure uses a multivariate analysis. The rinds of squash produce a distinctive, circular "scalloped" phytolith (Bozarth 1986). All other major tropical domesticates, including manioc (*Manihot escu-*

TABLE 14-1
SOIL SAMPLES ANALYZED AND ASSOCIATED CULTURAL PERIODS

Site	*Phase*	*Phytolith Content*
G-163-B3	Tronodora	Abundant
G-163-C2	Tronodora	Common
G-163-D1	Tronodora	Common
G-163-S3, stone feature 150cm BPGS	Tronodora	Rare
G-163-A6/1, from interior of vessel	Tronodora	Not common
G-163-I14, posthole #1	Tronodora	Rare
G-163-I14, posthole #2	Tronodora	Rare
G-163-R3, posthole #2	Tronodora	Common
G-163-W19, posthole #4	Tronodora	Rare
G-163-V33, on top of Aguacate Formation	Tronodora	Absent
G-163-R4, posthole #4	Tronodora	Absent
G-163-W20, posthole #5	Tronodora	Rare
G-175-B1	Arenal	Not common
G-175-B3	Arenal	Rare
G-175-B5	Arenal	Rare
G-175-B7	Arenal	Not common
G-164-W20, posthole #5	Arenal	Rare
G-164-B6, trash feature on top of burials	Arenal	Abundant
G-164-B7, below trash associated with burials	Arenal	Not common
G-155-C3	Tilarán	Rare
G-155-C1	Tilarán	Rare
G-161-B5	Arenal	Common
G-154-A2	Tilarán	Rare
G-154-I1	Tilarán	Rare
G-150-B5, elite graves?	Silencio	Rare
G-150-C4, elite graves?	Silencio	Abundant
G-150-D5, elite graves?	Silencio	Common
G-150-H1, large graveyard	Silencio	Rare
G-150-H4, large graveyard	Silencio	Rare
G-150-H6, large graveyard	Silencio	Abundant

lenta Krantz), otoe (*Xanthossoma* spp.), peppers (*Capsicum annuum*), sweet potato (*Ipomoea batatas*), and cotton (*Gossypium barbadense*), produce either no phytoliths or kinds also found in wild species. Although the phytolith record for crop plants is limited and we found no evidence on possible vegecultural systems, the presence or absence of maize and squash is very important to determine.

Many wild species, including palms (many of which were domesticated or tended prehistorically), and members of the Marantaceae (arrowroot family), Compositae (sunflower family), Cyperaceae (Sedge family), Moraceae (elm family), and Urticaceae (nettle family), produce identifiable phytoliths. Table 14-2 summarizes phytolith production and taxonomic significance in the fifteen hundred species that make up the modern phytolith collection.

TABLE 14-2
PRODUCTION AND TAXONOMIC SIGNIFICANCE OF PHYTOLITHS IN VARIOUS FAMILIES

Spore-bearing families in which phytolith production is high and taxonomy significant
Hymenophyllaceae, Polypodiaceae, Selaginellaceae
Monocotyledon families in which phytolith production is often absent
Alismaceae, Amaryllidaceae, Araceae, Butomaceae, Cyclanthaceae, Dioscoreaceae, Iridaceae, Liliaceae, Xyridaceae
Monocotyledon families in which phytolith production is often abundant and taxomony significant
Cyperaceae, Commelinaceae, Gramineae, Heliconeaceae, Marantaceae, Ochidaceae, Palmae
Dicotyledon families in which phytolith production is often absent or rare
Amaranthaceae, Bignoneaceae, Bixaceae, Caricaceae, Chenopodiaceae, Convulvulaceae, Labiatae, Lauraceae, Malvaceae, Malpighiaceae, Melastomataceae, Myrtaceae, Polygonaceae, Rhizophoraceae, Rubiaceae, Solanaceae
Dicotyledon families in which phytolith taxonomy is often not significant
Bignoniaceae, Bombacaceae, Chloranthaceae, Combretaceae, Euphorbiaceae, Labiatae, Leguminosae, Malvaceae, Melastomataceae, Rubiaceae, Sterculiaceae, Verbenaceae
Dicotyledon families in which production is often abundant and taxonomy significant
Acanthaceae, Annonaceae, Boraginaceae, Burseraceae, Chrysobalanaceae, Compositae, Cucurbitaceae, Dilleniaceae, Loranthaceae, Magnoliaceae, Moraceae, Piperaceae, Podostemaceae, Ulmaceae, Urticaceae

Note: Assessments of phytolith production and taxonomy are based on analysis of plants predominantly from lower Central America. Detailed descriptions and classifications of phytoliths can be found in Piperno (1985a, 1988). Phytoliths listed as not having taxonomic significance are defined as those not specific to at least the family in which a particular species is found.

ECONOMIC PLANTS

We recovered maize phytoliths from the following excavation units: G-175-B7, G-163-B3, G-163-C2, G-163-D1, and probably G-150-H6. We recovered phytoliths potentially diagnostic of maize of the "cross-shaped type" in substantial numbers from units G-163-A6/1, G-164-B6, and G-164-B7; however, their sizes and three-dimensional shapes are indicative of wild grasses, not maize. Table 14-3 contains the sizes and characteristics of cross-shaped phytoliths from these units.

The maize-bearing deposits from habitation sites G-163 and G-175 date to the Tronadora Phase and the Arenal Phase, respectively. G-150 is a large Silencio Phase cemetery. We collected the maize remains from operations located away from the main burial areas. We encountered maize pollen in three samples from G-150 and tentatively identified it in one sample from G-163 (Chap. 15). We retrieved macro-maize remains from sites G-150, G-154, and G-163 (Chap. 16).

Abundant maize phytoliths recovered from the Tronadora Phase site G-163 confirm the presence of this domesticate from the earliest dated sedentary occupation of the Arenal area. Because maize phytoliths are deposited by the decay of vegetative structures (leaves, husks, tassels, but in this case most probably leaves—see below), maize phytolith evidence indicates onsite cultivation. The presence of maize phytoliths from Arenal Phase occupations at G-175, where we retrieved neither pollen nor macrobotanical remains, indicates that maize cultivation continued during this phase.

The identification of maize phytoliths rests on the size and form of cross-shaped phytoliths found only in maize. These attributes are short axis length, three-dimensional structure, and percentages of cross-shaped phytoliths in leaf specimens. They have been determined for twenty-three races of maize, six races of teosinte, and thirty-nine wild grasses (Piperno 1984; Piperno and Starczak 1985; Piperno 1988).

To provide a measure of interpopulation variability of wild phytoliths, we studied two leaves from the same plant and four replicate samples of different plants, each from a different environmental region, in eight species in which cross-shaped phytoliths were most common. In five

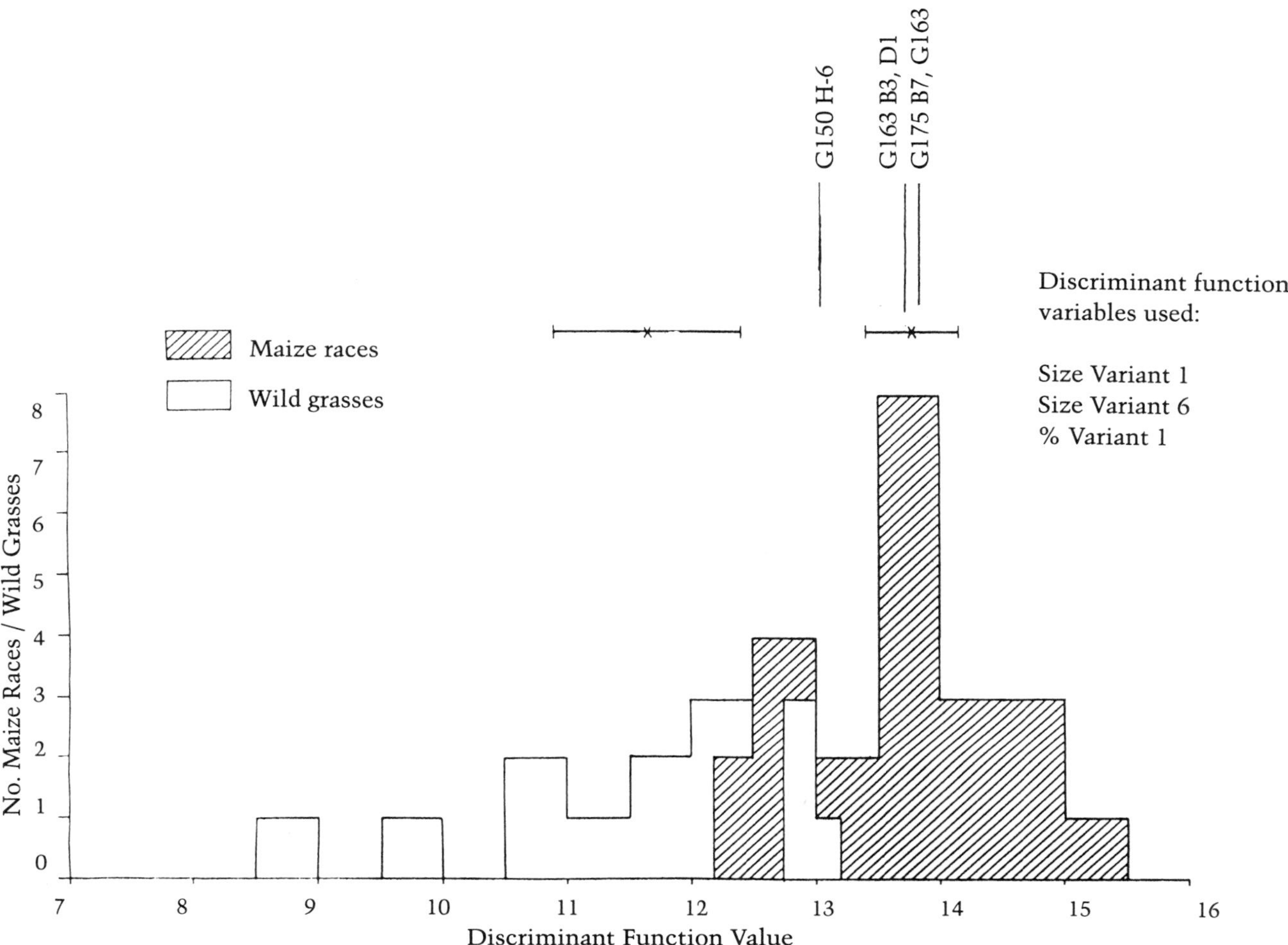

Figure 14-1.
Discriminant function values for maize and wild grasses, Arenal Project sites.

TABLE 14-3
CHARACTERISTICS OF CROSS-SHAPED PHYTOLITHS FROM THE SITES

Site	*% Variant 1*	*6*	*7*	*× Size Variant 1*	*6*	*N*
G-163-B3 (maize)	85	13	2	13.1	12.1	60
G-163-C2 (maize)	97	3	—	12.7	13.5	30
G-163-D1 (maize)	88	12	—	12.9	11.6	40
G-163-A6/1	50	50	—	11.4	11.4	10
G-175-B7 (maize)	73	27	—	13.6	11.9	15
G-150-H6	82	16	2	12.5	12.0	35
G-164-B6	87	13	—	11.7	12.0	15
G-164-B7	40	40	20	12.0	11.8	4

races of maize, we studied leaves, husks, and tassels of four replicate samples from distinct plants (Piperno and Starczak 1985; Piperno 1988).

There is no wild grass yet examined that, like maize, combines the following attributes: large-sized, cross-shaped phytoliths; dominant frequencies of "Variant 1" cross-shaped phytoliths; a three-dimensional form in which both sides of the phytolith are cross-shaped; and high percentages of cross-shapes among all short-cell (dumbbell and cross-shaped) types.

We tested these observations with a multivariate analysis using a discriminant function. The results (Fig. 14-1) indicate that modern maize and wild grasses can be separated into two groups based on these measurements. Fig. 14-1 shows two clusters, one corresponding to maize, shown in crosshatch, and the other to wild grasses in an open bar.

The results of the analysis for the archaeological cross-shaped phytoliths are shown above the results from modern grasses in Figure 14-1. This figure is based on the measurements summarized in Table 14-3. The discriminant function values for cross-shapes from G-163 (n = 130) and G-175 (n = 15) classify them clearly as maize, as they fall within the 95% confidence interval about the mean of modern maize. Cross-shapes from G-150 (n = 35) do not classify as wild grasses or as maize, because they fall outside of the 95% confidence intervals for both. I believe some of these phytoliths are from maize, but at this site, not enough maize was deposited to overwhelm the phytoliths from the wild Panicoid grasses present and give a definitive statistical picture of maize.

We based the multivariate analysis of the modern specimens solely on leaf phytoliths. Maize husks and tassels also contribute cross-shaped phytoliths, but in sizes and three-dimensional structures very different from those found in leaves (Piperno 1988) and uncharacteristic of the archaeological cross-shapes. I believe, therefore, that the archaeological maize phytoliths are predominantly from leaves and constitute evidence for on-site maize cultivation.

We recovered no squash phytoliths from the deposits. These phytoliths have a distinctive scalloped shape and are found in the rinds of various *Cucurbita* species. Testing of rinds from *Cucurbita* in Panama has indicated that not all squashes produce this kind of phytolith (Piperno 1988). Therefore, their absence in the Arenal deposits does not necessarily indicate the absence of *Cucurbita*.

OTHER ECONOMIC AND ENVIRONMENTAL RECONSTRUCTION

There is phytolith evidence of a number of other kinds of plants in the archaeological deposits, and their frequencies show marked changes from the earliest sedentary occupation (Tronadora Phase) to the latest (Tilarán Phase). Many other phytolith types not represented in the modern comparative collection also occur in the Arenal soils. I believe that many are from the seeds and leaves of arboreal dicotyledons because they occur in substantial frequencies in modern soils underneath five hundred–year-old rain forest on Barro Colorado Island, Panama (ibid.). As the modern phytolith collection is expanded, it should become possible to identify these forms.

Among the identifiable taxa are *Trichomanes* spp., ferns of wet forests; *Guatteria* spp., mature forest trees; *Chusquea* spp., forest bamboos; palms (the Palmae phytoliths are of a type found in genera such as *Scheelia, Manicaria*, and *Oenocarpus*); *Heliconia* spp., herbaceous plants of disturbed vegetation; wild grasses belonging to the Panicoid (tall grass), Chloridoid (short grass), and Festucoid (humid grasses) subfamilies; members of the Marantaceae, herbaceous plants of tropical forests, and the Chrysobalanaceae, mature forest trees.

Percentage phytolith frequencies from the deposits can be found in Table 14-4. Much of the diversity in the phytolith record occurs in assemblages from soils taken during the 1984 field season. Samples taken during the 1985 season are predominantly from postholes and other "low-energy" repositories, where pollen and phytoliths might have been subject to less grinding and crushing. In these samples, phytolith content is generally low, however, and when phytoliths are present in substantial numbers they are often of a uniform type from the grass family.

In Table 14-4, notable shifts in the occurrence and percentages of phytolith types are evident. Phytoliths from *Trichomanes* and *Chusquea*, which are indicators of mature wet forest, are found only in deposits from G-163, the Tronadora Phase site. Palm phytoliths are found in their highest frequencies here. *Guatteria* is more common in G-163 than elsewhere; the only other site where it occurs is G-154 (Tilarán Phase), where we found it in small numbers. Phytoliths that may be from the fruits of the Chrysobalanaceae, a family of wet forest trees, are common in G-163.

TABLE 14-4
PERCENTAGE PHYTOLITH FREQUENCIES OF MAJOR IDENTIFIABLE PHYTOLITH TYPES

Phytolith Type	*G-163*				*G-175*	
	B3	*C2*	*D1*	*R3*	*B1*	*B7*
Gramineae (total of weedy types)	45	39	47	5	50	89
Saddle-shaped	17	12	18	5	36	51
Dumbbell	27	23	28	—	14	27
Cross-shaped	1	4	1	—	4	6
Festucoid	—	—	3	—	—	—
Chusquea	1	*	*	No	No	No
Trichomanes	*	*	*	No	No	No
Palmae	4	24	4	7	No	No
Chrysobalanaceae	31	25	*	85	*	*
Heliconia	*	No	No	No	No	No
Guatteria spp.	No	*	No	No	No	No
Marantaceae	No	No	No	2	No	No
Unidentified forest types	*	*	*	No	No	No

	G-164		*G-150*			*G-161*
	B6	*B7*	*C4*	*D5*	*H6*	*B5*
Gramineae (total of weedy types)	98	93	51	74	88	83
Saddle-shaped	28	60	11	70	56	40
Dumbbell	65	30	37	3	20	42
Cross-shaped	2	2	1	1	9	—
Festucoid	3	2	2	—	—	1
Chusquea	No	No	No	No	No	No
Trichomanes	No	No	No	No	No	No
Palmae	No	2	No	No	No	No
Chrysobalanaceae	No	*	No	No	No	No
Heliconia	2	No	No	No	No	No
Guatteria spp.	No	No	No	No	No	No
Marantaceae	No	No	No	No	No	No
Unidentified forest types	No	No	No	No	No	No

Note: * indicates present in frequencies of less than 1%.

In addition, virtually all of the unknown phytoliths, which I believe may be from the fruits of arboreal dicots, occurred at this site.

The abundance of forest elements found in G-163, but not in deposits of later time periods, indicates that forested environments were common in the Tronadora Phase but were denuded by successive occupations of the area. The frequent occurence of arboreal fruit phytoliths earlier, but not later, may indicate a concurrent shift away from the use of arboreal resources, perhaps to a greater reliance on field and garden crops.

The frequency of phytoliths from weedy kinds of grasses increases from a minimum of 5%, found in a postmold sample from G-163-R3, to over 80% in Arenal and later-phase samples. Most of the other Tronadora Phase deposits show higher percentages of weedy grasses, but still substantially lower than in later deposits. It appears that some habitat modification was occurring near G-163, but not to the severe extent that occurred later.

There is significant negative evidence relevant to issues such as the chronology of the introduction of peach palm (*Bactris gasipaes*) and on the use of other kinds of palms. Notable for their absence in the palm phytolith record are conical-shaped forms, which are found in all species of such genera as *Bactris, Acrocomia, Astrocaryum, Geonoma*, and *Desmoncus*. My extractions of palm seeds, leaves, petioles, and trunks have shown that all parts of a single species produce large numbers of the same kind of phytolith (Piperno 1988). Palms are unique in doing so.

Quantitative analysis of phytolith content in seeds of peach palm reveals a value of 1.8% (of dry weight), an amount nearly equivalent to those found in grass leaves. The absence of conical palm phytoliths is strong evidence that peach palm and all of the foregoing genera were not consumed or utilized in the Arenal area at the sites investigated. The kind of phytolith isolated from the deposits is produced by such genera as *Scheelia, Oenocarpus,* and *Elaeis.*

SUMMARY

Phytolith analysis of sites from the Proyecto Arenal has revealed the presence of maize in Tronadora, Arenal, and Tilarán Phase occupations. We recovered no squash phytoliths, a finding that may have more to do with the particular varieties of squashes grown than with the absence of the domesticate.

Seed crop cultivation is the only form of agriculture that can be identified positively in the phytolith record. Root crops such as manioc and sweet potato leave no identifiable silicified remains; hence, the contribution of vegeculture to prehistoric subsistence systems in Arenal and other tropical regions remains difficult to ascertain. Corn's low dietary contribution, less than 12%, indicated by stable carbon isotope analysis, may provide evidence for vegeculture.

We have established the exploitation of tree crops with the macrobotanical record (Chap. 16). Further evidence for arboriculture may be found in the numerous palm phytoliths present at G-163, although it is not possible to distinguish wild and domesticated palm phytoliths. The phytolith record indicates that genera such as *Bactris,* which includes peach palm, *Acrocomia,* and *Astrocaryum,* were not exploited.

The phytolith record has also provided evidence that moist forested environments were present around the Tronadora Phase site, G-163. The absence or dramatic reduction of forest indicators, along with substantial increases in weedy grasses in the phytolith assemblages of later-phase occupations, show that tropical forest clearance accelerated after about 500 BC. Although the prehistoric inhabitants of the Arenal area remained economically self-sufficient and maintained low population densities, they, like other tropical forest peoples, exerted a considerable effect on their environment.

15

Pollen Evidence for Prehistoric Environment and Subsistence Activities

KAREN H. CLARY

INTRODUCTION

The Arenal Project has conducted interdisciplinary research in northwestern Costa Rica using specialists from biology, volcanology, pedology, agronomy, and chemistry to achieve project objectives focused on human ecology (Chap. 1). We collected forty-seven pollen samples from features such as postholes, vessels, and burials at nine sites and submitted them to the Castetter Laboratory for Ethnobotanical Studies (University of New Mexico-Albuquerque) for analysis (Table 15-1). The chronology of the sites ranges from the Tronadora Phase through the Tilarán Phase. The goals of the pollen analysis were to obtain evidence for the use of plant species by site inhabitants and to obtain evidence of vegetation extant during site occupation.

Analysis showed that the pollen was poorly preserved. Most of the samples contained fewer than one thousand pollen grains per gram of sediment. We noted few taxa. In spite of low pollen numbers, however, the analysis yielded evidence of prehistoric maize utilization and reflected vegetational disturbance that may have resulted from human impacts.

POLLEN EXTRACTION

The lab processed the samples using a modification of the method described by Mehringer (1967).

1. A 40-g soil sample was taken from the field sample.

TABLE 15-1
NUMBERS OF POLLEN GRAINS COUNTED IN SAMPLES FROM THE PROYECTO PREHISTÓRICO ARENAL

	POLLEN SAMPLE & LOCATION																	
		G-150 – surface pinch	G-150-B5	G-150-C4	G-150-C7b (insufficient pollen)	G-150-D3	G-150-D6	G-150-H1-30	G-150-H4-30	G-150-H5-60 (insufficient pollen)	G-154-A2	G-154-I1	G-155-C1 (insufficient pollen)	G-155-C3	G-161-B7 (insufficient pollen)	G-163-A6/1	G-163-B3 (insufficient pollen)	G-163-C2
Sedges and Grasses	Cyperaceae (sedges)		15	3			1				1							
	Poaceae (grasses)	6	49	53		9	17	6	5		7	12		5*				
	Zea mays L. (maize)	2	(2)				(2)	(1)										
Herbaceous Plants	Cheno-am (chenopod-amar)	2	8	5		1	(1)		(1)									2
	Asteraceae (high spine)	5	20	24		7	1		(1)									
	Asteraceae (low spine)			1					10			6						
	Asteraceae, Liguliflorae			1														
	Convolvulaceae (morning glory)		1					1			(1)							
	Malvaceae (mallows)		2															
	cf. *Phaseolus* sp. (cf. bean)							1			1							
	Polygonum sp. (smartweed)		1															
Herbs, Shrubs, Trees, and Vines	cf. Bauhinia sp. (orchid tree)		1															
	cf. Cycadaceae (cf. cycads)			3								2						
	Malpighiaceae (malpighs)											(1)						
	E-R-A	24	2															
	Euphorbiaceae (spurges)		1				(1)				(1)							1
	Juglandaceae (walnuts)			1														
	Mimosoideae (mimosas)		1															
	Melastomataceae (melastomas)			2														
	cf. *Mortoniodendron*	2										(1)						
	cf. *Persea schiediana*			1														
	Piperales (peppers)	6	1	4		1		2						1				
	Proteaceae (proteas)											(1)						
	Ulmus sp. (elm)		1															
	Pinus sp. (pine)						(2)									(1)		
	Urticales (nettles)	6		3							4	1						1
	Unidentified	11	20	12		8	7	4	1		10			4				2
	Unidentified, too weathered	9	11	29		4	2	3	4		6	3						
Sums	Total number	73	136	142		30	34	18	22		31	27		10		1		6
	Spore Type A		15	19		6	2	+	+		+	+						
	No. Spores	81	26	32		19	8	3	5		1	+		+		2		3
	No. grains per gram of sediment	13,560	3,251	11,095		9,190	395	1,952	514		308	648		2,948		70		1,161

Notes: Numbers in parentheses indicate that these pollen grains were found after the pollen grains had been counted, after sieving the pollen residue through a mesh screen.

G-163-D1	G-163H, posthole 1	G-163H, posthole 5	G-163-H30 (insufficient pollen)	G-163-I14, posthole 1	G-163-I14, posthole 2	G-163-K6, posthole 1	G-163-K7, posthole 1	G-163-R3, posthole 1 (insufficient pollen)	G-163-R3, posthole 3 (insufficient pollen)	G-163-R3, posthole 2	G-163-R4, intrusive fea (insufficient pollen)	G-163-R4, posthole 4 (insufficient pollen)	G-163-S3 (insufficient pollen)	G-163-V33 (insufficient pollen)	G-163-W19 (insufficient pollen)	G-163-W20	G-164-B6	G-164-B7 (insufficient pollen)	G-164-B8	G-164-E27 (insufficient pollen)	G-164-E30/1	G-164-E30/2 (insufficient pollen)	G-170-A6/3 (insufficient pollen)	G-175-B1 (insufficient pollen)	G-175-B3 (insufficient pollen)	G-175-B5 (insufficient pollen)	G-175-B7 (insufficient pollen)	G-182-A2/4	G-182-A2/5
				1		1											2		1										
(1)?																													
(1)																1					4								
				(5)																									
(1)																													
		(1)								2																			
(1)																													
	(1)				(1)					(1)									(1)									(1)	2
																												1	
					(1)		1																						
4	1	1		6	2	1	1			3						1	2		2		4							2	2
+	9	16		1	(1)	2										6			3									9	7
141	69	72		533	200	44	110			235						72	244		59		50							118	327

⁺the presence of the spores was noted

*aggregates of pollen were noted

2. The sample was washed through a 180-μm mesh brass screen with distilled water into a 600-ml beaker.

3. Tablets of fresh, quantified *Lycopodium* spores were dissolved in each sample to serve as a control for pollen degradation or loss during the process, and to calculate absolute pollen sums.

4. Carbonates were removed by adding 50 ml of 40% hydrochloric acid (HCl) to each beaker. When effervescence ceased, each beaker was filled with distilled water and the sediments were allowed to settle for at least 3 hours. The water and dilute HCl were then carefully poured off, and the rinsing process was repeated.

5. Beakers were filled one-third full with distilled water and, without creating a vortex, were stirred with clean stirring rods to suspend sediments and pollen. Five seconds after stirring stopped, the lighter soil particles and the pollen grains were poured off into a second clean beaker, leaving the heavier sand particles behind in the first beaker. The procedure was repeated several times.

6. Silicates were removed by adding 50 ml of hydrofluoric acid (HF) to each beaker. The beaker was allowed to sit overnight and the HF was poured off. Samples were rinsed twice with distilled water.

7. The sediments were transferred to 50-ml test tubes.

8. Organics were removed by the following process. The samples were rinsed with 30 ml glacial acetic acid, centrifuged, and poured off. A fresh acetolysis solution was prepared, of 9 parts acetic anhydride to 1 part sulfuric acid (H_2SO_4). Thirty ml were added to each test tube, stirred, and placed in a hot water bath for 10 minutes. Tubes were removed and cooled, then centrifuged, the liquid poured off, and the contents rinsed with glacial acetic acid. This procedure was repeated.

9. In order to cleanse the samples of acids, the centrifuge tubes were rinsed with distilled water, stirred, centrifuged, and poured off. This was repeated twice.

10. Droplets of the pollen-bearing sediment were placed on microscope slides and fixed with glycerine. A cover slip was placed on each slide and the slides were sealed with fixative.

11. The slides were examined with a Nikon microscope under magnifications of 200×, 400×, and 1,000×. Pollen identification was made using Erdtman (1952), Kapp (1969), Heusser (1971), Bartlett and Barghoorn (1973), Markgraf and D'Antoni (1978), and the comparative collection of fifteen hundred tropical pollen types in the Castetter Lab. To derive relative frequencies, an attempt was made to reach a count of at least 200 pollen grains for each sample (Barkley 1934).

12. When slide preparations were scanned with the microscope, it was found that some of the samples were still laden with humic debris and charcoal, making the location and identification of pollen difficult. These samples were further treated by "floating" the debris from the samples by use of a dispersant (trisodium phosphate in a 5% aqueous solution) followed by successive rinses with distilled water, increasing pollen concentrations by a factor of 2 to 3.

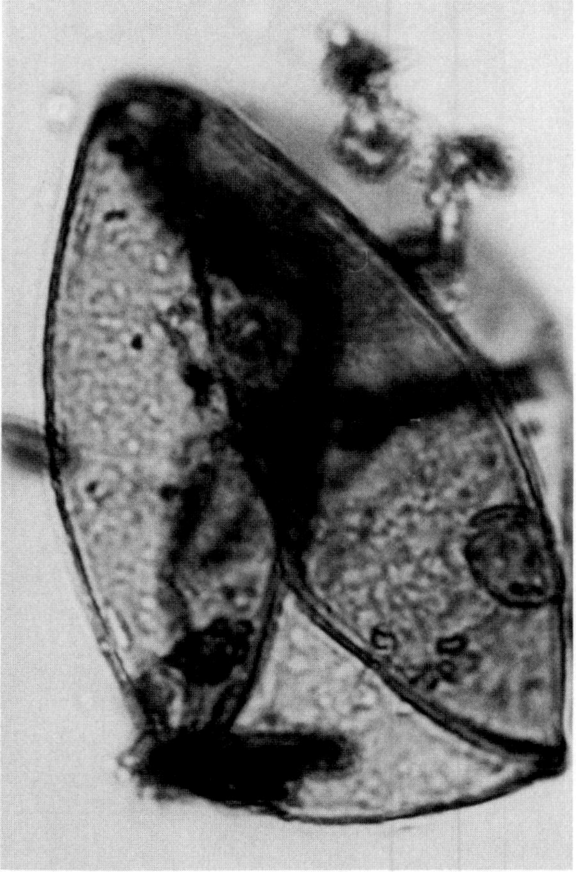

Figure 15-1.
G-150, B-5. Zea mays *L., size, 87.5 x 57.5 micrometers 400x, monoporate, pore in upper center of grain. Photograph by Karen Clary.*

13. The pollen was counted and the absolute pollen number was computed (Stockmarr 1971). The absolute pollen number is derived from the ratio between the number of grains counted and the *Lycopodium* control:

Absolute pollen number =

$$\frac{\text{no. fossil grains} \times \text{no. exotics added}}{\text{no. exotics counted} \times \text{weight (g) of sample}}$$

14. After attempting a 200-grain count, the pollen was examined specifically for maize and other pollen larger than 45 μm. This was accomplished by sieving the pollen residue through a 45-μm mesh screen. The residue was mounted on a microscope slide and examined. This method proved useful in detecting maize pollen in three samples from G-150.

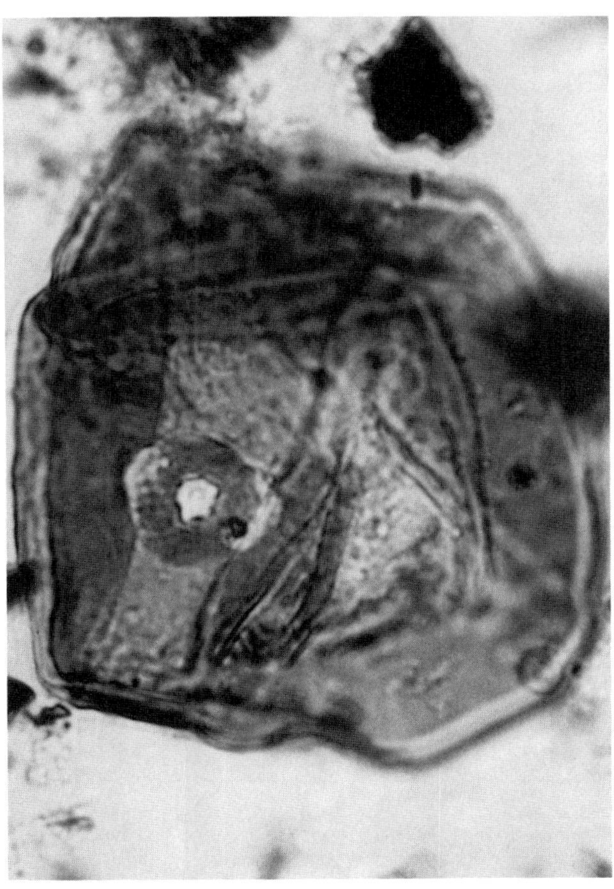

Figure 15-2.
G-150, D-6. Zea mays *L., size, 75 x 75 micrometers, 400x, monoporate, pore at lower left. Photograph by Karen Clary.*

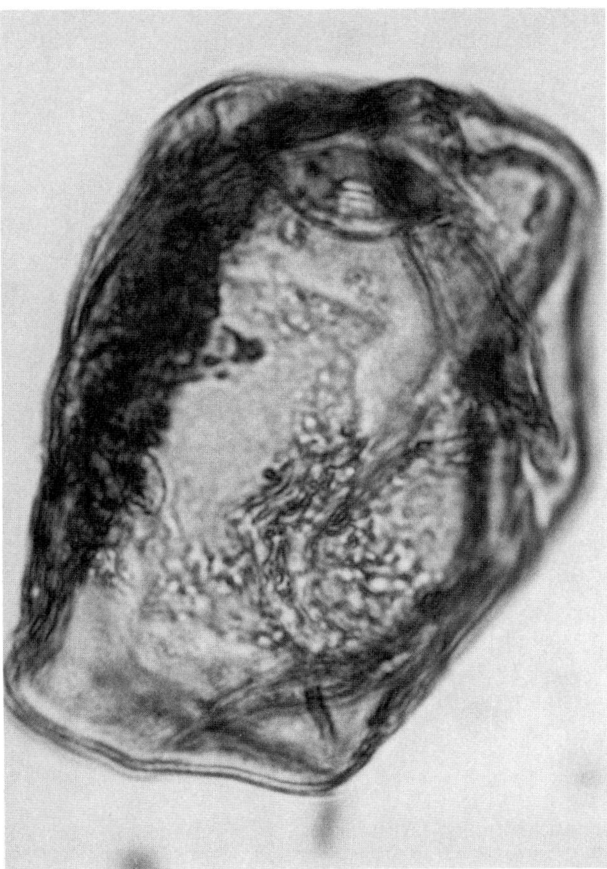

Figure 15-3.
G-150, B-5. Zea mays *L., size 80 x 50 micrometers, 400x, monoporate, pore near top center of grain. Photograph by Karen Clary.*

RESULTS

DESCRIPTION OF PLANT TAXA IN TABLE 15-1

Cyperaceae (Sedge Family)

In this large family of aquatic or terrestrial herbs, the majority of cyperaceous flowers are wind-pollinated. They are widespread and particularly numerous in higher latitudes, usually in wet places (Croat 1978: 151–152).

Poaceae (Grass Family)

The flowers are principally wind-pollinated (ibid.: 121). This category includes all members of the grass family with the exception of maize (*Zea mays* L.).

Zea mays *L. ssp.* mays *(Maize)*

Maize is wind-pollinated, but because of its large size, lack of buoyancy, and shape, the pollen grain does not travel far from its source. Since it falls to earth so rapidly (Leopold and Scott 1957), maize pollen is rarely distributed as evenly within the regional pollen rain as are other pollen types (Bryant and Holloway 1983: 195). The presence and relative frequency of maize pollen is useful in evaluating prehistoric maize field locations or areas of human activity in which maize may have been utilized.

We identified maize pollen by measuring size of the grain, the ratio of the dimensions of the outer ring of the annulus and the size of the inner annular pore related to the size of the grain, and the pattern of the spinules and columnellae as seen by phase contrast microscopy. Together these techniques are reasonably satisfactory for

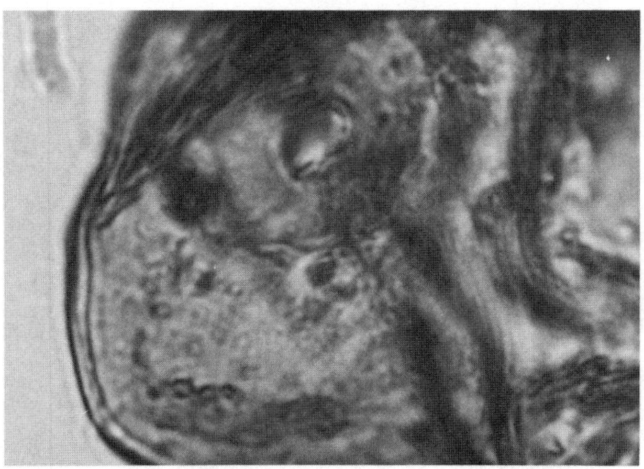

Figure 15-4.
G-150, B-5. Zea mays *L., close-up of pore and endexine (surface) of photo 3, 1000x. Photograph by Karen Clary.*

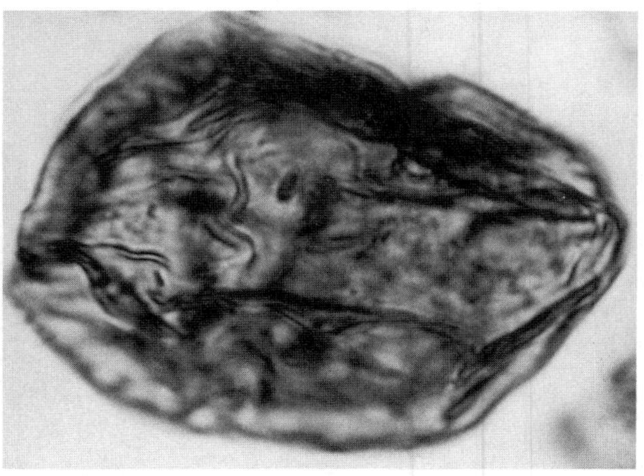

Figure 15-5.
G-150, B-5. Zea mays *L., size 80 x 60 micrometers, 400x, monoporate, pore at upper left. Photograph by Karen Clary.*

TABLE 15-2
COMPARISON OF COSTA RICAN MAIZE POLLEN (*ZEA MAYS* L. *SSP. MAYS*) FROM G-150 WITH MAIZE POLLEN FROM OTHER ARCHAEOLOGICAL CONTEXTS

		Mean (x) Measurements (μm)		
No. Pollen Grains Measured	*Description*	*Inner Annulus*	*Outer Annulus*	*Longest Dimension*
10	Coprolites from 11th-century AD Chaco Canyon, N.M.	5.20	14.30	86.50
46	Cueva Ladrones, Panama	5.20	15.20	86.90
4	Arenal Project, site G-150	6.00	14.30	80.62

TABLE 15-3
MEASUREMENTS OF MAIZE POLLEN (*ZEA MAYS* L.) FROM ARENAL PROJECT, SITE G-150

Provenience	*Longest Dimension × Perpendicular Dimension (μm)*	*Annulus (Outer × Inner)*	*Photo No.*
B-5	1. 80.0 × 60.0	15.0 × 5.0	1
	2. 87.5 × 57.5	12.5 × 5.0	3
	(close-up photo of endexine and annulus for maize in photo 2)		4
D-6	3. 75.0 × 75.0	15.0 × 9.0	2
	4. No measurement		
H-1	5. 80.0 × 60.0	15.0 × 5.0	5
Mean ×	80.62 × 63.13 ± 5.15 ± 8.0	14.38 × 6 ± 1.25 ± 5	

the identification of maize, except in making the important distinction between maize and teosinte (*Zea mays* L., ssp. *mexicana*) and in establishing the specific origin of grains that are atypically small in diameter (Tsukada and Rowley 1964:407).

The fossil maize pollen from G-150 (Figs. 15-1–15-5) compares well to fossil pollen of *Zea mays* L. ssp. *mays* (and not teosinte) from Anasazi coprolites (Chaco Canyon, New Mexico) and Ladrones Cave (Panama) in size (Table 15-2). Some fossil maize pollen grains are smaller than modern ones. Martin and Schoenwetter (1960) believe that fossil maize pollen from the Cienega, Arizona, archaeological site, which ranges in size from 55 μm to 104 μm in diameter, suggests an Archaic Period mixed maize population. Most fossil maize pollen grains are 60 μm to 85 μm in diameter, thus falling below the range for modern maize pollen of 85 μm to 125 μm (Tsukada and Rowley 1964:410). The encountering of maize macrobotanical remains in a maize pollen–bearing sample (D-6) from G-150 and the encountering of maize phytoliths from additional samples from G-150 provide complementary botanical evidence for the presence of maize in the samples examined (Chaps. 14 and 16).

At G-150, we measured four of the five maize pollen grains we encountered (the fifth grain was too crumpled for a useful measurement), with a size range of 75 μm to 87.5 μm. All of the grains were crumpled to some extent. Fully expanded, the grains would be larger in size (Table 15-3), and well within the size range of cultivated maize.

Asteraceae, High Spine (Sunflower Family)

These erect to decumbent herbs or vines, sometimes small trees or shrubs, are both insect- and wind-pollinated (Croat 1978:838). This taxon includes those members of the sunflower family whose pollen contains spines (echinae) 2.0 μm or longer (Kapp 1969).

Asteraceae, Low Spine (Sunflower Family)

This taxon includes those members of the sunflower family whose pollen contains spines (echinae) less than 2.0 μm in length (ibid.).

Convolvulaceae (Morning Glory Family)

These terrestrial herbaceous vines or lianas are without tendrils and have large, showy, funnelform flowers. Most species are bee-pollinated. A number of species probably depend on people for their seed dispersal (Croat 1978:720) and can be expected to occur in areas of human disturbance.

Malvaceae (Mallow Family)

In the Neotropics, this family appears as trees, shrubs, or herbs. Arenal Project pollen appears to be that of herbaceous, weedy mallows. The flowers produce copious pollen and are visited by bees, hummingbirds, and pollen-feeding insects (ibid.:579).

cf. **Phaseolus** *sp. (Beans)*

This pollen type is identifiable to genus level (Fig. 15-6). Wagner (1985:205, 218), in a study of the cultural geography of the Nicoya Peninsula, notes that the Conquest Period aboriginals grew many kinds of beans. During the period in which he performed his fieldwork (the 1950s), beans (black, red, and striped varieties) were an important native crop.

Polygonum *sp. (Smartweed)*

This widespread herb species is known to grow in water and in wet, dry, and moist forests (Croat 1978:379–380).

cf. **Bauhinia** *sp. (Orchid Tree [Caesalpinoideae])*

This is a widespread genus of trees, shrubs, or lianas (Allen 1977:136; Croat 1978:446).

cf. Cycadaceae (Cycad Family)

This gymnosperm family is morphologically distinct from all other gymnosperms because of its palmlike appearance. It is distributed throughout the tropics (Lawrence 1951:357).

Malphigiaceae (Malphig Family)

These are trees, shrubs, or scandent lianas, with the last most common. Flowers are insect-pollinated, and this tropical plant family is widespread (Croat 1978:869).

E-R-A

This pollen taxon comprises three plant families with pollen that has overlapping morphological characteristics (tricolporate, prolate, reticu-

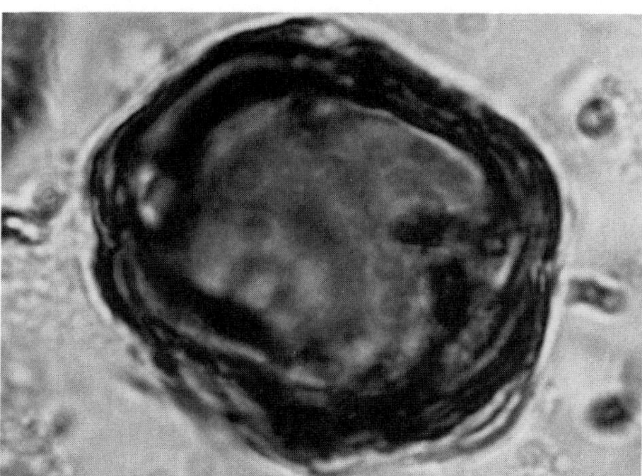

Figure 15-6.
G-150, H-1. cf. Phaseolus *sp., size, 30 micrometer diameter, pericolporate, reticulate, 1000x. Photograph by Karen Clary.*

late, 30–60 μm in length). E-R-A comprises herbs, shrubs, lianas, and trees. Species of Euphorbiaceae (Spurge family), Rubiaceae (Madder family) and Anacardiaceae (Sumac family) are widespread in tropical America (ibid.).

Euphorbiaceae (Spurge Family)

Most species of these are trees, shrubs, lianas, vines, or herbs and are probably insect-pollinated, although a few species are wind-pollinated. They are widely distributed (ibid.: 519–521).

Juglandaceae (Walnut Family)

This family comprises about sixty species, mostly of the north temperate zone, but with one distributional range extending through Central America, along the Andes, to Argentina (Lawrence 1951: 547).

Melastomataceae (Melastoma Family)

This family takes the form of shrubs and small trees, sometimes herbs, rarely vines. They are probably bee-pollinated and are widespread and abundant (three thousand to forty-five hundred species) in the tropics (Croat 1978: 662).

cf. **Mortoniodendron** *(Tiliaceae)*

This forest tree (P. Allen 1977: 268) is probably insect-pollinated (Croat 1978: 573).

cf. **Persea schiediana**

The genus *Persea* (avocado) consists of approximately 145 tropical and subtropical evergreen species worldwide, with the heaviest concentration of species in Brazil. Twenty-two species occur in Mexico and Central America, among them *P. americana*, the commonly cultivated avocado. *P. schiediana*, lesser known but also cultivated for its fruit, is native to Mexico and Central America. It attains a height of 20 m to 50 m and may be found growing from sea level to the highlands (K. Allen 1948). The scant presence of pollen that most closely resembles this species of avocado suggests that the species was present during prehistoric times as well and may have been used for food. Future studies employing additional pollen, phytolith, and macrobotanical analyses should confirm or deny this observation.

Piperales

This order is composed of the Saururaceae (lizard's-tail family), the Piperaceae (pepper family), and Chloranthaceae (Chloranthus family), with morphologically similar pollen. The plants are predominantly herbaceous, or small trees or shrubs (Lawrence 1951: 442–446; Croat 1978).

Pinus *sp. (Pine)*

The pine is wind-pollinated and its pollen is notable, since the distribution of pine is limited in the tropics and it is not currently native to Costa Rica. Three species of pine grow in Central America (*Pinus caribaea, P. oocarpa*, and *P. pseudostrobis*). *P. caribaea*, the southernmost Central American pine, extends southeastward in Nicaragua to 12° 10′ near Bluefields, 200 km distant from Lake Arenal (Denevan 1961: 296). The pollen records from Holocene cores from Costa Rica (Nicoya Peninsula), Panama (Gatun Lake and Parita Bay), and this study indicate that pine forests did not grow in the southern part of Central America (Bartlett and Barghoorn 1973; Clary 1986, in progress); however, the presence of scant pine pollen in the lower portions of the cores, excluding Gatun Lake, and in this study suggests that pine forests may have been more widespread in northern Central America than they are today. Future regionally focused research is needed to substantiate this pattern. Although pine is not naturally distributed in Costa Rica or southern

Nicaragua (Standley 1937:65), it is often planted as an ornamental and used in reforestation projects in Central America (Fig. 15-7).

Ulmus sp. (Elm)

These trees or shrubs are insect-pollinated.

Proteaceae

These shrubs and trees have aromatic wood. Roupala spp. grows in the mountains of Costa Rica (Standley 1937:402).

Urticales

Pollen of the Ulmaceae, Moraceae, and Urticaceae is morphologically similar (Lawrence 1951:461).

Unidentified

This category includes pollen of plant taxa that are not identifiable with the available reference material and that do not occur repeatedly.

Unidentified, too weathered

This is pollen from plant taxa that are deteriorated to the point that they no longer contain morphological characteristics useful for identification. They are noted as an aid in determining the relative state of preservation of pollen in the samples.

Spore Type A

This is a spore common to most of the samples. The palynomorph is spherical, echinate, heteropolar, with a trilete scar. Diameter is 45 μm.

POLLEN OF CULTIGENS

We encountered *Zea mays* L. (maize) in four samples from G-150 (Table 15-1). It is also tentatively identified in the sample from D-1, G-163. The pollen grain found in G-163 fits the size and ektexine requirement for maize (C. 80 μm, folded). This sample dates to the Tronadora Phase. Piperno (Chap. 14) encountered maize phytoliths from the same sample as well as from two other samples from G-163. Matthews (1984) encountered poorly preserved plant remains tentatively identified as a charred maize cupule and two fused maize kernels. Given the early age of the site, it would be especially meaningful to verify maize pollen here. In order to better evaluate the pollen components of the site, we analyzed another sample, but results were not conclusive.

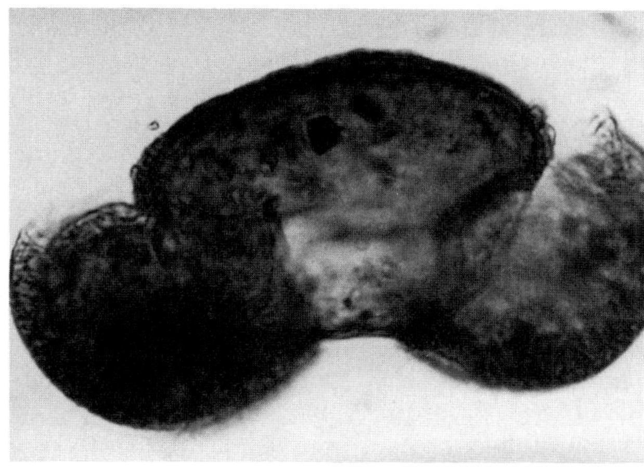

Figure 15-7.
G-150, D-6. Pinus *sp., 400x. Photograph by Karen Clary.*

The presence of both *Phaseolus* sp. (bean) at G-150, G-154 and *Persea schiediana* (avocado) at G-150 indicates the utilization of these taxa by site inhabitants. The samples date to the Silencio Phase (G-150) and the Tilarán Phase (G-154). The bean pollen was present in one of the three maize-bearing samples from G-150 (Sample H1-30), indicating that these two cultigens were utilized in tandem. The pollen of both beans and avocado may be expected to be rare in the pollen record. Bean plants produce low numbers of pollen grains relative to other species. The fragile avocado pollen exine does not easily weather the chemical washes used to extract pollen from soil (Alan H. Graham, personal communication, 1983). Because the pollen of both bean and avocado is scant in this record, the identification of these taxa serves primarily as a tenuous key to closer examination of samples from future excavations.

ENVIRONMENTAL INDICATORS

It is difficult to evaluate the Arenal Project pollen record for environmental indicators. First, we took the pollen samples from features at archaeological sites, where human activities such as vegetational disturbance and the importation of plants for food or economic use bias the pollen record. Second, preservation of fossil pollen in the soil samples is highly variable, between 0 and 11,095 pollen grains per gram of sediment. None of the samples contained sufficient pollen to attain a standard 200-grain pollen count, although the procedure was attempted for all samples.

In this analysis I have not calculated an arboreal/nonarboreal pollen ratio. Many of the pollen taxonomic categories (Table 15-1), such as the Euphorbiaceae, represent both arboreal and nonarboreal growth forms. A more diagnostic category is that of the grasses, since grasses attain only one herbaceous growth form and are here considered indicators of disturbance or succession (see Leyden 1987:411). Other useful disturbance indicators are the Cheno-ams, Asteraceae (sunflower family), and the Convolvulaceae (morning glory family) because they are primarily of a herbaceous growth form.

Grasses are present in over half of the pollen-bearing samples (N = 25) and they are the numerically dominant taxon in the majority of samples in which they are present (Table 15-1). The herbaceous plants that occur consist of some of the weeds encountered in soil disturbed by human activities such as on-site trampling, construction, and agriculture. Indicators of undisturbed forest conditions, or arboreal species, are poorly represented in comparison. At G-150, the presence of Cyperaceae, or sedge pollen, indicates a source of water nearby.

Overall, the scant pollen record is influenced by grasses and some indicators of vegetational disturbance, especially in the pollen records from G-150 and G-154, where the preservation of pollen is best. At G-150, this disturbance may be related to the practice of maize farming in the vicinity of the site locale, or to construction related to funerary practices.

SUMMARY AND CONCLUSIONS

Before beginning the pollen analysis we did not know if pollen could be recovered from the soils of the Arenal Project study area. The preservation of pollen in archaeological sites from the tropics is highly variable and unpredictable. The analysis of pollen from the Arenal Project was productive in establishing that pollen may be recovered from these sites, but that its preservation is differential. We encountered maize pollen in at least one site, G-150, and probably at G-163. Identifications of two other economic pollen taxa, bean and avocado, suggest utilization of these taxa as well. The environment of the site areas sampled is most obvious in the pollen record from G-150, where pollen was relatively well preserved. The pollen record indicates the presence of gramineous elements, some vegetational disturbance, and perhaps maize cultivation. The occurrence of arboreal pollen is low in comparison, indicating that tree species are not locally abundant, or that sampling error and differential preservation are contributing to a bias in the pollen record.

16

Macrobotanical Remains of the Proyecto Prehistórico Arenal

NANCY MAHANEY
MEREDITH H. MATTHEWS
AIDA BLANCO VARGAS

INTRODUCTION

In this chapter we will discuss the analysis of macrobotanical specimens collected by the Proyecto Prehistórico Arenal and implications regarding the prehistoric subsistence system. This study includes analyses of the macrobotanical remains from the 1984 and 1985 excavations of the Proyecto Prehistórico Arenal. Meredith Matthews conducted the analysis of the 1984 materials, with the help of Aida Blanco Vargas (Museo Nacional de Costa Rica) and Michael Snarskis (Universidad Nacional de Costa Rica). Aida Blanco Vargas analyzed the 1985 collections with help from Jorge Gómez Laurito (Herbarium of the Universidad Nacional de Costa Rica).

One of the goals of the Proyecto Prehistórico Arenal was to determine the subsistence strategies of the prehistoric inhabitants of the project area (Sheets 1983). We collected and analyzed pollen, phytolith, and macrobotanical samples in an attempt to identify utilized economic species and to gain a better understanding of the prehistoric environment (Chaps. 14 and 15). We conducted stable carbon isotope analysis of the human skeletal remains to determine the relative importance of maize agriculture (Friedman and Gleason 1984).

METHOD OF COLLECTION

We analyzed two categories of macrobotanical remains. The first consists of the larger, readily visible vegetal remains, which the field-workers collected during excavation. These materials make up the vast majority of the specimens analyzed. The second category consists of remains recovered by water flotation in the laboratory. Flotation was conducted in 1984 to test this method for the successful recovery of small-scale botanical remains. The technique was not very productive and therefore we did not utilize it in the 1985 season.

METHODS OF FLOTATION

The following discussion of flotation methodology and results is a summary of Matthews's 1984 study. For a more detailed discussion on this topic, see Matthews (1984).

We collected fourteen flotation samples from burials, strata containing cultural debris, and areas of high organic content at five sites. The size of the sample varied from 500 ml to 2.5 L. We employed a bucket and sieve flotation method, after which we air dried the materials, sorted, and analyzed them using a binocular microscope (10×–70×).

RESULTS OF FLOTATION

The results of the flotation analysis are summarized in Table 16-1. We processed fourteen flotation samples, resulting in the positive identification of six plant taxa. The majority of the specimens recovered were not charred. Because of the generally poor conditions for organic preservation in the project area, we believe that these specimens represent recent contaminants introduced by plant or animal activity (see Chap. 1). Only charred flotation specimens will be considered in the following discussion and conclusions.

LARGE-SCALE MACROBOTANICAL REMAINS

We obtained considerably better results from the collection and analysis of the large-scale vegetal remains (Table 16-2). The dominant type of specimen recovered at all sites was charred wood (Table 16-3), which we retrieved from twelve operations during 1984 and nine operations during 1985. Very few of the wood specimens retrieved in 1985 and none of the wood remains from 1984 are associated with specific features. Large quantities of wood not associated with features may be the result of contamination from historic or prehistoric clearing activities or prehistoric exploitation of wood resources.

Several hearths found at lower stratigraphic levels of site G-163 provide evidence for the use of firewood (Chap. 4). The presence of an intact Unit 50 Complex covering most of the site indicates that historic contamination is unlikely at these lower levels.

Operation B at site G-164 provided a greater variety and quantity of identifiable macrobotanical remains than any other single operation (Table 16-2). This greater concentration is not unusual in light of Hoopes and Chenault's interpretation that this is an area of cultural debris or midden (Chap. 5).

We recovered cultigens from both domestic and cemetery sites. The habitation sites from which we recovered cultigens include G-154, which produced four fragments of avocado seed (*Persea americana*), numerous corn (*Zea mays*) kernel fragments, and one cob fragment; G-163, which produced many corn kernels and one cob fragment; and G-169, which produced a bean cotyledon, and two pericarp fragments from an unidentified genus of *Cucurbitaceae* (squash). We found two maize cupules and a bean from the Silencio cemetery (G-150). We believe charred botanical remains in graves at G-150 to be inadvertent inclusions. It has been suggested that domestic materials can occur at large burial sites as the result of post-interment rituals that involve temporary habitation in the cemetery (Chap. 6).

CULTIVATED AND GATHERED RESOURCES

For the purposes of the following discussion, we have grouped the identified macrobotanical remains into two categories: cultivated, or encouraged, resources; and native, or gathered, resources. The first category is represented by the remains of *Zea mays* (maize), *Persea americana* (avocado), *Phaseolus vulgaris* (bean) (Fig. 16-1), and possible cucurbits. Richard Ford (1984:180) indicates that at least two of these crops (maize and avocado) were available to the prehistoric inhabitants of Central America via their migration from Mesoamerica to South America. We recovered only pericarp fragments from cucurbits, precluding the possibility of identification at the genus or species level. We believe that they were a

TABLE 16-1
RESULTS OF 1984 FLOTATION ANALYSIS

	Provenience													
	G-150						*G-154*		*G-155*		*G-161*	*G-163*		
Taxon / *Part*	*H3* #1	*D6–B5* #2	*H6* #3	*H4* #4	*H1* #5	*A2* #1	*I/A1* #2	*I/C1* #3	*C2* #1	*C3* #2	*B5 F1&2* #1	*B3 F1* #1	*D1 F2* #2	*C2* #3
Dicotyledoneae														
wood	x/C			x/C	x/C		x/C	x/C						
Caryophyllaceae														
Stellaria sp.														
seed									1/N				3/N	
Compositae														
achene	5/N	x/N		2/N	x/N				2/N		1/N			2/N
Gramineae														
fruit									1/N				1/N	
stem	1f/C													
Zea mays														
kernel								1f/C						
cupule		x/C												1f/C
Oxalidaceae														
Oxalis sp.														
seed									1/N		1/N			
Solanaceae														
Physalis sp.														
seed													2/N	
Indeterminate														
seed	1/C	1/N		1/N		1/N	2/N		4/N	5/N	3/N		1/N	4/N
fruit					1/N									
wood	x/C					x/C								
stem	1f/C													
Residue	r	r	r	r	r	r	r	r	r	r	r	r	r	r

Notes: Numbers and lower-case letters indicate quantity of specimen recovered. Upper-case letters indicate condition of specimen.
x—presence identified in sample
f—fragment identified in sample
r—residue resulting from flotation
C—specimen identified was charred
N—specimen identified was not charred

cultivated rather than a gathered resource. León has noted that "Cucurbitaceaes are among the oldest cultivated plants in America. They offered primitive man an abundant source of nourishment, which was quickly and easily propagated" (1968:423, translation by Mahaney).

The most frequently represented cultigen is *Zea mays*, which we found in twenty provenience units (lots) from five sites (Tables 16-1 and 16-2). Most of these remains consist of fragments of kernels and cupules. We recovered one ten-rowed cob fragment (Fig. 16-2) from G-161, a Tilarán Phase habitation site. The fragment measures 1.6 × 1.1 cm. The specimen is described by Matthews as being "in good condition" and it is thought that, by comparing it with identified cobs from contemporary sites, it may be possible to assign the cob to a race or variety.

Ten of the twenty provenience units with maize were at site G-163 (Tables 16-1 and 16-2). We retrieved kernels and cupule fragments from three hearths in Operations C and W associated with Tronadora Phase ceramics. We collected carbon samples from these features, but have not yet analyzed them. Some of the dates provided by other C-14 samples at this site are problematic because they are earlier than anticipated for the Tronadora Phase.

One C-14 sample associated with a maize kernel from site G-163, lot L10 yields a date of 3332

TABLE 16-2
RESULTS OF LARGE-SCALE MACROBOTANICAL ANALYSIS

	Provenience															
Taxon	*G-150*		*G-153*	*G-154*							*G-155*	*G-156*	*G-161*		*G-163*	
Part	*D6*	*H1*	*A*	*A2*	*D2*	*I1*	*I/A1*	*I/B1*	*I/C2*	*J1*	*NL*	*C2*	*C7*	*D2*	*B1*	*C1*
Bignoniaceae																
Crescentia alata																
fruit				2f*		x*	x*	x*	2f*					3f*		
Cucurbitaceae																
fruit							x									
Euphorbiaceae																
Croton sp.																
seed																
Gramineae																
Zea mays																
kernel				3f*	1f	1f			2f	4f					2*	
cob										1f			1f			1f
cupule	2															
Lauraceae																
Persea americana																
fruit																
seed					3f*				1f							
Leguminosae																
Phaseolus vulgaris																
seed		1														
Malpighiaceae																
Byrsonima crassifolia																
seed																
Palmae																
Unknown																
fruit																
seed					1*											
wood																
Bactris gasipaes																
seed																
Unidentified																
seed									1	1	1					
fruit			3	5	4					4	1					
wood		x		x		x						x				
other																

Notes:
x—presence noted
f—fragment
*—tenative identification
d—either *Elais oleifera* or *Scheelea rostrata*
NL—no lot/provenience

(3053) 2929 BC. Ceramics in northwestern Costa Rica had not previously been dated to before 2000 BC, but earlier dates for corn are not unexpected, given its presence in other Central American sites. *Zea mays* pollen from Panama has been dated from associated organic materials to 5350 ± 130 BC (Galinat 1980:175), and maize may have reached southeastern Guatemala by 4000 BC (McK. Bird 1984:46). Galinat has also suggested that, "if maize spread southward through Panama, early archaeological contexts of around 4000 BC for this cultivar in the area would seem to be in accord with the present evidence" (1980:175). McK. Bird has noted (1984:43), however, that very few archaeological specimens in Central America predate 500 BC.

Early C-14 dates associated with maize at G-163 indicate that the *Zea mays* remains recovered from the Arenal Project are the earliest recorded from controlled excavations in Costa Rica. These data appear to support Galinat's migration hypothesis. It is unfortunate that most of the early

TABLE 16-2
(continued)

G-163																*G-164*				*G-169*
G2	*I5*	*I24*	*J4*	*L10*	*L13*	*Q3*	*V8*	*V11*	*V25*	*V28*	*V33*	*V36*	*W7*	*W16*	*W35*	*B6*	*B7*	*C6*	*E19*	*NL*
			4f				1f									2f		1f		4f
																				2f
									1f	1f										
				1f	1f		1	1				1	1	2f		3f				
																				1f
																2f				
							1													
						1f										4fd	1fd			
	x	x									x									
2f										1f										
				1f																
																			1	
																				x
				1											4f					

maize specimens from the Arenal Project consist of single cupules, precluding identification of race or variety.

Macrobotanical remains of naturally occurring economic plants include *Byrsonima crassifolia* (nance), *Crescentia alata* (jícaro), *Croton* species, and possibly *Bactris gasipaes* (pejibaye). *Byrsonima crassifolia* produces an edible fruit and its range extends from Mexico to Paraguay in lowland savannas and open semideciduous woods (Anderson 1983:202).

The fruit of *Crescentia alata* (jícaro) is quite similar to that of the *Lagenaria siceraria* (calabaza). The hollowed-out fruit of either may be used as a container. During the course of this research we found no references indicating the use of jícaro as a food source. *Crescentia alata* has been recorded from Central Mexico to South America (Janzen 1983:222). We did not identify modern jícaro trees within the Arenal Project area. It has not been determined if the modern lack of *Crescentia alata* is due to historic distur-

Figure 16-1.
*Bean cotyledon (*Phaseolus vulgaris*) from G-150-H1. Length 0.9 cm, width 0.5 cm. Photograph by Meredith Matthews.*

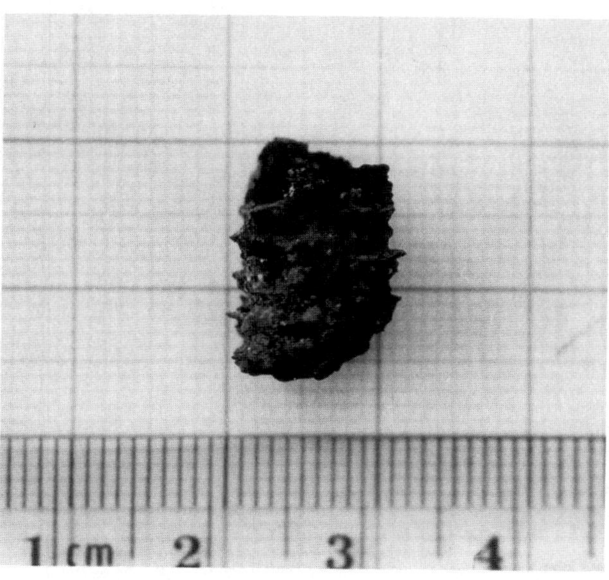

Figure 16-2.
Ten-rowed cob fragment of Zea mays *recovered from G-161-C7. Length 1.7 cm, width 1.15 cm. Photograph by Meredith Matthews.*

TABLE 16-3
PROVENIENCE OF UNIDENTIFIED CARBONIZED WOOD REMAINS

Sample Number	*Operation & Lot*	*Stratigraphic Level*	*Feature Designation*
1	G-163-G2	50u	
2	G-163-G4	64	
3	G-163-U2	54	
3	G-163-I5	60	
4	G-163-K4	60/61	
5	G-163-M3	60/64	
6	G-163-I5b	60	
7	G-163-G4	64	Intrusive pit
8	G-163-I9	52/53	
8	G-163-H11	64	
9	G-163-V2	50u	
10	G-163-S3	55/61	
11	G-163-Q3	60	
12	G-163-W2	54	
13	G-163-I6	65	
14	G-163-W16	60/61	Hearth
14	G-163-I6	65	
15	G-163-I1	30	
15	G-163-W14	60	
16	G-163-I4	54/55	
16	G-163-W18	61/64	
17	G-163-V25	60	
17	G-163-I6	65	
18	G-163-J1	30	
18	G-163-I18	50cd	
19	G-163-J4	54/55	
20	G-163-J5	60	
21	G-163-U3	64	
22	G-163-M2	54	Near vessel
22	G-163-V11	64	
23	G-163-M5	60/64	Posthole #2
24	G-163-T5	60	
25	G-163-W4	50	
26	G-163-W4	50	
26	G-163-L7	50cd	
27	G-163-L10	61	
27	G-163-I24	61	
28	G-163-V6	50abc	
28	G-163-G2	50u	
29	G-163-G2	50u	
29	G-163-V8	60/61	
30	G-163-V9	64	

n/a = no stratigraphic level assigned

bance or to inappropriate habitat. If the latter, then the presence of *Crescentia alata* in the archaeological record indicates that the resource was brought into the study area from an area with appropriate environmental conditions (Matthews 1984:196).

Croton, which includes more than one thousand species of trees, shrubs, and herbs, has a pantropical distribution. According to Record and Hess (1943:156), some species of *Croton* are fragrantly scented, some are used for dyestuffs, resins, and medicines, and a few species provide timber for various purposes. We could not identify the archaeological specimens to the species level; therefore, we cannot make conjectures regarding their use. For the purpose of this study and in the absence of information to the contrary, *Croton* will be considered to have been available prehistorically as a nonedible gathered resource.

The literature on *Bactris gasipaes* (pejibaye) in-

TABLE 16-3
(continued)

Sample Number	Operation & Lot	Stratigraphic Level	Feature Designation
32	G-163-V28	50b	
32	G-164-B6	54	
33	G-163-V28	50b	
35	G-163-V29	50c	
36	G-163-I13	60/61	
37	G-163-I14	64	
38	G-163-V32	60	
39	G-163-V21	50c	
41	G-163-V19	52/53	
42	G-163-H28	50	
43	G-163-V22	54/55a	
44	G-163-V42	50b	
45	G-163-V51	50a	
46	G-163-V34	64	
47	G-163-V34	64	
48	G-163-V33	61	
49	G-163-V36	65 INT	Posthole #3
50	G-163-V36	65 INT	Posthole #4
51	G-163-W16	60	
52	G-163-W14	60	
53	G-163-W17	61	Hearth
54	G-163-I6	65	
55	G-163-V24	60a	
56	G-163-V52	50b	
57	G-163-V37	64	
58	G-163-W17	61	Hearth
59	G-163-W7	54	
60	G-163-W5	51	
61	G-163-W18	61	
63	G-163-W18	61	Hearth
64	G-163-V56	60	
65	G-163-V47	60	
66	G-163-V55	60	
67	G-163-V57	61	
68	G-163-V58	64	
69	G-163-V48	61	
70	G-163-H34	50c	Extension #4
71	G-163-H33	50b	
72	G-163-I20	54/55	
74	G-163-H38	61	Extension #4
75	G-163-W17	61	Near Hearth
76	G-163-W35	54	Pit #1
77	G-163-W32	60	

TABLE 16-3
(continued)

Sample Number	Operation & Lot	Stratigraphic Level	Feature Designation
78	G-163-V49	64	
79	G-163-H48	50c	Extension #3
80	G-163-I25	65	
81	G-163-V31	60	
82	G-163-H43	65	Extension #4 Posthole #14
83	G-164-B6	54	
84	G-164-B6	54	
85	G-164-A8	n/a	Vessel interior
86	G-164-A8	n/a	Surface
87	G-164-A9	n/a	Vessel interior
88	G-164-A9	n/a	Surface
89	G-164-C8	64	
90	G-164-C6	50u	
91	G-163-W16	60	Hearth #2
92	G-163-W18	61	Posthole #5
93	G-164-A11	65 INT	
94	G-164-E6	55	
95	G-164-E10	64	
96	G-164-E14	50b	
97	G-164-D13	60	
98	G-164-B17	65 INT	
99	G-164-B17	65 INT	
100	G-164-B6	54	
101	G-164-E15	50c	
102	G-164-E16	50u	
103	G-164-B6	54	
105	G-164-B7	65 INT	
106	G-164-E17	61	
107	G-164-B6	54	
108	G-164-B8	65 INT	
109	G-164-B9	65 INT	
110	G-164-E13	50a	
111	G-164-A12	65 INT	
112	G-164-E19	50a	NW extension #3
113	G-164-A14	n/a	
114	G-164-E29	54	
115	G-164-E27	62	
116	G-164-E28	54	
117	G-164-E32	62	
118	G-164-E31	54	
119	G-164-E33	62	
120	G-164-B17	65 INT	

dicates that the plant is either native to Costa Rica (Dahlgren 1936:408) or was introduced from South America prior to Spanish contact (Prance 1984:87). Pejibaye, an important historic and modern food source, was under heavy cultivation at the time of Spanish contact in this area (Prance 1984:87). The time at which pejibaye began to be cultivated is difficult to determine, possibly because of weak selection for palms in the New World. C. E. Smith (1980:173) has indicated that, in modern Panama, indiscriminate discard of seeds, combined with a severe resistance to the removal of palm trees, may have resulted in a lack of selection for fruit or seed size. The continuity in seed size from preceramic to pre-Conquest times, which may have resulted from such practices, makes the development of *Bactris gasipaes* cultivation difficult to interpret.

The small representation of this plant in the macrobotanical assemblage, along with a lack of

TABLE 16-4
OCCURRENCE OF FOOD RESOURCES BY CERAMIC PHASE

Ceramic Phase Site/Lot/Strata	*Zea mays*	*Crescentia alata*	*Cucurbitacea species*	*Croton species*	*Bactris gasipaes*	*Byrsonima crassifolia*	*Persea americana*	*Phaseolus vulgaris*
Tronadora								
G-163-J4 -		X						
G-163-V8 -		X						
G-163-V25 -				X				
G163 L13 50cd	X							
G163 Q3 60	X							
G163 W16 60/61	X							
G163 L10 61	X							
G163 W36 61	X							
G163 V11 64	X							
G163 V36 65	X							
G163 B1 -	X							
G163 C2 -	X							
Mixed Arenal/Tronadora								
G163 W7 54	X							
Predominantly Arenal								
G163 V28 50b				X	X			
G163 G2 50u					X			
Late Arenal								
G164 B6 54	X	X				X		
G-164-C6		X						
Silencio								
G150 D6 62	X							
G150 H1 30								X
Tilarán								
G154 A2 30	X	X					X	
G154 D2 30	X							
G154 I1 30	X	X					X	
G154 IC2 30	X	X						
G154 J1 30	X							
G-154-IA1 -		X	X					
G-154-IB1 -		X						
G-161-D2 -		X						
G161 C7 -	X							
G169 general		X	X					X

representation in the phytolithic record (Chap. 14), may indicate that the fruit was carried into the study area. If the macrobotanical and phytolithic records are not biased, it appears that *Bactris gasipaes* was a gathered or encouraged resource in the study area.

The remaining macrobotanical materials recovered (Table 16-2) were not identifiable at the time of analysis. Further investigations may allow the identification of additional domesticated, encouraged, and wild plant resource.

SUMMARY AND CONCLUSIONS

The small, poorly preserved macrobotanical assemblage collected by the Arenal Project is of limited representative value. Therefore, we believe that there is not sufficient information for extensive reconstructions of subsistence strategies. By separating the occurrence of charred macrobotanical remains by time period, however, a trend in the representation of cultigens can be seen that may be indicative of a temporal change in the subsistence system (Table 16-4).

We recovered *Zea mays* from nine operations dating to the Tronadora Phase. This is the only resource identified for this phase. Undoubtedly, *Zea mays* was supplemented by gathered resources that are not represented here because of sampling error or differential preservation. *Zea mays* was also identified from several Arenal Phase operations along with *Bactris gasipaes* and *Byrsonima crassifolia*, which are both gathered food resources. Nonfood resources from the Arenal Phase operations include *Crescentia alata* and *Croton* species. A second cultigen, *Phaseolus vulgaris*, was identified in Silencio Phase deposits. We cannot determine whether the lack of gathered resources identified for this phase is indicative of poor preservation and sampling problems or a prehistoric decline in the use of gathered food sources. During the Tilarán Phase, *Persea americana* and unidentified cucurbits are added to the list of probable cultigens. Gathered resources are represented in this phase by *Crescentia alata*, which is considered nonedible.

Although the macrobotanical assemblage is characterized by very few remains that are represented over a long period of time, the information from this assemblage may indicate an increasing dependence on cultivated resources, with the introduction of new cultigens over time and an apparent decrease in gathered food resources over time. This change in subsistence strategies is substantiated by Piperno's phytolithic study, which indicates that "tropical forest clearance accelerated after about 500 BC" (Chap. 14). Such clearing activities were probably related to increased cultivation, resulting in localized tropical savanna environments. Boucher et al. (1983:72) state: "Savannas result from cutting and burning forests leaving only scattered trees in the resulting grassland. A characteristic set of trees is found in savannas throughout the Neotropics, including *Byrsonima crassifolia, Curatella americana, Crescentia alata*, and the palm *Acrocomia vinifera*. These species have in common their resistance to fire and the herbivory." This may explain the presence of *Byrsonima crassifolia* and *Crescentia alata* in the later phase occupations in an otherwise tropical savanna environment. The presence of macrobotanical remains of other species of trees may have been the result of deliberate encouragement of certain species through planting or protection during land clearing or may be the result of gathering and harvesting activities conducted in neighboring tropical forest environments.

Since *Zea mays* is represented in each of the occupation phases and represents the largest percentage of the nonwood macrobotanical remains, it would seem logical to assume that this cultigen provided a major dietary staple of the prehistoric inhabitants of this area. Stable carbon isotope analysis of human skeletal material has shown, however, that *Zea mays* probably composed less than 12% of the diet of the prehistoric inhabitants of the project area, at least during the Silencio Phase (Sheets 1984c:211). This may be an indirect indication that some portion of the remaining diet was composed of cultivated root crops, in spite of their lack of representation in the macrobotanical record. Root crops do not preserve well and are rarely represented in the archaeological record. Piperno (Chap. 14) has also noted the difficulty of identifiying the role of tubers in subsistence strategies due to their lack of identifiable silicified remains. Such negative information is often overlooked in the course of reconstructing prehistoric lifeways and may provide a very important link in understanding subsistence regimes.

Analysis of macrobotanical remains from the sites excavated in the Arenal area indicates use of cultivated/encouraged and gathered/wild plant resources over a long time. Although the data are limited, there appears to be a general trend toward the decreased relative importance of gathered resources. The macrobotanical data base was affected by differential preservation, which may have eliminated evidence for root crops and may have had an effect on representation of the other resources. Despite the limitations of the macrobotanical data, the information provided in this study may be regarded as a starting point in a diachronic reconstruction of the subsistence strategies of the prehistoric peoples of the Arenal area.

AKNOWLEDGMENTS

We would like to thank Michael Snarskis and Jorge Gómez Laurito for their help with the identification of unfamiliar botanical materials. The owners of the Hotel Grecia in Tilarán were very gracious in allowing us to locate our lab on their premises. Flor and Lidieth were valuable and much-appreciated lab employees. Thanks to Marilynn Mueller, Brian McKee, Mark Chenault, and Payson Sheets for advice on the manuscript and help with editing. Special thanks go to Dr. Sheets for his patience and guidance and to all the members of the project for their moral support.

17

Summary and Conclusions

PAYSON D. SHEETS

INTRODUCTION

The Proyecto Prehistórico Arenal conducted multidisciplinary research emphasizing archaeology, volcanology, and biology from 1984 through 1987 in northwestern Costa Rica. The objectives of the project included establishing volcanic and cultural sequences to aid the study of settlement, subsistence, and artifacts; exploring the effects of periodic explosive volcanism on societies; determining past adaptations to tropical environments; and exploring the integration of local societies into wider social and economic networks. Remote sensing by NASA provided an abundance of imagery that was surprisingly effective in detecting traces of prehistoric paths that connected sites with one another and with features and sources of materials.

Guanacaste, the northwestern province of Costa Rica (Fig. 1-3) has three principal physiographic zones: the Pacific Coast, the inland plains, and the mountains. The coast has been relatively well studied archaeologically, especially by Lange (1980a), resulting in a well-known sequence of sites and artifacts from about 500 BC to the Conquest. The inland plains have not received as much attention, but some projects have contributed significant adaptational and chronological information (e.g., Coe and Baudez 1961). Inland mountainous areas, locally called "la Cordillera," have been studied the least, with only a few preliminary publications (e.g., Finch 1982–1983; Norr 1982–1983; and Aguilar 1984). Comparative analyses are inhibited by the lack of published site reports for Guanacaste.

We chose the Arenal area for this project because Arenal Volcano was known to have erupted and buried artifacts beneath volcanic ash layers (Snarskis, personal communication, 1980; Sheets 1982–1983). Volcanological research by Melson indicates that Arenal Volcano erupted explosively at least nine times in prehistory (Melson and Saenz 1973; Melson 1984). The eruptive-depositional sequence offered good preservation of sites and features under volcanic ash, as well as a stratigraphic sequence of ash layers independent of ceramic and lithic analyses to assist dating. Further, the Arenal area could add to the comparative data base for exploring the nature of human adaptations to tropical areas experiencing explosive volcanism (Sheets 1983).

A theoretical framework for the project is provided by natural hazards research. Hazards research, involving physical and social sciences, explores the dynamic relationships between human societies and their changing environments. All human societies possess adaptive mechanisms for coping with environmental fluctuations, yet each has limits to its coping with changed circumstances by making in situ adjustments, and migrations or other radical actions may be necessary (Burton, Kates, and White 1978), or societies may fail. It is more difficult to compare hazards and human responses in prehistory than with contemporary or recent historic events; however, when we compare Costa Rican volcanism and societies with Salvadoran and Panamanian cases involving more complex societies, it appears that simpler societies were more resilient to the sudden impact of explosive eruptions. That may be because they were less dependent on an elaborate "built" environment, with complex economic systems, including occupational specialization, long-distance trade routes, and concentrated populations.

The Arenal-area environment is tropical, and elevations range from 300 m to 1,500 m. There is a marked gradient in mean annual precipitation, from over 6,000 mm (240 inches) near Arenal Volcano, down to 3,000 mm (120 inches) along the Continental Divide in the central part of the area, and only 1,300 mm (50 inches) near Cañas in the west. Seasonality of precipitation is minimal in the eastern end, but it is pronounced in the western end, with wet (May–November) and dry (December–April) seasons. Soil saturation in the wetter area discourages agriculture, particularly of seed crops. Most soils in the Arenal area were formed by weathering volcanic ash, and generally are fertile and porous, although they are low in available phosphorus, potassium, zinc, and manganese (Tosi 1980). The soils not derived from recent volcanic ash, either below Arenal Volcano's ash layers or beyond them, are more typical of tropical soils, with their high clay and aluminum-iron oxides content and relatively low fertility. Soil acidity follows the moisture gradient, with pH readings from about 4 in the eastern end to about 6 in the western end. The eastern area's greater cloud cover markedly decreases solar radiation, which averages only 4.4 hours per day, and mean temperatures. The area is extremely windy, with mean annual windspeeds along the lake of 23 km per hour; by comparison, Chicago, America's "windy city," averages 16 km per hour. Wind damage to crops is a problem for agriculturalists.

Of all terrestrial environments, tropical rain forests are known for maintaining the most stable of climatic conditions (humidity, temperature), and for having the highest standing biomass and species diversity (Richards 1966). The Arenal area stands out among Central American tropical forests for having a relatively rich flora and fauna (Tosi 1980). Tosi (ibid.) lists minimum species counts for the area as follows: 500 plants, 25 fish, 150 amphibians or reptiles, and 400 birds.

RESEARCH RESULTS

The Arenal research area, in the Cordillera, straddles the border between two defined prehistoric culture areas: the Greater Nicoya archaeological subarea to the west, and the Atlantic Watershed to the east (Lange 1984b: fig. 7.1). An assessment of the cultural materials, through time, recovered by the Arenal Project allows for a close examination of the nature of that border. We have found stylistic and technological characteristics of both areas during all sedentary, ceramic-producing phases in the Arenal area. The Tronadora Phase shares characteristics with La Montaña and Chaparrón in the Atlantic Watershed; comparisons with Guanacaste to the west are difficult because of the lack of early sites. During the Arenal and Silencio phases, the Arenal area shared more material culture with Greater Nicoya than with the Atlantic region. That relationship reversed itself during the Tilarán Phase. We believe that a Cordilleran subarea can be defined between Greater Nicoya and the Atlantic areas (Sheets 1984c). Its geographic extent is not clearly known, but it probably includes the chain of volcanoes and hills from Orosi Volcano in the north to Monteverde and perhaps Cerro Cedral in the south. It certainly includes the Naranjo River–Bijagua Valley (Norr 1982–1983) and the Hacienda Jericó (Finch 1982–1983). If defining a new cultural subarea is justified, the Arenal sites and others in the Cordilleran subarea are not merely peripheral derivatives of another cultural tradition, or a blend of two traditions, but a relatively independent tradition, only occasionally accepting and incorporating innovations made elsewhere.

PHASES OF OCCUPATION

The oldest artifact encountered during project research is a Clovis-style point (Chap. 11) made out of locally available chalcedony and found along the shore of Lake Arenal. This likely dates to approximately 10,000 BC and is evidence of the earliest known human occupation in the area. This find, along with the abundant Paleo-Indian artifacts from Turrialba in the wet Atlantic highland rain forest (Snarskis 1979) and the paucity of Paleo-Indian artifacts from the dry Santa María area of southern Panama (Cooke 1984), calls into question the assumption that Paleo-Indian peoples would have adapted better to the drier plains than to the humid forests.

Throughout all phases, from the Archaic to the Conquest, the Arenal area was characterized by an exceptionally high degree of cultural continuity, in settlement patterns, subsistence, and technology. Some basic elements of technology were established by 4000 BC and remained essentially unchanged to the Spanish Conquest, including core-flake technology, the primary means of generating cutting edges, and the use of cooking stones. Most of the villages established in the two millennia before Christ were still occupied in the final phase before the Conquest. Changes in chipped stone, ground stone, and ceramic technology were markedly slight. In contrast to many areas of Middle America, the Arenal area apparently never experienced rapid population increases or a shift into a subsistence reliance on a single staple. Villages maintained high degrees of economic self-sufficiency, in contrast to their Mesoamerican and Andean contemporaries, which became dependent on more centralized economies and long-distance trade networks. Such stability is even more remarkable in that it was maintained in a volcanically and tectonically unstable environment.

Throughout all sedentary phases, relatively flat ground near permanent streams was the favored locale for settlement. The greatest concentration of villages we encountered was along the ecotonal south shore of present Lake Arenal, against the foothills of the mountain massif, where people had access to a variety of ecological zones and resources. These include the lake with its mammals and fish, the upper Arenal River Valley, with its fertile volcanically derived soils, and the areas in the hills above them. The analyses of macrobotanical remains, pollen, and phytoliths indicate a mixed subsistence strategy including seed crops, tree crops, and probably some root crops and wild seeds, fruits, and berries.

The Fortuna Phase (4000–3000 BC) is known from surface finds, excavated debitage, and an excavated campsite. We found a stemmed "Fortuna point" (Sheets 1984b), along with debitage from well-controlled bifacial flaking of petrified wood, chalcedony, dacite, and other fine-grained, locally available materials. The campsite, with its two hearths, yielded dozens of cooking stones, evidently for stone boiling, along with fragments of stones that fractured as a result of the rapid temperature changes. The most common means of producing cutting edges was an informal core-flake percussion industry. Both the cooking stone and the core-flake technologies continued essentially unchanged until the historic era.

A troublesome gap of a thousand years, the third millennium BC, exists between the end of the Fortuna Phase and the beginning of the Tronadora Phase, as we have defined them. Unfortunately, we have not been able to separate these occupations based on stratigraphic, stylistic, or seriational analyses. The shift from a hunting and gathering life-style into sedentary villages with ceramics and heavy ground stone implements apparently occurred during that millennium.

The Tronadora Phase (2000–500 BC) begins with well-dated houses and ceramics at the Tronadora Vieja site (G-163). The site is likely one of many small villages scattered through the Arenal area in the second millennium BC. Preservation was facilitated by burial under the Unit 61 volcanic ash, evidently from the earliest eruption of Arenal Volcano, at about 1800 BC. Ceramics were well made and elaborately decorated by incising and painting (Hoopes 1984a, 1985, 1987; Chap. 10). Burials, probably secondary, apparently were in small rectangular pits between houses in the village, occasionally accompanied by pottery offerings. Although ground stone implements are rare, oval metates with three short legs are known. Structures were circular in plan, with poles supporting presumably thatch roofs, and floors were of tamped earth.

The ceramic sequence for the Arenal area is based on the analysis of over twelve thousand sherds from surface collections and stratigraphic excavations (Hoopes 1984a, 1987). Phase definitions derive from comparisions with existing sequences in Costa Rica and adjoining countries.

Tronadora Phase pottery from the site of Tronadora Vieja (Fig. 17-1) is the earliest dated ceramic assemblage in Costa Rica (Chap. 10). Radiocarbon dates indicate that it first appeared in the Arenal basin no later than 2000 BC, and it may have been hundreds of years earlier. Tronadora pottery has its strongest affinities with other early Costa Rican and Nicaraguan complexes: Chaparrón from the San Carlos region (Snarskis 1978), Dinarte from Ometepe Island (Haberland 1966, 1982–1983), Loma B from coastal Guanacaste (Lange 1980a), early Naranjo Phase pottery from the northern Cordillera (Norr 1982–1983), La Montaña and Barva from the Central Highlands (Snarskis 1978, 1984a), and Curre from the Diquis Valley (Corrales 1985). It is similar in many ways to contemporaneous assemblages in Mesoamerica and northwestern South America and shares modes with Barra and Ocós to the north (Coe 1961; Lowe 1975; Clark et al. n.d.), and Canapote, Barlovento, and other complexes of northern Colombia (Bischoff 1966, 1972; Reichel-Dolmatoff 1985) to the south. Tronadora, however, is not sufficiently similar to any of these assemblages for us to posit a direct relationship. Rather, the characteristics of Tronadora Phase pottery suggest that it represents a distinct manifestation of Early and Middle Formative ceramic technology, representing a facet of what was probably a widespread tradition of decorated ceramics throughout the Intermediate Area by the second millennium BC.

Tronadora Phase ceramic vessels are dominated by *tecomate*-shaped vessels, the most abundant of which are large with heavy bolstered rims. Other vessel forms include short jars and tall cylinders. Although red-painted rims and incised zones are common, plastic decoration predominates. This includes groove incision on vessel lips and exteriors, zones of heavy punctation, various types of shell stamping (including zigzag shell rocker stamping), and bold combinations of painted strip appliqué and incisions. Pastes range from fine to coarse and are tempered with fine tephra. Overall, the technology is well developed.

Given the wide geographic distribution of the earliest ceramic complexes in Costa Rica and the Tronadora Phase pottery's general similarities to Early Formative ceramics from both Mesoamerica and South America, it is difficult to characterize these ceramics as belonging to either northern or southern, Atlantic or Pacific cultural traditions. Their closest affinities are with Chaparrón, in the northern Atlantic Watershed (Snarskis 1978), and Dinarte, from Ometepe Island in Lake Nicaragua (Haberland 1966); surface finish and firing quality are more similar to Barra and Ocós than to Barlovento. Until the nature of the Early Formative occupation in Costa Rica is better understood, however, Tronadora stands out as a tightly regionalized ceramic complex in the Early and Middle Formative periods in the Intermediate Area.

The Arenal Phase (500 BC–AD 600) is the local manifestation of the Zoned Bichrome horizon in lower Central America (Hoopes 1987; Lange 1984b). Population density in the Arenal area, and likely the entire Cordillera, reached its peak during this phase. The numbers of sites, their sizes, and the frequencies of datable ceramics are all greatest during this phase. Cemeteries often were located on prominent ridges near villages. Domestic housing, with circular floor plans and presumably thatch roofs, remained unchanged. Large cooking hearths were located on the ground immediately outside the houses.

Our sample of Arenal Phase burials is from the Sitio Bolívar (G-164) cemetery; it evidently is representative of cemeteries during this phase, at least for the Arenal area, based on local residents' descriptions of illicit excavations of other cemeteries and on our inspections of many. Primary burials (judging from the size of the prehistoric pits) were in elongated pits and often were accompanied by grave goods. After the body was placed in the burial pit, the pit was filled with soil, elongated stones were lined up in a rectangle outlining the subsurface pit, and then tons of river rocks were exuberantly smashed into place. Many complete ceramic vessels and elaborate metates and manos were broken on top of the rock layer. A number of cobble mounds at other sites also date to this period.

Arenal Phase ceramics were dominated by necked jars, as neckless *tecomate* forms declined in importance. Vessels with both solid and hollow supports appear at this time, as do multiple-brushed painted decoration and the use of zoomorphic appliqué. There are strong stylistic ties between Greater Nicoya and the Arenal area at this time, and many Zoned Bichrome types (Lange et al. 1984) are common to both areas;

Figure 17-1.
The Tronadora Vieja site, the earliest sedentary village yet discovered in Costa Rica, dating to 2000 BC and before. It is located on a low, gently-sloping ridge overlooking the ancient Lake Arenal. Excavations are in progress in the center of the photograph. Photograph by Payson Sheets.

however, many traits also are shared with Atlantic Watershed assemblages.

The Arenal Phase is divided into two facets on the basis of cross-sequence comparisons and radiocarbon dating. Characteristics of the earlier facet (500 BC–AD 1) include bichrome painting (red-on-cream) bordered by heavy incision, multiple-brush painting in red, and bands of shell impressions. The later facet (AD 1–600) is characterized by more black painting on red-slipped vessels, fine incised decoration (predominantly geometric and guilloche decorations), resist decoration resembling Usulután, and the appearance of early polychromes toward the end of the phase. Overall, Arenal Phase ceramics are most similar to Greater Nicoya, but ties to the Atlantic Watershed are indicated by the use of red-on-cream decoration, zoomorphic appliqué, and decorated hollow supports. Trade ceramics from the Atlantic Watershed appear at the Bolívar site (G-164) and elsewhere in eastern Guanacaste (Ryder 1982–1983a) at about AD 300–600.

Ground stone artifacts became much more common and were used for utilitarian and religious or status purposes. Metates had ovoid grinding surfaces. Virtually all had three cylindrical or conical legs. Bar manos, with a long cylindrical shape, that often overhung the metate, were common. Celts were plentiful, with sides that were straight or flared to a wide bit, and they commonly were buried with the dead.

The Silencio Phase (AD 600–1300) witnessed a population decline, indicated by a decrease in the number of occupied villages and their sizes, although there were a few large sites. Polychrome pottery began to be made in the area, but lithic industries changed only slightly. Bifacial flaking of projectile points/knives, apparently suspended during the Arenal and most of the Tronadora phases, returned with the advent of the Silencio point; however, bifacial flaking of celt blanks continued uninterrupted from the Tronadora through the Tilarán phases. Cemeteries often were farther from villages than in other phases, many kilometers in the case of the Silencio cemetery (G-150), and burials were encased in stone cist tombs (slab boxes of flat-fracturing volcanic stone locally called "laja") and regularly were accompanied by grave goods. Construction techniques are virtually identical to stone cist tombs in the Central Highlands of Costa Rica (Snarskis 1984a). Graves in the Arenal area often included miniature polychrome vessels, gold pendants, or elaborate metates. This is the culmination of the trend, which began during the Tronadora and Arenal phases, of increasing distance between settlements and their cemeteries, and increasing complexity in tomb construction and burial furniture. Even though many cemeteries were located at considerable distances from villages and other features, remote sensing has allowed us to make direct connections between sites by the detection of small, erosional footpaths that directly link cemeteries with villages, springs, and special-activity sites. Remote sensing is considered in more detail below.

The ceramic evidence for strong contacts with Greater Nicoya cultures continues through the Silencio Phase. In Greater Nicoya there was a proliferation of elaborate, high-quality polychrome ceramic types about this time, and this is evident also in the Cordillera. We found abundant polychrome ceramics at the Silencio site (G-150), primarily cached in stone cist burials. Small polychrome vessels, perhaps manufactured in the Tempisque Valley to the west, appeared as burial offerings, sometimes in association with gold pendants. While a large number of sherds of Middle Polychrome Period types from Greater Nicoya at the Silencio site may represent items acquired from regions to the west through trade or exchange, the most common polychrome type (Jiménez) is manufactured locally. Its quality is not as good as Tempisque-area ceramics.

In addition to the appearance of polychromes, the Silencio Phase is characterized by an abundance of incised ceramics, a continuation of a very long-lived tradition in the area. Decoration in fine-line motifs, which often extend to the upper surfaces of flat vessel rims, includes geometric and guilloche patterns and hachured friezes, occasionally infilled with white pigment. Vessel forms include jars and open bowls with T-shaped rim profiles that carry polychrome, bichrome (red-on-cream), and incised monochrome decoration.

Metates change from ovoid grinding surfaces with rounded lines and longer tripod legs toward blocky, rectangular forms with shorter and thicker legs and more elaborate surface decoration. Decoration with zoomorphic and abstract motifs is common on edges and legs, and often on the grinding surface as well, indicating that they were not just utilitarian implements. Most metates have three legs. Manos are virtually unchanged from the previous phase, but celts exhibit change. Convex bits replace the straight bits of the previous phase. Flaring-sided celts continue.

The Tilarán Phase (AD 1300–1500) witnessed a continued population decline and saw a turn in cultural affiliation away from Greater Nicoya and toward the Central Highlands and the Atlantic Watershed. The change in ceramics is similar to the change away from Greater Nicoya noted by Creamer (1983) for the Gulf of Nicoya. Previous phases show only weak connections toward the east and southeast, as Cordilleran peoples maintained primary cultural affiliations with Greater Nicoya to the west. In contrast to the previous phase's settlement pattern of scattered small-to-medium-sized villages, the Tilarán Phase is characterized by many small hamlets widely dispersed across the countryside. The settlement pattern is more like that of the Tronadora Phase than any other. The ceramics, reflecting cultural changes, are no longer the elaborately painted polychromes, but are decorated by appliqué, modeling, and other plastic techniques (Hoopes 1984a). It is probable that the trend toward more elaborate funerary practices, evident in the previous three phases, did not continue in this phase, but we found no burials dating to this phase. Grave goods from this phase are rare in private collections, and local looters are not aware of cemeteries of this phase.

The pottery of the Tilarán Phase shows much less decorative variety than any preceding sedentary phase. There was a strong break with the elaborate polychrome traditions that continued to flourish in Greater Nicoya. Except for a few sherds, which may represent trade items, polychrome decoration disappears altogether in Arenal-area assemblages. Instead, local ceramics are unslipped monochromes, occasionally decorated by zoomorphic appliqués on handles and supports. In addition to the aesthetics, the quality of these ceramics in terms of texture and firing is worse than any other phase.

Curiously, we found no ground stone artifacts unequivocally dating to this phase. This probably means a decline in the frequency of ground stone artifact manufacture and use, but the sample size is small, as few excavations or surface collections were taken from purely Tilarán Phase sites. It is highly unlikely that they had no ground stone implements.

VOLCANISM

The 1968 eruption of Arenal Volcano was the most violent in Costa Rica's history. It killed about eighty-seven people and devastated mature tropical rain forest, some farms, ranches, and a town. Activity continued as of July 1991 and consisted of lava flows and occasional relatively small explosive eruptions. Arenal's eruptive history before the 1968 eruption is unknown, but the flurry of research during the past two decades has divulged at least nine explosive eruptions during the past 4,000 years (Melson 1984). The consistency of the contemporary trade winds, blowing from the east, is evident for the past few millennia. Tephra blankets throughout the sequence are thicker toward the west of Arenal Volcano than in other directions (Fig. 17-2).

The predecessor of Arenal Volcano was Cerro Chato, and it may have experienced a final, paroxysmal eruption at approximately 4000 BC. It is not yet well dated, however, and its effects on Archaic inhabitants are unknown.

The earliest tephra layer that affected villages in the research area is Unit 61, which fell about 1800 BC. It apparently came from the first major explosive eruption of Arenal Volcano and fell on the occupied countryside. It assisted in preserving the structures and activity areas at early village sites such as Tronadora Vieja (G-163).

The second tephra layer attributed to Arenal is Unit 55, which fell about 800 BC. It was a major eruption, and the ash layer resulting from it formed a relatively compacted surface in the area.

Two ash layers, called Units 53 and 52, fell at about the time of Christ. They were thinner than Units 61 or 55, and presumably they had lesser effects on the flora, fauna, and human settlements. Many of these ash layers, with soils formed on them, are visible in Figure 17-2, from a stratigraphic test pit excavated to the west of the G-150 Silencio cemetery.

Then, two relatively thick ash layers fell in the area, from two large eruptions that were closely spaced. We call them Units 41 and 40, and they fell at about AD 800 to 900. They appear to have been thick enough to have caused significant ecologic disruptions.

The last prehistoric eruption, and one of the most violent of all, deposited Unit 20 at about AD 1450. It is a very convenient stratigraphic marker that separates prehistoric from historic time spans, and it is readily recognizable in most of the research area.

Melson has studied the tephra of each of the major units at the type site of El Tajo, near the volcano (1984; Melson and Saenz 1973). He has been able to correlate most of the Arenal Project's archaeologically associated tephra units with that master chronology, but some questions remain.

EARLY EMERGENCE OF SEDENTISM

Survey of the present Lake Arenal shoreline during 1984 encountered Tronadora Phase ceramics at many sites, usually as minor components dominated by Arenal or other phase ceramics. The Tronadora Vieja site (G-163), however, had a predominance of those early ceramics, so it was selected for excavations in 1985. This is the earliest Formative village in Costa Rica excavated to date. Architecture, intravillage secondary burial pits, features, maize horticulture, and elaborate ceramics are all well dated to about 2000 BC and may extend a millennium earlier. Figure 17-3 is an artist's reconstruction of houses, a path through the village, cooking areas, an outbuilding perhaps used for storage, and a variety of activity areas inside and outside of houses. We found some Archaic artifacts at that site in the clay-laden reddish tropical soil that caps the Aguacate For-

Figure 17-2.
Volcanic ash layers (lighter) and soils formed on them (darker layers) at a stratigraphic test pit to the west of the Silencio cemetery. Seven separate volcanic eruptions are recorded at this location. Photograph by Payson Sheets.

mation. Those Archaic artifacts include the stemmed Fortuna point and some bifacial debitage, and they may be associated with the fourth millennium BC radiocarbon dates from the Aguacate Formation. We are not able to separate the late Archaic artifacts and charcoal from the early Tronadora Phase materials stratigraphically, so we do not know where within the 3000–2000 BC time span the Archaic/Formative boundary should be drawn. And, an abrupt boundary is an oversimplification of the ebb and flow of human culture change in shifting environmental and social contexts.

The explosive eruption that deposited Unit 61 at the site shortly after 2000 BC assisted the preservation of at least five houses, with their associated ceramics, lithics, and activity areas. Houses with fairly well preserved floors and postmolds were built with poles supporting (presumably) thatch roofs, round floor plans, and diameters of

Figure 17-3.
Artist's reconstruction of the Tronadora Vieja site, the earliest sedentary village yet excavated in Costa Rica. This scene shows thatched houses, a small outbuilding probably for storage, a path through town, and a variety of activity areas inside and outside of the structures. Arenal Volcano is visible in the distance. Drawing by Larry King.

5 m to 8 m. The doorways faced east, which is downslope and toward the lake. Internal post patterns suggest room dividers or elevated platforms for domestic activities. Smaller postmolds outside the houses may have been for storage or other small structures. Field testing for inorganic phosphates (Eidt 1984) assisted in identifying habitation areas.

The earliest circular houseplan previously known in Costa Rica is from La Fábrica near San José, dating to AD 500–900 (Snarskis 1981a:58, 1984a:221). Still earlier rectangular houses are known, such as at Severo Ledesma in the eastern lowlands dating to between AD 1 and 500, leading Snarskis (1984b) to suggest that the earliest Costa Rican house types are square in plan, and he thinks they are derived from Mesoamerica. The Arenal-area houses are at least two millennia earlier, however, and they are circular.

The ground plan of houses may not be a good cultural affiliation indicator. Household 1 at the clearly Mesoamerican Cerén site in El Salvador lived in one circular and three rectangular structures. Floors in the early Tronadora Phase houses were of tamped earth and were kept largely clean. Some bifacial implements were manufactured in or near the houses, and, in a holdover from the Archaic, cooking stones were used to boil water. The assumption that cooking stone technology would be replaced by cooking with ceramic vessels certainly is not applicable to the Arenal area, as both technologies coexisted for at least 3,500 years, until the Spanish Conquest. We found caches of cooking stones along with discarded fractured cooking stones outside the house walls. Sedentism was based more on exploitation of the rich floral and faunal diversity of the natural tropical rain forest than on domesticated staple foods.

SUBSISTENCE

We found maize in deposits of all sedentary phases, from Tronadora through Tilarán, in carbonized kernel, cob, pollen, or phytolith form. We also found grinding stones (i.e., manos and metates) in all phases following the Archaic except for Tilarán (Chenault 1984a). From these qualitative indicators one might conclude that a lot of maize was cultivated, processed, and consumed, or that maize was the staple. Maize, because of its hard shell, characteristic phytoliths, abundant pollen, and the fact that it is more often parched or roasted and thus more readily carbonized than are other foods, has a higher probability of being preserved than do most other foods, and thus it is easily overemphasized in subsistence reconstructions. For example, Coe and Baudez (1961) infer "intensive maize agriculture" for the Zoned Bichrome Period in northwestern Costa Rica, yet their evidence for maize cultivation is weaker than at Arenal. The frequencies of manos and metates (or ratios relative to sites, to ceramic artifacts, and to lithic artifacts) are much lower in the Arenal area than in eastern and southeastern Mesoamerica, as exemplified at Chalchuapa (Sharer 1978), Barton Ramie (Willey et al 1965), and the Zapotitán Valley (Sheets 1983). In contrast to the heavy use wear on most southeastern Mesoamerican metates, use wear is slight on most Arenal-area specimens. Although Arenal-area metates probably were used to grind maize, and likely some other materials, a major function may have been in the symbolic realm. This interpretation is strengthened by the fact that Arenal metates are more elaborately decorated, even on the grinding surface, than their quotidian contemporaries in Mesoamerica. Lange (1971:212–217) notes the paucity of use wear on legged, decorated metates from the Sapoa River area of extreme northwestern Costa Rica and argues that they were used more symbolically, as "seats of power" or symbols of office. In contrast, Snarskis (1984a:210) argues for quotidian use of most Costa Rican metates. Our data indicate that both interpretations probably are correct when applied to Arenal-area metates, but the relative amounts of utilitarian versus symbolic use are difficult to assess accurately.

The ratio of the stable C-13 to C-12 carbon isotopes in human bones (Van der Merwe 1982; Friedman and Gleason 1984) can be a dietary indicator. Our interpretation of the isotopic analyses is that less than 12% of the diet, at least in the Silencio Phase, was from C-4 photosynthetic pathway plants such as maize. Thus, the qualitative and quantitative subsistence evidence indicates maize use from the Tronadora Phase to the Conquest, but it appears to have composed only a small fraction of the diet. The lack of human bone preservation during most phases kept the sample small, unfortunately.

The maintenance of a broad-based subsistence strategy, including the avoidance of a maize staple, may have contributed to an adaptational stability greater than that achieved in Mesoamerica. Maize and beans provide an intensifiable subsistence base. As population increases, they can be planted and tended with greater inputs of human labor, yielding more per unit area, but societies face hazards of soil overexposure, erosion, leaching, drought, or pestilence. In contrast, reliance on diverse wild species and maintenance of populations at lower densities allows for greater demographic and adaptational stability. Harris (1973) argues that seed crop agriculture tends to be less stable than root crop or vegeculture because of its tendency to cause environmental degradation.

ECONOMICS

Arenal-area villages enjoyed greater economic self-sufficiency than their Mesoamerican counterparts. Arenal residents evidently were able to obtain virtually all their essential food, materials for housing, chipped- and ground stone materials, cooking stones, clay and temper for pottery, pigments, and other supplies from the environs of their settlements, without having to depend on elaborate procurement networks such as in Mesoamerica. A habitation and funerary site, G-169, illustrates the self-sufficient Arenal-area village, with access to the lake resources below, and the environmental diversity of an ecotone in the tropical rain forest (see Fig. 3-1). Production of cutting edges was minimal, in that the simplest percussion core-flake technology was performed in each household. The only common utilitarian items we found whose material came from outside the area were celts; the metamorphic raw materials (primarily a plagioclase-phyric andesite showing some hydrothermal alteration) are available in lowland Guanacaste some 40 km to 60 km to the west. Arenal residents could have obtained this material by down-the-line trade or by direct procurement. Given the durability of stone axes, and the evidence of resharpening, I would estimate that a trip by one person could easily supply the material for a village for a year.

Some goods, functioning more in the symbolic/ritual domain, came from moderate distances, including a variety of polychrome vessels (Hoopes 1984a) and gold pendants (Chenault and Mueller 1984; Chap. 13) in Silencio Phase tombs. The ceramics apparently came from lowland Guanacaste, and the gold pendants may have come from the Atlantic lowlands to the east, based on stylistic similarities with others found there. Gold occurs naturally in the Arenal area, however, and along the Pacific slope. Both ceramics and gold pendants could have been obtained by informal trade, gift exchange, or direct procurement. If the last, the search for symbols of power from distant localities by nascent chiefs might have been a major objective (Helms 1979).

Mesoamerican communities were more dependent on long-distance trade routes extending hundreds of kilometers for materials such as obsidian, vesicular basalt, metamorphic rocks, and perishable goods. Mesoamerican economic and political systems functioned by differentiation, occupational specialization, centralization of authority, and controlled redistribution; therefore, sites were characterized by diversity and interrelatedness instead of by the repetition of self-sufficient units of production and consumption across the countryside.

REMOTE SENSING

The Arenal area presents major challenges for remote sensing applied to archaeology for a number of reasons. The very heavy cloud cover and abundant atmospheric moisture interfere with many data-gathering techniques. The moist tropical climate has resulted in a mature tropical rain forest with exceptionally high biomass, or thick grass cover where it was cut for pasture. Arenal's eruptions have buried features under numerous volcanic ash layers. The human population density of the area was low at all times in prehistory, compared to similar-sized drainages in Mesoamerica or the Andean area, and the impacts of Arenal peoples on their prehistoric environments were relatively slight. Arenal-area societies were egalitarian at most times, as in the Gulf of Nicoya (Creamer and Haas 1985), with weak evidence of their having crossed the threshold into ranked or chiefdom societies during the Arenal or Silencio phases. Hence, they lacked the large-scale public constructions of more complex societies, which are detectable by remote sensing.

The project has benefited from an abundance of remotely sensed data obtained by the Earth Resources Laboratory of NASA. Two Landsat satellite scenes (Multispectral Scanner and Thematic Mapper instruments) recorded general environmental gradients, detected tropical rain forest variability (Joyce 1983), and traced the impact of the 1968 Arenal eruption on the research area. Four aircraft overflights contributed optical images in the form of color and color infrared aerial photography, and digital data from the laser profiler (Lidar), synthetic aperture radar (SAR; Wu and Sader 1987), and TIMS (Kahle and Goetz 1983; Sever and Wiseman 1985). In addition, numerous black-and-white prints were obtained from the 9 inch × 9 inch negatives at the Instituto Geográfico in Costa Rica; their detail, even when enlarged ten times, was of considerable assistance. They remain the most economical form of remotely sensed data available to the project.

Numerous linear anomalies have been discovered in the color infrared, color aerial, and black-and-white photography, and in the digital data, particularly from the TIMS and SAR instruments, and in the multiple passes of the Lidar instrument. With analysis and comparison with features of the contemporary landscape, many such as fence lines, cattle paths, or roads, are identifiable as historic or recent features. Many, however, connected prehistoric sites with other prehistoric sites or resource sources; for instance, lines leaving the Silencio cemetery lead directly to a spring, and another line connects the cemetery with repositories of flat-fracturing andesite used for tomb and wall construction and lead to the surface outcrop of that rock type, and other lines apparently lead to the villages supplying dead bodies to the cemetery.

The lines can only be considered anomalies until they are investigated in the field and until unequivocal evidence is collected that indicates that they are cultural and prehistoric. Many of the lines, investigated by excavating trenches across them, turned out to be prehistoric erosional footpaths. Examination of the stratigraphy indicated the means of formation and preservation. As use of the footpath began, soil compaction retarded vegetation growth and reduced rainfall infiltration. As rain fell, surface runoff and erosion began along the line of path use. Erosion formed a U-shaped trench along the path itself. As the path continued to be used and eroded, the banks became steeper; lateral erosion then formed a broad V-shaped trench containing the path. Along some steeper slopes where there was considerable foot traffic and greater downward and lateral erosion, the entrenchment reached a few meters in depth and extended more than 5 m on each side of the path. After path abandonment, revegetation stabilized the surface, inhibiting erosion and facilitating preservation. Later volcanic ash layers also aided preservation and facilitated our interpretation of the complex mixture of natural and cultural processes.

The tephra sequence established by Melson (1984) was of great assistance in dating path use. Path excavations indicate the stratum from which erosion began, giving an initiation date for path use, such as after that volcanic ash layer fell and developed a soil, but prior to the fall of the next ash layer. The uneroded ash layer above the path provides a dating of the cessation of path use. Lithic and ceramic artifacts provide independent data for dating path use. They are rare in most path trenches, however, and the lithics rarely are diagnostic of short time periods. If artifacts were the sole means of dating the paths, most trenches would have required extensive excavations, of many dozens of square meters, to generate an adequate sample.

A crucial element of remote sensing is field verification, and clear criteria must be established for an anomaly to be considered a prehistoric cultural feature. The reverse is also true, that the field methodology must clarify how anomalies can be identified as noncultural phenomena or as recent cultural features. In a few cases, we discovered linear anomalies in the imagery that had the form, color density, or spectral signature of previously confirmed prehistoric paths, yet, by examining stratigraphic relationships discovered during field investigations, we determined them to be historic or recent.

The detection of linear anomalies in the remote-sensing data and the confirmation (by excavations) of most anomalies as prehistoric footpaths are beginning to establish the network of human transportation and communication across the landscape. These prehistoric paths are much like the contemporary path network of the Kayapó Indians in the Amazon drainage of Brazil recorded by Posey (1983), which links villages, fields, and resources in a moist tropical rain forest environment.

CONCLUSIONS

The Proyecto Prehistórico Arenal was designed as a study of settlement and subsistence in the Costa Rican tropical rain forest under the occasional impact of explosive volcanic eruptions. We hoped that a habitation record spanning at least a millennium could be found to explore the resiliency to explosive volcanism of relatively simple societies in Costa Rica, so that they could be compared with more complex societies in northern Central America and elsewhere that were affected by sudden eruptions. The Arenal data base that we developed for exploring settlement, subsistence, and volcanism is geographically and chronologically more extensive than originally anticipated, ranging from the very wet Atlantic drainage to the drier monsoon climate on the Pacific drainage, and including evidence of Paleo-Indian and Archaic occupation prior to the emergence of sedentary village life sometime before 2000 BC.

As with comparable research done in El Salvador (Sheets 1983) and in Panama (Linares, Sheets, and Rosenthal 1975), our excavations, largely because of the difficulties of discovering and excavating deeply buried sites, focused on sites that were not buried by many meters of volcanic ash. Sites at the other extreme, with a mere dusting of ash, were avoided also, as they do not offer improved preservation of features, artifacts, structures, and recognizable tephra layers for dating purposes, and residents were not faced with significant adaptive problems when the ash fell.

Emphasizing sites buried by moderate amounts of tephra (1 m to 2 m) also confers advantages in comparability, as similar depths of airfall ash have similar effects on flora and fauna (Segerstrom 1950; Rees 1979), and the similarities and differences in human responses can be sought. A factor making comparisons more difficult is the scale of various eruptions; even though different sites can be buried by the same depth of ash from different eruptions, the magnitude of eruptions and the areas covered by varying ash depths need to be taken into account. Although we are far from understanding all significant variables and having sufficient cases to be considered adequate samples, we can propose some working hypotheses and initial generalizations.

The simpler Costa Rican societies seem to have been more resilient than the more complex Salvadoran societies to explosive volcanic eruptions. Prehistoric Salvadoran societies were more vulnerable to sudden eruptions, evidently because they relied more heavily on the built environment and on a domesticated staple crop. They had a more complex economy relying on commodities transported greater distances and involving redistribution, and the settlements were vertically organized into tiers that represented social, political, and economic centralization (Sheets 1983).

Although not as complex as Salvadoran societies, the Barriles chiefdom of western Panama was organized into two levels of villages, and at least some of the economy was under centralized control (Linares, Sheets, and Rosenthal 1975). Subsistence apparently was based on a maize staple, and alluvial soils were strongly favored for settlement and agriculture. The eruption of Baru Volcano depopulated the upper reaches of the Chiriqui Viejo River and may have been the impetus for settlement on the Atlantic slope north of the Continental Divide.

In both El Salvador and Panama the major eruptions (Ilopango and Baru, respectively) serve as phase or period boundaries because they were large enough to cause societal impacts evidenced in material culture change. Societies reoccupying the areas after the recovery of vegetation and soils were sufficiently different to warrant a phase or period boundary. Such is not the case in Costa Rica, even though Arenal's explosive eruptions occurred on an average of every four centuries, thus probably catching nearby people as unprepared as they were during its most recent eruption in 1968. There is not a single Arenal eruption that can be correlated with a phase boundary, and thus with a time of significant culture change. No Arenal eruption had a sufficient effect on nearby societies, whether by internal disruption, by ecologic impact, or by causing migration with culture change prior to reoccupation, to be recognizable in the cultural record. In contrast, the Baru tephra was thinner at occupied sites, yet it had a greater impact on prehistoric Panamanian villages. The Ilopango tephra was comparable in thickness to Arenal tephra layers at considerable distances from the source, and the relatively small eruptions of Laguna Caldera, Boquerón, and Playón provide comparative cases (Sheets [ed.] 1983).

The strongest effect of volcanism on settlement detected in the Arenal area occurred with the emplacements of Units 41 and 40, about AD 900, which may have caused a movement of people leading to a concentration of settlements in the Piedra River Valley. The ash layers were thinner in the valley than in the Arenal Lake-River area, and thus it may have served as a refuge area until soils and vegetation recovered in the areas closer to the volcano. In spite of the settlement changes, there appear to have been no detectable changes in material culture, and we have drawn no phase or period boundaries at that time. The general decline in population in the research area from the Arenal Phase to the Spanish Conquest does not seem to correlate with volcanic activity, and it seems to have been a more regional phenomenon.

We have defined five phases for the Arenal area, from the Fortuna Phase in the local Archaic through the Tilarán Phase just prior to the Spanish Conquest. It is significant that the degree of culture change represented by the phase boundaries is markedly lower than in Mesoamerican phase boundaries. The degree of continuity in settlement patterns, in basic technology, in artifact style and form, and in subsistence is striking. Their success in establishing village life by 2000 BC, with a basic technology of stone boiling and core-flake technology for production of cutting edges that derived from the Archaic, is impressive. A part of that success probably is based on a high degree of village self-sufficiency, maintained up to the Spanish Conquest. Subsistence stability probably was facilitated by a reliance on wild fruits, seeds, nuts, berries, game, and fish and avoiding the instabilities of intensifying a domesticated seed-based economy in a tropical wet environment.

Paleo-Indian occupation is evidenced by a Clovis point, made out of locally available chalcedony. Archaic occupation, locally identified as the "Fortuna Phase," is indicated by a campsite with two hearths, a large accumulation of cooking stones, and core-flake technology. The two latter elements of adaptive technology, beginning in the

Archaic if not earlier, continue essentially unchanged throughout all later phases up to the Spanish Conquest.

The beginning date of the earliest Formative settlements is unclear. Sedentism occurred sometime during the third millennium BC, or possibly slightly earlier, but it is clear that sedentary villages were well established by 2000 BC. The earliest eruption of Arenal Volcano buried house floors, features, and artifacts at the Tronadora Vieja site. Burials were placed in small rectangular pits near houses. Ceramics were sophisticated, being technically well made and elaborately decorated by painting and incising.

Ceramic traditions in the Arenal area did not develop in isolation. From the very beginnings of the Tronadora Phase, however, the sequence has decidedly local flavor throughout. Red-rimmed domestic vessels are predominant in all but the Tilarán Phase, and clear continuities in form are apparent from one phase to the next. Even during the Silencio Phase, when influence from Greater Nicoya was strongest, the predominant ceramic types are quite localized. The Silencio points may show a distant connection with the southward migrations of the Pipil and Nicarao populations from central Mexico into Central America, but the bulk of the lithic industries represent local solutions to local problems.

The ceramic sequence suggests that the region was characterized by continuity of population and culture, with little evidence for displacement, migration, or invasion. The quantity and distribution of ceramics does suggest some significant demographic trends through the sequence, however. Sites with Arenal Phase ceramics greatly outnumber those of other phases, suggesting a peak population in the region at this time. Cemeteries were in special locations beyond the edges of villages and marked with large numbers of river rocks and broken ceramic vessels and elaborate metates.

Although the numbers and sizes of sites generally declined during the Silencio Phase, cemeteries were often located even farther from villages, and the deceased were given still more elaborate treatment. Polychrome pottery began in the area and the Silencio point was an addition to the chipped stone inventory.

The final phase of prehistory, the Tilarán Phase, witnessed a break with Greater Nicoya in the primary affiliation of the Cordillera. Tilarán Phase artifacts show a generalized similarity with the cultures to the east and south. The settlement pattern is marked by smaller and more dispersed hamlets. Ceramics were decorated by plastic surface modification rather than painting, and the quality of production declined.

With its occasional explosive eruptions, Arenal Volcano applied periodic stresses on the flora, fauna, and societies living downwind. Those stresses decline with distance from the source, and become small at distances from 20 km to 30 km. Arenal has erupted at least nine times during the past 4,000 years, providing a series of time-stratigraphic horizon markers throughout much of the area.

In spite of occasional environmental instability, egalitarian societies in the Arenal area were able to maintain cultural stability for millennia. That achievement was assisted by the maintenance of relatively simple societies and broad-based adaptive strategies. The avoidance of a single staple crop, the avoidance of overdependance on the built environment, and economic independence of villages probably were key factors in social stability and recovery from occasional disasters.

ACKNOWLEDGMENTS

This chapter presents an overview of the objectives, methods, context, and results of the Proyecto Prehistórico Arenal, and thus it should be considered as a summary of the work of the entire project. I thank Brian McKee and an anonymous reviewer for the University of Texas Press for critiquing earlier drafts of this chapter.

References Cited

ABEL-VIDOR, S.

1980 The Historical Sources for the Greater Nicoya Archaeological Sub-Area. *Vínculos* 6(1–2):155–169.

1981 Ethnohistorical Approaches to the Archaeology of Greater Nicoya. In *Between Continents/Between Seas: Precolumbian Art of Costa Rica.* Edited by E. Benson, pp. 85–92. New York: Harry N. Abrams.

1988 Gonzalo Fernández de Oviedo y Valdés: His Work and His Nicaragua, 1527–1529. In *Costa Rican Art and Archaeology: Essays in Honor of Frederick R. Mayer.* Edited by Frederick W. Lange, pp. 261–290. Boulder: University of Colorado.

ABEL-VIDOR, S., C. BAUDEZ, R. BISHOP, L. BONILLA V., M. CALVO M., W. CREAMER, J. DAY, J. GUERRERO, P. HEALY, J. HOOPES, F. LANGE, S. SALGADO, R. STROESSNER, AND A. TILLET

1987 Principales tipos cerámicos y variedades de la Gran Nicoya. *Vínculos* 13(1–2):35–318.

ACCOLA, RICHARD

1978 Una revisión de los tipos de cerámica del período policromo medio en Guanacaste. *Vínculos* 4:80–105.

ADAMS, RICHARD E. W.

1977 *Prehistoric Mesoamerica.* Boston: Little, Brown and Co.

AGUILAR P., C.

1972 *Guayabo de Turrialba.* San José: Editorial Costa Rica.

1976 Relaciones de las culturas precolombianas en el intermontano central de Costa Rica. *Vínculos* 2(1):75–86.

1984 Introducción a la arqueología de la región del volcán Arenal. *Anales, Academia de Geografía e Historia de Costa Rica* (San José).

ALLEN, KAREN K.

1948 Lauraceae. Flora of Panama. Part V. Fascicle 1. *Annals of the Missouri Botanical Garden* 35:2–5.

ALLEN, PAUL H.

1977 *The Rain Forests of Golfo Dulce.* Stanford, Calif.: Stanford University Press.

ANDERSON, W. R.
1983 Byrsonima crassifolia (Nance, Nancite, Shoemaker's tree). In *Costa Rican Natural History*. Edited by Daniel Janzen, pp. 202–204. Chicago: University of Chicago Press.

ANDREWS V., E. WILLEYS, AND NORMAN HAMMOND
1990 Redefinition of the Swasey Phase at Cuello, Belize. *American Antiquity* 55(3):570–584.

BALSER, CARLOS
1974 *El jade de Costa Rica*. San José: Librería Lehmann.

BARKLEY, FRED A.
1934 The Statistical Theory of Pollen Analysis. *Ecology* 15(3):283–289.

BARTLETT, ALEXANDRA S., AND ELSO S. BARGHOORN
1973 Phytogeographic History of the Isthmus of Panama during the Past 12,000 Years. In *Vegetation and Vegetational History of Northern Latin America*. Edited by Alan H. Graham, pp. 203–299. New York: Elsevier Scientific Publishing Co.

BAUDEZ, CLAUDE F.
1967 Recherches archeologiques dans la vallée du Tempisque, Guanacaste, Costa Rica. *Travaux et Memoires de l'Institut des Hautes Etudes de l'Amerique Latine, no. 18*. Centre National de la Recherche Scientifique, Paris.

BAUDEZ, CLAUDE F., AND MICHAEL D. COE
1962 Archaeological Sequences in Northwestern Costa Rica. Akter, 34th International Congress of Americanists, pp. 366–373. Vienna.
1966 Incised Slate Disks from the Atlantic Watershed of Costa Rica: A Commentary. *American Antiquity* 31:441–443.

BERNSTEIN, DAVID
1980 Artefactos de piedra pulida de Guanacaste, Costa Rica: una perspectiva funcional. *Vínculos* 6(1–2): 141–154.

BINFORD, L. R.
1971 Mortuary Practices: Their Study and Their Potential. In *Approaches to the Social Dimensions of Mortuary Practices*. Edited by J. A. Brown, pp. 6–29. *Memoirs of the Society for American Archaeology*, no. 25.
1972 *An Archaeological Perspective*. Seminar Press, New York.

BISCHOF, HENNING
1966 Canapote—an Early Ceramic Site in Northern Colombia. Preliminary Report. *Actas y Memorias, 36 1/2 Congreso Internacional de Americanistas* 1:484–491. Seville.
1972 The Origins of Pottery in South America: Recent Radiocarbon Dates from Southwest Ecuador. *Proceedings of the 40th International Congress of Americanists* 1:269–281. Genoa: Tilgher.

BISHOP, RONALD L., F. W. LANGE, AND P. C. LANGE
1988 Ceramic Paste Compositional Patterns in Greater Nicoya Pottery. In *Costa Rican Art and Archaeology*. Edited by F. W. Lange, pp. 11–44. Boulder: University of Colorado Museum.

BLACK, KEVIN D.
1983 The Zapotitán Valley Archeological Survey. In *Archeology and Volcanism in Central America*. Edited by Payson D. Sheets, pp. 62–97. Austin: University of Texas Press.

BLANCO VARGAS, AIDA M., JUAN VICENTE GUERRERO MIRANDA, AND SILVIA SALGADO GONZÁLEZ.
1986 Patrones funerarios del policromo medio en el sector sur de Gran Nicoya. *Vínculos* 12(1–2): 135–158.

BLANTON, RICHARD E.
1972 Prehispanic Settlement Patterns of the Ixtapalapa Peninsula Region, Mexico. *Occasional Papers of the Department of Anthropology*, no. 6. University Park: The Pennsylvania State University.

BLONG, RUSSELL J.
1984 *Volcanic Hazards: A Sourcebook on the Effects of Eruptions*. New York: Academic Press.

BORGIA, A., C. POORE, M. CARR, W. MELSON, AND G. ALVARADO
1988 Structural, Stratigraphic, and Petrologic Aspects of the Arenal-Chato Volcanic System, Costa Rica: Evolution of a Young Stratovolcanic Complex. *Bulletin of Volcanology* 50:86–105.

BOUCHER, D. H., M. HANSEN, S. RISCH, AND J. H. VANDERMEER
1983 Agriculture; Introduction. In *Costa Rican Natural History*. Edited by Daniel H. Janzen, pp. 66–73. Chicago: University of Chicago Press.

BOZARTH, S.
1986 Morphologically Distinctive Phaseolus, Cucurbita, and Helianthus Phytoliths. In *Plant Opal Phytolith Analysis in Archaeology and Paleoecology*. Edited by I. Rovner, pp. 56–66. Occasional Papers No. 1 of the Phytolitharian, North Carolina State University.

BOZZOLI DE WILLIE, MARIA EUGENIA
1975 Birth and Death in the Belief System of the Bribri Indians of Costa Rica. Ph.D. dissertation (Anthropology), University of Georgia, Athens.

BRADLEY, JOHN
1984 The Silencio Funerary Sites. *Vínculos* 10(1–2): 93–114.

BRADLEY, JOHN E., JOHN E. HOOPES, AND PAYSON SHEETS
1984 Lake Site Testing Program. *Vínculos* 10 (1–2): 75–92.

BRAY, WARWICK
1978 An Eighteenth-Century Reference to a Fluted Point from Guatemala. *American Antiquity* 43: 457–460.
1981 Gold Work. In *Between Continents/Between Seas: Precolumbian Art of Costa Rica*. Edited by E. Benson, pp. 153–166. New York: Harry N. Abrams.
1984 Across the Darien Gap: A Colombian View of Isthmian Archaeology. In *The Archaeology of Lower Central America*. Edited by F. W. Lange and D. Z. Stone, pp. 305–340. Albuquerque: University of New Mexico Press.

BRUSH, C. F.
1965 Pox Pottery: Earliest Identified Mexican Ceramic. *Science* 149:194–195.
1969 A Contribution to the Archeology of Costal Guerrero, Mexico. Ph.D. Dissertation, Columbia University.

BRYANT, VAUGHN M., JR., AND RICHARD G. HOLLOWAY
1983 The Role of Palynology in Archaeology. In *Advances in Archaeological Method and Theory*, Vol. 6. Edited by Michael D. Schiffer, pp. 191–224. Orlando: Academic Press.

BURTON, I., R. KATES, AND G. WHITE
1978 *The Environment as Hazard.* New York: Oxford University Press.

CAMERON, H. L.
1958 History from the Air. *Photogrammetric Engineering* 24: 366–375.

CAPPER, COL. J. E.
1907 Photographs of Stonehenge as Seen from a War Balloon. *Archaeologia*: 571.

CARLSON, JOHN B.
1981 Olmec Concave Iron-Ore Mirrors: The Aesthetics of a Lithic Technology and the Lord of the Mirror. In *The Olmec and Their Neighbors.* Edited by Elizabeth P. Benson, pp. 117–148. Washington, D.C.: Dumbarton Oaks Research Library and Collections, Trustees for Harvard University.

CARR, M. J., AND J. A. WALKER
1987 Intra-eruption Changes in the Composition of Some Mafic to Intermediate Tephras in Central America. *Journal of Volcanic and Geothermal Research* 33: 147–159.

CARSON, M. A., AND M. J. KIRKBY
1972 *Hillslope Form and Process.* Cambridge: Cambridge University Press

CARSTENS, K. C., T. C. KIND, AND N. V. WEBER
1982 Using Remote Sensing in a Predictive Model: The Jackson Purchase Region, Kentucky. *Proceedings of Pecora VII Symposium,* pp. 494–507. Washington, D.C.: U.S. Dept. of the Interior.

CASTILLO-MUÑOZ, R.
1983 Geology. In *Costa Rican Natural History.* Edited by Daniel Janzen, pp. 47–62. Chicago: University of Chicago Press.

CATER, JOHN D.
n.d. Groundstone Artifacts from Site 5MT2, Yellow Jacket, CO. Manuscript. University of Colorado Museum, Boulder.

CHACÓN, JUAN BRAVO
1982 Geomorfología de la Hoja Fortuna. Trabajo de Investigación para el Grado de Licenciado en Geografía. Campus Omar Dengo, Heredia, Costa Rica.

CHANG, K. C.
1968 Toward a Science of Prehistoric Society. In *Settlement Archaeology.* Edited by K. C. Chang, pp. 1–9. Palo Alto, Calif.: National Press.

CHAPMAN, R.
1981 The Emergence of Formal Disposal Areas and the "Problem" of Megalithic Tombs in Prehistoric Europe. In *The Archaeology of Death.* Edited by R. Chapman, I. Kinnes, K. Randsborg, pp. 71–81. Cambridge: Cambridge University Press.

CHENAULT, MARK L.
1984a Ground and Polished Stone from the Cuenca de Arenal. *Vínculos* 10(1–2):167–186.
1984b Test Excavations at Neblina and Las Piedras. *Vínculos* 10(1–2):115–120.
1986 Technical Analysis of Precolumbian Costa Rican Jadeite and Greenstone Artifacts. M.A. thesis, University of Colorado.
1988 Jadeite, Greenstone and the Precolumbian Costa Rican Lapidary. In *Costa Rican Art and Archaeology: Essays in Honor of Frederick R. Mayer.* Edited by Frederick W. Lange, pp. 89–110. Boulder: University of Colorado.

CHENAULT, M., AND M. MUELLER
1984 Jewelry from the Cuenca de Arenal. *Vínculos* 10(1–2): 187–192.

CHIESA, S.
1987 Estudio de las capas piroclásticos (tefras) del Volcán Arenal (Costa Rica) con énfasis en la Unidada 20. Report no. 276, Instituto Costarricense de Electricidad.

CLARK, JOHN E., MICHAEL BLAKE, PEDRO GUZY, MARTA CUEVAS, AND TAMARA SALCEDO
n.d. Final Report to the Instiuto Nacional de Antropología e Historia of the Early Preclassic Pacific Coastal Project. Manuscript. New World Archaeological Foundation, Brigham Young University.

CLARY, KAREN H.
1986 An Analysis of Pollen from Core 2, from the Nacascolo Archaeological Area, on the Nicoya Peninsula, Northwestern Costa Rica. Manuscript. University Museum of Archaeology/Anthropology, University of Pennsylvania, Philadelphia.
In progress. Pollen Studies from Coastal Cores from the Bay of Parita, Panama.

COE, MICHAEL D.
1960 Archaeological Linkages with North and South America at La Victoria, Guatemala. *American Anthropologist* 62: 363–393.
1961 La Victoria, an Early Site on the Pacific Coast of Guatemala. *Papers of the Peabody Museum of Archaeology and Ethnology,* vol. 53. Cambridge: Harvard University.

COE, MICHAEL D., AND C. BAUDEZ
1961 The Zoned Bichrome Period in Northwestern Costa Rica. *American Antiquity* 26: 505–515.

COE, MICHAEL D., AND RICHARD DIEHL
1980 *In the Land of the Olmec.* Austin: University of Texas Press.

COE, MICHAEL D., AND KENT V. FLANNERY
1967 Early Cultures and Human Ecology in South Coastal Guatemala. *Smithsonian Contributions to Anthropology,* vol. 3. Washington, D.C.: Smithsonian Institution.

CONANT, F. P.
1976 Satellite Analysis of Human Ecosystems in the Sahel of East Africa. Proposal submitted to the National Science Foundation.

CONANT, F. P., AND T. K. CARY
1977 A First Interpretation of East Africa Swiddening Via Computer-assisted Analysis of 3 Landsat Tapes. *Proceedings, 1977, Machine Processing of Remotely Sensed Data Symposium,* pp. 36–43. West Lafayette, Ind.: Purdue University.

COOKE, R.
1984 Archaeological Research in Central and Eastern Panama: A Review of Some Problems. In *The Archaeology of Lower Central America.* Edited by F. Lange and D. Stone, pp. 263–302. Albuquerque: University of New Mexico Press.

COOKE, R. G., AND A. J. RANERE
1984 The Proyecto Santa María: A Multidisciplinary Analysis of Prehistoric Adaptations to a Tropical Watershed in Panama. In *Recent Developments in Isthmian Archaeology: Advances in the Prehistory of Lower Central America.* Edited by Frederick W. Lange, pp. 1–30. Proceedings of the 44th Congress of Americanists, Manchester, 1982. B.A.R. Series 212.

CORRALES, FRANCISCO U.
1985 Prospección y excavaciones estratigráficas en el Sitio Curré (P-62-Ce), Valle Diquis, Costa Rica. *Vínculos* 11(1–2):1–16.
1989 La ocupación agrícola temprana del sitio arqueológico Curré, Valle del Diquis. Tesis de Lic., Escuela de Antropología y Sociologia, Facultad de Ciencias Sociales, Universidad de Costa Rica, San José.

CRAWFORD, O. G. S.
1923 Air Survey and Archaeology. *Geographical Journal* 61:342–366.
1924a Archaeology from the air. *Nature* 114:580–582.
1924b Air Survey and Archaeology. *Ordinance Survey Professional Papers*, no. 7.
1929 Air Photography for Archaeologists. *Ordinance Survey Professional Papers*, no. 12.

CRAWFORD, O. G. S., AND ALEXANDER KEILLER
1928 *Wessex from the Air*. Oxford: Clarendon Press.

CREAMER, WINIFRED
1979 Preliminary Survey Near Upala (Alajuela), Costa Rica. Paper Presented at the 44th Annual Meeting, Society for American Archaeology, Vancouver.
1983 Production and Exchange on Two Islands in the Gulf of Nicoya, Costa Rica, A.D. 1200–1550. Ph.D. dissertation. Tulane University. Ann Arbor: University Microfilms.

CREAMER, W., AND S. DAWSON
1982–1983 Preliminary Survey near Upala, Alajuela, Costa Rica. In *Prehistoric Settlement Patterns in Costa Rica*. Edited by F. W. Lange and L. Norr. *Journal of the Steward Anthropological Society* 14(1–2): 161–166.

CREAMER, W., AND J. HAAS
1985 Tribe versus Chiefdom in Lower Central America. *American Antiquity* 50:738–754.

CROAT, THOMAS B.
1978 *Flora of Barro Colorado Island*. Stanford, Calif.: Stanford University Press.

CRUMLEY, CAROLE L.
1983 Archaeological Reconnaissance at Mont Dardon, France. *Archaeology* (May–June): 12–17.

DAHLGREN, B. E.
1936 Index of American Palms. In *Field Museum of Natural History Botanical Series* 14(35):406–409.

DAHLIN, B. H.
1980 Surveying the Volcán Region with the Post Hole Digger. In *Adaptive Radiations in Prehistoric Panama*, pp. 276–279. Peabody Museum Monograph 5. Cambridge: Harvard University.

DAY, J. S.
1984 New Approaches in Stylistic Analysis: The Late Polychrome Period Ceramics from Hacienda Tempisque, Guanacaste Province, Costa Rica. Ph.D. dissertation, University of Colorado. Ann Arbor: University Microfilms.

DECKER, R. W., AND D. HADIKUSUMO
1961 Results of the 1960 Expedition to Krakatau. *Journal of Geophysical Research* 66:3497–3511.

DENEVAN, WILLIAM M.
1961 The Upland Pine Forests of Nicaragua. *University of California Publications in Geography* 12(4): 251–320.

DEUEL, LEO
1969 *Flights into Yesterday: The Story of Aerial Archaeology*. New York: St. Martin's Press.

DILLON, BRIAN D.
1984 Island Building and Villages of the Dead: Living Archaeology in the Comarca de San Blas, Panama. *Journal of New World Archaeology* 6(2):49–65.

DROLET, ROBERT P.
1983 Al otro lado de Chiriqui, El Diquis: nuevos datos para la integración cultural de la región Gran Chiriqui. *Vínculos* 9(1–2):25–76.
1984a Investigations in Diquis. In *The Archaeology of Lower Central America*. Edited by Frederick W. Lange and Doris Stone, pp. 33–60. Albuquerque: University of New Mexico Press.
1984b Community Life in a Late Phase Agricultural Village, Southeastern Costa Rica. In *Recent Developments in Isthmian Archaeology: Advances in the Prehistory of Lower Central America*. Edited by Frederick W. Lange, pp. 123–152. Proceedings of the 44th Congress of Americanists. B.A.R. Series 212, Manchester.

EARLE, T., AND A. W. JOHNSON
1982 Research and Technology: Annual Report Fiscal Year 1982. National Space Technology Laboratories, National Aeronautics and Space Administration. NSTL Station.
1987 *The Evolution of Human Societies: From Foraging Group to Agrarian State*. Stanford, Calif.: Stanford University Press, Stanford Earth Resources Laboratory.

EASBY, ELIZABETH K.
1968 *Pre-Columbian Jade from Costa Rica*. New York: Andre Emmerich.
1981 Jade. In *Between Continents/Between Seas: Precolumbian Art of Costa Rica*. Edited by E. Benson, pp. 135–151. New York: Harry R. Abrams.

EBERT, JAMES
1984 Remote Sensing Applications in Archaeology. In *Advances in Archaeological Method and Theory*, vol. 7. Edited by Michael B. Schiffer, pp. 293–362. Orlando, Fla.: Academic Press.

EBERT, JAMES, AND THOMAS R. LYONS
1983 Archaeology, Anthropology, and Cultural Resources Management. In *Manual of Remote Sensing*. Edited by Robert N. Colwell, pp. 1233–1304. Vol. II, Interpretation and Applications. Falls Church, Va.: American Society of Photogrammetry.

EDIENE, BERNARD
1956 Une Méthode practique pour la detection aerienne des sites archaeologiques, en particulier par la photographie sur films en couleurs et sur films infrarogues. *Bulletin de la Société Prehistorique Française* 53:540–546.

EIDT, R. C.
1984 *Advances in Abandoned Settlement Analysis: Application to Prehistoric Anthrosols in Colombia, South America*. Milwaukee: University of Wisconsin–Milwaukee, Center for Latin America.

EINHAUS, C. SHELTON
1980 Stone Tools from La Pitahaya (IS-3). In *Adaptive Radiations in Prehistoric Panama*. Edited by Olga Linares and Anthony Ranere, pp. 429–466. Peabody Museum Monograph 5. Cambridge: Harvard University, Peabody Museum.

ERDTMAN, G.
1952 *Pollen Morphology and Plant Taxonomy. Angiosperms*. Waltham, Mass.: Chronica Botanica Co.

FANALE, R.
1974 Utilization of ERTS-1 Imagery in the Analysis of Settlement and Land Use of the Dogon of Mali. M.S. thesis (Anthropology), Catholic University.

FERRERO, A. L.
1977 *Costa Rica Precolombina.* San José: Editorial Costa Rica.
1981 *Costa Rica Precolombina.* 4th edition. San José: Editorial Costa Rica.

FINCH, WILL O.
1982–1983 A Preliminary Survey of Hacienda Jericó. In *Prehistoric Settlement Patterns in Costa Rica.* Edited by F. W. Lange and L. Norr. *Journal of the Steward Anthropological Society* 14(1–2):97–104.

FINDLOW, FRANK J., M. J. SNARSKIS, AND P. MARTIN
1979 Un análisis de zonas de explotación relacionadas con algunos sitios prehistóricos de la vertiente atlántica de Costa Rica. *Vínculos* 5(2):53–71.

FLANNERY, KENT, ED.
1976 *The Early Mesoamerican Village.* New York: Academic Press.

FLANNERY, KENT, AND JOYCE MARCUS
1983 *The Cloud People: Divergent Evolution of the Zapotec and Mixtec Civilizations.* New York: Academic Press.

FONSECA Z., OSCAR
1981 Guayabo de Turrialba and Its Significance. In *Between Continents/Between Seas: Precolumbian Art of Costa Rica.* Edited by E. Benson, pp. 104–111. New York: Harry N. Abrams.

FORD, JAMES A.
1969 A Comparison of Formative Cultures in the Americas: Diffusion or the Psychic Unity of Man? *Smithsonian Institution Contributions to Anthropology,* vol. 2. Washington, D.C.: Smithsonian Institution.

FORD, RICHARD I.
1984 Prehistoric Phytogeography of Economic Plants in Latin America. In *Pre-Columbian Plant Migration.* Edited by Doris Stone, pp. 175–183. Papers of the Peabody Museum of Archaeology and Ethnology, vol. 76.

FOSHAG, WILLIAM
1957 Mineralogical Studies on Guatemalan Jade. *Smithsonian Miscellaneous Collections* 145(5).

FRIEDMAN, I., AND J. GLEASON
1984 C^{13} Analysis of Bone Samples from Site G-150, El Silencio. *Vínculos* 10(1–2):113–114.

FUDALI, R., AND W. G. MELSON
1972 Ejecta Velocities, Magma Chamber Pressure, and Kinetic Energy Associated with the 1968 Eruption of Arenal Volcano, Costa Rica. *Bulletin Volcanologique* 35(2):383–401.

GALINAT, W. C.
1980 The Archaeological Maize Remains from Volcan Panama—A Comparative Perspective. In *Adaptive Radiations in Prehistoric Panama.* Edited by Olga Linares and Anthony Ranere, pp. 175–180. Peabody Museum Monograph 5. Cambridge: Harvard University, Peabody Museum.

GARNETT, D. (ED.)
1938 *The Letters of T. E. Lawrence.* London: Spring Books.

GEOLOGICAL SOCIETY OF AMERICA
1948 *Goddard Rock Color Chart.* Boulder: Geological Society of America.

GOLDSTEIN, LYNNE
1981 One-Dimensional Archaeology and Multi-Dimensional People: Spatial Organization and Mortuary Analysis. In *The Archaeology of Death.* Edited by R. Chapman, I. Kinnes, K. Ransborg, pp. 53–69. Cambridge: Cambridge University Press.

GRAHAM, MARK
1981 Traditions of Costa Rican Stone Sculpture. In *Between Continents/Between Seas: Precolumbian Art of Costa Rica.* Edited by E. Benson, pp. 113–134. New York: Harry N. Abrams.

GREEN, DEE F., AND GARETH W. LOWE
1967 Altamira and Padre Piedra, Early Preclassic Sites in Chiapas, Mexico. *Papers of the New World Archaeological Foundation,* no. 20.

GUERRERO, J.
1982–1983 Recientes investigaciones en el Valle de Nosara, Guanacaste. In *Prehistoric Settlement Patterns in Costa Rica.* Edited by F. W. Lange and L. Norr. *Journal of the Steward Anthropological Society* 14(1–2):369–386.

GUERRERO, J., AND A. BLANCO
1987 La Ceiba: un asentamiento del policromo medio en el Valle del Tempisque con actividades funerarias. Thesis (Anthropology and Sociology), University of Costa Rica, San José.

GUERRERO, J., A. BLANCO, AND S. SALGADO
1986 "Patrones funerarios del policromo medio en el sector sur de Gran Nicoya." *Vínculos* 12:135–157.

GUMERMAN, GEORGE J., AND JAMES A. NEELY
1972 An Archaeological Survey of the Tehuacán Valley, Mexico: A Test of Color Infrared Photography. *American Antiquity* 37:520–527.

HABERLAND, WOLFGANG
1966 Early Phases on Ometepe Island. *Actas y Memorias, 36 1/2 Congreso Internacional de Americanistas* 1:399–403.
1969 Early Phases and Their Relationship in Southern Central America. *Proceedings and Transactions of the 38th International Congress of Americanists* 1:229–242.
1978 Lower Central America. In *Chronologies in New World Archaeology.* Edited by R. E. Taylor and C. W. Meighan, pp. 395–430. New York: Academic Press.
1982–1983 Settlement Patterns and Cultural History of Ometepe Island, Nicaragua: A Preliminary Sketch. In *Prehistoric Settlement Patterns in Costa Rica.* Edited by F. W. Lange and L. Norr. *Journal of the Steward Anthropological Society* 14(1–2): 369–386.
1983 To Quench the Thirst: Water and Settlement in Central America. In *Prehistoric Settlement Patterns: Essays in Honor of Gordon R. Willey.* Edited by E. Vogt and R. Leventhal, pp. 79–88. Albuquerque and Cambridge: University of New Mexico and Peabody Museum Press.

HABICHT-MAUCHE, JUDITH, JOHN W. HOOPES, AND MICHAEL GESELOWITZ
1987 Where's the Chief?: The Archaeology of Complex Tribes. Paper Presented at the 52nd Annual Meeting of the Society for American Archaeology, Toronto, May 6–10.

HAGGETT, PETER
1965 *Locational Analysis in Human Geography.* London: Arnold.

HAMMOND, NORMAN, DUNCAN PRING, RICHARD WILK, SONA DONAGHEY, FRANK P. SAUL, ELIZABETH S. WING, ARLENE V. MILLER, AND LAWRENCE H. FELDMAN

1979 The Earliest Lowland Maya? Definition of the Swasey Phase. *American Antiquity* 44(1)92–110.

HARNER, MICHAEL J.

1970 Population Pressure and the Social Evolution of Agriculturalists. *Southwestern Journal of Anthropology* 26:1–106.

HARRIS, D.

1973 The Prehistory of Tropical Agriculture: An Ethnoecological Model. In *The Explanation of Culture Change*. Edited by C. Renfrew, pp. 391–417. London: Duckworth.

HARTMAN, C.

1901 *Archaeological Researches in Costa Rica*. Stockholm: Royal Ethnographical Museum.

1907 Archaeological Researches on the Pacific Coast of Costa Rica. *Memoirs, Carnegie Museum*, no. 3.

HARTSHORN, G.

1983 Plants: Introduction. In *Costa Rican Natural History*. Edited by D. Janzen, pp. 118–157. Chicago: University of Chicago Press.

HEALY, PAUL

1974 Archaeological Survey of the Rivas Region, Nicaragua. Ph.D. dissertation (Anthropology), Harvard University.

1980 *Archaeology of the Rivas Region, Nicaragua*. Waterloo, Ontario: Winfred Laurier University Press.

1988 Greater Nicoya and Mesoamerica: Analysis of Selected Ceramics. In *Costa Rican Art and Archaeology*. Edited by F. W. Lange, pp. 291–302. Boulder: University of Colorado Museum.

HEIZER, ROBERT F., AND JONAS E. GULLBERG

1981 Concave Mirrors from the Site of La Venta, Tabasco: Their Occurrence, Mineralogy, Optical Description, and Function. In *The Olmec and Their Neighbors*. Edited by Elizabeth P. Benson, pp. 109–116. Washington, D.C.: Dumbarton Oaks Research Library and Collections, Trustees for Harvard University.

HELMS, M.

1979 *Ancient Panama: Chiefs in Search of Power*. Austin: University of Texas Press.

HERTZ, ROBERT

1960 *Death and the Right Hand*. Translated by Rodney and Claudia Needham. Glencoe, Ill.: Free Press.

HESTER, T.

1986 On the Misuse of Projectile Point Typology in Mesoamerica. *American Antiquity* 51:412–415.

HEUSSER, CALVIN J.

1971 *Pollen and Spores of Chile*. Tucson: University of Arizona.

HOOPES, J.

1979 Recent Archaeological Investigations at the Site of La Guinea, Tempisque River Valley, Guanacaste, Costa Rica. B.A. thesis, Yale University.

1980 Archaeological Investigations at the Site of La Guinea, Tempisque River Valley, Guanacaste, Costa Rica. MS on file, National Museum of Costa Rica.

1984a A Preliminary Ceramic Sequence for the Cuenca de Arenal, Cordillera de Tilarán Region, Costa Rica. *Vínculos* 10(1–2):129–148.

1984b Prehistoric Habitation Sites in the Río Santa Rosa Drainage. *Vínculos* 10(1–2):121–128.

1985 El Complejo Tronadora: cerámica del período formativo en el cuenca de Arenal, Guanacaste, Costa Rica. *Vínculos* 11(1–2):111–118.

1987 Early Ceramics and the Origins of Village Life in Lower Central America. Ph.D. dissertation (Anthropology), Harvard University. Ann Arbor: University Microfilms.

n.d. Early Formative Cultures in the Intermediate Area: A Background to the Emergence of Social Complexity. Manuscript.

1988 The Complex Tribe in Prehistory: Sociopolitical Organization in the Archaeological Record. Paper presented at the 53rd Annual Meeting of the Society for American Archaeology, Phoenix, April 27–May 1.

HORDER, ALAN (ED.)

1971 *The Manual of Photography*. Philadelphia: Chilton.

HORTON, R. E.

1945 Erosional Development of Streams and Their Drainage Basins: Hydrophysical Approaches to Quantitative Morphology. *Bulletin of the Geological Society of America* 56:275–370.

HUMMER, ANNE G.

1983 Ground Stone of the Zapotitán Valley. In *Archeology and Volcanism in Central America*. Edited by Payson D. Sheets, pp. 229–253. Austin: University of Texas Press.

HUNTINGTON, RICHARD, AND PETER METCALF

1979 *Celebrations of Death: The Anthropology of Mortuary Rituals*. New York: Cambridge University Press.

IMESON, A. C., AND M. VIS

1982 Factors Influencing the Erodibility of Soils in Natural and Semi-Natural Ecosystems at Different Altitudes in the Central Cordillera of Colombia. In *Applied Geomorphology in the Tropics*. Edited by I. Douglas and T. Spencer, pp. 91–106. Berlin: Gebruder.

JANZEN, DANIEL H.

1983 Crescentia alata (Jicaro, Guacal, Gourd tree). In *Costa Rican Natural History*. Edited by Daniel H. Janzen, pp. 222–224. Chicago: University of Chicago Press.

JENSEN, JOHN R.

1986 *Introductory Digital Image Processing: A Remote Sensing Perspective*. Englewood Cliffs, N.J.: Prentice-Hall.

JESSUP, T.

1981 Why Do Apo Kayan Shifting Cultivators Move? *Borneo Research Bulletin* 13(1):16–32.

JOYCE, A.

1983 *Remote Sensing of Forest Dynamics in Tropical Regions*. Washington, D.C.: NASA Office of Space Science and Applications.

KAHLE, A. B., AND A. F. H. GOETZ

1983 Mineralogic Information from a New Airborne Thermal Infrared Multispectral Scanner. *Science* 222:24–27.

KAPP, RONALD O.

1969 *Pollen and Spores*. Dubuque, Ia.: Wm. C. Brown.

KENNEDY, WILLIAM J.

1968 Archaeological Investigations in the Reventazón River Drainage Area, Costa Rica. Ph.D. dissertation (Anthropology), Tulane University.

KIDDER, A. V.
1929 Air Exploration of the Maya Country. *Bulletin of the Pan American Union* 63:1200–1205.
1930a Colonel and Mrs. Lindbergh Aid Archaeologists. *Masterkey* 3(6):5–17.
1930b Five Days over the Maya Country. *Scientific Monthly* 30:193–205.

KIDDER, A. V., JESSE D. JENNINGS, AND EDWIN M. SHOOK
1946 *Excavations at Kaminaljuyu, Guatemala.* Carnegie Institution of Washington, Publication 561. Washington, D.C.

KIRKBY, M. J.
1969 Erosion by Water on Hillslopes. In *Introduction to Fluvial Processes.* Edited by Richard Chorley, pp. 229–238. Suffolk: Mithuen.

KNIGHTLEY, P., AND C. SIMPSON
1971 *The Secret Lives of Lawrence of Arabia.* New York: Bantam Books.

LANGE, F.
1971 *Culture History of the Sapoa River Valley, Costa Rica.* Occasional Papers in Anthropology, no. 4. Beloit, Wisc.: Logan Museum, Beloit College.
1976 Bahías y valles de la Costa de Guanacaste. *Vínculos* 2:45–66.
1978 Coastal Settlement in Northwestern Costa Rica. In *Coastal Adaptations: The Economy of Maritime Middle America.* Edited by B. Stark and B. Voorhies, pp. 101–119. New York: Academic Press.
1980a The Formative Zoned Bichrome Period in Northwestern Costa Rica (800 BC to AD 500), Based on Excavations at the Vidor Site, Bay of Culebra. *Vínculos* 6(1–2):33–42.
1980b Una ocupación del policromo tardio en sito Ruiz, cerca de Bahía Culebra. *Vínculos* 6(1–2):81–96.
1982–1983 The Guanacaste/San Carlos Corridor Project. In *Prehistoric Settlement Patterns in Costa Rica.* Edited by F. W. Lange and L. Norr. *Journal of the Steward Anthropological Society* 14(1–2):93–96.
1984a Cultural Geography of Pre-Columbian Lower Central America. In *The Archaeology of Lower Central America.* Edited by F. Lange and D. Stone, pp. 33–60. Albuquerque: University of New Mexico Press.
1984b The Greater Nicoya Archaeological Subarea. In *The Archaeology of Lower Central America.* Edited by F. Lange and D. Stone, pp. 165–194. Albuquerque: University of New Mexico Press.

LANGE, F. (ED.)
1980c *Vínculos,* Vol. 6. Special issue on the Bahía Culebra Area, Guanacaste.

LANGE, F., AND S. ABEL-VIDOR
1980 The Formative Zoned Bichrome Period in Northeastern Costa Rica (800 BC to AD 500). *Vínculos* 6:33–42.

LANGE, F., S. ABEL-VIDOR, CLAUDE F. BAUDEZ, RONALD L. BISHOP, WINIFRED CREAMER, JANE S. DAY, JUAN VICENTE GUERRERO M., PAUL F. HEALY, SILVIA SALGADO G., ROBERT STROESSNER, AND ALICE TILLET
1984 New Approaches to Greater Nicoya Ceramics. In *Recent Developments in Isthmian Archaeology: Advances in the Prehistory of Lower Central America.* Edited by F. W. Lange. Proceedings of the 44th International Congress of Americanists. Manchester, 1982. B.A.R International Series 212:199–214 (Oxford).

LANGE, F., AND RICHARD M. ACCOLA
1979 Metallurgy in Costa Rica. *Archaeology* 32(5): 26–33.

LANGE, F., AND RONALD L. BISHOP
n.d. Papers of the Greater Nicoya Ceramic Conference. Manuscript, Smithsonian Institution.
1982–1983 A Search for Jade Sources and Prehistoric Settlement on the Santa Elena Peninsula. In *Prehistoric Settlement Patterns in Costa Rica.* Edited by F. Lange and L. Norr. *Journal of the Steward Anthropological Society,* vol. 14, nos. 1 and 2. University of Illinois, Urbana.

LANGE, F., AND T. MURRAY
1972 Archeology of the San Dimas Valley, Costa Rica. *Katunob* 7(4):50–91.

LANGE, F., AND L. NORR (EDS.)
1982–1983 *Prehistoric Settlement Patterns in Costa Rica. Journal of the Steward Anthropological Society,* vol. 14, nos. 1 and 2. University of Illinois, Urbana.

LANGE, F., AND C. RYDBERG
1972 Abandonment and Post-Abandonment Behavior at a Rural Central American House-Site. *American Antiquity* 37(3):419–431.

LANGE, F., AND K. SCHEIDENHELM
1972 The Salvage Archaeology of a Zoned Bichrome Cemetery. *American Antiquity* 37(2):240–245.

LANGE, F., AND D. STONE (EDS.)
1984 *The Archaeology of Lower Central America.* Albuquerque: University of New Mexico Press.

LAWRENCE, GEORGE H. M.
1951 *Taxonomy of Vascular Plants.* New York: Macmillan.

LEÓN, JORGE
1968 *Fundamentos botánicos de los cultivos tropicales.* San Jose: Instituto Interamericano de Ciencias Agrícolas de la O.E.A.

LEOPOLD, E. G., AND R. A. SCOTT
1957 Pollen and Spores and Their Use in Geology. *Annual Report of the Smithsonian Institution* 1957:303–323.

LEYDEN, BARBARA
1987 Man and Climate in the Maya Lowlands. *Quaternary Research* 28:407–414.

LILLESAND, THOMAS M., AND RALPH W. KIEFER
1979 *Remote Sensing and Image Interpretation.* New York: John Wiley and Sons.

LINARES, O., AND A. RANERE (EDS.)
1980 *Adaptive Radiations in Prehistoric Panama.* Peabody Museum Monograph 5. Cambridge: Harvard University.

LINARES, O., AND P. SHEETS
1980 Highland Agricultural Villages in the Volcán Baru Region. In *Adaptive Radiations in Prehistoric Panama.* Edited by O. Linares and A. Ranere, pp. 44–55. Peabody Museum Monographs, no. 5. Cambridge: Harvard University.

LINARES, O., P. SHEETS, AND J. ROSENTHAL
1975 Prehistoric Agriculture in Tropical Highlands. *Science* 187(4172):137–145.

LIND, A.
1981 Applications of Aircraft and Satellite Data for the Study of Archaeology and Environment, Mekong Delta, Vietnam. In *International Symposium on Remote Sensing of Environment,* Proceedings, vol. 3:1529–1537.

LINDBERGH, C. A.
1929 The Discovery of Ruined Maya Cities. *Science* 70:12–13.

LINES, JORGE A.
1936 Una huaca en Zapandí. Notas preliminares tomadas a propósito de las excavaciones arqueológicas hechas a raíz de la inundación del Río Tempisque en 1933, Filadelfia, Provincia de Guanacaste, Península de Nicoya, Costa Rica. San José: Imprenta Lehmann.

LOTHROP, SAMUEL K.
1926 *Pottery of Costa Rica and Nicaragua*. Contributions from the Museum of the American Indian, no. 8. 2 vols. New York: Heye Foundation.
1950 Archaeology of Southern Veraguas, Panama. *Memoirs of the Peabody Museum of Archaeology and Ethnology* 9(3). Cambridge: Harvard University Press.
1963 Archaeology of the Diquis Delta, Costa Rica. *Papers of the Peabody Museum of Archaeology and Ethnology*, vol. 51. Cambridge: Harvard University.
1966 Archaeology of Lower Central America. In *Archaeological Frontiers and External Connections*. Edited by Gordon R. Willey and Gordon F. Ekholm, pp. 180–208. *Handbook of Middle American Indians, Volume 4*. Austin: University of Texas Press.

LOWE, GARETH W.
1959 Archaeological Exploration of the Upper Grijalva River, Chiapas, Mexico. *Papers of the New World Archaeological Foundation*, no. 2.
1971 The Civilizational Consequences of Varying Degrees of Agricultural and Ceramic Dependency within the Basic Ecosystem of Mesoamerica. In *Observations on the Emergence of Civilization in America*. Edited by Robert F. Heizer and John A. Graham, pp. 212–248. Contributions of the University of California Research Facility, no. 11:212–248. Berkeley and Los Angeles: University of California Press.
1975 The Early Preclassic Barra Phase of Altamira, Chiapas: A Review with New Data. *Papers of the New World Archaeological Foundation*, no. 38.
1978 Eastern Mesoamerica. In *Chronologies in New World Archaeology*. Edited by R. E. Taylor and C. W. Meighan, pp. 331–393. New York: Academic Press.

LYONS, T. R., AND T. W. AVERY
1977 *Remote Sensing: A Handbook for Archeologists and Cultural Resource Managers*. Washington, D.C.: National Park Service.

MACARTHUR, R. H.
1972 *Geographical Ecology: Patterns in the Distribution of Species*. New York: Harper and Row.

MACNEISH, RICHARD S., ANTOINETTE NELKEN-TERNER, AND IRMGARD W. JOHNSON
1967 *The Prehistory of the Tehuacán Valley, Vol. 2: Nonceramic Artifacts*. Austin: University of Texas Press.

MACNEISH, RICHARD S., F. A. PETERSON, AND K. V. FLANNERY
1970 *The Prehistory of the Tehuacán Valley, Vol. 3: Ceramics*. Austin: University of Texas Press.

MACNEISH, RICHARD S., JEFFERY K. WILKERSON, AND ANTOINETTE NELKEN-TERNER
1980 *First Annual Report of the Belize Archaic Archaeological Reconnaissance*. Andover, Mass.: Robert E. Peabody Foundation for Archaeology, Phillips Academy.

MADRY, SCOTT L. H.
1983 Remote Sensing in Archaeology. *Archaeology* (May–June): 18–20.

MALAVASSI, E.
1979 Geology and Petrology of Arenal Volcano. M.A. thesis, University of Hawaii.

MARKGRAF, VERA, AND HECTOR L. D'ANTONI
1978 *Pollen Flora of Argentina*. Tucson: University of Arizona Press.

MARTIN, P. S., AND J. SCHOENWETTER
1960 Arizona's Oldest Cornfield. *Science* 132:33–34.

MASON, J. ALDEN
1927 Mirrors of Ancient America. *The Museum Journal* 18(2):201–209. Museum of the University of Pennsylvania, Philadelphia.
1945 Costa Rican Stonework: The Minor C. Keith Collection. *Anthropological Papers of the American Museum of Natural History* 39.

MATTHEWS, MEREDITH H.
1984 Results of Macrobotanical Analysis for the Proyecto Prehistórico Arenal: Preliminary Evidence of Resource Use and Subsistence Strategies. *Vínculos* 10(1–2):193–205.

MCK. BIRD, ROBERT
1984 South American Maize in Central America. In *Pre-Columbian Plant Migration*. Edited by Doris Stone, pp. 39–66. Papers of the Peabody Museum of Archaeology and Ethnology, vol. 76.

MEGGERS, BETTY J., CLIFFORD EVANS, AND EMILIO ESTRADA
1965 Early Formative Period of Coastal Ecuador. *Smithsonian Institution Contributions to Anthropology*, vol. 1. Washington, D.C.: Smithsonian Institution.

MEHRINGER, P. J.
1967 Pollen Analysis on the Tule Springs Site, Nevada. In *Pleistocene Studies in Southern Nevada*. Edited by H. M. Wormington and D. Ellis, pp. 130–200. Carson City: Nevada State Museum Anthropological Papers 13.

MELÉNDEZ, CARLOS
1984 Papel de los Zopilotes en la religión de los indios del Pacífico Sur de Costa Rica. In V° Centenario de Gonzalo Fernández de Oviedo, Memoria del Congreso sobre el Mundo Centroamericano de su Tiempo, pp. 79–87. San José, Costa Rica: Editorial Texto Ltda.

MELSON, W.
1978 Eruption of Arenal Volcano, Costa Rica, 1968–1973. *National Geographic Society Research Reports*, pp. 433–446.
1982 Alternation between Basaltic Andesite and Dacite in Historic and Prehistoric Eruptions for Arenal Volcano, Costa Rica. Manuscript. Washington, D.C.: Smithsonian Institution.
1984 Prehistoric Eruptions of Arenal Volcano, Costa Rica. *Vínculos* 10:35–59.

MELSON, W., J. BARQUERO, R. SAENZ, AND E. FERNÁNDEZ
1986 Erupciones explosivas de importancia en volcanes de Costa Rica. *Boletín Volcanología* 16:15–22.

MELSON, W., AND R. SAENZ
1968 The 1968 Eruption of Arenal Volcano, Costa Rica: Preliminary Summary of Field and Laboratory Studies. November 7, report. Smithsonian Institution Center for Short-lived Phenomena.
1973 Volume, Energy, and Cyclicity of Eruptions of Arenal Volcano, Costa Rica. *Bulletin Volcanologique* 37(3):416–437.

MELTZER, D. J., D. D. FOWLER, AND J. A. SABLOFF (EDS.)
1986 *American Archaeology Past, Present, and Future.* Washington, D.C.: Society for American Archaeology and Smithsonian Institution Press.

MINAKAMI, T., S. UTIBORI, AND S. HIRAGA
1969 The 1968 Eruption of Volcano Arenal, Costa Rica. *Bulletin of Earthquake Research* 47:783–808.

MUELLER, MARILYNN
1984a Laguna de Arenal Shoreline Survey. *Vínculos* 10 (1–2):61–74.
1984b Appendix A. The Silencio Stratigraphic Sequence. *Vínculos* 10(1–2):51–55.
1986 Settlement in the Cuenca de Arenal, Northwestern Costa Rica. M.A. thesis, University of Colorado.

MURRAY, THOMAS A., AND EDWARD W. JESS
1976 Preliminary Report of the Río Sabalo Valley Survey. Manuscript, Dept. of Anthropology, SUNY, Binghamton.

MYERS, THOMAS P.
1978 Formative Period Interaction Spheres in the Intermediate Area: Archaeology of Central America and Adjacent South America. In *Advances in Andean Archaeology.* Edited by D. L. Browman. The Hague: Mouton.

NEWHALL, C. G., AND W. MELSON
1983 Explosive Activity Associated with the Growth of Volcanic Domes. *Journal of Volcanic and Geothermal Research* 17:111–131.

NOLAN, MARY LEE
1979 Impact of Paricutin on Five Communities. In *Volcanic Activity and Human Ecology.* Edited by P. Sheets and D. Grayson, pp. 293–338. New York: Academic Press.

NORDENSKIÖLD, ERLAND
1926 Miroirs convexes et concaves en Amerique. *Journal de la Société des Americanistes de Paris* 18:103–110.

NORR, LYNETTE
1979 Stone Burial Mounds and Petroglyphs of the Zoned Bichrome Period. Paper presented at the 44th Annual Meeting of the Society for American Archaeology, Vancouver.
1982–1983 Archaeological Site Survey and Burial Mound Excavations in the Río Naranjo–Bijagua Valley. In *Prehistoric Settlement Patterns in Costa Rica.* Edited by F. W. Lange and L. Norr. *Journal of the Steward Anthropological Society,* vol. 14: 135–156.

NORWEB, ALBERT
1964 Ceramic Stratigraphy in Southwestern Nicaragua. *Proceedings and Transactions of the 35th International Congress of Americanists* 1:551–561.

ODIO, EDUARDO
1989 La Pochota: un sitio temprano en el Valle de Tempisque. Manuscript, Museo Nacional, San José.

PASZTORY, ESTHER
1983 *Aztec Art.* New York: Henry N. Abrams.

PEARSALL, D. M.
1989 *Paleoethnobotany: A Handbook of Procedures.* San Diego: Academic Press.

PEARSON, G. W., J. R. PILCHER, M. G. L. BAILLIE, D. M. CORBETT, AND F. QUA
1986 High-Precision C^{14} Measurement of Irish Oaks to Show the Natural C^{14} Variations from AD 1840–5210 BC. *Radiocarbon* 28(2B):911–934.

PEARSON, G. W., AND M. STUIVER
1986 High-Precision Calibration of the Radiocarbon Time Scale, AD 1950–500 BC *Radiocarbon* 28(2B): 805–838.

PERALTA, M. M.
1883 *Costa Rica, Nicaragua y Panamá en el siglo XVI, su historia y sus límites según los documentos de archivo de las Indias de Sevilla, del Simancas, etc., recogidos y publicados con notas y aclaraciones históricas y geográficas.* Madrid: Librería de M. Murillo.

PIPERNO, D.
1984 A Comparison and Differentiation of Phytoliths from Maize and Wild Grasses: Use of Morphological Criteria. *American Antiquity* 49:361–383.
1985a Phytolith Analysis and Tropical Paleo-Ecology: Production and Taxonomic Significance of Siliceous Forms in New World Plant Domesticates and Wild Species. *Review of Paleobotany and Palynology* 45:185–228.
1985b Phytolith Taphonomy and Distributions in Archaeological Sediments from Panama. *Journal of Archaeological Science* 12:247–267.
1985c Phytolithic Analysis of Geological Sediments from Panama. *Antiquity* 59:13–19.
1988 *Phytolith Analysis: An Archaeological Perspective.* San Diego: Academic Press.

PIPERNO, D., AND V. STARCZAK
1985 Numerical Analysis of Maize and Wild Grass Phytoliths Using Multivariate Techniques. Paper presented at the 2nd Phytolith Research Workshop, Duluth.

PLOG, FRED
1968 Archaeological Surveys: A New Perspective. M.A. thesis, University of Chicago.

POSEY, D.
1983 Indigenous Ecological Knowledge and Development in the Amazon. In *The Dilemma of Amazonian Development.* Edited by E. Moran, pp. 225–257. Boulder, Colo.: Westview Press.

PRANCE, GHILLEAN T.
1984 The Pejibaye, Guilielma gasipaes (H.B.K) Bailey, and the Papaya, Carica papaya L. In *Pre-Columbian Plant Migration.* Edited by Doris Stone. Papers of the Peabody Museum of Archaeology and Ethnology 76:85–104.

RECORD, SAMUEL J., AND ROBERT W. HESS
1943 *Timbers of the New World.* New Haven: Yale University Press.

REES, J.
1979 Effects of the Eruption of Paricutin Volcano on Landforms, Vegetation, and Human Occupancy. In *Volcanic Activity and Human Ecology.* Edited by P. Sheets and D. Grayson, pp. 249–292. New York: Academic Press.

REICHEL-DOLMATOFF, GERARDO
1955 Excavaciones en los conchales de la costa de Barlovento. *Revista Colombiana de Antropologia* 4: 249–272.
1965a *Columbia. Ancient Peoples and Places.* New York: Praeger.
1965b *Excavaciones arqueológicas en Puerto Hormiga, Departamento de Bolívar.* Publicaciones de la Universidad de Los Andes, Antropología 2 (Bogotá).
1985 *Monsú: un sitio arqueológico.* Bogotá: Fondo de Promoción de la Cultura del Banco Popular.

REINING, P.
1973 *Utilization of ERTS-1 Imagery in Cultivation and Settlement Site Identification and Carrying Capacity Estimates in Upper Volta and Niger.* Springfield, Va.: National Technical Information Center.
1974a Human Settlement Patterns in Relation to Resources of Less Developed Countries. *Proceedings: COSPAR Meetings,* São Paulo, Brazil. On file at International Office, American Association for the Advancement of Science, Washington, D.C.
1974b Use of ERTS-1 Data in Carrying Capacity Estimates for Sites in Upper Volta and Niger. Paper presented at the 1974 Annual Meeting of the American Anthropological Association, Mexico City.

RICHARDS, P.
1966 *The Tropical Rain Forest: An Ecological Study.* Cambridge: Cambridge University Press.

RICHARDSON, FRANCIS B.
1940 Non-Maya Monumental Sculpture of Central America. In *The Maya and Their Neighbors.* Edited by C. L. Hay et al., pp. 395–416. New York: D. Appleton-Century.

RICKETSON, OLIVER, JR., AND A. V. KIDDER
1930 An Archeological Reconnaissance by Air in Central America. *Geographical Review* 20(2).

RITTER, DALE F.
1986 *Process Geomorphology.* Dubuque, Ia.: W. C. Brown.

ROWE, JOHN HOWLAND
1953 Technical Aids in Anthropology: A Historical Survey. In *Anthropology Today.* Edited by Alfred L. Kroeber, pp. 895–940. Chicago: University of Chicago Press.

RYDER, PETER
1982–1983a Hacienda Mojica. In *Prehistoric Settlement Patterns in Costa Rica.* Edited by F. W. Lange and L. Norr. *Journal of the Steward Anthropological Society* 14(1–2):105–120.
1982–1983b Guayabo de Bagaces. In *Prehistoric Settlement Patterns of Costa Rica.* Edited by F. W. Lange and L. Norr. *Journal of the Steward Anthropological Society* 14(1–2):121–134.

SABINS, FLOYD F., JR.
1987 *Remote Sensing: Principles and Interpretation.* 2d ed. New York: W. H. Freeman.

SABLOFF, J. A., AND R. E. SMITH
1969 The Importance of Both Analytic and Taxonomic Classification in the Type-Variety System. *American Antiquity* 34(3):278–285.

SAENZ, R.
1976 Erupción del Volcán Arenal en el año 1968. *Revista Geográfica de América Central* 5:149–188.

SAENZ, R., AND W. MELSON
1976 La erupción del Volcán Arenal, Costa Rica en julio, 1968. *Revista Geográfica de América Central* 5:55–148.

SAXE, A.
1970 Social Dimensions of Mortuary Practices. Ph.D. dissertation, University of Michigan. Ann Arbor: University Microfilms.

SCHIFFER, MICHAEL D.
1987 *Formation Processes of the Archaeological Record.* Albuquerque: University of New Mexico Press.

SCHWONGERDT, R.
1983 *Techniques for Image Processing and Classification in Remote Sensing.* London: Academic Press.

SEGERSTROM, K.
1950 *Erosion Studies at Paricutin.* U.S. Geological Survey Bulletin 965-A. Washington, D.C.: Government Printing Office.

SEVER, T., AND J. WISEMAN
1985 Conference on Remote Sensing: Potential for the Future. Manuscript. NASA Earth Resources Library Report, NSTL Station, Miss.

SHARER, R. (ED.)
1978 *The Prehistory of Chalchuapa, El Salvador.* 3 vols. Philadelphia: University of Pennsylvania Press.

SHAZLY, E. M.
1983 Space Borne Imagery Interpretation of Mega Features Related to Egyptian Archeology. *International Geoscience and Remote Sensing Symposium,* vol. 1. New York: Institute of Electrical and Electronic Engineers.

SHEETS, PAYSON D.
1978 Artifacts. In *The Prehistory of Chalchuapa, El Salvador,* vol. 2. Edited by R. Sharer, pp. 2–133. Philadelphia: University of Pennsylvania Press.
1982–1983 Preliminary Reconnaissance of the Cuenca de Arenal 1981–1982. In *Prehistoric Settlement Patterns in Costa Rica.* Edited by F. W. Lange and L. Norr. *Journal of the Steward Anthropological Society* 14(1–2):157–159.
1983 Settlement, Subsistence, and Volcanism near Arenal, Costa Rica. Proposal submitted to the National Science Foundation.
1984a Proyecto Prehistórico Arenal, an Introduction. *Vínculos* 10(1–2):17–30.
1984b Chipped Stone Artifacts from the Cordillera de Tilarán. *Vínculos* 10(1–2):149–166.
1984c Summary and Conclusions. *Vínculos* 10(1–2): 207–223.

SHEETS, PAYSON D. (ED.)
1983 *Archeology and Volcanism in Central America: The Zapotitán Valley of El Salvador.* Austin: University of Texas Press.

SHEETS, PAYSON D., AND M. MUELLER (EDS.)
1984 Archeological Investigations in the Cordillera of Tilarán, Costa Rica, 1984. Special issue of *Vínculos* 10(1–2).

SHEETS, PAYSON D., E. J. ROSENTHAL, AND A. J. RANERE
1980 Stone Tools from Volcán Baru. In *Adaptive Radiations in Prehistoric Panama.* Edited by Olga F. Linares and Anthony J. Ranere, pp. 404–428. Peabody Museum Monographs No. 5. Cambridge: Havard University.

SIEGEL, B. S., AND A. R. GILLESPIE
1980 *Remote Sensing in Geology.* New York: Wiley.

SMITH, C. E.
1980 Plant Remains from the Chiriqui Sites and Ancient Vegetational Patterns. In *Adaptive Radiations in Prehistoric Panama.* Edited by Olga F. Linares and Anthony J. Ranere, pp. 151–174. Peabody Museum Monographs No. 5. Cambridge: Havard University.

SMITH, R. E., G. R. WILLEY, AND J. C. GIFFORD
1960 The Type-Variety Concept as a Basis for the Analysis of Maya Pottery. *American Antiquity* 25(3):330–340.

SNARSKIS, MICHAEL J.
1976 La vertiente atlántica de Costa Rica. *Vínculos* 2:101–114.
1978 The Archaeology of the Central Atlantic Watershed of Costa Rica. Ph.D. dissertation, Columbia University.
1979 Turrialba: A Paleo-Indian Quarry and Workshop Site in Eastern Costa Rica. *American Antiquity* 44:125–138.
1981a Archaeology of Costa Rica. In *Between Continents/Between Seas: Precolumbian Art of Costa Rica.* Edited by E. Benson, pp. 15–84. New York: Harry N. Abrams.
1981b Catalogue. In *Between Continents/Between Seas: Precolumbian Art of Costa Rica.* Edited by E. Benson, pp. 178–227. New York: Harry N. Abrams.
1982 *La cerámica precolombina en Costa Rica/Precolumbian Ceramics in Costa Rica.* Bilingual ed. San José: Instituto Nacional de Seguros.
1984a Central America: The Lower Caribbean. In *The Archaeology of Lower Central America.* Edited by F. Lange and D. Stone, pp. 195–232. Albuquerque: University of New Mexico Press.
1984b Prehistoric Microsettlement Patterns in the Central Highlands–Atlantic Watershed of Costa Rica. In *Recent Developments in Isthmian Archaeology.* Edited by F. Lange. B.A.R. International Series, 212:153–178 (Oxford).
1985 Symbolism of Gold in Costa Rica and Its Archaeological Perspective. In *The Art of Precolumbian Gold.* Edited by Julie Jones, pp. 22–33. London: Weidenfeld and Nicholson.

SNARSKIS, MICHAEL J., AND AIDA BLANCO
1978 Dato sobre cerámica policromada guanacasteca excavada en la Meseta Central. *Vínculos* 4:106–114.

SOUTHWARD, JUDITH
1982 Identifying Food-Preparation Activities Using Ethnographic and Archaeological Data Bases. M.A. thesis, University of Colorado, Boulder.

SQUIER, EPHRAIM GEORGE
1860 Some Account of the Lake of Yojoa or Taulebe, in Honduras, Central America, *Journal of the Royal Geographical Society* 30:58–63.

STANDLEY, PAUL C.
1937 *Flora of Costa Rica.* Field Museum of Natural History, Botanical Series, vol. 18, Chicago.

STOCKMARR, JENS
1971 Tablets with Spores Used in Absolute Pollen Analysis. *Pollen et Spores* 13(4):615–621.

STONE, DORIS
1972 *Pre-Columbian Man Finds Central America.* Cambridge, Mass.: Peabody Museum Press.
1977 *Precolumbian Man in Costa Rica.* Cambridge, Mass.: Peabody Museum Press.

STONE, DORIS, AND CARLOS BALSER
1965 Incised Slate Discs from the Atlantic Watershed of Costa Rica. *American Antiquity* 30:310–329.

STRAUSS, JOYCE R.
n.d. A Mirror Tradition in Pre-Columbian Art. M.A. thesis, University of Denver.

STUIVER, M., AND G. W. PEARSON
1986 High-Precision Calibration of the Radiocarbon Time Scale, AD 1950–500 BC. *Radiocarbon* 28(2B): 805–838.

SWAUGER, JAMES L., AND WILLIAM J. MAYER-OAKES
1952 A Fluted Point from Costa Rica. *American Antiquity* 17:264–265.

SWEENEY, JEANNE W.
1975 *Guanacaste, Costa Rica: An Analysis of Precolumbian Ceramics from the Northwest Coast.* Ph.D. dissertation (Anthropology), University of Pennsylvania. Ann Arbor: University Microfilms.

TAINTER, J.
1973 The Social Correlates of Mortuary Patterning at Kaloko, North Koua, Hawaii. *Archeology and Physical Anthropology of Oceania* 8:1–11.
1977 Modeling Change in Prehistoric Social Systems. In *Formal Theory Building in Archaeology.* Edited by L. Binford, pp. 327–351. New York: Academic Press.
1978 Mortuary Practices and the Study of Prehistoric Social Systems. In *Advances in Archaeological Method and Theory,* no. 1. Edited by M. B. Schiffer, pp. 105–143. New York: Academic Press.

TARTAGLIA, LOUIS J.
1977 Infrared Archeological Reconnaissance. In *Remote Sensing Techniques in Archeology.* Edited by T. R. Lyons and R. Hitchcock, pp. 35–50. Albuquerque: Chaco Center.

TOLSTOY, P., AND S. FISH
1975 Surface and Subsurface Evidence for Community Size at Coapexco, Mexico. *Journal of Field Archaeology* 2: 97–104.

TOSI, J.
1980 *Estudio ecológico integral de las zonas de afectación del Proyecto Arenal.* San José: Centro Cientifico Tropical.

TSUKADA, MATSUO, AND JOHN R. ROWLEY
1964 Identification of Fossil Maize Pollen. *Grana Palynologica* 5(3):406–412.

VAILLANT, G. C.
1930 Excavations at Zacatenco. *Anthropological Papers,* vol. 32: Pt. 1. New York: American Museum of Natural History.

VAN DER MERWE, N.
1982 Carbon Isotopes, Photosynthesis, and Archaeology. *American Scientist* 70:596–606.

VOORHIES, BARBARA
1976 The Chantuto People: An Archaic Period Society of the Chiapas Littoral, Mexico. *New World Archaeological Foundation Paper,* no. 41.

WAGNER, PHILIP L.
1985 Nicoya, a Cultural Geography. *University of California Publications in Geography* 12:193–250.

WALLACE, HENRY, AND RICHARD M. ACCOLA
1980 Investigaciones arqueológicas preliminares de Nacascolo, Bahía Culebra, Costa Rica. *Vínculos* 6 (1–2):51–67.

WEILAND, DORIS
1984 Prehistoric Settlement Patterns in the Santa María Drainage of Central Panama: A Preliminary Analysis. In *Recent Developments in Isthmian Archaeology: Advances in the Prehistory of Lower Central America.* Edited by F. W. Lange, pp. 31–53. Proceedings of the 44th Congress of Americanists. B.A.R. Series 212, Manchester.

WEST, R., AND J. AUGELLI
1966 *Middle America: Its Lands and Peoples.* Englewood Cliffs, N.J.: Prentice-Hall.

WILLEY, G.
1971 *An Introduction to American Archaeology, Volume 2: South America.* Englewood Cliffs, N.J.: Prentice-Hall.
1984 A Summary of the Archaeology of Lower Central America. In *The Archaeology of Lower Central America.* Edited by F. Lange and D. Stone, pp. 341–378. Albuquerque: University of New Mexico Press.

WILLEY, G., W. BULLARD, J. GLASS, AND J. GIFFORD
1965 *Prehistoric Maya Settlements in the Belize Valley.* Peabody Museum Papers, vol. 54. Cambridge: Harvard University.

WILLEY, G., AND C. R. MCGIMSEY
1954 *The Monagrillo Culture of Panama.* Peabody Museum Papers, vol. 54. Cambridge: Harvard University.

WILLEY, G., AND J. SABLOFF
1971 *A History of American Archaeology.* San Francisco: Freeman.

WINTER, MARCUS C.
1976 The Archaeological Household Cluster in the Valley of Oaxaca. In *The Early Mesoamerican Village.* Edited by Kent V. Flannery, pp. 25–31. New York: Academic Press.

WU, S., AND S. SADER
1987 *Multipolarization SAR Data for Surface Feature Delineation and Forest Vegetation Characterization.* IEEE Transactions on Geoscience and Remote Sensing, vol. GE-25, no. 1. New York: Institute of Electrical and Electronic Engineers.

YOUNG, R. A., AND C. K. MUTCHER
1969 Soil Movement on Irregular Slopes. *Water Resources Research* 5:1084-1089.

ZEITLIN, R.
1984 A Summary Report on Three Seasons of Field Investigations into the Archaic Period Prehistory of Lowland Belize. *American Anthropologist* 86: 359–369.

ZEVALLOS MENÉNDEZ, CARLOS, W. C. GALINAT, D. W. LATHRAP, E. R. LENG, J. G. MARCOS, AND K. M. KLUMPP
1977 The San Pablo Corn Kernel and Its Friends. *Science* 196(4288):385–389.

Notes on Contributors

AIDA BLANCO VARGAS is an archaeologist working in Costa Rica.

JOHN E. BRADLEY is a Southwestern archaeologist.

MARK L. CHENAULT is receiving his Ph.D. at the University of Colorado and is an archaeologist with SWCA, Inc., Environmental Consultants, in Tucson, Arizona.

KAREN H. CLARY is a botanist at the University of Texas, Austin.

JOHN W. HOOPES is an associate professor of anthropology at the University of Kansas.

BRIAN R. MCKEE is enrolled in the Ph.D. program in anthropology at the University of Arizona.

NANCY MAHANEY is an assistant curator in anthropology at the Arizona State Museum in Tucson and does contract archaeology in the U.S. Southwest.

MEREDITH H. MATTHEWS is a contract archaeologist working in the U.S. Southwest.

WILLIAM G. MELSON is a volcanologist at the Museum of National History, Smithsonian Institution.

MARILYNN MUELLER is a contract archaeologist working in Hawaii.

DOLORES PIPERNO is a phytolith analyst with the Smithsonian Tropical Research Institute in Panama.

THOMAS L. SEVER is a senior research scientist at the Earth Resources Laboratory, Stennis Space Center, NASA.

PAYSON D. SHEETS is a professor of anthropology at the University of Colorado.

Index